Second Edition

Gender Stereotypes

Traditions and Alternatives

Second Edition

Gender Stereotypes

Traditions and Alternatives

Susan A. Basow
Lafayette College

Brooks/Cole Publishing Company
Monterey, California

Consulting Editor: *Lawrence S. Wrightsman*

Brooks/Cole Publishing Company
A Division of Wadsworth, Inc.

Printed in the United States of America

10   9   8   7   6   5   4   3   2

**Library of Congress
Cataloging-in-Publication Data**

Basow, Susan A., 1947–
    Gender Stereotypes.

    Rev. ed. of: Sex-role stereotypes, c1980.
    Bibliography: p.
    Includes index.
    1. Sex role.   2. Stereotype (Psychology)
I. Basow, Susan A., 1947–
Sex-role stereotypes.   II. Title.
HQ1075.B36   1986   305.3   85-30145
ISBN 0-534-06474-4

Sponsoring Editor: *Claire Verduin*
Production Services Coordinator: *Joan Marsh*
Production Editor: *Stacey C. Sawyer, San Francisco*
Manuscript Editor: *Toni Haskell*
Permissions Editor: *Mary Kay Hancharick*
Interior and Cover Design: *John Edeen*
Interior Illustration: *Mary Burkhardt*
Typesetting: *Omegatype, Champaign, Illinois*
Cover Printing: *Malloy Lithographing, Inc.*
Printing and Binding: *Malloy Lithographing, Inc.*

To Jade, who belongs to the future,
and to Jay, with love

Preface

Masculinity. Femininity. These words engender clear pictures of two opposite sets of behavior and personal attributes. To some degree, we all know what these characteristics are. In fact, one of the most impressive aspects of these images is the extent to which we Americans share them. Men should be strong, rational, aggressive; women should be weak, emotional, submissive. And yet, to what extent do these images fit the majority of real-life people? That is, do men and women really conform to these images, or are these images stereotypes? If men and women do not conform to the stereotypes, how did such stereotypes come into being? Once established, how are the stereotypes maintained and transmitted? Once transmitted, how do these stereotypes affect women and men in our society? Once affected by the stereotypes, how does one break free, and toward what does one change? This book is dedicated to answering these questions.

The following chapters will demonstrate that there is little physical or psychological evidence to support gender stereotypes as clear-cut distinctions between the sexes. Yet the stereotypes are firmly entrenched in our individual and cultural psyches and are passed to future generations directly and indirectly via every socializing agent in society (parents, teachers, the media, religion, and so on). The effects of these stereotypes are pervasive, intense, and generally damaging to all individuals (both women and men), to their relationships, and to society as a whole. To break free of stereotypes is a difficult yet beneficial process, which is aided by the concept of androgyny, which is a flexible integration in one person of instrumental/active and expressive/nurturant attributes.

To explore these areas, this book is divided into five parts: Part 1 explores the stereotypes; Part 2 discusses the current findings in the area of sex similarities and differences; Part 3 deals with the origins of sex roles and the stereotypes; Part 4 delves into the effects of the stereotypes; and Part 5 considers alternatives to the stereotypes.

The format and overall approach are similar to the first edition of this book, published in 1980. Yet, there have been a number of changes including the updating of the information and of the references; the second edition also has a broader perspective. Research in the area of sex roles has increased dramatically since the first edition was written in 1979. As a result, more than one-half of the information in this book is new, and more than 1500 new references have been included. Some new topics have been added—for example, moral development, computer usage, gender schema theory, homosexual relationships, and feminist theory. Coverage of other topics has been expanded—for example, the sections on research methodology and the history of patriarchy, and information on Blacks and other minorities, female friendships, and crimes by females. A concerted effort was made to be more sensitive to issues of race, class, and sexual preference. In general, I think that this edition is more interdisciplinary and more balanced with regard to minorities than was the first edition.

This book still is a viewpoint book, perhaps even more than was the first edition. I feel very strongly that the gender stereotypes are imposed by society, not by physiology. People differ, yes. But they do not differ in most cases on the basis of sex. In those cases where sex differences are found, they arise mostly in interaction with a particular situation. Thus, this book takes an interactionist point of view with regard to gender behaviors; they are the product of the person as well as the situation. I also believe that gender stereotypes restrict individuals, their relationships, and society as a whole from maximizing their potential. The perspective is a feminist one. I hope that by putting this bias up front, I can aid the reader in evaluating in an objective manner the material presented.

This book is designed to be used as a text in psychology and sociology courses on sex roles, sex differences, gender, and women. Because of its interdisciplinary nature, it also can be used in courses on women's or men's studies. Sections of the book can be used as a supplement in broader psychology, sociology, or interdisciplinary courses that have units on sex roles, sex differences, human sexuality, or male-female relations. The book also can supplement traditional social psychology texts. The book was written to appeal to both introductory level and advanced students.

Many people have assisted me in bringing this second edition into being. I owe much to the original Women's Studies faculty development group at Lafayette College—Lynn Van Dyke, Maryann Valiulis, Stacey Schlau, Beth Ferris, and Debbie Byrd. From them I learned to get beyond my narrow disciplinary perspective and to expand my awareness of the issues of class, race, and sexual preference. The support, challenge, and encouragement of Stacey Schlau, in particular, helped me to grow both intellectually and personally. I also would like to thank those people who worked with me on various parts of the manuscript—Florence Campanile on the references, Amy Shultis on the references and the name index, Nancy Silberg on the references and library research, and Lisa Konoplisky on the cover idea, references, library research, typing, and editorial comment. Their help lightened my load immeasurably. Lisa's competence and sense of humor, in particular, helped keep me sane as we frantically raced against deadlines.

I would also like to thank the following reviewers of the text for their helpful comments: Mary Booth, Grossmont College; Cynthia Burnley, East Tennessee State University; Suzanne Kessler, SUNY/College at Purchase; Edward LaFontaine, Keuka College; Abigail Stewart, Boston University; and Lawrence S. Wrightsman, University of Kansas, who is also consulting editor for this book.

I also appreciate the support of the Brooks/Cole editorial staff, especially Claire Verduin, who provided just the right balance of understanding and firmness. Most of all, I would like to thank my friends and family, particularly Jay K. Miller, for putting up with my single-minded concentration on the book, often at their expense.

Susan A. Basow

Contents

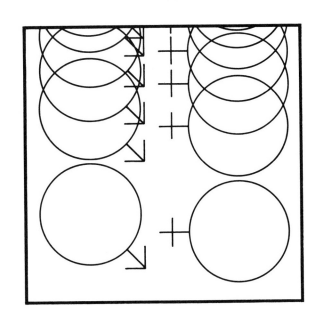

Part 1
Introduction

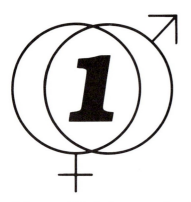

Gender Stereotypes

A boy and his father were involved in a serious automobile accident. The father was killed instantly; the son was severely injured. An ambulance rushed him to the nearest hospital, and a prominent surgeon was summoned to perform an immediate operation. Upon entering the operating room, however, the surgeon exclaimed "I can't operate on this boy. He's my son." Question: how can this be?

If this apocryphal story is unfamiliar to you, and you came up with answers involving a stepfather, adopted father, reincarnation, a mistake, and so on, you are part of the majority of Americans who think of surgery as a male occupation. The answer to the above riddle is simple: the surgeon is the boy's mother. The fact that most people do not guess that answer demonstrates the pervasiveness and strength of certain gender stereotypes—in this case, occupational ones.

This book will examine gender stereotypes—their bases, transmittal, consequences, and alternatives. It will be argued that such stereotypes are based on few actual sex differences and that, more importantly, such stereotypes seriously limit individual functioning and have a negative effect on relationships as well as on society.

Definition

There are other gender stereotypes in our daily lives besides the occupational ones. For example, if you were giving a toy to a child, would you give a doll to a boy or to a girl? a catcher's mitt? a chemistry set? a coloring book? Such choices tap our basic assumptions about boys and girls, males and females. Although for a particular child your choice may not reflect the typical female/male pattern of responding to the above questions, how about your response

for an unknown boy or girl? If that distinction made a difference, you have come face-to-face with the meaning of the term *stereotype*. According to Wrightsman (1977), a stereotype is "a relatively rigid and oversimplified conception of a group of people in which all individuals in the group are labeled with the so-called group characteristics" (p. 672). That is, stereotypes are strongly held overgeneralizations about people in some designated social category. Such beliefs tend to be universally shared within a given society and are learned as part of the process of growing up in that society. Not only may stereotypes not be true for the group as a whole, because they are oversimplifications (most boys may *not* want a chemistry set), but they also are unlikely to be true for any specific member of the group (Johnny Doe, in particular, may not want a chemistry set). Even when a generalization is valid (that is, it does describe group averages), we still cannot predict an individual's behavior or characteristics. For example, if we know that men are taller than women, we still don't know necessarily that Jane Doe is shorter than John Doe. Stereotypes, because they are more oversimplified and more rigidly held than such generalizations, have even less predictive value.

When we speak of gender or sex-role stereotypes, we are speaking of those oversimplified conceptions pertaining to our behavior as females or males. A *role* is "a cluster of socially or culturally defined expectations that individuals in a given situation are expected to fulfill" (Chafetz, 1978, p. 4). Thus, roles are defined by society, are applied to all individuals in a particular category, and are well-learned responses by individuals. For example, the masculine role is currently defined by American society as involving aggressiveness, independence, nonemotionality, and so forth. It is applied to all individuals labeled male and is

3

learned by the person during his early socialization experiences. The same is true with the feminine role. The fact that the definitions of the terms *masculinity* and *femininity* are different in different cultures and have changed over time, even in American culture, demonstrates their learned, as opposed to innate, nature. Thus, what we term masculine and feminine is not linked in any biological sense to being a male or a female but rather is established by society.

For example, in the United States, dentistry is viewed as a male profession; and, indeed, most dentists today are men. In Sweden and the Soviet Union, however, most dentists are women, and the profession is viewed as a female one. Clearly, then, the skills involved in dentistry are not inherently male or female related but are so labeled by a society.

Children in every culture need to learn their roles and the behaviors that go with them. They need to learn what a child, a student, a brother/sister, son/daughter, man/woman should do. With sex roles, as with other roles, the expectations are not always clear, nor does everyone adopt them to the same degree. For example, the male role in many working-class families involves being physically aggressive and settling disagreements by a show of physical strength; in many middle- and upper-class homes, the expectation for men is to be verbally and intellectually aggressive and to settle disagreements through the use of reasoning powers. Yet there are many working-class men who disdain physical violence and many upper-class men who use it. The former group, particularly, are likely to be accused of not being "masculine" enough. Such charges reveal the operation of specific role expectations.

Combining the definition of *stereotype* and the definition of *role*, we can view sex-role or gender stereotypes as the rigidly held and oversimplified beliefs that males and females, by virtue of their sex, possess distinct psychological traits and characteristics. Such overgeneralizations tend to be widely shared in a particular culture and rigidly held. It is worth noting, however, that not all researchers agree with this definition. Ashmore and DelBoca (1979) do not think stereotypes are by definition rigidly held or that they imply consensus. Our definition refers primarily to cultural stereotypes, and Ashmore and DelBoca prefer to draw a distinc-

tion between personal and cultural stereotypes. A personal sex-role stereotype refers to "structured sets of inferential relations that link personal attributes to the social categories female and male" (Ashmore & DelBoca, 1979, p. 225). In this sense, sex-role or gender stereotypes can be viewed as a type of implicit personality theory (Ashmore & Tumia, 1980; Del Boca & Ashmore, 1980). As such, the topic fits in with a wide range of research and theory on psychological processes.

Because roles are learned, there is always the possibility that they can be unlearned and the definitions of the roles themselves redefined. The possibility of such changes is important to bear in mind as we examine the specific sex-role or gender stereotypes in more depth.

Evidence of Gender Stereotypes

There is considerable experimental evidence to support the existence of gender stereotypes in the United States. Studies conducted during the late 1960s and early 1970s with nearly 1000 males and females (Broverman, Vogel, Broverman, Clarkson, & Rosenkrantz, 1972; Rosenkrantz, Vogel, Bee, Broverman, & Broverman, 1968) have demonstrated that there exists strong agreement about the differing characteristics of men and women. This consensus is found regardless of the age, sex, religion, educational level, or marital status of the respondents. More than 75% of those asked agreed that 41 traits clearly differentiated females and males. Table 1-1 lists these traits in the two categories suggested by statistical analysis: 29 male-valued items (Competency Cluster) and 12 female-valued items (Warmth-Expressiveness Cluster). Although these studies are somewhat dated, more recent research (for example, Canter & Meyerowitz, 1984; Del Boca & Ashmore, 1980; T. Ruble, 1983; P. Smith & Midlarsky, 1985; Spence & Sawin, 1985) still finds that both sexes view the typical man and woman as distinctly different from each other on such "masculine" and "feminine" traits. Children as young as seven years make these distinctions (Davis, Williams, & Best, 1982; Hensley & Borges, 1981), and even cross-cultural research

Table 1-1

Stereotypic Sex-Role Items (Responses from 74 College Men and 80 College Women)

Competency Cluster: Masculine Pole is More Desirable

Feminine	Masculine
Not at all aggressive	Very aggressive
Not at all independent	Very independent
Very emotional	Not at all emotional
Does not hide emotions at all	Almost always hides emotions
Very subjective	Very objective
Very easily influenced	Not at all easily influenced
Very submissive	Very dominant
Dislikes math and science very much	Likes math and science very much
Very excitable in a minor crisis	Not at all excitable in a minor crisis
Very passive	Very active
Not at all competitive	Very competitive
Very illogical	Very logical
Very home oriented	Very worldly
Not at all skilled in business	Very skilled in business
Very sneaky	Very direct
Does not know the way of the world	Knows the way of the world
Feelings easily hurt	Feelings not easily hurt
Not at all adventurous	Very adventurous
Has difficulty making decisions	Can make decisions easily
Cries very easily	Never cries
Almost never acts as a leader	Almost always acts as a leader
Not at all self-confident	Very self-confident
Very uncomfortable about being aggressive	Not at all uncomfortable about being aggressive
Not at all ambitious	Very ambitious
Unable to separate feelings from ideas	Easily able to separate feelings from ideas
Very dependent	Not at all dependent
Very conceited about appearance	Never conceited about appearance
Thinks women are always superior to men	Thinks men are always superior to women
Does not talk freely about sex with men	Talks freely about sex with men

Warmth-Expressive Cluster: Feminine Pole is More Desirable

Feminine	Masculine
Doesn't use harsh language at all	Uses very harsh language
Very talkative	Not at all talkative
Very tactful	Very blunt
Very gentle	Very rough
Very aware of feelings of others	Not at all aware of feelings of others
Very religious	Not at all religious
Very interested in own appearance	Not at all interested in own appearance
Very neat in habits	Very sloppy in habits
Very quiet	Very loud
Very strong need for security	Very little need for security
Enjoys art and literature	Does not enjoy art and literature at all
Easily expresses tender feelings	Does not express tender feelings at all easily

From "Sex Role Stereotypes: A Current Appraisal," by I. Broverman, S. R. Vogel, S. M. Broverman, F. E. Clarkson, and P. S. Rosenkrantz, *Journal of Social Issues,* 1972, *28*(2), 59–78. Copyright 1972 by the Society for the Psychological Study of Social Issues. Reprinted by permission of the author and publisher.

finds considerable generality in those characteristics seen as differentially associated with women and men (Ward, 1985). For example, in all twenty-five of the countries sampled by Williams and Best (1982), men were associated with such traits as "adventurous" and "forceful," whereas women were associated with such traits as "sentimental" and "submissive."

However, despite general agreement on a number of sex-stereotypic traits, cultural variations in the complete stereotype do occur (Lii & Wong, 1982; Romer & Cherry, 1980; P. Smith & Midlarsky, 1985; Williams & Best, 1982, 1984). For example, Whites[1] are more likely than Blacks to see women as passive, status conscious, emotional, and concerned about their appearance. Compared with Blacks, Whites are more likely to see men as unexpressive of emotions, aggressive, competitive, independent, and status conscious. In addition, the stereotypes of Afro-American males and females are more similar to each other in terms of expressiveness and competence than are the stereotypes of Anglo-American males and females. Furthermore, there are social class differences, age differences, and occupational differences in the gender stereotypes as well (Cazenave, 1984; Del Boca & Ashmore, 1980; L. Lewis & Deaux, 1983).

Recent research suggests that in the 1980s, two distinct stereotypes for women actually exist—one of a traditional woman, and one of a liberated woman (Cartwright, Lloyd, Nelson, & Bass, 1983; Lii & Wong, 1982). The liberated woman stereotype incorporates such stereotypically masculine traits as aggressiveness, ambition, and self-confidence. Some might argue that there is a liberated man stereotype as well, which incorporates such stereotypically feminine traits as gentleness and sensitivity (Doyle, 1983; Ehrenreich, 1984; Pleck, 1981b). Still, when most people think of a typical man or typical woman, they apparently have the traditional (White) stereotype in mind.

Although the gender stereotypes appear to have considerable generality and to be quite strong and stable, there is some indication that people's attitudes about socially desirable traits for men and women may be changing. For example, Thomas Ruble (1983) found that although college students believed that the typical female and male differed on nearly 53 traits, these students also believed that it was desirable for males and females to differ on only 12 traits (such as aggressiveness and neatness). Women appear to perceive fewer characteristics as desirable for one sex only than do men (Canter & Meyerowitz, 1984). Thus, men appear to view gender stereotypes as more appropriate than do women, a finding that will reappear repeatedly in different contexts throughout this book.

Measuring gender stereotypes involves some problems, which will be discussed next. This discussion will be followed by an examination of some important issues related to the gender stereotypes.

Problems

There are a number of problems with studies of gender stereotypes. One problem relates to the *methodologies* of the studies themselves (Cicone & Ruble, 1978; Pleck, 1981b). Asking questions about how males differ from females may yield information about the attributes that are viewed as differentiating the sexes but not necessarily about how people see typical males and females themselves. In other words, most questionnaires ask about relative, rather than absolute, beliefs. For example, males and females may be thought of as similar in honesty, intelligence, and helpfulness but different in aggressiveness and warmth. Because only the differences are considered, the similarities are minimized.

In addition, most studies of gender stereotypes use *checklist* responses rather than self-generated descriptions. Checklists encourage responding from one's beliefs about the characteristics of males and females rather than from one's actual experience with the sexes. Thus, less stereotyping is found when people are asked to give their own description of males and females than when they are asked to check an adjective list (Cicone & Ruble, 1978; Deseran & Falk, 1982; Kite & Deaux, 1984).

---

[1]The racial descriptors "White" and "Black" are capitalized to indicate that the terms refer to designated social categories and not to physical characteristics.

Bearing in mind that the research on stereotypes may present an exaggerated picture of people's beliefs about the sexes, it still is notable how consistent the stereotyped differences are. Even in an open-ended questionnaire, the single most common description of women is in terms of interpersonal sensitivity. In general, women most often are characterized as being warm, expressive, and people oriented; men are seen as active, levelheaded, dominant, and achievement oriented.

Another problem with research on gender stereotypes is that such stereotypes are *not unitary* (L. Bernard, 1981; Deaux & Lewis, 1984; Myers & Gonda, 1982b; P. Smith & Midlarsky, 1985; Spence & Sawin, 1985). There appear to be at least four identifiable components of gender stereotypes that operate relatively independently. One can talk about masculine and feminine traits (such as independence and gentleness, respectively), about masculine and feminine roles (such as head of household and caretaker of children, respectively), about masculine and feminine occupations (such as truck driver and telephone operator, respectively), and about masculine and feminine physical characteristics (such as broad-shouldered and graceful, respectively). A graceful individual could be male or female, independent or gentle, a head of household or a caretaker of children, and a truck driver or a telephone operator. Although the components of gender stereotypes are related, they appear to function differently under different conditions. Research that looks at gender stereotypes as unitary may overstate their connection to the labels "male" and "female" and simplify what appears to be a complex process. With regard to actual behavior as well, sex role traits, attitudes, and behaviors appear to be relatively independent (Orlofsky, 1981b).

A number of issues regarding gender stereotypes merit further consideration: their social desirability, their implied opposition, and their all-or-none categorizing.

Issues

The general *social desirability* of masculine and feminine traits is related to gender stereotypes. When people in the Broverman and Rosen-

krantz studies (1972, 1968) were asked to rate the social desirability of each trait, the researchers found that the masculine poles were considered by both men and women to be more socially desirable than the feminine poles for any adult, regardless of sex. It is possible that this negative bias regarding women is an artifact of the specific items the Broverman group used. However, the fact that these 41 traits were themselves chosen as particularly characteristic of the sexes from a larger number of traits suggests that there may indeed be an uneven evaluation of the two sex roles.

Other researchers have found similar evidence of a negative bias toward feminine traits, although one investigator, Sandra Bem (1974), also found that a few feminine traits were rated more highly than any masculine ones (for example, "sensitive to the needs of others"). Williams and Best (1982, 1984) argue that the stereotypic male traits they studied were viewed as more active and strong but not as more favorable per se than the stereotypic female traits. Yet, to the extent that active and strong traits are viewed more positively than passive and weak traits, masculine traits appear more socially desirable than feminine traits. Another point is that, since the late 1970s, females at least seem to have a more positive view of femininity than did females in previous decades, and than do males (Lii & Wong, 1982; P. Smith & Midlarsky, 1985; Werner & LaRussa, 1985). Furthermore, there seems to be more flexibility within the feminine than the masculine role (Ruch, 1984). For example, a person may be "feminine" by exhibiting some but not necessarily all of the feminine sex-typed traits. But, to be "masculine," one needs to display most or all of the masculine sex-typed traits. As we will see throughout the book, this greater rigidity of the male sex role has important implications for boys and men. In many cases, this rigidity can lead to a constant "proving" of one's masculinity. On the balance, however, more negatively valued traits are typically attributed to the feminine role than to the masculine role. The implications are far reaching. How does it feel to be thought of as submissive, very emotional, easily influenced, very sneaky, and not at all ambitious? How does it feel to share the feeling that such traits are undesirable? How does it affect one's self-image, one's opinion of women, and one's attitude toward female professionals? Such consequences of the gender stereotypes will be examined in Part Four.

The traits listed in Table 1-1 reveal another common finding related to gender stereotypes: The characteristic traits for men and women are commonly viewed as being *opposite* each other. Thus, whereas males are thought of as dominant and objective, females are thought of as submissive and subjective. This all-or-none distinction may have been a function of the questionnaire used by the Broverman group. The items were presented as two end points on a line, and each respondent was asked to check where on the line the typical male or female could be placed. Thus a female could only be rated as either submissive or dominant, not as more or less submissive, or more or less dominant. (See Brannon, 1978, for an excellent critique of such studies.) Even when responses are free form, however, nearly identical lists and distinctions emerge; for example, males are strong, females weak; females are emotional, males are unemotional. Furthermore, as many researchers (Deaux & Lewis, 1984; Foushee, Helmreich, & Spence, 1979) have found, most people think that masculinity and femininity are negatively related—that is, that being low on masculine traits implies being high on feminine traits.

If sex-typed traits were opposites, we would expect a strong inverse relationship between how a person scores on masculine traits and how she or he scores on feminine traits; that is, being high on one dimension (for example, masculine) would mean being low on the other dimension (for example, feminine). However, research that has correlated individual scores on the masculinity and femininity scales has found little relationship between the two (Bem, 1974; Inoff, Halverson, & Pizzigati, 1983; Orlofsky, 1981b; Spence & Helmreich, 1978). How masculine someone scores is unrelated to how feminine he or she scores. Thus, the bipolar model of masculinity and femininity, which postulates that instrumentality and expressivity fall at opposite ends of a single dimension, is incorrect.

The *all-or-none* categorizing of gender traits is misleading. People just are not so simple that they either possess all of a trait or none of it.

This is even more true when trait dispositions for groups of people are examined. Part A of Figure 1-1 illustrates what such an all-or-none distribution of the trait "strength" would look like: All males would be strong, all females weak. The fact is, most psychological and physical traits are distributed according to the pattern shown in Part B of Figure 1-1, with most people possessing an average amount of that trait and fewer people having either very much or very little of that trait. Almost all the traits listed in Table 1-1 conform to this pattern. To the extent that females and males may differ in the average amount of the trait they possess (which needs to be determined empirically), the distribution can be characterized by *overlapping normal* curves, as in Part C of Figure 1-1. Thus, although most men are stronger than most women, the shaded area indicates that some men are weaker than some women and vice versa. The amount of overlap of the curves generally is considerable.

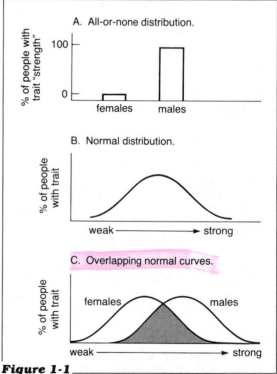

Figure 1-1

Three types of distributions for the trait "strength."

Another attribute related to overlapping normal curves is that differences within one group are usually greater than the differences between the two groups. Thus, there is more variation in the strength trait within a group of men that there is between the "average" male and the "average" female. Most of the stereotypic traits in Table 1-1 fit this pattern. For example, although males on the average may be more aggressive than females on the average, there may be greater differences among males than there are between males and females.

This concept of overlapping normal curves is critically important in understanding gender stereotypes because it undermines the basis of most discriminatory regulations and laws. Although most men are stronger than most women, denying women access to jobs requiring strength simply on the basis of sex is unjustified, because *some* women are stronger than some men (see shaded area in Part C of Figure 1-1). Thus, if most of the stereotypic traits are actually distributed in normal curves along a continuum (that is, people may be more or less dominant, more or less submissive) rather than distributed in an all-or-none fashion—dominant *or* submissive—then setting up two opposite and distinct lists of traits for females and males is entirely inappropriate and misleading.

Not only is it inaccurate to view traits as all-or-none; it may also be inaccurate to view gender stereotypes in terms of personality *traits*. As noted above, recent research on gender stereotypes suggests that most people think of the terms *masculinity* and *femininity* as related to biological sex (male, female), sex-appropriate physical characteristics (muscular, petite), and appearance descriptors (handsome, pretty) more than to personality traits (dominant, submissive). Thus, most of the scales used to measure sex typing (that is, people's conformity to gender stereotypes) may be inadequate.

Furthermore, there is strong debate over whether personality can be viewed in trait terms altogether. Despite their popularity, trait theories of personality have little empirical validity (for example, Chaplin & Goldberg, 1985). People are simply not as consistent in their behavior across a variety of situations as one might like to believe. Mischel (1968) concludes that cross-situational consistencies rarely produce correlations greater than +.30. That is, a person does not usually exhibit the same trait to the same degree in every situation. Rather, human behavior is a function of both the person and the situation. The situation, in many cases, accounts for more than 90% of the variability in a person's behavior. For example, one's behavior during a church service or at a red light is almost entirely a function of the situation. As another example, how assertively a person acts depends not only on the person but on the situation itself. This can be readily verified from one's own experience. An individual can be very assertive in one situation (for example, in a class or group meeting) and markedly unassertive in another (for example, with a close friend).

Of course, some people may be more consistent than others in their behaviors in general and with respect to specific behaviors in particular (D. Bem & Allen, 1974). That is, some people may generally be more predictable than others across a wide range of situations. For example, people who strongly identify with a sex role are more predictable because they more often act according to sex-role expectations than people who don't identify with such a role (Bem, 1975b, 1984). And some people are more consistent than others with respect to a particular behavior (for example, "You can always count on Mary to be assertive"). On the whole, however, the trait approach to personality needs to be modified. Specific people interact with specific situations and produce specific behaviors; generalized traits rarely apply.

With reference to gender stereotypes, then, it can be concluded that: (1) people cannot be viewed as simply collections of consistent traits, because situations are also important; (2) males and females specifically cannot be viewed as having unique traits that are opposite each other; and (3) whatever attributes are thought of as distinctly masculine or feminine are also possessed by at least some members of the other sex.

Therefore, if women and men are not accurately described as a collection of feminine and masculine traits, respectively, and, in fact, if the application of trait terms to personality is generally not appropriate, how can behavior be understood and how can the seeming differences in actual behavior between the sexes be accounted for?

Alternative to Sex Typing

What is needed is a new conceptualization of personality that both allows and accounts for behavioral inconsistency. An answer may lie in the concept of *androgyny*, a term put forth by Sandra Bem denoting the integration of masculine and feminine traits within a single individual (Bem, 1974, 1975b, 1976, 1981b, 1984). Androgynous people tend to characterize themselves, for example, as strongly understanding, compassionate, and affectionate *and* as strongly self-reliant, assertive, and independent. Sex-typed individuals, on the other hand, characterize themselves as strongly having *either* the first *or* last three characteristics but not all of them. The complex characteristics of androgynous individuals can be evidenced, depending on the situation, all in a single act or only in a number of different acts. Thus, a person may be an empathic listener when a friend has a problem, an assertive leader propelling a group to action, and an assertive and sensitive boss when an employee needs to be fired. Being androgynous does not mean being neuter or imply anything about one's sexual orientation. Rather, it describes the degree of flexibility a person has regarding gender stereotypic behaviors.

Sex typing also relates to the degree of salience gender per se has for an individual (Bem, 1981b, 1984). Sandra Bem recently developed a theory about how sex-typed people acquire a gender schema, through which they see themselves and others (discussed further in Chapter 7). Sex-typed individuals seem to be more aware than non-sex-typed individuals of such gender-related issues as the number of men and women in a room, whether the topic discussed is masculine or feminine, and whether an occupation is sex-role-appropriate or not

(Frable & Bem, 1985; C. Miller, 1984; Mills, 1983).

Non-sex-typed individuals may be androgynous, or undifferentiated (Spence, Helmreich, & Stapp, 1974). People who fall into the undifferentiated category generally ascribe a balance of masculine and feminine traits to themselves but only to a limited degree. They do not perceive themselves as strongly having any sex-typed traits. Thus, although they are not sex typed, such individuals are clearly different from the androgynous group.

The concept of androgyny, which will be discussed in greater depth in succeeding chapters, suggests a new way of looking at behavior and also serves as an alternative to strict sex typing. However, there are a number of problems associated with the concept of androgyny that warrant some discussion before we proceed.

Problems

Some of the problems with the concept of androgyny are theoretical, some empirical. Theoretically, androgyny may be a self-defeating concept in the sense that it depends on the existence of two separate sets of traits—the masculine and the feminine. Thus it may serve to perpetuate the gender stereotypes themselves. One solution to this problem is to refer to masculine and feminine traits by their qualities—instrumental/agentic and expressive/nurturant—rather than by their stereotyped labels (Spence & Helmreich, 1980; Spence, 1983). Another solution is to go beyond the concept of androgyny altogether and speak in terms of sex-role transcendence (Rebecca, Hefner, & Olenshansky, 1976). This issue will be discussed further in the last chapter.

Another theoretical issue that will be discussed further in Chapter 9 is whether androgyny is just the sum of its parts—that is, a combination of instrumental and expressive traits, or whether it is really a unique quality—greater than the sum of its parts. Research has not resolved this issue, and the uniqueness of androgyny has not been clearly established (Harrington & Andersen, 1981; Lee & Scheurer, 1983; Lubinski, Tellegan, & Butcher, 1981;

Markus, Crane, Bernstein, & Siladi, 1982; Spence, 1983; Taylor & Hall, 1982; Whitley, 1983, 1984). For example, people with high instrumental/agentic traits (both masculine sex-typed individuals and androgynous individuals) appear to be higher in self-esteem, creativity, and psychological adjustment than do individuals low in these traits. Androgynous individuals, by virtue of also having high expressive/nurturant characters, are not uniquely "better."

A second problem with androgyny relates to the use of this concept in research. At least three different scales have been used to measure androgyny—the Bem Sex Role Inventory (BSRI; Bem, 1974), the Personal Attributes Questionnaire (PAQ; Spence et al., 1974, and the extended version, EPAQ, Spence, Helmreich, & Holahan, 1979), and a rescoring of the Adjective Check List (ACL, Heilbrun, 1976). There is increasing evidence that the different instruments used to measure androgyny may not be measuring identical concepts (Locksley & Colten, 1979; F. Wilson & Cook, 1984). Furthermore, different scoring methods yield different results and imply different definitions of androgyny (Handal & Salit, 1985; Locksley & Colten, 1979; Pedhazur & Tetenbaum, 1979; Sedney, 1981; Spence & Helmreich, 1979b; Strahan, 1981). Another research problem is that the concepts measured are factorially more complex than some researchers have acknowledged (Bem, 1979; Pedhazur & Tetenbaum, 1979; Ruch, 1984; F. Wilson & Cook, 1984). For example, factor analytic studies have shown that current scales, particularly the Bem Sex Role Inventory (BSRI) may involve up to two masculinity factors—assertiveness, dominance, or instrumentality, and independence—and up to two femininity factors—interpersonal sensitivity, or caring, and immaturity. Lenney (1979a, 1979b) identifies three additional research problems: too rigidly held values about what androgyny and sex typing mean, too many atheoretical research projects, and too little integration of androgyny research with more traditional personality and social psychology research. All these problems can be resolved and may be viewed as reflecting the increasing maturity of androgyny research.

There also has been some concern about the validity of the various measures of an-

drogyny and sex typing; that is, do the scales measure what they are supposed to measure? Do they predict behavior in meaningful ways? As we will see throughout the book, androgyny and sex-typing categories indeed have been related to behavior in predictable ways (for example, Bem & Lenney, 1976; La France & Carmen, 1980; Senneker & Hendrick, 1983; Spence & Helmreich, 1980; Taylor, 1984; Tunnell, 1981). However, many questions about the scales' validity still remain (Lubinski, Tellegen, & Butcher, 1983; Myers & Gonda, 1982a; Uleman & Weston, 1984). Remember that personality traits in general tend to be relatively independent of attitudes and, in some cases, behaviors. Thus, the general independence of sex-role traits, attitudes, and behaviors found in some studies should not be surprising (Orlofsky, 1981b; Spence & Helmreich, 1980). Sex typing may only be related to behavior that requires instrumental and/or expressive traits.

A third major problem with androgyny is that the concept may become the new standard of mental health, replacing sex-typed behavior. Everyone then would be expected to acquire thoroughly both agentic and expressive characteristics in equal amounts. This new standard essentially would double the pressure people already are under. Instead of acquiring thoroughly one set of characteristics (their own sex role), they now must acquire two sets of characteristics. Thus a little boy might be pressured to play with dolls and with trucks and to be aggressive and sociable. The main point about androgyny is that any standard of behavior, if it is prescribed rigidly, is restrictive and inimical to effective functioning. People need to be allowed to develop their natural qualities and aptitudes without the restrictions of any stereotypes. If that means some people are more expressive and others more agentic, so be it. But, and this is the major point, these distinctions are unlikely to divide solely on the basis of physical sexual characteristics. That is, most males are unlikely to be purely agentic and most females are unlikely to be purely expressive. The differences will be individual ones, not sex-linked ones.

The percentage of people who could be classified as androgynous varies as a function of many factors: the specific population studied, the measuring instrument and the scoring procedure used, and even the year in which a study is done. For example, males seem to have increased their level of androgyny during the 1970s compared to the 1960s, whereas females showed higher levels of androgyny in the 1960s (Heilbrun & Schwartz, 1982). One should note that there are no absolute cutoff points for the categories of androgynous and sex-typed individuals. Rather, the cutoffs are based on the median scores of a particular sample. In general, about one-third of college populations are classified as androgynous, and there may be more androgynous males than androgynous females. About half of all college students describe themselves as possessing traits more characteristic of one sex than the other; that is, they are categorized as either sex-typed or cross-sex-typed. Another 15–20% are characterized as undifferentiated. The fact that a goodly number of people describe themselves as operating in terms of the gender stereotypes gives one pause. If the stereotypes are indeed overgeneralizations and oversimplifications, and if people cannot justifiably be described by trait terms in general, why do so many people characterize themselves in gender stereotypic terms?

Bases of Gender Stereotypes

Perhaps these stereotypes have some empirical validity; that is, perhaps there are real differences in behavior between the sexes that the stereotypes just exaggerate. This approach suggests that the differences exist first and that the stereotypes simply reflect them. In this case, what have been called stereotypes would not be stereotypes at all—that is, simplified overgeneralizations—but simply generalizations. It is only if a trait is not strongly possessed by a particular sex but is perceived by others as being possessed by that sex that the trait can be called a stereotype.

A study of Unger and Siiter (1975) examined this question and found that, at least in the area of values, most of the gender stereotypic traits were indeed oversimplifications and exaggerations of minor group differences. Polling 240 college students, Unger and Siiter found a striking agreement between males and females on the values they considered most important for themselves and members of the same sex. For example, both men and women felt it was important to be honest, responsible, and broadminded, and they thought other individuals of their sex felt similarly. Thus, the strong sex differences suggested by the gender stereotypes did not fit self- or same-sex perceptions. When it came to predicting the values of members of the other sex, however, the stereotypes operated quite strongly. Women exaggerated the importance of achievement-oriented values for men, and men, to the same degree, exaggerated the importance of nurturant-oriented values for women. Such misperceptions of the other sex (that is, views of the other sex as believing more strongly in stereotyped values than they actually do) can have far-reaching effects. Gender stereotypes, thus, may not be based on statistically significant differences between the sexes but, at best, are exaggerations of a grain of truth. Most of the research on actual differences in behavior, attitudes, or traits between the sexes that we will review in the next four chapters show few if any differences (Deaux, 1984; Inoff, Halverson, & Pizzigati, 1983; Maccoby & Jacklin, 1974: C. Martin, 1984). Those that exist are small in magnitude. Yet people continue to exaggerate the number and magnitude of differences between the sexes (see also Davis, Williams, & Best, 1982; Gilbert, Deutsch, & Strahan, 1978; Spence, Helmreich, & Stapp, 1975; Williams & Best, 1982).

Another way gender stereotypes become validated is through the observation that men and women, girls and boys, frequently engage in different activities. Males are likely to play with guns, know how to change a flat tire, mow the lawn well, and be employed when they are adults. Females are likely to bake well, change diapers, play with baby dolls, and be homemakers as well as employed when they are adults. As Canter and Meyerowitz (1984) found, college men and women report greater ability, enjoyment, and performance of such gender stereotypic behaviors. As we will see in Part Three, boys and girls are encouraged in many ways to learn such stereotypic behaviors. Once acquired, however, people may look at the differences in behavior and conclude that they are a product of different innate traits or abilities, rather than a product of learning. Thus the stereotypes themselves become strengthened. Further strengthening the stereotypes is the tendency for people to overestimate the frequency with which gender-stereotypic behaviors occur (Hepburn, 1985). It appears likely that people's expectations of the major activities of women and men affect the strength of their gender stereotypes. For example, Eagly and Steffen (1984) found that people's beliefs that females possess more communal (concerned with others) and less agentic (masterful) qualities than men are a result of perceiving women as homemakers and men as employees. When women are specifically described as employees, they are perceived as more similar to men in terms of communal and agentic qualities.

Effects of Gender Stereotyping

Rather than reflecting real behavioral differences, then, it is more likely that belief in the stereotypes may give rise to some behavioral differences. If the stereotypes function as part of the sex-role expectations, then people will learn them and be influenced by them. Even though sex-typed distinctions between the sexes may not fit individuals, stereotypes themselves have power as standards to which to conform, against which to rebel, or with which to evaluate others.

One way stereotypes operate is by setting up a *self-fulfilling prophecy*. If females are viewed as having more negative characteristics than males, some females may view themselves this way and may, in fact, develop those very characteristics. For example, if females are expected to be less rational than males, some may view themselves that way and not participate in problem-solving activities or take advanced math courses, since such behaviors are not sex-role appropriate. As a result, some females may indeed develop fewer problem-solving abilities

than some males who have had those experiences, thereby fulfilling the stereotypes. Such beliefs can powerfully influence behavior in either a negative way, if the expectations are negative, or positive way, if the expectations are positive (Snyder, Tanke, & Berscheid, 1977).

An example of the critical role of other people's expectancies on our own behavior was demonstrated by Skrypnek and Snyder (1982). In a laboratory study, males were led to believe that they were paired with either another male or a female in a task requiring a division of labor. Males selected more gender stereotypic activities for themselves and for their partner when the partner was thought to be female than when the partner was thought to be male. More important, the female partner later chose more stereotypic "feminine" tasks when her partner believed that she was female, even though she wasn't informed directly of his expectations. Thus, other people's expectations become fulfilled.

As this study suggests, another way gender stereotypes affect us is through *impression management*. All of us, at some level, want to be socially acceptable, at least to some people. To the extent that we desire such approval, we may engage in impression-management strategies in order to obtain it. That is, we will try to present ourselves (our image) in a way that we think is acceptable to another person. Zanna and Pack (1975) found that female Princeton undergraduates when meeting a man they viewed as a desirable partner would present themselves as extremely conventional women when the ideology of the man was conventional and as more liberated women when his ideology was nontraditional. When the man was viewed as undesirable, his views did not have much impact on the images presented by the women.

In a similar study by von Baeyer, Sherk, and Zanna (1981), 53 female undergraduates acted as job applicants and were interviewed by a male confederate who supposedly held either traditional or nontraditional views of women. The women who saw the traditional interviewer presented themselves in a more traditional way (they wore makeup and clothing accessories, talked to and gazed at the interviewer less, and gave more traditional answers to a question concerning marriage and children) than the women who saw the nontraditional interviewer. These changes were unrelated to the women's own degree of sex typing. Thus, one way the gender stereotypes function is to define expected gender behavior and thereby shape people's self-presentations. This is as true for men as it is for women. As the stereotypes change, so might gender behaviors. Such changes, however, may simply define new images rather than reflect a general reduction in impression management.

In recent years, gender stereotypes have been undergoing change. For example, Pleck (1976b, 1981b) points out that males traditionally have been expected to be instrumental, focusing on achievement, lacking in interpersonal and emotional skills, and relating to women in a dominant way. The modern version of the male role requires more interpersonal and intellectual skills than physical strength, as well as an egalitarian companion-style relationship with women. Yet men's emotional expressiveness still is restricted, and work still is the primary determinant of a man's self-esteem. Thus, although the content of the stereotype may be shifting (see also Doyle, 1983; Dubbert, 1979; Ehrenreich, 1984; Solomon & Levy, 1982), some stereotypes of masculinity remain. Similarly, Gilbert and colleagues (1978) found that, although descriptions by college students of the ideal woman and man tended to be more androgynous than in the past, such descriptions still remained sex typed. This was especially true of the "ideal woman" description given by college men. To the extent that individuals, male or female, are stereotyped, realization of their full human potential in all its complexity is impeded.

Note that stereotypic expectations can be overcome by specific information about an individual (Deaux & Lewis, 1984; Dobbins, Stuart, Pence, & Sgro, 1985; Locksley, Borgida, Brekke, & Hepburn, 1980). In this sense, stereotypic beliefs appear to operate as intuitive estimates for the probabilities of traits in social groups. If we know nothing else about a person except that she's female, we're likely to guess that she's expressive, nurturant, dependent, and so on. But when we learn more about her, we will use the specific information instead of gender stereotypes to make predictions. Even if people aren't stereotyped, the expectations that they should be can cause conflict. For example, Lynne Davidson (1981) has found that both men and women experience each other as demanding gender stereotypical behavior, yet both men and women would like to change. The conflicts for women were actually greater than they were for men.

Looking Ahead

Where do these stereotypes come from? What are the differences and similarities that exist between the sexes? How many of the differences are innate and how many are learned? These questions are important to examine before looking at the actual effect of these stereotypes on people's lives.

Recommended Reading

Bem, S. L. (1981). *Bem Sex-Role inventory, professional manual.* Palo Alto, Calif.: Consulting Psychologists Press. A description of the development, administration, and scoring of the Bem Sex Role Inventory for the measurement of androgyny and sex typing.

Brannon, R. (1978). Measuring attitudes toward women (and otherwise): A methodological critique. In J. Sherman & F. Denmark (Eds.), *The future of women: Issues in psychology.* New York: Psychological Dimensions. An excellent critique of measurement studies.

Deaux, K. (1984). From individual differences to social categories: Analysis of a decade's research on gender. *American Psychologist, 39,* 105–116. A review of recent research on sex and gender, with specific attention to sex both as a subject variable and as a social category. Research on individual differences in sex-typing and androgyny also is covered.

Ruble, D. N., & Ruble, T. L. (1982). Sex stereotypes. In A. G. Miller (Ed.), *In the eye of the beholder: Contemporary issues in stereotyping* (pp. 188–252). New York: Praeger. An overview of research on sex-role stereotypes: Their origins, development, and consequences.

Part 2
Current Findings

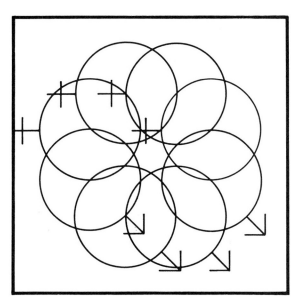

An infant girl is in the babbling stage of development. An observer laughingly remarks, "A typical female. You can't keep them from talking."

After hearing how his son was sent home from school for being disruptive in class and fighting with other boys, a father remarks, with a smile, "Well, boys will be boys."

In both these incidents, certain assumptions are made regarding emotional and behavioral differences between females and males. Boys are assumed to be more active, unruly, and aggressive; girls are assumed to be more emotional, talkative, and passive. Our very use of the term *opposite sex* assumes that females and males are diametrically different from each other not only in their sexual characteristics but in their behaviors as well. In order to understand these stereotypic expectations, it is important to know what differences between the sexes actually do exist—that is, on what the stereotypes are based. Are any of the stereotypic differences listed in Chapter 1 based on fact? If so, which ones are factually based and to what degree? This section will attempt to answer these questions by examining the current findings related to male and female characteristics in four major areas: physical, cognitive, social, and sexual.

Controversy often surrounds even the most mundane of "facts," and what is accepted today may be questioned tomorrow. Human behavior is not fixed; it is not a direct product of biological factors. Therefore, because the environment can exert a major influence on behavior, research results are often quite complex and, at times, inconsistent. The clearest summary statement that can be made is that nearly all behavior is a function of situational forces that may interact with biological predispositions. The relative weighting of the two components varies with the particular behavior, the particular person, and the particular situation, as well as with more general cultural factors.

Because the research on gender stereotypic behaviors and characteristics is so complex, some attention to research methods and problems is needed before the findings themselves can be looked at in detail. The remainder of this introductory section will examine such problems. By necessity, the discussion will be brief. The interested reader is encouraged to read the Summer 1981 issue of the *Psychology of Women Quarterly*, Unger (1983), or Wallston and Grady (1985) for further elaboration of research problems.

Research Methods and Problems

In many of the studies reported in this book, certain research problems occur that serve to place limits on the reported results. Problems regarding basic assumptions of the researchers, choice of subjects, experimental design and methodology, and interpretation of the results are liable to occur in any research area. The areas of sex-role behaviors and sex differences are particularly vulnerable to such problems, because these areas are very personal and, in many ways, political. It is thus necessary to highlight some of the possible

problems, so that the reader can keep them in mind in reviewing the research presented in this book. First, however, it is important to get a general idea of the ways in which psychologists and other social scientists ask and answer questions about behavior.

Research Methods

In psychological research, scientists make hypotheses about how people will behave in certain situations. These hypotheses, or guesses, generally are based on theories about why behavior occurs. The actual testing or verification of these hypotheses can be done in a variety of ways, each with its own advantages and disadvantages. The four most common research methods are case history, survey, naturalistic observation, and experiment.

In the *case history* method, one or a few individuals are studied in depth. For example, Freud based his entire theory of human behavior on intensive examination of a few patients and himself. The advantages of this method are that a great deal of information can be collected in a short time and in a relatively natural setting. However, because the people examined are so few, the information obtained may not be generalizable to others. Therefore, this method's value is to help in developing hypotheses and theories, not in definitively testing them.

The *survey* uses a standardized questionnaire or interview to obtain information from a large sample of people. The advantage of this method is that a great deal of information from many people can be gathered in response to the same questions. For example, questions relating to menstrual discomfort and emotional changes can be given to a large number of people in a relatively short amount of time. However, people also may respond in ways to make themselves look good (responding in a way to seem socially desirable), or to please the experimenter (responding to what is expected of them, called *demand characteristics*). People also may not remember their behavior. Therefore, this method's value is in getting rough estimates of people's attitudes or in obtaining preliminary information to guide later research.

Naturalistic observation involves studying people's reactions to naturally occurring events in natural settings. For example, a researcher may put video cameras in nursery schools and observe how teachers react to male and female children. The advantages to this method are that it allows firsthand observation rather than retrospective reporting; people are more likely to respond naturally because demand characteristics are not obvious; and natural environments are most likely to elicit behavior as it usually occurs. However, naturalistic observations may be difficult to analyze precisely because responses are wholistic and not easily broken down into discrete components; results are difficult to verify because natural events seldom reoccur in exactly the same way, and such observations cannot establish cause-and-effect relationships. Just noting that two events co-occur does not mean that one causes the other. For example, finding that the amount of attention each student gets from the teacher is positively correlated with the child's performance on problem-solving activities does not mean that teacher attention causes improved problem solving. Good problem solvers may elicit more attention from teachers. Or, both factors could be related to a third unmeasured one, such as the child's level of intelligence. In general, naturalistic observations are valuable in providing important information that then can be tested in experiments.

The *experiment* is the sine qua non of scientific methodology. In an experiment, a researcher directly manipulates one variable, called the *independent variable*, while measuring its effects on some other variable, called the *dependent variable*. In doing so, the researcher also must *control* for all other factors that might possibly influence the results. For example, a researcher may be interested in the effects of training on visual-spatial performance. Subjects are randomly assigned to either the experimental group, which receives the specific training, or to a control group, which performs some unrelated activity for

the same amount of time. The two groups then are tested and the results are statistically analyzed to determine how likely it is that the group difference is due to chance. The generally accepted standard is that if the difference between the two groups has less than a 5% likelihood of being due to chance, the findings are termed *statistically significant*. The experimental hypothesis then is supported, and the *null hypothesis* (that there is no difference between the two groups) is rejected. Rigid controls must occur in an experiment: subject selection must be unbiased and assignment to groups random; subject's expectations must be controlled to avoid demand characteristics. This may mean some deception. For example, subjects may not know that their training was intended to improve their performance or that the experimenter expects males to do better. *Experimenter bias* also needs to be controlled—for example, by the tester not knowing which group had received specific training, or by the trainer not knowing the hypotheses. The advantages of experiments are that ideally they can establish cause-and-effect relationships, they are repeatable by anyone who replicates the conditions, and they can be used to analyze the variables precisely. However, experiments also have disadvantages: subjects know that they are being studied, and too much control may make the situation very artificial regarding both the independent and dependent variables. An experiment conducted outside the laboratory (field experiment) may solve some of these problems, but is not always practical.

Thus, no one method is perfect. A finding supported by more than one method is more persuasive than one obtained by just one method. For example, case studies of married couples may reveal that husbands seem to have more difficulty than wives communicating their feelings to their spouse. Husbands also seem to have more difficulty picking up and understanding emotional messages from their spouse than do wives. Naturalistic observations of couples waiting to talk to their child's teacher at parent-teacher conferences may confirm this observation. Surveys that ask husbands and wives how often they tell their spouse how they feel, how well they feel understood by their spouse, and so on may provide some ideas about how common a problem this may be. Laboratory studies may reveal more information about the dynamics of the whole communication process. For example, it may be nonverbal forms of expression that husbands have the most difficulty understanding; or certain feelings that are the most difficult to communicate; or that it is mainly unsatisfactory marriages that show this communication problem. Thus all methods have something to offer, and our understanding of people can be furthered when different approaches point to the same conclusion. (More discussion of marital communication patterns are in Chapter 10.)

Now let us look at some of the research problems that are particularly important in research on sex roles. The reader interested in specific guidelines for nonsexist research would do well to obtain those written by the Division 35 Task Force in 1981. (Division 35 of the American Psychological Association is the division of the Psychology of Women.)

Basic Assumptions

Perhaps the most basic problem in examining the research on sex differences is the underlying assumption that sex differences exist and that these differences are important. As Kaplan and Bean (1976) point out, because researchers study areas already thought to reflect male/female differences, such as hormonal cyclicity, the data reflecting these differences may be exaggerated. For example, much research has been done on the effect of female hormone cyclicity on moods; very little has been done on the effect of male hormones (Parlee, 1973; Ramey, 1972). The implication is that hormones play a larger role in female behavior than they do in male behavior. Similarly, Peterson (1983) observed that as research reveals fewer sex differences in cognitive abilities than previously had been thought, more and more research is done on the few remaining areas that do suggest a gender difference. Thus we get an exaggerated picture of a male/female dichotomy and

a limited understanding of the full range of human potential.

This emphasis on sex differences, as opposed to similarities, is further perpetuated by the policy of most journals to publish only statistically significant findings. The null hypothesis, meaning that there is no difference between groups, can never be proved. The strongest statement that can be made is that the null hypothesis cannot be rejected. Therefore, findings reflecting no difference usually do not get reported in the literature. Additionally, because journals have limited space, they have to reject a high percentage of submitted articles, and they naturally tend to accept those with positive findings. Signorella, Vegega, and Mitchell (1981), in studying sex-related variables in research published from 1968 to 1970 and from 1975 to 1977, found an increase in the number of studies testing for sex differences. Such an increase may result in more chance findings of differences being reported. Furthermore, journals select articles on the basis of "importance" of the research topic. Although published research on topics related to the psychology of women has increased in mainstream journals over the last 20 years from 2–5% to 11–14% (Lott, 1985), the percentage still is a small one. (Perhaps coincidentally, the percentage of women on editorial boards of professional journals in psychology increased markedly during the 1970s, although women were and are underrepresented. The gains were reversed in the 1980s [White, 1985].) In addition, most of this research is on gender differences or sex-typing differences, so the differences again are highlighted. Thus basic assumptions and theories operating in psychology are difficult to challenge and revise.

Another basic assumption in research on sex roles is that sex differences can be attributed to either nature (biology) or nurture (environment). Even calling this topical area "sex differences" suggests that the underlying reason for any differences found is likely to be biological (related to sex) rather than cultural (related to gender) (see Unger, 1979, for a discussion of this distinction). As many writers have noted, it is nearly impossible to separate the influences of biology and environment in humans because socialization begins at birth, and humans have such a tremendous capacity for learning (Division 35, 1981; Lott, 1985; Lowe & Hubbard, 1979). As we shall see in the upcoming chapter, even gender identity is formed through a complex interaction of biological, psychological, and sociocultural factors (DeBold & Luria, 1983; Rogers & Walsh, 1982; Sherif, 1979). All these factors need to be taken into account when examining human behavior. The tendency of some feminist researchers to reject biological factors is as much to be deplored as the tendency of other researchers to accept complete biological determinism (see Newcombe, 1983; Sherif, 1979, for a discussion of this issue). The recent upsurge of interest in sociobiological theories demonstrates that belief in pure biological determinism still has appeal (Bleier, 1984; Lowe & Hubbard, 1979). An interactionist perspective is needed, and we must determine the way this interaction operates for various behavior patterns in various contexts.

The third basic assumption influencing research is that what males do is the norm; what females do, if it is different from what males do, is deviant. Thus McClelland and colleagues (1953) based an entire theory of achievement motivation primarily on male subjects. The fact that this theory did not fit females as well as males did not invalidate the theory nor limit its generalizability. Similarly, Kohlberg (1969) based a theory of moral development almost entirely on male subjects, yet females have been shown not to conform to his theory as well (Gilligan, 1982a, 1982b). Indeed, Grady (1981) reports that males appear as subjects in research nearly twice as often as do females. The important point here is that theories based solely or primarily on males have been generalized to "people in general" even though the theories do not fit 51% of the human race. When women's behaviors and thoughts are included, the theories themselves will be drastically revised. Such work is just beginning.

All these assumptions fit in with a positivist empiricist model of research in psychology, one that restricts analysis to a few clearly observable units of behavior (Unger, 1983). Such a model shapes research questions, findings, and interpretations. Yet this model ignores the inevitable effects of social constructs, such as status and power, on the research process itself. Unger (1983) suggests a more reflexive model of research, which requires an understanding of the reciprocal and interactive relationship that exists between the person and reality, and therefore between the experimenter and the "subject."

Choice of Subjects

Research problems arise in choosing whom to study. Some researchers have used animals, because human experimentation in the biological area presents serious ethical and practical problems. The choice of which animals to study, however, is often a product of the experimenter's assumptions and biases. Thus, rhesus monkeys, who show different behaviors by sex, are studied more frequently than gibbons, who do not show such differences; yet gibbons are evolutionarily closer to humans than rhesus monkeys (M. Rosenberg, 1973). The ability to generalize findings with animals is also questionable, because humans are unique in their development of the neocortex and of the plasticity of their behavior. Human behavior is extremely modifiable by experience. Although there may be similarities in behavior between humans and animals, the antecedents of behaviors may be quite different. It is curious, in this regard, to note the overwhelming number of studies on aggression that have used nonprimates, particularly rats and mice, and that have been generalized to humans. (See Bleier, 1979, for an excellent discussion of this topic.)

Subjects may be selected to fit preexisting assumptions. For example, in examining the effect of menopause on women, one study simply excluded from the sample all women who worked outside the home, apparently on the grounds that such women were "deviant" (Van Hecke, Van Keep, & Kellerhals, 1975). Similarly, studies of attachment in infants nearly always look at mothers rather than fathers, on the assumption that infant-mother attachment is more important. Another example of bias in subject selection is the fact that 90% of all research on aggression has used male subjects, whereas females have been involved in only half the studies (McKenna & Kessler, 1977). As noted previously, males more often are used to represent all human beings, despite the frequent importance of gender on the topic studied. Indeed, significant self-selection may occur in some studies. Signorella and Vegega (1984) have found that women are most interested in signing up for experiments on "feminine" topics, such as revealing feelings and moods, whereas men are most interested in signing up for experiments on "masculine" topics, such as power and competition. Results from such studies may be biased and thus limited in generalizability.

Studying people with some abnormality or who need some form of treatment is also problematic, because by definition, these are individuals whose development differs from normal. Women who consult doctors for menstrual problems, for example, are a select group and cannot be assumed to represent women in general. Other people may be brought up differently because of parental knowledge of their problems, or research may be designed to specifically highlight their differences (for example, Stoller, 1968). Such problems limit the ability to generalize findings.

The cultural relativity of many findings is important, too. Thus, although Tiger (1969) argues that greater male strength and size determine male dominance, this has not been supported in other cultures (for example, Mead, 1935). Physical activity and nutrition are often of greater importance than sex in determining physical attributes (Barfield, 1976), and religion has been found more important than hormones in determining menstrual discomfort (Paige, 1973).

Most research has used White middle-class subjects, often college students, which severely limits the ability to generalize findings. For example, White women appear to be less assertive than Black women, and male-female relationships among Blacks tend to be more egalitarian than male-female relationships among Whites (Adams, 1983; Reid, 1984). Thus results found using White women are not necessarily the case for all women, yet researchers rarely make such limitations explicit.

Some behaviors seem to be situation- or age-specific. Thus Maccoby and Jacklin (1974) found that boys are more active in the presence of their peers, especially male peers, than are girls or than are boys when alone. This may contribute to the conflicting data on activity level. The sex of the experimenter has been shown to be a very influential contextual variable, yet it is rarely even reported (Basow & Howe, 1982; Rumenik, Capasso, & Hendrick, 1977). Also not frequently reported is age of subject in topical areas where age may be influential. For example, menstrual problems appear to be age-related (Golub & Harrington, 1981). Clearly, such variables are important to control and need to be borne in mind when generalizations are made from research findings.

A major problem in many studies is the lack of an adequate control group (see Parlee, 1981). For example, female behavior during the menstrual cycle has been extensively studied but rarely compared to male behavior during a similar length of time. Stein & Yaworsky (1983) found no difference between males and females on a memory task assessed over a four-week period, which suggests, on this measure at least, that female behavior is not more variable than male behavior, despite female hormonal changes. Dan (1976) demonstrated that, although females increased their activity preceding ovulation, there were no differences between wives and husbands in overall variability of activities. Similarly, although Dalton (1969) found correlations between premenstrual phase and commission of certain asocial behaviors, such as crimes and suicide, these behaviors were still less common in females than in males.

Design

In addition to choosing subjects, researchers also choose one particular method or design to use in their research. Related problems in design are the lack of precise objective definitions of the behavior studied, selective perception of raters, and shifting anchor points. This last problem refers to the fact that we often evaluate male and female behavior differently. For example, what is seen as active for a boy may be different from what is seen as active for a girl. This may also depend on the rater (Maccoby & Jacklin, 1974; Rogers & Walsh, 1982). The use of different definitions of a behavior as a function of the sex of the ratee may also be a function of the sex of the rater. Imprecise measures of behavior may also limit a study's findings. Besides the premenstrual syndrome having various definitions, actual physiological measures of cycle phase have varied enormously from study to study, some relying on self-reports, others relying on varying physiological measurements taken at varying intervals (Parlee, 1973). The fact that the testosterone level has been difficult to measure in males may have contributed to the lack of attention paid to it (Hatton, 1977).

Three research designs used in studying sex differences have serious limitations (see Brannon, 1981; Grady, 1981; Unger, 1981, for a more detailed summary):

1. Correlation studies do not demonstrate causation, although they are frequently interpreted that way by unsophisticated readers and, at times, by researchers themselves. Thus, a correlation between anxiety and the premenstrual phase has led many to assume that hormones determine mood in females, although such a relation may be caused by a third variable such as expectation of amount of flow (Paige, 1971). The causation also may occur in the opposite direction. For example, anxiety can bring on menstruation (see Parlee, 1973).

2. Retrospective questionnaires suffer from reliance on an individual's memory. For example, Golub and Harrington (1981) and Parlee (1982) found complaints of mood impairment during or before menstruation by adolescent girls when mood was assessed retrospectively, but no evidence of such mood changes on scales given at the time menstruation actually occurred. Questionnaires may also selectively lead the respondent to provide certain information, for example, by asking only about negative mood changes as a function of menstrual phase.

3. Self-reports or observations have serious problems with people's need to respond in a socially desirable way. As an example, males may be reluctant to admit mood changes, because they contradict societal gender stereotypes. These methods also have a problem with selective perception or selective reporting by the respondent. For example, only negative mood changes may be observed or admitted in females, because that is the cultural and/or the experimental expectation (Koeske & Koeske, 1975; Ruble, 1977).

An important problem in all psychological research, especially in this area, is the effect on the results of the experimenter's beliefs. Robert Rosenthal (1966, Rosenthal & Jacobsen, 1968) has ingeniously demonstrated that in unconscious, nonverbal ways, experimenters can influence the outcome of an experiment to conform to the experimental hypotheses. Thus, in studies in which the experimenter expects to find moods varying with menstrual phase, she or he may indeed find them (Moos et al., 1969). Because most researchers have been male, they unconsciously may have misperceived certain situations with humans and animals to put males in the better light. For example, Harry Harlow's (1962, 1965) research with monkeys has contributed a great deal to our understanding of attachment behavior. But reading some of Harlow's observations of the behavior of monkeys sometimes resembles viewing a soap opera with females "scheming" and acting "helpless" and males acting "intelligently" and "strongly."

Using an appropriate baseline, or standard, when measuring sex differences is imperative but not frequently found. Thus, Parlee (1973) argues that an interpretation of a midcycle syndrome of positive traits and behaviors (that is, improved performance and feelings about oneself during the ovulatory period of the menstrual cycle) is as justifiable as a premenstrual syndrome of negative traits (that is, impaired performance and negative moods directly preceding menstruation). Such an interpretation has rarely been offered.

Interpretation

Statistical reporting and analysis are often a function of an experimenter's hypotheses and biases. To illustrate, although Dalton (1969) found that 27% of her female subjects got poorer grades before menstruation than at ovulation, she ignored the 56% who had no changes and the 17% who actually improved.

Another reporting problem arises in reviews such as those by Garai and Scheinfeld (1968) and Maccoby and Jacklin (1974). Although the studies that were reviewed varied greatly in quality, both reviews simply tabulated the results without giving greater emphasis to the better research. Therefore, a finding of a high percentage of studies reporting no difference in an area may be due to there being no difference, or it may be due to a large number of inadequate experiments. More use of the statistical technique of meta-analysis is needed in order to truly integrate the findings in this area. This technique provides us with two estimates: one of effect size and one of degree of variability. Because a sex difference can be significant in the statistical sense yet still unimportant in a practical sense, such estimates can provide much needed information. With increasing use of this technique in recent years, many of the findings cited in Maccoby and Jacklin have been qualified greatly (see Cooper, 1979; Eagly & Carli, 1981; Hyde, 1981; Linn & Petersen, 1983, for examples). Still, meta-analyses can include studies that may be inadequate on grounds previously mentioned.

Stephanie Shields (1975) has documented how interpretation of facts has sometimes deter-mined the facts themselves. When the frontal lobes of the brain were regarded as the main area of intellectual functioning, research studies found men had larger frontal lobes, relative to the parietal lobes, than did women. When parietal lobes were regarded as more important, the findings themselves changed. Men now were "found" to have relatively larger parietal lobes, relative to their frontal lobes, than did women. Today, there is no firm evidence of sex differences in brain structures or proportions, so interest has turned to sex differences in brain organization, following a predictable pattern. When men were thought to be less lateralized than women, that was thought to be superior. When men were thought to have more brain lateralization than women, that then was thought to be superior (see Alper, 1985; Star, 1979). As we will see in Chapters 2 and 3, the research on sex differences in brain lateralization is so confounded with methodological and interpretational problems that we cannot draw any meaningful conclusions at this point.

To summarize, in examining the studies on female and male behaviors and characteristics, one must be aware of the many research problems that can invalidate the results. Science is constructed by people, and people are never value-free or impervious to social forces. Therefore it is incumbent upon all researchers to understand the implications of such a "constructivist perspective" of science (Wittig, 1985a). With this caution in mind, we will examine the current findings.

2 Physical Characteristics

The examination of the differences and similarities between the sexes in the area of physical characteristics requires a clear understanding of some complicated physiological phenomena. How sex is determined needs to be understood, as do the specific areas in which sex differences have been found or suggested: anatomy, physiological processes, brain organization, physical vulnerability, and activity levels. Because some people cite biology as the ultimate justification for stereotypes such as "Boys will be boys" or "Girls are just naturally more passive than boys," it is necessary for us to understand just what is biologically "given" and how biology and the environment may interact.

Sex and Gender

To begin an examination of the physical differences between the sexes, it is important to understand the distinction between sex and gender. *Sex is a biological term*; people are termed either male or female depending on their sex organs and genes. *Gender is a psychological* and cultural term, referring to one's subjective feelings of maleness or femaleness (*gender identity*). Gender may also refer to society's evaluation of behavior as masculine or feminine (*gender role*). It is quite possible to be genetically of one sex with a gender identity of the other. Such may be the case of people born with ambiguous reproductive structures (anatomical *hermaphrodites*) or with other unusual physical conditions. A mismatch between sex and gender identity also occurs in *transsexuals*, who often report feeling "trapped in the wrong body" (Kessler & McKenna, 1978; Stoller, 1968). The degree to which a person identifies with societal definitions of "masculinity" or "femininity" is referred to as *gender role identity* or *sex typing*

(Spence & Sawin, 1985). It is possible, indeed common, for women and men to vary in their adoption of sex-typed characteristics. This is discussed in Chapter 1 with regard to research on androgyny.

The distinction between sex and gender, explored in the research of John Money and others (see Freimuth & Hornstein, 1982; Money & Ehrhardt, 1972) is important precisely because it points out that one's behavior—indeed, one's basic identity as a female or male—is not directly determined by one's genes or hormones; that is, by one's biological sex. Through the study of sexually anomalous individuals (people born with ambiguous sex organs or with organs that do not correspond to

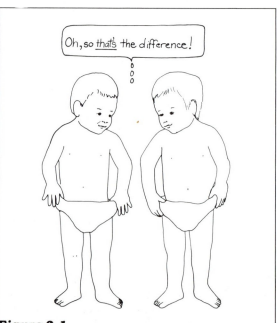

Figure 2-1 _____
The basic sex difference.

their genetic sex), it becomes clear that "the predominant part of gender-identity differentiation receives its program by way of *social transmission* from those responsible for the reconfirmation of the sex of assignment in the daily practices of rearing" (Money & Ehrhardt, 1972, p. 4, italics added). That is, a person's gender identity, for the most part, conforms to the sex according to which the parents rear that person, regardless of the person's genes or hormones or sexual equipment. In fact, some researchers view gender as a completely social construction, independent of objective criteria (Kessler & McKenna, 1978; Rogers & Walsh, 1982; Sherif, 1982).

Note that what is referred to as "sex" is both an independent as well as a dependent variable (Unger, 1979); that is, people can be classified as either male or female and their behaviors explained as a function of this classification. This is a typical research paradigm. But one's sex also is something to which people respond differentially; thus gender-related behaviors may result from the expectations and/ or the behaviors of others. This social aspect of gender and its implications too often have been ignored by researchers in the field. The current trend is to use the term *gender* instead of *sex* to acknowledge the social construction of male and female roles. In this book, we will try to reserve the term "sex" for discussions of biological distinctions.

How sex can be viewed as a social construct will be clearer after examining the variables that determine one's biological sex. For most people, the determination of sex seems strikingly simple and obvious. The *obvious* refers to one's external genitalia. Other criteria are internal genitalia, hormones, and chromosomes. Although these indices are usually in concordance, in some cases they are not. It is these unusual cases, these sexual anomalies, that shed light on the process of sexual differentiation.

Chromosomes

Usually, two X chromosomes produce a female, and an X and a Y chromosome produce a male. This initial sex determination occurs at the moment of conception and remains the only difference between male and female fetuses until the sixth to eighth week after conception. At this time, the internal reproductive organs develop from an undifferentiated state. Generally, if a Y chromosome is present, the gonad (sex gland) of the fetus will develop into a testis; if a Y chromosome is not present, the gonad will develop into an ovary. Thus, the fetus is basically *bipotential*, capable of developing with male or female organs. Indeed, in one sense, the basic course of development is female in that female sex organs will develop unless a Y chromosome is present. This fact has led some writers (for example, Sherfey, 1974) to state that the fundamental form is female; males represent a deviation. To form a male, something must be added: in the first fetal stages, a Y chromosome; in the next stage of fetal development, the hormone androgen.

Besides the normal genetic patterns of XY for males and XX for females, anomalies occasionally occur in which individuals are produced with just one X chromosome (XO), three Xs (XXX), an extra Y (XYY or XXY), or other variations. Again, the presence or absence of the Y chromosome determines the development of the sex organs. A person with either an XYY- or an XXY-chromosome pattern will develop a testis, and an XO or an XXX person will develop an ovary.

Current endocrinological research suggests that the X chromosome is molecularly more information-packed than the Y chromosome (Gordon, 1983; Probber & Ehrman, 1978). However, it is not clear what this means, just as it is not clear what the exact influence of genes on behavior is. Indeed, research on genetic influence is quite controversial. We will continue to examine this topic in this and the next three chapters. What can be said here is that the fact that males typically have just one X chromosome makes them susceptible to any recessive X-linked disorder they might have inherited, such as color blindness and hemophilia. Females, having two X chromosomes, are usually protected by the second X chromosome from developing such recessive disorders. Of course, if both X chromosomes carry such an ailment, the female will also manifest the disorder. In other cases, however, the female will merely be a carrier of the disorder. This genetic process has been thought to account partially for males' greater physical vulnerability.

Hormones

Prenatally, hormones have been found to be extremely important in the sexual differentiation of a fetus. After the first six to eight weeks of embryonic development, the internal reproductive organs (testes or ovaries) develop in response to either the presence or absence of the Y chromosome. Once these organs develop, hormone production begins, and further differentiation of the fetus occurs. Figure 2-2 shows the ensuing sexual differentiation.

During the third prenatal month, if the hormone testosterone (one of the androgens) is produced, the male external organs (urethral tube, scrotum, and penis) and the male ducts

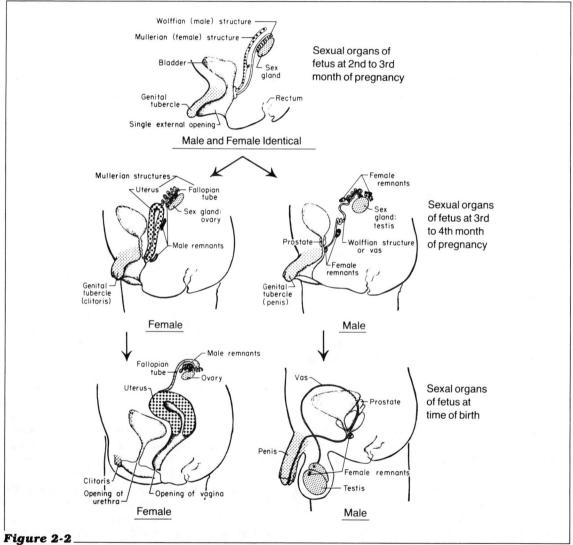

Figure 2-2

Sexual differentiation in the human fetus. Note the early parallelism of sex organs. From Man and Woman, Boy and Girl, *by J. Money and A. A. Ehrhardt. Copyright 1972 by The Johns Hopkins University Press. Reprinted by permission.*

(seminal vesicles, vas deferens, and ejaculatory ducts) will develop, and the female ducts will regress. If testosterone is not produced, female sex organs (labia minora, labia majora, and clitoris) and female ducts (uterus, fallopian tubes, and upper vagina) will develop, and male ducts will regress. Once again, unless something is added—in this case, the hormone testosterone—female structures will develop. Anatomical development of the female fetus does not seem to require any special hormones (Gordon, 1983; McCoy, 1977). The critical period for this development occurs between the second and third prenatal months.

If hormone production or hormone sensitivity is impaired, or hormones are externally administered to the mother during this critical period, an infant with sexual anomalies may develop (Hines, 1982; Money & Ehrhardt, 1972). Thus if a genetically female fetus is exposed to androgens, structural development will proceed along male lines; that is, male external sex organs will develop. This occurs in the *adrenogenital syndrome*, caused by excessive fetal androgen production signaled by an abnormally functioning adrenocortical gland, and in *progestin-induced hermaphroditism*. This latter disorder arises in some cases in which the mother is given the synthetic hormone progestin early in pregnancy to avert the danger of a miscarriage. Conversely, if a genetically male fetus is deprived of the androgens either through an inherited androgen insensitivity or through a metabolic error, a female system will be produced. From these cases it is clear that genes only predispose, not guarantee, the development of the corresponding reproductive structures.

During the critical period for the differentiation of the external sex organs, another major differentiating development occurs, at least in animals, in response to the presence or absence of testosterone (Gordon, 1983; Money & Ehrhardt, 1972). This differentiation is in the brain in the area called the *hypothalamus*. This region is located at the base of the brain and controls the release of hormones at puberty by the attached pituitary gland. When testosterone is present during this prenatal period, the pituitary will function at puberty to cause a regular production of androgens and sperm. The presence of testosterone causes the pituitary gland to function at puberty with low levels of continuous hormone release. When testosterone is absent during the prenatal period, the pituitary will function at puberty to cause high levels of cyclical hormonal activity, which result in ovulation and menstruation. These differences in pattern of hormone production do not appear until the full functioning of the pituitary gland at puberty, yet the patterns seem to be set during the second to third month of gestation. The effect on performance and emotions of such differences in hormonal patterns is negligible in most cases and unclear in others (see "Physiological Processes" below). Again, hormonal errors during this critical period of gestation will affect pituitary functioning at puberty unless corrective hormones are administered after birth. It must be emphasized, however, that most of the evidence for brain differentiation is based on work with animals. Such differentiation in humans remains speculative at this time.

According to the above information, after eight weeks male and female fetuses can be differentiated by hormonal production. After birth, however, and until the child is about eight years old, hormonal production is negligible. Hormones, therefore, do not differentiate the sexes during this period. At puberty there is an increased production of all sex hormones in both sexes. Males generally have a greater increase in androgen production than do females, and the production of androgens becomes fairly regular and continuous. Females generally have a greater increase in estrogen and progesterone production at this time than do males, and this production becomes cyclic (the menstrual cycle). Hormones at this time result in the development of the secondary sex characteristics, such as facial and ancillary hair, enlarged genitals, and deeper voice in males, and development of breasts and menstruation in females.

It is important to note that these hormone differences are not absolute. Both sexes have all the hormones, are receptive to all the hormones, and, as is the case with most other human attributes, individuals differ greatly in the relative amounts and proportion of the sex hormones they possess. An overlapping normal curve distribution for all hormones demonstrates that some genetic females may have more androgen than some genetic males, at least some of the time. Distinctions between the sexes based on hormonal production are proportional, not absolute (Briscoe, 1978; Gordon, 1983; Money & Ehrhardt, 1972).

The effects of prenatal hormones on later behavior is a subject of great debate. A recent hypothesis put forward by Norman Geschwind (in Marx, 1982) is that excess testosterone or unusual sensitivity to testosterone during fetal life can affect brain anatomy and consequently can affect a variety of later behaviors including left-handedness, dyslexia, immune system disorders, and mathematical genius, all apparently found more often in males. Some support for this hypothesis has been found (see Kolata, 1983), but it is too soon to call this hypothesis anything but speculative.

Another suggestive line of research has investigated the relationship between testosterone concentration and personality traits (Baucom, Besch, & Callahan, 1985). At this time, it appears that prenatal hormones, by affecting certain areas of the brain, may influence the ease with which certain behaviors (such as nurturant behaviors and rough-and-tumble play) are acquired. The behaviors themselves would still be markedly affected by environmental factors (DeBold & Luria, 1983; Ehrhardt, 1985; Money, 1978; Reinisch & Karow, 1977). However, even this seemingly interactionist statement has been contested by some (Briscoe, 1978; Hines, 1982; Rogers, 1983; Rogers & Walsh, 1982). Because hormones, as well as genes, can never be fully separated from environmental and sociocultural factors, at least in humans, we never can know the "pure" effects of hormones or genes.

Genitalia—Internal and External

The external sex organs are the primary means by which sex is determined at birth. Males have an external penis and scrotum; females, a clitoris and vagina. Until the second to third month of pregnancy, however, the external genitalia, as well as the internal reproductive organs and tracts, are in an undifferentiated state

(see Figure 2-2). Differentiation begins during the second to third month as a result of the presence or absence of the Y chromosome, which determines the internal organ development. Differentiation then proceeds during the third month as a function of the presence or absence of the hormone testosterone, which determines the external organ development. At each stage, development can go either way— toward the male form or toward the female form. That is, development is bipotential.

This bipotentiality continues at birth. With the doctor's pronouncement, based on external genitalia, that the infant is a boy or a girl, two different patterns of infant-adult interactions begin. These differentiating behaviors can be observed in the giving of blue or pink blankets, in the naming and handling of the infant, and in verbalizations to the infant. Again, it is the sexually anomalous individual who sheds light on the development of gender identity. Studies of hermaphrodites, pseudo-hermaphrodites (those born with external genitalia of the other sex), and children who suffered from surgical accidents that affected their genitals (for example, damage to the penis during circumcision) vividly demonstrate that the single most important variable in the development of gender identity is the sex of assignment; that is, the sex one's parents raise one to be (Money & Ehrhardt, 1972). This influence can override other influences of genes, hormones, and external organs and demonstrates very fundamentally how plastic and malleable is human behavior.

A striking example of the bipotentiality of the human infant is the case of identical twin boys, one whose penis was severely injured by an electrical needle during circumcision (Money & Ehrhardt, 1972). Rather than attempt reconstructive surgery, which would have been complicated and time consuming and would have had a low probability of success, the doctors recommended that the boy be given an artifical vagina, which was a simpler operation, and be raised as a girl. The parents agreed, and follow-up studies at ages 5–6 showed the two children to be clearly differentiated in terms of activities, toy preferences, and mannerisms as a result of different child-rearing practices. In fact, these children were more clearly differentiable than are most girls and boys. However, genetic and prenatal hormonal effects on behavior cannot be dismissed: a report from the girl's psychiatrist in 1982 describes a very gender-confused adolescent (Diamond, 1982). There may be many nonbiological reasons for such confusion, not the least of which may be knowledge of what happened to her after birth, but it behooves us to be properly open-minded until research findings are more conclusive.

As for other stages of development, there appears to be a critical period for the postnatal development of gender identity—up to 18 months or the time the child acquires language (Money & Ehrhardt, 1972). This identity becomes consolidated by ages 3 to 4, depending on the consistency of child-rearing experiences. Any attempt to change sex assignment after a child has acquired language is usually unsuccessful and may lead to later emotional problems. It is interesting, in this regard, that transsexuals do not seem to have formed a gender identity of their biological sex at this stage. Whether this deficit is due to parental upbringing, to rigid societal gender stereotypes, or possibly to a prenatally determined predisposition is unclear at this time (Finney, Brandsma, Tondoro, & Lemaistre, 1975; Money & Ehrhardt, 1972; Raymond, 1979).

Having detailed the differentiation of sex in a fetus and in an infant and examined some problems that may arise, it remains to be emphasized that for the vast majority of infants all physiological sex characteristics are in agreement. That is, most babies with female external genitalia also have female internal genitalia, have an XX chromosome pattern, and will produce a preponderance of female sex hormones at puberty. Of these indicators, the external genitalia are the most important because they determine the sex of assignment. It is the sex of assignment that has been found critical in determining an individual's gender identity.

The research in this area has two major implications. The first is that research that searches for simple biological reasons for sex-role stereotypes is misdirected. Given the enormous plasticity of human behavior and the fact that biological and environmental factors never can be fully separated in humans, the question of whether any particular behavior or trait is caused by nature or nurture is unanswerable. Indeed, the nature/nurture question is moot in the area of gender development as well as in virtually all aspects of human functioning. What is in question is the relative weights of the experiential and physiological influences. Money's studies (1963, 1978; Money & Ehrhardt, 1972) demonstrate that postnatal experiential factors can override prenatal, physiological ones in the majority of cases. Although Money's research has been criticized as biased and methodologically flawed, his conclusion regarding the overriding influence of sociocultural factors has been supported (Rogers & Walsh, 1982).

The second implication is that human beings are bipotential in their psychosexual identity and behavior at each stage of development. Which path (male or female) is followed at each stage depends on both the internal and external environment. A fetus can develop male or female gonads, depending on its chromosomes; male or female external genitalia and possibly brain (hypothalamic) differentiation, depending on its hormones; and a male or female gender identity, depending on sex of assignment. There is a critical period for each stage of development to occur, after which the male or female path is relatively fixed. The sex of the infant usually is fixed by birth; its gender, by 18 months. After this time, people ordinarily do not change their image of themselves as male or female, although what traits and behaviors are implied by those terms may change. What is important to note is that even on a biological level, many sex differences are differences in degree, not kind (Freimuth & Hornstein, 1982). On a behavioral level, this is even more the case.

Physical Functioning

Some physical differences do exist between the sexes, although their implication for behavior is unclear and many differences are culturally determined. First let us examine the findings. We will look specifically at anatomy, physiological processes, brain organization, physical vulnerability, and activity levels. Remember: there is a tremendous amount of overlap in virtually all human traits and characteristics.

Anatomy

Clearly, the most basic difference between the sexes at birth lies in their external genitalia. These organs usually determine the sex of assignment, and some writers, especially Freud, think they determine the personality structure of the child as well ("anatomy is destiny"; see Chapter 5). Although the possibility of getting pregnant, as opposed to impregnating, probably has meaningful consequences for one's personality, these consequences will surely vary with the individual, the family, the culture, and other external forces to such a degree that a mere deterministic explanation is simply untenable.

The sexes also typically differ in size and weight at birth, males generally being slightly larger, although these differences are minimal until age 13 or 14. Indeed, because female puberty begins two years earlier than male puberty on the average, for two years girls generally surpass boys in height and weight (Monagan, 1983). Females have a wider pelvic outlet, narrower shoulders, less cardiovascular power, and tend to have a greater body fat-to-muscle ratio than do boys at all ages (Hatton, 1977; McDonald, 1984). These differences all increase significantly during and after puberty and contribute to males generally having more strength, more ease in running and overarm throwing, less flexibility, and poorer ability to float and withstand cold. These are average differences, of course, and may also be a function of athletic training.

Training and experience have been found to eliminate sex differences in many physical and athletic endeavors. Hall and Lee (1984) found that after one or more years in a coeducational physical education program, prepubescent girls and boys performed at similar levels on most physical fitness test items. Improvement by girls over the years was significant, and by the last year of testing, girls actually performed better than same-age boys from the previous two years. Similarly, the army found in 1977 that, when 825 women were given regular basic training and compared to men, there was little difference in relative performance ("Arms," 1977). Another example of the effect of training is the fact that between 1970 and 1982, women's best performance in the marathon run improved by a little over 20% whereas the men's record improved by .1%. In the 1983 Boston Marathon, Joan Benoit's women's world-record time would have beaten the 1961 male winner in the race.

These relative differences in size and strength may have accounted for certain sex-role distinctions in the past or resulted from such distinctions, such as certain forms of hunting that required strength. However, they certainly have little importance in our modern technological society. Most work that formerly required brute strength is now performed with the aid of equipment, levers, and push buttons.

Physiological Processes

Generally, females mature faster than males. This difference can be observed as early as the seventh week of embryonic life and continues through puberty. Girls also tend to have a slightly lower metabolic rate and consume fewer calories than do boys. After puberty, boys tend to have greater respiratory volume and higher systolic blood pressure than do girls. It currently is debatable as to which sex is capable of more physical endurance, males with their better ability to use oxygen, or females with their extra fat, more efficient heat regulatory system, and higher amounts of estrogen that may increase blood circulation (McDonald, 1984; Monagan, 1983).

There do not seem to be major sex differences in sensation, although females may have a slight edge in sensitivity to touch and pain (McGuinness & Pribram, 1978; Maccoby & Jacklin, 1974; Reinisch, Gandelman, & Spiegel, 1979; "Women have," 1984). Females after puberty also seem to have a more acute sense of smell than do men, perhaps due to their higher estrogen level. Most research finds no differences in vision or audition (Maccoby & Jacklin, 1974), although work with electrical potentials in the brain suggests that women may be more sensitive to visual stimuli (Goleman, 1978).

One major process in which the sexes do differ is in hormonal functioning and production after puberty. Differences occur in actual hormone levels, in the pattern of secretion, in the sensitivity to particular hormones, and in the sources of hormone production (gonads or adrenals). Males tend to have continuous androgen secretion; females have cyclical hormonal fluctuations as part of the menstrual cycle. The different patterns of hormonal production represent reproductive fertility for the adolescent and result in the development of secondary sex characteristics (for example, facial hair in males, breast development in females).

Menstrual Cycle.   The menstrual cycle has been the focus of much research and will consequently be described in some detail. The beginning of the cycle, which averages 28 days but which may range from 15 to 45 days, is usually set at the day menstruation begins. From that time, estrogen production increases to a high point around the 12th day. During this first part of the cycle, the lining of the uterus thickens to prepare it to receive the fertilized egg. On the basis of a 28-day cycle, an egg is released from an ovary around the 14th day and travels down a fallopian tube to the uterus. During its transit, if the egg encounters a sperm, it will most likely become fertilized. The fertilized egg will then become embedded in the

thickened lining of the uterus. If fertilization does not occur, estrogen production decreases, and production of progesterone increases. Both hormones drop precipitously a few days before actual menstruation (the shedding of the uterine lining) begins. A new cycle then starts. Figure 2-3 charts the hormonal changes for one average 28-day cycle, although it should be emphasized that such an "average" cycle occurs in no more than 16% of the female population (Ryan, 1975).

These hormonal changes that occur during the menstrual cycle may be related to some physical changes, but there are large individual differences in this area. Most common are reports of fluid retention and slight weight gain premenstrually and increased basal temperature and smell acuity around ovulation (Dan, 1979; Hatton, 1977). Ruble (1977) has found, however, that even physical-symptom reports can be heavily affected by psychosocial factors. She found that, by misleading college undergraduates as to their actual cycle phase, she could obtain reports of severe physical symptoms, such as water retention and pain, if the subjects believe they were premenstrual, even though they were not really in that phase. Thus, learned associations or beliefs could lead a woman to exaggerate or overstate a feeling.

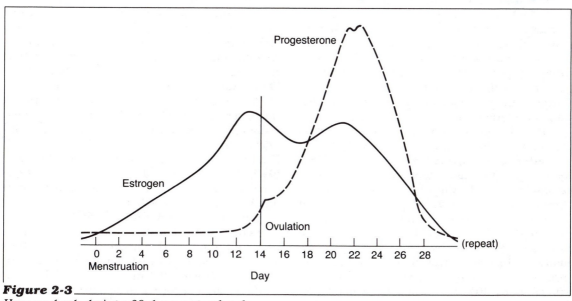

Figure 2-3

Hormone levels during a 28-day menstrual cycle.

Such results must temper any conclusions based on self-report data regarding the magnitude of menstrual-related changes as well as the physiological bases of such changes.

Much attention has been paid to the psychological changes, especially of mood, thought to be associated with the menstrual cycle. These supposed changes, including anxiety, irritability, unrest, and depression, were called the *premenstrual syndrome* (or PMS) by Dr. Katharina Dalton in 1948. PMS has received much recent attention because of its use as a legal defense for murder, especially in England (Sommer, 1984). However, its existence as a syndrome has been severely questioned, because research on this topic has suffered from serious deficiencies in definition, measurement, design, and interpretation (Hopson & Rosenfeld, 1984; Parlee, 1973, 1982). Some females do experience an increase in anxiety premenstrually, although such anxiety seems related more to the amount of the anticipated flow and to expectations than to the hormone levels themselves (Paige, 1971; Parlee, 1982). Some females do experience an increase in hostility levels premenstrually that may be related to the amount of a certain chemical, monoamine oxidase (MAO) in the blood (Ward, Dworkin, Powers-Alexander, & Dowd, 1983). (MAO increases with progesterone levels and has been implicated in certain affective disorders.) Negative mood changes also may be due to lowered progesterone levels and/or lowered endorphin (a natural brain opiate) levels (Briscoe, 1978; Hopson & Rosenfeld, 1984). Other personality changes that occur during the cycle appear to be exaggerations of existing traits and can occur at any time of the month, not just premenstrually (Landers, 1977). Furthermore, many studies do not find mood changes as a function of the menstrual cycle at all (for example, Golub & Harrington, 1981), and some find changes opposite to those expected (for example, Parlee, 1982). Indeed, the only general statement that can be made is that all females do not show similar changes with reference to their menstrual cycle; rather, they show only those consistent with the individual's own behavior pattern.

More to the point, the variability of moods in females has not been found significantly different from the variability of moods in males matched for lifestyles. Dan (1976) found that, when husbands and wives kept track of their daily moods over a period of months, there were no significant differences in moods between spouses. This occurred even though the wives were experiencing hormonal changes related to their menstrual cycle. Indeed, environmental events and social variables have been found to account for more of the variance in mood than does cycle point (Good & Smith, 1980; Landers, 1977).

Despite the preceding facts, both men and women in Western cultures do believe that negative moods are related to the premenstrual phase and attribute and interpret such moods accordingly (Clarke & Ruble, 1978; Curtis, 1981; Koeske & Koeske, 1975; Ruble, Boggiano, & Brooks-Gunn, 1982). This expectation may become a self-fulfilling prophecy, either creating the moods themselves or causing them to be more noticed. Positive moods, because they are not expected, may pass unnoticed, thereby preventing disproof of the belief. This negative expectation regarding menstruation is culturally determined. As cross-cultural researchers have discovered (for example, Sanday, 1981a), menstruation is viewed quite positively in a number of cultures.

Besides moods, the menstrual cycle also has been thought to affect behavior. In particular, premenstrual women have been thought to perform more poorly on cognitive tasks than women in other cycle phases, and than men. However, empirical research has failed to support this belief (Curtis, 1981; Stein & Yaworsky, 1983). Interestingly, some women think they perform more poorly, which again may be a function of the stereotypes surrounding menstruation.

The effect of the menstrual cycle on women's sexual desires and activity is also complicated by expectations, but only heterosexual women have been investigated. It has been found that heterosexual women's sexual desires appear to peak around ovulation for all but two groups of women: those taking oral contraceptives, suggesting a hormonal link, and those using the rhythm method of birth control, suggesting a psychological factor (Adams, Gold, & Burt, 1978). Gold and Adams (1981) also found a peak of sexual activity postmenstrually, around cycle day 8, probably as a result of sexual abstinence. Because increases in estrogen and androgen occur after that time, hormone levels cannot account for such activity.

Androgens have been associated with increased libido, or sexual desire, and increased erotic reactivity, but this is true for both females and males (Money & Ehrhardt, 1972; Rosenberg & Sutton-Smith, 1972) and is not a consistent finding even in animals (M. Rosenberg, 1973). To the extent that males, on the average, have larger amounts of androgen than females, some may argue that the male sex drive is greater. As will be discussed in Chapter 5, human sexuality is so much a function of learning and of social forces that a simple, biologically deterministic approach would be completely inappropriate. In addition, it is worthwhile to repeat that individuals differ in androgen levels and the distributions for females and males overlap.

The interest in the hormonal cycle and its correlates in females has obscured the fact that cycles are a part of all living things, and that both males and females have similar hormonal endowment and a pattern of cyclical secretion of sex hormones (Briscoe, 1978; Hatton, 1977). This neglect of males is evidence of how societal stereotypes (males are "unemotional" and "rock-steady") may affect the questions researchers ask. Because males have no external indication of cycles like menstruation, such questions have been easy to ignore. Those few studies that have examined this area have indicated that male behavioral and mood variability does exist, but its determinants and pattern are unclear (Dan, 1976; Doering, Brodie, Kramer, Becker, & Hamburg, 1974; Petersen, 1979). Testosterone levels, correlated with aggression in some animals, do not have a clear causative effect and, in some cases, may be a result of aggressive behavior (Rose, Gordon, & Bernstein, 1972). In humans, the findings regarding the effects of hormones on males have been mixed (Doering et al., 1974; Ramey, 1973). In one recent study of adolescents, the effect of hormones on behavior appeared to be stronger for boys than for girls ("Teen," 1985). The clearest statement that currently can be made is that further study is needed.

In sum, hormones have complicated effects on humans, and hormonal activity constantly interacts with social and psychological factors. Individual differences in moods and behavior are the norm, and this is true for males as well as females—even for such hormonally influenced events as menstruation, pregnancy, postparturition, and menopause (Bram, 1983; Howell, 1981; Notman, 1981).

Brain Organization

Since 1974, research has accumulated suggesting that men's brains may be organized differently from women's for certain tasks and activities. It had previously been suggested that each side of the brain was specialized and functioned differently. Language and language-related skills were thought of as being contained in the left hemisphere; nonverbal and spatial skills, in the right hemisphere. More recent research suggests that although this may be true for most right-handed men, it does not seem true for left-handed individuals or for many women (Bryden, 1979, 1983; Hines, 1982; Kupke, Lewis, & Rennick, 1979; McGlone, 1980).

For right-handed individuals, a sex difference in perceptual asymmetry appears fairly regularly. Using both visual and auditory modalities, more males than females tend to have their verbal abilities primarily in their left hemisphere, and their spatial abilities primarily in their right hemisphere. For more females than males, however, performance of verbal and spatial tasks seems to involve *both* hemispheres. This does not mean that females are less lateralized than are males, as some researchers have concluded. Rather, the difference is in the distribution of left- and right-hempispheric receptive processes, not in their magnitude. For example, whereas 90% of right-handed males show a right-side advantage (showing left-hemispheric activity) for verbal materials, only 80% of right-handed females show right-side advantage (Bryden, 1983). As a result of such asymmetries, females may have greater flexibility between hemispheres (Jorgenson, Davis, Opella, & Angerstein, 1979; Witelson, 1976), a hypothesis supported by recent findings of a sex difference in the size of the corpus callusum, a part of the brain that connects the two hemispheres. De Lacoste-Utamsing and Holloway (1982) report that this brain part is 40% larger in women than men. More females than males also may have bilateral representation of language functions, although this is not firmly established (Bryden, 1983; McGlone, 1980).

These differences in brain organization may be genetic, or they may be influenced by different prenatal sex hormones (Bryden, 1979; Carter & Greenough, 1979; Hines, 1982; Hines & Shipley, 1984; Marx, 1982). Such differences in genes and/or hormones themselves may reflect a long historical adaptation to sociocultural mandates. However, it is not known whether sex differences in laterality are present at birth or develop over time. There is some evidence supporting the latter possibility (Turkewitz & Ross-Kossak, 1984). Therefore, it is possible that sex differences in brain functioning result from differential socialization practices (Petersen, 1982). Even if such differences are somehow inherent from birth, differential treatment still will drastically affect the development of each sex. In particular, socialization appears to influence the type of cognitive strategies each sex develops. These strategies may then interact with cerebral organization to cause different patterns of behavior (Bryden, 1979; Star, 1979).

The finding of small sex differences in brain organization is still tentative and may prove a result of methodological problems. Furthermore, the implications of the findings are unclear. Differences in brain organization may contribute to sex differences in verbal, mathematical, and visual-spatial skills, which are discussed in the next chapter, and to sex differences in discerning emotions, discussed in Chapter 4. However, it should be kept in mind that all such differences are average differences, not absolute ones, and, as the percentages in Bryden's (1983) research reveal, focusing on differences obscures the basic similarities between the sexes. Because of the relatively small intersex variation in cognitive function, and the lack of an adequate theory to explain such a small variation, Alper (1985) argues that focusing on sex differences in brain asymmetry cannot lead to significant scientific progress in understanding either sex differences or brain functioning.

Physical Vulnerability

Another physical area that has been thought to differentiate the sexes is physical vulnerability. At every stage of life, males, particularly Black males, are more vulnerable than are females to disease, physical disorders, and death (Cordes, 1985; J. Harrison, 1978). The life span of females is nearly universally longer than that of males. In the United States in 1980, the average female life span for Whites was 78.1 years and for others, 73.6; the average male life span for Whites was 70.7 and for others, 65.3 (U.S. Dept. of Commerce, 1984). In 1900, the average life span for women and men was 48.3 and 46.3 years, respectively. Although the X and Y sperm appear to be produced in equal numbers, between 108 and 140 males are conceived for every 100 females. At birth, the ratio of males to females in the United States is reduced to between 103 and 106 to 100. In India the ratio is 98 males to 100 females. This lower birth rate of males is accounted for by the fact that four times as many males as females are miscarried or stillborn and that 54% more males than females die of birth injury. Of those born, 18% more male infants have congenital malformations than do female infants. In the first year of life, more male than female babies die: 44% more for Whites, 28% more for Blacks (U.S. Dept. of Commerce, 1984). By ages 20 to 25, females outnumber males in the United States (Hatton, 1977), and the differences increase with age: After age 65, there are about 150 women to 100 men. These ratios fluctuate as a function of societal changes. (See Guttentag & Secord, 1983, for an interesting discussion of this point.)

Males are more vulnerable than females to a wide range of physical handicaps that are genetically linked. As was previously discussed, because males have one X chromosome, if that chromosome carries genes related to any one of a possible 62 specific recessive disorders, ranging from hemophilia to color blindness, males will manifest it. Females, with a second X chromosome to balance out the abnormal one, would not develop the disorder. Males are also more susceptible to degenerative and infectious diseases and to death from them.

Males also show a greater incidence than

females of a wide range of developmental problems, ranging from enuresis to minimal brain damage and autism. Stuttering is two to ten times as common among males; reading disabilities are four to six times as common, depending on how *disability* is defined, to cite two examples (Harris, 1977; Maccoby & Jacklin, 1974).

In examining the major causes of death in 1972, James Harrison (1978) found that in four of the five major causes—the four being diseases of the heart, malignant neoplasms, accidents, and influenza and pneumonia—the death rate for males exceed the death rate for females. Only in deaths from cerebrovascular diseases (the third most frequent cause) did the rate of female deaths exceed that of males. The 1980 data presented in Table 2-1 show an identical pattern. In addition, certain other causes of death show a strikingly high male-to-female death ratio: homicide caused the death of nearly four times more males than females; suicide resulted in the death of more than three times more males; bronchitis, emphysema, and asthma killed more than two times more males, and diseases of the liver took nearly twice as many males.

This greater physical vulnerability of males goes against one of our most basic stereotypes—that of the strong male and weak female. Perhaps the stereotype needs to be restricted to muscular strength, although muscle strength is distributed normally in the population, indicating that some females are stronger than some males. Perhaps the stereotype refers to the greater strength surviving males must have over their less fortunate brothers. Or perhaps the stereotype of strength is a cognitive defense against this very vulnerability.

It is important to examine possible explanations for this difference in physical vulnerability. It has been suggested that, because the basic fetus is female and something—chromosome and gonadal hormones—must be added to make the fetus male, more can go wrong with the developing male embryo (Barfield, 1976; Money & Ehrhardt, 1972; Reinisch et al., 1979). Other evidence suggests that female hormones may be protective. Risk of heart disease, for example, increases in females as estrogen decreases (Barfield, 1976); progesterone has anticonvulsive properties (Oakley, 1972). It may be that ability to withstand infection is transmitted via the X chromosome or that females' lower metabolic rate contributes to their superior capacity for survival (Hatton, 1977; McCoy, 1977).

Another possible explanation for superior female survival is that males may be more active, more subject to stress, and therefore more likely to have accidents, to be exposed to germs, to die of stress-related diseases, and to be victims of war. We shall see in the next section that the research on exploratory behav-

Table 2-1

Major Causes of Death (1980 Data)

	Percentage of All Deaths	Ratio of Males to Females
Diseases of the heart	38.3	1.21
Malignant neoplasms	20.9	1.25
Cerebrovascular disease	9.6	0.74
Accidents	5.3	2.59
Bronchitis, emphysema, and asthma	2.8	2.34
Influenza and pneumonia	2.7	1.08
Diabetes mellitus	1.8	0.74
Cirrhosis, diseases of the liver	1.5	1.94
Arteriosclerosis	1.5	0.69
Suicide	1.4	3.38
Homicide	1.2	3.84
Certain causes in infancy	1.1	1.42

From U.S. Department of Commerce, 1984.

ior does not support the explanation that boys are more active than girls simply because of biology. Nonetheless, it is true that male children are usually allowed more freedom of movement than are females and often are encouraged to take risks and be more aggressive, thereby increasing their exposure to accidents and illnesses.

J. Harrison (1978) and others (Jourard, 1971; Perry, 1982) have asserted that it is the male sex role itself that is dangerous to men's health. The emphasis on conformity to the male role and on achievement may give rise to anxiety about failing. This anxiety may lead to the development of certain compensatory behaviors that are health hazardous. Examples include taking risks, exhibitions of violence, smoking, and excessive consumption of alcohol. Other aspects of the male role encourage the development of aggressive, competitive behaviors, also known as Type A, or coronary-prone behaviors. Research has shown that Type A personality traits are significantly correlated with measures of instrumental (stereotypically masculine) traits (Blascovich, Major, & Katkin, 1981; DeGregorio & Carver, 1980; Grimm & Yarnold, 1985). Additional stress may occur because males are expected not to show their emotions and therefore must suppress most feelings. All of these patterns would lead to the major causes of death listed in Table 2-1. In fact, Waldron (1976) has estimated that three-quarters of the difference in life expectancy between males and females (currently about eight years) can be attributed to behaviors related to sex role. One-third to one-half of the difference is due to smoking alone. For Black males, there is the added stress of racism.

Thus we see an example of the negative effects of our socialization practices on males. Indeed, as females begin to experience many of the same stresses and behaviors that males do, like smoking, their susceptibility to stress-related diseases also increases (Barfield, 1976; Waldron, 1976). As an example, 15% of both teenage girls and boys now smoke, and in the last three decades deaths from lung cancer among women have increased fivefold (compared to a twofold increase among men), because women have taken up the smoking habits of men (M. Unger, 1984; U.S. Bureau of the Census, 1982).

Some of the differences in physical vulnerability probably reflect aspects of Western society. Yet not all; across a variety of cultures with different stresses, males still seem to die earlier and have a greater incidence of chromosomal abnormalities than do females (Fitzgerald, 1977). It seems likely that a biological predisposition interacts with social factors in unclear ways to make males more physically vulnerable.

Activity Levels

Studies investigating the amount of activity shown by male and female infants have been plagued by methodological problems, an example being the definition and measurement of activity, and thus have produced inconsistent results (Maccoby & Jacklin, 1974; McCoy, 1977). Generally, females and males during infancy evidence equal amounts of total activity; but males show more large body movements, and females show more refined and limited movements. This difference in type of movement may be due to the differing rates of maturation of females and males.

Male infants tend to be more fretful and wakeful than females. Although in some cases this tendency may be a result of more male birth problems or the effects of circumcision (Barfield, 1976; Maccoby & Jacklin, 1974), a well-controlled study by Phillips, King, and DuBois (1978) found a similar disparity between female and male fretfulness. During the two days following birth, 14 uncircumcised males and 15 females matched for physical and demographic variables were observed, and males evidenced significantly higher levels of wakefulness, facial grimacing, and low-intensity motor activity (hand and foot movements) than did females. This difference in fretfulness has implications for parent/infant interactions, because an infant's irritability may lead to decreased parental contact (Lewis & Weinraub, 1979; Segal & Yahraes, 1978). Research on parent/infant interaction is unclear, but it does suggest another way biology and culture may interact.

As children and adolescents, males tend to be slightly more active than females in regard to participation in rough-and-tumble play and physical exertion (Maccoby & Jacklin, 1974;

Tauber, 1979). This is true of other primates as well (Harlow, 1962, 1965). Females are also active but in different activities—for example, playing house and hopscotch—thus making a quantitative distinction difficult (Fitzgerald, 1977). Such differences may be a function more of socialization than of hormones.

Some writers suggest that androgen may be involved in activity levels. This involvement is indicated by the increased display of tomboy behavior (more physical activity) in females who experienced prenatal androgen produced either internally, as in the adrenogenital syndrome, or externally, as when the mother is given progestin to avoid a miscarriage (Ehrhardt, 1985; Money & Ehrhardt, 1972). Because masculinization of the genitals also occurs in some of these cases, it is possible that the parents of these children may have expected more such behaviors in these girls, thereby subtly reinforcing them. In support of this interpretation is Hine's (1982) conclusion from a review of the literature that when research involved individuals who were exposed to unusual hormones prenatally but who were born without physical abnormalities, many studies failed to find evidence of "masculinized" play comparable to that reported for androgenized girls. Additionally, because most females engage in tomboy behaviors (estimates range from 51% to 78%, according to Hyde, Rosenberg, & Behrman, 1977), the use of this index to define a "masculine" activity pattern is highly questionable. Indeed, some recent writers have taken issue with the definitions Money and his colleagues used to determine "masculine" play styles (for example, girls not wearing dresses), as well as these researchers' methods of data collection and use of control groups (Hines, 1982; Rogers & Walsh, 1982). In conclusion, the role of prenatal androgen in activity level and style still is unclear, but the evidence points strongly to the more important role of socialization (Ehrhardt, 1985).

Summary

The physical underpinnings of gender stereotypes are complex. We have seen that even sex differentiation is not simple. It occurs in stages, first influenced by chromosomes, then by hormones prenatally, then by genitalia and socialization postnatally. At each stage, the developing fetus is bipotential; that is, it can develop along either female or male lines. Furthermore, differences between the sexes even on a physical level are usually differences in degree, not differences in kind. The most critical factor in gender identity (one's concept of oneself as a male or a female) is culture, which can override the biological factors, as demonstrated in cases of sexual anomalies. We need not argue about nature or nurture. It is logical that an interaction occurs, with nature possibly predisposing, and nurture either reinforcing or contradicting that predispostion. Most of the research evidence is consistent with this interactionist position.

This interaction is true in the areas of physical functioning as well. Although, on the average, males tend to be bigger and stronger than females, nutrition and athletic training can decrease the gap. In physiological processes, females tend to mature faster and are slightly more sensitive to touch and maybe to smell than males, and they have cyclical hormonal fluctuations after puberty. The consequences of these differences are dependent on socialization and societal expectations, as depicted clearly in the research on menstrual cycle and the lack of research on male cycles. Particular mental functions may be organized more specifically in some male brains than in some female brains. Males tend to be more physically vulnerable to disease, death, and physical disorders than females, although these differences also can be affected by the environment. Differences in activity levels may exist but these, too, depend on the environment and the researcher's definition of activity.

In summary, the only "basic irreducible element of sex differences which no culture can eradicate, at least not on a large scale, [are that] women can menstruate, gestate, and lactate, and men cannot" (Money & Ehrhardt, 1972, p. 14). For their part, men can impregnate, and women cannot. The explanation for nearly all other human behaviors is "not in our genes" (see Lewontin, Rose, & Kamin, 1984).

Recommended Reading

Alper, J. S. (1985). Sex differences in brain asymmetry: A critical analysis. *Feminist Studies, 11,* 7–37. An excellent review of the current research on sex differences in cognitive functioning. Emphasis is on the role played by the nonscientific presupposition that the category of sex is important for understanding human diversity.

Freimuth, M., & Hornstein, G. A. (1982). A critical examination of the concept of gender. *Sex Roles, 8,* 515–532. An interesting view of gender as a continuum rather than two discrete categories.

Harrison, J. (1978). Male sex role and health. *Journal of Social Issues, 34*(1), 65–86. A persuasive argument describing how the male sex role is hazardous to men's health.

Hines, M. (1982). Prenatal gonadal hormones and sex differences in human behavior. *Psychological Bulletin, 92,* 56–80. An excellent though complex review of recent research on the effects of prenatal sex hormones.

Parlee, M. B. (1982, September). New findings: Menstrual cycles and behavior. *Ms.,* pp. 126–128. A review of research on menstruation for the lay audience.

3 Cognitive Abilities

- Boys are smarter than girls.
- Girls can't do math.
- Boys are more analytical than girls.
- Girls are better at simple repetitive tasks, like filing; boys, at "higher level" tasks, like making decisions.

These misconceptions of the cognitive abilities (the thinking and reasoning powers) of the sexes are widely held in our culture (see also Figure 3-1). Despite the popularity of such misconceptions, however, research has provided little support for these hypothesized sex differences. In fact, few clear-cut differences between the sexes have been found in any cognitive behavior despite numerous attempts to find them. What is so striking in reviewing research in this area is how much attention has been paid to the very few and very small sex differences in cognitive functioning, especially those differences in which males, as a group, may show an advantage.

This chapter will examine the current status of the research in this area. Comparisons of male and female performance have been made in the area of learning and memory, intellectual abilities, and creativity. Alternative explanations of these findings will be examined in turn.

Learning and Memory

One common belief is that girls learn best by simple memorization or association (that is, by rote), and boys by some advanced form of reasoning. Maccoby and Jacklin (1974), in their comprehensive review of more than 2000 books and articles, concluded that, in the area of learning and memory, there is no sex difference. Both boys and girls are equally capable of responses calling for inhibition of various responses, such as saying the word *red* when the

letters b-l-u-e are written in red ink and the instructions require naming the color, and both are equally proficient in simple repetitive tasks. McGuinness and Pribram (1978), after a similar review of the current literature, conclude that women process information faster than men, particularly in tasks, like neurosurgery, that require rapid choices. Females also generally are superior to males in perceptual speed and accuracy tests (Antill & Cunningham, 1982).

In some situations, one sex may find some things easier to learn or to remember. When such a sex difference is found, the reason is likely to be a sex difference in familiarity and interest, not in ability. For example, there has been some suggestion that girls have better social memory than boys; that is, girls are better at remembering people's names and/or faces. Although there has been some support for this hypothesis among adults (for example, Borges & Vaughn, 1977; Hamilton, 1983), sex differences in social memory have not been found consistently among preschoolers (Etaugh & Whittler, 1982). Such a pattern of results suggests that socialization factors probably account for whatever difference in social memory exists, rather than any biological differences in memory capacity or efficiency. As we shall see in the next chapter, girls tend to be encouraged more than boys to develop interests and skills in the social area.

Supporting this hypothesis that socialized interest patterns may affect memory is the finding that "masculine" words, such as *sword* and *jump*, were better recalled by males, whereas "feminine" words, such as *song* and *jelly*, were better recalled by females (Brown, Larsen, Rankin, & Ballard, 1980). (The words selected had been sex-typed by other college students in another study). Each sex may remember information about same-sex others more accurately (Halpern, 1985). Bem (1984) suggests

Figure 3-1
Stereotyped picture of a cognitive sex difference, from a pencil package. (Courtesy of Reliance Pen & Pencil Corp.)

that some individuals (sex-typed ones) tend to perceive and process the world in terms of a gender schema. This gender schema then accounts for some findings of differential recall by males and females of gender-related information. Both boys and girls seem to recall sex-stereotyped people and activities better than nonstereotyped people and activities, and this memory preference is most marked for students with strong gender stereotypes (Cann & Garnett, 1984; Hepburn, 1985; Liben & Signorella, 1980).

Intellectual Abilities

Intellectual abilities can be examined with regard to overall IQ as well as with regard to such specific abilities as verbal, quantitative, visual-spatial, and analytic skills. An unavoidable problem with research in this area is the fact that intellectual ability cannot be measured directly but only indirectly, through performance. And performance is affected by many factors other than innate ability, such as mood, motivation, expectations, and social factors. For example, Golden and Cherry (1982) found that average-ability 11th- and 12th-grade girls performed better on verbal and math tests when they thought their results would not be made public than when they thought their results would be publicized. In contrast, high-ability girls as well as all boys showed no difference in performance across conditions. Thus, even when performance differences do appear between males and females, the cause of the difference is not always clear.

Are boys smarter than girls? According to research, the answer is "no". There are no known differences between males and females in overall intelligence after age 6, an unsurprising finding, because IQ tests were specifically designed to eliminate sex differences (Maccoby & Jacklin, 1974; V. Stewart, 1976); that is, test items were selected that specifically did not show differential responding by males and females, because it was assumed there were no sex differences in intelligence. Furthermore, although there is much evidence that IQ is partially inherited, there is no strong evidence that IQ is related to the X chromosome (Wittig, 1979) or to prenatal hormones (Hines, 1982).

There are differences in intellectual performance as a function of sex-role conformity, however. Nonconformity to gender stereotypes is positively related to IQ scores (Maccoby, 1966). Thus, the more assertive and active the female, the greater her intellectual abilities and interests; the less active and aggressive the male, the less developed his physique and the greater his intellectual abilities and interests. Here is a possible example of how conformity to gender stereotypes may limit one's capabilities.

Evidence also exists that intellectual development in boys is more closely tied to parental behavior and environmental circumstances than is the case for girls. For example, Bee and colleagues (1984) found, in their longitudinal study of 193 infant-parent pairs, that a boy's IQ at age four years was fairly well predicted by previous verbal stimulation from adults, sufficient and appropriate toys, and the absence of unpredictable stimulation, such as repeated change in caregivers. For girls, environmental and parental factors during the first 18 months of life were less powerful in predicting intelligence at age four.

In studies of specific abilities, only three differences appear fairly consistently: girls excel in verbal skills, and boys excel in quantitative abilities and in visual-spatial skills. Even these differences are small, however, and do not show up until after age eight (Maccoby & Jacklin, 1974; McGuinness & Pribram, 1978; Petersen, Crockett, & Tobin-Richards, 1982). No differences have been found in concept mastery or reasoning ability except for mechanical reasoning. On mechanical reasoning tests, males generally perform better than females, although this gender difference apparently is explained by the stronger differences found

when students are classified by sex type (Antill & Cunningham, 1982). "Masculine" subjects of both sexes performed highest on this task, "feminine" subjects the lowest. In one area where sex differences have been assumed—intuition—research has not even been done (Petersen, 1983). Unfortunately, the literature abounds with studies of the differences, not the similarities, so that a reader gets the impression that these differences are large and very important.

Verbal Skills

Clearly, verbal skills are salient in our society, but, because there is considerable overlap in verbal performance between the sexes and because studies are sometimes contradictory, one wonders why only the differences are stressed. Research on ways to close the gap is also underrepresented.

Picture the winner of a seventh-grade spelling bee. If your winner was a girl, then you are aware that overall females have been found to excel in a wide variety of verbal abilities (Hyde, 1981; Maccoby & Jacklin, 1974; McGuinness & Pribram, 1978; Petersen et al., 1982). They acquire language earlier than boys, as measured by acquisition of phonemes, amount of vocalization in infancy, age of use of first word, vocabulary size, articulation, comprehensibility, and fluency. From age 3 to about age 11, sex differences are minimal. After that time, including old age (Cohen & Wilkie, 1979), females again excel in grammar, spelling, word fluency, comprehension, and production, although, again, the size of the difference is small. The exception to this pattern of fluctuating female superiority is the population of underprivileged children, where females maintain their advantage throughout childhood. This female advantage in underprivileged groups may result from the exaggeration of males' general physical vulnerability, through poor nutrition and medical care. For boys, the frequency of reading problems and speech difficulties is greater than for girls throughout the school years, although this may be due more to emotional-behavioral problems than to verbal ones.

Thus, although there are no sex differences in intelligence, the sexes on the average do show a different pattern of intellectual skills. The pattern of female superiority in verbal abilities is a common one, yet it is not always found (see Benbow & Stanley, 1980, 1983). Furthermore, the size of the sex difference actually is very small, accounting for only about 1% of the variation in scores (Hyde, 1981); that is, 99% of a person's score on verbal tests is determined by factors other than a person's sex. The practical implications of such small sex differences are virtually nil. For example, one might expect, given that females as a group have higher verbal abilities than do males, that more women than men would be employed in language-related occupations, such as writing and publishing. That this is not the case demonstrates how elements other than ability, such as social and political factors, play a major role in people's vocational choices.

The reasons for this apparent female advantage in verbal abilities appear to be primarily social, although biological factors also may play a role. Let us examine these two types of explanations separately, bearing in mind that in actual practice, the explanations probably interact.

Biological Explanations. As was noted in Chapter 2, there is some suggestion that a small sex difference may exist in degree of brain lateralization, probably as a result of prenatal hormones. The exact nature of the difference still is debatable, with some researchers arguing that females are more cognitively specialized than males, at least for language (Carter-Saltzman, 1979; Levy & Reid 1978; Star, 1979), whereas other researchers argue that more males than females show strong lateralization of functions, with the left hemisphere excelling at verbal processing, and the right at spatial processing (Bryden, 1983; Hines, 1982; Star, 1979).

Because females mature faster than males, the functional specialization of language in the left hemisphere may occur earlier for them, giving females a lead in childhood language skills. Owing to this earlier lead, girls may use language more in their processing of their environment, whereas boys develop language abilities later than other cognitive abilities. Thus, more girls than boys may use their left hemisphere when processing both verbal and spatial information, thereby appearing to be both cognitive specialists and less strongly lateralized.

Because boys' shift to linguistic skills occurs later, more language-related disorders may arise, as has been found. The finding that there is a higher correlation between verbal abilities and spatial skills for girls than for boys supports this hypothesis, as do findings that spatial ability is related to the degree of lateralization. Eventually, language may play a more important role in a female's intelligence and in her social interactions than in a male's, as some evidence suggests.

This line of research is suggestive but certainly not conclusive at this time. The precise relationship between degree of hemispheric specialization and performance of a particular skill is still an open question, and not all results have been confirmatory (for example, Alper, 1985; Bryden, 1979; Sherman, 1979; Waber, 1979). Remember that the size of the sex difference is very small in brain lateralization as well as in verbal skills. Furthermore, it is not known whether sex differences in laterality are present at birth or develop over time. Prenatal hormonal factors, which have been implicated in brain lateralization patterns, have not been found predictive of verbal ability (Hines & Shipley, 1984). Even if sex differences in brain organization were in some way inherent, social factors could still be important in the development of particular abilities. Acceptability of, motivation to use, and strategies in implementing a behavior are all affected by the environment.

Social Explanations. The environment can affect the development of sex differences in children in different ways, through differential treatment by parents and others, and through differential sex-role expectations. The finding that sex differences in verbal skills appear most strongly before age three years and after age 11 except for underprivileged children suggests social factors may be operating on such differences.

Picture a parent holding a three-month-old infant. First picture the infant as a girl; then picture the infant as a boy. If your picture changed, you understand the basis of the differential-treatment approach. Evidence of differential parental treatment according to the sex of the child has been substantial although not unquestioned (Bee et al., 1984; L. Harris, 1977; M. Lewis, 1972; Maccoby & Jacklin, 1974). Males appear to be handled more often and more vigorously than females during the first six months of life, whereas females are more frequently vocalized to, especially by mothers. More frequent parental vocalizations to daughters may *lead to* increased vocalization on the part of female infants. Conversely, these differences in parental treatment may *result from* female infants' more frequent vocalizations. Evidence for both positions is available, and it is highly likely that these factors interact to strengthen each other from the earliest days of the child's life.

Other evidence for social factors operating on the small sex difference in verbal skills can be found in cross-cultural studies. There is some evidence that female superiority in language skills may not occur in every culture (L. Harris, 1977). In cultures where reading is considered to be male-appropriate (for example, England and Germany), males' reading and vocabulary performance is generally the same as or superior to that of females (Finn, 1980; D. Johnson, 1973). In the United States, socioverbal and artistic skills are seen as "feminine" beginning in the second grade, just before sex differences in verbal skills become noticeable (Hill, Hobbs, & Verble, 1974; Nash, 1979). Boys, especially, may begin to feel intense pressure not to do well in such a "feminine" area, because doing anything vaguely feminine becomes increasingly threatening to boys during grade school.

Teachers' expectations regarding what subject matters are more appropriate to each sex also may be important, as well as their own modeling of academic interests. Some studies report that males perform better when tested and/or taught by males, particularly when verbal materials are presented, and females perform better when tested and/or taught by females (Nash, 1979; Shinedling & Pedersen, 1970).

In sum, research on verbal abilities indicates that some females perform better than some males in the first three years of life and after age 11. These differences are extremely small and are likely to be due to differences in the socialization process interacting, perhaps, with differences in brain organization.

Quantitative Abilities

There has been tremendous interest in the last few years in the area of gender differences in mathematical ability. In general, there are few gender differences in mathematical achievement until about the seventh grade (ages 11–13). At that time, males generally move ahead in mathematics achievement, although there are wide individual variations and the actual differences are small (Benbow & Stanley, 1982; Fox, 1981; Hyde, 1981; Maccoby & Jacklin, 1974). Children from poor families constitute an exception; among them, girls are superior to boys at all ages. Another exception is on computation subtests, where females frequently perform better than males. Furthermore, girls in some cases still get better math grades in school (Benbow & Stanley, 1982; De Wolf, 1981). The size of the gender difference in this area frequently is overlooked. For example, only between 1% and 5% of the variation in quantitative performance can be accounted for by gender alone (Hyde, 1981; Rossi, 1983). Yet, the public has been bombarded in recent years with reports of "large" and "sizable" sex differences (Benbow & Stanley, 1980, 1983). Another problem with research in this area is that the amount of exposure each sex has had to mathematics, such as from courses taken, has rarely been controlled for.

Most of this recent interest in quantitative performance by males and females has been generated by researchers Camilla Benbow and Julian Stanley (1980, 1982, 1983) who have examined mathematically gifted youth each year since 1972. In a nationwide search, these Johns Hopkins University researchers tested almost 50,000 seventh and eighth graders, seeking those who scored in at least the top 2 to 5% on standardized math and verbal achievement tests. These select students then were given the Scholastic Aptitude Test (SAT) math and verbal subtests, more usually taken by high school juniors and seniors. The results have been quite striking and quite controversial. More than twice as many boys as girls have math scores greater than 500 on the SAT, where the highest possible score is 800, and boys have an average score at least 30 points higher than that of girls. Score differences are the greatest between highest scoring boys and girls. For example, among students who scored greater than or equal to 700, boys outnumber girls 13 to 1.

These results have been criticized for exaggerating the differences between the sexes, since group differences using the entire sample were almost nonexistent (Rossi, 1983). Furthermore, as stated previously, gender differences still accounted for less than 5% of the total variance. Also not noted by Benbow and Stanley was the tremendously high variability of the males' performance—in one year, 19% of the boys scored higher than the highest girl; in another year, only 0.1% of the boys outperformed her (Tobias, 1982). The use of the SAT as a "pure" measure of aptitude has been questioned as well, because these tests also involve knowledge of particular techniques (Fox, 1981; Tobias, 1982).

But perhaps more controversial than Benbow and Stanley's findings have been the reasons invoked to explain the findings. These explanations again fall generally into two groups: those that primarily emphasize biological factors, and those that primarily emphasize social factors.

Biological Explanations. Although Benbow and Stanley (1980) suggested that male superiority in mathematics was probably due to both biological and social factors, the media picked up mainly on the former (for example, in *Time*, Dec. 15, 1980, males were described as "naturally abler than females"). Yet no strong evidence for genetic influence on sex differences in mathematics has been found (Petersen, 1983; Sherman & Fennema, 1978). Even the pattern of results belie a genetic factor, since consistent female inferiority among the mathematically talented was not found (Tobias, 1982).

An alternative hypothesis that involves prenatal hormones to explain "math genius" has been put forward by Geschwind (see Kolata, 1983; Marx, 1982). Geschwind proposes that brain anatomy can be altered during fetal life due to excess testosterone or unusual sensitivity to testosterone. The right hemisphere of the brain then will become dominant for language-related abilities as well as for mathematical and spatial abilities. The result is either mathematical genius or learning disorders, depending on

whether some delicate balance had been obtained. Further implications of such prenatal hormone activity are that such people should be more likely to be left-handed (right-hemispheric dominance) and more prone to immune system disorders (which have been found linked to testosterone production and sensitivity). As already noted, males do seem more likely than females to be math geniuses and to suffer from learning disorders. They also are more likely than females to be left-handed and to have immune system disorders, such as allergies and asthma. When Benbow and Stanley contacted those students who scored above 700 on the SAT math test, they found that 20% were left-handed, twice the percentage expected in the general population, and 60% had immune system disorders, five times the incidence in the general population. In contrast, when average scorers were examined, the incidence of left-handedness and of immune system disorders was the same as in the general population. These findings, while quite provocative, need more research support. They do, however, provide a possible mechanism that may underlie math genius in some cases. For most individuals, however, such a mechanism would not be operating, and we need to look at other factors that might explain why some males score higher than some females.

Social Explanations. Researchers in this area generally agree that most of the difference in math performance between males and females can be explained by environmental factors. Even biological factors can be modified by a child's surroundings. Among the most powerful social influences are the attitudes of the students, parents, and teachers toward mathematics performance, as well as actual differences in mathematics-related behaviors.

The most common and reliable finding in this area is that females tend to take fewer math courses than males as soon as such courses become optional, usually in high school (Benbow & Stanley, 1982; De Wolf, 1981; Fox, 1981; Sherman, 1978, 1981). According to a study of high school seniors in 1978 by the College Entrance Examination Board, approximately 63% of college-bound males but only 43% of the females had taken four or more years of high school mathematics (Fox, 1981). These women are effectively shut out of many of the highest-paying jobs, those in technical and scientific areas (Fox, 1981; Sells, 1980). Interestingly, when amount of math courses taken has been controlled for, sex differences in math achievement usually are greatly attenuated or eliminated (DeWolf, 1981; Fennema & Sherman, 1977). It thus is encouraging to note that the sex difference in participation in math courses appears to be decreasing (Chipman, Brush, & Wilson, 1985). Although differences in course taking did not account for the sex differences in mathematical achievement among the gifted seventh and eight graders in Benbow and Stanley's research (1980, 1983), these students may have had different math-related experiences outside of school. For example, Fox and Cohn (1980) found that more boys than girls in the Johns Hopkins program reported that they had systematically studied mathematics and science textbooks with a parent or teacher before entering the talent search. Other reports also suggest that parents of mathematically gifted children are more likely to work with and encourage their sons than their daughters (Fox, 1981; Tobias, 1982).

Why do girls tend to take fewer math courses than boys? Julia Sherman (1981, 1982a, 1982b, 1983a, 1983b) has tried to answer that question by following students from eighth grade through high school graduation. Sherman measured both attitudes and performance. For boys, the best predictors of enrolling in four years of college preparatory mathematics were, in order of their importance: (1) confidence in learning math, (2) math achievement, (3) vocabulary scores, and (4) perceived attitude of father toward one as a learner of math. For girls, the best predictors in order were: (1) vocabulary scores, (2) confidence in learning math, (3) spatial visualization scores, (4) perceived usefulness of math, (5) math achievement, and (6) effectance motivation in math (joy in problem-solving activities). Given the importance of these factors, it is interesting to note that girls generally score lower than boys in spatial visualization scores (see next section), confidence in learning math, and perceived usefulness of math (Chipman et al., 1985; Eccles [Parsons], 1983). For example, boys appear more likely than girls to attribute success in

math to ability and less likely than girls to attribute failure in math to lack of ability (Eccles [Parsons], Adler, & Meece, 1984; Parsons, Meece, Adler, & Kaczala, 1982; Stipek, 1984). Thus, boys may become more confident after math successes and less discouraged after math failures than do girls (Fox, Tobin, & Brody, 1979). Related to sex differences in self-confidence in learning math is the fact that math generally is viewed as a male subject area beginning around puberty, especially by boys (Boswell, 1985; Fox, 1981; Nash, 1979; Sherman, 1979). Sherman (1978, 1982b) found that for girls but not for boys, perception of math as a male domain was related to lower self-confidence in learning math scores. Such perceptions also were related to actual math performance for girls, especially during grades six to eight, when gender identity issues become particularly salient. The finding that math is perceived as a male subject area also may account for the finding that girls who do well in this area tend to have more sex-role conflicts than do girls who do not do as well (Sherman, 1982a, 1982b).

Attitudes of significant others have also been found important in math achievement. Fox (1981) reviews studies that find that many teachers view math as a male domain and convey this attitude both directly and indirectly; for example, by giving males and females different kinds of feedback. Sherman (1982a) also found teacher attitude to be important in girls' pursuit of math, especially when intellectual ability was held constant. Furthermore, math teachers tend to be male, especially those teaching more advanced courses. As was found with verbal tests, both sexes test better with same-sex teachers/examiners (Nash, 1979). Parental expectations also are critical and may be even more important than a child's previous math achievement in predicting achievement attitudes and expectations (Parsons, Adler, & Kaczala, 1982). Parents tend to have lower expectations for girls than boys and to foster self-confidence and an interest in taking math courses less for girls than boys (Fox, 1981). Fathers' attitudes may be particularly important (Sherman, 1978, 1983a). Peer pressure too can influence course taking and achievement in math by girls (Fox, 1981). One way this may occur is through boys ignoring or devaluing any interest in math shown by girls. For example, Webb (1984) observed junior high school math classes where students worked in small groups (about four students) to learn different math units. Results showed that females tended to seek help from males more than females, despite no difference in previous ability. However, males tended to ignore females' requests for help, especially in groups where there was only one female. Overall then, females received less help than did males, which impeded their learning of the unit.

Other social factors can affect math performance. For example, problem content has been found to have an effect on math performance. Female mathematical performance is facilitated when problems describe experiences with which females may be more familiar, such as cooking, as opposed to baseball (Dwyer, 1979; Graf & Riddel, 1972; Nash, 1979). Girls' attitudes toward math and their math performance also appear to benefit from accelerated classes and programs (Fox, 1981). It appears girls need extra support and encouragement for them to feel as confident and take the types of courses their male peers do.

In sum, a variety of social factors impinge on females to undermine their confidence in their mathematical ability. This may lead them to take fewer math courses than their male peers, which then may lead to differential math achievement. Although math genius may have a biological foundation, social factors appear to be the most powerful and pervasive factors with regard to math achievement for most individuals. These factors can account for the small

gender differences generally found after age eleven.

Visual-Spatial Abilities

Look at Figure 3-2. If finding the simple figure in the complex figure is a relatively easy thing for you to do, it is likely that you have good visual-spatial ability. These abilities refer to the visual perception of objects or figures in space and the way they are related to each other. Such perception usually requires some mental transformation of the object, as in disembedding a visual figure from its context (Embedded Figure Test—Figure 3-2) or in solving mazes. The Rod-and-Frame test (see Figure 3-3) also taps this ability, sometimes referred to as *field dependence* or *field independence* (Witkin, Dyk, Faterson, Goodenough, & Karp, 1962).

Of all the research done on gender differences, one of the two most consistent findings has been a male advantage in visual-spatial abilities after age 8 (Cohen & Wilkie, 1979; Connor & Serbin, 1985; L. Harris, 1981; Keyes, 1983; Maccoby & Jacklin, 1974; Petersen et al., 1982; Wattanawaha & Clements, 1982). (The other consistent gender difference occurs in aggressive behaviors, discussed in Chapter 4.) This male superiority in visual-spatial ability after age 8 is one gender difference that appears across social classes and in most cultures, and is maintained through old age.

Once again, it is important to bear in mind that the actual size of the difference is small. Hyde (1981) estimates that gender differences account for less than 5% of the variability of

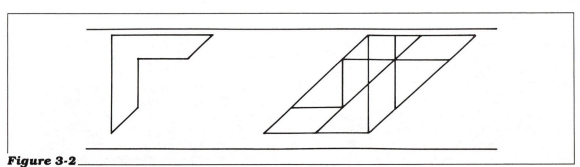

Figure 3-2

The Embedded Figures Test. Find the simple shape (on left) in the complex shape (on right).

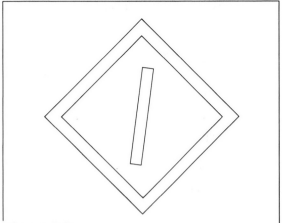

Figure 3-3

The Rod-and-Frame Test used to measure field dependence and field independence. The center rod must be aligned to the true vertical despite the tilt of the frame.

scores on visual-spatial tests, although Rosenthal and Rubin (1982) argue that such a difference does have practical significance. Furthermore, gender differences in visual-spatial (and other cognitive) abilities appear to be decreasing (Becker & Hedges, 1984). And the tests themselves have been criticized as not uniformly measuring visual-spatial ability (Linn & Petersen, 1983; Wattanawaha & Clements, 1982). Indeed, the whole notion of "spatial abilities" recently has been called into question (Caplan, MacPherson & Tobin, 1985).

In a meta-analysis of research studies performed since Maccoby and Jacklin's review (1974), Linn and Petersen (1983) conclude that there actually are three subtypes of spatial ability, only one of which shows strong gender differences. The largest group of studies used measures of spatial visualization, such as the Embedded Figures Test (Figure 3-2). These tasks require analytic ability for solution, and do not demonstrate significant gender differences.

A second subtype of spatial ability involves measures of horizontality/verticality, as in the Rod-and-Frame Test (see Figure 3-3), where the subject must adjust a luminous rod inside a luminous frame to the true vertical. Both the frame and the rod are tilted, and, since the room is darkened, the subject has few cues with

which to align the rod. Those who are accurate in their judgment of the true vertical are termed field independent; those who are inaccurate are termed field dependent (theoretically, they are assumed to be influenced by the frame or "field"). In general, females were considered to be field dependent; males, field independent (Witkin et al., 1962). More recent work casts doubt on this simple distinction. Furthermore, the terms *dependent* and *independent* suggest the possibility of interpretive bias.

Field independence, because it involves responding to a stimulus without being distracted by its context, actually refers to more than visual-spatial ability. It is the same ability used in selective listening, such as listening to one voice in a noisy room, and in tactual discrimination, such as feeling a certain pattern amidst many others. This qualification has frequently been overlooked, however, and many researchers glibly equate visual-spatial ability with field independence. Although Witkin and colleagues originally (1962) thought that both the Rod-and-Frame Test and the Embedded Figures Test were similar, they more recently concluded that the two tests measure distinct abilities (Witkin & Goodenough, 1981). Linn and Petersen (1983) came to the same conclusion: The Rod-and-Frame Test requires the use of primarily kinesthetic cues for solution; and the Embedded Figures Test primarily requires analytic ability. Although males do have a slight edge over females on these tasks, the differences are small, beginning about age eight and becoming stronger after age 18.

The third subtype of spatial abilities determined by Linn and Petersen (1983) were tests involving mental rotation of pictures. This subtype was the only one to show moderate gender differences in favor of males. For example a two- or three-dimensional figure is presented, and questions are then asked that require the observer to picture the figure from a different perspective. (Imagine how Figure 3-2 would look upside down.) These tests appear to require rapid analog processing for the achievement of high scores. Gender differences, which occur by age ten, may reflect differential strategy usage, differential rate of rotation, or differential caution. Wattanawaha and Clements (1982), using Australian seventh to ninth graders, came to a similar conclusion—that male superiority on spatial tasks occurs primarily on questions requiring three-dimensional thinking or mental manipulation of visual images. These researchers also found that the results depended in part on the manner in which an answer had to be presented. Males did better on questions in which the final visual image had to be drawn or reproduced rather than simply identified.

In sum, some males appear to have an advantage over some females on tasks that require mental rotation of objects. The implications of this finding are unclear because such a specific ability is not required for many tasks except perhaps map reading (Linn & Petersen, 1983). Yet, as Petersen (1983) notes, more and more research is being done to explore this sex difference, and more research is using measures most likely to find this difference. Thus, it is likely that sex differences in this area will become highly exaggerated in the future, while the implications of the differences will become increasingly obscured.

Visual-spatial ability, as a general skill, does appear to be used in some aspects of engineering and architecture. However, other factors play a larger role in achievement in those fields, particularly social factors. For example, although gender differences in this ability are small, more than 98% of all engineers in the United States were men in 1978. This male domination should become slightly less overwhelming in future years because females are entering engineering in increasing numbers. In 1981, women comprised 17% of all first-year undergraduate engineering majors, in contrast to just 2% in 1967 ("Big rise," 1984).

Visual-spatial ability also has been linked to performance in math and science, but these correlations have been challenged as not uniformly accounting for sex differences in these areas (Connor & Serbin, 1985; Linn & Petersen, 1983; Pattison & Grieve, 1984; Sherman, 1983a). For example, Sherman (1983a) found that girls' visual-spatial skill in the eighth and ninth grades predicted their continuation of math for four more years. However, such skills were not predictive of males' continuing with math. Nor did such skills account for gender differences in math performance.

Because this skill, or set of skills, appears to be the one area where the most gender differences are found, much attention has been paid to the reasons for such differences. Interestingly, there has been much more research on biological than on social processes affecting gender differences in this area and little emphasis on the fact that the differences themselves are small and do not occur on all tasks measuring this ability. (See Caplan et al., 1985; Newcombe, 1982, for critiques of these approaches.)

Biological explanations. A number of biological factors have been examined in the search for explanations of the small gender difference in visual-spatial abilities—genetic, hormonal, and brain lateralization factors. The research still is inconclusive, and none of it rules out the likelihood of interactions with social factors.

There has been substantial research into genetic influences on visual-spatial ability, but most research fails to find any connections (see Linn & Petersen, 1983, and Vandenberg & Kuse, 1979, for excellent reviews of this research). Although there is some inferential evidence that genetic control over this ability may be recessive and carried on the X chromosome, the research frequently has been flawed with regard to statistical techniques, age corrections, and types of tasks used. When Linn and Petersen (1983) reviewed the evidence for X linkage in visual-spatial ability by breaking the tasks into the three subtypes discussed above, more of the studies failed to support the hypothesis than supported it. Even if genetic factors operate here, the contribution of cultural and environmental factors is not ruled out, because genetic transmission of a trait is quite complex and the gender differences mentioned are only sex influenced, not sex limited. The latter qualification means that, even though more males than females have good visual-spatial ability, not all males do. Furthermore, the actual demonstration of ability is a function more of contextual factors than of innate ones, as a glance at any engineering school will demonstrate.

Hormones have been examined as possible mediators of gender differences in this area, but the evidence is inconsistent and largely negative (Hines, 1982; Hines & Shipley, 1984; Linn & Petersen, 1983). Petersen (1983) suggests that androgen levels may be related to spatial ability, but the relationship appears to be curvilinear rather than linear, as would be expected on the basis of gender differences; that is, some intermediate level rather than a high level of androgen at the time of testing has been associated with higher scores on spatial ability tests. More research using direct measurement of hormones is needed, and it should be recalled that wide individual differences exist in the exact amount of hormones circulating in each individual at any one point in time. Furthermore, gender differences in visual-spatial ability appear as early as age eight, before pubertal hormonal changes make the sexes more hormonally distinct. It should be noted, however, that gender differences in visual-spatial ability do appear to increase at adolescence (Nash, 1975).

Prenatal hormones may have a more indirect effect on sex differences in this area by affecting brain organization and lateralization, as discussed in Chapter 2 and in the section on verbal abilities earlier in this chapter. Fewer females are as strongly lateralized as are males, yet females appear to be more lateralized for language than are males. Spatial ability, primarily located in the right hemisphere and generally nonlinguistic in nature, may require use of the right hemisphere without the left, which may be more difficult for some females than some males; that is, it may be easier for females than men to combine spatial and linguistic skills, as in "reading" a person's facial expressions, than it is to separate them (Goleman, 1978). Yet Hines and Shipley (1984) did not find that women who were prenatally exposed to a synthetic estrogen had differences in visual-spatial ability, although there was a difference in brain lateralization pattern. Furthermore, the research in this area suffers from serious methodological and interpretive flaws (Bryden, 1979; Caplan et al., 1985; Petersen, 1982, 1983; Star, 1979). For example, the differences in laterality could also be a result of socialization experiences and/or differences in cognitive strategies. Thus, even if evidence that males and females differ in brain organization becomes better established, we still will not know whether this difference is due to prenatal hor-

monal factors, or postnatal environmental ones.

Another physiological process that might account for some gender differences in visual-spatial abilities is differential maturation rates. In her research, Waber (1976, 1977) found that, regardless of sex, later maturing children scored better than early maturing children on spatial-ability tasks. No relationship was found between performance on verbal tests and maturational rate. With early maturers, predominant use of the left hemisphere before localization is fully complete may interfere with an individual's ability to handle spatial information. Because males usually mature later, they may have a different brain organization that leads to sex differences in verbal and spatial abilities. Waber (1979) argues that, rather than viewing neuropsychological maturation as a linear process of increasing hemispheric specialization, it would be more accurate to view neuropsychological maturation as a process of repeated reorganization of functions. The developmental changes are qualitative as well as quantitative.

Not all research supports Waber's hypothesis (Bryden, 1983; Petersen, 1976). Furthermore, because degree of brain lateralization may be established at birth or at least by age five (Bryden, 1979, 1983; Petersen, 1979), there may be no causal relationship between maturation rate and degree of lateralization. A causal relationship between maturation and spatial ability also has not been established. For example, Newcombe and Bandura (1983) found that although spatial ability in 11-year-olds was significantly related to timing of puberty, it also was significantly related to other psychological variables that accounted for more of the variance in spatial ability than did the maturation factor (37% compared to 5%). (The psychological variables assessed certain personality traits typically associated with males, such as instrumentality and math/science interests.) Thus, either the biological factors or the psychological factors could be causal mechanisms, or they could interact to lead to gender differences in spatial ability. More attention needs to be paid to those factors that appear to be more powerful than the biological ones.

Social Explanations. Of all the social factors studied, the greatest amount of evidence has accumulated regarding the positive effects of experience and practice on visual-spatial skills for both females and males (Connor & Serbin, 1985; Newcombe, Bandura, & Taylor, 1983; Stericker & LeVesconte, 1982). For both sexes, participation in spatial activities positively correlates with high scores on tests of spatial ability, and both sexes benefit from specific training in visual-spatial skills. Thus, the general group sex difference found in visual-spatial abilities is likely to be due to the differential experience the two sexes have in using this ability. More male sex-typed toys and activities have been found to involve visual-spatial skills than female sex-typed toys and activities. For example, using hand tools and building models are "masculine" activities and are highly correlated with spatial ability. Furthermore, as might be expected, males have more experience with such activities than do girls.

The question remains, however, of why boys have more experience with toys and tasks involving visual-spatial ability; that is, is their greater experience with such activities a determinant of good visual-spatial abilities, or might such experience result from some greater ability or interest? The fact that differential experience with such activities begins by preschool whereas gender differences in ability are observed somewhat later suggests that experience itself may be the causal factor (Serbin & Connor, 1979). However, longitudinal studies clearly are needed. A related point is that more of the toys and activities labeled "masculine" involve such abilities. Most children are encouraged to play at gender-appropriate activities; therefore, perhaps regardless of ability or interest, boys may have more experience with those types of toys and activities.

Sex typing of activities thus is another important factor in the gender difference in visual-spatial abilities. More spatial activities tend to be masculine rather than feminine sex-typed, thereby accounting for the frequent observation that masculine sex-role orientation is associated with higher spatial ability (Jamison & Signorella, 1980; Nash, 1975; Newcombe & Bandura, 1983). Cultural norms may interact with individual personality traits to determine experiences and abilities. For example, in Hong Kong, expectations for male and female behavior are quite marked and distinct. In that cul-

ture, no significant correlation between sex-role identification and cognitive ability was found, perhaps because regardless of aptitudes or gender identity, the sexes engaged in quite different activities and courses (Keyes, 1983).

The importance of cultural factors in visual-spatial ability and experiences is important to remember. Schools, teachers, parents, and peers all work together to encourage males and females to engage in different activities, especially during adolescence. Such activities may be associated with differential use of kinesthetic cues and may provide differential practice in mental rotation images; for example, juggling, pole vaulting, soccer, carpentry, knitting, writing, and cooking all use different visual-spatial skills (Linn & Petersen, 1983). People, especially teachers, also may respond differentially to males and females, as will be discussed in Chapter 7. In particular, boys usually are reinforced for problem-solving behavior whereas girls appear to be praised more randomly, or for "good behavior." In one culture where the sexes have not been found to differ in visual-spatial ability—the Canadian Eskimos—the sexes also receive similar encouragement in autonomy, a trait that has been found linked to good visual-spatial ability (Berry, 1966; Coates, 1974; MacArthur, 1967).

In sum, males as a group tend to perform better than females as a group on visual-spatial tasks, at least those that involve mental rotation of images. These differences are small and variable, and can best be explained by differential experience with tasks involving those abilities. Such experience differences may give rise to or interact with biological differences in brain organization to yield a small gender difference in performance. The implication of such small and specific differences in ability for life tasks and activities remains highly questionable.

Analytic Ability

In research focusing directly on analytic ability, few gender differences have been found. In one controversial study, Broverman and associates (1968) argued that females perform better on simple, overlearned perceptual-motor tasks that involve little thinking, whereas males perform better on tasks requiring inhibition or perceptual restructuring—a "higher" cognitive process. Following this argument, some might conclude that women are more suitable for typing and filing and men for managing businesses. The Broverman group also attributed these differences in cognitive processing to hormonal differences.

Numerous critics have attacked the assertions made by Broverman and colleagues (for example, Dan, 1979; Maccoby & Jacklin, 1974). Among the many problems found in the work of the Broverman group are the following: the group selected and interpreted only those studies that conformed to their hypothesis, ignored the tremendous amount of overlap in male and female performance, and confused analytic functioning with a basically perceptual phenomenon—visual-spatial ability. There are no differences in analytic ability when verbal or auditory materials are employed, nor when spatial ability is controlled (Petersen & Wittig, 1979). Furthermore, in the more recent research of Linn and Petersen (1983), even tests of visual-spatial ability that involve an analytic strategy for solution, such as the Embedded Figures Test, have not shown any gender difference.

Thus, even though males take more math, science, and computer courses than do females, the sexes do not appear to differ in analytic ability. This conclusion has important implications for the burgeoning area of *computer literacy*. Although there is much evidence that males have dominated the computer field, especially with regard to video games, computer courses, and computer camps, there are no gender differences in ability that would justify such a disparity (Kerr, 1985; Kiesler, Sproull, & Eccles, 1983; "Notes," 1984; Vredenburg, Flett, Krames, & Pliner, 1984). Rather, cultural factors and expectations seem to keep girls out of the video arcades and away from computers.

Evidence for the influence of cultural factors on computer usage is the finding that interest in computers seems to decrease with age. Lovett Gray (1984) cites research that shows that among first-graders, girls were as interested as boys in learning to program computers. By the sixth grade, however, boys interested in computers outnumbered girls 2 to 1, and by the ninth grade, more than four-fifths of the interested students were males. One reason for this

decrease in interest by girls over the years may be because computers are often introduced into schools in math programs. As is the case with math, girls seem to prefer other activities to computing, perhaps because of societal expectations, or because of their own value system (L. Gray, 1984; "Notes," 1984). For example, more girls than boys may prefer to spend their free time with friends, rather than with a computer. (Gender differences in values will be discussed in the next chapter.) Females and males both believe computers to be essentially masculine (Vredenburg et al., 1984), and this may be another reason girls steer clear of them. Furthermore, most of the computer games, and even most educational programming, involve such "masculine" themes as sports, war, and violence. Research has shown that with specific encouragement and female role models, girls will spend as much time on the computer as boys, and learn as readily (L. Gray, 1984; Kiesler, Sproull, & Eccles, 1983; Van Gelder, 1985). However, without such encouragement, girls tend to shy away, a trend that has serious implications for future career opportunities.

How do males and females approach the solution to a problem? There has been some suggestion in the past of sex differences in cognitive strategies in *problem solving*, but these differences may be based on differential visual-spatial abilities (Maier & Casselman, 1970; Sherman, 1967). Boys, when presented with a pattern to reproduce, performed better and utilized more visual cues than did girls. It may be that females use a general, less specialized strategy than do males for solving cognitive problems (Carter-Salzman, 1979). Allen and Hogeland (1978) found that, while both sexes use the same pattern of approaches to problems, women use spatial strategies less effectively and give up more easily than do men. Recent research on computer usage also shows gender differences in programming styles (Turkle, 1984). Boys appear to prefer use of logic and control; girls prefer a more intuitive style, which may appear to be "just fooling around."

Many of these findings suggest that experience is important in problem-solving ability. Boys generally receive more practice in, and reinforcement for, problem-solving behavior from parents and teachers than do girls, making boys more familiar with such activities and more proficient at them (Beck, 1977; Coates, 1974). Interestingly, Berger and Gold (1979) have found that, among individuals under age 25, sex differences in problem solving no longer exist (see also Gold & Berger, 1978). These researchers suggest that the more supportive atmosphere in recent years for female achievement and the reduced emphasis on male achievement have served to eliminate sex differences in this area. Other research has indicated that sex differences can be minimized by changing the testing conditions, the problems used, or the sex of the experimenter (Hoffman & Maier, 1966) and by controlling for occupational affiliation (Berger & Gold, 1979).

Sex roles also may be important with regard to cognitive strategies. Rotter and O'Connell (1982) found that androgynous and cross-sex-typed college students were more cognitively complex than undifferentiated students (using the Bem Sex-Role Inventory for classification). (Cross-sex-typed people are those who are sex-typed in traits appropriate for the other sex.) Cognitive complexity was defined as: (1) openness to conflict and new experience, (2) only a minimal amount of categorical thinking, and (3) relative independence of thought. This finding implies that to avoid being traditionally sex-typed one must have a different way of approaching experience.

Creativity

Another area in which cognitive differences have been thought to exist is creativity. A problem here is with the definition and tasks used to measure the construct. When creativity is measured by the number of responses produced to a stimulus (for example, "List all the possible uses of a paper clip") or by the uniqueness of the responses, females are superior, especially if verbal materials are used (Kershner & Ledger, 1985; Maccoby & Jacklin, 1974). When creativity is measured by career accomplishments, however, males excel, because most awards and recognition go to males.

The relationship between sex role and creativity is unclear. There is some evidence that

androgynous individuals show more creativity than sex-typed individuals, perhaps because for both males and females instrumental traits are strongly correlated with seeing oneself as creative (Harrington & Andersen, 1981; Lott, 1978). However, this relationship appears clearer for males than for females. Sex-role conflicts for women may result in different ways of expressing creativity than have been examined.

Summary

In examining a wide range of cognitive gender differences, the only consistent findings lie in a general small female superiority in verbal abilities after age 11 and a general small male superiority in quantitative abilities after age 11 and in visual-spatial abilities after age 8. There are no differences in how the sexes learn, in overall intelligence, in analytic ability, or in creativity (unless measured verbally). There may be some differences in cognitive strategies in certain situations.

A variety of physical and environmental explanations have been suggested to account for the three differences that have been found. There is little evidence for a genetic basis for any of these differences. Hormones do not appear directly involved in cognitive functioning, although prenatal androgen exposure may produce differential brain functioning. The effects of differential brain functioning and of differential maturation rates on cognitive processes are unclear at this time, although preliminary findings are provocative.

Two environmental factors that seem to be involved in the three small cognitive differences are differential treatment by parents and differential experiences. There are, of course, wide individual and class differences in child-rearing practices. A direct effect of particular parental practices on particular cognitive skills has not been demonstrated. Other evidence of the importance of environmental factors can be found if one examines gender differences in societal expectations of cognitive performance. Such differences are demonstrated by finding cultural differences in cognitive functioning, by examining specific gender stereotypes and their behavioral consequences, by studying those individuals not strongly sex typed, and by demonstrating conditioned anxiety in people who engage in activities deemed appropriate for the other sex.

Some sort of interactional hypothesis seems warranted. It seems likely that some biological predisposition, possibly due to prenatal hormones, interacts with the environment to determine whether the ability itself will be actualized. The environment can either reinforce or discourage such actualization, depending on the behavior's sex appropriateness in that society. The fact that most gender differences are not apparent in early childhood and emerge before puberty undercuts a purely physiological explanation. Expectations of performance shape a child's behavior, and these expectations vary along sex lines.

An important question to keep in mind as we continue to look at reported sex differences involves the implications of such differences. Because individual differences are so broad and because adult achievement and performance involve so much more than pure ability, no clear-cut predictions on the basis of sex are possible. The similarities between the sexes are as notable as, if not more notable than, the differences.

Recommended Reading

Caplan, P. J., MacPherson, G. M., & Tobin, P. (1985). Do sex-related differences in spatial abilities exist? A multilevel critique with new data. *American Psychologist, 40,* 786–799. A comprehensive criticism of the research to date that purports to find evidence of gender differences in spatial ability. The construct of spatial abilities itself is questioned.

Chipman, Susan F., Brush, Lorelei R., & Wilson, Donna M. (Eds.) (1985). *Women and mathematics: Balancing the equation.* Hillsdale, N. J.: Lawrence Erlbaum. Twelve articles reporting on ten research projects funded by the National Institute of Education's special research grants program on women and mathematics.

Maccoby, E. & Jacklin, C. N. (1974). *The psychology of sex differences.* Stanford, Calif.: Stanford University Press. The now classic examination of the research on sex differences in cognitive and social areas up to 1973. Annotated bibliography.

Wittig, M. A., & Petersen, A. C. (Eds.) (1979). *Sex related differences in cognitive functioning: Developmental issues.* New York: Academic Press. An excellent compilation of findings on cognitive sex differences and of explanations, primarily the biological, for such differences.

4 Personality and Social Behavior

Generally, when we talk about masculinity and femininity, we are talking about certain personality and social characteristics. Females are seen as very emotional, very submissive, very talkative, very aware of others' feelings, and so forth; males are seen as possessing opposite traits. Figure 4-1 exemplifies one part of the stereotype.

In examining the factual bases for stereotypes in the areas of personality and of social behavior, a number of difficulties arise. First is the problem, discussed in Chapter 1, of thinking of traits as consistent characteristics of an individual in all situations at all times. As has been noted, there is little support that traits are so consistent. Situational factors interact with individual factors in determining behavior, and this is especially the case with social behaviors. For example, a person in isolation is not assertive. Assertive behaviors occur in a social setting and depend on that setting for their expression. Furthermore, a person may feel assertive but choose not to act that way in a particular situation.

Figure 4-1
Illustrative sex "difference" in personality?
(Copyright 1973 by Bülbül. Reprinted by permission.)

There is also the problem of definitions. Although cognitive differences, such as verbal ability, can be measured by a variety of paper-and-pencil tests (for example, spelling, reading comprehension), it is much more difficult operationally to define and measure concepts like *dependence*. An operational definition gives information regarding how a particular construct can be measured. *Dependence*, for example, can be measured in terms of *clinging behaviors, social responsiveness, number of friends,* and so forth. To illustrate, if one researcher looks at clinging behaviors of preschoolers and another looks at the number of friends a group of 8-year-olds have, the results would be difficult to compare. To complicate matters further, some researchers do not state explicitly which definition they used in their research, making comparisons among studies difficult (Maccoby & Jacklin, 1974).

Differently aged subject groups are also a problem when comparing study results, especially if developmental issues specifically are not discussed. This is particularly troublesome, because so much research is done with college students, generally aged 18 to 22. Results are often generalized to "all adults." Developmental issues are even more salient for children. Thus, comparisons of help-seeking behavior in children revealed gender differences for 3- to 6-year-olds but not for 7- to 11-year-olds (Whiting & Edwards, 1973).

A related problem with regard to generalizing from research subjects to the whole population has been the tendency on the part of some researchers to see the male as the norm for human beings. Thus Lawrence Kohlberg (1969) developed an entire theory regarding stages of moral development based only on evidence from male subjects. Carol Gilligan's (1982a, 1982b) revolutionary research suggests that females do not conform to his model as well as do males, not because they are less "moral" than males, but because their moral development may proceed along a different path. Clearly a theory of *human* moral development must incorporate findings from both females and males.

The applicability of research on White subjects to people of different racial and ethnic backgrounds also needs to be addressed. Most research is on White subjects, yet when research does include Blacks, different patterns frequently are found. In particular, race and sex may interact with respect to a number of social behaviors, such as assertiveness and dominance, yet this interaction often is overlooked in research design and interpretation (K. Adams, 1980, 1983).

Another problem that interferes with understanding the bases of the stereotypes is the effect of social expectations on an individual's behavior. This effect may take the form of a self-fulfilling prophecy, or it may be reflected in observer bias. For example, because girls are not expected to be aggressive, they do not develop aggressive behaviors, or their behavior might be mislabeled or misinterpreted. These and other research problems severely handicap an objective researcher (if one exists). It is important to keep such problems in mind as we evaluate the studies.

Also important to remember is the tremendous amount of overlap in behaviors between the sexes. This overlap makes any clear-cut difference between males and females difficult to find and of little use in predicting an individual's performance.

The behaviors discussed in this chapter can be grouped into four major areas: personality and temperament, communication patterns, person-related behaviors, and power-related behaviors. This four-part division is somewhat artificial because all social behaviors, including those that are power-related and those that are communication- and person-related, overlap considerably. Still, these categories do tap the stereotypic view of women as being more "interpersonal" and of men as being more "agentic/active." We will come across a number of common themes: the importance of gender as opposed to sex, the importance of person-situation interactions, and the importance of race of subject.

Personality and Temperament

The term *personality* refers to the distinctive character of an individual, which includes traits, behaviors, emotions, and thoughts, whereas *temperament* refers to emotional mood or disposition only. Both areas have been assumed to have gender differences. Most personality theorists, however, emphasize individual, rather than sex-specific, differences. (Freud and the neo-Freudian theorists are exceptions but their position will be discussed in the next chapter.) For our purposes here, a brief look at personality development as related to sex typing will prove instructive.

Personality Development

When one talks about personality development, the distinction between stereotypic gender differences and true gender differences often is difficult to determine. As was noted in Chapter 1, people generally are in a great deal of agreement as to what constitutes the gender stereotypes and these stereotypes are learned by ages three to five. However, children do not necessarily behave accordingly. Of interest here is the common finding that boys are behaviorally sex typed much earlier and more strongly than are girls (Maccoby & Jacklin, 1974; Payne, 1981; Stericker & Kurdek, 1982; Urberg, 1982). Between ages 3 and 11, it is very unusual for boys to prefer activities or toys ascribed to girls. On the other hand, it is quite common for girls to choose "boys'" toys and activities as often as, if not in preference to, those ascribed to girls. In fact, between ages 6 and 9, most girls prefer "male" activities, perhaps because such activities have also been rated as more interesting and more fun (Donelson, 1977a).

The degree of agreement between sex-role expectations and self-descriptions varies with age and, apparently, with gender. Davis, Williams, and Best (1982) found that third-graders attribute gender stereotypic traits to their peers, but not always to themselves. Third-grade boys, in particular, were more likely than girls to see themselves in terms of both male and female stereotypic traits. Third-grade girls generally saw themselves in terms of female stereotypic traits only. Stericker and Kurdek (1982), in their study of third- to eighth-graders, found a similar pattern of results with the two youngest groups. This gender difference may be due to the nature of the male stereotype,

which is relatively more "adult" and perhaps "unnatural" than the female stereotype. For example, the independent, assertive, and unemotional parts of the male stereotype would be difficult for most children and, perhaps, for most adults.

From grades six to twelve there is increasing consistency between self-description and sex-role expectations (Donelson, 1977a). By adolescence, these female/male distinctions strongly appear (Feather, 1984). These gender differences have been quite stable despite societal changes over the last 30 years (Baldwin, 1984). These female/male distinctions have been variously labeled by different writers. Parsons and Bales (1955) speak of expressive (emotional, people-oriented) and instrumental (active, doing) orientations. R. Carlson (1965) speaks of people (other-involved) and individualistic (self-involved) orientations. Bakan (1966) speaks of communion (involving cooperation and receptivity) and agency (involving self-assertion and ego enhancement) orientations. These similar terms all describe stereotypic gender differences in personality and social behavior, but the research findings just cited refer only to self-descriptions and ideal self-descriptions, not to behavioral differences. With gender stereotypes being as pervasive as they are, it is not surprising that most people see themselves as behaving in gender appropriate ways. Whether they actually behave this way is a different matter. Stericker and Kurdek (1982) make a similar point when they argue that due to intense peer pressure to conform to accepted stereotypic behaviors during childhood and adolescence, gender self-concept may be a poor predictor of behavior. Canter and Meyerowitz (1984) find that both female and male college students expect and report sex-stereotypic behaviors, but this expectation is stronger for males than for females. Any gender differences that may arise in behavior are thus as likely to reflect differences in learning opportunities and societal rewards as to reflect differences in personality.

Another issue concerns developmental aspects. Although most research concentrates on children and college students, personality development appears to be a continuous process. A number of studies report that people tend to become more androgynous (that is, combine both expressive and agentic competencies) as they mature from late adolescence to middle adulthood (Fischer & Narus, 1981b; Levinson, 1978; Moreland, 1980; M. White, 1979). Men, in particular, may become more acceptant of stereotypically cross-sex characteristics with age. Thus it is important to speak cautiously of gender differences in personality across the life span.

Life-cycle stages appear to affect an individual's level of "masculinity" and "femininity" (Cunningham & Antill, 1984). Employed women have been found to score lower on the "feminine" scale of the Bem Sex-Role Inventory than did nonemployed women, regardless of their marital or parental status. Furthermore, the male partners of employed women tended to score lower on the "masculine" scale than did the male partners of nonemployed women. These data do not demonstrate that female employment causes personality changes, for certain personality traits may differentiate those women who seek employment from those who do not. However, it is likely that employment does have some effect on a woman and her partner, and this effect apparently is stronger than the effect of having children.

Temperament

With regard to temperament, females have often been thought to be more passive than males. As Maccoby and Jacklin (1974) note, however, the term *passivity* has a variety of possible definitions: submissiveness, lack of sexual interest, dependence, inactivity, and so on. Because it covers such a broad range of behavior, passivity per se will not be examined here. From the research on the possible components of passivity, however, it is clear that there is little support for the assumption that females are uniformly more passive than males.

Emotionality. In the area of emotionality (another vague term), studies of infants show few consistent gender differences, but male infants do appear to be more irritable, emotionally labile, less attentive, and less socially responsive than female infants (Haviland & Malatesta, 1982; Maccoby & Jacklin, 1974;

Phillips et al., 1978). The situations that occasion emotional outbursts are different for boys and for girls from ages 3 to 5. Boys react most to frustration situations, conflicts with adults, and fear-inducing situations; girls respond most to conflicts with other children. Girls also decrease their total emotional responsiveness at a faster rate than do boys (Fitzgerald, 1977; Maccoby & Jacklin, 1974).

In terms of fearfulness, the evidence is contradictory, partly due to different measurement techniques. Regarding infants' fear of strangers, which occurs in less than 50% of all infants (Fitzgerald, 1977), males more frequently evidence this fear, although females respond more intensely and at an earlier age to it. Observational studies of behavior do not show females, in childhood and adolescence, to be more timid than males of that age, although teacher ratings and self-reports usually do show more timidity in females (Brody, 1984; Maccoby & Jacklin, 1974). The one area where more fearfulness in females than in males actually has been observed in adults is in fear of spiders (Cornelius & Averill, 1983). However, this fear appears to be more like revulsion than a specific concern about danger.

This apparent gender difference in fearfulness may be a function of sex-typing since self-rated fears were found to be correlated significantly with femininity scores (Krasnoff, 1981). The difference in fearfulness also may be a function of gender expectations. A problem with self-reports, as was noted in the introduction to Part 2, is that people tend to respond in a socially desirable way, or they may respond to the demand characteristics of a situation. Thus, girls, especially those high in "feminine" traits, may be more likely to admit to fear or anxieties because such admissions are more socially acceptable from, and more expected of, them. In this regard, Birnbaum and colleagues (1980, 1984) found that preschoolers had marked stereotypes about sex differences in emotionality. Females were more associated with fear, sadness, and happiness, and males were more associated with anger. Similar stereotypes were held by parents, and were reflected in television programming. Parents, in practice, accepted anger in boys more than in girls, and accepted fear in girls more than in boys. Thus, girls actually may show more fear than boys because fear is more socially acceptable for girls than boys. These stereotypes may also lead more females than males to report fearfulness.

In test-taking situations, females generally have higher anxiety levels than males, a condition that may interfere with complex problem solving (Maccoby, 1966; Unger & Denmark, 1975). This anxiety in test-taking situations may be related to deviation from gender norms (achieving on a test may be viewed as unfeminine) rather than from chronically higher levels of anxiety in females. If this explanation were true, males who engage in cross-sex activities should also be more anxious. Bem and Lenney (1976) have found support for this prediction with college students.

A curious aspect of research in this area is defining emotionality as *fear* or as *the number of emotional upsets*. Emotions, of course, cover a wide range of feelings, including hostility. Yet, although more males display hostile feelings than do females, males are rarely termed "emotional," as illustrated in Figure 4-1. Again, a sexist bias in research questions, definitions, and conclusions is apparent.

In general, then, we cannot conclude simply that females are more emotional or more timid than males. Early childhood studies show few consistent differences between the sexes; after early childhood, differences that emerge seem more a consequence of gender stereotypes rather than a basis for them. In this regard, it is interesting to note that Buck (1977) found that boys between ages 4 and 6 increasingly inhibited and masked their overt reactions to emotion-producing situations (in this case, slides depicting emotion-laden scenes). Girls, however, continued to respond relatively freely to such situations. Such differences, becoming more extreme during adolescence, clearly conform to gender stereotypes of females as being emotional. As noted, this may mean only that more females than males show their emotions, not that more females have emotions. The most common example is in crying behavior. Females report crying significantly more frequently and intensely than do males, and in a wider variety of situations (Lombardo, Cretser, Lombardo, & Mathis, 1983). However, both males and fe-

males agree on the kinds of situations in which crying is most likely to occur.

Research on brain lateralization suggests that women and men typically process emotions differently (Star, 1979). Whereas men tend to use their left hemisphere in processing emotions (that is, the side more associated with analytical thinking), women tend to use both their hemispheres in processing emotions. Furthermore, when asked to think about something without emotion, men were less able to do so than women, contradicting the gender stereotype of females as more likely than males to let their emotions "interfere" in their thinking. Cherulnik (1979) concluded from his research with undergraduates that, although women may be more emotionally expressive than men, especially facially, women do not appear to experience emotions more strongly than men. Evidence of this difference in emotional disclosure shows up clearly in gender differences in communication patterns.

Communication Patterns

The stereotype of female emotionality may be related to the greater frequency with which females display or communicate their emotions. The area of communication is an extremely important one in the study of gender differences, since most of our information and knowledge of others comes through their verbal or nonverbal cues. Until recently, however, few researchers have examined gender differences in this area. In ground-breaking work, Nancy Henley (1977; Mayo & Henley, 1981) has found gender differences in communication patterns to be pervasive in both verbal and nonverbal behaviors.

Verbal Communication

Contradicting the "talkative female" stereotype, Henley found that males talk more and for longer periods of time than do females. Males interrupt other speakers more, control conversations more as to topic, make more jokes, and speak less in standard English (that is, they use slang more). Females talk at a much higher pitch, ask tag questions (for example, "Isn't that so?") rather than make statements, allow themselves to be interrupted, listen more, and disclose more personal information to others. Female speech is more "polite" than male speech and is expected to be so, regardless of the gender of the person addressed or the content of the speech (Kemper, 1984). In contrast, males are expected to modify their speech as a function of the sex-appropriateness of the content, and the gender of the addressee. For example, it is rarely all right for women to use profanity, but men can use it as long as they don't use it with women. During the 1984 presidential campaign, vice-presidential candidate Geraldine Ferraro could never have gotten away with the expression "kick a little ass" as her opponent George Bush did. The only negative comments about Bush's use of the expression centered on its utterance in "mixed" company. The use of profanity by males appears to demonstrate a degree of social power that women do not have (Selnow, 1985).

Differences in content of conversation are not clear because males and females often engage in different activities and occupations. Content differences also are unclear because content of conversation appears to depend not only on the gender of the speaker but also on the gender of the listener (A. Haas, 1981; Hall & Braunwald, 1981). Among White middle-class children, boys talk more about sports to both boys and girls, and girls talk to girls more about school, identity, and wishing and needing. When girls talk to boys, they are more verbally compliant and they laugh more. When boys talk to girls, they use more direct requests. In general, males more often are talked about by both sexes, perhaps a reflection of their greater importance or interest.

Women are stereotyped as gossips, yet research does not completely support this image (Levin & Arluke, 1985). Although college women have been found to talk more frequently about a third person than do college men, there is no gender difference in the frequency of derogatory remarks about that person. Furthermore, derogatory remarks constitute only 25% of the type of comments made about a third person.

In general, males tend to dominate verbally, whereas females tend to listen more and to disclose intimate information about themselves more. Even among preschoolers, males tend to talk more than females (Cook, Fritz, McCornack, & Visperas, 1985). Henley's (1977) work has been supported by numerous other studies (Gerdes, Gehling, & Rapp, 1981; Haas, 1979; Parlee, 1979; Reis, Senchak, & Solomon, 1985). The finding that women are more self-disclosing than are men relates specifically to intimate topics, such as personality and bodily matters, at least when such topics are seen as "feminine" (Derlega, Durham, Gockel, & Sholis, 1981). When personal topics are considered "neutral," such as tactfulness, and even when they are considered "masculine," such as aggressiveness, no sex difference regularly appears. On such topics as opinions, interests, and work, men disclose more than women (Rosenfeld, Civikly, & Herron, 1979). The reluctance of males in general to disclose intimate information about themselves, especially to strangers, is most likely a reflection of the strong social norms against doing so. For example, Derlega and Chaikin (1976) found that self-disclosing males were perceived as significantly more psychologically maladjusted than non-self-disclosing males. The reverse effect was found for females. That is, the non-self-disclosing females were seen as significantly more maladjusted.

The general pattern of gender differences in verbal communication must be qualified by research that finds stronger differences as a function of sex typing than as a function of gender per se. Thus, it is specifically "masculine" and "undifferentiated" males, not androgynous males, who markedly limit the personal information they reveal (Lavine & Lombardo, 1984; Lombardo & Lavine, 1981; Narus & Fischer, 1982). Androgynous people of both sexes appear to be flexible with regard to self-disclosure, responding more to their partners' level of disclosure and to the nature of the topic than do their sex-typed peers (Gerdes et al., 1981; Sollie & Fischer, 1985).

Nonverbal Communication

In studies of nonverbal behavior, the observed gender differences are of even greater importance than in the verbal behaviors just noted, since the impact of nonverbal communication is so much stronger and so much more subtle than verbal communication (Henley & Thorne, 1977). Generally, females are more restricted in their demeanor and personal space, have more frequent eye contact during conversations (but avoid eye contact otherwise), smile more when it is unrelated to happiness, touch less but are touched more, and are more sensitive to nonverbal cues than are males (Berman & Smith, 1984; Hall, 1985; Henley, 1977; Mayo & Henley, 1981). Many of these general findings must be qualified by situational, cultural, age, and sex-typing factors, however.

For example, the finding related to females' skill at decoding nonverbal cues is complex. Research has found that this superiority is present mainly when the nonverbal message appears to be intentional and overt, such as in facial expressions, rather than more covert or unintended, such as in body position (Blanck, Rosenthal, Snodgrass, DePaulo, & Zuckerman, 1981; Rosenthal & DePaulo, 1979). The interpretation of this pattern has been in terms of "politeness"; that is, females learn to refrain from effectively decoding the less controllable cues of the sender. The finding that this pattern increases with age from the years nine to 21 suggests that this phenomenon results from social learning; that is, girls may be trained through modeling and rewards to develop this decoding pattern.

The research on the relationship between sex-typing and decoding has been inconsistent. Some studies find an advantage for individuals high in expressive characteristics (both androgynous and feminine-typed groups) (Heilbrun, 1984). Other research finds little relationship between sex typing and decoding skill, with small differences favoring those higher in instrumental qualities (Hall & Halberstadt, 1981). The critical variable may be the amount of attention paid to the communicator, which may vary with many personal and situational factors. In general, women appear to pay more attention to visual nonverbal cues than do men, which may be a function of their lower status, a point that will be discussed below.

As was found with verbal behaviors, males are less expressive nonverbally than are females, a gender difference that appears regularly among adults but inconsistently among children (Buck, 1977; Hall, 1980, 1985; Haviland & Malatesta, 1982; Yarczower & Daruns, 1982). This age pattern suggests that learning this skill is part of learning one's gender role, a hypothesis supported by finding a stronger relationship between encoding skill and sex typing than between encoding skill and sex (Zuckerman, DeFrank, Spiegel, & Larrance, 1982). Accuracy of encoding intentional nonverbal cues is positively correlated with "femininity" (expressive) traits, and negatively correlated with "masculinity" (instrumental) traits.

The importance of sex typing with respect to nonverbal behavior is clearly illustrated by a study conducted by LaFrance and Carmen (1980; LaFrance, 1982). Androgynous and sex-typed male and female undergraduates were observed in same-sex pairs in either a situation requiring instrumental qualities (debating an abstract issue) or expressive qualities (sharing feelings about starting college). Some nonverbal behaviors were coded as feminine (for example, smiling, gazing) and some were coded as masculine (for example, interrupting, vocalizing while pausing ["uh . . .", "mmm . . ."]). Both types of nonverbal behaviors were present in androgynous individuals, whereas sex-typed students were more restricted to sex-consonant behaviors, regardless of the topic. In this regard, it is interesting that "feminine" language styles have been found to contribute to a communicator's credibility, perhaps because listeners interpret sharing feelings, smiling, and gazing as linked to personal openness. In contrast, "masculine" language styles appear to contribute to the perception of the communicator as extroverted, perhaps because frequent and constant vocalizations are interpreted as a desire to affect the listener (Berryman-Fink & Wilcox, 1983). Thus it may be an advantage to use different speech modes in a flexible fashion, as androgynous individuals seem to do.

One must keep situational cues in mind when discussing all social behaviors, especially nonverbal ones. For example, the gender of the person to whom one talks may be as or more important than the gender of the person communicating (Davis & Weitz, 1982; Hall & Braunwald, 1981). Such factors also are important in research on personal space (Berman & Smith, 1984; Hayduk, 1983; Riess & Salzer, 1981), and in research on touching (Berman &

Smith, 1984; Major, 1982; Schmidlin & Major, 1983; Stier & Hall, 1984). Another important variable is culture. Females tend to sit closer than males during conversations, but the actual distance varies as a function of cultural background and the language being spoken (Sussman & Rosenfeld, 1982). Black women appear to show some nonverbal behaviors in same-sex pairs that are unique to their gender-race group (A. Smith, 1983): they do not smile more often than Black male pairs, they look at one another less often than White female pairs, and they move together in synchrony more often than both White female and Black male pairs.

Still, the general pattern of research suggests that females nonverbally display more submission and warmth and males display more dominance and high status cues (Frieze & Ramsey, 1976). Physiological factors and gender-related traits have been suggested to explain some of these findings. The main physiological explanation rests on research in hemispheric processing of the brain (see Chapters 2 and 3). The female advantage in discerning the emotions of others may be due to women's greater use of both hemispheres to understand emotion, whereas men appear to rely primarily on one hemisphere, although there is some controversy as to which hemisphere it is. Safer (1981) reports it is the right hemisphere, Star (1979) reports it is the left hemisphere. In any case, women appear to have greater access to left-hemisphere verbal codes for emotion. This gender difference, which is quite small, may reflect innate differences in brain structure, or it could come from early conditioning. The age patterns suggest the latter. Because males generally are discouraged from acknowledging their emotions verbally as part of their sex role, fewer males than females may build the necessary hemispheric connections.

It is likely that some innate factors interact with social factors to cause this gender difference, when it occurs (Haviland & Malatesta, 1982; Trotter, 1983). Male and female infants may present different patterns of emotional reactivity and different forms of signaling behaviors very early in life. Parents, particularly mothers, may view these behaviors differently as a function of infant gender, with girls' expressions viewed more positively, boys' more negatively. Furthermore, high maternal expressiveness may overstimulate highly reactive infant males. Perhaps as a consequence of these factors, mothers appear to be more restrictive in the range of emotions they express toward and encourage in their sons than in their daughters. The result would be girls' enhanced understanding of emotional expression.

Although physiological and learning factors may be important in understanding nonverbal behavior, the most persuasive explanation lies in the power and status differences between males and females. This explanation rests on the assumption that males and females hold different statuses and have differential access to power in our culture. Differences in nonverbal behaviors, then, reflect differences in status and power, and are not specific to gender.

The first to propose this kind of analysis was Helen Mayer Hacker (1951, 1975) who compared women to other minority groups, specifically to Blacks. She found striking similarities in behavior (flattering or deferential manner, fake shows of helplessness/ignorance), ascribed attributes (inferior intelligence, irresponsibility), rationalizations of status (each has his or her "place"), discrimination (limits on job and educational opportunities), and problems (unclear roles, role conflict). This analysis is still valid more than 35 years later and has received experimental support from different lines of research.

Nancy Henley (1977; Mayo & Henley, 1981) has analyzed sex differences in verbal and nonverbal behavior as particularly reflecting differences in status. These differences and her comparisons are summarized in Table 4-1. Thus, females' politeness, smiling, emotional expressiveness, smaller personal space, less frequent touching and talking, and greater frequency of being interrupted all reflect their subordinate status. Females' greater sensitivity to nonverbal cues may reflect a survival mechanism. Because a female's well-being is likely to depend on her "superior's" moods or desires, it is to her advantage to learn to read them well, especially because these "superiors" try to hide them. Henley's analysis has received wide but not unequivocal support (M. Davis & Weitz, 1982; Forden, 1981; Porter & Geis, 1982; Schmidlin & Major, 1983; Snodgrass, 1985; Stier & Hall, 1984). Her conclusions apply mainly to adults, and are situation specific.

Table 4-1
Gestures of Power and Privilege. (*Examples of some nonverbal behaviors with usage differing for status equals and nonequals, and for women and men.*)

	Between Status Equals		Between Status Nonequals		Between Men and Women	
	Intimate	Nonintimate	Used by Superior	Used by Subordinate	Used by Men	Used by Women
1. Address	Familiar	Polite	Familiar	Polite	Familiar	Polite
2. Demeanor	Informal	Circumspect	Informal	Circumspect	Informal	Circumspect
3. Posture	Relaxed	Tense (less relaxed)	Relaxed	Tense	Relaxed	Tense
4. Personal space	Closeness	Distance	Closeness (option)	Distance	Closeness	Distance
5. Time	Long	Short	Long (option)	Short	Long	Short
6. Touching	Touch	Don't touch	Touch (option)	Don't touch	Touch	Don't touch
7. Eye contact	Establish	Avoid	Stare, ignore	Avert eyes, watch	Stare, ignore	Avert eyes, watch
8. Facial expression	Smile?	Don't smile?	Don't smile	Smile	Don't smile	Smile
9. Emotional expression	Show	Hide	Hide	Show	Hide	Show
10. Self-disclosure	Disclose	Don't disclose	Don't disclose	Disclose	Don't disclose	Disclose

From *Body Politics: Power, Sex, and Nonverbal Communication,* by N. M. Henley.
Copyright 1977 by Prentice-Hall, Inc. Reprinted by permission.

An advantage of a status analysis rather than a role analysis is that it allows the incorporation of traditional theories of nonverbal behavior with theories on gender oppression. It points to the problem as being one of unequal status and not sex roles per se, and it suggests ways to change by breaking down the "body-power barrier." For example, women can stop smiling when they are not happy and start staring people in the eye. Men can stop interrupting and start displaying some emotion. The implications of these patterns are important. Because females (or feminine- and androgynous-sex-typed individuals) generally use more self-disclosure, display greater eye contact and smiling behavior, have smaller personal space, and exhibit greater listening and attending skills than males, they generally facilitate close personal interactions. Rosenthal and colleagues (1979) have determined that people who are more skillful at decoding nonverbal cues are more effective in their interpersonal relationships. Because more women have this skill and use it politely, their proficiency in interpersonal situations would be strengthened. Males (or masculine-sex-typed individuals), who have greater domination of conversations, space, and touching, and have minimal self-disclosure, would generally impede close personal interactions but would facilitate interpersonal control. These differences in spheres of influence (personal interactions versus power interactions) again reflect stereotypic differences.

Person-Related Behaviors

As noted above, females generally are assumed to be more concerned with person-centered interactions than males, who are assumed to be more concerned with power-centered interactions. Although this generalization is true to some extent, both types of interactions are composed of a wide range of behaviors, and not all of these behaviors show clear-cut sex differences. Person-centered interactions encompass such behaviors as dependency, affiliation, empathy, nurturance, altruism, morality, and equity/equality.

Dependency

Dependency is a trait commonly associated with females. As with passivity, however, dependency has multiple meanings and is neither clearly unitary nor clearly the opposite of independence (Sherman, 1976).

When dependency is defined as seeking the presence of others or as resistance to physical separation, no consistent sex difference for this trait emerges during the childhood years, although parental behavior toward the child may differ during different situations and at different periods (Fitzgerald, 1977; Maccoby & Jacklin, 1974; Wasserman & Lewis, 1985). Males may receive more physical contact during the first six months; females seem to receive more contact after that time. This differential treatment by parents may make males less amenable to social reinforcement and more autonomous than are females. In contrast, the greater parental contact females receive may strengthen the interpersonal bonds between the child and other people.

When dependency is defined as social interest or social responsiveness, some differences do appear, although they are subtle. Maccoby and Jacklin (1974) found no consistent differences during the first two years of a child's life in social responsiveness to either live people, faces, or voices. Similarly, Etaugh and Whittler (1982) found that preschool boys and girls did not differ in their ability to remember the faces of their peers. During childhood and adolescence, boys appear more sociable than do girls in the sense that they have more friends, chat and play with them more frequently, show off with them, and depend more on them for values, support, and activity (Lott, 1978; Maccoby & Jacklin, 1974; Strommen, 1977). Young girls are more likely to play alone or to relate to nearby adults. Although there may be some similarity in friendship patterns for the sexes

(Kandel, 1978), the relationships themselves seem qualitatively different during childhood and adolescence. Girls have fewer, but more intense, friendships that provide emotional support in personal crises. Boys have more friends of a less intimate nature (a "gang") who provide support in case of conflict with adults. (Friendships will be discussed at greater length in Chapter 10.)

This tendency of males to form groups has rarely been defined as dependency, however. Rather, it sometimes has been viewed as the basic element of society (see Tiger, 1969). Tiger argues that males have an innate tendency to bond together and form close groups and suggests that this bonding serves to maintain social order and accounts for male leadership and all-male clubs. However, although males do tend to have more friends, female friendships appear closer than male friendships. And no sex difference has been found in the tendency to belong to single-sex groups (Booth, 1972).

Thus, there is no evidence that females are more dependent than males when dependency is defined as proximity seeking or social responsiveness. An argument can be made that boys are more dependent when dependency is measured by numbers of friendships. These findings again illustrate the frequently biased nature of research questions and definitions.

The importance of consistent research definitions cannot be sufficiently stressed. In a cross-cultural study of 3- to 11-year-old American, Western European, and African children (Whiting & Edwards, 1973), younger girls (ages 3 to 6) were found to be more dependent than boys only when dependency was defined as seeking help and physical contact. Older boys (ages 7 to 11) were more dependent when dependency was defined as seeking attention. Across six cultures, sex differences were found to be a reflection of style and of task assignment (more away-from-home chores for males, more domestic chores for females) rather than a reflection of innate sex differences. In a similar vein, Lott (1978), in her study of four-year-old New Zealanders, found that children of both sexes smiled, asked for help, and followed adult instructions with equal frequency although gender differences had been predicted by adults. Such differences in expectations may lead adults to treat the sexes differently, such as to treat girls as more dependent. This differential treatment may have direct and indirect effects; for example, it may lead girls to believe they cannot do things by themselves. There is no evidence, however, to support popular notions that women have a "hidden fear of independence" (Dowling, 1981).

Situational and sex-typing factors also are important. For example, the willingness to seek and receive help is affected by the gender and sex-typing of the help-seeker, and the gender of the helper (Nadler, Maler, & Friedman, 1984). Males, especially "masculine" ones, were most affected by the gender of the helper, expressing more willingness to seek help from a female than a male. Females, especially "feminine" ones, showed the most consistent help-seeking behaviors. These results show the powerful effect of gender norms in moderating social behaviors.

Affiliation

When interest in, and concern about, other people is assessed after childhood, females tend to show a greater interest in affiliation and more positive feelings about social interactions than do males (Ickes & Barnes, 1977; Maccoby & Jacklin, 1974; Pollak & Gilligan, 1982; Swap & Rubin, 1983; Veroff, Depner, Kulka, & Douvan, 1980). For example, when adolescents were asked to rank a number of concerns in the order of the importance they felt each had for them personally, both sexes ranked identity and sexuality as the top two items. For the third item, however, a gender difference appeared. Girls ranked interpersonal relationships as the third most important concern to them, whereas boys ranked autonomy third (Strommen, 1977). It already has been noted that females compared to males express feelings more, verbally and nonverbally, and are more perceptive of the nonverbally expressed feelings of others. Thus, there does seem to be a gender difference here, corresponding to gender expectations, although it does not show up until adolescence and is thus more likely to be a consequence, not a cause, of the gender stereotypes.

Interestingly, this greater "need" for affiliation on the part of females has led many to assume that females are more dependent on males for love and fulfillment than males are

dependent on females (for example, Dowling, 1981). Men, on the average, actually fall in love more quickly and easily, become more upset at the end of a relationship, are more likely to remarry, and generally are in worse emotional and physical shape when unmarried than are women (for example, Gove, 1973, 1979). Thus simple generalizations of females "needing" others are unwarranted.

The reasons for this gender difference in interpersonal orientation appear very similar to those given for gender differences in nonverbal behavior, particularly status differences. High interpersonal orientation may develop as an adaptation to "a chronic position of relative powerlessness" (Swap & Rubin, 1983). Because low-power people are more likely to be affected by the actions of other people than are high-power people, it is to the advantage of low-power people to pay close attention to others.

Empathy

One component of empathy is the degree of sensitivity to others' thoughts and feelings. Females and feminine-sex-typed individuals, as it was previously discussed, tend to be better than males and masculine-sex-typed individuals at interpreting nonverbal cues, perhaps because they have greater eye contact or because they take more of an interest in people. When other forms of empathy are examined, however, as in responding to people with problems or in describing the feelings or plans of characters in a story or picture, no consistent sex differences emerge (Bem, Martyna, & Watson, 1976; Brehm, Powell, & Coke, 1984; Eisenberg & Lennon, 1983; Maccoby & Jacklin, 1974). Rather, people tend to be more accurate about people of the same sex and about situations with which they are familiar. Females tend to be more empathic when self-report measures are used, but not when nonobtrusive measures are used, perhaps because of gender-related expectations. Supporting this hypothesis is the finding that sex-typing affects empathy scores. Masculine-sex-typed people appear less empathic than either androgynous- or feminine-sex-typed people (Bem et al., 1976), paralleling the findings for nonverbal communication. If one views empathy as a positive trait, masculine sex typing is a handicap. There is no support for the hypothesis that self-report differences in empathy are due to an innate mechanism or predisposition (Eisenberg & Lennon, 1983).

Another factor affecting interpersonal sensitivity is the status of the participants. People in subordinate roles tend to be more sensitive to the feelings of another person than do people in leadership roles (Snodgrass, 1985). To the extent that women are more likely to be in a subordinate role than are men, a gender difference in interpersonal sensitivity is likely to be found which, in actuality, is a status difference.

Nurturance

Females traditionally have been thought to possess exclusively the capability of nurturing others—facilitating the development of others or, more generally, helping others. This belief has been an outgrowth of the fact that only women can bear and nurse children. Because only women can bear and nurse them, it might follow that women must "naturally" be more qualified to take care of them and, by extension, take care of others. The problem with this assumption is twofold. First, there is no evidence at all of a maternal instinct. Second, there is no evidence that females are consistently more nurturant than are males. In responses to infants and other vulnerable creatures, males and females have been found capable of equally nurturant behavior (Bem et al., 1976; Berman, 1980; Maccoby & Jacklin, 1974). Males and females do differ, however, in their self-report of their reactions to infants, and indeed in their behavioral reactions when observed or when assigned the caretaking role (Berman, 1976, 1980; Nash & Feldman, 1981). These differences, which appear to increase with age and are more marked during adolescence, seem primarily a response to gender expectations, because there is no gender difference in physiological responding to infants and children, nor in behavior when the individuals are not directly observed or evaluated.

The important variables related to nurturant behaviors seem to be: (1) contact with a newborn during a critical period after birth (first 24 hours, especially the first 45 minutes) (Bronfenbrenner, 1977; Maccoby & Jacklin, 1974; Money & Ehrhardt, 1972), (2) experience (fe-

males are usually given more preliminary practice with such behaviors—for example, playing with dolls, babysitting), and (3) gender expectations (Rossi, 1985). For example, Bem and colleagues (1976) found that androgynous college men were just as responsive to a kitten and to a human baby as were college women, but masculine-sex-typed men were not as responsive. Thus, sex typing may restrict nurturing behavior in males. Another interesting finding in the Bem study is that, when nurturant behavior necessitated active initiation of a response, feminine-sex-typed college women were less nurturant than androgynous women and androgynous men. Thus, because feminine women are behaviorally constricted in instrumental functioning, they were less able to be nurturant when the situation also required assertion.

Although there is no such thing as a maternal instinct, there is some indication that it is easier to trigger the response of parental care in females than in males. This may be a function of prenatal hormonal history (Ehrhardt, 1985; Hines, 1982; Money & Ehrhardt, 1972). Specifically, exposure to androgens seems to inhibit such behavior. Although most studies have been done with animals, studies of adrenogenital females show them to be less interested in rehearsing parental behaviors, such as babysitting and playing with dolls, during childhood. This, of course, may be a function of competing athletic interests and/or socialization and not a consequence of prenatal hormone exposure. These girls do eventually marry and have children; so again the hormonal effect seems, at most, to make parental behaviors easier to learn. Hormones clearly do not make parental behaviors inevitable, as evidenced by numerous cases of child abuse and infanticide in the general population. Nor do hormones prevent males from learning nurturing behaviors.

The fact that women are more likely to be in nurturant roles in our society (mothers, nurses, social workers, and so forth) is more a consequence of gender stereotypes than a direct reflection of any fundamental sex difference in nurturing ability. As Whiting and Edwards (1973) found in their cross-cultural study, differences in nurturance did not show up until ages 7 to 11, and then they were a clear function of differential socialization pressures. In those cultures where girls do not engage in infant care as well as in cultures where boys do care for infants, fewer sex differences in behavior are found. For example in Fiji, both sexes are involved in infant care and there is no difference in sex-typing between males and females (Basow, 1984a).

Altruism

Because females are expected to be more concerned about others, one might also expect them to be more altruistic—that is, to live and to act for the good of others, as in helping someone in distress. Indeed, girls do score significantly higher than boys on measures tapping their reputation for altruistic behaviors (Shigetomi, Hartmann, & Gelfand, 1981; Zarbatany, Hartmann, Gelfand, & Vinciguerra, 1985). However, on measures that assess actual helping behavior, no consistent sex differences appear. Where differences are found, it more often is in the direction of greater male than female helpfulness (Brehm, Powell, & Coke, 1984; Maccoby & Jacklin, 1974; Piliavin & Unger, 1985).

There are many mediating factors with regard to helping behavior. Among the important variables here are: (1) the nature of the response required (men are more likely than women to help if some initiative on the part of the respondent is required); (2) the nature of the task (females are more likely than males to perceive a situation as dangerous; males are more reluctant than females to engage in activity inappropriate to sex-role), and (3) the gender of the person requiring help (other-sex helping behaviors are more likely than same-sex ones). Helper sex typing may be another important factor, although the evidence is inconsistent (Basow & Crawley, 1982; Senneker & Hendrick, 1983). In some situations, high scorers on instrumental traits ("masculine" and androgynous individuals) are more likely to help than low scorers. In other situations, where embarrassment is possible, high scorers on instrumental traits are less likely to help than low scorers (Tice & Baumeister, 1985). All these variables point to the importance of social factors in determining helping behavior.

Morality

Since the 1960s, moral development has been conceptualized as a series of stages that children pass through. These stages relate to a child's level of cognitive development. As Kohlberg (1969) describes the six stages grouped into three levels, children move from a level of preconventional morality (concern with obedience and punishment as well as instrumental considerations) to a level of conventional morality (concern with social acceptance and following authority), and then perhaps to a level of postconventional morality (concern with individual rights and with individual principles). Although not everyone achieves the highest of the six stages, the sequence was seen as invariant. From Kohlberg's research as well as that of others, males typically score around Stage 4 (concern with authority) whereas females typically score around Stage 3 (concern with feelings and social opinions). These findings supported the belief, based on Freudian theory, that females were less developed morally than were males, although Kohlberg's focus was on cognitive development, while Freud emphasized emotional development.

This theory of moral development had fundamental flaws, not the least of which was that it was based entirely upon the study of male subjects responding to male protagonists in a story. Using Kohlberg's original stories but varying the sex of the protagonist, Bussey and Maughan (1982) found that males reasoned differently as a function of the protagonist's sex: they scored at Stage 3 when the character was female, but at Stage 4 when it was male. Females did not change their reasoning as a function of the sex of the protagonist. These results indicate that: (1) Kohlberg's original stories were biased toward males, (2) that gender stereotypes probably affect the responses of males, and (3) that males' moral reasoning is more responsive to external cues than is females' (or at least to these particular external cues).

Carol Gilligan (1977, 1982a, 1982b), in attempting to correct the male bias in Kohlberg's research by talking with women and girls, discovered that women conceptualize morality very differently and that Kohlberg's stages do not capture the ways some women think about moral problems. When people talk about a personal moral dilemma, men seem more concerned than women with the "right" thing to do whereas women seem more concerned than men with the "responsible" thing to do. Rather than abstract principles of justice, women were much more concerned than were men with the social context and with the feelings of others when thinking about real personal dilemmas. Blake and Cohen (1984) in their meta-analysis of sex differences in moral development verified Gilligan's claim that there are two different orientations for describing moral development. Determining which approach is more "moral" is clearly a subjective evaluation. Gilligan's approach is that the two paths to morality are different and equal and that these differences should be recognized and accepted. A new theory of morality, which incorporates the experiences of both men and women, thinking about both real and hypothetical moral problems, clearly needs to be developed. Moral thinking needs to be defined to include both justice and care. Indeed, longitudinal studies by Gilligan suggest that over time, people move from a single focus on one ethic or the other, toward a dual focus on both (Cordes, 1984b).

Equity/Equality

Numerous studies have indicated that males in general appear to subscribe to a norm of equity, allocating rewards according to inputs, whereas females appear to subscribe to a norm of equality, allocating rewards equally regardless of inputs (Kahn & Gaeddert, 1985; Reis & Jackson, 1981). It has been hypothesized that these differences are due to: (1) differences in personal orientation (males being more competitive, females more social), (2) differences in status (high-status people use equity, low-status people use equality), (3) attributions for performance (males may be more likely to use internal attributions, females may be more likely to use external attributions), and (4) gender stereotypes (Kahn & Gaeddert, 1985; Kahn, Nelson, & Gaeddert, 1980; Major & Adams, 1984; Stake, 1985). Careful examination of the research reveals, however, that this gender difference may be exaggerated due to experimental artifacts. Situational factors appear to be

critical in determining reward allocation patterns by providing cues as to the appropriate behavior for women and men in that setting (Major & Adams, 1984). Sex typing also may be involved, because individuals high in instrumental qualities have been found to allocate rewards equitably whereas individuals high in nurturant/expressive qualities tended to allocate rewards more equally (Olejnik, Tompkins, & Heinbuck, 1982).

Power-Related Behaviors

In the area of power-centered interactions, males generally are thought to be more proficient than females. Such interactions encompass the behaviors of aggression, assertion, dominance, competition/cooperation, and independence/compliance.

Aggressiveness

Of all assumed gender differences, the most commonly and strongly held assumption concerns males' greater aggressiveness. Although this assumption has been repeatedly substantiated across many situations and cultures (Frodi, Macaulay, & Thome, 1977; Hyde, 1984b; Maccoby & Jacklin, 1974; Whiting & Edwards, 1973), the size of the difference actually is quite modest. In her meta-analysis of gender differences in aggression, Hyde (1984b) found that the size of the difference was only about one half a standard deviation in scores. Furthermore, gender accounted for only 5% of the variation in scores. As with gender differences in spatial ability, which are approximately of the same magnitude, it is easy to overestimate the importance of the difference by exaggerating the frequent findings of a difference.

Besides the size of the gender difference being relatively small, there also are important methodological qualifiers. A primary qualification is again in definition. Moyer (1974) has differentiated at least eight different types of aggression, some of which are more common in females. Of the different types, boys tend to aggress in physical and destructive ways, girls in verbal and disobedient ways (Barfield, 1976; Hyde, 1984b). Gender differences are largest in physical aggression. Gender differences also are larger in naturalistic studies than in experimental ones, and larger when aggression is directly observed or reported by peers than when it is reported by self or adult others (Hyde, 1984b). Males also tend to be more aggressive than females when some form of initiative, such as getting up to do something, is required; no difference occurs when just a response, such as pushing a button to deliver a shock after having been shocked by the target person, is called for (Deaux, 1976). There also are age trends, with larger differences among young children, especially preschoolers, than among adults (Hyde, 1984b). Interestingly, there are generational trends as well, with larger differences found in studies before 1973 than after 1978.

In addition to these methodological qualifiers, there also are important situational qualifiers. In this regard, it is important to differentiate behavioral aggression from both the ability to aggress and the propensity to aggress. Although males seem to have a greater readiness to respond in aggressive ways (Maccoby & Jacklin, 1974), they still must learn the behavior and choose to display it. As Bandura (1973) has demonstrated, girls learn aggressive behavior to about the same degree as boys but are more inhibited in performing those behaviors. When the social situation allows it, however, girls exhibit the same amount of aggression as boys. Other important situational variables affecting the display of aggression in both males and females are sex of victim and observer, empathy, guilt, aggression anxiety, amount of provocation, attitude toward women, sex typing of the situation, and affective assessment of aggressive acts (Frodi, Macaulay, & Thome, 1977; Richardson, Vinsel, & Taylor, 1980; Slife & Rychlak, 1982; H. Thompson & Richardson, 1983; Towson & Zanna, 1982). For example, women are less often the victim of retaliatory aggression than are males, and both sexes advocate more aggressive responses when the situation is gender-congruent than when it is gender-incongruent.

All these qualifications lead to the conclusion that males and females are more similar than different in their aggressive behavior. However, the modest differences that do exist suggest that males in general may have a somewhat greater tendency than females in general to respond to certain situations with behavioral aggression. Most explanations for this difference center either on physiological or social factors, although it is probably more accurate to say that these factors interact.

Physiological explanations have centered primarily on the role of hormones, especially prenatal, although some researchers also have suggested that chromosomes may be important. The evidence with regard to chromosomes is very unclear. Meyer-Bahlburg's (1974) finding of a higher percentage of males with an extra Y chromosome (XYY instead of XY) in mental-penal institutions than in the general public gave rise to speculation that the extra Y chromosome may make these individuals hyper-aggressive. Further studies did not support such a linkage. For example, such individuals did not commit more aggressive crimes than their XY counterparts, and males with an extra X chromosome (XXY) are comparable behaviorally to those with an extra Y chromosome (Barfield, 1976). Thus, the question of chromosomal influence on aggression still is unresolved. Indications are that environmental conditions may interact with abnormal genetic conditions to make certain deviant behavior patterns, including aggression, more likely.

With regard to role of prenatal hormones, the evidence is more suggestive although still not conclusive. Male fetuses during the third prenatal month normally produce androgen, which sets the brain for a fairly regular production of hormones at puberty. Evidence from studies on animals and humans has suggested that testosterone (an androgen) is related to aggressiveness (Barfield, 1976; Maccoby & Jacklin, 1974; Money & Ehrhardt, 1972). This relationship is not clear-cut, however. Firstly, the relationship is not unidirectional. High levels of testosterone may increase aggressiveness, but aggressiveness may also increase testosterone levels (Rose, Gordon, & Bernstein, 1972). Secondly, the relationship between the two is not found in all animals, nor have significant correlations been found between testosterone level and hostility or aggression in human males

(Doering et al., 1974; Moyer, 1974). Thirdly, studies of genetic females exposed to prenatal androgens (those with the adrenogenital syndrome) have found higher levels of rough-and-tumble play and self-assertion, but not always aggression (Hines, 1982; Money & Ehrhardt, 1972). Not surprisingly, human behavior appears to be multidetermined.

On the other hand, sex differences in aggression in rhesus monkeys do seem to have a hormonal component, since even infants raised with cloth and wire "mothers" exhibit sex differences in aggressive play (Harlow, 1965). In addition, administration of hormones postnatally can sometimes increase aggression (Barfield, 1976).

The most parsimonious explanation of these findings is that prenatal exposure to androgen may predispose an individual to behave aggressively. Such a predisposition may increase sensitivity to certain stimuli, like rough contact, or may make certain patterns of reactions, such as large muscle movements, more rewarding and thus more likely to occur (Hamburg & Lunde, 1966). This predisposition may arise through the effect of androgens on the amygdala, a structure in the limbic system of the brain that appears to affect aggressive behavior. For this predisposition to be actualized, however, various social influences are needed.

The importance of social factors in the expression of aggression can be seen clearly in the previously cited research on the innumerable situational and methodological factors that affect aggressive behavior. Regardless of any physiological predisposition, society plays the determining role in the development of aggressive behavior, a point dramatically illustrated by the classic cross-cultural studies of Margaret Mead (1935). Rather than males always being more aggressive than females, she found one New Guinean tribe where both sexes were aggressive as adults (Mundugumor); one, where both sexes were nonaggressive (Arapesh); and one, where females were aggressive and males passive (Tchambuli). In more Western-oriented cross-cultural research, Block (1973) found that aggression in males is particularly encouraged in the United States, more so than in England and Scandinavia. Parents seem more tolerant of aggression in their sons than in their daugh-

ters, although this varies with the type of aggression displayed and the object of the aggression. Somewhat surprisingly, Maccoby and Jacklin (1974) found that boys are actually punished more often for physical aggression than are girls. This may occur because boys engage in physical aggression more often than do girls. Observations of toddler play groups confirm that boys act more aggressively than do girls (Fagot & Hagan, 1985). Interestingly, boys more often than girls were reinforced by their peers for their aggressive behavior, making it likely that boys would continue to demonstrate such behaviors in the future. A major factor in American culture encouraging aggressive behavior in males is the media. As will be discussed in Chapter 8, television in particular is filled with images of males acting aggressively. Such images dramatically affect the behavior of many viewers (for example, Slife & Rychlak, 1982).

Thus, even a behavior with a possible physiological basis, such as aggression, can be influenced by cultural norms, being either augmented or diminished. Other evidence indicates that this environmental and biological interaction is true with animals as well. Aggressive behavior is influenced by rearing, previous encounters, situational factors, and amount of fighting experience (Bleier, 1979).

In conclusion, males may have a greater predisposition to act aggressively than do females, but aggressive behavior is determined primarily by situational factors and previous learning history. The implications of this predisposition are not clear, since, in industrialized societies, physical aggressiveness does not necessarily help one survive or achieve high status. Rather, physical aggression may be maladaptive for the individual as well as for society if it leads to violence and crime. These societal effects of aggression will be discussed in Chapter 12.

Assertiveness

Although the terms *assertiveness* and *aggressiveness* are frequently confused, they refer to different verbal and nonverbal behaviors. Whereas aggressiveness refers to behaviors meant to enhance the self at the expense of the other, assertiveness refers to the ability to speak up for oneself while continuing to respect the other person. Assertiveness can also be differentiated from passivity, which in this regard refers to letting oneself be put down by someone else (Alberti & Emmons, 1978; Phelps & Austin, 1975). In studies of this variable, females have been found generally to be less assertive than males. We previously noted that women let men dominate conversations, allow themselves to be interrupted, and are less likely to initiate actions. However, this general lack of assertiveness may be true only for White women. Black females have been found to have little difficulty asserting themselves with Whites or Blacks, males or females (Adams, 1980).

Sex-typing also may be related to assertiveness. A number of studies have found that androgynous individuals, both female and male, were the most effective in situations involving both positive (commendatory) assertions and negative (refusal) assertions (Bem, 1975a; Darden, 1983; Kelly, O'Brien, & Hosford, 1981). The least assertive individuals were the undifferentiated, low on both expressive and instrumental traits. In other research, however, sex typing had little effect on conventional assertiveness (Crosby, Jose, & Wong-McCarthy, 1982).

Gender stereotypes have clearly associated "femininity" with nonassertiveness and "masculinity" with assertiveness. Such stereotypes have been found to influence judgments of assertiveness (L. Wilson & Gallois, 1985). As early as the fourth grade, children have been found to view assertive behaviors as more desirable for males and passive behavior as more desirable for females (Connor, Serbin, & Ender, 1978). Concomitantly, these same children express greater approval of gender-consonant behaviors. Thus we find that by the college years, women in particular view assertive behavior as more aggressive when engaged in by a female than the identical behavior when engaged in by a male (Freundl, 1981). This social perception may make some women hesitate to engage in such behaviors.

Situational factors are quite important with regard to assertive behaviors, as they are to most social behaviors. Some people may find it easier to be assertive with friends than with strangers; some may find it easier to be assertive with same-sex rather than other-sex individuals. And there are different types of assertions. In some contexts, such as expressing negative feelings to a close friend of the other sex, assertion by females is viewed as even more appropriate than is assertion by males (Linehan & Seifert, 1983). Other research suggests that it is only in mixed-sex groups, especially ones that are structured, that one can observe lower female than male assertiveness (Kimble, Yoshikawa, & Zehr, 1981). In such groups, a female may be reluctant to be assertive due to expected social rejection for her behavior and/or due to her lower social status. Social status has been found influential in terms of behavior in groups, especially for females (Freundl, 1981; Lockheed & Hall, 1976).

Assertiveness is an important area of research. While many of the positive aspects of power, such as standing up for one's rights, displaying leadership, and so forth, have been associated with the trait of aggressiveness, they are really assertive behaviors. Because aggression may be biologically based, some people have assumed that males more "naturally" are leaders. This is totally unwarranted, since most leadership behaviors involve assertiveness, and assertiveness is definitely learned and has been successfully taught (Alberti & Emmons, 1978). Indeed, some have argued that males more than females need to be trained in assertiveness in order to modify their more typical aggressive social behaviors (Smye & Wine, 1980).

Dominance

The image of males as the more dominant sex is strongly held in our culture. Think of the standard picture of our prehistoric ancestors— a caveman dragging a cavewoman about by the hair. Dominance refers to a relationship in which one member of a group has control and influence over the behaviors of others (Frieze & Ramsey, 1976). As noted in the discussion of communication patterns, males clearly dominate conversations and physical space. Males also dominate when behaviors are related to physical toughness and force, as in children's play groups. However, even here there is a considerable amount of overlap between the behavior of the sexes (Maccoby & Jacklin, 1974). These early differences in dominance may be related to differences in aggression, which, in turn, may be related to androgen production. However, Money and Ehrhardt (1972) found in their study of adrenogenital females that, although these girls did compete more in the dominance hierarchy of boys than did other girls, they did not compete for the top positions, a suggestion that social factors may also be operating. In addition, other researchers have found that aggression does not automatically lead to dominance even in animals, although the two may be correlated (Leibowitz, 1979; Rose, Holaday, & Bernstein, 1971).

One problem with research in this area has been the narrowness or lack of specificity of the definition of dominance behavior. Control and influence over others can be for selfish ends, such as self-assertion or self-enhancement. This kind of dominance is called *agentic* or *egoistic* (for example, persuading one person to perform another person's menial tasks). However, control and influence over others also can be for the furthering of group goals or group harmony. This kind of dominance is called *communal* or *prosocial* (for example, by settling disputes among group members) (Buss, 1981; Whiting & Edwards, 1973). Male undergraduates have been found to judge agentic dominance as more desirable than communal dominance, but to engage in both types of dominant behaviors (Buss, 1981). In contrast, female undergraduates rate communal dominance as more desirable than agentic dominance, and they express dominance primarily in group-oriented communal ways. Such distinctions are important in order to understand the dominant behaviors of males and females, because many research designs assess only one kind of dominant behavior. Furthermore, the differential evaluation of dominance activities by males and females suggests there have been different patterns of socialization regarding such activities and different degrees of social support for engaging in different types of dominant behaviors.

Males and females also may form different types of dominance relationships in same-sex groups. Although traditionally, a relatively linear dominance hierarchy has been expected, with a strong leader and clear ranking of sub-ordinate positions, such a pattern has been based on all-male rather than all-female groups. As we have seen with other research topics, using the male as the norm biases the findings for females and the conclusions about "people in general." More current research (for example, Paikoff & Savin-Williams, 1983) suggests that female groups tend to be less structured and less linear than male groups, with usually two people in the top positions. These groups also tend to be more cohesive than all-male groups, at least among late adolescents. The term *cohesive dyarchy* better characterizes all-female groups while the more traditional *dominance hierarchy* better characterizes all-male groups.

In same-sex groups, females have not been found to be less dominant in conversations than are men (Kimble, Yoshikawa, & Zehr, 1981). However, in mixed-sex groups, the picture typically is quite different, at least among Whites. In laboratory settings and in society at large, males more often are leaders in mixed-gender, cooperative, and task-oriented groups. By adolescence, leadership has little to do with force and much to do with status, norms, and expertise. As some researchers have argued (Kanter, 1977; Lockheed & Hall, 1976; Thompson, 1981), males generally have higher status than females, and this higher status structures the power and prestige of a group unless steps are taken to alter the power structure. This status factor of sex may interact with race, as Adams (1980) has noted. In her research, Black females consistently were more dominant than White females regardless of the race of their partner, whereas Black males became dominant only with partners of their own race. These complex findings emphasize the importance of not generalizing from research on Whites to the behavior of other races, as well as the importance of considering situational variables and person variables in assessing social behavior.

One situational variable that may be important in mixed-sex task-oriented groups is the sex typing of the group task. Male undergraduates were more likely than female undergraduates to emerge as leaders when the group task was "masculine" (how to invest $10,000) and neutral (how to spend $10,000 on entertainment items). When the task was a "feminine" one (how a young woman should spend $10,000 on her wedding), women were more likely than men to assume the leadership role (Wentworth & Anderson, 1984).

Becoming a leader depends upon being seen as a leader. One group of researchers (Porter & Geis, 1982; Porter, Geis, & Jennings [Walstedt], 1983) found that women simply were unlikely to be seen as leaders in mixed-sex groups despite the presence of customary leadership cues, such as sitting at the head of the table. This was true regardless of the observer's sex, sex typing, or feminist ideology. Such perceptions, then, appear to be cultural stereotypes that operate on a nonconscious level. Even when a woman and a man engage in similar group behaviors, observers are more likely to view the man as the leader than the woman (Butler & Geis, 1985; Porter, Geis, Cooper, & Newman, 1985). Even equally participating group members are likely to view only the men as leaders, unless they've been exposed to a number of women in positions of authority (Geis, Boston, & Hoffman, 1985).

Similarly, Nyquist & Spence (in press) found, in a dyad situation, that when college women were paired with male peers, only 38% of the women assumed leadership despite women scoring higher than their partners on dominance, as measured by the California Personality Inventory. However, in same-sex dyads, the high-dominant individual assumed leadership 74% of the time. Similar findings have been reported by other researchers (Fleischer & Chertkoff, in press; Golub & Canty, 1982; Megargee, 1969). Again, the findings suggest that sex role, rather than dominance, is related to leadership in mixed-sex groups. Recent research by Porter and colleagues (1985) offers additional support for the importance of sex roles in determining leadership. Male dominance was the norm in small mixed-sex groups of undergraduates except when androgynous individuals were present and received support for sharing leadership.

In intimate relationships, men and women appear to use different power strategies to get their way, depending on the type of relationship involved and their own sex-typing (Cowan, Drinkard, & MacGavin, 1984; Falbo, 1982; Falbo & Peplau, 1980). Among heterosexual couples, men are more likely than women to report using bilateral and direct strategies, such as bargaining and reasoning. Individuals high in instrumental traits also were likely to use bilateral direct strategies, in contrast with unilateral and indirect strategies, such as evasion and using negative affect like crying. Such strategies were more often used by women and those low in instrumental traits. However, among homosexual couples, and among friends, women and men do not use different power strategies. These findings parallel those of people who preferred, and perceived themselves to have, more power than their partner in the relationship. Those with more power also were more likely to use bilateral and direct strategies, but were less likely to receive such strategies. From this line of research, we again are forced to acknowledge the important role of differential status in determining social behaviors, in this case, use of power.

It is not true that women are simply less dominant, less task-oriented, or less active than men or that they naturally assume a more social-expressive role rather than an instrumental role in a group (Kimble et al., 1981; Lockheed & Hall, 1976). Rather, peer interactions and expectations for competence tend to socialize males and females to play different roles in groups. With appropriate interventions, such as by reinforcing competent behaviors of low-status individuals, or by de-emphasizing the task orientation of the group, this imbalance can be remedied, and females can be equally effective as leaders (Fleischer & Chertkoff, in press; Kimble et al., 1981; Lockheed & Hall, 1976). (The issue of women as leaders will be discussed again in Chapter 11.)

Competitiveness

According to gender stereotypes, males are generally more competitive than females. This is certainly true in sports and perhaps in business, but, in laboratory settings, sex differences are not found consistently (Kahn, 1979; Maccoby & Jacklin, 1974). In observations of young children's behaviors, sex differences in competitiveness also generally do not appear (Lott, 1978). Moely, Skarin, and Weil (1979) found an interesting developmental pattern in their study of competitive and cooperative behavior in children aged 4 to 5 and 7 to 9. Both sexes in the younger age group were most competitive with other-sex partners; in the older age group, however, only girls retained this response selectivity. Boys aged 7 to 9 showed a general tendency to compete regardless of partner sex and instructional set.

What do emerge from a variety of studies are differing patterns of performance for the sexes, with males being more likely than females to be concerned with winning, especially if money is concerned, and in surpassing an opponent. Females appear more concerned than males with interpersonal aspects of the situation, such as minimizing losses (Deaux, 1976). Furthermore, women's performance but not men's was particularly affected by peer approval or disapproval of competition (Alagna, 1982). These differences, of course, parallel sex-role expectations of instrumental versus expressive behaviors, and they probably reflect the marked differences the sexes experience in athletic training and play activity. Supporting this interpretation is the finding that "masculine" and androgynous individuals had better performance and greater perceived success under competitive conditions than did "feminine" and "undifferentiated" individuals (Alagna, 1982). Other variables affecting competitive performance are the nature of the task, group composition, significance of the behavior, training, race and racial ideology of participants, and so forth (Deaux, 1976; Jackson, 1982; Kahn, 1979; Lockheed & Hall, 1976; Maccoby & Jacklin, 1974). During college, males seem to maintain a generalized competitive approach, whereas females appear to reduce their competitiveness if their partner is a male peer (Bunker, Forcey, Wilderom, & Elgie, 1984).

Independence/Compliance

From a large number of literature reviews and meta-analyses, it appears that across all subject matters and sources of influence, females are not more compliant, suggestible, or conforming than are males (Cooper, 1979; Eagly, 1983; Eagly & Carli, 1981; Eagly & Wood, 1985; Maccoby & Jacklin, 1974; Sohn, 1980). There also is no gender difference in the degree to

which male and female college students are influenced by other people in making certain life decisions (Basow & Howe, 1979a). When gender differences are found in the literature, however, they usually are in the direction of greater female conformity, although the effect sizes are quite small (less than a quarter of a standard deviation), and the differences appear to be due to a number of situational and methodological variables. Findings of a gender difference in influenceability depend on the nature of the task itself, on the presence of others, on the gender of the researcher, on the sex typing of the individual, and on the race and status of the participants.

When a task is familiar or gender appropriate, both sexes show independence; when it is unfamiliar or gender inappropriate, both sexes are more likely to conform (Feldman-Summers, Montano, Kasprzyk, & Wagner, 1980; Karabenick, 1983; Morelock, 1980; Sistrunk & McDavid, 1971). The sex typing of the topic appears to interact with the source of the majority influence such that when the source and the topic are sex-congruent, there is greater conformity (Feldman-Summers et al., 1980; Morelock, 1980). For example, when the issue is female related and the source of the majority influence is female, subjects conformed more.

When subjects in laboratory studies on conformity are being observed, males tend to conform less than do females (Eagly & Carli, 1981; Eagly, Wood, & Fishbaugh, 1981). However, when subjects are not observed, few gender differences appear. These findings parallel those found with situations involving group pressure (for example, Asch, 1956). When there is no group pressure, females are no more likely to conform in their opinions than are males; when group pressure exists, and in face-to-face encounters, females are more likely to conform than are males. The change appears more at the level of behavioral expression than at the level of a genuine change of opinion. These results suggest that males view nonconformity/independence of thought as part of their sex role and therefore are less likely to show conformity in the presence of others. It also is possible that female conformity in such situations is due to their greater concern about interpersonal harmony. However, Eagly, Wood, and Fishbaugh (1981) found no support for this last hypothesis.

Men's greater nonconformity in the presence of others also may reflect their relatively higher status. This hypothesis has been supported by a number of studies (Eagly, 1983; Eagly & Wood, 1982, 1985). Women are expected to hold lower-status positions than men, and lower-status individuals tend to conform more than higher-status individuals, especially in the presence of others. Men, by virtue of their sex role, occupy a higher status than women. This higher status creates expectancies regarding social behaviors that affect social interactions in ways that then confirm the expectancies. For example, males are expected to exert greater influence than females. They then act in influencing ways, and females and other low-status individuals act in more conforming ways; the outcome is greater male influence and greater female conformity, at least in some situations. A prime illustration of this dynamic is Eagly and Carli's (1981) finding from their meta-analysis of social influence studies. Male researchers, who were 79% of the authors of such studies, obtained large gender differences in the direction of greater persuasibility and conformity among females. Female researchers generally found no gender difference. The importance of the sex of the researcher needs to be given greater weight in evaluating social behavioral research. Also needing more recognition is the important interaction between race and sex in research design. As noted in the previous section, Black females appear less easily influenced and more assertive than either their Black male or White female peers (Adams, 1980, 1983).

Sex typing is another important factor in conformity research. In general, feminine-sex-typed college students appear most conforming, and androgynous and "masculine" individuals least conforming (Bem, 1975b; Brehony & Geller, 1981). These results may be especially true for females and may be related to the individual's locus of control. The more students saw themselves as responsible for their behavior, the less conforming they were, and androgynous individuals were more likely to see themselves as responsible for their behavior than were "feminine" individuals.

Gender does interact with situations in such a way that, during childhood, girls comply more than boys with directives from parents and teachers; boys comply more than girls with peer pressure (Maccoby & Jacklin, 1974). It is possible that girls may be more socialized for adult approval than are boys. In any case, it does seem true that females receive more requests from adults than do boys, making the cause and effect sequence here very unclear.

Summary

In this chapter, we have reviewed a wide range of social behaviors and have found very few clear-cut sex differences except for aggressiveness (more frequent in males) and for communication patterns (males tend to dominate). Most differences that appear in the literature seem to be differences in quality, not quantity, as in moral behavior and dominance patterns; that is, females and males appear to have different patterns of behavior. Yet, there is a considerable amount of overlap in all areas surveyed.

In general, girls do not seem more fearful than boys, although they are more willing to admit fears; they are not more dependent when dependency is defined as seeking a caretaker or as number of friends. In fact, by the latter definition, boys are more dependent, since they have more friends and rely on them more for their values. Females do express a greater interest in affiliation during and after childhood than do males but they are not more responsive to social rewards.

In almost all areas of social behavior, situational factors either alone or in interaction with gender are the major determinants of behavior. Interactions between the situation and the gender of the participant, or between the situation and the sex typing of the participant are the major findings in the following areas: communication patterns, nurturance, empathy, equity, altruism, aggressiveness, assertiveness, competitiveness, and compliance.

In reviewing explanations for the few gender differences, there is some evidence that a predisposition for aggressiveness may be related to prenatal androgen levels and is thus more common in males. But the specific behaviors must be learned by each individual, and society can either encourage or discourage the development of behaviors in one sex or in an individual. Similarly, prenatal androgen exposure may inhibit parental behavior in adults, but this behavior is more clearly a function of learning than of hormonal predisposition.

Differences in verbal and nonverbal communication, compliance, and in leadership patterns seem to reflect differences in the status of males and females in U.S. society. Male behavior is consistent with males' higher status; female behavior is consistent with the subordinate status of females.

The strong sex-by-situation and sex-typing-by-situation interactions for certain behaviors emphasize the influence of social forces (parental behavior and societal expectations), as do developmental patterns.

In summary, social factors and status factors seem to play the major roles in determining social behaviors and personality functioning. Biological predispositions, however, may be involved for aggression and nurturant behaviors in particular.

Recommended Reading

Adams, K. A. (1983). Aspects of social context as determinants of black women's resistance to challenges. *Journal of Social Issues, 39,* 69–78. An important article urging the consideration of race and gender variables as interacting factors in social behavior.

Eagly, A. H. (1983). Gender and social influence: A social psychological analysis. *American Psychologist, 38,* 971–981. A comprehensive review of the literature on influenceability and its implications.

Gilligan, C. (1982a). *In a different voice: Psychological theory and women's development.* Cambridge, Mass.: Harvard. A ground-breaking book describing women's moral development and the ways in which it differs from that of men.

Hall, J. A. (1985). *Nonverbal sex differences: Communication accuracy and expressive style.* Baltimore: Johns Hopkins University. Thorough review and analysis of the extensive research literature on nonverbal sex differences among infants, children, and adults. Possible explanations are evaluated.

O'Leary, V. E., Unger, R. K., & Wallston, B. S. (Eds.) (1985). *Women, gender, and social psychology.* Hillsdale, NJ: Lawrence Erlbaum Associates. Excellent collection of review articles on most of the major topics in social psychology research today, with special attention to methodological issues.

Sexual Behavior

Perhaps no area in the study of sex differences and similarities is more clouded by misconceptions than is the area of sexual behavior. Part of this confusion is due to the very private nature of sexual experiences in our culture. Although a person's social behaviors are observed by many people, an individual's sexual behaviors are viewed by very few others—perhaps by only one other person in the course of a lifetime. This clearly limits factually based generalizations.

In the United States especially, there has been a taboo against talking about sexual feelings and behaviors. This is particularly true for females. This limits the information one can obtain from others. When one does obtain information from self-reports, it is difficult to know its accuracy, which is a general problem. Kinsey's surveys in the 1950s (Kinsey, Pomeroy, & Martin, 1948; Kinsey, Pomeroy, Martin, & Gebhard, 1953), Masters and Johnson's laboratory research (1966, 1979), Hite's surveys of female and male sexuality (1976, 1981), and Pietropinto and Simenauer's survey of male sexuality (1977) have added tremendously to our knowledge of sexual functioning, but research problems still abound.

A major problem in sex research has been researcher bias. Because people have so many preconceived notions of sexual behavior, it is not surprising that these assumptions manifest themselves in the research questions asked. For example, women's reactions to visual stimuli have rarely been studied, since there is a pervasive myth that women do not get turned on by erotica. Similarly, some researchers generalize about human sexuality from animal data despite the fact that nonhuman female primates have no hymen, no orgasm, no menopause, and no voluntary birth control. In addition, nonhuman primate sexuality is determined by the female estrus cycle. The extent to which such researcher biases can influence our attitudes and beliefs is clearly demonstrated in the case of Freud, who postulated the vaginal orgasm as an index of a woman's psychological maturity. Despite the fact that there is no such thing as a vaginal orgasm (scientists now agree that all female orgasms result from clitoral stimulation), Freud was believed for 50 years and is still believed today by many people.

Another research problem is in the use of volunteers. As Abraham Maslow (in Seaman, 1972) demonstrated, people who willingly participate in sex research without financial compensation are usually freer in their sex lives than most people and are less inhibited and more self-actualizing. Consequently, surveys may be using biased samples. Masters and Johnson, however, did pay their subjects and carefully screened them for psychological abnormalities; so such bias in their studies is reduced. One might argue, however, that people who would allow their sexual behavior to be studied in a laboratory still constitute an unrepresentative sample.

Gender of the researcher is also an important variable. Male anthropologists often get data only on the male sex life in other cultures either because of their own bias or because females will not talk with them about sexual matters. Israel and Eliasson (1971) found an effect of interviewer bias that resulted in each sex giving more traditional answers to same-sex interviewers. This bias certainly would affect survey responses.

Once results are obtained, the data often are interpreted according to prevailing assumptions. Although there is a striking amount of similarity in male and female sexual responses, only the differences have been stressed. Thus, based on the findings that more males than females engage in masturbation, it has been concluded that females are uninterested in sex for its own sake. Yet the same studies also show that more than half of the females do masturbate and achieve orgasm, contradicting the woman-as-asexual image.

Keeping these research problems in mind, we will review the current findings regarding sexual behavior. Because sexual behavior is so complex and, in some ways, hard to break into its component parts, the explanations put forth to explain individual aspects of sexual behavior have a great deal of overlap. Consequently, it will make more sense to examine these explanations after we first examine the findings.

Current Findings

Perhaps the first area to consider is that related to the physiology of sexual responses. We will then examine the findings on sexual desires, responses to erotic stimuli, homosexuality, and masturbation.

Physiology of Sexual Responses

In Masters and Johnson's revolutionary work (1966), the authors shattered the myth of sex differences in sexual responding. In their laboratory study of 382 women and 312 men, they discerned four phases of human sexual response, each of which is virtually identical in males and females. These phases are summarized in Table 5-1.

The four phases are as follows:

1. The *excitement* phase is characterized by sexual stimulation producing vasocongestion (filling of the blood vessels). This vasocongestion results in lubrication and clitoral erection in females in 5 to 15 seconds and penile erection in males in 3 to 8 seconds. This response occurs for any kind of effective sexual stimulation, physical or mental.

2. The *plateau* phase results in sexual tension increasing if effective sexual stimulation continues. Both sexes experience generalized skeletal muscle tension, rapid breathing, fast heart rate, and, in some, a body flush. In females, the clitoris retracts while remaining ex-

tremely sensitive to traction on the clitoral hood, the vaginal passageway constricts, and the inner two-thirds of the vagina balloons out. In the male, the glans of the penis increases in diameter and the testes are pulled up into the scrotum.

3. In the *orgasmic* phase, a sequence of rhythmic muscular contractions occurs about every .8 seconds, markedly reducing the vasocongestion built up by stimulation. Breathing increases at least three times normal, blood pressure increases by one-third, and heart rate more than doubles. In males, semen is ejaculated. In females, muscular contractions continue longer, and many females can have a further orgasm immediately with continued stimulation. This repeated orgasm is very rare in males.

4. The *resolution* phase completes the cycle, with muscular tension subsiding and the body gradually returning to its preexcitement state. The speed with which this occurs is related to the speed with which excitement occurred—the more slowly the excitement builds up, the more slowly it recedes. If orgasm does not occur, the resolution phase is prolonged, giving rise to a tense, uncomfortable feeling. This is true for both males and females. Males experience a refractory period in which they are temporarily unresponsive to sexual stimulation; females experience no refractory period.

These reactions occur in the same sequence regardless of the type of stimulation (manual, oral, genital) or the source of stimulation (fantasy, masturbation, homosexual stimulation, heterosexual intercourse). However, many people's sexual responses do not fit neatly into these phases (Zilbergeld, 1978). Furthermore, intensity and duration of sexual responses vary. Women generally have more intense and quicker orgasms from manual clitoral stimulation, especially from their own stimulation, than from heterosexual intercourse. In fact, as Kinsey and colleagues (1953) found, during masturbation, a woman takes the same length of time to reach an orgasm as does a man— from two to four minutes. The fact that it usually takes a woman longer to achieve orgasm during intercourse is most often a function of poor coital technique and of poor communication between partners regarding what is most stimulating.

Table 5-1

Four Phases of Human Sexual Response in Males and Females

Male	Female

Excitement Phase

Male	Female
Erection of penis	Vaginal lubrication
Nipple erection	Nipple erection
Partial elevation of testes	Lengthening and distention of vagina

Plateau Phase

Male	Female
Fast heart rate (100–175 beats per minute)	Fast heart rate (100–175 beats per minute)
Rapid breathing	Rapid breathing
Elevated blood pressure	Elevated blood pressure
Sex flush (25% incidence)	Sex flush (75% incidence)
Glandular emission of lubricating mucus from penis	Glandular emission of lubricating mucus into vagina
Sometimes deepened color change in head of penis (glans)	Vivid color change in labia minora
Increased circumference in ridge at the penile glans	Decrease in size of vaginal opening
Full elevation of testes	Elevation of uterus
	Retraction of clitoris

Orgasmic Phase

Male	Female
Rapid breathing	Rapid breathing
Fast heart rate (110–180 beats per minute)	Fast heart rate (110–180 beats per minute)
Increased blood pressure elevation	Increased blood pressure elevation
Rhythmic penile contractions, beginning at .8 second intervals	Rhythmic vaginal contractions, beginning at .8 second intervals

Resolution Phase

Male	Female
Return to normal breathing, heart rate, and blood pressure	Return to normal breathing, heart rate, and blood pressure
Loss of vasocongestive size increase in penis, scrotum, testes	Loss of vasocongestive size increase in vagina, labia majora, and labia minora
Rapid disappearance of sex flush	Rapid disappearance of sex flush
Perspiring reaction (33% incidence)	Perspiring reaction (33% incidence)
Refractory period—temporary loss of stimulative susceptibility	No refractory period—capable of repeated orgasm if stimulated

Data from *Human Sexual Response,* W. H. Masters and V. Johnson. Boston: Little, Brown, and Company, 1966.

Masters and Johnson's research and that of others proved a variety of ideas about sexuality to be false. They found the following facts:

1. Women have sexual responses similar to men except that women are capable of multiple orgasms. This finding is contrary to the belief that women are less sexual than men or that they are even asexual.

2. Women arouse and reach orgasm as quickly as men when stimulation is appropriate, contrary to the belief that women are inherently slower to respond than are men.

3. Women, as well as men, may respond with physical discomfort to not reaching an orgasm, contrary to the belief that an orgasm doesn't matter for a woman.

4. Women can achieve full sexual satisfaction without genital intercourse, contrary to the belief that a woman's sexual enjoyment depends on a man. Vaginal penetration may stimulate the Grafenberg spot, which is located within the anterior wall of the vagina. This "G spot" appears to be erotically sensitive in some women and may lead to female ejaculation (Perry & Whipple, 1981). Hite (1976) and others did find that, with vaginal penetration, orgasm is more diffuse (felt less specifically over wider areas of the body) than without it. This can be either more or less pleasurable for a woman, depending on individual preference.

5. Women have only one kind of orgasm, based in the clitoris, although contractions are felt in the vagina. This is contrary to Freud's distinction between a vaginal and a clitoral orgasm, the former, according to Freud, being more "mature." However, some researchers now are suggesting that stimulation of the Grafenberg spot leads to a different type of orgasm than does pure clitoral stimulation (Perry & Whipple, 1981). At this point, such a suggestion still is unproven.

6. The subjective experience of orgasm is essentially the same for females and males. This was confirmed in an experimental study in which people closely concerned with sexual behavior (for example, psychologists, obstetricians/gynecologists, medical students) were unable to distinguish the sex of a person from that person's written description of his or her orgasm (Proctor, Wagner, & Butler, 1974). Further gender similarities in the experience of orgasm lie in the recent findings that some women may ejaculate through their urethras upon orgasm (Belzer, 1981; Perry & Whipple, 1981).

These findings have altered traditional thinking about female sexuality, but changes in awareness have come slowly. Hite (1976) found that, ten years after Masters and Johnson's research was published, many women still believed the traditional view of their sexuality, even though they knew that they did not conform to it. She found that most women have more intense, quicker orgasms with masturbation than with intercourse but that they feel they should not do so. Articles in women's magazines from 1950–1970 frequently condemned a married woman's masturbation as "disloyal" to the marriage. These same articles advised a woman to focus all her sexual energies on her husband and to fake orgasm as well. The consequences of holding a traditional view of female sexuality may be feelings of insecurity and inferiority (LoPiccolo & Heiman, 1977). As Hite notes, there is no great mystery about why a woman has an orgasm. The key is adequate stimulation, and, for most females, this is simply not supplied by intercourse, since clitoral stimulation, if it occurs, is usually indirect.

Helen Singer Kaplan (1979) offers an alternative to Master and Johnson's four-stage model of human sexual response. Kaplan proposes a three-phase model: the desire phase, the excitement phase (which combines Masters and Johnson's excitement and plateau phase), and the orgasmic phase. It is in the stage of sexual desire that some sexual dysfunction may arise, and it is in this stage that gender differences are the most commonly expected. A close examination of this phase is needed.

Sexual Desires

One misconception resistant to refutation is that of men's stronger sex drives. It is important to differentiate among sexual desire, sexual interest, and sexual experience. Some evidence indicates that males generally have more sexual experiences (summing all types of experiences together) than do females (Griffitt & Hatfield, 1985; Kinsey et al., 1948, 1953), but this is a function of age and social factors, such as social class. For males, the highest point of sexual activity occurs around the age of 18; for women, around the age of 30. Sexual activity also varies with marital status for females but not for males. Zilbergeld (1978) stresses that although males tend to have more sexual experiences than do females, male sexuality tends to be focused solely on penile penetration. In contrast, female sexuality tends to include more variety in terms of enjoyable body parts and types of stimulation.

Few studies have directly examined women's sexual desires. From the studies that have dealt with female desires, confusing or contradictory results have emerged. There is some suggestion that women may have a peak of sexual desire at a specific phase of their menstrual cycle. For some women, the peak corresponds to their ovulatory phase; for others, the menstrual phase; and for still others, the postmenstrual phase (Adams, Gold, & Burt, 1978; Gold & Adams, 1981; Money & Ehrhardt, 1972). This finding is far from conclusive and depends, at least in part, upon the form of birth control used.

Mancini and Orthner (1978) studied recreational preferences among more than five hundred middle-class wives and husbands. They found that wives were more likely to prefer reading a book to sexual and affectional activity (37% preferred the former; 26%, the latter). Husbands, on the other hand, preferred sexual and affectional activities over attending athletic events and reading books (45%, 41%, 33%, respectively). If women are less interested in sex than are men, some writers (Hite, 1976; Zilbergeld, 1978) suggest that it is most likely because they do not expect to achieve orgasm from it. Intercourse may not be a particularly satisfying experience for many women. The fact that this dissatisfaction results from inadequate stimulation and not from a personal or female-related defect is usually neither known nor acknowledged.

One problem with assessing sexual desires is that self-reports of sexual feelings strongly reflect sexual attitudes. It is in the area of attitudes toward sexual activity that major changes over the last 30 years have been observed. As a whole, U.S. society has become more sexually permissive, especially of premarital sexual intercourse (Fink, 1983; Glenn & Weaver, 1979). This permissiveness is most marked for individuals aged 18–29 and for those with some college education. For example, a Louis Harris and Associates poll taken in 1983 (Fink, 1983) found that 79% of men and 70% of women aged 18–29 thought it was all right for regularly dating couples to have sex. These percentages contrast sharply with those of men and women aged 50–64. In the older age group, 55% of the men and only 40% of the women thought such behavior was all right. Showing a similar pattern, only 22% of

the men and 27% of the women in the 18–29-year-old age group thought it was important for a woman to be a virgin when she marries, whereas in the 50–64-year-old group, 41% of the men and 64% of the women thought premarital female virginity was important. What is striking in the findings for the younger age group is the similarity between the attitudes of the men and women, suggesting a decline in the double standard regarding sexuality.

This shift in attitude toward premarital sexual activity and decline in the sexual double standard have manifested themselves in behavior. Since the 1950s, there has been an increase in premarital sex among women to the extent that, of married couples 18 to 24 years of age, 95% of the males and 81% of the females have had premarital sex (Hunt, 1974). This can be compared to 92% of the male, and 65% of the female, partners in married couples in the age group of 25 to 34 years old. Hopkins (1977), in his review of surveys conducted between the 1930s and the 1970s on the sexual behavior of adolescents, concludes that a larger number of college-age people are sexually experienced now than in earlier generations. There has been a greater increase in the incidence of premarital intercourse for college females than for males (from about 25% of all college females in the mid-1960s to about 70% to 85% in the mid-1970s), although most surveys still report a higher absolute incidence for males. These findings suggest that the younger generation of women may be more interested in sex, or at least its manifestation in intercourse, than previous generations. Virginity is no longer a necessity for marriage for young women, and, therefore, fewer feel compelled to retain it or to say they have retained it.

Despite the marked increase in sexual behavior and more permissive attitudes toward sexual activity, there are some signs that promiscuous sexual activity is beginning to decline, especially for women. This shift away from casual sex is occurring among both heterosexuals and homosexuals (Lyons, 1983; "The revolution," 1984). Furthermore, the shift is reflected in the most recent surveys of sexual attitudes (Astin, 1985; Hendrick, Hendrick, Slapion-Foote, & Foote, 1985). For example, in a 1984 nationwide representative survey of college freshmen, less than one-third of the women in contrast to nearly two-thirds of the men thought it was all right for people who like each other to have sex (Astin, 1985). After examining five different types of sexual attitudes among college students, Hendrick and colleagues (1985) conclude that women are moderately conservative in sexual attitudes, whereas men are moderately permissive. This shift in attitudes and behaviors may reflect the increasing conservatism of America in the early 1980s, along with a kind of retrenchment from the "sexual revolution" of the 1960s and 1970s. Some of this retrenchment may be a response to fears about herpes and AIDS.

Interestingly, men's interest in sex may be less important than once was believed. In a survey of 1990 men conducted by Louis Harris and Associates for Playboy Enterprises (reported by Brozan, 1979), slightly less than half (49%) of the men surveyed considered sex as "very important" for life satisfaction. Of greater importance, in order of preference, were health, love, peace of mind, family life, work, friends, respect from others, and education. Only religion and money, in that order, figured lower than sex.

Yet, despite the preceding findings—the more permissive attitudes regarding sex and the nearly equal numbers of males and females currently engaging in sexual activity—the belief persists that men have stronger sex drives than do women (Byrne, 1977; Gross, 1978). Because the male sex drive is believed to be stronger than the female drive, sex is perceived by both females and males as being more important and enjoyable for men than for women. This belief is particularly evident in married and dating couples (see reviews by Gross, 1978; Peplau, Rubin, & Hill, 1977).

Males usually do seem to take the lead in heterosexual activities, both in initiating sexual contact and in controlling the sexual interaction itself (Blumstein & Schwartz, 1983; Grauerholz & Serpe, 1985; Masters & Johnson, 1979; Safilios-Rothschild, 1977). Women appear to exert more negative control; that is, they may resist or encourage sexual advances but may not initiate them. This double standard regarding sexual initiative still remains strong, although attitudes about its acceptability may be changing (Blumstein & Schwartz, 1983; Peplau et al., 1977; Quante, 1981; Zilbergeld, 1978).

Meaning of Sex. Regardless of similarities or differences between the sexes in sexual interest, there does seem to be an important difference between males and females in the meaning attached to sex (Carroll, Volk, & Hyde, 1984; Glass & Wright, 1985; Gross, 1978; Hendrick et al., 1985; Keller, Elliott, & Gunberg, 1982; Peplau et al., 1977). Indeed, gender differences in this area may turn out to be the strongest of all gender differences. Carroll et al. (1984) estimate that gender accounts for 29% of the variability in attitudes toward casual premarital sex, a percentage much higher than the variability accounted for by gender in aggressive behaviors, and in visual-spatial skills (around 6%).

The gender difference in the meaning of sex can be summarized as follows: females generally connect sex with feelings of affection and closeness; males often see sex as an achievement, an adventure, a demonstration of control and power, or a purely physical release. Various studies have found that women generally have fewer partners than do men. Their first experience is usually with someone with whom they are romantically involved. They are also more likely to use sex to get love, rather than using love to get sex. This is true before, during, and outside marriage and for homosexual relationships as well as heterosexual ones. Hite (1976) found also that the chief pleasures of sex and intercourse for women are the shared feelings, the emotional warmth, and the feeling of being wanted and needed, not the physical sensations per se. Men, on the other hand, tend to isolate sex from other aspects of relationships and are more likely than women to view any heterosexual relationship in a sexual-romantic framework (Gross, 1978).

Other studies question these conclusions, however. Pietropinto and Simenauer (1977), after surveying over 4000 men, conclude that most men, like most women, prefer having love and sex together, although men, perhaps, are more likely to separate them. Masters and Johnson (1979) found that, contrary to belief, both heterosexual men and heterosexual women are preoccupied with attaining orgasm, especially when contrasted with homosexuals of both sexes. Levine and Barbach (1984) report that some men fake orgasm when they engage in sexual intercourse without really wanting to. Such faking commonly occurs among heterosexual women. For example, in the 1982 *Playboy* survey of sex on campus, 54% of the women said they had faked orgasm. However, the reasons for faking appear to be different for women and men. Whereas women may fake orgasm to enhance their partner's ego, men appear to fake orgasm to maintain the myth of an omnipresent male sexual interest.

These differences in the meaning of sex may be due to the fact that intercourse often is not satisfying for females or is less satisfying than is masturbation. Hence, the secondary gains of intimacy may be the only benefit some females experience. These differences may also be a function of the different socialization experiences for males and for females in our society. As Gross (1978) and others have noted, sex is commonly viewed as a major proving ground of a male's masculinity. Quantity, more than quality, is stressed, with many negative consequences as a result.

Some of the negative consequences manifest themselves in sexual dysfunction. For males, problems with impotence or premature ejaculation often arise from pressure to perform and from an exclusive goal orientation, both being parts of the male role. As Masters and Johnson (1974) note, this very pressure can be self-defeating. In females, sexual dysfunction often takes the form of inability to have an orgasm. In the past, such women were termed *frigid*. Now they are called *preorgasmic,* because it is understood that, with proper stimulation, any female can have an orgasm. Instruction on self-stimulation has been markedly effective in this regard. Modern sex therapists treat sexual problems more as learning and communication problems than as a reflection of physiological problems, although the latter sometimes occur. These physiological problems, too, usually can be successfully treated.

Response to Erotic Stimuli

Another strong belief in our society is that males are sexually aroused, especially by vi-

sual stimuli and by their own fantasies, more frequently and more easily than are females. Females in particular appear to overestimate the degree of sexual arousal experienced by males in response to erotic material (Veitch & Griffitt, 1980). This belief regarding arousal is part of the male stereotype of a stronger sex drive. In fact, females do get aroused by erotic material, and females do have sexual fantasies.

Research on reactions to erotic stimuli generally has used only male subjects or has used materials with explicit sexual content aimed almost exclusively at heterosexual males. Hence, accurate data on female responsiveness have been minimal. However, a few well-controlled studies have confirmed that females do respond to erotic and erotic/romantic stimuli (stories, pictures, films) with levels of arousal equal to that of males (Fisher & Byrne, 1978; Heiman, 1975; Masters & Johnson, 1966; Schmidt, 1975; Veitch & Griffitt, 1980). In one study (Schmidt & Sigusch, 1973), from 80% to 91% of the men were aroused, while 70% to 83% of the women were aroused, with considerable intragroup differences in responding. There is some suggestion that males may respond more than women to posed pictures of the other sex, but this may be due to differences in pictures or to differences in experience. Certainly the female form has been pictured more frequently in sexual poses in advertising and pornography than has the male form. (See Figure 5-1). Fisher and Byrne (1978) found that the females in their experiments had less contact with erotica and had more negative beliefs about it than did the males. Despite these differences, when actually exposed to erotic films, the sexes reported equal levels of arousal.

A disturbing implication of males' greater experience with erotic material is the finding that exposure to such material can have adverse effects on judgments of one's mate (Gutierres, Kenrick, & Goldberg, 1983). Men, but not women, who were exposed to nude photographs taken from *Playboy, Penthouse,* and *Playgirl* later rated their mate as less sexually attractive than a control group who saw pictures of abstract art. Such findings suggest that exposure to such erotica may not be as benign as some people think. As will be seen in Chapter 12, the effects

Figure 5-1
Men have more experience with erotica because of the pervasive use of the female form in advertising products unrelated to the female form. (Courtesy of Sanders Bootmakers.)

of pornography that is more hard-core are even more negative.

A problem with some of the older studies on responses to erotica (for example, Kinsey et al., 1948, 1953) is that they relied purely on self-reports. As Heiman (1975) documented, women sometimes do not know when they are physiologically aroused, or else they feel reluctant to report this arousal. This reluctance may be due to conditioning and also to the fact that female sexual arousal (vaginal lubrication) is much less noticeable to the woman herself than is male arousal (erection) to the man. The conditioning explanation is supported by the finding that it is mainly women who feel guilty about sex who tend to report low sexual arousal while viewing an erotic videotape (Morokoff,

1985). Such self-reports contradict the objective finding that such women also tend to show greater physiological arousal during erotic videotapes than do women low in sex guilt. Guilt may make women inhibit their conscious sexual arousal to erotic material, yet this inhibition actually may make such women more arousable.

Another finding from the post-Kinsey studies is that females do not respond more to romantic stories than to erotic ones, as Kinsey had hypothesized. Rather, both sexes respond most to explicit sex stories, women sometimes responding more than men (Fisher & Byrne, 1978; Heiman, 1975). Furthermore, women do not respond only to dominance or submission story themes. Rather, they seem to respond equally to descriptions of aggressor and victim fantasy themes and gender-equal fantasy themes (Mader & Pollack, 1984).

In regard to erotic fantasies, it appears that both sexes are able to arouse themselves through fantasy (Heiman, 1975), and the majority of both sexes do arouse themselves in this way (Kinsey et al., 1948, 1953; Knafo & Jaffe, 1984). Women and men apparently spend equivalent amounts of time fantasizing about sex, although the kinds of fantasies created by men and women differ (Knafo & Jaffe, 1984). Women tend to have more submission fantasies than do men, whereas men tend to have more performance fantasies than do women.

Homosexuality

Homosexuality commonly is thought of as fundamentally "sexual" in nature. This is a misconception that ignores the complexity of individual lives. Homosexuals frequently are thought of as interested in sex all the time, whereas heterosexuals are acknowledged to be interested in many things, such as work, friends, play, and so on, in addition to sex. Homosexuality refers only to sexual orientation: preferring same-sex partners rather than other-sex partners for the satisfaction of emotional and sexual desires. In most aspects of living, homosexuals and heterosexuals are similar and indistinguishable from each other. However, because there is a stigma against homosexuality in American society, homosexuals seem very different in the eyes of the majority culture. Indeed, the stigma attached to homosexuals may cause some homosexuals to be different in some ways—for example, by being more secretive about their private lives and more paranoid regarding people's reactions to them. Although it is difficult to obtain precise figures, in our culture, more males than females are apt to have had a homosexual experience or be exclusively homosexual (Hunt, 1974; Kinsey et al., 1948, 1953; Moses & Hawkins, 1982).

One difficulty in obtaining precise estimates derives from the fact that homosexuality is not an exclusive identification. Homosexuality and heterosexuality are points on a continuum of sexual orientation, with many points in between. For example, some people have homosexual fantasies but have had no corresponding experience; some have had a homosexual experience but prefer heterosexual ones; and so on. Consequently, classifying people as either heterosexual or homosexual depends on the definitions of these terms that are used. The number of people in each category will vary accordingly. Another difficulty in obtaining accurate figures is that, because homosexuality is such a stigma in our society (Lehne, 1976; Morin & Garfinkle, 1978), many people are reluctant to admit to engaging in any homosexual behaviors.

It does appear, however, that sexual attraction between same-sex members is common and that, by age 45, approximately one-third of all men and one-sixth of all women have had at least one homosexual experience (Hunt, 1974; Kinsey et al., 1948, 1953; *Playboy,* 1982). The number of exclusive homosexuals after age 15—from 3% to 16% of all males and from 1% to 5% of all females—is much smaller than the figures cited above for homosexual experiences (Hunt, 1974; Kinsey et al., 1948, 1953; Marmor, 1980). About 25% of the men and 13% of the women studied by Kinsey and his colleagues had sexual histories that would best be described as bisexual. These findings are approximate.

In our culture, there is a greater stigma attached to male homosexuality and greater persecution of male homosexuals than is the case with their female counterparts (see Morin & Garfinkle, 1978, for a review of such studies).

This difference in social opinion may reflect the greater importance and status our society attaches to anything "masculine." Therefore, a deviation from "masculine" behavior is more disapproved of than is a deviation from "feminine" behavior. Supporting evidence for this hypothesis comes from the observation that, among male homosexuals, it is those who are more effeminate who receive the most harassment and disapproval, even from other homosexuals (Chafetz, 1978). Similarly, disapproval of homosexuality is much stronger among males than females. A 1984 national survey of college freshmen (Astin, 1985) found that 58% of the men, in contrast with 38% of the women, thought homosexual relations should be prohibited.

Although homosexuality is often considered a mental disorder (the American Psychiatric Association removed it from its classification system only in 1973), most controlled research has indicated that homosexuals as a group are as emotionally stable as heterosexuals. (See Riess & Safer, 1979, for a review.) In fact, some homosexuals may have even stronger ego controls than heterosexuals (Freedman, 1975; Thompson, McCandless, & Strickland, 1971). Yet, psychotherapists still tend to view a hypothetical client (male or female) who holds a homosexual orientation as less psychologically healthy than an identical person with a heterosexual orientation (Garfinkle & Morin, 1978). When emotional problems *are* found in individuals with a homosexual orientation, one major cause of those problems often is the heavy stress under which such individuals are placed by an antihomosexual society. Being labeled *deviant* may give rise to feelings of anxiety, depression, anger, and/or alienation.

Interestingly, gender differences in homosexual behavior seem to reflect the same gender differences in sexual functioning as was previously noted for heterosexuals. Males tend to have more sex with more partners and in the context of more short-term relationships than do females (Bell & Weinberg, 1978; Kinsey et al., 1948, 1953; Meredith, 1984; Peplau, 1981). Male homosexuals also tend to act on their sexual feelings earlier than do female homosexuals (Riddle & Morin, 1977), just as heterosexual males act earlier than do heterosexual females. Female homosexuals appear to emphasize the importance of emotional attachments over sexual behaviors more than do male homosexuals (Blumstein & Schwartz, 1983; deMonteflores & Schultz, 1978; Moses & Hawkins, 1982; Peplau, 1981), again in keeping with the heterosexual pattern. For example, a study of ads in personal columns in newspapers (Deaux & Hanna, 1984) revealed that men, whether homosexual or heterosexual, showed more concern with objective and physical characteristics than did either homosexual or heterosexual women. In contrast, the women were more interested in the psychological aspects of a potential relationship than were the men.

These same patterns are found as well for bisexuals (those who relate sexually to both males and females under some circumstances) (Blumstein & Schwartz, 1977). These results concerning homosexuals and bisexuals indicate that sex-typed sexual behaviors occur regardless of the sexual orientation of the person.

Interestingly, research on the nature of homosexual relationships has found a great deal more equality and less role playing in such relationships than in heterosexual relationships (Deaux & Hanna, 1984; Maccoby & Jacklin, 1974; Peplau, 1981). Despite the stereotype that in a homosexual couple, one plays the "male" and one the "female," this pattern actually characterizes only a minority of such couples. Role playing is commonest among those who are older, at lower socioeconomic levels, and among men—groups least influenced by gay liberation and lesbian feminism. Most homosexual couples resemble best friendships more than husbands and wives, and satisfaction generally runs very high.

Masturbation

Sex differences are also found when individuals sexually stimulate themselves—that is, in masturbation. More males engage in masturbation more frequently than do females, although, with increased sexual awareness on the part of females, these numerical differences seem to be changing (Abramson & Mosher, 1979; Mosher & Abramson, 1977). Virtually all men and two-thirds of all women have masturbated (Hunt, 1974; Kinsey et al., 1948, 1953).

The fact that some women never masturbate is important in light of the findings that masturbation is strongly related to the ability to have coital orgasms (Kinsey et al., 1953).

Explanations

Because sex is necessary for the reproduction of the species and because it involves many physiological responses, some researchers lean toward a physiological explanation of sexual behavior. Others stress psychosocial factors and status differences. As will be demonstrated, all these factors interact. The strongest factors, however, seem to be the environmental ones.

Physiology

"Men are just naturally more interested in sex than women." "Men's urges are stronger, you know." These comments reflect the belief that physiological factors underlie differences in sexual behavior. Explanations invoking physiological processes center on hormones, anatomy, and evolutionary development.

Hormones. Sexual interest, or libido, for both males and females has been related both prenatally and postnatally to the hormone androgen (Barfield, 1976; Money & Ehrhardt, 1972). Androgen secretion appears to lower the threshold of arousal and to increase the energy with which sexual activity is pursued in both humans and animals. Even in animals, however, social factors and past experience play the more important role (Barfield, 1976). In humans, behavior is more variable and freer from direct hormonal control than is the case with animals. Consequently, the effect of experience is even greater. Even in individuals who reach puberty earlier than usual due to hormonal changes, sexual behavior still appears at the appropriate age and in the appropriate way (Hamburg & Lunde, 1966). Therefore, although generally higher androgen levels in males may tend to lower their arousal threshold, social factors could either encourage or discourage related sexual behavior. In our society, such behaviors are encouraged in males but not in females. It bears repeating that there is wide individual variation in androgen secretion, and some females secrete more androgen than do some males.

Changes in women's sexual desires as a function of menstrual cycle, although not consistently found, have been related by some researchers to changes in hormones (for example, Adams et al., 1978). However, the data have been contradictory, and social factors have been so important that it now seems clear that at least for pre- and postmenstrual rises in sexual behavior, a hormonal explanation is not satisfactory (Gold & Adams, 1981). The best explanation of the postmenstrual peak is as a rebound phenomenon if couples abstain from sexual behavior during menstruation. A peak in desire premenstrually may relate to anticipated sexual abstinence during menstruation if such abstinence occurs, to increased vasocongestion, or to the unlikelihood of conception at the time.

Although hormones may affect the amount of sexual energy, they do not affect the choice of sex partner. There is no known correlation between homosexuality and either prenatal or postnatal sex hormones (Barfield, 1976; Bleier, 1979; Hines, 1982; Money & Ehrhardt, 1972). Genetic females (those with two X chromosomes) who were exposed to androgen prenatally are no more likely to be homosexual than females not exposed to androgen during that period. In determining sexual orientation and other aspects of sexual behavior, learning and social factors are the most important.

Similarly, the age difference in sexual peaks for males and females does not appear to be due to any difference in hormones. It is now generally agreed that such peaks reflect differences in social training.

Anatomy. The fact that males and females have different sex organs has been held by some to account for the sex differences in sexual behavior. By this reasoning, the greater visibility and accessibility of the penis (as opposed to the clitoris) and the use of the penis in urination may orient a boy to handling it and discovering its pleasurable qualities. This may account for males' greater likelihood of masturbation. At puberty, a male's attention is further

focused on his genitals by the increased frequency of erections and by the start of seminal emissions. Female genitals, on the other hand, are easier to ignore, often remaining unlabeled (referred to only as "down there"), and their signs of arousal are subtler. As Heiman (1975) found, some women misread their physiological arousal. This may occur because females have relatively less experience in producing and identifying such states than do males, since they tend to masturbate less than males. Furthermore, since masturbation is clitoral, it would be difficult to imagine vaginal intercourse as pleasurable. Puberty for females is marked by menstruation, which has reproductive, rather than sexual, significance and which is often surrounded by fear or mystery. Thus, anatomical differences may lead to differences in attention being paid to genitalia. This differential attention may be further socialized into two different scripts (behavioral blueprints) concerning sexual behavior for males and females (Gagnon & Simon, 1973; Laws & Schwartz, 1977).

Freud (1905/1964c, 1924/1964a, 1924/1964b) spelled out the anatomy-is-destiny approach quite comprehensively and is most closely identified with it. In brief, he posited that a child's gender development is based on unconscious reactions to anatomical differences. When a little boy (age 3 to 6) discovers that a female does not have a penis, he becomes afraid of losing his. This *castration anxiety* forces him to repress his desire for his mother and to identify with his father. By identifying with the father, the little boy's fear of punishment for his incestuous desire is reduced, because he believes that the father would not punish someone so much like him. This male form of resolution of the *Oedipus complex* leads to the development of a strong superego (through fear of punishment) and a strong male gender identification.

A little girl, however, on discovering she does not have a penis, envies a male and feels inferior. She rejects her mother because the mother also is "inferior" and looks to her father for a replacement penis. The resolution of her "Oedipus" complex (called the *Electra complex* by neo-Freudians) occurs when she accepts the impossibility of her wish for a penis and compensates for it by desiring a child. This *penis* envy on the part of females has enormous consequences for their personality development, according to Freud. He concluded that, firstly, females have weaker superegos than males, because their Electra complex is resolved by envy, not fear. Secondly, he concluded that females feel inferior to males and consequently develop a personality characterized by masochism, passivity, and narcissism. Thirdly, he believed that females give up their clitoral focus in masturbation and begin to prepare for adult gratification via vaginal stimulation.

Freud's theory has been criticized on a variety of grounds. What concern us here are the criticisms of penis envy and its consequences. As was noted previously, there is no evidence that females are more passive or masochistic than males, or that they have inferior superegos. In addition, the vaginal/clitoral orgasm differentiation is incorrect. All orgasms are clitorally based regardless of stimulation. There is also no evidence that little girls believe they are anatomically inferior to boys or that they blame their mothers for lack of a penis, and so on. Freud's theory reflects a strong male bias: he regards sexuality itself as male, he bases his theory on a patriarchal society, and he assumes that everyone recognizes a penis as inherently superior (see Millet, 1970, for an interesting critique). If young girls do envy boys, they more likely are envying males' higher status and greater power rather than the male anatomical appendage (Horney, 1922/1973). In support of this status interpretation, Sharon Nathan (1981) found in her cross-cultural analysis of dream reports, that the occurrence of "penis envy" in a dream was a function of the status of women in that culture. Where the status of women was low, dream reports showed penis envy; where the status of women was higher, dream reports showed less penis envy. Furthermore, an equally persuasive argument can be made for male *womb envy*. This envy is theoretically manifested in the way males develop rituals and develop a greater achievement orientation as compensation for their inability to conceive (see Bettelheim, 1962; Chesler, 1978; Collins, 1979). Thus, although anatomy may influence an individual's sexual development, Freud's "destiny" edict is greatly overstated and very male biased. Indeed, Horney (1922/1973) suggests

that Freud's ideas regarding female thoughts and feelings are really projections of Freud's own feelings and thoughts about girls.

Evolution. Before leaving physiological explanations, the explanation based on evolutionary development merits consideration. Mary Jane Sherfey (1974) argues that women have a biologically based inordinate sexual drive. As evidence, she cites women's potential for multiple orgasms, and she includes the fact that the more orgasms a woman achieves, the more she can achieve. This sexual capacity may have evolved because the more erotic primates bred more and therefore reproduced more than the less erotic primates. In humans, however, women's inordinate sexual drive had to be suppressed if family life and agricultural economies were to develop, since the female sex drive interfered with maternal responsibility and the establishment of property rights and kinship laws, all elements vital to modern civilization. Thus, Sherfey (1974) describes how men had to suppress female sexuality in order to establish family life and maintain their own position of power and the power of patriarchy.

There are many problems with Sherfey's theory. In the first place, there is no conclusive evidence that female hypersexuality ever existed, even in tribal hunting societies (Tavris & Offir, 1977). Also, her theory cannot account for societal differences. As we shall see, female sexuality is not universally suppressed. In addition, the theory itself reflects a curious patriarchal bias in which men are viewed as coming to the rescue of society and in which women are viewed, in terms of their sexuality, as being unable to control themselves. Thus, although provocative, Sherfey's theory remains in the realm of speculation. It does highlight, however, the greater, often unused, potential that females have for sexual enjoyment.

Another type of explanation based on evolutionary development is the sociobiological one. Donald Symons (1979) has argued that differences in sexual conduct between women and men relate to different reproductive strategies in the sexes. These different strategies ultimately are dependent on the differences between sperm and egg cells. Because men produce a large number of sperm, their reproductive strategy is to have many sexual partners and transient relationships. Women, because they have a small supply of eggs and must carry a child for at least 9 months, require stable relations with a good provider. Symons uses this theory to explain the greater number of sexual partners men have than do women, the greater interest in casual sex by men than by women, and the greater arousability of men than women to visual stimuli. Symons argues that in homosexuality we see the true nature of male and female sexuality—multiple involvements for men, committed relationships for females.

Symons's arguments, albeit provocative, involve much speculation and ignore contradictory evidence that currently is available (for example, the research on responses to erotic stimuli). Symons also bases his entire explanation on sexual conduct in the United States, despite the fact that sexual behavior varies widely in different cultures. Therefore, although his explanation has a certain simplistic appeal, it does not appear to be well substantiated. (See Bleier, 1984, and Lewontin et al., 1984 for critiques of sociobiology.) The male-female dichotomy in sexual behavior can be explained better by social factors than by genes.

In sum, physiological factors do not clearly explain male and female sexual behavior. Psychosocial factors also need to be examined.

Psychosocial Factors

Evidence for the importance of psychosocial factors in the development of sexual behavior comes from four major sources: parent-child relationships, sex typing, sexual scripting, and cross-cultural studies.

Parent—Child Relationships. The viewpoint that parent-child relationships are important in determining a child's eventual sexual behavior is an outgrowth of Freud's theory of personality development and the particular importance of the phallic stage (ages 3 to 5). It is during this stage that the resolution of the Electra and Oedipus complexes occurs. "Deviant" sexual behavior, including homosexuality, was seen as a result of some problem with resolving this stage. There is little support for this aspect of Freud's theory. For example, re-

search on both male and female homosexuals does not consistently find a particular family constellation or particularly deviant or traumatic childhood experiences (Bell, Weinberg, & Hammersmith, 1981; Moses & Hawkins, 1982; Pleck, 1981b). However, parents can affect their children's sexual behavior and orientation. M. Johnson and colleagues (1981) found that heterosexual women were more likely to perceive their fathers as affectionate, involved, and accepting of anger, than were lesbians.

Fleishman (1983a, 1983b) has proposed a more controversial theory—that sexual orientation is acquired before age three through physical contact with adults. Her theory rests on the following findings: that parents touch their daughters and sons differently, that infants respond to sexual stimulation and discriminate between the sexes, and that homosexuals in infancy were psychosocially and presumably physically responded to as children of the other sex. This theory is quite speculative at this time but suggestive of ways in which parental behavior may affect a child's sexual development (see Simari & Baskin, 1983, for a critique).

Sex Typing. An individual's sex typing and attitudes toward sex roles also affect her or his sexual behaviors and attitudes. Contrary to Freud's assertions that traditional femininity, meaning passivity, is associated with female sexual satisfaction, research has found no significant relationship between "femininity" and sexual satisfaction (Kirkpatrick, 1980). Rather, such "masculine" characteristics as assertiveness and self-confidence seem important for both male and female sexual fulfillment (Maslow, 1942; Oakley, 1972). Being low in both instrumental and expressive traits is associated with low sexual satisfaction and responsivity among women (Snow & Parsons, 1983). Positive attitudes toward non-gender-stereotypic roles and behaviors also are associated with female sexual satisfaction (Kirkpatrick, 1980).

Given the different sexual scripts for females and males, it is not surprising that sexuality in males and females is perceived differently. Luis Garcia (1982; Garcia & Derfel, 1983) found that females who displayed nonverbal behaviors associated with males (for example, direct gazing), were perceived as more sexually experienced and more sexual in general than if they had displayed nonverbal behavior typically associated with females. Furthermore, in another study, females described as sexually experienced were more likely to be perceived negatively than were females described as low in sexual experience, especially by sex-typed raters. For male targets, no such differences were found.

Both men and women appear to associate gender characteristics with sexual orientation despite there being no relationship between the two variables (Kite & Deaux, 1984; Pleck, 1981b; Storms, 1980). Thus Storms and colleagues (1981) found that women described as "masculine" (for example, competitive) were perceived by others to be homosexual, and women described as homosexual were perceived to be masculine sex-typed. "Feminine" homosexual women and "masculine" heterosexual women were seen as having confused sexual identities. Such perceptual distortions and stereotypes have a great effect on interpersonal judgments. All but the "feminine" heterosexual women were stigmatized, a powerful factor in producing sex-role conformity.

Despite the influence of sex typing on sexual behavior and attitudes, Allgeier (1981) concludes that gender actually is a stronger and more consistent variable. Thus the sexual scripts of women and men appear to override individual personality characteristics.

Sexual Scripts. In our society, as in most societies, females and males have different sexual scripts (Gagnon & Simon, 1973; Laws & Schwartz, 1977; Zilbergeld, 1978). In the United States, parents expect the adolescent son, but not the daughter, to have overt sexual activity. They therefore are more restrictive of the daughter's behavior, which retards her sexual experimentation. Consequently, adolescent rebellion in girls usually consists of sexual "offenses," whereas adolescent rebellion in boys usually does not involve sex. In fact, the labeling of adolescent female sexual activity as deviant or as an offense is itself an example of the sexual double standard. Such behavior in adolescent males is expected and often encouraged. For adolescent females to have sexual experiences, they often deliberately have to reject their families. This is not true for boys.

Because females can become pregnant, their socialization typically emphasizes this consequence of sexual activity. Females usually learn about sex as connected to reproduction, family life, and emotional ties. They are thereby trained to think about "catching" a mate, using sex as a bait if necessary. Females' limited sexual exploration, combined with their minimal experience with masturbation, may cause some females to mature without having had any sexual gratification. It therefore may be difficult for them to connect heterosexual sex activity with pleasure. Female sexuality is never spoken of as valuable or worthwhile in and of itself, but only as a means to an end. Many females learn to use their sexuality in this way and become quite manipulative. One-fourth of the women answering a 1972 survey in *Psychology Today* magazine reported using sex to bind a person into a relationship; two-thirds admitted to faking an orgasm to make their partner feel good and avoid rejection (Tavris, 1973.)

Such sexual scripting also affects lesbian relationships, with sex being more tied to love than it is among gay men (Meredith, 1984; Peplau, 1981). The devaluation of female sexuality is also evident in our double standard of shamefulness. Female genitals are either unlabeled or derogatorily labeled (for example, "down there," "cunt"). Indeed, few girls learn correct anatomical names for female genitalia. Gartrell and Mosbacher (1984) found that whereas the correct names for male genitalia were learned by 40% of boys and 29% of girls, the correct names for female genitalia were learned by 18% of boys and only 6% of girls. Girls are encouraged to conceal "their privates" with clothes, leg positions, and deodorant. It is therefore not surprising that some women never touch their genitals or learn to masturbate.

Boys, however, are taught to view sex as a way of proving their masculinity. This emphasis reflects the pressure on males to consistently achieve in all areas of their lives (Fasteau, 1974; Gross, 1978; O'Neil, 1981b; Zilbergeld, 1978). In the sexual area, this may result in the males' trying to "score"—that is, have many sexual experiences with many partners and, for the "modern" male, bring their partners to many orgasms. Numbers matter, not the quality of the experience. Such an impersonal orientation toward sex is strikingly evident among many male homosexuals, whose promiscuous behaviors greatly resemble the fantasized sexual life of many heterosexual men (Meredith, 1984).

This exclusive goal orientation may be a result of early male masturbatory experiences in which the focus is solely on producing an orgasm. As a result of this achievement focus, females are often viewed solely in their sexual roles (for example, "a piece of ass"), and sex itself is viewed as a conquest rather than as a form of communication. (See Figure 5-2.) In the 1973 (Tavris) survey previously cited, more than half of the men that were questioned admitted to using deception in order to have sex. A 1985 survey of college men reached a similar conclusion: 42% of the men admitted to saying things they didn't mean to obtain sex from a woman against her will (Greendlinger & Byrne, in press). Furthermore, many men apparently misinterpret or ignore women's sexual willingness. In a study involving nearly 4000 college

women, 70% reported having had a man misinterpret the degree of sexual intimacy they desired ("Casualties," 1983). Some men apparently go even further than deception to "obtain sex." As will be discussed in Chapter 12, about one-third of all men admit that they might rape a woman under some circumstances (Malamuth, 1981). Nearly half of all women will be a victim of an attempted or actual rape (Riger & Gordon, 1981).

Males are also expected to be in control, to take the lead, in sexual areas particularly. This control may sometimes be a burden. In one study (Carlson, 1976), nearly half of the husbands felt that the responsibility for sexual initiation should be equal between husband and wife. Yet women feel uncomfortable as the initiator, perhaps because they sense men's ambivalence about losing control (Komarovsky, 1976; Safilios-Rothschild, 1977). In one study of college students (Grauerholz & Serpe, 1985), only those women who were aware of sexual

Figure 5-2

A cartoonist's view of male and female communication about sex. (Copyright 1973 by Bülbül. Reprinted by permission.)

inequality and who had relatively liberal attitudes toward masturbation, instructing one's sexual partner, and so on, were likely to feel comfortable initiating sexual activity. Actually, men appear more accepting of sexually assertive women than women in general perceive them to be (Quante, 1981). Furthermore, men appear more accepting than women in terms of their attitudes toward sexual assertiveness in women. However, male attitudes toward sexually assertive women are related to their attitudes toward women in general; men who hold traditional views of women hold unfavorable views of sexually assertive women. So the double standard of sexual behavior still exists in some form, especially for women. As Warren Farrell (1982) notes, women and men never will be truly equal until the risk of sexual rejection is shared. When men take all such risks, defensive and protective attitudes commonly develop, such as depersonalizing the woman, de-emotionalizing sex, and developing anger and resentment toward all women.

The consequences of the male sexual role are many. The unstated permission to masturbate may limit male sexuality to the genitals and make sex entirely goal oriented, thus limiting the pleasure of a sexual experience. The pressure to appear in charge may also make men hesitate to reveal ignorance or uncertainty, thereby inhibiting open communication between partners about sexual interactions (Gross, 1978; Masters & Johnson, 1979; Zilbergeld, 1978). The constant pressure to achieve may lead to impotence, since anxiety is inconsistent with sexual arousal (Masters & Johnson, 1970). Yet, if sexual difficulties occur, a man is more likely to be censured by other men for his "inadequacies" than is a woman with similar difficulties to be censured by other women (Polyson, 1978). Women do not show this same negative attitude toward sexually troubled men, although men may not be aware of, or believe, that. Thus, open communication with one's partner may be restricted.

If we consider the two different cultural scripts for males and females, we can better understand why more males express interest in, and participate in, sexual activities than do females. They must be more interested if they are "real men." Sex for many is another area

of achievement or of power, unconnected to feelings of intimacy. Similarly, we can understand why some women never learn to enjoy their own sexuality. They haven't had the experience, and, besides, they shouldn't enjoy it if they are "good girls." Sex is all right only in the context of a relationship, only as a means to an end. In this respect, Evans (1984) has found that college females have much greater sex guilt than do college males, and these differences were most marked for sex-typed students. Furthermore, college women with a high degree of sex guilt tend to use contraception less frequently than do college women low in sex guilt (Gerrard, 1982). For such women, use of contraception may suggest that they thought about engaging in a sexual activity ahead of time, and were not just "swept away" by emotions. Thus, acceptance of the cultural sanction against enjoyable and premeditated sex for women actually may lead to unplanned pregnancies.

These sexual expectations, or cultural scripts, combine with both a societal preoccupation with sex and a social taboo against talking about sex, especially for females. The results are serious misunderstandings, dishonesty ("scoring," "faking it"), and a lack of full sexual enjoyment for both sexes, particularly for females. Hence, we find greater numbers of women who can achieve orgasm through masturbation rather than through genital intercourse.

Liberating men from their stereotype as sex agents and liberating women from their stereotype as sex objects will result in a sexuality based on authentic concern for the persons involved, whether it be part of play, affection, or love. This form of sexuality will undoubtedly be deeper and more rewarding for those concerned than the manipulative form of sexuality we now often have.

Cross-Cultural Studies. Nowhere can the social bases of our sexual behavior be more clearly seen than in comparisons with other cultures. When different cultures have different forms of sexual behavior, it is apparent that these behaviors cannot have a primarily physiological basis. In observing such behaviors in a wide range of cultures, enormous variability has been found.

Cultures vary on a number of factors related to sexual behavior:

1. The amount of sexual play permitted between children varies between cultures. For example, Trobriand Islanders (Malinowski, 1932) and the Yolngu in Australia (Money & Ehrhardt, 1972) encourage such play; the U.S. strongly discourages it.

2. The permissibility of intercourse before marriage is strongly encouraged in Mangaia, Polynesia (Marshall, 1971), and by Pilagá Indians in Argentina (Money & Ehrhardt, 1972), but is strongly discouraged in the Batak culture of northern Sumatra (Money & Ehrhardt, 1972) and in the U.S.

3. The latitude of sexual activity after marriage varies widely, from strict monogamy among the Batak, to serial monogamy in the U.S., to extramarital relations in Mangaia.

4. The importance attached to sexual activity itself ranges from highly desirable, as in the Truk Islands (Malinowski, 1932) and among Mangaians, to very unimportant and secondary, as among the Arapesh of New Guinea (Mead, 1935).

5. The extent to which sexual desire is seen as dangerous varies from the Manus (Malinowski, 1932), who encourage restraint, to the Balinese, who view the sex drive as very weak (Malinowski, 1932).

6. The acceptance of homosexuality differs from encouragement during certain ages in the Batak culture, to acceptance by American Mohave Indians (Devereaux, 1937), to nearly total rejection in the U.S. and Nicaragua.

7. The expectation of gender differences in sexual behavior ranges from no expectation of a difference, as in Southwest Pacific societies like Mangaia (Marshall, 1971), to an expectation that the female sex drive is stronger, as among Trobriand Islanders and the Kwoma and Mataco (Malinowski, 1932), to an expectation that the male sex drive is stronger, as in Latin America.

In those societies where the sexes are seen as equal in sexual potential (for example, Mangaia), the sexes do not have different sexual peaks, sex is not linked necessarily to love for women, and frigidity and premature ejaculation are rare. Thus, the cultural relativity of our sexual sex-role standards and their consequences are readily apparent.

Status

Another way of explaining gender differences in sexual behavior is by examining the differences in status and power between the sexes in our culture. We live in a patriarchy, in which men hold economic and material power. This holds several direct consequences for sexual behavior.

One major consequence of patriarchy, as Millet (1970) points out, may be that, for females to obtain economic and material security, they must barter their sexual availability either through marriage or prostitution. Thus, females may use sex as a means to an end, subordinating their own desires to those of the male, distorting their self-image and personality in the process. Men end up distrusting women and being afraid of getting "hooked." Hite (1976) found that, for several reasons, women were very reluctant to create their own orgasms either through masturbation or by requesting certain behaviors from their partner: habit, fear of losing their man's "love," and, especially, fear of economic recrimination. In our marriage laws, a woman is required to have sexual intercourse with her husband; she need not enjoy it, and many do not enjoy it. If a woman is financially and emotionally dependent on a man, she is not in a good position to demand equality in bed.

Another consequence of patriarchy is men's control of women's biological functioning. Laws and institutions regulating contraception, pregnancy, and childbirth are made and run by men. Thus, many women are prevented from controlling their own bodies. Their sexuality remains tied to their reproductive functioning, whereas men's sexuality is not tied to reproduction. This may limit more than a woman's sexuality—such dependence limits career and educational plans as well. Since the late 1960s, there have been increasing challenges to this aspect of patriarchy, but the continuing battle over abortion laws and contraceptive availability indicate that the struggle is far from over.

Patriarchy also restricts female behavior and activities, including sexual behavior. This is clearly shown by the various conceptions of sexuality and of healthy, versus dysfunctional, behavior held by scholars throughout Western history (LoPiccolo & Heiman, 1977). For example, Freud (1924/1964b) wrote that "masturbation at all events [*sic*] of the clitoris is a masculine activity, and the elimination of clitoral sexuality is a necessary precondition for the development of femininity." Patriarchy further restricts sexuality, both female and male, through "compulsory heterosexuality" (Rich, 1980). The possibility of individuals finding emotional and sexual satisfaction with same-sex partners in egalitarian relationships is threatening to a system that relies on dominance of men over women. Consequently, homosexuals are viewed as deviant and are heavily stigmatized.

Women's major role in our culture has been to serve the needs of others, particularly the needs of men and of children. Thus, women have been oriented to satisfy men's sexual needs without any thoughts about their own needs or about any expectation of reciprocity. The double standard of sexual behavior is very much ingrained in America. Men are supposed to need, want, and enjoy sex; women are not supposed to do any of these things. As Hite (1976) notes, "Lack of sexual satisfaction is another sign of the oppression of women" (p. 420).

A related consequence for females of a patriarchal society is defining sexuality using the male as the norm. Thus, sexuality in our culture is *phallocentric;* that is, sex is defined as genital intercourse and male orgasm. Female satisfaction occurs in foreplay or in afterplay, if it occurs at all, but it is not the main point of sexual activity (Rotkin, 1972). Many people still believe in vaginal orgasms because such orgasms require a penis; a clitoral orgasm does not have that requirement. Other evidence of phallocentrism can be seen in the following facts: (1) A female generally is considered to be a "virgin" as long as she has not had genital intercourse; (2) the clitoris usually is defined as a miniature penis rather than the penis being defined as an enlarged clitoris, though the latter definition is phylogenetically more accurate (see Chapter 2); (3) premature ejaculation is sometimes viewed as the cause of female frigidity, although the penis does not provide the best mode for producing female orgasms.

The effects of phallocentricity are far-reaching for females and for males. Females often give up expecting sexual satisfaction and use sexual contacts to secure affection and security rather than for sexual pleasure. Or they feel guilty about their desires and think they are abnormal, immature, and so on. Men, on the other hand, are under increased pressure to identify themselves with their penis, and some see in it the answer to all problems. (See Figure 5-3 for one example.) Thus, any sexual difficulty for either the male or the female partner reflects on the male's masculinity, on his psychological effectiveness, and on his personal identity (Polyson, 1978; Zilbergeld, 1978). In addition, as females increase the substitute demands of love and commitment, males become more confused, more guilty, and more alienated. This further reduces compatibility (Masters & Johnson, 1974; Rotkin, 1972).

One way to avoid these consequences is to redefine sexuality. This is a major undertaking because sexuality is both so personal and so political, and it is hard to examine it directly. Recent writings by feminists (see Greer, 1984; Snitow, Stansell, & Thompson, 1983; Vance, 1984) have begun such an examination and have revealed tremendous diversity of opinions and approaches. At the very minimum, the clitoris needs to be recognized as equal with the penis as a center of human sexuality. Females need to be recognized as having separate sexual centers for gratification (clitoris) and for reproduction (vagina). Whereas reproduction requires intercourse, gratification does not, although intercourse may well provide secondary pleasures. A liberation from constricting sex roles is needed as well as a change in the patriarchal system. As Masters and Johnson (1974) note, "The most effective sex is not something a man does to or for a woman but something a man and woman do together as *equals*" (p. 84).

Summary

It can be said, in summary, that there are some similarities between the sexes in sexual behavior, and there are some differences. Male and female sexual responses are virtually identical with one exception: females are capable of multiple orgasms, and most males are not. Both

Figure 5-3

An often proposed solution to female unhappiness.
(Copyright 1973 by Bülbül. Reprinted by permission.)

sexes have sexual fantasies and become aroused by erotic material, although most material is aimed solely at heterosexual males. In our culture, males generally are more sexually active and express greater interest in sex than do females, although females are far from inactive. Fewer females than males have orgasms. Orgasms experienced during masturbation are more frequent and usually are more intense for females than those experienced during intercourse. There is generally a qualitative difference in sexual behavior for males and females, whether heterosexual or homosexual—sex tends to be tied more to love and affection for females and more to achievement for males. A minority of individuals of both sexes partake in some homosexual activity, and sex differences in such activities are similar to those for heterosexuals. More males apparently engage in homosexual activity and in masturbation than do females.

Physiological factors do not adequately account for the differences between males and females in sexual behavior, although they may provide the basis for different socialization experiences. Culture puts a value on certain behaviors and characteristics, endowing some characteristics with more status and more power than others. In most cultures, males have the power. From the different experiences and scripts for the sexes, different sexual behaviors develop.

Recommended Reading

Blumstein, P., & Schwartz, P. (1983). *American couples.* New York: William Morrow. The results of the most comprehensive study of American couples to date, including both heterosexual and homosexual pairs.

Masters, W., & Johnson, V. (1966). *Human sexual*

response. Also (1970). *Human sexual inadequacy.* Boston: Little, Brown. Two ground-breaking works in the area of sexual functioning.

Rich, A. (1980). Compulsory heterosexuality and lesbian existence. *Signs, 5,* 631–660. A challenging and influential article delineating the political nature of the lesbian lifestyle, and female sexuality in general.

Vance, C. (Ed.) (1984). *Pleasure and danger: Exploring female sexuality.* Boston: Routledge & Kegan Paul. A highly controversial collection of papers from the 1982 Barnard conference on sexuality. Examines the nature of female sexuality, in all its manifestations.

Zilbergeld, B. (1978). *Male sexuality: A guide to sexual fulfillment.* Boston: Little, Brown. A sensitive and humorous examination of male sexuality, and how sexual and sex-role myths interfere with sexual fulfillment.

Part 2: Summary

After reviewing the current findings related to gender differences and similarities, certain general conclusions can be stated. Summary Table 1 summarizes the information in the physical, cognitive, personality, social, and sexual areas.

As the table indicates, there are very few clear-cut differences between males and females. Males, compared to females, tend to be more physically vulnerable, aggressive, and sexually active, to excel in visual-spatial and quantitative skills after age 8, and to dominate communications. Females, compared to males, tend to mature faster, to have cyclic hormonal production, to have greater hemispheric flexibility, to excel in verbal skills after age 11, to be more interested in people after adolescence, and to be capable of multiple orgasms.

Far more numerous than the areas of gender difference are the areas in which no overall gender differences have been found. These areas include activity level, hearing, learning, memory, general intelligence, analytic ability, concept mastery, creativity, emotionality, dependence, empathy, nurturance, altruism, assertiveness, compliance, dominance, competition, suggestibility, sexual responsiveness, and response to erotica. In a few areas, the differences are unclear, such as sense of touch, pain, vision, and smell; cognitive style; and fearfulness.

Of the few gender differences that seem to exist, the differences themselves are small, and there is wide individual variation. The distribution of these behaviors for the sexes overlaps considerably. Thus, the differences in Summary Table 1 reflect group averages and are not predictive of individual behavior.

Table 1
Summary of Gender Comparisons

Physical

Anatomy: Females have a uterus, ovaries, a clitoris, and a vagina. Males have testes, a penis, and a scrotum. Males tend to be bigger and more muscular.

Processes: Females mature faster, have slower metabolism. Differences in sensation are unclear; females may be more sensitive to touch, pain, and visual stimuli. Hormonal production is cyclic in females after puberty (ovulation and menstruation); it is mostly continuous in males.

Brain organization: Females may have greater hemispheric flexibility.

Vulnerability: Males are more vulnerable to disease, physical disorders, and early death.

Activity level: No differences in the amount of activity, although differences in type of movements and activities are found.

Table 1   *(continued)*

Cognitive

Learning and memory: No difference.
Intelligence: No difference in level of intelligence.
    Verbal: Females tend to excel up to age 3 and after age 11.
    Quantitative: Males tend to excel after age 12.
    Visual-spatial: Males tend to excel after age 8.
    Analytic: No difference.
    Concept mastery: No difference.
Cognitive style: Differences are unclear.
Creativity: No difference with nonverbal material; females tend to excel with verbal material.

Personality and Temperament

Self-description: Females are more people-oriented; males are more achievement-oriented.
Emotionality: No difference during childhood.
Fears: The evidence is contradictory; females report more fears.

Social Behavior

Communication patterns
    Verbal: Males dominate; depends on situational and sex-typing factors.
    Nonverbal: Males dominate; females may be more sensitive to cues; depends on situational factors.

Person-Centered interactions

Dependency: Depends on the definition used and situational factors.
Affiliation: No difference during childhood. After adolescence, females tend to be more interested in people.
Empathy: Depends on situational and sex-typing factors.
Nurturance: Depends on experience, situational, and sex-typing factors.
Altruism: Depends on situational and sex-typing factors.
Morality: Females seem more concerned with "responsibilities," males with "rights."
Equity/equality: Males seem more concerned with equity, females with equality.

Power-Centered interactions

Aggression: Males tend to be more physically aggressive after age 2; depends on definitions used and situational factors.
Assertiveness: Depends on situational and sex-typing factors.
Dominance: Depends on situational and definitional factors.
Competition/cooperation: Depends on situational and sex-typing factors.
Compliance: Depends on situational and sex-typing factors.

Sexual Behavior

Response: No difference; females are capable of multiple orgasms.
Interest: Males express more and have more experiences. Meaning of sex may be different for the two sexes.
Response to erotica: No difference.
Homosexuality: Reported more in males.
Masturbation: Reported more in males.

Another important finding that appears in examining research on gender differences is the tremendous importance of situational and personal factors, such as social expectations, the nature of the task, the presence and characteristics of other people, the age of the subjects, and, especially, the sex typing of the subjects. In most cases, these variables interact with an individual's gender in determining performance. Such situational factors need to be acknowledged more and trait terms need to be relied upon less.

It is important to note that many of the gender differences that are found do not appear until adolescence or later. This suggests that they might be a consequence, rather than a cause, of the gender stereotypes.

In looking at explanations of the differences, environmental factors (learning, expectations, and status differences) seem to be the most powerful influences on gender differences, although biological predispositions may play a role in some cases. Even in these cases, however, nature and nurture interact, with environmental factors usually overpowering the biological factors, shaping the behavior to conform to cultural expectations. We are all born with different physical, intellectual, and emotional potential, but these differences are not distributed by gender. The potentials that become actualized depend on the environment in which we are raised. And social factors in our environment often do differ on the basis of gender.

The question remains as to why the gender stereotypes discussed in Chapter 1 remain and are so strongly believed when there is little factual basis for them. To understand stereotypes' tenacity, one needs to understand the nature of the stereotypes themselves. Once believed, stereotypes become confirmed and strengthened whenever someone behaves in the expected way. For example, whenever a female expresses fearfulness, an observer may remark "That's just like a woman." The observer's belief in the stereotype then becomes stronger. On the other hand, when someone acts in a way contrary to the observer's expectation, instead of weakening the stereotype, the behavior in question is more likely to go unnoticed or to be classified as an exception. Thus, if a female does not act fearful, an observer might simply brush off the observation as unusual ("Oh, she's different"), if an observation is made at all. The stereotype itself remains inviolate and protected from refutation. Thus, we have the case where active athletic behavior on the part of girls is called atypical ("tomboyish") even though the majority of girls behave that way.

To challenge stereotypes, we need to get to the individual before he or she learns them; that is, we need to change the content of our gender socialization. In the next section, we will review how gender socialization occurs and how very difficult instituting such change would be.

Part 3
Origins of Sex Roles and Gender Stereotypes

As was shown in Part Two, there are few basic differences between the sexes aside from the purely physical. Given that few differences are inherent, how do sex roles and gender stereotypes get transmitted to members of a society? The following three chapters are devoted to answering this question.

Before examining the transmission of sex roles and stereotypes from one generation to another, we might first ask how the sex roles began. Did a division of traits, behaviors, and activities always exist between the sexes? If so, on what was a division based, since there are so few innate differences between the sexes and since the gender stereotypes themselves differ to some degree cross-culturally? Does such division necessarily imply differing statuses? To answer these questions, anthropological evidence is needed as well as an evolutionary and historical perspective. These will be covered in Chapter 6.

Given an evolutionary and historical background, we then can examine how children develop their sex roles and how they learn the gender stereotypes appropriate to their culture. *Socialization* is the process by which children are inculcated with the values and mores of their society. Four different theories of how gender socialization occurs, together with evidence regarding specific socializing agents, are reviewed in Chapter 7, and various socializing forces are discussed in Chapter 8.

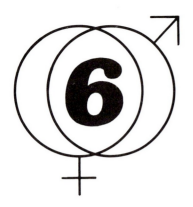

6

Historical Perspectives

A survey of a broad cross-section of cultures over the course of human history reveals that male dominance and a division of labor between the sexes are nearly universal. The precise division of labor, however, varies from one society to another, as does the rigidity with which such divisions are held (Blumberg, 1977, 1979; J. Brown, 1976; Ortner & Whitehead, 1981; Sanday, 1981a). In most cultures, males are primarily responsible for hunting, fishing, and warfare, and females for gathering foods, cooking, and child care. Yet this division is not true for all cultures. For other activities, such as preparing soil and tending and harvesting crops, the cultural variations are considerable.

Like the division of labor between the sexes and male dominance, the presence of gender stereotypes is nearly universal. In a 30-nation study, John Williams and Deborah Best (1982) found that nearly everywhere, males are characterized as adventurous, forceful, and independent, and females are characterized as sentimental, submissive, and superstitious. In all countries studied, the characteristics associated with males were stronger and more active than the characteristics associated with females.

Although Williams and Best studied gender stereotypes and not behavior, other cross-cultural research suggests that there are similar pancultural differences between women and men in actual behavior and in subjective world view. For example, a frequent finding is that males more often see the world in more instrumental and agentic ways and act in more aggressive, dominant, independent, and achievement-oriented ways than do females. Females more often see the world in expressive and communal ways and act more nurturantly, responsibly, obediently, and expressively than do males (Ember, 1981; Munroe & Munroe, 1980; Stockard & Dougherty, 1983; Welch & Page,

1981). Such difference in behavior and world view may result from biological and/or social factors, in particular, the division of labor between the sexes.

In this chapter, we will examine briefly the sex-based labor division patterns in various societies and review the explanations proposed to account for the patterns. How these patterns relate to the status of females and males within a society is another important issue that will be discussed. Much controversy surrounds all research in this area, with many conflicting theories and interpretations of findings. Although this chapter will not do justice to the breadth of research relating to the origins of sex roles, it will summarize some of the major approaches. The interested reader should examine sources listed at the end of the chapter for further information.

Patterns of Labor Division and Male Dominance

In nearly all cultures, women and men perform different tasks. The exact division of tasks depends on three factors: the particular subsistence base of a society, the supply of and demand for labor, and the compatibility of the needed tasks with child rearing. This last factor accounts for the fact that women's contributions to the subsistence activities of their society vary more than men's. Across all cultures, however, women contribute about 44% of their society's subsistence (Blumberg, 1977).

In this section, we will examine the various patterns of labor division by sex as a function of the technoeconomic base of the society. There are four major bases: hunting and gathering, horticulture, agriculture (wet and dry), and industry. Societies based on hunting and gathering and on horticulture are characteristic of almost all of the last three to four million years of human history, and in most of these societies, women were the primary producers (Blumberg, 1979).

Hunting and Gathering Societies

In hunting and gathering societies, which are the original form of social grouping, both sexes may work together to hunt and gather where game is close; this is the case, for example, with the Mbuti pygmies of the African Congo. Where game is available at a distance and vegetables are available nearby—as among the !Kung Bushmen of Africa—the sexes are segregated. Men hunt and provide protein for the group; women gather roots and berries, thereby contributing most (60–80%) of the food supply. This pattern is the most common. Where hunting is the only food source, men provide all the food. This pattern, which is found, for example, among the Eskimos, is quite rare (Friedl, 1975). Except in the latter case, women are generally full economic partners in hunting and gathering societies. Although males still retain some degree of dominance in other areas, relations between the sexes tend to be warm, cooperative, and relatively egalitarian, and women tend to be unrepressed sexually (Blackwood, 1984; Blumberg, 1977; Etienne & Leacock, 1980). This type of society apparently characterized all human groups for several million years— 98% of all human history (Blumberg, 1979; Collins, 1979).

Most hunting and gathering societies have been nonterritorial and have focused around the activities of both men and women, not solely around men as has sometimes been claimed (Bleier, 1979; Gough, 1975; Leibowitz, 1983). For example, in the !Kung society, groups of siblings and their offspring of both sexes band together, share food with all members of the group, and migrate to a new setting when any conflict arises (Lee, 1972). In such a society, women enjoy relatively high status, relative autonomy, and some ability to influence group decisions (Kolata, 1974). Fathers also tend to

have a great deal of contact with children, including infants (Collins, 1979).

Horticultural Societies

Societies in which food is cultivated by hoe emerged in the Middle East about 10,000 years ago and are primarily found today in sub-Saharan Africa and islands of the Pacific. Here, the amount of subsistence contributed by women is a direct function of the amount of warfare in that society and of certain natural environmental conditions (J. Brown, 1976; Sanday, 1973, 1981a). In general, because hoe cultivation is compatible with child care, women tend to make the predominant contribution. Indeed, it is now thought, though not widely acknowledged, that women rather than men probably invented agriculture (Bleier, 1979). In Africa, 75% of the cultivation is in the hands of women (Sciolino, 1985). Because neither sex automatically controls food, there is considerable flexibility in sex roles and some equality between the sexes on certain life options. For example, in the South Pacific nation of Fiji, male and female Melanesians are strikingly similar in instrumental and expressive characteristics (Basow, 1984a). Neither sex is sextyped according to U.S. standards, and both sexes can be described either as androgynous or undifferentiated. Both sexes also tend to have similar attitudes toward women's roles in society, although these attitudes appear to be relatively traditional (Basow, 1984b). In general, horticultural societies tend to be relatively egalitarian (as opposed to completely male-dominated), with status in many cases being based on principles other than gender (Ortner, 1981).

Agrarian Societies

When a group begins to lay claim to land and increase its food supplies through plow cultivation and the domestication of animals, certain social changes occur as well. Because land becomes property to be owned, defended, passed on, and bartered, inheritance factors, such as legitimacy of offspring, become very important. Thus, with the rise of agrarian societies five or six thousand years ago in the valleys of the

Tigris-Euphrates, Nile, and Indus rivers, patriarchy (societal organization based on the supremacy of the father in the family and the reckoning of descent and inheritance in the male line) and men's control of women's sexuality became firmly established. Women were not to engage in any sexual activity with men other than their husbands in order to ensure the legitimacy of their children. Consequently women's behaviors and lives became more restricted. Thus, with the development of private property, male dominance became institutionalized. Many writers, particularly those holding to traditional Marxism, view the development of private property as the beginning of all inequalities, sexism as well as classism (for example, Engels, 1972; Meillassoux, 1981). For other writers, sexism has itself been viewed as the prototype of all other inequalities (Firestone, 1970). In this latter viewpoint, sexism precedes the development of private property.

In the overwhelming majority of agrarian societies, men tend to dominate the division of labor, and exploitation of women's reproductive processes is much more common than in foraging societies (Blumberg, 1979; Meillassoux, 1981). The division of labor seems to be based on the fact that, because plow cultivation is more efficient, such work generally requires fewer people than does horticulture. In addition, because the activities required for plow cultivation range far from home, they are generally not compatible with child care. The !Kung offer a case in point (Kolata, 1974). Although foragers for over 11,000 years, more and more of the !Kung have now begun to live in agrarian villages since the 1960s. In 1974 fewer than 5% were still nomadic hunter-gatherers. Their society has changed dramatically as a result. Women have less mobility and contribute less to the food supply. Children now play in single-sex and -age groups as opposed to all playing together. Such segregated play encourages segregated roles. Aggression has increased because of such segregation, less supervision by adults, and less ability to leave the area. Fertility has also increased because of earlier age of menarche as a result of changing diet. All these factors have led to a marked drop in women's status.

In cultures that use wet irrigation—for example, for the cultivation of rice, as in Southeast Asia and Indonesia—more labor is required in a smaller area. There, women (at least those of the working class) contribute a great deal to the economy in the paddies and the market place. Consequently, their status is relatively high. In dry agrarian regions, however—for example, in northern India and the Middle East—there is a surplus of labor, and women's economic importance is minimal. This, too, is reflected in their status (Blumberg, 1977).

In sum, the status of women in agrarian societies is low because of patriarchy, institutionalized male dominance, and the division of labor. Interestingly, every one of today's industrialized societies sprang from an agrarian base (Blumberg, 1979).

Industrial Societies

The Industrial Revolution, begun about 1800 in England and northwest Europe, transformed basically agrarian societies but did little to improve the status of women. In fact, the position of women declined as men took over tasks formerly done by women and transferred these tasks from the home to the factory (Boserup, 1970). Men then assumed dominance of the public sphere with women relegated to the private sphere, which now decreased in societal importance as the means of production moved outside the home. It's important to note, however, that from another perspective, the work women did (and still do) in the home is vitally important both to the family and to society.

Because factory work is not compatible with continuous child care, women were not encouraged to do such work except when their labor was needed and/or when they needed the money. Thus, it was mostly poor women who worked and then mainly in low-status sweatshop activities. Women were viewed as a cheap and often nonessential labor pool. They were still viewed this way after World War II in the late 1940s and 1950s when service sector and low-level information-processing jobs boomed. In the early 1960s in the United States, the combination of these new jobs and a period of inflation pushed large numbers of White married women into the labor force (M. Harris, 1981). However, because these jobs were just as dead-end and low-level as the previous ones at the turn of the century, they did not improve women's status. Furthermore, women were not seen as competing with men, because the jobs women moved into were those that had long been dominated by women rather than men. Today, although women constitute from one-quarter to one-half of the labor force in industrialized societies, they still are not viewed as an integral or permanent part of the labor force (Blumberg, 1977).

This pattern of viewing women as cheap temporary labor when a society begins industrializing is strikingly evident in many Third-World countries today (see Nash & Fernandez-Kelly, 1983). Many manufacturing industries, especially textiles and electronics, have transferred production to export-processing zones in the Third World. These industries have shown an overwhelming preference for female workers who are viewed as a cheap, abundant, and politically docile labor force.

In the transition from a subsistence to a market economy in the United States, which accelerated with the Industrial Revolution, specialized roles for men and women arose. For women, particularly middle- and upper-class women, the new role created by the Industrial Revolution during the mid-19th century in the United States was that of *True Womanhood* (Wetter, 1966). As more men became involved in an increasingly materialistic society, the traditional values of piety and purity became viewed as the province of women almost exclusively. In addition to the values of piety and purity, the cult of True Womanhood involved the values of submissiveness and domesticity. Although rarely lived up to in their most extreme forms, these values served to constrain women's lives and to foster feeling of guilt and confusion in women.

Whereas the cult of True Womanhood existed mainly until the latter part of the 19th century, the new role for men, that of the *Good Provider,* lasted much longer. Bernard (1981) dates the Good Provider role in the United States from the 1830s to the late 1970s, when more than half of all married women were in the labor force. This role created a heavy burden on men to achieve in the work force to support their families. This role also increased

women's dependence on men and transformed marriage itself.

Although birth control and modern child-care and educational practices free a mother from having to structure her life solely around childbearing and child-rearing activities, such traditional activities still often are used to bar women from equal employment opportunity and equal pay. To some extent, then, industrialized society's low view of women's productivity and status may be a carry-over from its agrarian heritage. Attitudes have not yet caught up with current realities.

Explanations of Labor Division and Male Dominance

Why are men almost always the hunters and warriors and women the gatherers and domestics? The reason for the nearly universal division of labor by sex has, at various times, been attributed to physical, psychological, and functional factors.

Physical Factors

The *physically* based explanations argue that, because men are "naturally" bigger, stronger, and more aggressive, and women are "incapacitated" by childbearing, men are assigned the more strenuous, dangerous, and important societal activities. Marvin Harris (1977b) has gone so far as to say that a woman's most "essential characteristic" is her ability to make eggs, and this ability lays the groundwork for all differences between women and men in all societies for all times. This is part of the sociobiological viewpoint discussed in the previous chapter, which essentially holds that fundamental human behavioral similarities are based on genetic blueprints because they have some evolutionary significance.

The size difference between males and females that exists among almost all primates may play some role in the division of labor and the status of the sexes. Hrdy (1981) argues that large males were evolutionarily functional because males must be able to compete with each other for mates, but large females were not functional, because they would have less food to spare for babies. The result was male physical dominance, which, she argues, has led to the subjugation of women in patriarchy, where laws were made and enforced by men to secure paternity. Similarly, Steven Goldberg (1974) argues that males' greater aggressiveness, which he assumes to be physiologically based, could alone explain patriarchy, male dominance, and male attainment of high-status roles.

In contrast to the size and aggressiveness hypotheses is the lactation hypothesis (Lancaster, 1985). A slowly developing, large-brained infant requires much parental investment of time and energy. The greater fat deposits on female primates than male primates enable the mother to lactate nearly continuously. Lactation, then, may lead to different male and female behaviors.

The difficulties with pure physical explanations are numerous (Bleier, 1979; Leibowitz, 1979, 1983; Mitchell, 1971): (1) Physical differences between the sexes do not exist until puberty, and they vary considerably. In fact, such differences are often a function of different activities rather than a cause of them. (2) Motherhood does not require giving up work, not even in the paid labor force. (3) Women's activities require a great deal of physical strength and energy (for example, carrying water or lifting a 30-pound child). (4) Women generally do contribute substantially to a society's economic base. (5) In some societies, parenthood restricts male activities. For example, in some extreme cases, fathers—not mothers— are expected to have labor pains and a long recovery period after birth (Paige & Paige, 1973). (6) Male dominance and aggression is not universal, even among primates, and is not necessarily associated with better breeding opportunities.

As Mitchell (1971) argues, it is not physical coercion or physical weakness that has led to the subjugation of women but rather social coercion interacting with the division of labor based on biological capacity. The bearing and nursing of children do have significance for what women can do in societies where life expectancy is short, no efficient birth-control methods are available, and the family is entirely responsible for the socialization of its young. In most primitive societies and in India until 1920, the average age at death was 20. Until about 1800, the average age at death in most countries was only 35 (Youssef & Hartley, 1979). In such societies, women spend most of their lives either pregnant or breast-feeding. Thus, women's activities must be compatible with simultaneous child care. Therefore, the natural reproductive differences between the sexes may have led to some division of labor, which in agrarian and industrialized societies led to status differences (Firestone, 1970). This will be commented on further in the subsequent section "Functional Factors."

Another physically based explanation relates to how the brain is organized. As was noted in Part Two, females appear to have superior verbal skills and ability to read nonverbal cues. These characteristics seem well suited to the traditional mother's role and may be based on nonspecific localization of function in female brains. Males, in contrast, appear to have superior visual-spatial skills—traits that are appropriate to roaming in search of food and that may be based on more specific localization of function in male brains. Division of labor, then, may have followed from genetic blueprints. However, this explanation is based on much speculation; a sex difference in perception of nonverbal cues is not that clear, nor are any of the sex differences absolutes. Furthermore, the understanding of brain organization and localization of functions is very limited at this time, and any difference may be a result of different experiences, rather than different genes or hormones.

Psychological Factors

Many theorists have argued that there are fundamental psychological differences between the sexes based on anatomical and/or reproductive differences that underlie the division of labor. For example, Freud (1933/1965) described how a girl's recognition that she is missing a penis shapes her personality development by age five in the direction of passivity, inferiority, vainness, and masochism. Even feminist psychoanalytic thinkers like Chodorow (1978) argue that early experiences with a female fig-ure (mother) shape the personalities of boys and girls in different directions. Girls, who form a personal identification with their mother that is reinforced by later role expectations of personal relationships with children, develop a personality based on personalism and sub-jectivity. Boys, who identify originally with mother but then must shift to a more abstract identity with a remote male figure, develop a personality based on abstractness and objec-tivity. Similar basic personality differences have been argued by others as well (Gilligan, 1982a; O'Brien, 1981; Ortner, 1974). As a result of these basic psychological differences, fe-males become more associated with nature and the private sphere, whereas males become more associated with culture and the public sphere. These psychological differences need not be assumed to be innate but can result from probably universal socialization experiences (that is, children brought up by women). Thus, psychological differences may be the result rather than the cause of the division of labor.

Viewing psychological factors as the ex-planation of the division of labor and of male dominance is extremely controversial. Although certain gender stereotypes appear in a wide variety of cultures, as do certain sex-linked behaviors, most researchers conclude that there is no evidence of basic psychological differences between females and males. Mead (1935) and other cross-cultural researchers have noted that the sexes are quite variable on a number of different traits—jealousy, depen-dency, artistic interests, aggressiveness, and so on. Specific cultures may encourage the devel-opment of different traits in females and males, but these differences then are culturally, not biologically, derived.

Functional Factors

Functional explanations of the division of labor between the sexes stress the practicality of such divisions for a society. Claude Lévi-Strauss (1956) suggests that, by having men and women responsible for different tasks in a society, mu-tual dependency between the sexes is estab-lished. This dependency serves to strengthen marriage and family ties. Although interesting, this theory does not account for the specific division of tasks by sex (J. Brown, 1976).

Another functional explanation involves women's childbearing capacity (Blumberg, 1979; Friedl, 1975; Leibowitz, 1983). Since women do bear and nurse children, it is more functional to have them perform tasks that are compatible with such activities in societies where no alternative exists. Because hunting, fishing, and warfare occur irregularly, last for unpredictable lengths of time, and require long-distance travel, these activities are not very compatible with childbearing and early child care; however, if hunting activities occur near home, women can and do participate in hunting, without detriment to their child-care activities (Goodman, Griffin, Estioko-Griffin & Grove, 1985). Carrying young children around for a long distance is cumbersome, and leaving them home to be cared for by others is unfeasible when the children are still nursing, although in many societies, wet nursing (nursing by other women) is customary.

In addition, it would be impractical to train everyone to become hunters. Game is an un-certain commodity. Therefore, some members of society must be responsible for a more reli-able food supply, such as berries and roots. Since foraging activities, hunting small game, and cultivating the land are perfectly compat-ible with childbearing and early child care, women became primarily responsible for these food-producing activities. Men, in turn, were assigned other tasks, perhaps by default, or because of their expendability (Meillassoux, 1981; Sanday, 1981a).

Thus, the most persuasive explanation of the division of labor involves an interaction of functional distinctions between the sexes and the economic bases of specific cultures. Tasks are divided according to the compatibility of tasks with child care, the subsistence base of the society, and the labor supply and demand. This still occurs today (M. Harris, 1981; Wojcicka-Sharff, 1981).

As is evident from the previous discussion, different scholars have seen status differences as a cause, a concomitant, or a consequence of the division of labor. Hence, a closer examina-tion of this complex variable is warranted.

Status and Its Relation to the Division of Labor

Men having a higher status than women in terms of power and prestige is a nearly universal occurrence. Even in modern societies in which women hold what we, in the United States, would consider high-status jobs, their actual status is low. For example, most doctors in Russia are women, but practicing medicine is considered a low-status job there.

Although there is some controversy regarding the universality of male dominance, most writers agree that the status differential between the sexes seems to have existed in varying degrees since prehistoric times (Chafetz, 1984; Flax, 1981; M. Harris, 1977b; Ortner & Whitehead, 1981). Does this status differential arise from the division of labor between the sexes, or does the differential give rise to the division of labor? There is evidence for both of the above positions. Figure 6-1 gives a humorous example of one way status and labor division are related.

Status as a Cause of the Division of Labor

Ortner (1974; Ortner & Whitehead, 1981) suggests one way status factors may have affected the division of labor. She believes that people tend to put a higher value on things they can control than on things they cannot control. Thus, all activities that are regulated by humans (activities of a society, such as hunting) are viewed as more valuable than all activities regulated by nature (for example, childbirth). Because women, by virtue of their reproductive functions, are more controlled by nature than by their culture, their work and their status as people become devalued. Men, who do not seem as subject to natural forces as do women, are considered to be more in control of themselves. Therefore, they and their activities become more highly valued.

Ortner's thesis, although controversial (see MacCormack & Strathern, 1981), has been extended by other anthropologists. After examining more than 150 tribal societies, Sanday (1981a) concludes that male dominance is not universal but most likely occurs in societies severely stressed by migration, food shortages, or colonialism. In such circumstances, public and private life become split, and public life, that part separate from child rearing and family activities, becomes synonymous with the male collective. Etienne and Leacock (1980) put forth a similar view—that much of the male dominance found today in many societies is actually the result of the hierarchical relationships brought by the agents of colonialism (for example, priests, bureaucrats, and military personnel).

Figure 6-1 _____
One relationship between status and the division of labor. (B. C. by permission of Johnny Hart and Field Enterprises, Inc.)

From the above, it is clear that status factors may play a role in assigning tasks within a society. Status may also accrue from task divisions, depending upon which sex is dominant in a task.

Status as a Consequence of the Division of Labor

Marvin Harris (1977a) proposes that male supremacy existed since prehistoric times as a way to counter the threat of overpopulation and to counter the threat of depletion of resources that such overpopulation would bring. Warfare was one means of controlling overpopulation as well as of controlling the resources. Because, during prehistory, muscle-powered weapons (clubs, bows, and arrows) were relied upon and because of the greater average strength and height of the human male, men were everywhere the principal, if not exclusive, combatants. To prepare to risk one's life in battle took years of mental and physical training via competitive sports and physical ordeals. Since a female's life cycle after puberty was constantly interrupted by pregnancy and breast feeding, males were the logical sex to undergo such training.

The consequences of only males' being responsible for warfare were enormous. To get males to risk their lives and their comfort, a powerful system of rewards and punishments was needed. Sex was the reward; ostracism, the punishment. "If wives and concubines were to be the chief inducement for men to become masculine, women had to be trained from birth not for combat but for acquiescence to male demands" (Harris, 1977b, p. 117). Patriarchy, patrilocality (place of residence determined by males), exchange of women, polygamy, aggressiveness in males, passivity in females, and male chauvinism and supremacy all follow from assigning responsibility for warfare solely to males.

The division of labor in other areas of society followed the initial division for combat. Harris further states that males' hunting specialty arose from their warfare training. The weapons of hunt were the same as the weapons of war. Therefore, women were assigned all the remaining tasks. Because maleness was associated with power and prestige through warfare, whatever men did was considered of high status. Because females were trained to be subordinate, whatever they did was considered of low status. This relationship between male status and female status continues into the present. Touhey (1974) found that the status of an occupation declined when respondents (female and male) thought more females than males would enter that occupation in the future. When more males than females were predicted as entering an occupation, the status of the occupation increased. Although more recent replications of Touhey's study using expectations of changing sex proportions have not found the same results (for example, Suchner, 1979), the bias still appears to exist when actual increases in proportions of women in various occupations occur.

Because Harris sees the threat of overpopulation and the assignment of warfare exclusively to males as the cause of male supremacy, he foresees the development of safe contraceptives and the integration of women into the military as the way to end this domination by males. Not everyone shares his optimism or his thesis. In the first place, as previously noted, not all societies were focused around warfare or hunting, nor were all societies patrilocal. Secondly, men's relatively greater strength may have been a consequence of men's roles as warriors and hunters and not a cause of the role assignment. Thirdly, some control over contraception, although unrefined, did exist in some primitive societies. For example, the !Kung of Africa breast-feed each child for about four years (Friedl, 1975). Breast feeding often inhibits ovulation, thereby facilitating a certain amount of spacing between children. Of course, nursing itself does impose some restrictions on a woman's activities. On the whole, however, Harris's thesis is provocative and supported by current findings in Israel. In that country, once the army stopped using women in combat, women's status in the military and in society regressed ("Israeli," 1982).

The degree to which a woman contributes to the economic base of her society generally parallels her status in that society; that is, the greater her contribution, the higher her status, up to a point. As was noted above, female contributions tend to be greater in horticultural societies than in other societies. Their status in horticultural societies also tends to be higher than in other societies. In agrarian societies, in which women's contributions are low, their status is also low. Yet this relationship is not perfectly linear. Even when women contribute greatly to a society, their status still tends to be lower than men's. For example, in 1985, African women made up 60–80% of the agricultural labor force, yet their status vis-à-vis men remained low ("African," 1985).

A key factor in determining status levels is the control of the most valued resources (Chafetz, 1984; Collier & Rosaldo, 1981; Leacock, 1978; Sanday, 1981a). Blumberg (1979), in examining 61 preindustrial societies, found that participation in production, by itself, was not directly related to control of certain life options, such as freedom to initiate and end a marriage. The strongest influence on female equality was women's relative degree of economic control over the group's productive resources and surpluses. For example, Iroquois women have an unusually high status in their society. They contribute about 50% of the subsistence of their society (basically vegetables, fish, and game). But in other societies in which women contribute more, as in the Tikopia and the Azande societies, their status remains low (Sanday, 1974). What differentiates the Iroquois from these other groups is that, in the past, the Iroquois women also controlled the distribution of food because their men were frequently away hunting or at war for years at a time (J. Brown, 1970). Being in charge of food distribution was a form of power, and Iroquois women used this power in political areas as well. In societies where women do not have control of the food distribution, even though they contribute 60% to 70% of the food supply, their status is low. In most societies, it is usually game that gets distributed among tribal members. Because men are in charge of hunting, they are generally in charge of the food distribution. The vegetables and berries gathered by women are usually directed more toward family, rather than toward tribal, consumption (Friedl, 1975). Hence,

women generally have less power and status than men.

A number of researchers have found that the economic power of women in society is further enhanced by their being strategically indispensable and by kinship arrangements that take females into account (Blumberg, 1979; Leibowitz, 1983; Mendonsa, 1981; Sanday, 1981a). Strategic indispensability arises when there is no reserve labor pool—such as slaves or homemakers, when specific expertise is needed, and when work is autonomous, as in the case of African marketing. Strategic indispensability also occurs when there are fewer women than men in a society over a period of time (Guttentag & Secord, 1983; Secord, 1983). In societies where inheritance passes through the mother's side of the family or where the family residence is with the wife's family, women also tend to have considerable economic power. Economic power can be translated into political power and into some immunity to physical force. Thus, for full sexual equality, economic power by women is imperative.

In modern societies, the same pattern of economic power seems to exist as has been described for more primitive cultures. Even though women constitute nearly half the labor force, their status remains lower than men's. This may be because the goods and services produced by women (for example, social services and clerical work) are not valued as highly as those produced by men (for example, manufacturing and managerial work) (Chafetz, 1984). Gender inequality may decrease only if women move into male-dominated professions with higher prestige. Furthermore, because men are assigned the role of breadwinner, they usually are in charge of the distribution of their earnings. Even if the wife works outside the home, men's generally higher salaries mean the men still are in control. The battle for equal pay for equal work has important ramifications for the balance of power in a family, as both opponents and supporters of the equal-pay position are well aware.

Another reason men have had more power and status may be that they are in charge of the relatively more vital and rarer resources. Since protein can be considered more vital and rarer than vegetables, and since meat is protein, men's contributions from hunting have been more highly valued than women's contributions from gathering.

Still another explanation builds on the Marxist economic position that whoever controls the means of production has the most power and status. This explanation asserts that, because of women's role in reproduction, the situation of women is unique (Eisenstein, 1979; Firestone, 1970; Flax, 1981; Janssen-Jurreit, 1982; Mitchell, 1971; O'Brien, 1981). With the advent of the concept of private property and of men's discovery and recognition of their role in reproduction (paternity), women were reduced to "factors of production" in the recreation of the human labor supply. Men "appropriated" the children and built institutions to support female chastity and monogamy. Custom and ideology then developed that promoted the idea of female inferiority and supported and reinforced a still shaky sense of male power. Reproduction also removed women from the arena of production—which occurred outside the home—in agricultural and industrialized societies. This later developed into an emphasis on the socialization—in the home—of children by their mother. Such an emphasis on maternal child care serves to decrease women's influence in their community, as Werner (1984) found among the Mekranoti of Central Brazil. In that group, child care did not interfere with a woman's contribution to subsistence, but it did interfere with a woman's ability to acquire the personal connections needed to exercise influence. For example, although mothers still helped provide food, their interactions with men other than their husbands were severely restricted, and even their interactions with other women tended to be circumscribed by child-care responsibilities. To achieve equality, women must participate equally not only in the economic/production process, but they must gain control of the reproductive process as well as transform societal norms regarding socialization.

In summary, males' high status can be viewed as both a cause and a consequence of the division of labor between the sexes. The legacy of male dominance, however, has continued far past its initial justification.

Summary and Overview

The difference in status between the sexes, so visible in our society, seems to be a carry-over from the division of labor in societies that preceded ours. This division of labor was initially necessary because of women's child-bearing function and was determined by environmental conditions. Thus, the precise activities allocated to women were determined by the activities' compatibility with child care, with the supply and demand of labor, and with the subsistence base of the society. In hunting and gathering societies, men were the hunters; women, the gatherers. Men had slightly higher status because their activities were more dangerous, more vital for their tribe's survival, and because their activities gave men more power in the distribution of the food. But women and their economic contribution were very important. In horticultural societies, females generally contributed a great deal and also tended to have high status. Because males were the warriors, however, their status still tended to be higher. In agrarian societies, women's economic contribution dropped, as did their status. In industrialized societies like our own, the division of labor and the lower status of women have continued despite the fact that such divisions and status levels no longer are justified culturally.

Thus, although childbearing is an unchangeable sex difference, the implications of this biological fact are different today in the United States from previous times in other societies. With the advent of birth control, women no longer need to become pregnant frequently and unpredictably. Most women now use some form of birth control, plan on having fewer children, and are having them at a later age than in the past. Because of smaller family sizes and longer life expectancies, motherhood, if entered at all, occupies a much smaller proportion of an American woman's life than it used to. In advanced countries, less than one-seventh of a woman's average lifetime is spent bearing children. In addition, because many child-care responsibilities previously borne by the family alone are now borne by society, such as by schools and day-care centers, there is no longer any justification for a division of labor based on sex.

One implication from the above brief survey of labor division and status is that, although productive labor does not automatically lead to equality, it does lead to economic power, at least in the form of control of a paycheck. This economic power, in turn, is the strongest determinant of a woman's freedom and status. Economic power is not, however, the only determinant. Political and military power are of even greater importance in determining the status of members of a society. Women's presence in these areas is just beginning.

Recommended Reading

Harris, M. (1977). *Cannibals and kings.* New York: Random House. A fascinating, albeit controversial, examination of how societal needs shape the norms and mores of a society and the behaviors of the sexes in particular.

Lowe, M., & Hubbard, R. (Eds.) (1983). *Woman's nature: Rationalizations of inequality.* New York: Pergamon. A stimulating series of essays examining the roots of female subordination, and the myths surrounding it.

O'Brien, M. (1981). *The politics of reproduction.* Boston: Routledge & Kegan Paul. A provocative book that creates a theoretical model of the role of reproduction in human history, using a Marxist analytical framework.

Ortner, S. B., & Whitehead, H. (Eds.) (1981). *Sexual meanings: The cultural construction of gender and sexuality.* Cambridge: Cambridge University Press. An excellent collection of articles representing the symbolic anthropological approach to the understanding of gender. The major thesis is that culture determines gender through the workings of status and prestige hierarchies.

Sanday, P. R. (1981). *Female power and male dominance: On the origins of sexual inequality.* Cambridge: Cambridge University Press. An attempt to link cultural ideas about sex roles to the shifting ecological environments in which "sex-role plans" are created. In Sanday's view, there is no universal pattern of male dominance in tribal societies.

Socialization: Theories and Agents

In Part Two, a strong case was made for the overriding importance of socialization over biological factors in determining an individual's sex-typed behaviors. In Chapter 6, the origins of the gender stereotypes were found to be rooted in the division of labor based on economic and biological conditions present in a society. Although such a division based on biological sex is no longer either practical or necessary, the traditional pattern remains and gets transmitted to each succeeding generation as part of its socialization. Because socialization is such an important factor, it is productive to examine more closely how such a socialization process occurs, who the socializing agents are, and what other forces operate.

In this chapter, three traditional theories of gender identity development—psychoanalytic theory, social learning theory, and cognitive-developmental theory—will be reviewed and evaluated. As with other research in this area, the evidence is complex and contradictory, partly because of methodological problems and partly because of the complexity of human development itself. In general, some combination of the above theories is needed to account for the complex interaction among biological factors, the learning environment, and the level of cognitive development of the child. One promising new theory that attempts such integration—gender schema theory—will be discussed. Reviews of research on the major socializing agents, which include parents, teachers, and peers, will follow, along with a summary of their influence. Chapter 8 will focus on the influence of other socializing forces in American society.

Theories

There are three traditional theories of gender development—psychoanalytic, social learning, and cognitive developmental. Each emphasizes different aspects of development and makes different predictions as to the sequence of development. Many of these models focus on early childhood, although a number of writers have been urging a life-span approach to the topic of sex roles, gender stereotypes, and gender socialization (for example, DelBoca & Ashmore, 1980; Fischer & Narus, 1981b; Katz, 1979). This life-span approach, which will be discussed in the section on cognitive-developmental theory, should be kept in mind as we review the different theories.

Psychoanalytic Theory

Psychoanalytic theory stresses the importance of biological (including anatomical) factors and parental identification. As was discussed in Chapter 5, through the resolution at age 5 to 6 of the Oedipus and Electra conflicts brought on by the recognition that only boys have penises, children become motivated to identify with the same-sex parent. Each child is thought to have incestuous desires that cause guilt and anxiety. Each views the same-sex parent as either responsible for the absence of a penis, in the case of girls, or able to remove the penis, in the case of boys. Identifying with the "aggressor" is thus a way to allay this anxiety. The fear of penis removal is considered stronger for males than is penis envy for females, because girls have already "lost" the coveted penis. Consequently, males' gender identity is viewed as stronger than females' gender identity. For Freud, same-sex identification is critical for healthy adjustment and for the development of masculine and feminine personalities. He viewed the sequence of development as innate and biologically based, proceeding from an awareness of the anatomical sex difference to identification with same-sex parent and eventually to adoption of sex-typed behaviors.

There is little empirical support for the above assertions of traditional psychoanalytic theory, although Silverman and Fisher (1981) argue that the effects of the Oedipus complex on adult males can be discerned through careful laboratory testing. We have already reviewed evidence of the nonuniversality of Freudian personality concepts, stages, and interpretation (see Chapter 5). In addition, contrary to psychoanalytic predictions that females should have a weaker identification with their same-sex parent than do boys, Lynn (1979) cites research that shows the reverse to be true. More females than males do seem to prefer other-sex activities (for example, Connor & Serbin, 1978), but interpretations other than "penis envy" are more likely. Some females may prefer male-related activities because of males' generally higher status and greater power. Or they may prefer such activities because of the intrinsic qualities of the activities themselves. For example, engaging in sports or playing with an Erector Set simply may be more fun than playing with dolls.

The prediction that identification with the same-sex parent is critical for mental health also has not been verified (Pleck, 1981b; Williams, 1973), nor has the importance of having appropriately sex-typed parents. Spence and Helmreich (1978) found that the most healthy homes (those in which children are able to function effectively and achieve a sense of worth) are homes in which both parents are perceived as androgynous. Following closely in this same rating for health are homes in which only one parent is perceived as androgynous.

Part of Erik Erikson's (1964) extension of Freudian theory emphasizes how the shape of one's genitals affects one's sense of space. This conclusion, resulting in the description of males as more outer-space oriented and females as more inner-space oriented, was based on one poorly controlled study of 11- to 13-year-olds. These children were asked to build a scene out of a selection of toys. Erikson observed that boys tended to build towers, girls tended to build enclosures. However, no controls were exerted on previous experience or on the types of toys chosen. More recent attempts at replication reveal that no difference in constructions emerge when children use the same toys (Budd, Clance, & Simerly, 1985; Karpoe & Olney,

1983). Children of both sexes make "feminine" constructions with "girl" toys such as dolls, and "masculine" constructions with "boy" toys such as trucks.

As noted in Chapter 6, there are current feminist psychodynamic thinkers (for example, Chodorow, 1978; Flax, 1981) who break with Freud on the anatomy-is-destiny part of his theory but who concur that psychodynamic principles are the prime shapers of an individual's gender identity. In particular, being brought up primarily by a mother or other female figure causes boys and girls to develop different cognitive orientations and personalities. Girls, who continue a personal identification with the female socializer, develop a more personal and embedded style of being, whereas boys, who must shift to an abstract identification with a more distant and diffuse male figure, develop a more abstract and impersonal style of being. Boys also must reject their personal identification with the mother, which leads to rejecting everything connected with her—that is, everything female and feminine. Although the agentic/expressive, impersonal/personal, objective/subjective distinctions between males and females characterize the gender stereotypes, there is a great deal of individual variability in these traits not accounted for by the theory. Furthermore, the tremendous influence of social factors (besides the mother) on behavior is relatively ignored here, as it is in all psychodynamic theorizing. Although there is some support for the idea that it may be more difficult for boys to form their gender identity than it is for girls, explanations other than a psychodynamic one can account for this. For example, there may be fewer male figures for a boy to model.

In summary, psychoanalytic theory does not completely account for the development of an individual's gender identity.

Social Learning Theory

One theory that contrasts strongly with the psychoanalytic approach is social learning theory. Instead of viewing gender identity as an innate, biologically determined development, social learning theory views gender identity as a product of various forms of learning. This theory, put forth by Mischel (1966), Bandura and

Walters (1963), Lynn (1969), and others, emphasizes the importance of the environment on a child's gender development. The child learns his or her role directly through differential treatment, rewards, and punishments, and indirectly through observational learning and modeling.

If a boy is punished for clinging and is rewarded for working on his own and doing things, he is more likely to develop autonomous and independent behavior than is his sister who receives the opposite treatment. In addition, because powerful, nurturant, and similar models are most likely to be imitated (Bandura, 1969), children tend to model their same-sex parent (the one most similar to themselves), thus learning gender-appropriate behavior through observation.

Of course, models other than parents, if present in the child's environment, would have a similar effect (for example, television characters). Males, who are viewed by children as more powerful and strong than are females (DelBoca & Ashmore, 1980; Williams & Best, 1982), may be particularly important models for young children. For example, Koblinsky and Sugawara (1984) found nursery school children to be more affected by the gender-related behavior of the male teacher than they were by the behavior of the female teacher. However, same-sex modeling also occurred.

According to the social learning theory, because sex typing begins at birth, same-sex modeling precedes, and gives rise to, the formation of a stable gender identity. Because different behaviors get reinforced and modeled by the different sexes, children develop an awareness of the two sex roles very early, starting in the first year of life (DelBoca & Ashmore, 1980; Lewis & Weinraub, 1979). Their own behavior becomes shaped to accord with one of these roles, and they then develop a stable gender identity. In other words, "I do girl things; I must be a girl."

Lynn (1959, 1969), in an expansion of this theory, posits that, since the father is frequently absent from the home and since masculine-sex-typed activities are not directly observable by the child, boys have a more difficult time than girls in establishing their gender identity. They are forced to develop a more abstract identification with the male role, while girls identify directly with their mothers, who are observable. This early abstraction may account for sex differences in cognitive style and in males' greater attachment to a culturally defined masculine role. Although cognitive style differences have not been found consistently and can be explained better by differences in experience (see Chapter 3), there is some support to Lynn's hypothesis that a son's identification with his father is qualitatively different from a daughter's identification with her mother. For example, Lynn (1979) has summarized studies finding greater mother-daughter similarity than father-son similarity. Also, boys clearly attend to same-sex models, when available, although girls do not always do so (Connor & Serbin, 1978). Boys also may imitate same-sex models more closely than do girls and are more likely than girls to reject other-sex behaviors and objects (Bussey & Bandura, 1984; Bussey & Perry, 1982; Downs, 1983; Raskin & Israel, 1981). Girls may be more flexible because they are less consistently reinforced than are boys for imitating only same-sex adults (Kagan, 1964).

More support for social learning theory comes from studies indicating that knowledge about gender stereotypes increases with age from ages 2½ to college (DelBoca & Ashmore, 1980; Leahy & Shirk, 1984; Williams & Best, 1982). In one study (Vener & Snyder, 1966), children 5 years old were found to have an 84% accuracy rate in matching certain artifacts with adult sex roles (for example, "Who uses lipstick? Who smokes a pipe?"). Even children 2½ years of age showed 75% accuracy, although another study (Myers, Weinraub, & Shetler, 1979) found less than chance accuracy in children under age 3. The examples used in the studies, of course, assumed a clear dichotomy in usage of items. Such an assumption may be unwarranted, especially when stereotyped behaviors are becoming more flexible. Also supportive of social learning theory are findings that the number of sex-typed traits increases with age (Silvern, 1977). Further support for social learning theory is the finding that both sexes, as early as age 3 years, emulate same-sex models more than other-sex models (Bussey & Bandura, 1984).

Although there is much evidence that people can and do learn through reinforcement and imitation, social learning as the sole explanation of the development of gender identity is insufficient. Firstly, like all learning theories, social learning theory views the child as relatively passive in the learning process. Other evidence suggests complex parent-child interactions. For example, if female infants begin vocalizing earlier than males, parents may respond with more vocalizations to females. This parental response further reinforces the infants' vocalizations, and a sex difference in language development may ensue.

Secondly, research on direct reinforcement has been equivocal. Clearly, it would be impossible for parents consistently and deliberately to reward and punish each behavior according to its gender appropriateness. Maccoby and Jacklin (1974), reviewing a large body of research, concluded that, at least in parental self-reports and in laboratory observations, there is surprisingly little differentiation in parent behavior according to the sex of the child. The one exception to this finding is that boys are subject to more intense socialization pressures than are girls. Some differences in parent behavior do emerge outside laboratory settings, but not enough differences occur to account for the clear differences in gender expectations that boys and girls have.

Thirdly, a problem with social learning theory concerns the importance placed on imitation of the same-sex parent in the acquisition of sex-role behavior. Although identification can account for the acquisition of more behavior than can differential treatment, the evidence again is only partially supportive. Maccoby and Jacklin (1974) found that children do not always select same-sex models, that they do not necessarily resemble the same-sex parent, and that the sex-typed behavior, such as it is, is not a direct copy of adult behavior but tends to be more stereotyped and exaggerated. Maccoby and Jacklin did not take into account imitation of models other than parents. However, even in such situations, same-sex modeling does not always occur (Raskin & Israel, 1981).

The criticism regarding the extent of imitation by a child has been addressed by Perry and Bussey (1979). These researchers demonstrated that the imitation process is more complex and abstract than previously assumed. Children learn gender-appropriate behaviors by observing differences in the frequencies with which female and male models, as groups, perform various behaviors in given situations. Children are more likely to imitate a model if that model usually displays sex-appropriate behavior than if that model usually does not display such behaviors. Furthermore, boys appear to be more affected than girls by the gender appropriateness of the model's behavior (Eisenstock, 1984; Raskin & Israel, 1981). Hence, a child may imitate a same-sex parent or other model, but only if the parent or model is seen as representative of other members of his or her sex. Since Perry and Bussey's modification of social learning theory involves a significant amount of abstracting ability, such as in noticing that the sexes differ in their frequency of performing some behaviors, a child's cognitive capacities need to be fairly well developed for this imitation process to occur. It is important to note that research supporting this theory used 8- to 11-year-old children. Factors other than imitation must be involved in earlier sex differences.

Age is a crucial factor in sex-role behavior acquisition. There is a trend toward same-sex modeling that increases from nursery school through high school and adulthood, especially for boys (Bussey & Bandura, 1984; Connor & Serbin, 1978). These findings agree with Perry and Bussey's (1979) reformation of social learning theory. However, the degree of gender stereotyping also varies with age but not in the same way. For example, with regard to occupational gender stereotypes, sex-typed attributions were minimal during preschool, increased until first or second grade (ages 6 to 8), and then decreased after fourth grade (Garrett, Ein, & Tremaine, 1977; O'Keefe & Hyde, 1983; Tremaine, Schau, & Busch, 1982). A similar pattern is found regarding other aspects of the gender stereotypes (Burleigh, 1983; Plumb & Cowan, 1984). In fact, stereotyped sex-role behavior and attitudes may be most pronounced around age 5 or 6 years (Kohlberg & Ullian, 1974; Urberg, 1982). After these ages, definitions of appropriate sex-role behaviors become less rigid, especially for girls. Social learning theory would predict increasing strength of stereotypes with age, because there would be increased exposure to the stereotypes. Thus research on age patterns does not fully support social-learning theory.

Social learning theory does offer an explanation of how modeling and reinforcement may interact, with the former process being involved in the acquisition of behavior and the latter determining the performance of the behavior. For example, Bandura (1965) found that boys were more likely than girls to act aggressively after viewing an aggressive model. When incentives for behaving aggressively were introduced, however, the sex difference was wiped out. This study demonstrates that both sexes may learn aggressive responses, but girls are less likely to perform them because of their reinforcement history. Similarly, Perry and Bussey (1979) found that 8- and 9-year-old children were unaffected by the sex of a model in recalling a model's behavior, even though the sex of the model was an important variable with regard to whether the children actually imitated a behavior.

What is needed is a theory that can take into account the different cognitive abilities of young children. These abilities are likely to mediate any experiences young children have. Cognitive-developmental theory provides one way of acknowledging these factors.

Cognitive-Developmental Theory

Cognitive-developmental theory, put forth by Kohlberg (1966; Kohlberg & Ullian, 1974) emphasizes the active role of the child in acquiring sex-role behaviors. As Piaget has delineated, children go through various discrete stages in their cognitive development. They first perceive the world in relation to their sensorimotor abilities, such as crawling and sucking. Then they learn how to categorize the world. Later they become capable of performing concrete operations on that world as in taking both the height and width of an object into account when estimating its size. Finally, they become capable of abstract reasoning, but not usually until after age 8. A child's reality, then, is qualitatively different from an adult's.

Based on Piaget's theory of stages of cognitive development, Kohlberg argues that the way children learn their sex role is a function of their level of understanding the world. Before about ages 4 to 7, children do not have an understanding of physical constancy. For example, they don't understand that water poured from a narrow glass to a wide glass is still the same amount of water. Therefore, before about age 5, they cannot have a firm gender identity. After that age, however, the permanence of gender is grasped, and this self-categorization (one's label of self as girl or boy) becomes an organizing focus of future behaviors. The child begins valuing same-sex behaviors and attitudes and begins devaluing other-sex ones. He or she then seeks out models and situations in accordance with this categorization in order to remain self-consistent; that is, after establishing what they are (female/male), children look around to find out what people with that label do. It is at this point, when gender identity is already established, that a child may identify with the same-sex parent, reversing the sequence proposed by social learning theorists. This identification is not important to cognitive-developmental theorists, however. A child can acquire information about appropriate sex-role behaviors from many sources—adults, peers, stories, TV, and so forth. Table 7-1 contrasts Kohlberg's proposed sequence of development with that proposed by psychoanalytic and social learning theorists. Kohlberg's theory posits that the establishment of gender identity guides the perception of gender stereotypes and the consequent development of gender attributes.

Because their cognitive development is still tied to concrete operations, children aged 6 to 7 often have very simplistic and exaggerated pictures of the two sex roles and have sharp gender stereotypes. It is only with further cognitive development that these stereotyped conceptions can become modified to incorporate exceptions and personal preferences. Thus, a cognitive-developmental theorist would explain the findings of Garrett and associates (1977) that fifth-graders held fewer occupational stereotypes than did first- and third-graders by suggesting that the older children were at a cognitively more sophisticated level of classification competency than were the younger children. They were able to use multiple classification schemes and did not need to rely on extreme either/or categories.

There is evidence for a rapid and early increase in the accuracy of gender differentia-

Table 7-1

Theoretical Models of Gender-Identity Development: Sequence of Events

Psychoanalytic

Awareness of anatomical differences	→ Identification with same-sex parent	→ Gender identity	→ Sex-typed behaviors

Social Learning

Exposure to sex-typed behaviors	→ Imitation of same-sex model	→ Sex-typed behaviors	→ Gender identity

Cognitive Developmental

Awareness of sex categories	→ Gender identity	→ Identification with same-sex model	→ Sex-typed behaviors

tion and labeling from ages 2 to 5 years as well as evidence for important cognitive development changes relating to the recognition of gender constancy during ages 2 to 8 years (Coker, 1984; Kuhn, Nash, & Brucken, 1978; Leahy & Shirk, 1984; Reis & Wright, 1982). For example, prior to achieving gender constancy (say, at age 4), children might say that a pictured girl would be a boy if she wore "boy's" clothing or had a "boy's" haircut. After constancy is achieved, however, the girl would still be considered a girl no matter how she looked or what she wore.

Slaby and Frey (1975) have identified three sequential aspects of gender identity formation related to a child's cognitive development. This process of gender identity formation begins around age 3 with an awareness that two sexes exist, followed by an awareness that gender remains the same over time (stability). This awareness of stability is then followed by an awareness that gender remains fixed across a wide range of situations and behaviors (constancy). This constancy, critical for the attainment of true gender identity, occurs between the ages of 4½ and 5½. As gender constancy increases, children spend more total time attending to models and therefore become more sex-typed. Sex-typed preferences also increase after age 6 years and seem related to acquisition

of gender stability, at least in part (Emmerich, Goldman, Kirsch, & Sharabany, 1977; O'Keefe & Hyde, 1983). Research that has directly examined conservation of objects has found that such an ability precedes gender constancy and occurs about age 7 or 8 (Marcus & Overton, 1978). With increasing age from 3 to 8, children also have a qualitatively different view of gender stereotypes, a view that is correlated with other measures of cognitive flexibility (Coker, 1984; Leahy & Shirk, 1984). This orderly age progression in the attainment of gender stages has been supported by cross-cultural research as well (Munroe, Shimmin, & Munroe, 1984). All these findings support a cognitive-developmental perspective.

Some of the strongest support for Kohlberg's theory comes from studies that find that children, boys more so than girls, do value their own sex more highly (Albert & Porter, 1983; Bussey & Perry, 1982; Etaugh, Levine, & Mennella, 1984; Munroe et al., 1984; Tremaine et al., 1982; Urberg, 1982). This preference facilitates the modeling process and the acquisition of gender appropriate behavior. For example, McArthur and Eisen (1976) found that more than 90% of nursery school children preferred same-sex characters of a story. When asked why they had this preference, the children usually indicated some form of identification with that character (for example, "because I'm a girl [boy]"). Since children view same-sex characters as more similar and more likeable, it is not surprising that they imitate them.

The age at which gender identity is established is critical in cognitive-developmental theory. Although there is strong evidence that, by age 6 or 7, gender identity is firmly established, a significant amount of sex typing does seem to occur before this age. Thus, Money and Ehrhardt (1972) found that changing a child's assigned sex up to age 2 was easy, but after age 4 it was usually unsuccessful. Also, as was noted previously, by nursery-school age, children do prefer same-sexed toys in comparison to other-sex toys, boys more so than girls, and they are quite knowledgeable about sex roles (Downs, 1983; Garrett et al., 1977; Maccoby & Jacklin, 1974; Smetana & Letourneau, 1984; Urberg, 1982). In fact, in children as young as 20 months of age, sex-typed toy preferences and labeling have been observed (Kuhn et al., 1978; Lewis & Brooks-Gunn, 1979). The age at which children actually acquire a gender identity is further complicated by the suggestion that Kohlberg's age estimates may be inaccurate. Lewis and Weinraub (1979) point out that Kohlberg's estimates were based on data that may have confounded gender knowledge with language sophistication.

Kohlberg's idea that cognitive development is associated with changes in sex-role concepts and gender identity has prompted a number of researchers to extend Kohlberg's model beyond early childhood (Block, 1973; Condry, 1984; DelBoca & Ashmore, 1980; Parsons & Bryan, 1978; Ullian, 1976). In Table 7-2, three of these theoretical models are presented. In all the models, the child is viewed as going through a number of stages with varying degrees of rigidity. These stages are a function not only of cognitive development, but also a function of biological and sociocultural pressures. Following the rigidity of the 5- to 7-year-old period is a period of gender conformity and same-sex play. During early adolescence, there is a return to rigidity of gender conceptions, based on psychological and sociocultural concerns. Middle and late adolescence is a time of striving to develop a secure personal gender identity in a social context. In all models, there

theoretically is a final stage of sex-role transcendence or integration, where "masculine" and "feminine" traits and values are integrated into an individualized androgynous sex-role definition. Although everyone does not reach the highest level of maturity, those who do seem to be androgynous, and those who are androgynous seem to be older (Block, 1973; Fischer & Narus, 1981b; Sinott, 1984; Waterman & Whitbourne, 1980). Kohlberg's theory relates only to the first three stages—the gradual development of gender identity, gender stereotypes, and conformity. However, there is support for the existence of later stages as well (for example, O'Keefe & Hyde, 1983).

One problem with cognitive-developmental theory is that Kohlberg used only male examples and interviews to support his theory (Weitz, 1977). Thus, the theory can explain why boys should see a physical size difference between men and women and learn to value it and, by extension, other males. But how do females learn to value the female role? Only recently has Ullian (1984) suggested that young children, who are at the preoperational level of cognitive development, view sex-role concepts as rooted in physical characteristics. For boys, this means that being a man involves strength and dominance. For girls, being a woman involves nurturance as well as physical vulnerability. Furthermore, young girls see themselves as similar to adult women in that both groups are relatively small and powerless and potential mothers. Therefore, girls develop interests, skills, and values that correspond to this emerging female identity. The double-conception of women as both nurturant and fragile causes girls to develop a "need to be good," meaning a need to be nurturant and empathetic, as well as a "fear of being bad," meaning a fear of being hurt and hurtful. As a result of these two psychological forces, the female child develops an identity very different from that of the male child.

There are other problems with Kohlberg's theory as well. For example, Martin and Halverson (1983) have shown that the age gender constancy appears may be a function of the type of test used. When responding to a real as opposed to a pretend situation, children as young as age 3 manifest gender constancy, a

Table 7-2
Models of Sex-Role Development

Approximate Age (in years)	Kohlberg (1966)	Block (1973)	Ullian (1976)	Parsons & Bryan (1978)
0–2				Undifferentiated
2–4	Own gender label, gender identity (2–3 yr); Gender labeling of others, biological basis (3–4 yr)	Gender identity, self-expression, self-interest		Hyper-gender role differentiation (3–7 yr)
5–7	Gender stereotypes (5–6); Moralizing gender stereotypes (5–8 yr)	Extension of self, self-enhancement	Sex roles as biologically based (6 yr)	
8–11		Conformist, sex-role stereotypes, bifurcation of sex roles	Sex roles as separable from biology (8 yr); Sex roles as essential for social order (10 yr)	Gender role differentiation (7–11 yr)
12–14		Self as sex-role exemplar vis-à-vis internalized values	Sex roles as social roles seen as arbitrary (12 yr)	Transition phase I: return to rigidity
15–18		Differentiation of sex role, coping with conflicting aspects of self	Sex roles as essential for mental health (14–16 yr)	Transition phase II: developing stability of gender identity
18 +		Individually defined sex role; integrated, androgynous sex-role definition	Personally defined gender identity	Gender role transcendence

finding more in line with social learning theory. Similarly, a number of researchers have found that sex-stereotyped preferences exist before the development of gender constancy (Bussey & Bandura, 1984; O'Keefe & Hyde, 1983; Smetana & Letourneau, 1984). Furthermore, Kohlberg's specific prediction that the acquisition of gender constancy leads a child to become more sex-typed afterward and more likely to prefer same-sex activities and objects has not always been confirmed (Leahy & Shirk, 1984; Marcus & Overton, 1978; Urberg, 1982). Indeed, Ur-berg (1982) found gender conservation to be associated with decreased sex-typing, perhaps because the children were more secure in their gender identity. Although this finding does not support Kohlberg's theory, it does recognize the importance of a child's level of cognitive development in the development of gender identity and gender stereotypes.

One way of resolving these conflicting findings is to posit that early acquisition of sex-typed behaviors is due to differential reinforcement and observational learning, as social learning theory predicts, whereas later sex typing, after gender constancy has been acquired, may be due to same-sex modeling, as cognitive developmental theory predicts. In this regard, it is possible that sex-role preference and adoption are not the same as gender identity. This will be commented on further below. Cognitive-developmental theory, although not ruling out learning principles, subordinates them to inborn cognitive processes.

Integration: Gender Schema Theory

Some coordination of the three theories discussed above seems required to account for the complexity of sex-role development. Such a coordinated explanation would include an active role for children in developing concepts of masculinity and femininity and in organizing their world consistent with their level of cognitive development. In this process, differential treatment by primary socializing agents and observation of different models all add to the information the child gathers about appropriate gender behaviors. Interacting with this input are the affectional bonds formed with one or both parents and any biological predispositions the child may have.

A number of integrative theories of sex-role development have been proposed (Cahill, 1983; Constantinople, 1979; Kagan, 1964). The most promising one is Sandra Bem's (1981b, 1982, 1983, 1984) *gender schema theory*. Gender schema theory contains features of both social learning and cognitive-developmental theories, as well as acknowledging the importance of cultural factors. In this theory, sex typing derives in large part from gender-schematic processing, a readiness on the part of the child to encode and to organize information according to the culture's definition of the sex roles. By observing the distinctions made between males and females in their culture, children learn not only the specific content of the sex roles but also that gender and gender distinctions are important. This acquired gender schema is a cognitive structure that serves to organize and guide an individual's perception. Sex typing then results, in part, from the assimilation of the self-concept to the gender schema. For example, a child may observe that boys generally are described as "strong," "big," or "brave," whereas girls more often may be described as "good," "nice," and "cute." What this child learns is that the sexes not only differ but that certain attributes are more relevant for one sex than the other. By matching one's behaviors and attributes against the developing gender schema, one learns to evaluate one's adequacy as a person. In this way, cultural stereotypes can become self-fulfilling prophecies.

People differ in the degree to which they use gender schema in processing the world: Those who perceive the world, including themselves, in gender-specific terms, are considered sex-typed; those who do not process information primarily on the basis of gender are considered non-sex-typed, such as androgynous individuals. This theory is noteworthy in its emphasis on the acquired nature of gender schema. If cultures did not make such broad distinctions between the sexes so that nearly everything is divided into "masculine" and "feminine" (for example, toys, speech, walking styles, personality traits, clothes, even colors and food: "Real men don't eat quiche"), then children would not develop or use such strong gender schemas. As was discussed in Chapter 6, cultures do vary in the degree to which gender distinctions are made, although nearly all cultures make distinctions that go beyond the biological.

Bem's theory has received empirical support (Bem, 1981b, 1983, 1984; Frable & Bem, 1985; Mills, 1983), although more work is needed. For example, sex-typed individuals show more clustering of gender-relevant items in a free recall memory test than did non-sex-typed individuals, suggesting that sex-typed individuals do organize and process information in terms of gender schema. In addition, sex-typed individuals respond more quickly and have better recall for gender-congruent than for gender-incongruent words, whereas non-sex-typed individuals show no difference in recall. Furthermore, sex-typed individuals appear more likely than non-sex-typed individuals to organize other people into "feminine" and "masculine" categories. In fact, sex-typed individuals appear particularly likely to confuse members of the other sex with each other.

Gender schema theory has been criticized as needing to take situational variables more into account (Mills & Tyrrell, 1983). For example, not all situations apparently elicit gender schematic processing. Another criticism suggests that one need not posit a separate gender schema to explain sex typing (Crane & Markus, 1982; Markus, Crane, Bernstein, & Siladi, 1982; C. Miller, 1984; Spence & Helmreich, 1981). Rather, a general self-schema of which gender is just one part may be sufficient to account for sex typing. Yet, these criticisms have not negated the major thrust of the theory—that is, that people do process the world in terms of schema and that sex-typed individuals are particularly likely to use a gender schema as their primary way of organizing their world and self-concept.

Research Problems

Clear empirical support of any of these theories has been difficult to obtain because of the many research problems in the area. Discussed in previous chapters were problems of assumptions, definitions, methodology, choice of subjects, and interpretation. These are equally present in the area of sex-role development. A few examples will suffice.

Although all theories use gender identity as a key concept, the term *gender identity* is not *defined* the same by all researchers. As Lynn (1959) notes, there are important distinctions to be made among the following terms: (1) *sex-role preference,* the desire to adopt certain behaviors associated with one sex, which is measured by asking the child, (2) *sex-role adoption,* the performing of behaviors characteristic of one sex, which is measured by observation, as of play behavior, and (3) *sex-role* or *gender identification,* the actual incorporation of a role and the unconscious reactions characteristic of it, which is measured by figure drawings and parent-child similarities. These measures may be independent of each other and may operate differently for girls and for boys. Thus, girls can prefer male activities and toys and adopt male behavior, like wearing pants and playing ball, and still have a female identification, as in drawing themselves as a female. This, in fact, seems to be true more often for girls than is its complement for boys (Downs, 1983; Maccoby & Jacklin, 1974). Thus, males are generally considered to be more strongly sex-typed at an earlier age than are girls. Studies that do not use these distinctions are confusing. Experiments using toy preference as a measure of gender identity actually are measuring only sex-role preference, which is another dimension altogether. This preference may develop early, beginning by age 2, whereas true gender identity may develop later, around age 5 to 6, as Kohlberg suggests. Furthermore, in research using toys, most studies report results only for sex-typed toys. Yet Downs (1983) found that elementary school–aged children preferred non-sex-typed toys to sex-typed toys if given the opportunity to play with them, a finding that throws sex-typed toy preferences into a different light.

Another research problem lies in the *measurement* instruments used. For example, the It Scale for Children (D. Brown, 1956), a projective test frequently used to measure sex-role preference, may be biased in the male direction. The "neutral" stick figure has been found to be more easily interpreted as a male figure, which may account for the frequent findings of girls' "preferring" male sex-role activities. They may simply be matching a perceived male figure with male activities and not indicating their own preference at all (Fling & Manosevitz, 1972). When a new test of sex-role preference was used, both sexes preferred same-sex activities (Brinn, Kraemer, Warm, & Paludi, 1984). Furthermore, some statistical analyses of data produced by the IT scale have been found to be flawed (Paludi, 1984a).

Another serious methodological problem is the frequent use of *self-reports* of both parents and children. When people describe behaviors related to sex roles, it is often difficult to separate out socially desirable responses from an individual's true preferences or behavior. Thus, studies that find few parental differences in admitted treatment of sons and daughters (see Maccoby & Jacklin, 1974) may reflect more a parental ideal than actual parental practices. In addition, much parental behavior may occur beyond the parents' level of awareness or even intention and is thus difficult to measure.

Similarly, *laboratory studies* of parent-child interactions may not reflect what actually goes on in the home. Bronfenbrenner (1977) concludes from surveying a number of studies that interactions in the laboratory are substantially and systematically different from those in the home. Laboratory settings tend to increase anxiety and decrease behaviors showing social competence. This effect may be even more profound on working-class families, for whom the laboratory setting is especially likely to be anxiety arousing. For example, parents may be so anxious about doing the "right" thing or being "good" subjects that they may refrain from punishing their child in the laboratory, although they do so at home. Thus, generalizations from laboratory observations may be quite limited. Even home observations may be flawed. Fagot (1985) found that parents interacted with their child very differently during the first couple of hours of observation than they did during later observations. These and other research problems should be kept in mind as the research related to socializing agents is presented.

From our review of socialization theories, it is clear that both people and social forces, including social institutions, affect the developments of sex typing and gender stereotypes. Although people and social forces operate together, for convenience we will discuss them separately, keeping their integration in mind.

Socializing Agents

Clearly, because of the prolonged interaction, the differences in power, and the intense bonds between parents and children, parents serve as the initial and major socializing agents in our society. The term *parents* here refers to a child's biological parents or to anyone who has major caretaking responsibilities, such as a grandparent or a regular baby-sitter. Little research has been done with these latter groups, although similar socialization procedures probably operate. Similarly, the influence of siblings has been markedly neglected.

A child also receives input from people outside the home. Once school begins, teachers and peers become increasingly important. These agents will be examined following a discussion of the role parents and siblings play in the socialization of children.

Parents

In order to understand how parents transmit gender stereotypes to their children, it is important to look at parental treatment, at the role of the father, at cross-sex effects, and at parent-child interactions.

Parental Treatment. Parents are aware of the gender stereotypes and begin to apply them to their child at the moment a sex determination is made. Rubin, Provenzano, and Luria (1974) interviewed 30 first-time parents within 24 hours after their child's birth and found that a significant amount of sex typing already had begun. Girls were seen as softer, finer, and littler; boys, as firmer, stronger, and more alert. These differences were posited even though hospital data indicated that the infants did not differ on any health or physical measure. Fathers made even more stereotyped ratings of their newborn than did mothers, a finding that has received confirmation in other studies (Barry, 1980; Block, 1973; Lynn, 1979). Perhaps because a father's contact with a newborn is generally less than is a mother's or maybe because males generally are concerned more about sex roles than are females, fathers fill in their lack of knowledge with more stereotyped expectations. In any case, it seems clear that sex typing and gender socialization begin at birth and may affect the way parents actually treat their children. If boys are viewed as stronger, they may be handled more roughly than girls, and girls may be protected more. There is some evidence that this does occur (Condry et al., 1983; Culp, Cook, & Housley, 1983; Frisch, 1977). For example, a crying infant is responded to more quickly by young women if it is thought to be a girl rather than a boy. Infant girls also are expected to be cuter than infant boys, and this expectation may affect the evaluation as well as the treatment of an infant (Hildebrandt & Fitzgerald, 1979).

Actually, sex typing may begin even before birth in the form of differential preference for, and value attached to, a male or female child. Hoffman (1977) and Williamson (1976) summarize data to show that, in the United States today, most couples prefer male children to female children and base this value preference on assumed sex differences, such as boys carrying on the family name and girls helping around the house. Although such preference for males is considerably less in this country than in other countries, especially in less industrialized areas like Asia and India, a striking difference remains that cannot help but be reflected in the way the sexes are treated by their parents.

In studying how parents actually treat their children, a somewhat confusing picture emerges. Strong differences in sex typing are not found consistently (Bee et al., 1984; Bellinger & Gleason, 1982; Shepard, 1980). However, depending on the population studied and method used, certain differences do emerge. Many parents perceive girls as more vulnerable and fragile and treat them accordingly. They dress the sexes differently (girls wear dresses; boys, pants), assign different household tasks (girls help set the table; boys help Dad in the yard), and provide different toys in line with the gender stereotypes (toys for girls, like dolls, relate to the mother role; those for boys, like trucks, the work role). Parents strongly discourage their children, especially boys, from engaging in other-sex activities. Picture Johnny playing with a dollhouse and tea set. Imagine his parents', particularly his father's, reactions. Parents encourage boys' independent explorations and pressure them more for achievement. They give boys both more praise and more punishments than they give to girls (Hoffman, 1977; Maccoby & Jacklin, 1974).

The direct effects of these differences in parental treatment on a child's behavior are not always apparent. However, the steering of girls to dolls and of boys to trucks, for example, and the generally more intense socialization that boys receive cannot fail to convey some message to a child struggling to organize his/her world. This message may be that boys are more important, since more attention is paid to them. Also, the message may be that the sexes are really opposite, since strong distinctions are made between them. Such behaviors by parents toward children may also lead to some of the gender differences discussed in Part Two.

In addition, although parents say they treat their daughters and sons similarly, they do admit to having different expectations of females and males and to having different emphases in child rearing (Block, 1973; Fagot, 1981b; Maccoby & Jacklin, 1974). In an examination of 110 different societies, a consistent pattern of sex differences in child-rearing behaviors emerged (Zern, 1984). Males were much more likely than girls to be socialized toward such agentic variables as self-reliance and achievement. Less consistently, girls were more likely than boys to be socialized toward nurturance and obedience. These differential expectations (of agentic qualities for boys and communal qualities for girls) may be communicated in more subtle ways than can be measured in a laboratory or by a questionnaire. One way these value differences may be communicated is through parental reactions to their children's behavior. Parents have been found to react more positively when sex-typed toys were used by children of the appropriate sex, especially boys, than when they were used by the other sex (Fagot, 1977). Furthermore, mothers and fathers may model different behaviors, with mothers more involved than fathers with home and child-care activities and with low-status occupations, and fathers may be more involved than mothers with play activities, competitive, aggressive, directive, and analytic behaviors, and with high-status occupations (Bellinger & Gleason, 1982; Bronstein, 1984a; Goldman & Goldman, 1983; Shepard, 1980).

In other studies, race and class have been found to be important mediators of gender socialization (Canter & Ageton, 1984; Cazenave, 1984; Lynn, 1979; McBroom, 1981; Weitzman, 1975). Working-class families tend to differentiate between the sexes even more sharply than do middle-class families, and they tend to be particularly restrictive toward girls. Research on the influence of parents on young Black females is minimal. What research exists suggests that Black parents tend to socialize their daughters to be more independent than do White parents, and Blacks seem to use a different female stereotype—that of the "strong Black woman"—in their training (Gump, 1980; Lynn, 1979; Malson, 1983; E. Smith, 1982; Wallace, 1979). Indeed, the "traditional" female role probably does not exist for Black women. Instead, a female role involving both employment and homemaking and child-care activities is most typical. Such differences need to be borne in mind in examining research findings, especially since most of the research has been on middle-class Whites. The ability to generalize such findings, therefore, may be limited.

In general, according to all studies of parental behaviors, boys seem to have the more intense socialization. Compared to girls, they receive more pressure against engaging in gender-inappropriate behavior, they receive more punishment and also more encouragement and praise, and they receive more attention in general (Feinman, 1981, 1984; Maccoby & Jacklin, 1974; Spence & Helmreich, 1978). This is true in other cultures as well (Welch & Page, 1981). Girls receive intensified role pressures from puberty on, but these are centered around their sexual identity and around finding a mate (Katz, 1979).

Why this differential pressure exists is not clear. As Maccoby and Jacklin (1974) suggest, perhaps males' greater strength and aggressiveness make their adequate early socialization much more important. Or perhaps males simply are more valued, and, therefore, more attention is paid to them. This is supported by findings regarding parental sex preferences and other research which shows that sex is a status variable, with males having the higher status (Feinman, 1981, 1984). Another reason for differential pressure involves the greater demands of the masculine sex role. To get a child to accept the masculine role, as in suppressing his feelings, socialization must be intense. Or perhaps establishing a male identity is harder to do because of absence of male models; so socialization must be more intense to compensate.

The explanations with the most support involve the differential value being placed on the male sex role and the greater demands attached to it. The rigidity of the male sex role can be seen in the four basic themes of masculinity (David & Brannon, 1976; Pleck, 1981b): (1) rejecting all "feminine" behaviors and traits, (2) being strong, competent, and independent, (3) acquiring success and status, and (4) demonstrating aggressiveness and dar-

ing. Regardless of which explanation for differential pressures is accepted, such differential pressures have important consequences for a child's personality development and the child's relationships with others. These consequences will be discussed in Part Four.

Aside from specific treatment, however, the behavioral characteristics of the parents also influence a child's sex typing. A number of researchers have investigated the relationship between college students' current sex typing and certain behaviors of their parents (Jackson, Ialongo, & Stollak, 1983; Kelly & Worell, 1976; Orlofsky, 1979). Despite the limitations of retrospective reports, the results are interesting. In all three studies, the effects of certain parent behaviors depended on the gender of the child. For males, parental warmth and involvement were critical factors in determining their sex typing; for females, cognitive encouragement and consistent discipline were most important. However, the particular parental patterns associated with each sex type differed from one study to the other. Overall, each parent plays an important part in the sex-role development of their child, with the influence of each parent varying as a function of the child's gender.

Parental sex typing is related in complex ways to the personality development of the child. Traditional gender traits in parents (that is, agentic traits in fathers and expressive traits in mothers) is significantly associated with their young child's stereotyping of toys and occupations (Repetti, 1984). Parental sex typing also appears to be associated with other parental behaviors. For example, Spence and Helmreich (1978) found that families in which one or both parents were androgynous were rated highest in parental warmth and supportiveness and in encouraging achievement and a sense of self-worth in the children. "Undifferentiated" couples were rated the lowest in the above qualities; the traditional "masculine-feminine" couples were rated at an intermediate level.

All the studies just referred to indicate the importance of both parents in a child's development. Yet traditionally, the father role generally has received short shrift. It will therefore be instructive to focus on the father role in some detail.

Father's Role. Fathers, as specific socializing agents, have rarely been studied in the past. As with other aspects of gender research, preconceived notions about the "naturalness" of maternal behavior have led many fathers to avoid child care and have led many researchers to avoid studying fathers. Results from research conducted with fathers demonstrate that fathers are active in and indeed important for their children's development, especially the children's gender identity and gender stereotype development, academic achievement, and moral development (Baruch & Barnett, 1981; Biller, 1981b; Booth & Edwards, 1980; Bronstein, 1984a; B. Carlson, 1984; M. Hoffman, 1981; Lamb, 1979; McBroom, 1981; Radin, 1981). Figure 7-1 depicts a father actively involved in his daughter's motor development.

There are some problems with earlier studies. Few were of actual fathering behavior (Kotelchuck, 1976). Rather, most of these studies were conducted with children whose fathers were absent. Unfortunately, differences in social class between father-absent and father-present homes were seldom taken into account. More recent research suggests that the key factors in father-absent homes may be the additional stresses a family experiences when a father is absent rather than the absence per se (Biller, 1981a; Shinn, 1978).

The effect of fathers on the gender identity development of their children actually is unclear. In general, fathers tend to show more sexism than do mothers, especially overtly (Barry, 1980). And traditional gender attitudes in fathers are significantly associated with traditional gender attitudes in their sons (Emihovich, Gaier, & Cronin, 1984). Most studies have focused on the father's role as an identification figure or as a model for his son. With few exceptions, the literature has failed to support the hypothesis that "masculine" fathers will have "masculine" sons or that boys raised in homes without fathers will be less "masculine" (Biller, 1981a, 1981b; Jackson et al., 1983; Lamb, 1981b; Maccoby & Jacklin, 1974). Such studies are complicated by methodological problems with the techniques used to assess masculinity and similarity, as well as by failure to control for important variables, such as socioeconomic

Figure 7-1

Many fathers are actively involved in the development of their children.

status. Fathers do seem to be the primary role models of young boys, but only when the fathers are nurturant and the father-child relationship has been affectionate (Biller, 1981b; Radin, 1981). Paternal nurturance appears to be associated with the development of androgyny and cognitive competence in sons more than in daughters. Orlofsky (1979) found that a father's behavior was more important than a mother's in determining the sex typing of a male. Spence and Helmreich (1978) found that males were more likely to exhibit the socially desirable characteristics of their fathers than of their mothers. Females, on the other hand, were likely to exhibit desirable characteristics of either parent regardless of their gender appropriateness. Thus, fathers do appear to have a particular influence on their sons as well as on their daughters. Fathers indeed may be more influential for sons than daughters in some areas, for example, moral socialization, although the amount of influence here is small (M. Hoffman, 1981).

Somewhat surprisingly, the impact of fathers on the sex-role development of their daughters has been found to be quite strong, particularly when contrasted with paternal effects on sons. "Femininity" of daughters is greatest when fathers are nurturant and participate actively in child rearing. In addition, acceptant relations between fathers and daughters seem critical for the daughters' personality development and for heterosexual behaviors in particular (Bannon & Southern, 1980; Biller, 1981b; Johnson et al., 1981; Lynn, 1979; McBroom, 1981). Cognitive development, too, may be enhanced by particular father behaviors, but the results are complex and somewhat contradictory (Radin, 1981). For example, specific father interest in a daughter's academic progress facilitates her intellectual growth, although some distance and autonomy from the father also appear to be important. In contrast, moral development in daughters appears to be unrelated to the father's influence (M. Hoffman, 1981).

Cross-Sex Effects. The finding that, in some areas, fathers have particularly strong effects on daughters rather than on sons is paralleled by findings that mothers have particularly strong effects on sons rather than on daughters. These cross-sex effects have been found to be stronger than the sex of the child alone in influencing parent-child interactions; that is, all sons are not treated one way and all daughters another. Cross-sex effects also appear stronger than the sex of the parent alone in influencing parent-child interactions; that is, all mothers do not treat children one way and all fathers treat them another. Rather, it appears that mothers tend to treat their sons, and fathers tend to treat their daughters, in specific and different ways.

In general, fathers tend to be more favorable toward, and permissive with, girls in regard to aggressive, dependent, and achievement behaviors than they are with boys. For mothers, the opposite is true—they tend to be more favorable toward, and permissive with, boys than with girls (Bronstein, 1984a; Gurwitz & Dodge, 1975; Maccoby & Jacklin, 1974; McElroy, 1983). Not all studies find this pattern, however (Mulhern & Passman, 1981). For example, Bearison (1979) found that parents tend to be most role conscious and rule conscious with their offspring of the other sex. Thus, fathers tend to reinforce gender stereotypes in their daughters and mothers tend to reinforce such stereotypes in their sons. These differences appear as early as the first grade. Parents were also found to cuddle other-sex newborns more than same-sex ones (Rubin et al., 1974). Because mothers are often the only parent studied, these results may account for the predominant findings in the literature that boys receive more praise, are subject to stricter socialization, and are held more at birth than are girls. In the home, with father present, these effects may be counterbalanced. However, because most fathers do not spend an equal amount of time with their children as do mothers, girls may grow up receiving less positive treatment and more restrictiveness than do boys in general. As noted above, there is some evidence that this is the case.

The reasons for this cross-sex effect are unclear, but it may result from a variety of sources. It may be a reaction to the other-sex child as a member of the other sex, or it may be a reaction to the same-sex child as a rival. It may also be a reminder of the parents' own negative impulses, which they then punish. In any case, such effects certainly need to be taken into account in drawing conclusions about parental behavior. It would be inappropriate to conclude, however, that the relationship between a parent and same-sex child is less important than that between a parent and other-sex child. Rather, both relationships appear important, but in different ways. For example, in divorce cases, children living with the same-sex parent appear better adjusted than children living with the other-sex parent (Santrock & Warshak, 1979). This finding may explain why boys tend to have a more difficult time adjusting to parental divorce than do girls, because more than 90% of the time, child custody is awarded to the mother alone. (Most fathers don't ask for custody.)

Parent–Child Interactions. Another major consideration regarding parents as socializing agents is the interaction between the child and the parent. Research has shown that such exchanges go two ways: not only does a parent shape a child's behavior, but a child's characteristics can influence a parent's behavior as well (Bronfenbrenner, 1977; Maccoby, Snow, & Jacklin, 1984; Segal & Yahraes, 1978; Wasserman & Lewis, 1985). Studies have found that parents tend to handle male infants more frequently than females at 3 weeks of age, but the reverse is true for infants at 6 months of age (Moss, 1967). Parents also tend to vocalize more to female than to male infants (Cherry & Lewis, 1976; Wasserman & Lewis, 1985). These parental behaviors may stem from the greater fussiness of male infants and from the more frequent vocalization of girls. When infant fussiness was controlled for, some of these sex differences disappeared (Moss, 1967). It is thus possible that the greater fussiness of male infants leads to greater maternal contact, but, when such comforting does not quiet the child (as it seems not to), mothers begin cuddling less. This, in turn, may encourage earlier independence in sons than in daughters. Similarly, girls' earlier and greater vocalizations may be more reinforcing for the parent and may lead to more parental vocalization to daughters than to sons, further reinforcing the difference.

Child-parent interactions continue to occur throughout childhood (Barry, 1980). For example, children appear to be more potent reinforcers for the other-sex parent than for the same-sex parent (Mulhern & Passman, 1981). This differential value as a reinforcer may lead to the parents being more responsive to their other-sex child than their same-sex child, as previously discussed.

Regarding interactions other than those between parent and child in the home, a number of studies find that *siblings* play an important role in the sex-role development of a child, both directly, through their behavior with the child, and indirectly, through their effect on the parents (Barry, 1980; Bronfenbrenner, 1977; Cicirelli, 1982). For example, having older siblings is associated with enhanced gender stereotyping. The sex of siblings also may be important. Tauber (1979) found that cross-sex play among 8- and 9-year-olds was more common among children who came from single-sex families than among those coming from both-sex families. Her finding lends support to the idea of role diversification in families. Human behavior functions as part of a whole system, each part of which undoubtedly influences another.

Teachers

However influential parents and other household members may be in the child's development, once school begins, other people share the responsibility for socialization. Teachers, in particular, are important.

From the time a child starts school, which for some children occurs as early as 3 years of age, teachers provide additional messages regarding sex-role development through provision of activities, reinforcement, modeling, and subtler forms of communication. In most cases, these messages reinforce those received at home, strengthening the sex typing. Even when teacher messages contradict parental messages, their influence is enormous and sometimes is greater than parental influence, especially if the messages are supported by other socializing forces.

In general, teacher influence has been found to be very strong, albeit very subtle (Honig & Wittner, 1982). In an observational study of 15 nursery school teachers by Serbin and colleagues (1973), the teachers were found to reinforce boys for being aggressive and girls for being dependent. Teachers responded three times more often to boys who were disruptive than to girls. They also responded more to girls who clung or stayed nearby than to boys who exhibited similar behaviors. Teachers also actually taught boys more than girls. Boys were given more individualized instruction, thereby making them more capable of fending for themselves and more capable in problem solving. In general, boys were given more attention for their behavior, whether such behavior was appropriate or not. Fagot (1984) also found that nursery school boys were given more positive feedback from their teachers than were girls for engaging in tasks appropriate to academic behaviors. For girls, only sex-stereotyped behaviors brought consistent positive feedback from teachers.

A similar pattern was found by researchers who observed more than a hundred fourth-, sixth-, and eighth-grade classes over a three-year period (Sadker & Sadker, 1985). Boys consistently and clearly dominated classroom interactions at all grade levels, in all communities, and in all subject areas. Teachers tended to call on boys more often than girls and to encourage boys more. For example, if a girl gave an incorrect answer, the teacher was likely to move on to another student, whereas if a boy gave an incorrect answer, the teacher was likely to help him discover the correct answer and then praise him. Even when a girl gave a correct answer, she was more likely to receive a simple acceptance ("OK") than praise ("Excellent"). Thus, boys tended to receive a more specific and intense educational interaction. Furthermore, when a boy called out in class without first raising his hand, the teacher probably would accept his answer. However, when a girl called out in class, she was likely to receive a reprimand. These teacher behaviors sent the message that girls should keep quiet and be passive learners, whereas boys should be academically assertive and active.

Other researchers have supported these findings (Dweck & Bush, 1976; Dweck, Davidson, Nelson, & Enna, 1978). For example, in elementary school, girls have been found to receive most of their positive feedback for nonacademic behaviors—such as doing neat work—and most of their negative feedback for academic work. Black girls, in particular, appear to be discouraged from achievement-related academic behaviors by their teachers ("Study of," 1985). Instead, Black girls from kindergarten through third grade tend to receive praise from teachers for nurturing behaviors. The consequences of this pattern of teacher behaviors on both White and Black girls may be quite serious: Girls learn to give up on academic work after a failure more quickly than do boys. This learned helplessness by girls may stay with them throughout their school years.

The greater attention and encouragement given to boys have been found related to problem-solving ability and may explain boys' greater mathematical skills (Fox, 1981; Hess & Shipman, 1967). The lack of accurate and continuous feedback for girls may interfere with girls' realistic appraisal of their abilities. It may also interfere with the development of self-confidence and of achievement motivation.

The indirect reinforcement of aggressiveness in boys may also explain the higher incidence of behavior and learning problems in school-age boys than in girls, since such behaviors interfere with learning.

The differences in teacher behavior, supported by other studies (Cherry, 1975; Guttentag & Bray, 1977), parallel those found in parents. Boys receive more attention, more praise, and more punishment than do girls. These findings are especially striking because teachers were not aware that they were treating boys and girls differently even when faced with direct evidence. For example, in the Sadkers' (1985) elementary school study, the researchers asked teachers and administrators to view a film made of a classroom discussion. In response to a question as to which sex was talking more, the teachers overwhelmingly said the girls were. In fact, the boys in the film outtalked the girls at a ratio of three to one. Without awareness, changing differential teaching practices is impossible.

The generally favorable treatment of male as compared to female students may be restricted to a White population. Taylor (1979) found that Black males, when compared with females of both races and with White males, received the most unfavorable teacher treatment, such as the fewest response opportunities. Because the students in Taylor's study were hypothetical, actual student characteristics could not account for the differences in teacher behavior. Thus, race may interact with sex in affecting teacher behavior. Unfortunately, very few studies have even examined race as a variable.

Teachers, especially males, do admit to believing that boys and girls behave differently and need to be treated differently. However, in at least one study, child-care workers expected fewer sex differences in preschool children's behaviors than did parents (Fagot, 1981b). It may be that the exposure teachers have to the wide individual differences among children may minimize some of their own gender-related expectations. Still, teachers have been found to interpret a child's behavior as a function of the child's sex (Anderegg & Chess, 1983; Guttentag & Bray, 1977).

In addition, more teachers, especially females, admit to preferring male students, although teachers felt females were less of a discipline problem (Ricks & Pyke, 1973). Female teachers also were likely to rate fourth- and fifth-grade girls as higher than boys in self-esteem-related behaviors, although male teachers showed the opposite pattern (Loeb & Horst, 1978). Such beliefs and behaviors on the part of teachers undoubtedly affect the children's behaviors and feelings both about themselves and about each other. Perhaps female conformity in school (see Chapter 4) is an attempt to win teacher approval, a tactic that never quite succeeds.

Teachers also serve as important role models for children. For very young children, male teachers may be more salient sources of information about sex-role behaviors than are female teachers, perhaps because young children have limited opportunities to observe and interact with adult males (Koblinsky & Sugawara, 1984). In this respect, it is unfortunate that male teachers tend to believe in the gender stereotypes even more strongly than do female teachers (Fagot, 1981b). Just the presence of a teacher in a particular area of the room has been shown to affect the likelihood of a preschool child playing with toys in that area (Serbin, Connor, & Citron, 1981). If preschool teachers are mostly female and stay in feminine-typed areas (for example, the kitchen), each sex may have little encouragement to play with other-sex-typed toys. In later grades, especially college, female teachers serve as strong sources of influence on female students, perhaps because the educational environment becomes more male-dominated (Basow & Howe, 1979a, 1979b, 1980; Erkut & Mokros, 1983; Gilbert, 1985). The effect of female teachers on female students is striking not because it is stronger than that of male teachers but because of the marked lack of effect of female teachers on male students.

Peers

Age-mates also serve as strong socializing agents. They become increasingly important during the school years. In many cases, peer pressure is stronger and more effective than parental or other adult pressure, particularly during adolescence (Hartup, 1983; Katz, 1979; Strommen, 1977). Even during preschool years,

however, peers influence the sex-role behaviors of their friends.

Fagot (1984) found that preschoolers gave fewer reactions, in general, and more negative reactions, in particular, to classmates who did not play much with either masculine- or feminine-sex-typed toys. In addition, boys who preferred feminine-sex-typed toys received less positive feedback and were more likely to play alone than were other boys in their class. The findings from this and other studies (Fagot, 1977, 1978) suggest that children who adopt traditional forms of sex-role behavior are more socially acceptable to their peers than those who do not adopt traditional behaviors. This may be particularly true for boys, and it serves as another example of their more intense socialization and more rigid sex role.

The intense peer pressure toward gender conformity may be one reason why there is so little cross-sex-typing in elementary school children, even though the categories of "tomboys" and "sissies" exist (Hemmer & Kleiber, 1981; Stericker & Kurdek, 1982). Rather than denoting cross-sex-typing or androgyny, these labels seem to be used pejoratively by young children for peers who are regarded as socially difficult and antisocial. Given the more rigid sex role for males and the greater importance attached to the male sex role, it is not surprising that the term *sissy* is far more pejorative than the term *tomboy*. When self-defined, tomboyism may represent the beginnings of androgyny for women (Plumb & Cowan, 1984).

Three behaviors, in particular, seem affected by peer responses—aggressiveness, assertiveness, and passivity. Connor and associates (1978) found that 9- to 14-year-old girls expect less disapproval from their peers for passive behavior and more disapproval for aggressive behaviors than do their male classmates. Such expectations were indeed justified. Assertiveness is also regarded as more desirable for males than for females. Such gender stereotypes may influence the way children respond to other children and may influence their willingness to use other children as models.

Beginning in preschool years, boys and girls increasingly separate into same-sex groups, a process that intensifies once a child enters school. As was noted in Chapter 4, boys tend to have larger friendship groups than do girls and tend to be more influenced by them. Hartley (1959) suggests that a peer group is more important to a male because he has to look to them for information about the male role, since adult males are less available than adult females. Because his peers have no better source of information than he, the information the child obtains is likely to be distorted and oversimplified. Males' conceptualizations of appropriate behavior therefore are often extremely rigid and stereotyped.

Male bonding, as it emerges during late childhood and early adolescence, plays a very important role in male lives. Such bonding serves to reinforce a male's identity as male, meaning separate from female. Such bonding also gives rise to and reinforces a sense of male dominance over females. This dominance usually is achieved by degrading all that is female (as in, "Girls have cooties," etc.). Boys often feel great pressure to prove their masculinity through athletic skill, physical strength, acts of daring, and, later, sexual conquests (Fasteau, 1974; Stockard & Johnson, 1979). Pressure to prove their femininity does not exist for girls until adolescence, when they are often pressured to find a mate. Peer status for girls then becomes contingent on their popularity with boys (Chafetz, 1978; Weitz, 1977). For both sexes, gender-consistent behavior is a major factor in peer acceptance (Hartup, 1983; Parsons & Bryan, 1978). Adolescents with traditional gender attitudes appear to be more influenced by peers than adolescents with more nontraditional attitudes (Canter & Ageton, 1984).

In summary, peers play an important role in socializing children and adolescents into gender-appropriate behaviors and attitudes.

Summary

Children are strongly affected by socializing agents—parents, teachers, and peers—and generally learn the gender stereotypes early and well. By school age, children know what girls and boys "should" and "shouldn't" do and tend to behave accordingly, boys more so than girls. Boys tend to receive the more intense socialization pressures and consequently behave in more stereotyped ways than do girls. One future implication of this differential socialization pressure is that androgyny may be more difficult for males, since they are more committed to the masculine stereotype.

Both directly and indirectly—through modeling and reinforcement—and as a function of their level of cognitive development, children are steered toward different modes of behavior through a developing gender schema. Boys are steered toward the agentic—achievement, competition, independence—and girls toward the communal—nurturance, sociability, dependence.

Although the effects of socializing agents are enormous, socializing agents alone cannot account for the entire socializing process. Children formulate their conceptions of sex roles from a wide range of social forces acting on a more impersonal level, such as from the media, from the educational system, from religion, and so forth. It is to an examination of these forces that we now turn.

Recommended Reading

Bem, S. L. (1983). Gender schema theory and its implications for child development: Raising gender-aschematic children in a gender-schematic society. *Signs, 8,* 598–616. An excellent description of gender schema theory for nonpsychologists with an instructive section on child-rearing implications.

Chodorow, N. (1978). *The reproduction of mothering: Psychoanalysis and the sociology of gender.* Berkeley: University of California Press. An interesting feminist psychoanalytic view of the development of sex roles, which has had tremendous impact on feminist researchers in a number of areas.

Lamb, M. E. (Ed.). (1981). *The role of the father in child development,* 2d ed. New York: Wiley. An excellent collection of articles by the most prominent researchers in the area of paternal effects on children.

Lynn, D. B. (1979). *Daughters and parents: Past, present, and future.* Monterey, Calif.: Brooks/Cole. General review of the research on parental influences on the development of women.

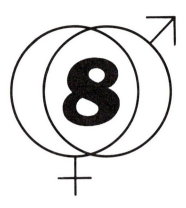

8 Socialization: Social Forces

A 6-year-old child is overheard by her mother explaining to a friend that only boys can be doctors and only girls can be nurses. The mother remarks "But, Sally, you know I'm a doctor." Sally replies "You're no doctor; you're my mother."

This story illustrates not only the simplistic categories children use to understand their world but also the fact that children acquire information about the world from sources outside the home. This chapter examines the sex-role messages the child's world contains.

That social contexts are crucial in understanding human behavior has been amply demonstrated by social psychologists. Under certain nonthreatening, innocuous conditions, people can be made nearly to kill other humans, while under other conditions they cannot be made to do so (Milgram's obedience experiments, 1965). People appear to react to their state of physiological arousal, induced by adrenalin, with either euphoria or anger depending upon their expectations and the behavior of another person (Schacter & Singer, 1962). Students can sometimes get better grades if their teachers expect them to be intelligent (Rosenthal & Jacobson, 1968). Given these findings, Weisstein concludes that "a study of human behavior requires a study of the social contexts in which people move, the expectations as to how they will behave, and the authority that tells them who they are and what they are supposed to do" (Weisstein, 1969, p. 58).

The influence of social contexts need not be direct or, in fact, deliberate. As Daryl and Sandra Bem (1970) suggest, this training of people to know "their place" is a function of a nonconscious ideology that can be seen most clearly in the socialization of the female. Whereas when a boy is born, it has been difficult to predict his life (job, interests, activities) 25 years later, when a girl is born, we could be fairly confident of how most of her time would be spent—in homemaking activities. Her individuality, her unique potential all have been irrelevant. The majority of women have ended up in the same role—homemaker—regardless of individual factors. If they have been employed, they most likely have been in one of four low-status, low-salary jobs—clerk, salesperson, waitress, hairdresser—and have done homemaking in addition. This restrictiveness has not been true for males.

An examination of the social context in which a child develops is thus important to fully understand how gender stereotypes and gender expectations develop and are maintained. Messages about gender-appropriate behavior can be found in our language, play activities, the media, school, religion, and the workplace. Of all, language is perhaps the most subtle.

Language

From the moment a child begins to understand the spoken word, she or he also begins to receive messages about the way society views sex roles. Language plays a major role in defining and maintaining male power over women. Sexism in the English language takes three major forms; ignoring, labeling, and deprecating (Henley & Thorne, 1977; Lakoff, 1975; Thorne, Kramarae, & Henley, 1983).

Ignoring

The most striking way of ignoring females is by using the masculine gender to refer to human beings in general—for example, "chairman;" "best man for the job;" "mankind;" "the working man;" "everyone should do his best." This use of the male term to refer to all humans makes maleness the norm and femaleness the exception. That people do, in fact, perceive the use of the masculine form to refer predominantly to males has been demonstrated by a number of researchers (Briere & Lanktree, 1983; Fisk, 1985; Hyde, 1984a; Mackay, 1980; Moulton, Robinson, & Elias, 1978). For example, when students from first grade through college were asked to make up a story about the average student in a school, only 12% who had read the pronoun *he* told a story about a female. When the pronoun encountered was *they,* only 18% told a story about a female, but when the pronoun was *he or she,* 42% of the stories were about females (Hyde, 1984a). Clearly, then, the use of male pronouns is not sex-neutral. Furthermore, most children in elementary school don't even know that "he" is "supposed to" include females (Hyde, 1984a). Children who are exposed to a constant flow of information about "he" appear to conclude that the typical person is male. Even the seemingly neutral pronoun "they" conveys mainly males, as do other apparently gender-neutral terms like "person" and "adult" (Wise & Rafferty, 1982). These results hold for adults as well. Thus, use of the generic "he" allows many people to ignore the female half of the population.

Labeling

Language also defines women by labeling what is considered to be the exception to the rule ("*lady* doctor," "*career* girl"), thereby reinforcing occupational stereotypes. The message appears to be that the typical adult/person is male—in other words, that being female is atypical. This implication that women are atypical is likely to be encoded into a child's developing gender schema. There may be important consequences for a child's self-esteem and self-confidence, as we will see in the next chapter. Another consequence may be in terms of career aspirations. For example, when a job description used only male pronouns, elementary and college students rated females as least able to do that job (Hyde, 1984a; Shepelak, Ogden, & Tobin-Bennett, 1984). Thus, use of the generic "he" is not just an arbitrary custom, but a continuing statement about the societal roles of

women and men. In one study (Dayhoff, 1983) such linguistic sexism affected readers' evaluations of a female candidate for public office.

Females are defined by the group with which they are linked. For example, the frequent group of "women and children" suggests a similar dependent status. Females also are defined by the order in which they are usually referred to—"he and *she*", "boys and *girls*"— that is, in second place. Women also are predominantly referred to by relationships—"Jane Doe, wife of John Doe and daughter of Mr. and Mrs. Joseph Smith." When women marry, they lose their name (identity) and take on that of their spouse; thereafter, they are "Mrs. John Doe." Until recently, marriage ceremonies pronounced a couple "man and *wife*." He maintains his personhood; she becomes a role. Women also are referred to as possessions, as in "pioneers moved West, taking their *wives* and children with them."

Deprecating

A third sexist aspect of language is the way it deprecates women. One way to do this is by trivializing them ("*poetess,*" "*girl*" for woman). Another way to deprecate women is to sexualize them. For example, *dame* and *madam* have double meanings, while their male counterparts, *lord* and *sir,* do not. A third means of deprecation is to insult women. One researcher found 220 terms for a sexually promiscuous woman, compared to 22 terms for a sexually promiscuous male (Henley & Thorne, 1977). Women of ethnic minority status are especially likely to have sexually derogatory epithets applied to them (Allen, 1984). These women appear to be doubly stigmatized on the basis of both their sex and their race. A fourth form of deprecation is depersonalization ("chick," "piece of ass," "cunt," "broad").

Even the American Sign Language system used by most deaf people in this country mirrors gender stereotypes. For example, references to men and masculine pronouns refer to the top portion of the head. This part of the body is also the reference point for signs depicting intelligence and decision making. References to women and feminine pronouns, however, are signed in the lower part of the face, the part of the body associated with signs for the emotions and feelings (Jolly & O'Kelly, 1980).

As was noted in Chapter 4, the sexes also are thought to use language differently. Lakoff (1975) suggests that women more than men use tag questions ("It's hot, isn't it?"), qualifiers ("maybe," "I guess"), and compound requests ("Won't you close the window?" rather than "Close the window"). These three speech style differences are assumed to indicate a lack of assertiveness and more politeness on the part of females. Research on parental directives to young children suggests that children learn these different linguistic styles from their parents (Bellinger & Gleason, 1982). For example, fathers appear to issue more direct commands than do mothers ("Put the screw in."), and mothers appear to issue more indirect requests than do fathers ("Can you put the screw in?"). Although not all researchers find strong gender differences in these speech styles (for example, McMillan, Clifton, McGrath, & Gale, 1977), there is evidence that speakers who do use the "female" speech style are more often viewed as less assertive, more polite, and warmer than speakers who use the "male" speech style (Mulac, Incontro, & James, 1985; Newcombe & Arnkoff, 1979). Furthermore, children are taught that girls do not curse, talk too loudly, or issue demands but that boys do. This greater permissiveness for boys is reflected in male dominance in verbal and nonverbal interactions—talking more, interrupting more, and touching more, and more often using a familiar form of address (first name, "honey") when talking to a female than would a female talking to a male.

Changing Language

These aspects of the English language convey to young children important messages—that females are less important and less interesting than males, that males are dominant and forceful—that are reinforced by other aspects of socialization. To begin to change these stereotypes, our language and our use of it must change. (See Blaubergs, 1978, for a review of types of changes.) Publishers are finally beginning to issue guidelines for eliminating sexism in writing (Scott, Foresman & Co. was among

the first in 1972). For example, use "he or she" instead of "he;" recast pronouns into the plural ("their" instead of "his"); neuterize occupation terms ("police officer" instead of "policeman").

Changes in our use of language clearly can be done. Witness the change of the word "Negro" to "Black" and the acceptance of "Ms." by most businesses and organizations. Anything that makes people more aware of sexist language may become an impetus for language change (Adamsky, 1981). It may be hard to change, it may be awkward until a new habit develops, and it may be superficial compared to needed economic and social changes. But it is important. As Blaubergs (1978) notes, "Although language may be only one of the reflections of societal practices, nevertheless it is a reflection, and as such provides continuing inspiration for sexism" (pp. 246–247).

Social and linguistic changes are interactive, each promoting change in the other. For example, Munroe and Munroe (1969), in their study of ten cultures, found a significant relationship between structural sex bias in a culture, such as marital residence and inheritance regulations, and the proportion of male to female gender nouns in use. To develop a more egalitarian society, a more egalitarian language is needed.

A positive sign of change can be seen in the 1982 edition of Roget's *Thesaurus,* a book of synonyms and antonyms first published in the 1850s. The most recent edition eliminates sexist words, such as changing "mankind" to "humankind." Also in that year, the American Psychological Association mandated nonsexist language use in its journals and conference presentations. Although much change has occurred since the 1970s, it probably will take another generation for the changes to be fully incorporated into the language. Furthermore, unless the new language regulations actually are enforced, institutional compliance tends to be minimal (Markowitz, 1984).

Play

Language is only one vehicle through which gender stereotypes are taught. As soon as children start to play, they receive another lesson.

Picture a group of children playing with blocks. Picture another group playing "house." What is the sex composition of these groups? Now picture a high school athlete who has just received a school letter for excellence in basketball. Does a boy or does a girl come to mind? From all these play activities—toys, games, and sports—children receive messages about gender-appropriate behavior that affect their lives.

Toys

As was noted previously, by the time girls and boys are 4 years old, they play with and prefer different toys. Boys play with trucks, building blocks, robots; girls, with dolls, household goods, stuffed animals. In general, girls' toys do not make many cognitive demands or prepare girls for any occupational future except the role of motherhood. Boys' toys, on the other hand, tend to be more varied, expensive, and creative—for example, scientific kits (Hoffman, 1977). These differential experiences convey important occupational messages to young children. One message is that careers are not important for girls but are important for boys. Another message is that child care is not important for boys but is important for girls. One consequence of playing with different toys may well be the development of different abilities, such as verbal abilities for girls (playing "house" involves a great deal of talk) and visual-spatial and manual abilities for boys.

The choice of sex-typed toys among preschoolers has been found to be associated with other sex-typed social behaviors (Cameron, Eisenberg, & Tryon, 1985). For example, a young boy who spends time interacting with his peers is also likely to prefer "masculine" toys, such as airplanes, and reject "feminine" toys, such as beads. (Socializing with peers is more common among young boys than among young girls.) Whether toy choice encourages or just reflects children's other sex-typed behaviors is unclear.

Language plays a role here as well: children are more likely to play with and be interested in toys that are labeled as gender-appropriate rather than gender-inappropriate (Bradbard & Endsley, 1983; Cobb, Stevens-Long, & Goldstein, 1982; Downs, 1983). This is true for boys more so than for girls. Such labeling may be used by advertisers, parents, other children, and particularly by salespeople (Ungar, 1982). Advertisers rarely show a sex-typed toy being played with by a child of the nonstereotypic sex (Schwartz & Markham, 1985). Parental concern that playing with toys labeled gender-inappropriate will later make their children maladjusted has proven unfounded (Collins, 1984). Rather, parental attitudes about toy playing and traditional sex typing appear more important with regard to a child's adjustment than the child's playthings. For example, a parent who expresses alarm at their son's enjoyment of a doll will do more to affect their child's adjustment than the doll itself.

Games and Sports

The games that boys and girls play also differ. Girls spend more time in individual activities that require little competition and have few rules—for example, jumping rope, playing "house" (Hennig & Jardim, 1977; Lott, 1978; Maccoby & Jacklin, 1974). Sports considered appropriate for females, such as skating, swimming, and horseback riding, also have few rules and usually involve no competition. The emphasis is on quality of performance, not on winning. Boys, on the other hand, are more likely to play in situations that involve sociability and coordinated action (Lott, 1978). They also are strongly encouraged to play in highly organized, complex, competitive team sports such as baseball, football, and basketball. Through such team sports, boys learn how to set goals and work with others to achieve those goals. They learn a degree of emotional detachment necessary in choosing players for a team. Boys come to understand and respect rules, and they learn to be persistent. They also learn the importance of winning and come to view it as a personal or team achievement. Failure can be spread among team members, keeping the individual ego protected (Hennig & Jardim, 1977).

These games may have direct consequences for future occupational performance. As David Riesman comments, "The road to the board room leads through the locker room" ("Comes the Revolution," 1978, p. 59). Hennig and Jardim (1977), in their book on women in management, attribute male dominance of business to early sports experience. Males transfer to the business world in an effective way what they learned from team sports—competition, emotional detachment, teamwork, and ego protection from failure. Females, however, usually have not learned these things. They are not used to delegating responsibility, tolerating people who do not perform well, or focusing on winning. Hennig and Jardim found that women who have "made it" in the business world have one thing in common—they were raised free from gender stereotypes. Other research (Rohrbaugh, 1979) has found that female participation in sports enhances females' general sense of confidence and well-being.

Sports and sport terms play another important role in future occupational performance. Many analogies used for business and political processes are based on sports—for example, *one-on-one, blitz, strike out.* People unfamiliar with the jargon, as are many women, are often at a loss to understand the messages being communicated. This lack of understanding further increases their difficulty in operating in traditionally masculine fields (Fasteau, 1974). In addition, many social activities and conversations revolve around sports, such as the business golf game, Monday night football. People who are not interested in, or are not familiar with, such activities, such as many women, often are left out.

There are, however, many negative consequences of sports participation, especially when athletics are overemphasized. This overemphasis is more often the case for males than females. Intense competitiveness may limit personality growth, instill feelings of inadequacy, inhibit close relationships, and lead to violence (Fasteau, 1974; Ogilvie & Tutko, 1971; Pleck, 1976a). Excessive competitiveness may even impair performance (Reis & Jelsma, 1978; Spence & Helmreich, 1978). Furthermore, the emphasis on, and preoccupation with, high-level performance and winning may cause an athlete to play while in great pain or when injured (Hyland, 1978; Stein & Hoffman, 1978). The male role, however, does not allow the male either to acknowledge or to give expression to such pressures and pain. This puts great strain

on the athlete and may cause lasting physical problems. In addition, the focus on top players (the star system) generates problems of cooperation among team members.

For male nonathletes, the pressure and strain of sports are even more severe. As Stein and Hoffman (1978) and others (Fasteau, 1974, Pleck, 1976a) note, the overemphasis on male athletic skill can be devastating to boys with limited athletic ability or interest. One result of this overemphasis on sports is role strain and feelings of failure and inferiority for not living up to male sex-role expectations. A. Wittig (1984) reports that "feminine" males show very high levels of sport competition anxiety, whereas "masculine" males show very low levels of such anxiety. Picture a clumsy boy who gets ridiculed for dropping the ball. One of the worst things he could hear would be "You play like a *girl!*" Such boys get left out of many male groups and consequently may feel like, and be, outcasts. Another consequence for the nonathlete of the overemphasis on male athletic skill is total disdain for sports and feelings of distance from his body.

The intimate association between athletics and masculinity is especially obvious in the resistance expressed by males when females try to join their games. Some writers even argue that such resistance to coed sports is necessary for boys to form an adequate male gender identity (for example, Monagan, 1983). Figure 8-1 shows an example of such resistance as well as an involved participant's view. (These letters to the Editor were written in response to *Time*'s cover story on women and sports.) The uproar over admitting qualified girls to Little League baseball teams and the concern about female "fragility" may reflect a belief in the masculinity-destroying prospects of female competition. To get beaten by a girl has been viewed as a major humiliation for boys because girls clearly are thought to be inferior. If they were not considered inferior their competition would be welcomed. One indication of the relationship between sports participation and traditional sex roles is the finding that male varsity athletes in college demonstrate a significantly more negative attitude toward nontraditional sex-role behaviors than do male nonathletes (Hirt, Hoffman, & Sedlacek, 1983). The issue

Your profiling women's participation in sports is like encouraging a snail to enter a foot race. Let's face it, women just aren't made right to enter a man's realm of sports.

They have cluttered up the baseball diamonds and football fields, and now they have invaded and completely tied up our handball courts with their sissy game of racquetball.

Thank you for your article on women in sports. I'm a twelve-year-old girl going to a school that doesn't really give girls a fair chance in sports. In eighth grade next year, I want to play flag football with the boys, but I'll never get permission from our school board or superintendent. Most of the boys try to discourage me and tell me to go back to cheerleading. Now, with the help of your article, I may be able to win over the boys and (I hope) the superintendent.

Figure 8-1

Two reactions to women in sports, the one on the left by a male, the one on the right by a female. (Letters to the Editor of Time *magazine in response to an article on women in sports. Copyright 1978 Time Inc. All rights reserved.)*

of female athletics at the college level taps more than attitudes, however. A division of money is at stake there in addition to the political and psychological ramifications.

Because athletics and the male sex role are so closely related, many women have hesitated to become involved in sports for fear of becoming, or being labeled, "masculine" (Matteo, 1984). However, recent research suggests that some of the stigma attached to female participation in sports may be diminishing (Basow & Spinner, 1984; Hoferek & Hanick, 1985; Rao & Overman, 1984; Rohrbaugh, 1979). Rather than being "masculine," females who participate in sports, especially traditionally "unfeminine" sports, tend to have more liberal gender-role attitudes and to be more androgynous than both women who compete in "feminine" sports and than female nonathletes. Male athletes, however, do tend to be masculine sex-typed. Thus, although sports are more closely associated with males, sports participation does not make females "masculine." We need to separate sports from the male sex role so that both sexes can receive the benefits of athletic participation.

Female's participation in sports is increasing. Between 1971 and 1978, the number of girls in interscholastic athletics in secondary schools jumped by more than 600% ("How Title IX," 1984). In 1980–1981, 36% of the country's 5.1 million high school athletes were girls. On the college level, women's participation in intercollegiate athletics more than

doubled between 1971 and 1976. By 1981–1982, 30% of all intercollegiate athletes were women. Even the recruiting of female high school athletes for university athletics programs is reaching the intensity of the recruiting of male athletes (Lichtenstein, 1981). In professional sports also, the growth of women's participation has been phenomenal and can be measured in dollars. For example, in 1970 there was only $200,500 available in prize money on the tennis circuit. In 1980 the corresponding figure was about $9.2 million (Seidman, 1979).

Although females' participation in sports is approaching that of males' in numbers, the meaning of sports still may be different for the sexes. Reis and Jelsma (1978), in their survey of 48 male and 47 female college varsity athletes evenly distributed among four sports (basketball, lacrosse, swimming, and tennis), found that there were important differences in the way each sex approached sports. The males scored significantly higher than females on all questions dealing with the importance of competition; the females scored significantly higher than males on all questions dealing with the importance of social interactions. These responses parallel, and perhaps reflect, the stereotypic sex difference in interest areas. There were no significant sex differences in enjoyment of the sport or in the desire to perform well. Other research supports the finding that males display greater competitiveness and assertiveness with regard to sports participation than do females (Croxton, Chiacchia, & Wagner, 1984).

The sex differences in attitudes toward sports may be related to the participants' sex typing. Myers and Lips (1978) found that feminine-sex-typed athletes may participate in sports for noncompetitive reasons whereas androgynous and masculine athletes may participate for competitive reasons. Unfortunately, the direct effect of attitudes on athletic performance was not examined.

The increased participation of females in athletics has been due in large part to the passage of the Title IX regulation of the Education Amendments Act of 1972, implemented in 1975. Title IX prohibits schools and colleges receiving federal funds from discriminating on the basis of sex in any educational program or activity. As a result of this legislation, some of the grossest inequities in budget allocations to male and female athletic activities have been reduced. For example, before Title IX, no colleges or universities offered athletic scholarships to women. Since Title IX, the number of college sports scholarships offered to women has skyrocketed—from 5,000 in 1978 to 15,000 in 1982 ("How Title IX," 1984). In 1972–1973, the average budget for women's athletics at Division I colleges and universities was $7,000; by 1976–1977, it was $71,000, and in 1980–1981, it was $338,000 (D. Tucker, 1983). Yet the figure for Division I men's athletic programs in 1980–1981 was nearly 10 times more, $3.2 million. Many of the gains made in educational equity since Title IX was passed have been halted since 1980. During the Reagan administration, enforcement of Title IX regulations has been lax. Furthermore, since the 1984 Supreme Court decision, *Grove City College* v. *Bell,* Title IX provisions can be applied only to programs that directly receive federal aid, not to the whole institution. Thus, if only the financial aid program receives federal aid, only that program is covered by Title IX. The institution can discriminate elsewhere in its programs— for example, in athletic budgets. (At press time, Congress was considering a bill that would reverse the decision.)

In summary, although sports participation appears important in the development of many positive skills, and although female participation in sports is increasing, the overall picture still shows inequities. Females in sports still remain handicapped by lower expenditures, unavailable facilities, lack of encouragement, absence of role models, and parental and societal suppression of female competition (Ames, 1984; P. Griffin, 1984; U.S. Commission on Civil Rights, 1980).

It is hoped that increasing visibility of female role models such as Martina Navratilova, Válerie Briscoe-Hooks, and Nancy Lopez will help. Figure 8-2 shows one way such models may help break down gender stereotypes.

Figure 8-2
How sports models can break down gender stereotypes. (Copyright 1973, G. B. Trudeau. Reprinted with permission of Universal Press Syndicate. All rights reserved.)

Media

Of all the sources of gender stereotypes, the media are the most pervasive. Television, books, films, songs, art—all communicate messages about sex roles that are far from subtle. Females and males are presented, for the most part, in stereotyped ways, usually with deviations from the stereotypes depicted negatively. Because the media both reflect and shape society, they are extremely influential, especially for young children who cannot clearly differentiate fantasy from reality. The 1980s have seen some improvement in the images of women presented in the media. However, the overall picture still is far from balanced.

Television

It has been estimated that children spend one-third of their lives at home and/or sleeping, one-third at school, and one-third in front of a TV set. Almost all households in the United States (98%) own at least one television set (Nielsen, 1985). TV usage averages more than 7 hours a day in the average TV household. Half of the 12-year-olds in the country watch this amount or more, although the average child watches between 3½ to 4 hours a day (Gerbner & Gross, 1976; Nielsen, 1985). By the time a child is 16, she or he has spent more time in front of a TV set than in a classroom. Children from blue-collar families and from minority groups spend even more time watching TV than White middle-class children. Consequently, whatever effects TV viewing has should be particularly strong for such children (Women on Words and Images, 1975a).

Children's Shows. The world that children see on TV is a sex-typed and White male-oriented one. Children's TV, for example, has been found to depict more than twice as many male as female roles. The behaviors of the female and male characters are strikingly different, as are the consequences of these behaviors (Feldman & Brown, 1984; Sternglanz & Serbin, 1974). Male characters are more likely to be aggressive, constructive, direct, and helpful and to be rewarded for their actions than are female characters. Females are more likely

to be shown as deferent and as being punished for displaying a high level of activity. Females also use indirect manipulative strategies to get their way (for example, acting helpless or seductive). In general, female behavior has no environmental consequence. This pattern parallels the practices of socializing agents: males get more attention and reinforcement; females are usually ignored and are expected to be passive and sedate.

Even in educational and "innovative" programs like "Sesame Street," males and females are depicted as having different activities. Men's work is outside the home; women's work is inside (Bergman, 1974). Furthermore, the major characters on "Sesame Street," the Muppets, all have male names or voices or both. These puppets not only are the mainstays of the show but also are prominent in books, toys, and other commercial articles. As Cobb, Stevens-Long, and Goldstein (1982) have demonstrated, puppet figures can have tremendous influences on children's sex-typed behaviors. They found that children aged 4 to 6 would not play with non-sex-typed toys that had been labeled by two Muppets as appropriate only for the other sex. This behavior change occurred after only 5 minutes of TV exposure.

Prime-Time TV. Sexism on prime-time TV has been amply documented since the late 1960s (Dominick, 1979; Downs & Gowan, 1980; Hodges, Brandt, & Kline, 1981; Kalisch & Kalisch, 1984; U.S. Commission on Civil Rights, 1977, 1979). These studies have shown, for example, that 65% to 75% of all leading characters have been White males. This percentage has remained relatively constant for 25 years. In exciting adventure shows, such as "The A Team," males constitute 85% of the major characters. Occupationally, twice as many jobs have been depicted for the major male characters as for the major female characters. Males can be police officers, detectives, lawyers, doctors, psychologists, and so on. Employed females usually have been nurses, secretaries, or teachers. Men also have been three times more likely than women to be depicted as wage earners, and women have been more than twice as likely as men to be depicted as nonwage earners. Since the 1950s, the makeup of the television-depicted labor force consistently has shown no relationship to the real-life employment patterns of women. Females are more often identified by their relationships to males—girlfriend, wife, mother—than males are identified by their relationship to females. Blacks and other minority groups, both females and males, scarcely have been represented at all on television (Seggar, Hafen, & Hannonen-Gladden, 1981). Figure 8-3 indicates some of the typical female roles on TV.

Although the number of male and female characters on TV conveys an important message to viewers, even more powerful are the qualities such characters portray (Williams, LaRose, & Frost, 1981). The preceding studies have shown that behaviorally, females were three times more likely than males to be depicted in a negative light, especially on adventure shows. For example, the only women in a number of "Mike Hammer" episodes, except for the secretary, were prostitutes or dope addicts. Women also were twice as likely as men to show incompetent behaviors. For example, even in a show where a woman is a major character ("Miami Vice"), she often must be rescued from a difficult situation by her male partner. Men, however, although depicted somewhat negatively on situation-comedy shows, are more than twice as likely as women to be shown as competent (independent, skilled, leaderlike, self-confident). Men on TV also are more likely than women to be older, more serious, and more likely to hold prestigious jobs, such as Trapper John. The family time concept was introduced in 1975 to eliminate violence and sex from programs shown between 7 and 9 P.M. A perhaps unintended by-product of this concept was the increase in stereotypic female characters, especially in programs aimed at younger viewers (Peevers, 1979).

Prime-time TV recently has begun to show some changes in their portrayal of women (Kerr, 1984). Of the 22 series making their debut in 1984, eight featured women in strong leading roles. Although not all the series survived, there are many more nonstereotypic roles for women and men on prime-time TV than ever before. Women are police officers ("Cagney & Lacey," "Hunter"), executives ("Dynasty"), lawyers

("Hill Street Blues," "Cosby Show"), even breadwinners ("Who's the Boss?"). Women have close and supportive female friendships ("Kate & Allie"). Network research has found that such strong female characters appeal especially to women between ages 25 and 54 with incomes of more than $30,000. Such viewers are highly desirable to advertisers. Although not all the portrayals of strong women have been positive ones ("V," "Falcon Crest"), their increasing presence might eventually reduce the current male dominance of the airways.

In news programs, the percentage of female network news correspondents has increased dramatically from 1977 when 79% of the newsmakers were White males, 10% White females, 8% non-White males, and 3% non-White females (U.S. Commission on Civil Rights, 1977, 1979; J. Wilson, 1984). In 1984, women constituted over 33% of the anchors on broadcast news programs. In fact, network research shows that most Americans would prefer to see a man and a woman anchoring the network news ("Progress," 1985). Minorities, however, still are seriously underrepresented, and the percentage of women in management positions still is small. For example, women were only 11% of all news directors in 1983, although this was an improvement over 1972, when less than 1% of the news directors were women. Women's progress in attaining a newscaster's job may belie the fact that only 10% of the nightly news stories actually were filed by female correspondents in 1984. Furthermore, female correspondents may be expected to be younger, more attractive, and more deferential than are male correspondents, as Christine Craft's 1983 suit against Metromedia, Inc. attested. Whether having more women both behind and in front of the camera would actually affect what news is transmitted is debatable (J. Wilson, 1984). However, the predominance of males in authoritative positions conveys its own message to viewers—that is, that men are important and knowledgeable and that women are not.

Commercials. The gender stereotypes are even more explicit in TV commercials than in regular programming (Courtney & Whipple, 1983; Downs & Harrison, 1985; Mamary &

I am a psychotic/mute/Indian/ Chicana who is restored to normalcy and neatness by a young, attractive, white, middle class doctor from the east. (Lots of flashbacks showing me whipped, raped, and force-fed)

I am the sister/daughter of an unjustly imprisoned man or else the witness to a mafia crime. I am also the client of a blind freelance insurance investigator. I scream often and inopportunely. I always fall and twist my ankle when the investigator and I are fleeing the bad guys.

I am a black/white cop. I have a short snappy name. I am tough but feminine. I like to follow my own instincts about a case. This frequently gets me into trouble; I am inevitably rescued by my male, fellow officers, who are devoted to me . . . I never rescue them.

I am the woman behind the man. I spend a lot of time keeping dinner warm for my crusading policeman/coroner, lover/husband. Sometimes I nag about being left alone so much. Sometimes I am kidnapped by mafia thugs. This makes a welcome break in my routine.

Figure 8-3

Memorable television role models. (From I'm in Training to Be Tall and Blonde, *by Nicole Hollander. Copyright 1979 by Nicole Hollander. Reprinted by permission of St. Martin's Press, Inc.)*

Simpson, 1981; Pingree, 1978). In order of frequency, women are depicted as predominantly concerned with their appearance, their housework, and family matters. In contrast, men are more likely to be shown working, playing, eating, or being nursed. Relations between the sexes are portrayed in strictly traditional ways. For example, one detergent commercial shows a man engaged in bird-watching. A woman next to him notices grime on his shirt and repeatedly remarks in an irritating, sing-song voice "Ring around the collar." The scene immediately shifts to the aghast wife and her subsequent efforts to rectify the "humiliating" occurrence. Men are almost always (96%) the authoritative, dominant voice-overs in commercials, even when the products are aimed at women. Thus again, males are depicted as the competent working authority; females as vain homemakers and consumers.

Even in toy commercials, more boys are depicted than girls, and girls are more likely than boys to appear in a passive role (Feldstein & Feldstein, 1982). Indeed, commercials aimed at boys have a different format than commercials aimed at girls. Commercials aimed at boys have rapid action, frequent cuts, loud music, sound effects, and frequent scene changes. In contrast, commercials aimed at girls contain many fades and dissolves, background music, and female narration (Welch, Huston-Stein, Wright, & Plehal, 1979). Children as young as 6 years of age recognize these distinctions, which means that even if the content of a commercial doesn't sex-type a product, the style in which it is produced might (Huston, Greer, Wright, Welch, & Ross, 1984).

Soap Operas. In daytime soap operas, viewed primarily by women, characters also are presented in traditional and stereotypic ways, although the subject matter has become more contemporary in recent years (Cantor & Pingree, 1983). Women on such shows as "All My Children" and "General Hospital" more often are depicted as nurturant, hopeless, and displaying avoidance behaviors than are men on these shows. Men, more than women, are depicted as directive and problem solving, although at least one study suggests that neither sex demonstrates competent coping strategies on such shows (Hodges et al., 1981).

Effects. The message one hears on TV is that there are more men around than women and that men are more important, competent, dominant, authoritative, and aggressive than women. Women are depicted in far fewer situations, are less likely to be working, and more often are shown in a negative way. Modeling is an important process in sex-role development, and the models presented on TV are stereotyped to the extreme. Even adults may be affected. Being exposed to a constant barrage of a TV world of gender stereotypes may help to reinforce adults' own sex-role training. Even if one's training had been nontraditional, TV may encourage more traditional conceptions of the sex roles.

This concept of "mainstreaming," whereby TV creates a homogeneous commonality of outlooks, suggests that the effect of TV is likely to be strongest among those who otherwise are least likely to hold traditional sex-role views. Michael Morgan (1982), in a two-year study of the relationship between TV viewing and gender stereotypes in sixth- through tenth-graders, found support for this hypothesis. For males, high TV viewing did not predict sexism scores one year later, but for girls, amount of TV viewing was associated significantly with sexism scores one year later. This finding suggests that for girls, greater sexism was a result of watching a great deal of TV. Because girls, especially middle-class girls, were less sexist than boys to begin with, watching TV may affect them the most. Curiously, early sexism on the part of boys was a strong predictor of TV watching one year later, suggesting that those with strong stereotypes may enjoy the reinforcement of those attitudes that occurs on TV.

Other research supports the preceding finding that TV is a powerful source of influence on viewers' attitudes and behaviors. This influence appears to be particularly strong for children, who, as a group, are not as skilled as adults in distinguishing fantasy from reality (Eysenck & Nias, 1978).

The amount of time children spend watching TV has been found to be directly and positively related to their degree of acceptance of traditional sex roles as early as kindergarten age (Gross & Jeffries-Fox, 1978; McGhee & Frueh, 1980; Sprafkin & Liebert, 1978; Zuckerman, Singer, & Singer, 1980). Furthermore, whereas among light viewers of TV, the perception of male stereotypes declines with increasing age, among heavy viewers no such decline occurs. Parents' sex-role attitudes may be important factors here, as may be a child's intelligence. These factors may interact with the amount of TV viewing in such a way as to ameliorate TV's sex-typing effects. And not all TV shows are alike. Children who watched more educational TV programs tended to demonstrate less sex-stereotyped attitudes than children who watched little educational TV (Repetti, 1984). However, even among college students and older adults, the amount of TV viewing of stereotyped programs has been found to be significantly and positively correlated with the amount of gender stereotyping in self-descriptions (Ross, Anderson, & Wisocki, 1982). Of course, especially in adult groups, the positive correlation may mean that sex-typed people prefer watching sex-typed shows. Still, frequent viewing is likely to be a powerful reinforcer of gender stereotypes.

Children's sex-role attitudes have been found to be directly affected by media messages. Pingree (1978) found that, by showing third- and eighth-grade children commercials of either traditional women (housewives and mothers) or nontraditional women (professional business people), she could affect children's attitudes about women. All children, except eighth-grade boys, who saw the nontraditional commercials and who were told that the women were real people, became less traditional in their attitudes about women. And this was after only 5 minutes of viewing! Other research supports the idea that the portrayal of non-stereotyped characters can expand gender consciousness among children, although "masculine" boys appear to be the hardest to reach (Eisenstock, 1984). However, nonstereotyped portrayals may be disregarded. For example, among first- and fourth-graders, one study found that a brief presentation of a male nurse and a female doctor was misremembered in a stereotyped direction (Drabman, Robertson, Patterson, Jarvie, Hammer, & Cordua, 1981); that is, children reported having viewed a female nurse and a male doctor. Clearly, children can learn from TV, although what they learn may be unintentional and unpredictable. TV's

effect may also vary as a function of the cognitive developmental level of the child.

In an interesting series of experiments at the University of Delaware, Florence Geis and colleagues (Geis, Brown, Jennings, & Corrado-Taylor, 1984; Geis, Brown, Jennings, & Porter, 1984; Jennings, Geis, & Brown, 1980) have demonstrated the powerful effect TV commercials can have on college student viewers. These researchers first videotaped replicas of four network commercials showing traditional gender divisions. They then produced four matching commercials with the sex roles reversed. In their first study, Geis et al. (1984) found that the gender stereotypes depended more on role than on actor sex. For example, actors playing the authoritative role (males in the traditional version, females in the reversed-role version) were rated as more rational, independent, dominant, and ambitious than actors playing the supportive role. In their other studies, these researchers found that women who viewed the reversed-role version of the commercials later showed greater self-confidence, more independence of judgment, and higher achievement aspirations than women who viewed the traditional version. Since children see about 20,000 traditional commercials a year, it is clear how TV can contribute to important sex differences.

Books and Magazines

Sex-role messages are clearly found in children's books, in magazines, and in fiction. Each of these categories will be discussed in turn.

Children's Books. Women on Words and Images (1972, 1975b) has compiled impressive statistics on the world depicted in elementary school readers. Table 8-1 shows the results of both their 1972 survey of 2760 stories in 134 books from 14 different publishers and their 1975 update using 83 readers published since 1972.

As shown in the table, 75% of the textbooks focus on male characters. Although there was some improvement in the number of female biographies and occupations presented in the 1975 update, the ratio of boy-centered to girl-centered stories increased further.

Table 8-1

Sexism in Children's Readers, 1972 and 1975

Content	1972	1975
Boy-centered stories to girl-centered stories	5:2	7:2
Male biographies to female biographies	6:1	2:1
Male occupations to female occupations	6:1	3:1
Adult male main characters to adult female main characters	3:1	*
Male animal stories to female animal stories	2:1	*
Male folk or fantasy stories to female folk or fantasy stories	4:1	*

*Not calculated in the 1975 update.

Data from *Dick & Jane as Victims,* by Women on Words and Images. Princeton, N.J.,
 1972, 1975b.

In addition to this quantitative male bias, there was also a qualitative male bias evident in both samples. Males predominated in situations with active mastery themes (cleverness, bravery, adventure, and earning money), and females predominated in situations with "second-sex" themes (passivity, victimization, and goal constriction). For example, Jane watches as John fixes a toy. This portrayal of the sexes has been found in studies of other children's books as well (A. Davis, 1984; Saario, Jacklin, & Tittle, 1973).

This stereotyping continues in textbooks throughout the school years. In fact, the stereotypes become even more pronounced with increasing grade level. Saario and associates (1973) report that, from first- to third-grade readers, the total number of female characters declined sharply, and the number of significant sex differences increased. Knopp (1980) found a similar pattern in West German readers from Grades 1 through 4. Interestingly, gender bias was significantly less common in East German readers, although it still occurred. Socialist literature appears to be promoting gender equality to a greater degree than does capitalist literature, probably a reflection of different societal ideologies regarding sex roles.

One of the tragedies of the male bias in children's stories is that such stories not only teach values but also influence behavior. McArthur and Eisen (1976) report that nursery school boys persist longer on a task (a measure of achievement motivation) after hearing a story depicting achievement behavior by a male character than after a story depicting the same behavior by a female character. The trend was in the opposite direction for girls. This change occurred after hearing just one story. Given that 75% of the central characters in children's books are males and that females, when depicted, are rarely shown in achieving roles, it is not surprising that women have been underrepresented in achieving roles in our society. Similarly, Ashton (1983) found that preschool children exposed to a stereotypic picture book subsequently chose a sex-stereotypic toy more often than a nonstereotypic one, whereas those who were exposed to a nonstereotypic picture book more often selected a nonstereotypic toy.

Clearly, children can be affected by what they read. In this sense it is somewhat encouraging that a number of nonsexist preschool picture books have been published since the late 1960s, although they are not always as nonsexist as they purport to be. For example, Albert Davis (1984) found that, compared to more conventional book characters, females in nonsexist books were more independent and males were less aggressive. However, females still were more nurturant, emotional, and less physically active than were males.

Magazines. In other written material as well, gender stereotypes abound. Magazines aimed at men focus on themes of sexuality *(Playboy)*, sports *(Field and Stream)*, and daring *(Road and Track)*. Franzwa (1975) found in her study of women's magazine fiction from 1940 to 1970 that the ideal female goal was to be a homemaker and mother. Women are shown as passive and dependent. Their lives revolve around men, and their activities are limited to the home. More recent examinations of women's magazines, including *Ms.*, find a similar emphasis on women striving to please or help others (Ferguson, 1983; Phillips, 1978). In most magazines, "a man" is still a woman's most important goal.

However, the 1970s did bring a change in one gender message. Nearly all magazines for women portray women working outside the home and such women are portrayed in a positive light (Geise, 1979; Ruggiero & Weston, 1985). One impetus for this change is the advent in the 1970s of a number of specialized magazines for women, such as *Working Mother, Working Woman,* and *Savvy.* In such magazines, compared to the more traditional ones, the women who are profiled are more likely to represent nontraditional occupations for women and to have power and influence over others (Ruggiero & Weston, 1985).

Advertisers, however, appear to be the last to acknowledge that women are multidimensional. For example, although women account for 39% of new car purchases, and participate in buying another 42% of all new cars and trucks, automobile companies spend less than 3% of their advertising money in women's magazines ("Family Circle," 1982; "Study: Women's," 1985). Advertisements that do appear in magazines reinforce gender stereotypes. Erving Goffman (1979) found numerous examples of genderisms that illustrate the position of men and women in our society: function ranking (male taller, in front, and in authoritative position), ritualization of subordination (for example, a woman at a man's feet), snuggling, mock assault games, and an overabundance of images of women on beds and floors. Females are also more likely to smile than are males. Figure 8-4 is an example of function ranking—the man is pictured seated above, and leaning over, the woman. Men also are more likely than women to be depicted with their faces prominent, as opposed to their bodies (Akert & Chen, 1984; Archer, Iritani, Kimes, & Barrios, 1983). Such "face-ism" has been documented in periodicals both in the United States and in 11 other cultures, in artwork over six centuries, and in TV interview shows. This difference in facial prominence affects the viewers's perception of the person; for example, a person is perceived more favorably and is rated as more intelligent when the face is prominent than when it is not.

Advertising featuring men has been moving gradually toward a decrease in gender stereotypes (Skelly & Lundstrom, 1981). For example, men are becoming more "decorative" and less authoritative. In contrast, the image of women in advertising has not changed much since the early 1970s (Courtney & Whipple, 1983). Women still are predominantly shown as housewives and mothers, whereas males are seen in many occupations. Women also are three times more likely than men to be shown inside the home. Advertising still has a long way to go before it is sex fair.

Fiction. In the traditional American novel, Snow (1975) found a consistent duality presented for women—purity versus evil. American bitch versus Mother-savior (for example, Philip Roth's *Goodbye Columbus* and Steinbeck's *Grapes of Wrath*). Much more so than men, women are depicted symbolically and simplistically, perhaps because most writing in the past was done by men. Since the early 1970s, however, books by and about women have increased. The stories now often depict strong women and the changes the authors have gone through with respect to their sex roles (for example, *The Color Purple,* by Alice Walker). Along with this more realistic trend, though, is another trend—the romantic historical novel, written and read primarily by women (for example, Gothic novels). In these stories, the heroine is usually helpless or dependent upon a man to bring meaning to her life, although recent heroines have been more nontraditional in attitudes and behavior than in the past, and relationships are more often ones between equals (Toth, 1984; Weston & Ruggiero, 1978). Indeed, Radway (1984) argues that modern romances, despite their confirmation of traditional female roles in a patriarchal society, also convey another message—that it is all right for women to be assertive, and for men to be nurturing and gentle. Indeed, it is this message that may account for their appeal among

Figure 8-4
Example of function ranking in magazine advertising.
Note how the man is seated above, and leaning over,
the woman. (Photo courtesy of Kenyon & Eckhardt
Advertising, Inc., New York.)

women made anxious about changing gender definitions.

Popular books and fiction aimed at men, on the other hand (for example, James Bond thrillers), tend to present the male going off for some adventure, unencumbered by family ties. Themes of aggression predominate, and if females are presented, they are usually cast in a stereotyped sexual role (Weitz, 1977). Much male fiction is pornographic, with interconnected themes of sexuality, dominance, and violence against women (Dworkin, 1981; Griffin, 1981). (Pornography will be discussed at greater length in Chapter 12.)

Newspapers. As with the other media, newspapers show a sexist bias both in the treatment of women and men, in the language used,

and in the comic strips that are serialized. Women reporters generally have a difficult time making the front page with their stories, because women generally do not cover foreign, White House, or important news beats ("Survey," 1985). In a survey of the front pages of 11 leading newspapers, the National Organization for Women found that women by-lined fewer than one-quarter of the signed articles, from a low of 10% at *The New York Times,* to a high of 42% at *USA Today.*

Foreit and colleagues (1980) documented that coverage of women was more likely to include mention of personal appearance, marital status, and spouse than was the coverage of men. The fact that more men than women are in the news, and that women are more likely than men to be written about in the "family" (that is, "women's") section, did not account for the difference in the treatment of the sexes. This differential coverage was especially evident in the 1984 vice-presidential campaign of Geraldine Ferraro. Her clothes, hairstyle, and behaviors, as a mother and a wife, were frequently profiled.

Many newspapers, including *The New York Times,* persist in using sexist language and in using "Miss" or "Mrs." to describe women rather than "Ms." As Dayhoff (1983) has shown, such language causes women candidates for elective office to be negatively evaluated, at least for offices perceived to be "masculine" or "neutral." In this sense, the refusal by *The New York Times* to refer to candidate Ferraro by her preferred designation "Ms." had more than grammatical implications.

Comic strips also perpetuate gender stereotypes. Men, especially White men, are represented far more than their proportion in the population warrants, whereas women are underrepresented (Chavez, 1985). Furthermore, men are given preferential treatment in terms of number of appearances and number of careers depicted. Although many male and female characters are described in equally favorable or unfavorable terms, sex-typed characteristics often are emphasized for females (Potkay & Potkay, 1984; Potkay, Potkay, Boynton, & Klingbeil, 1982). For example, women often are depicted either as a housewife or a sexpot (Blondie Bumstead, Miss Buxley).

Films

Like books and television, films present stereotyped images of the sexes. As in the American novel, American films generally have presented two images of women. These were clearly exemplified in the 1950s and 1960s as the brainless sexpot (for example, Marilyn Monroe) and the feminine homebody (for example, Doris Day). It was only during the late 1930s and early 1940s, with the increased number of women in the labor force spurred by the Feminist movement of the 1920s and by World War II, that successful, achieving images of women emerged (as in the case of Katharine Hepburn). This ended when the war ended. When men reclaimed their jobs, women were pushed back

to the home in films as well as in reality. The New Woman of the late 1960s and 1970s, although sexually active and more independent than her predecessors, usually was depicted in a negative way, or she was punished for her sexuality (Mellen, 1973). For example, in *Looking for Mr. Goodbar,* the main character gets killed by someone she met in a singles' bar. The spurt of films in the mid- and late-1970s presenting women as credible human beings, as in the movies *Alice Doesn't Live Here Anymore, An Unmarried Woman, Julia, Turning Point,* was thought to presage an acceptance of women's attempts to break out of the confines of their sex role (Mellen, 1978b; J. Wilson, 1977).

The 1980s have seen some films that continue to challenge traditional sex roles or that make fun of traditional sex-role conventions (such as *Desperately Seeking Susan*). However, the 1980s also have seen a backlash (Haskell, 1983, 1984; McKelvey, 1984). The top ten box office stars of 1983 were all male, and popular films, such as *Terms of Endearment,* evoke once again the earth mother or the bitch images for women. Black women have been particularly neglected in films, and this has been true throughout the history of filmmaking. The return of the sexy, brainless young woman to the screen (for example, *The Woman in Red, Flashdance*) and the relative absence of the strong-willed woman may be explained by the fact that the average moviegoer is a male between ages 14 and 24, and it is his fantasies that are being catered to. This contrasts with the finding that the prime viewers of TV are women (Nielsen, 1985).

Cinematic images of masculinity also have held strongly to the gender stereotype. Whereas the realms of domesticity and sexual allure have been reserved for women, those of aggression, as in Westerns, war, and gangster movies, moral superiority, and intelligence, as in detective and mystery movies, have been reserved for men (Weitz, 1977). Because the male stereotype has more positive characteristics than the female one and because male characters usually are developed to a far greater degree than are female characters because of their central role, men have not fared too badly in film. However, the overemphasis on violence and the depiction of superficial sexual encounters as the norm has tended to distort men's human characteristics. Mellen (1978a) argues that men, like Clint Eastwood and Charles Bronson, in some 1970s' films are even more violent and brutal than were their predecessors in older films.

At the same time, a new image of masculinity started to emerge in the 1970s—the emotionally competent hero (Starr, 1978). This new character is not the archetypal, old-fashioned hero, like John Wayne or Gary Cooper, or the intensely emotional hero, like Marlon Brando and James Dean, or the counter-culture anti-hero, like Dustin Hoffman in *The Graduate* and Jack Nicholson. Rather, he is strong and affectionate, capable of intimacy, unthreatened by commitment, and firm without being dominant. He is exemplified by Jon Voight in *Coming Home*, Alan Bates in *An Unmarried Woman,* and Kris Kristofferson in *Alice Doesn't Live Here Anymore*. Not coincidentally, the latter two films have been recognized as depicting women in nonstereotyped ways as well. However, in the 1980s, men, regardless of personality type, resumed their dominance of the film world, even taking over what were once considered female issues; for example, single parenting *(Kramer vs. Kramer),* and problems of divorce *(Starting Over)*. Even *Tootsie,* a film praised for its perceptive insights into sex roles, can be analyzed as conveying another message as well—that men make better women than do women. Relationships between women and men show active confusion about sex roles and, in many cases, explicit male anger and hostility directed at women (for example, Clint Eastwood's *Tightrope*) (Maslin, 1984). Hollywood still has a long way to go before there is true equality on, and behind, the silver screen. The same can be said for Broadway (Rich, 1984).

Popular Songs and Rock Videos

In popular songs, gender stereotypes are again observable. Women are frequently depicted as deceitful, excessively emotional, supportive, sentimental, illogical, frivolous, dependent, and passive. Men frequently are depicted as sexually aggressive, rational, demanding, nonconforming, adventuresome, and breadwinning

(Reinartz, 1975). Although in three genres of contemporary music—Country, Soul, and Easy Listening—the portrayal of female roles is generally positive, albeit stereotypic, the same cannot be said for the images in rock music (Freudiger & Almquist, 1978). In rock music, mostly written and performed by men, negative images of women abound.

The most striking displays of rock misogyny can be seen in rock video vignettes, where gratuitous violence against women and female-as-sex-object images appear quite frequently. For example, in Tom Petty's "Don't Come Around Here No More," an Alice-in-Wonderland-type female is terrorized by both men and women and eventually eaten. In Don Henley's, "All She Wants to Do is Dance," a Third-World woman is portrayed as sexual and hedonistic while a revolution is going on. Men glare at her and step on her image in a mirror. In Van Halen's "California Girls," dozens of skimpily clad attractive young women bound around and display themselves. There are less objectified images of women presented in rock videos, but they are few in number and usually performed by women. For example, Donna Summer's "She Works Hard for Her Money" shows the difficult life many employed women have. Cyndi Lauper's "Time After Time" shows an eccentrically dressed female character going off alone to seek her fortune. On the whole, however, stereotypic images of women and men abound in rock videos.

Art

In art, too, females have been depicted in the double image of either virgin or whore, with characteristics of either purity or sexuality. In recent years, the latter image has prevailed, with females almost completely becoming erotic images, often in an obsessive or distorted way (L. Brown, 1975; O'Kelly, 1980). For example, Tom Wesselman's *Great American Nude* is all grin and nipples and sprawl. Although male nudes also have appeared, they are more often presented as the ideal of humanity and not as objects of pleasure. For example, Michelangelo's paintings and sculptures of nude men emphasize their muscularity, solidity, and sense of proportion (as in the statue of David), whereas paintings of nude women, like Manet's *Olympia,* emphasize women's sensuality.

Of course, most artists have been male because of restrictions on training, encouragement, and economic support. Until this century, women were socially prohibited from seeing nude men. Drawing them was unheard of. Many of the paintings signed "Anonymous" have actually been done by women, and much artwork done by women has been devalued due to the artist's sex and to the use of male-normed criteria (Broude & Garrard, 1982; Russell, 1981). For example, the classification of painting and sculpture, which women traditionally had little access to, as "high" art, and pottery, needlework, and quilting, which primarily women did, as "low" art, shows a distinct male bias regarding esthetic standards. Only recently have female artists moved away from being evaluated primarily as a "woman artist," and instead are evaluated more appropriately as an "artist" (Russell, 1983). However, prejudice is not extinct. Many female artists still have to fight battles for time, space, recognition, and acceptance that male artists generally do not have to fight. Black female artists in particular may be discriminated against (Russell, 1983).

Summary

In all forms of media, gender stereotypes are conveyed often in the most exaggerated way. Since children are trying to understand gender-appropriate behavior and the world around them, they are especially vulnerable to these distorted images. That these images in no way reflect reality can be seen particularly in the media depiction of women and work. Although TV, magazines, and children's readers continually depict a world in which nearly all women stay at home as housewives, in the real world, most women are employed outside the home. Of women who have school-age children, nearly 60% are in the labor force. Even women who do stay home are concerned about more than waxy buildup on their floors. The male image, too, is far from realistic. Boys generally do not fight grizzly bears, cannot solve all problems with a show of physical force, and certainly experience emotions other than anger. To the extent that children are aware of the discrepancy between the TV world and their own experience, they are as likely to view their own experience, such as their employed mother, as abnormal as they are to consider the TV image to be erroneous unless corrective measures are taken—for example, learning how to view TV with a skeptical eye.

School

Unfortunately, the stereotypes perceived in the media are often echoed in another major socializing force in children's lives—school. As noted in the last chapter, teachers are a major source of gender stereotypes. Other aspects of school life are influential as well: textbooks, curricula, counseling, school organization, and general atmosphere. These factors come together to form a hidden curriculum on sex roles. This curriculum conveys the message, often without the conscious awareness of either the students or the teachers, that there are strong stereotypic sex differences. One way to discern this hidden curriculum is suggested by the Project on the Status and Education of Women (1982), a division of the Association of American Colleges. They have published a brochure that can help students, educators, and administrators assess whether their classroom climate is "chilly" toward women.

Raphaela Best (1983) observed an elementary school for four years and concluded that there actually are three curricula of sex-role learning—the academic curricula, with its sexist materials and sex-typing of academic skills; the behavioral curricula, with different roles and activities for girls and boys; and the sexual curricula, with explorations of sexuality guided by different ideologies (for example, flirting for girls, and "getting it" for boys). The title of her book, *We've All Got Scars,* conveys her sense that elementary school experiences negatively affect both girls and boys.

Textbooks

The absence of women in textbooks is found increasingly through grade school, high school, and college. Weitzman and Rizzo (1974) found that women are rarely mentioned as important historical figures, as government leaders, or as great scientists. This stereotyping is most extreme in science textbooks, in which only 6% of the pictures include adult women. Even when a scientist like Marie Curie, who won two Nobel Prizes, is presented, her achievements are likely to be minimized. (One text described Madame Curie as a "helpmate" of her husband.) Even in college, there is a striking absence of women both in textbooks and in the curriculum (Banner, 1977). The absence of women in textbooks can encourage readers to view the field depicted, particularly science, as a prototypic masculine endeavor. This may discourage females from entering the particular fields being studied, thereby perpetuating the stereotypes portrayed.

Schau and Scott (1984) examined over 40 studies involving the effects of sex-typed and sex-neutral instructional materials. They concluded that most materials still are sexist and that they seriously affect the sex-role attitudes of students from elementary school through college. One way these materials affect students' attitudes is through the use of male generic language. As noted earlier in this chapter, use of such language results in gender associations that predominantly are male. In contrast, use of gender-specified language referring to both females and males seems to lead to the most gender-balanced associations. A second way instructional materials affect students' sex-role attitudes is through the portrayal of the sexes in stereotypical roles. Such exposure appears to increase sex-typed attitudes, especially among young children. In contrast, exposure to sex-equitable materials and to same-sex characters in nontraditional roles results in less sex-typed attitudes among students of all ages. This kind of attitude change increases with increased exposure to nonsexist materials. Other important findings of Schau and Scott were that exposure to sex-equitable materials does not decrease student interest in the materials, nor does it adversely affect either males' or females' comprehension of the material.

Clearly, textbooks need to be rewritten with the elimination of sexism in mind. California was one of the first states to take systematic action in this regard, passing a code in 1977 requiring a balancing of traditional and nontraditional activities for each sex in textbooks used in state schools. Because California purchases huge quantities of books, the state's code has had some impact in all states. Change is slow, however, since replacing texts is expensive. As was reviewed previously, even recent books incorporate stereotypes, although not to as great a degree as before. However, there are many supplementary materials now available to teachers to help them promote sex equity in the classroom (S. Klein, 1985).

Curricula

Who takes home economics? Who takes shop classes? Either formally or informally, the different curricula and activities prescribed for each sex are powerful conveyors of gender stereotypes. Beginning in kindergarten, activities usually are segregated by sex. Boys and girls play different games, form different lines, carry out different classroom tasks, and learn different things.

Different curriculum requirements for girls and boys, where they occur, serve automatically to limit the choices children can make both while they are in school and later in life. Although Title IX has broken institutionalized "tracking," many school systems, parents, and peers still exert informal pressure to keep it going. In 1978, a nationwide study (U.S. Department of Health, Education, & Welfare, 1979) found that girls represent 75% of the students in consumer and homemaking courses, occupational home economics, health, and office occupations. In contrast, boys represent 75% of the students in agricultural, technical, trade, and industrial programs. This tracking system keeps students from learning many skills needed in their home as well as in their occupational lives. For example, girls don't learn how to make home repairs, and boys don't learn cooking and domestic skills. The consequences of this tracking are particularly pernicious, since such tracking prepares females for only a few jobs, which have low status and low salaries.

The Education Amendments of 1976 to the Vocational Education Act of 1963 went into effect in October 1977. They are helping to change some of the inequities just discussed. The new law requires educational institutions to initiate programs to overcome sex discrimination and sex stereotyping in vocational education programs and to make all courses accessible to everyone. When given the opportunity, women do move into male-dominated, higher paying fields. For example, the number of bachelor degrees awarded women in the computer and information sciences area increased more than sixfold, from 4.6% in 1965 to 30% in 1980 ("College degrees," 1981; "Proportion of degrees," 1978).

Even traditional courses of study have been shown to suffer from and reflect a male bias (Fiske, 1981; Langland & Gove, 1981). Since the women's studies movement began in the late 1960s, traditional scholarship has been challenged, new findings discovered, academic fields revised, and textbooks rewritten. For example, history books traditionally have divided the past into periods based on men's lives— wars, political regimes, and so on. Yet women's lives and experiences typically have been neglected completely. This neglect can be seen in discussions of the Renaissance. This period usually has been viewed as a great step forward in terms of humanistic inquiry and values, yet it represented a step backward in the status of women (Kelly-Gadol, 1977). If half the population regressed, how can the time period legitimately be viewed as a rebirth for all? Yet changing the curricula is slow, because it involves the revision of nearly all the academic disciplines and typically meets with strong resistance.

How-to manuals for help in implementing such curriculum change projects are available (Fritsche, 1985). The kinds of changes that would decrease gender stereotyping have been of great concern. Guttentag and Bray (1975, 1977) set up a 6-week curriculum designed to make kindergarteners and fifth- and ninth-graders more flexible in their assumptions about the sexes in occupational, familial, and socioemotional roles. These researchers designed curricula with the different developmental concerns and cognitive levels of the three grades in mind. Students read stories, saw films, acted out plays, and worked on special projects to accomplish the study's goals. Teachers were trained to use the materials and to treat boys and girls equally. The results were mixed. Attitude change was found to be a function of grade level, student sex, teacher attitude, background variables, and the particular stereotypes highlighted. Kindergarteners decreased their occupational stereotypes but not the socioemotional ones. Girls were more willing than boys to accept the nonstereotyped ideas. Ninth-grade girls showed the greatest decrease in stereotyped attitudes; ninth-grade boys showed the greatest increase in stereotyped attitudes. The key factor seemed to be the degree to which the teacher implemented the curriculum effectively. With an enthusiastic teacher, even ninth-grade boys changed to nonstereotyped views in many areas.

This study, as well as many others (Best, 1983; Fox, 1981; Kahn & Richardson, 1983; Koblinsky & Sugawara, 1984), illustrate the complexity of the school environment as well as the potential for change. Changing curricula can be effective when implemented early and when the new curricula coincide with the teacher's attitudes. Modeling, however, may be more important than specific lessons in the acquisition and maintenance of gender stereotypes. For example, decreases in stereotypic knowledge and preferences by young children were greatest when a nonsexist curriculum was presented by a same-sex teacher (Koblinsky & Sugawara, 1984). Male teachers may be particularly effective in this regard, perhaps because males are perceived to be both more sex-stereotyped and more privileged.

Counseling

In a variety of ways, school counselors support gender stereotypes. They so do by their career and personal counseling orientations and by their use and interpretation of achievement tests.

Vocational Counseling. Until the 1970s, different tests, scores, and interpretations for boys and girls were used in counseling and testing for aptitudes and interests. For example, the Strong Vocational Interest Blank had separate male and female versions (printed on blue and pink forms, respectively) with different occupations for each sex. The revised Strong-Campbell Interest Inventory removes some of the sex bias but still uses single-sex criterion groups for some occupations, such as language teacher (female) and photographer (male). Other attempts to eliminate sex bias in interest measurement also have not been entirely successful, although they show promise (for example, Lunneborg, 1979).

In addition, the problem of interpretation remains. Counselors often interpret test results on the basis of sex and provide verbal and nonverbal messages that discourage the student from pursuing nontraditional careers. For example, Thomas and Stewart (1971) found that high school counselors rated female clients who expressed an interest in traditionally masculine occupations as being more in need of counseling than women with more traditional interests.

A greater number of females than males graduate from high school with generally higher grades. Yet, until the 1980s, fewer females than males have gone on to college. Such figures suggest that a sex bias was operating in career counseling (Harway, 1980; Harway & Astin, 1977). Still, as education level increases, the proportion of women decreases. In 1986, 50% of all B.A.'s and 53% of all M.A.'s were awarded to women, but only 37% of the Ph.D.'s and 32% of the first professional degrees were awarded that year to women (National Center for Education Statistics, 1985). University admission practices may contribute to these figures as well. There is some evidence that higher entrance examination scores and grade point averages have been required for women seeking admission than for men, at least in the past (Harway & Astin, 1977). Bias in financial aid awards also may contribute to fewer women in higher education. A study during the 1981–1982 academic year by the National Commission of Student Financial Assistance found that while women college students tend to need more student aid than their male counterparts, they typically do not get it (Project on the Status and Education of Women, 1984).

Black women in particular may suffer from both racial and sex bias in the area of vocational counseling (E. Smith, 1982). Although Black females have higher scholastic achievement at the high school level than Black males, by col-

lege, their educational and occupational aspirations are lower than those of Black males. Furthermore, their choices of careers are markedly gender stereotyped, particularly if they had gone to a predominantly White liberal arts high school as opposed to a more integrated vocational high school (Chester, 1983).

Even available vocational materials have some bias. Women on Words and Images (1975c) analyzed 100 nationally distributed career education materials. In the materials, they found that males dominate the depicted field of work—five males to every two females. In the work force, the ratio is actually less than three to two. The occupations presented for each sex, for the most part, also were traditional and stereotyped. For example, men were depicted in administrative jobs, whereas women were depicted in clerical jobs.

Achievement Testing. In addition to career counseling, counselors also are responsible for much of the achievement testing done in schools. In such tests, too, sex bias is present. Saario and colleagues (1973) found frequent stereotypic portrayals in the content of test questions. For example, women were typically homemakers; men, responsible workers. There also was sex bias in the language used in the tests. Analysis showed more frequent use of male pronouns and referents than female pronouns and referents, since male characters predominated. Such a masculine orientation in tests has been shown to depress the scores of many females, thereby giving an inaccurate picture of their abilities. As with the findings on textbooks, stereotypic portrayals in achievement tests, particularly in the mathematics sections, intensify as grade level rises. Similar bias exists in college admissions testing programs and may account partially for the poorer performance of the average female than the average male on the mathematics portions of these tests.

Sex bias on the part of counselors is not surprising, since it is so prevalent in society at large. An investigation of counselor training (Harway & Astin, 1977) revealed three potential sources of sexism: (1) of all counselor educators, 85% are men, (2) textbooks used in counselor training appear biased, and (3) there is a paucity of courses on counseling girls and women as a group with special needs. Counseling procedures, then, are another part of the school environment that demonstrates a male bias. In a related area, Lacher (1978) notes that on the college level as well, academic advisors traditionally have been insensitive to the special concerns of female undergraduates.

Organization

From the very organization of the school itself, students receive messages regarding gender-appropriate behaviors and career opportunities. What they observe are men in positions of authority—coordinators, principals, superintendents—and women in positions of subservience—teachers and aides. The percentage of male teachers generally rises with grade level, as does their status, and the percentage of female administrators decreases. In a nationwide survey of public schools in 1978, women were found to account for nearly 70% of all classroom teachers but only 10% of all school administrators ("Survey finds," 1979). In elementary schools, 89% of the teachers were women, while 82% of the principals were men. At the secondary level, 98.5% of the principals were male, as were 99.5% of school district superintendents. At the college and university level, 90% of the presidents were men in 1984 (Watkins, 1985). The number of women presidents doubled between 1975 and 1984. College campuses averaged one senior woman administrator apiece, and most were academic deans or deans of women or student affairs ("Women gaining," 1985).

The percentage of women on college faculties has remained low despite a great deal of talk about Affirmative Action. In 1982–1983, the percentage of women on college faculties was 27%, slightly higher than 22.5% in 1974–1975 (National Center for Education Statistics, 1983). As rank increases, the percentage of women decreases. The percentage of women faculty by rank can be seen in Table 8-2.

There are findings that female college teachers may be particularly important role models for female students in their choice of careers and in their productivity. Therefore, the small number of faculty females, especially in the higher ranks, is disturbing (Basow & Howe, 1980; Gilbert, 1985; Gilbert, Gallessich & Evans, 1983; Goldstein, 1979). Without viable female career role models, female students may be further limited in their recognition of the career alternatives open to them.

Atmosphere

The number of women teachers in a school contributes to the total school atmosphere. And the school atmosphere is another way in which gender messages get communicated.

Elementary school classrooms primarily are the province of female teachers. Some writers argue that the predominance of women, plus the emphasis on obedience and conformity instead of on more active learning, makes the early school environment a feminine one (Fagot, 1981a; Sugg, 1978). This feminine atmosphere may account for the many school difficulties that boys have, especially in the early years, since such an atmosphere goes

Table 8-2
Percentage of Women Faculty by Rank, 1975–1976, 1982–1983

Rank	1975–1976	1982–1983
Instructor	47.2	51.7
Assistant professor	26.0	36.1
Associate professor	17.0	22.0
Full professor	9.8	10.7

Data from National Center for Education Statistics, 1983.

counter to the socialization boys receive elsewhere. Researchers (Hill et al., 1974) have found that children do classify reading as a feminine subject. Best (1983) suggests that this incongruence between the student role and the sex role for boys contributes to their generally poorer academic performance. In high school and in college, the student role and the male sex role become more congruent because of the clearer linkage between academic achievement and future success. It is then that male academic performance substantially improves. The picture for females is nearly the reverse. In elementary school, there is no incongruence between the female sex role and the student role. Both roles require obeying adults and being orderly. Females, therefore, do well in elementary school. As school achievement becomes more competitive and linked to future career achievements, however, the two roles for females become increasingly incongruent. Females' academic performance consequently declines.

The thesis that elementary schools are feminine and that they "feminize" boys can be criticized on a number of grounds. Firstly, the writers who equate femininity with passivity and equate masculinity with activity tacitly accept stereotyped definitions of sex-role behavior. Secondly, there is much evidence, reviewed before, that boys actually receive more teacher approval, attention, and direct instruction than do girls. Thirdly, boys' poorer achievement in grade school may reflect the intense and often contradictory pressures on boys at that time. To be aggressive, independent, and athletic may be viewed as more important for a boy during grade school than is achievement.

There is some support for the idea that at the preschool level, more girls than boys may feel comfortable in school. The kinds of activities girls prefer (for example, doll play and art activities) appear to receive the most positive teacher reinforcement (Fagot, 1981a). These female-preferred behaviors were more closely associated with school performance than were those behaviors preferred by boys (for example, block and sandbox play). However, scholastic performance in later school years is better predicted by play with traditionally masculine ac-

tivities than by play with traditionally feminine activities. Thus the early school years may indeed emphasize "feminine" styles of play and behavior, although the benefits for girls are short-lived. Both sexes need to be encouraged to play with and experience a wide variety of toys and activities in the early school years.

Because most elementary school teachers are females, a question arises as to how much their gender influences the atmosphere of the classroom. Research with preschool teachers has found that male preschool teachers gave more positive comments to, and were more physical with, both boys and girls than were female teachers (Fagot, 1981a). However, the presence of male teachers has not been found to have major effects on boys' academic achievement, school adjustment, or gender identification (Gold & Reis, 1982; Pleck, 1981b). The most positive effects appear to be with very young boys. Girls do not seem to be affected by the presence of male teachers at all. The difficulty boys experience in school appears more related to the incompatible demands of the male sex role and the student role, rather than the sex of the teacher. Boys also are more likely than girls to enter school with information-processing difficulties and disturbing aggressive behaviors (Anastas & Reinharz, 1984). These two gender differences may make school a more difficult place for boys than girls.

At the college level, school atmosphere also may affect the behavior of students. At traditionally male-dominated colleges, especially those that went coed in the 1970s, women are urged to achieve at the same time as they are pressured to conform socially to the male-dominant style. Such pressures may lead to lower female achievement (Tidball, 1976). The campus climate outside the classroom appears to preserve, rather than reduce, gender stereotypic differences between women and men (Hall & Sandler, 1984). College women often are made to feel like interlopers or "guests" on campuses where the social life, health services, athletic opportunities, and so on are focused predominantly around male needs and male interests. Black women at predominantly White institutions suffer from the pressures of both racism and sexism (Fleming 1983; E.

Smith, 1982). Such women tend to be particularly self-reliant and assertive, whereas in predominantly Black colleges, the sex-role norms encourage a social passivity on the part of Black women.

Because of the sex-role pressures at coed institutions, many young women are choosing single-sex schools, which have been attracting greater numbers of applicants since 1975 (Hechinger, 1981; Ingalls, 1984). At those colleges, female role models abound because women now represent the majority of college presidents (71%) and of the tenured faculty (51%). Even at the high school level, single-sex schools for females may facilitate girls' learning in such predominantly "masculine" areas as science (Finn, 1980).

School, then, serves as a powerful socializing force, especially with regard to sex-role development. Another major force in some children's lives is religion.

Religion

To the extent that a child has any religious instruction, he or she receives further training in the gender stereotypes. Virtually all major religions of the world, including the Judeo-Christian religions dominant in America, have strong emphases on the two sexes acting in ways consistent with traditional patriarchal society (Daly, 1974; Fiorenza, 1983; Ruether, 1983).

In the Old Testament, God clearly is perceived as male, creating first a male human and then a female helpmate to be subservient to the male. The Adam and Eve story can be viewed as a rationalization of patriarchy. Because of Eve's gullibility and treachery, she brings about the downfall of Adam and of succeeding generations. Consequently, she is condemned to suffer childbirth, to work hard, and to be a faithful and submissive wife. In earlier versions of the Old Testament, however, God was depicted as creating a man (Adam) and a woman (Lilith) at the same time. Because Adam would not accord Lilith equal treatment, she went into exile, emerging, in later mythology, as the snake who tempts Eve (Cantor, 1983). Such a version of the Creation gives a picture of the status of the sexes that is very different from the one currently promulgated.

In various references throughout the Bible, females clearly are depicted as secondary to males and are often the subject of derogatory statements, especially about their reproductive functioning (for example, menstruating women are "unclean"). In the New Testament, a double image of woman as Madonna (Virgin Mary) or whore (Mary Magdalene) is conveyed with all its double messages about female sexuality. Feminists have been challenging the traditional interpretation of scriptures since at least the early 1800s. In 1895, Elizabeth Cady Stanton wrote *The Women's Bible*. More recently, feminists have expanded their critique not only to document and trace male ideological bias, but also to discover an alternative history and tradition that supports the inclusion and personhood of women (Fiorenza, 1985; Heschel, 1983; Ruether, 1985).

In the religious hierarchies, power and prestige have been reserved exclusively for males. Until recently, only males could be priests, ministers, rabbis. The Catholic Church still does not have female clergy, although Roman Catholic women now are participating in the Mass as lectors and in the distribution of the Eucharist. Nuns also are becoming more visible and involved with the community and there is a strong movement for equality in the Church (Vecsey, 1979). In various Protestant and Jewish sects, female clergy have made some headway—the first female cleric was ordained in 1970; first female rabbi, in 1972; first female Episcopal priest, in 1976. Their position, however, is still controversial, although their numbers are increasing.

The degree to which different religions afford women equality is related to both occupational choice and attitudes toward women held by college students (Rhodes, 1983). In a study of a nationwide sample of college students in 1973, those students who identified themselves as Seventh Day Adventists, Mormons, or Baptists, particularly if they were White, showed the greatest sex differences in occupational choices and disapproval of careers for married women. Those students who identified themselves as Quakers, Unitarians, or of no religious preference showed the fewest sex differences in those two areas. Thus religious training may affect gender-related attitudes and training, even if it is not, as John Wilson (1978) states, "the single most important shaper of sex roles" (p. 264).

Another recent change in male-dominated religious messages has been the rewriting of hymns, creeds, and prayers to remove sexist words. In 1983, *An Inclusive Language Lectionary*, put out by the National Council of Churches, was released. This book marked the first formal effort to revise Bible passages in order to eliminate patriarchal terminology and exclusively male metaphors for God. In substituting *humanity* for *mankind, community* for *fellowship, Creator* for *Father*, and *Father* and *Mother* for *God*, and so on, the new guidelines should go a long way in reducing the predominance of male imagery in religion. But, as Dr. Bruce Metzger of Princeton Theological Seminary, revision committee chairperson of the Revised Standard Version of the Bible (due in the late 1980s) has found, the committee cannot alter passages that reflect a historical situation in a "masculine-oriented" and "male-dominated" society ("New edition," 1977). Religions, as they currently exist, still reflect that male dominance and not all religious personnel want that dominance to change.

Employment

Children also perceive sex-role messages in the world around them, particularly with regard to what occupations people have. One key source of influence on children's future plans is the behavior of sex-role models. As has been noted above, the image children get from the media (TV, books, songs) and from school is one of men primarily as wage earners in a wide range of occupations and of women primarily as housewives and mothers. If women are employed, their range of occupations is extremely narrow. For example, in children's readers, males were depicted in 195 different occupations; females, in only 51, with one being a fat lady in a circus and another being a witch (Women on Words and Images, 1975b). These

images certainly can influence what a child considers appropriate for males and females to do. These depictions are not accurate, since more than half of all women are employed and more than 90% of all females will be employed at some point in their lives. Yet, real differences do exist in the occupations of women and men. This difference, too, influences children's future plans and their conception of gender-appropriate behavior.

As will be discussed in Chapter 11, women are concentrated in predominantly low-paying, low-status jobs. Even when women achieve high-status positions typically held by men, they still are often depicted stereotypically. Figure 8-5 is an example of a newspaper's stereotyped portrayal of female politicians.

Children see the small number of women in certain professions and the small number of men in certain others and draw conclusions about which jobs are appropriate for themselves. In addition, seeing men in the higher-status, better paying jobs also affects children's conceptions of the status of the sexes. Since this is in line with other messages the child receives, it strengthens his or her gender stereotypes.

One reflection of the images of the sexes that children receive is the finding that adolescents, both female and male, White and Black, have nearly three times more heroes than heroines (Balswick & Ingoldsby, 1982). Athletes and actors were the most popular category of heroes. The only type of heroine that ranked high were family members, perhaps a comment on the images of women presented by the outside world compared to "real" women at home.

One result of these varied images of employed women and men is the finding that young children starting in preschool show sex typing of occupations both in general and for themselves (Franken, 1983). Such sex-typed choices are more characteristic of boys than of girls, of children from lower- to lower-middle-class schools than of children from middle- to upper-middle-class schools, and of younger (preschool) than of older (fifth-grade) children. Thus, as other research has found, girls appear to be broadening their own horizons as well as their images of men and women in the labor force. Boys, unfortunately, are lagging behind

Wynona Lipman

Pretty political

Time was when the presence — the mere presence — of a woman in the chambers of the State Legislature caused considerable raising of eyebrows, if not downright alarm.

But times, fortunately, have changed in Trenton and elsewhere around the nation's state capitol buildings.

When eyebrows are raised today, it may well be a woman legislator raising her own — such as in the case of Sen. Wynona Lipman (D-Essex).

And before New Jersey's lawmakers begin another day of debate and demur, it's not uncommon to witness typically feminine gestures from these assemblywomen:

Barbara Curran (R-Union) applying lipstick; Mary Scanlon (D-Essex) powdering her nose; Jane Burgio (R-Essex) combing her bangs, and Marie Muhler (R-Monmouth) applying a fresh scent of perfume.

Barbara Curran

Marie Muhler

Mary Scanlon

Jane Burgio

Photos by Edward N. Stiso

Figure 8-5

Stereotyped portrayal of female politicians. (From
The Newark Star-Ledger, *May 16, 1978, p. 15. Reprinted by permission.)*

and may need greater help to overcome their sex-typed images of the world.

Summary

What is most striking from this review of socializing forces is the consistency of the gender stereotypes conveyed. Through the structure of the English language itself, through play activities, media depictions, the school environment, religious messages, and career models, the two sexes are depicted as differing widely in behavior and status. Females typically are characterized as unimportant, incompetent, passive, and nurturant homebodies and homemakers; males, as important, competent, active, and aggressive wage earners and athletes. Throughout a child's developing years, these images are emphasized through continuous repetition. With this type of socialization, the high degree of concordance found regarding the gender stereotypes is understandable. Everyone knows and agrees with the stereotypes despite the fact that there are few actual sex differences in behaviors and attitudes.

Recommended Reading

Butler, M., & Paisley, W. (Eds.) (1980). *Women and the mass media: Sourcebook for research and action.* Beverly Hills, Calif.: Sage. A thorough discussion of sexism in media content and structure. Includes suggestions for change.

Fiorenza, E. S. (1985). *Bread not stone: The challenge of feminist biblical interpretation.* Boston: Beacon. One of a number of excellent revisionary accounts of Christianity. The argument is made that the Bible should be read as a historical document that must be reassessed and evaluated from a feminist perspective.

Hall, R. M., & Sandler, B. R. (1984). *Out of the classroom: A chilly campus climate for women?* (1982). Washington, D.C.: Association of American Colleges. This report, together with its predecessor, *The classroom climate: A chilly one for women?,* provides a concise overview of how higher education negatively affects women. Both reports include self-evaluation checklists.

Langland, E., & Gove, W. (Eds.) (1981). *A feminist perspective in the academy: The difference it makes.* Chicago: University of Chicago Press. An excellent summary of the contributions women's studies have made to several academic disciplines.

Stein, P. J., & Hoffman, S. (1978). Sports and male role strain. *Journal of Social Issues, 34* (1), 136–150. An interesting discussion of how the emphasis on sports for males produces role strain for athletes and nonathletes alike.

Thorne, B., Kramarae, C., & Henley, N. (Eds.) (1983). *Language, gender, and society.* Rowley, Mass.: Newbury House. Ten clearly written and perceptive studies that analyze the politics of language. Annotated bibliography.

Part 3: Summary

In Part Three, an answer to the question of how gender stereotypes are acquired has been explored on two levels—historical derivations and current socialization practices. Initially, the stereotypes arose from the division of labor by sex in previous societies as a function of the subsistence base of the society, the supply of labor, and the functional requirements of childbearing. Even though a division of labor is no longer functional or even practical, the stereotypes remain.

In each generation, a child experiences, from the moment of birth, socialization pressures based on her or his sex that, in most cases, incorporate the gender stereotypes. From parents, teachers, and peers and from the social forces of language, play, media, school, religion, and work, the child develops a gender schema and acquires a gender identity. This socialization process occurs through direct reinforcement, modeling, and imitation, as a function of the cognitive development of the child, and as a function of the gender distinctions the child's society makes. Boys, especially, receive intense socialization pressures and are particularly strongly sex typed.

The consequences of such rigid sex-role images are numerous and, as will be shown in Part Four, almost overwhelmingly negative. This does not mean that children should not form a separate and distinct gender identity. Clearly, they need to do so as part of their developing self-identity and for future reproductive functioning, if they so choose. But, as Money and Ehrhardt (1972) note, nature supplies the basic, irreducible elements of sex differences (women can menstruate, gestate, and lactate; men, impregnate). Sharply differing behaviors for the two sexes are simply unnecessary to accomplish the goal.

Provided that a child grows up to know that sex differences are primarily defined by the reproductive capacity of the sex organ, and to have a positive feeling of pride in his or her own genitalia and their ultimate reproductive use, then it does not much matter whether various childcare, domestic, and vocational activities are or are not interchangeable between mother and father [Money & Ehrhardt, 1972, p. 14].

What is being argued here is that rigid sex typing is neither necessary nor functional to the individual, to her or his relationships, or to society as a whole. Part Four will discuss these consequences in detail.

Part 4
Consequences of Gender Stereotypes

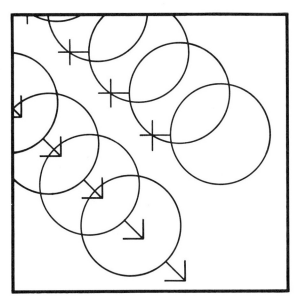

In the preceding chapters, the development of the gender stereotypes and their transmittal to successive generations were shown to occur despite little demonstrable support for the existence of the traits depicted by the stereotypes. Except for aggressive behavior and for mathematical and verbal abilities, the sexes differ very little during childhood; indeed, there appear to be more differences *among* members of a sex than *between* the sexes. Yet, once the stereotypes and gender identity are acquired by age 5 or 6, certain sex differences sometimes do emerge. Because the acquisition of gender stereotypes by a child occurs through individual instruction, interpersonal observation, and more generalized social forces, it is important to examine the consequences of the gender stereotypes on these three levels—that is, on the personal, interpersonal, and societal levels.

Even if the existence and knowledge of the stereotypes—what females and males are "supposed to be" like—do not change behavior, they can have many consequences. As will be shown in the next four chapters, the effects of the stereotypes are far-reaching and, for the most part, are negative to both females and males. Some of these negative consequences are a result of trying to live out the stereotyped sex roles to some degree. Other negative consequences are a result of the inconsistencies between actual behavior and characteristics, and expected sex-role behaviors and characteristics. Thus both gender stereotypes and stereotyped sex roles frequently result in unpleasant consequences.

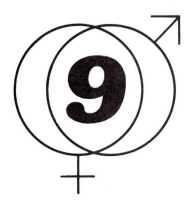

Individual Consequences

The effects of gender stereotypes can be seen most clearly on the individual level. The stereotypes affect an individual's self-concept, behavior, mental health, and physical health. In fact, there is almost no aspect of human functioning that the gender stereotypes do not, in some way, affect.

Self-Concept

A great golf course is like a good woman. Beautiful . . . and a little bit Bitchy.

—advertisement in a golf magazine

The quotation above reveals one concept of womanhood. Such conceptions of the sex roles are important insofar as they relate to an individual's *self-concept*—the way in which individuals view themselves. This concept incorporates several other concepts: (1) how one thinks of oneself, known by the term *self-esteem,* which itself incorporates self-acceptance and self-regard, (2) an estimate of one's abilities, referred to as *self-confidence,* and (3) a sense of control over one's life, including the *attributions* that one makes, called *locus of control.* These three aspects of self-concept—self-esteem, self-confidence, and locus of control—will be examined in some detail below, with the concept of the *ideal self* considered as incorporated within self-esteem. Other aspects of self-concept, such as self-image and body image, will not be discussed specifically. Findings in these last two areas, as well as in the areas that will be discussed, indicate that, overall, females have a somewhat more negative self-concept than do males (Loeb & Horst, 1978; Wise & Jay, 1982).

Because the gender stereotypes contain more negative characteristics of females than of males, as seen in this chapter's opening quote, such a finding of lower female self-concept should not be surprising. Yet it would not be correct to assume that all females have a more negative self-concept than all males in all situations. These findings depend on whether the sexes are comparing themselves to members of the same sex or to the other sex, on methodological variations in measuring the self-concept, and on what task is involved. A major variable in the findings concerns which aspect of the self-concept is being tapped—self-esteem, self-confidence, or locus of control.

Self-Esteem

When self-esteem (the degree of negative or positive regard one has for oneself) is examined, the sexes show surprisingly few differences. After examining a broad range of studies that used standardized paper-and-pencil questionnaires, a number of researchers have concluded that males and females, from kindergarten to college, generally indicate equivalent levels of self-esteem (Lerner, Sorell, & Brackney, 1981; Loeb & Horst, 1978; Maccoby & Jacklin, 1974). This is surprising, because society seems to value men so much more than it values women. How then can females think of themselves equally as positively as do males? The answer involves four possibilities: developmental differences, different standards, sex typing, and the nature of the tests used.

Developmental Differences. There is some indication that, starting in late elementary school, males may score increasingly higher than females in self-esteem. For example, beginning in the late 1970s, 900 students were interviewed every year from sixth to tenth grades to determine their level of self-esteem

(Schmich, 1984). By the time they reached seventh grade, fully half of the girls had low self-esteem compared with only a third of the boys. Similar results had been found in another study ten years earlier. These results support the hypothesis that during adolescence, girls start receiving conflicting messages about achievement and popularity, and this causes them to doubt themselves. Of course, it also is possible that boys inflate their self-esteem scores, whereas girls may not do so. This hypothesis concerning inflated scores is supported by the finding that, although fourth- and fifth-grade boys rated themselves higher in self-esteem than did their female classmates, teachers of these students rated the girls as higher in behaviors related to self-esteem. (Loeb & Horst, 1978). (Problems with the measurement instrument will be commented upon below.) In general, studies that use different age samples may obscure possible sex differences.

Different Standards. Another reason males and females do not differ in their levels of self-esteem may be because of their use of different standards for themselves; that is, females may compare themselves to the ideal female and males compare themselves to the ideal male, rather than both sexes comparing themselves to some absolute standard. In this case, both sexes would be accepting the roles society has assigned them and thus would have equal self-esteem.

The *ideal self* does seem to differ slightly for men and women. A number of researchers have compared self-descriptions of college students with their descriptions both of the typical female or male, and/or of the ideal female or male (Deseran & Falk, 1982; Lerner et al., 1981; D. Scher, 1984; Silvern & Ryan, 1983). When given either a free choice or a list of descriptors, females and males generally describe themselves relatively similarly and relatively androgynously. Similar results have been found for men and women age 60 and older (Sinott, 1984). The "ideals" of both sexes also tend toward androgyny, although college men picture the ideal man as having more masculine than feminine attributes. Yet for both sexes, the "typical man" and "typical woman" were described as relatively sex-typed. Thus,

there do seem to be different standards that the sexes may use to evaluate themselves, especially if they are using the typical member of their sex as a referent. Furthermore, for women as a group, self and ideal descriptions generally match, but for men as a group, self-descriptions were lower on instrumental traits than they had considered ideal. This self-ideal discrepancy may lead some males to have lower or more defensive self-esteem than women in some areas.

Self-esteem among Black adolescents may be complicated further by whether the ideal self-standard of comparison is based on Black or White norms. As discussed in Chapter 1, the gender stereotypes held by Whites and Blacks vary somewhat, with generally fewer sex differences expected by Blacks than Whites. In predominantly White institutions, gender stereotypes held by Whites may be the norm. Supporting this hypothesis is Chester's (1983) finding that in predominantly White liberal arts high schools, the self-esteem of Black females is significantly lower than that of Black males, whereas in a more racially integrated vocational high school, the sexes did not differ in self-esteem level. Overall, however, Black and White students generally do not differ from each other in global self-esteem (Jenkins, 1982; Porter & Washington, 1979).

In general, there is evidence that adolescents who feel successful in the realm they consider appropriate (sociability for many girls; achievement, leadership, and strength for many boys) have high levels of self-esteem (Hodgson & Fischer, 1981; Tucker, 1983a, 1983b). What the person views as central to her or his self-concept is important. With adults, these personal standards may not correspond to the gender stereotypes.

The key to understanding this area of self-concept seems to be to take into account both the discrepancy between the real and ideal self-concept and the salience of sex roles in the individual (Garnets & Pleck, 1979). Thus, for those for whom sex roles are important, gender conformity should be related to self-esteem. For those for whom sex roles are not that salient, there may be no relationship. Research has not yet examined the importance of sex-role salience as related to self-esteem.

Sex Typing. A number of studies have investigated the relationship between sex typing and self-esteem. In general, the more instrumental ("masculine") characteristics that are present, the higher the individual's self-esteem. There is some developmental trend in this regard.

In high school, self-esteem appears correlated with sex-typed role performance, especially for females (Connell & Johnson, 1970; Hodgson & Fischer, 1981). However, by late adolescence, self-esteem appears correlated mainly with instrumental, agentic traits. This means that androgynous individuals—those who score high on both instrumental and expressive traits—along with masculine-sex-typed individuals (both male and female) have the highest self-esteem (Gauthier & Kjervik, 1982; Hoffman & Fidell, 1979; Kimlicka, Cross, & Tarnai, 1983; Spence & Helmreich, 1978; Zeldow, Clark, & Daugherty, 1985). (See Whitley, 1983, for a meta-analytic review of such research.) Feminine-sex-typed women have significantly lower self-esteem than do androgynous and masculine groups. The "undifferentiated" individual (low on instrumental and expressive traits) appears to have the lowest level of self-esteem. This pattern has been found in other cultures as well (Basow, in press; Carlson & Baxter, 1984).

Although there are a number of methodological and situational factors that affect the relationship between sex typing and self-esteem (Flaherty & Dusek, 1980; Heilbrun, 1981; Whitley, 1983), the beneficial effect of agentic instrumental traits is clear, especially as an individual matures. This relationship between agentic instrumental traits and self-esteem may reflect societal values on agentic, as opposed to communal or expressive, qualities. The strong relationship between sex typing and self-esteem may serve to obviate sex differences in this area.

Test Instrument. Another possible explanation of the equal self-esteem levels found for females and males may lie in the test instrument itself. As Deaux (1976) reports, the questions used on self-esteem scales generally contain two distinct classes of items: those tapping *self-acceptance,* the degree to which one accepts oneself as one is, and *self-regard,* the degree to which one actively affirms one's worth and abilities. If females score higher on the former items and males score higher on the latter items, then their total scores would be equal, even though they are responding positively to different items. There is some indirect support for this interpretation.

Females generally make more realistic estimates of their abilities and have lower aspirations than do males (Erkut, 1983; Gitelson, Petersen, & Tobin-Richards, 1982; Stake, 1983). Using another indirect measure of self-esteem—how much people pay themselves for work done—a number of researchers have found that females, from first-graders through college students, consistently paid themselves less than did their male counterparts, at least when no social comparison information was available (Callahan-Levy & Messe, 1979; Kahn, O'Leary, Krulewitz, & Lamm, 1980; Major & Adams, 1983; Major, McFarlin, & Gagnon, 1984). These findings together suggest that females may have higher self-acceptance and lower self-regard than do males, at least as related to the abilities measured. Males, in contrast to females, have higher expectations of their abilities and tend to overestimate them, suggesting a higher self-regard and lower self-acceptance. One possible conclusion from these studies then is that although the sexes do not seem to differ in overall level of self-esteem as measured by questionnaires, the bases for self-esteem may be different and may be related to sex roles.

Other evidence supporting the hypothesis that the sexes have different bases for self-esteem comes from two studies by Stake (1979; Stake & Orlofsky, 1981). After reviewing factor analytic studies of self-esteem measures, Stake concluded that self-esteem is multidimensional, made up of at least two factors: performance and social self-esteem. Using a new scale to measure these two factors in a college sample, these researchers found that sex-typing differences overshadowed gender differences on both performance and social self-esteem. "Masculinity" scores correlated significantly with performance self-esteem whereas "femininity" scores correlated significantly with social self-esteem. Thus, sex-typed individuals may base their self-esteem on different qualities and behaviors. In summary, the sexes may have different bases for self-esteem, but this conclusion depends on how the bases of self-esteem are defined. When self-regard is a basis, sex differences usually occur.

Self-Confidence and Expectations

The research on self-regard, at least as related to task expectancy, is part of a considerable body of research on self-confidence. It is in this area that striking sex differences are observed. Males, on the average, consistently predict, over a wide range of ages and tasks, that they will do better than females predict for themselves (Erkut, 1983; Gitelson et al., 1982; Gold, Brush, & Sprotzer, 1980; McMahan, 1982; Vollmer, 1984). This gender difference becomes evident after the third grade.

Males in general have higher expectations of themselves and more confidence than do females in general, although this pattern may not hold among Black adolescents (E. Smith, 1982). This tendency leads many males to overestimate their abilities. However, it is also likely that it leads them to attempt more tasks. Such attempts give them more opportunities to increase their skill and to be rewarded. Females, who tend to underestimate their ability, may take themselves out of the running, refraining from attempting or continuing with new activities, thereby limiting their world and potential. It is important to note, however, that, although the sexes predict different levels of performance, there is little difference in actual performance. For example, Wallace and Richardson (1984) found that high self-confidence ratings in fourth- and sixth-grade boys correlated significantly with good performance in a competitive situation; for their female peers, self-confidence and performance were unrelated. Yet there was no sex difference in actual performance. Differences appear then only in how the two sexes think and feel about their performance. Many girls seem to exaggerate negative aspects of a situation; boys, the positive aspects (Donelson, 1977a). Indeed, in many ways, the aspirational level of boys seems much

less tied to situational factors, such as past performance and performance feedback, than does the aspirational level of girls (Monahan, 1983). This may result in very real differences in the way the sexes evaluate current behavior and in the way they derive their expectancies of future performance. For example, in a study of more than 3000 students at six top universities in the Northeast, women were found to underestimate consistently their academic ability and to have lower career aspirations than men, even though the grades of the women and men were relatively equivalent ("College Women," 1978).

The nature of the task used in testing is critical in laboratory studies. Because most experimental tasks are masculine in orientation—that is, related to the masculine stereotype, such as achievement—it is not surprising that males have higher expectancies of their abilities and that females have lower expectancies. O'Leary (1974) summarizes research that shows a positive relationship between self-esteem and exhibition of gender-appropriate behavior. To the extent that an individual's self-esteem has incorporated the gender stereotypes, it is likely that that individual would be hesitant to engage in gender-inappropriate behavior. Research has found that sex differences in level of aspiration are strongest on tasks that are labeled "masculine" or that appear to be male-appropriate, such as tasks requiring spatial ability (Gitelson et al., 1982; Lenney, 1981; McMahan, 1982; Mednick, Carr, & Thomas, 1983). This pattern appears to be true for Blacks as well as for Whites. Even tasks neutral on sex typing show a sex difference in level of aspiration. However, when the task is labeled "feminine" or is female-linked, women frequently expect to do as well as men expect to. The fact that women don't make higher predictions than do men may reflect the "masculine" nature of competency and achievement themselves. This may explain why in some research, even a "feminine" task or topic does not eliminate the more typical sex difference in self-confidence (Lippa & Beauvais, 1983).

An example of how sex differences in self-confidence manifest themselves in response to situational factors is a recent study of 627 female and male graduate students in science, engineering, and medicine at Stanford University ("Graduate," 1985). This study found that the women feel less self-confident and less sure of their ability than their male counterparts. Yet, the women's qualifications were equal, if not better, than the men's. An important factor was the presence of other women in their field. In departments where women were present in the largest number (biological and medical sciences), the women demonstrated the least amount of self-doubt and reticence to assert themselves.

Thus, although females appear to have a set of lowered generalized expectancies about their achievement potential, it would be inaccurate to conclude that females always have less self-confidence than males in all achievement situations. As we have seen, situational variables, such as specific ability area, availability of performance feedback, and the emphasis on social comparison, all affect females' self-confidence in such situations (Kimball & Gray, 1982; Lenney, 1981; Lenney, Gold, & Browning, 1983; Monahan, 1983; Stake, 1983). When the ability tapped relates to feminine behaviors (such as social skills), or is simply labeled as "feminine," no sex difference in self-confidence in achievement settings is found. Similarly, sex differences generally disappear when clear performance feedback is available or when social comparison is not made salient.

While the sex difference in self-confidence is consistent and stable under certain conditions, its antecedents are unclear. One reason for this discrepancy may be a result of differential reinforcement history for females and males. Males may be rewarded for being confident; females may be rewarded for being modest about their abilities. Or this difference between the sexes in self-confidence may be caused by differential sensitivity to rewards and punishments on the part of females and males. A third possibility to account for the difference may be linked to the different cultural norms that permit females more than males to admit to low self-confidence. Evidence was reviewed in Part Three supporting all these factors, the most powerful of which is the first—namely, the differential behavior on the part of the major socializing agents in line with the gender stereotypes (Parsons et al., 1976). For change to occur, then, the female stereotype

must be divested at the most basic level—the family—of its implied incompetence. To do this requires deliberate efforts by parents not to reinforce the stereotypes and not to give subtle cues that convey lower expectancies for girls than for boys, such as showing excessive concern for girls' safety. Parents also must give appropriate feedback and strategies for improving performances and provide competent female models.

In general, the research on expectancies demonstrates that females have lower self-confidence than do males, especially in male-oriented situations and activities. This pattern could contribute to a negative self-image in some females.

Locus of Control and Attributions

If you were given a choice between playing a game of luck, such as a "one-armed bandit" slot machine, or a game of skill, such as darts, which would you choose? Deaux and colleagues (1975) found that nearly 75% of the men studied chose a game described as requiring skill, whereas only 35% of the women did so. Women preferred games of chance, suggesting that they see themselves as less skilled than men and as having less control over the outcomes of their behavior.

Other research on *locus of control* (the expectation that one's behavior will lead to desirable goals and reinforcements) has found similar results (Johnson & Black, 1981; Lefcourt, 1976). The generally external locus-of-control orientation of females is associated with feelings of helplessness, with an avoidance of task-oriented behaviors, with fear of success, and with a preference for situations where luck, rather than one's degree of skill, determines the outcome (Savage, Stearns, & Friedman, 1979).

A recent longitudinal examination of locus of control in four large representative national samples of women and men aged 14–59 found that women of all ages became strikingly more external than men in their locus of control in the mid-1970s (Doherty & Baldwin, 1985). This divergence between the sexes in locus of control may be due to the fact that by the mid-1970s, women had become aware of the many external constraints (for example, discrimination) on their ability to achieve their goals in the labor force and elsewhere. Such awareness may explain why Blacks typically tend to show a different attribution pattern than do Whites. (*Attribution pattern* refers to the reasons given as to why something happened.) More Black adolescents than White adolescents appear to construe control as a mixture of both internal and external factors, rather than as one or the other. Black females, in particular, are likely to construe control as a mixture, perhaps an accurate reflection of real constraints imposed as a function of race and sex (Brown, Fulkerson, Furr, Ware, & Voight, 1984; Lykes, Stewart, & LaFrance, 1981).

The findings of sex differences in the area of locus of control and attribution patterns depend, to a large extent, on such personal variables as age, sex typing, and race of the individual, and on such situation variables as the performance outcome (success or failure), and the gender of an opponent. For example, although sex differences in attribution patterns usually have been found for adults and adolescents, they generally have not been found among very young children (Cotten-Huston & Lunney, 1983). Subject sex typing also has been linked to attributional pattern, with some studies finding a relationship between "masculinity" and internal locus of control, especially for males (Crombie, 1983; Hoffman & Fidell, 1979; Johnson & Black, 1981; Lee & Scheurer, 1983; Zeldow et al., 1985).

Whether a person has succeeded or failed at a task may be the most important situational variable affecting locus of control and attribution of control. Table 9-1 illustrates the three dimensions most frequently used to classify causal attributions for success and failure—whether the cause is seen as due to internal or external factors, to controllable or uncontrollable factors, or to stable or unstable factors.

In general, many females, especially Black females, tend to attribute their successes to external causes, like luck, or to unstable internal causes, like effort. In contrast, failures tend to be attributed to lack of ability or to another stable cause (Brown et al., 1984; Crombie, 1983; Erkut, 1983; Gitelson et al., 1982; McMahan, 1982; Stipek, 1984). For example, when students are asked why they received a 90 on a test, females are more likely than males to say they were lucky, that the test was easy, that the teacher liked them, or that they studied very hard. Males are more likely to say they received such a high grade because they knew the material or because they were smart. In contrast, when a low grade is received, females are more likely to say it was because they didn't know the material or were "dumb," whereas males are more likely to say it was because the test was unfair, the teacher didn't like them, or

Table 9-1

Three-Way Classification of Causal Attributions

	Attributions	
	Internal	External
	Controllable	
Stable	Effort (stable)	Others help or interfere consistently
Unstable	Effort (temporary state)	Others help or interfere in this situation only
	Uncontrollable	
Stable	Ability	Task ease or difficulty
Unstable	Fatigue	Luck

Adapted from Wittig, 1985.

because they didn't try. These tendencies are evident throughout the school years and become particularly striking in adolescence.

With the type of attribution process described above (attributing success to unstable or external factors and failure to lack of ability), it is very difficult for some females to feel good about themselves. Without taking credit for their successes, females cannot increase their self-confidence. With continued personal blame for their failures, females can only decrease their self-confidence further. Dweck and colleagues (1980) found that girls showed greater discouragement than boys after failure both in a laboratory and in a classroom setting. This discouragement continued despite changes in the task and the teacher. Such a generalized low expectancy may lead to withdrawal from achievement situations, when possible, for many females. For example, Brewer and Blum (1979) found that feminine-sex-typed, female college freshmen felt less control over their achievement in mathematics and science than did male respondents or androgynous females. This lack of control on the part of "feminine" females was translated into a low expectancy of success in math and science courses. This low expectancy might discourage persistence and lead to fewer women enrolled in math and science courses. Supporting this hypothesis is the finding that at Harvard University, only half the women who planned to major in science actually did so ("Female science," 1984). In contrast, more than two-thirds of the men who planned to major in science did so, despite the fact that the women and men had similar SAT scores and academic backgrounds. A suggestive finding is that the women were more likely than men to blame themselves for difficulty in class work.

In contrast to the characteristic attribution pattern of many females, the attribution pattern of many males (attributing success to ability and failure to external causes) is very protective. In the face of failure, this attribution pattern protects a person's self-confidence and self-image; in response to success, this pattern increases a person's self-confidence and self-image. However, this pattern may have nega-

tive consequences, too, by making it difficult for many males to learn from their mistakes or to admit failure. For example, some researchers have found males, in general, to be more defensive than females following failure in sports events (Croxton & Klonsky, 1982). Another negative consequence of this pattern for many males is their increasing frustration when they discover that they have less ability than they had assumed. A male may unrealistically expect to receive a 90 on a test and be extremely disturbed and frustrated when a 70 is received instead. This frustration itself may have serious negative consequences, such as increased aggressive behavior.

Yet, such an attribution pattern does serve to increase males' continued striving. This, in turn, increases the probability of future success. Given the pressure on males to achieve, their self-protective attitude is facilitative. Furthermore, if males do have an internality bias, attributing most consequences both positive and negative to themselves, as some research suggests (Frieze, Whitley, Hanusa, and McHugh, 1982; Sweeney, Moreland, & Gruber, 1982), then their feeling of control and power would be enhanced. Girls deliberately need to be taught to attribute their success to internal and stable causes, such as their ability, rather than to be taught to be "modest." (Women apparently think it makes a better impression on others to make more modest attributions for success [Berg, Stephan, & Dodson, 1981]). Girls likewise need to be taught to attribute their failures to unstable yet controllable causes, like lack of effort.

Such attributions *can* be taught (Dweck, 1975). However, it is important to note that although sex-related attribution patterns frequently are found, especially males' preference for ability attributions and general reluctance to use luck attributions, the size of the sex difference is small in magnitude and not always found (Croxton et al., 1984; Frieze et al., 1982; Sohn, 1982). Furthermore, the number of situational, methodological, and personal factors affecting the attribution patterns is large (Kaufman & Shikiar, 1985; Levine, Gilman, & Reis, 1982; McHugh, Frieze, & Hanusa, 1982;

Travis, Burnett-Doering, & Reid, 1982; Wittig, 1985). For example, some research suggests that apparent sex differences in attribution patterns really are sex differences in self-presentational goals, or in sex-role norms, or occur only among low expectancy or low ability students. Thus it is important to examine aspects of female and male achievement behavior other than attribution patterns in order to fully understand sex differences in this area.

Summary

The picture drawn with respect to the consequences of the gender stereotypes on males' and females' self-concepts suggests that females, in general, tend to have a more negative image of themselves than do males; they have less self-regard, less self-confidence, and less feeling of responsibility for their successes. This negative self-concept is offset by their being more self-acceptant than are males. Males, on the other hand, tend to have a very positive, though somewhat unrealistic, self-image. They have a high regard for themselves, are overconfident of their abilities, feel responsible for their successes, and attribute their failures to external causes. They are, however, notably less self-acceptant. These varying self-concepts on the part of the sexes have direct consequences for behavior and for evaluation of others.

Behavior

Gender stereotypes, even if we do not conform to them, affect us directly as *standards* of behavior. They also affect us indirectly through effects on our self-concept. One consequence of the stereotypes can be seen in the flexibility of our behavior—that is, how comfortable and effective we are in engaging in a wide variety of behaviors. A more specific consequence of the stereotypes is the manner in which we engage in certain behaviors. One area of behavior that has been the focus of much study has been the area of achievement and achievement motivation. This area will be examined first, followed

by a review of the research on behavioral flexibility.

Achievement

History books amply demonstrate that women have not been considered major contributors to Western Civilization beyond their role of reproduction and family matriarch. Although the reasons for this fact may lie in the biases of historians themselves, in institutionalized sexism, in the lack of effective means of birth control, and in other social forces, at least one reason may lie within the individual herself. The reason most often suggested for the discrepancy in achievement level between females and males is that females do not have as great a *need for achievement* as do males.

In school, girls generally outperform boys in all subjects. These differences narrow from elementary school to high school to college (Maccoby & Jacklin, 1974; Stewart, 1976). In high school, girls fall behind in certain subjects, including social studies, mathematics, science, and citizenship. Although more girls graduate from high school than do boys, fewer go on to college, and still fewer go on to graduate and professional schools. Because there is no evidence that the sexes differ in intelligence, differences in school achievement more likely point to personality and social factors. Boys may find the student role incompatible with the stereotyped male role during childhood but find it increasingly compatible with the male role during adolescence. At that time, its linkage with occupational success becomes stronger and clearer. The reverse may be true for females, who are often actively discouraged from planning careers (Katz, 1979; Locksley & Douvan, 1979).

Do men have a greater need for achievement than do women? Since the original work of McClelland and associates in 1953 on achievement motivation as measured by projective techniques, a vast amount of data has accumulated showing that males and females have equal amounts of motivation to achieve (Maccoby & Jacklin, 1974; Veroff et al., 1980). The lack of sex differences in need for achievement has been noticeable particularly since the late 1960s. In two representative national surveys of adults regarding basic motives, one in 1957 and one in 1976, Veroff and colleagues (1980) found that the motive for achievement in women had increased while the same motive for men remained stable.

Strong sex differences emerge, however, when achievement behavior is examined as a function of the achievement motive. The results of studies with males on the relationship between need for achievement and achievement behavior have been theoretically consistent. Yet, results with females show a contradictory and confusing picture. For example, males increase their need-for-achievement imagery as a function of "arousing" appeals to competence and mastery (McClelland, Atkinson, Clark, & Lowell, 1953); females do not increase in the same way (Lesser, Kravitz, & Packard, 1963; Veroff, Wilcox, & Atkinson, 1953). Male achievement behavior is a direct function of motive to achieve, expectancy of the consequences of success, and the value attached to such consequences; female achievement behavior is not a direct function of these factors (Atkinson & Feather, 1966).

As a result of the failure of many women to conform to the proposed theoretical model of achievement behavior, they simply were neglected from study for many years (an example of the sexist nature of science). More recently, however, sufficient data have accumulated that throw light on achievement motivation and achievement behavior in many females. The recent studies focus on problems with measurement, competing needs, fear of success, gender-appropriate behavior, and definitions of achievement.

Measurement. The standard measurement of achievement motivation has been based on projective techniques, such as stories about a picture card, has been scored using a system developed on male data, and has been collected in response to male competitive cues (O'Leary, 1974). Thus, it is not surprising that such measures do not predict well for many females, because many females may operate under a different definition of achievement than do many males. In addition, Entwisle (1972), summarizing the research on such projectives,

found that the scoring categories did not cover the full range of the women's responses. This possibly may lower intercorrelations. Furthermore, the projective measure's low reliability (.30 to .40) may account for its lack of predictive validity.

Helmreich and Spence (1978) developed a nonprojective questionnaire (Work and Family Orientation Questionnaire) to measure achievement motivation and aspiration. In their instrument, achievement motivation is conceived of as four factors: Mastery (preference for challenging tasks), Work Orientation (desire to work hard), Competitiveness (enjoyment of interpersonal competition), and Personal Unconcern (lack of concern over others' reactions to one's success). McClelland (1980) argues that such an instrument taps achievement values rather than the more unconscious need for achievement. In any case, validity studies have been impressive. The pattern of motives or values most conducive to actual achievement, as measured by grades, salaries, and so on, is high Mastery and Work Orientation and low Competitiveness, at least in the United States. In other cultures, different patterns may exist (Basow, 1984b; Helmreich & Spence, 1978; Spence & Helmreich, 1978, 1983). Most research finds similarities between males and females with regard to the structure of their achievement motivation or values, but males generally score higher than females in Competitiveness, and slightly higher in Mastery. Females generally score slightly higher than males in Work Orientation. It is interesting that males' generally high Competitiveness scores may not be facilitative of actual achievement. Sex typing is a stronger factor than gender with regard to the four achievement motives, with high masculinity scores (instrumental traits) being strongly related to the Mastery, Work Orientation, and Competitiveness scales. The highest scorers on Mastery and Work Orientation generally are androgynous individuals.

Other recent research suggests that in addition to different types of achievement motives, there are different styles of achieving. Lipman-Blumen and colleagues (1983) suggest that there are direct (confronting a task directly), instrumental (using self or others as the means to goals), and relational (achieving through the accomplishments of another) styles of achieving. Each style can further be divided into three substyles. Individuals differ both in their preferred style as well as in their flexibility in using different styles. Such differences as exist between males and females in achievement thus may be related to their different styles of achieving, rather than differences in need for achievement or even in achievement values. For example, Licht and Dweck (1984) found that boys are more likely than girls to have a mastery orientation. Such an orientation is important in dealing with confusing and difficult subject matter, such as math.

Research studies on achievement must be quite clear regarding the measurement instrument used as well as its implications. Needs, values, and styles tap different dimensions and all need to be examined to understand the complex area of achievement behavior.

Competing Needs. Problems with measuring achievement behavior in females also may have to do with some females having needs that compete with achievement needs for actualization. Specifically, research has focused on females' somewhat greater need for affiliation as compared to males' need. Because females, as a group, are more needful of social approval, they supposedly do not strive to achieve. Veroff and colleagues (1980) found that the gap between females and males in affiliation motives has widened since the 1950s due to the decrease in this motive among men.

Role orientation is an important factor with regard to the relationship between affiliation and achievement motives. College women who did not believe in traditional roles for women displayed high achievement motivation under standard instructions aimed at challenging their intelligence (Gralewski & Rodgon, 1980). In contrast, traditional women did not respond to such instructions. Rather, traditional women displayed greater achievement motivation under instructions aimed at arousing their affiliative motives.

It is important to note here that, although some females may be more needful of social approval, there is no evidence to support the contention that females are more influenced than are males by social reinforcements (Mac-coby & Jacklin, 1984; Van Hecke, Tracy, Cotler, & Ribordy, 1984). A survey of 848 tenth and twelfth grade students revealed that boys were even more sensitive than girls to anti-intellectual influences from their peers (Schneider & Coutts, 1985). Nor is there anything intrinsically conflicting in the two needs. The important variable seems to be the consequences of achievement behavior. Thus, although males and females have similar needs for achievement, because some females have a stronger need for affiliation and because achievement behavior in females traditionally has been socially disapproved, females may limit their own achievement or channel it to different areas (Elder & MacInnis, 1983). Black females in particular may be steered toward social goals and away from achievement goals ("Study of," 1985).

Recognition by Matina Horner (1968) that women's achievement might be a function of the perceived consequences of success transformed psychology's understanding of female achievement behavior by invoking another motive—a motive to avoid success.

Fear of Success. Although not an entity unto itself, the concept of a motive to avoid success has added much to our understanding of achievement behavior. This motive, however, also has been the focus of considerable controversy, some of which is due to a misinterpretation of its nature (Horner, 1978). It will be instructive to review the development of the concept and then the controversy surrounding it. Used appropriately, it appears to be a meaningful and valuable construct.

Horner (1968, 1970, 1972) asked students to write stories about the following sentence: "After first term finals, Anne (John) finds herself (himself) at the top of her (his) medical school class." Horner found that roughly 65% of women college students, but only 10% of the men, told stories indicating fear of success. Fear of success was defined as denial of success, unhappiness about it, or negative consequences that followed it. For example, fear of success would be scored for responses such as the following: "A mistake has been made. Anne is not really at the top of the class" and "Anne is ugly, studies all the time, and will never get married."

Not only did more females than males demonstrate this motive to avoid success using a projective technique, but Horner also found this fear to predict behavior in competitive achievement situations. Females high on fear-of-success imagery performed better in noncompetitive situations than did females low in such imagery. Males in general performed better in competitive situations. From these findings, Horner concluded that fear of success was "a stable personality trait" and was caused by the negative consequences expected to follow success.

As a result of the research that this concept generated, however, it soon became apparent that this simple, clear explanation was insufficient to account for all the data. The problems are multiple—methodological, empirical, and theoretical. (See Paludi, 1984b, and Tresemer, 1977, for a review of the research.) Some of the criticisms, however, are based on a misunderstanding of the concept.

Methodological measurement of fear of success as a psychological trait has been markedly unreliable and lacking in validity. Research (Condry & Dyer, 1976; Paludi, 1984b) has shown fear of success to lack consistency across various cues, across various cue contexts, and across judges. For example, when "Anne" is put at the top of her *nursing* school class (Alper, 1974) or when her medical school class is composed of 50% women (Lockheed, 1975), women respond with less fear-of-success imagery. Horner (1978), however, never implied that fear of success functioned by itself. Rather, the critical factor is an expectation of negative consequences for success when one desires or expects success. Thus, in the nursing and coed-class situations, negative consequences might not have been expected.

A more serious problem with the measurement of fear of success is the finding of Sadd, Lenauer, Shaver, and Dunivant (1978) that fear of success is not a unitary concept. Factor analysis of five measures of fear of success and two measures of fear of failure revealed five separate factors, only one of which came close to Horner's definition regarding fear of success— that is, concern about the negative consequences of success. The other four factors were: self-deprecation and insecurity, test anxiety, attitudes toward success in medical school, and

extrinsic motivation to excel. Unfortunately, Sadd et al. found the only factor to correlate highly with Horner's original measure was factor four, attitudes toward success in medical school—a very limited definition of fear of success, indeed. Other research too suggests that different measures of fear of success result in different findings (Gelbort & Winer, 1985; MacDonald & Hyde, 1980; Orlofsky, 1981a; Paludi, 1984b).

Additionally, research on the *empirical* validity of Horner's measure of fear of success has been sufficiently contradictory to cast some doubt on it. Although there has been some tendency to find higher levels of this motive among women at elite, highly competitive colleges (Fleming, 1977), this is not a consistent finding. Nor is it always the case that such a fear actually reduces achievement attempts on the part of females (Condry & Dyer, 1976; Fleming, 1982; Lentz, 1982; MacDonald & Hyde, 1980; Paludi, 1984b). Studies involving mixed-sex competition demonstrate that women's achievement behavior is different in those situations than it is in same-sex competitive situations. However, such changes are not clearly related to fear of success (for example, Makosky, 1976; Swanson & Tjosvold, 1979).

A more telling criticism of fear of success involves the *theoretical* assumption that respondents are projecting their own motives onto the story. This assumption is the basis of all projective techniques. Horner had females and males write stories using only the same-sex character, Anne or John, because she assumed respondents needed a same-sex character to facilitate projection. When people respond to both Anne and John cues, however, males and females in the early 1970s frequently invoked more fear of success images for Anne than for John (Feather & Raphaelson, 1974; Monahan, Kuhn, & Shaver, 1974). These findings suggest that cultural stereotypes regarding appropriate achievement behaviors of females and males and regarding the actual consequences of such behaviors, not any deep-seated "motive," may be tapped by the stimulus cues. In fact, in the studies before 1979, when Anne was the cue, men told even more fear-of-success stories (68%) than did women (51%). In other words, more people may predict negative consequences for a female who is at the top of her medical school class than for a male because she is engaging in gender-inappropriate behavior and/or because such women actually do meet with more negative consequences than do their male counterparts. Fear of success as a motive may have little, if anything, to do with it.

Another criticism often aimed at fear of success as an explanation of female achievement behavior is that fear of success also occurs in many males. Horner (1978), however, never proposed that the motive to avoid success was either sex linked or related to a particular sex-role orientation, but rather, that it would arise in anyone whenever a desire or expectation of success was present alongside an expectation that success would have negative consequences. Research has indeed found that, under those conditions, males as well as females do seem to express such fears (Bremer & Wittig, 1980; Cherry & Deaux, 1978; Garland & Smith, 1981; Janda, O'Grady, & Capps, 1978). The specific cue used is the important variable. When no situation is given (for example, when the cue is "Anne [or John] succeeded"), no difference occurred in the amount of fear of success projected by college females and males (Gravenkemper & Paludi, 1983). Paludi, in her 1984 summary of 64 studies, found that the proportion of fear of success in females ranged from 6% to 93%, the median being 49%. In males, percentages ranged from 7% to 95%, with the median being 45%. Thus, there does not seem to be a unique motive to avoid success that distinguishes women from men.

Fear of success in females and males, however, may have different causes. In women, fear of success may be caused by fear of social rejection. In men, it may be due to questioning the value of success. That is, the stories women create seem to involve the social consequences of success (no dates, dislike by classmates), whereas the stories men create seem to involve the worth of success itself (the emptiness of achievement, not having any future goals).

In summary, there is little to support Horner's statement that fear of success is a stable personality trait, although there is evidence that it does arise in females and males in conjunction with specific expectations and values. Perhaps a more satisfactory explanation of the research findings can be made by viewing fear of success as a *situational variable*—that is, as a realistic appraisal of negative consequences that may result from success in specific situations. As will be shown, such an explanation can account for existing findings as well as for other problematic ones.

Gender Appropriateness. The critical factor in understanding achievement behavior in men and women is the gender-appropriateness of the behavior. As was discussed in Chapter 7, children learn by age 5 or 6 the cultural norms for gender-appropriate behavior and begin to alter their values, attitudes, and behaviors in response to them. Deviation from these norms has negative consequences both internally, in terms of anxiety and low self-concept, and externally, in terms of others' reactions. As cited above, research indicates that men sometimes show even more negative consequences in response to Anne's success in medical school than do women. Men prefer to work alone rather than to work with their steady dates in competitive situations (Peplau, 1976). And men are less likely than women to choose to hire a gender-inappropriate person (for example, a female engineer) than a gender-appropriate person, at least in research studies (Lips & Myers, 1980). Therefore, given no other information, the fear of negative consequences as a result of success that many females have, at least in male-defined situations, may be quite reasonable, albeit counterproductive. For example, the behavior of some female athletes suggests that many may feel that success threatens their "femininity" (Rohrbaugh, 1979). This ambivalence may limit their sports potential.

Thus, more fear-of-success imagery and more blocking-of-achievement behavior may have been found in females because most studies have used male-appropriate achievement situations, such as medical school or competition. If achievement is defined in a female-appropriate situation, such as in nursing school, or in feminine-defined tasks, the opposite results would be expected; that is, more males would be found restricting their achievement behavior and showing high fear of success. This prediction has received consistent empirical support. As noted above, numerous researchers have found that both sexes write more fear-of-success stories to gender-inappropriate cues than to gender-appropriate cues.

Examining fear of success as the motive to avoid what is considered role-inappropriate is useful in explaining the inconsistent results on fear of success among Blacks (Fleming, 1978, 1982; Mednick & Puryear, 1975). In general, Black women, perhaps due to their greater involvement in the labor force, demonstrate less fear of success than White women. However, Black women who do have high fear of success appear to channel their achievement into more gender-appropriate professions than do Black women low in fear of success. Research on Black men is scarcer, with some suggestion of greater fear of success for them than for either Black women or White men. This finding, if confirmed, may relate to the strong racial stereotypes of Black men as unreliable and unproductive. Therefore, they may see any success as role-inappropriate. Even middle-class Black men may have conflicts over achievement (Cazenave, 1984; Cordes, 1985). Such conflicts may lead to a lack of striving. Certainly there are strong societal barriers to achievement for Blacks as well as possible internal barriers.

As Deaux (1976) concludes, both men and women will avoid success if the consequences of that success seem likely to be unpleasant. Conversely, both men and women will seek success/achievement if the consequences are likely to be pleasant. Thus, if males get more rewards by achieving in academic and competitive situations, they will be more oriented in academic and competitive directions. If females get more rewards for achieving in cooperative, interpersonal situations and in the domestic sphere, they will be more oriented in those directions. If these positive consequences are coupled with negative consequences for deviation, it is quite clear how the above results could be obtained.

As was reviewed in Chapters 7 and 8, the sexes generally are rewarded differentially during childhood for different behaviors, and they perceive different achievement behaviors in the models presented to them in the media, at home, and at school. Girls and boys appear to learn to value certain behaviors and tasks differently, and these sex differences in subjective

task value have been found to be the strongest mediator of sex differences in achievement (Eccles, 1983; Eccles et al., 1984; Sherman, 1982b). For example, some academic disciplines such as math and science are perceived as male domains. Achieving in such areas may become a particular source of conflict for adolescent girls, especially because during adolescence, most girls are expected to develop social skills. As a result, many girls develop neither confidence nor adequate achievement skills, particularly in math and science. Many boys, on the other hand, are encouraged to be achievement oriented. They are reinforced for being independent and for conquering challenging tasks. They also perceive many models of male achievement.

By college, a young woman who is intellectually equal or superior to her male peers may suppress her achievement behavior because she has learned to be more interested in affiliation. And affiliation, she has also learned, may be threatened by her achieving (Donelson & Gullahorn, 1977; Komarovsky, 1946). For example, Michelini and colleagues (1981) found that college students expected a success-oriented woman to have more difficulty in getting married than a non-success-oriented woman. A young man, on the other hand, may feel compelled to achieve and may be afraid to express or act upon more tender feelings or affiliative needs. In general, achieving situations do appear to represent danger to women more so than to men. In contrast, men are more likely than women to perceive danger in affiliative situations (Benton et al., 1983; Pollak & Gilligan, 1982, 1983).

From these findings, it can be predicted that the more traditional an individual is in sex-role attitudes, the more his/her achievement behavior would be affected by situational factors. A number of researchers have found that gender conceptions in female undergraduates play a central role in mediating the effects of situational factors on achievement-related expectations. In general, women with traditional female orientations, attitudes, and beliefs scored lower on achievement-motivation measures than did women with nontraditional female orientations, at least using traditional measurement techniques (Canter, 1979; Gralewski & Rodgon, 1980). In studies using measures of sex typing such as the Personal Attributes Questionnaire and the Bem Sex Role Inventory, low career achievement and fear of success, especially as measured by objective scales, are associated with low "masculinity" scores and feminine sex typing (Cano, Solomon, & Holmes, 1984; Major, 1979; Orlofsky, 1981a; Orlofsky & Stake, 1981; Sadd, Miller, & Zeitz, 1979; Wong, Kettlewell, & Sproule, 1985).

In general, the more instrumental "masculine" characteristics an individual admits to, the fewer achievement conflicts he or she is likely to have. Somewhat surprisingly, most recent studies have not found a relationship between measures of expressive "feminine" traits alone and achievement conflicts (Orlofsky & Stake, 1981; Sadd et al., 1979; Savage et al., 1979). This lack of a consistent relationship between expressive traits and fear of success may mean that the "femininity" scale measures traits that have little to do with achievement. It should be recalled that it was the instrumental/"masculinity" scale, not the expressive/"femininity" scale, that was found to relate strongly to achievement orientation (Spence & Helmreich, 1978). It now seems that the "masculinity" scale relates to achievement conflicts as well.

More recent research in the area of achievement conflicts suggests that some change is occurring. As more women are entering traditional male-dominated fields (in 1984, one-third of all law and medical school students were women), the stigma against female achievement is lessening, at least among high-ability females and for high-prestige occupations (Garland & Smith, 1981; Golden & Cherry, 1982). For example, in a 1981 study, no sex difference was found in achievement motivation or fear of success imagery for high-prestige masculine occupations, although for middle-prestige occupations, both males and females evidenced higher achievement motivation toward gender-appropriate jobs.

Definition of Achievement. Because females who achieve in male-defined areas often do meet with negative consequences, it is no wonder that many females do not demonstrate achievement in such areas but prefer interper-

sonal situations. Social areas may represent achievement for females, not a way to satisfy affiliation or social approval needs, as previously thought. It is not that females have no need for achievement; this motive is equally present in females and males. It is not that females are blocked by a unique fear of success; this does not differentiate males and females across situations. Rather, it must be concluded that males and females are basically similar in their achievement behavior; only their areas of striving and the consequences of that striving may differ as a result of traditional gender socialization. Females who accept achievement behavior as part of the female role respond like males to achievement-instigating conditions, whereas traditionally role-oriented females display high achievement motivation only under affiliative arousal conditions (Gralewski & Rodgon, 1980). Longitudinal research suggests that young women with a high need for achievement have two different life paths available: either a worklife-career path, in which work and family interests are combined in the traditionally masculine way, or a social-marital path, in which achievement is directed toward marital and family interests (Elder & MacInnis, 1983).

Achievement motivation and behavior in women may need to be conceptualized differently than it is for men. For example, Daniel Levinson (1978) in his study of the lives of White middle-class men, found that most of these men formed a "dream" regarding career goals in early adulthood. They then single-mindedly strove to attain this "dream." Women's lives do not appear to follow this same course (Baruch, Barnett, & Rivers, 1983). Family life stages appear to play a more important role for women then they do for men. Women with young children may find the importance of achievement lessened as the importance of nurturance increases (Krogh, 1985). As their children get older, achievement goals may become more important for women.

Thus, the definition of achievement may be different for females and for males. As discussed above, achievement may be viewed as encompassing three major styles—direct, instrumental, and relational (Lipman-Blumen et al., 1983). The definition of achievement used for most achievement measures may be tapping achievement only in its traditional, male-oriented sense: direct achievement, vocational aspirations and attainments, competitive games, and so forth (Spence & Helmreich, 1978). Besides being more interested in social achievements than are some males, many females also appear to be more interested than many males in self-directed improvement for the sake of mastery rather than for the impact such mastery would bring (Depner & Veroff, 1979; Goldberg & Shiflett, 1981). That is, many females seem more autonomous in their achievement strivings, whereas many males seem to respond more to normative pressures for performance. Indeed, Spence and Helmreich (1978) found in their investigation of the antecedents of achievement motivation that girls are expected to be devoted to hard work for its own sake, whereas boys are expected to work hard in order to be better than others.

More women than men also may try to satisfy their achievement needs through a relational style of achieving, especially the vicarious substyle. That is, some women may choose indirect achievement satisfaction through the successes of important males in their lives (husbands, sons, fathers, brothers, bosses) rather than direct satisfaction through their own success (Lipman-Blumen & Leavitt, 1976).

A further point needs to be made regarding achievement and male sex-role behavior. Whereas the underemphasis on achievement behavior for females may be counterproductive for effective human functioning, its overemphasis for males may lead to the same result. Analysis of the male sex role reveals that it is primarily defined by success and status gained through working and achieving (Brannon, 1976; Cicone & Ruble, 1978; Doyle, 1983; O'Neil, 1982). All that counts is the material rewards of achieving—money, possessions, power, and "winning" in sexual and athletic areas. In contrast to many women, many men achieve more for the social rewards of achieving than for the personal rewards of mastery. Success for many men means only economic success (Goldberg & Shiflett, 1981). This emphasis on achieving may prevent the development of other human abilities—sensitivity to others, nurturance, emotional expressiveness, and formation of relationships.

As Pleck (1976b) points out, although the area in which men are expected to achieve may be changing (more intellectual and interpersonal skills as compared to physical strength skills are now positively sanctioned), the fundamental stress on achievement remains. The very nature of the male role, both traditional and modern, may be dysfunctional because it contains inherent role strain between role demands and more fundamental personal needs. In addition, in a competitive society like America, only a few can win or come out on top in terms of success or status. Even when success is obtained, it usually lasts for only a limited time, because there is always either something else to achieve or someone else who achieves more. Consequently, many males spend their lives competing endlessly with little possibility of reaching their goal. Furthermore, because masculinity is so tied to working and achievement, when unemployment occurs, some men also may experience damaging losses of self-esteem. Research confirms that an unsuccessful man is downgraded much more than an unsuccessful woman (Fogel & Paludi, 1984). All these pressures may give rise to frustration, aggression, and/or depression, among other consequences.

Summary. Achievement behavior for women and men is a function of both achievement motivation and gender expectations. Achievement itself may have multiple meanings, referring to both process and impact dimensions. In general, women have been discouraged from achieving in male-defined areas such as medicine and mechanics, and men have been discouraged from achieving in female-defined areas, like nursing and clerical skills.

Flexibility of Behavior

How comfortable and effective do you feel in situations requiring assertiveness? empathy? mechanical skills? nurturance? physical aggression? social skills? leadership? intuition? The wider the range of behaviors, the more flexible one is in one's behaviors. Gender stereotypes markedly affect this range through the impact of socialization practices.

In order to examine how the stereotypes affect the range of behaviors in which we feel comfortable engaging, a closer look at the effects of the socialization processes involved in sex typing is warranted. Following the consideration of socialization processes, a review of the original work by Sandra Bem and her associates on sex typing and behavioral flexibility will be undertaken together with some assessment of the current status of their work.

Socialization.   As was reviewed in Part Three, males appear to receive more intense socialization than do females. Males are both punished and rewarded more than females, particularly with regard to gender-appropriate behaviors. One result of this intensity of socialization is that such differential pressures lead to differential attachment to gender stereotypes and to sex-typed behaviors.

Males, starting at age 3 and continuing into adulthood, are generally found to be more sex typed and to be more reluctant to express a preference for, or engage in, other-sex activities than are females (Canter & Meyerowitz, 1984; Helmreich, Spence, & Holahan, 1979; Maccoby & Jacklin, 1974; Plumb & Cowan, 1984; Stericker & Kurdek, 1982). This strong preference for sex-typed tasks has been found especially in masculine-sex-typed males. Females, on the other hand, generally appear to have greater role flexibility than do males. They frequently prefer and adopt male roles and activities throughout childhood; hence, the common phenomenon of "tomboy" behaviors in girls between ages 6 and 9. During the elementary school years, boys' preferences become more stereotypically masculine, while girls' preferences become less stereotypically feminine (Marcus & Overton, 1978; Nadelman, 1974).

These differences may reflect differences in the consequences of sex-role deviation; that is, boys seem to be more punished than are girls for engaging in gender-inappropriate behaviors. These differences in role flexibility also may reflect differences in the intrinsic nature of the roles themselves, with the male role and male-identified activities seen as being more desirable and suitable for establishing personal competence. Indeed, if girls are to acquire any sense of competence, assertiveness, or achieve-

ment behaviors, they must identify, to some extent, with males and male characters in stories. This is so because males appear three times as often as do females in stories, and they are the main ones displaying such behaviors (see Chapter 8).

From grades 5 through 12, both sexes show increasing consistency with gender stereotypes in their self-description (Silvern, 1977; Stericker & Kurdek, 1982). The frequency of cross-gender self-concepts is generally low, although androgynous self-concepts characterize about one-third of young children and preadolescents. For females, increasing gender conformity means experiencing greater restrictiveness than previously experienced. This may cause role conflict and strain (Katz, 1979; Locksley & Douvan, 1979). At puberty, girls may be pressured subtly to give up outside interests (sports, academic achievement, and so on) and to concentrate on finding a mate. It is at this point, in high school and especially in college, that academic performance by females declines. Girls may start acting "dumb" to make themselves more desirable. Their hours and their personal environment are restricted more than that of their male peers, and this restrictiveness continues into adulthood. Some results of this restrictiveness may be a confused self-identity, lessened self-esteem, and/or high anxiety. In general, strong socialization narrows the options available to women, whereas it increases the options available to men (Block, 1973). Women often must choose between a family and a career. If they choose a career, they traditionally have been restricted to a few female-dominated occupations, such as teaching or nursing. Men, on the other hand, can have both a family and a career and have a wider variety of careers from which to choose.

The consequences of socialization for men, however, are not all positive. As mentioned above, males hold to their gender identity very rigidly and are punished for deviations. This intense socialization causes a great deal of anxiety over anything vaguely feminine and leads males to deny certain aspects of themselves that have been associated with femininity, particularly feelings of dependence and vulnerability. As Fasteau (1974) notes, this denial sets up a classic scapegoating process whereby what is feared becomes disliked, and those who display the feared behavior become hated and ridiculed. That boys often express dislike and contempt for girls is a common observation ("yech, girls!"), but Fasteau remarks that this early misogyny never really disappears but only becomes more subtle and disguised. This scapegoating obviously will affect relationships between the sexes.

In a number of articles, James O'Neil (1981a, 1981b, 1982) has described how men's gender-role socialization and the masculine stereotype combine to create a fear of femininity in many males. As illustrated in Figure 9-1, this fear may manifest itself in six major ways: restrictive emotionality, homophobia, socialized power issues, restrictive sexual and affectionate behavior, obsession with achievement and success, and health care problems. The major consequence on the personal level is gender-role conflict and strain. Using a questionnaire designed to measure these dimensions of gender-role conflict and strain, O'Neil et al. (1984)

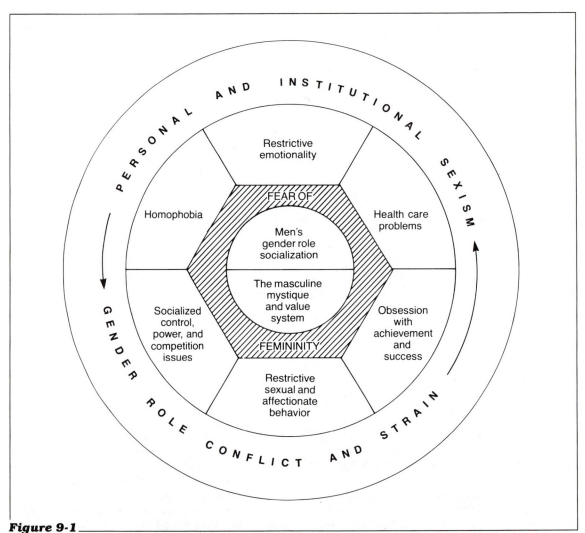

Figure 9-1

Six patterns of gender-role conflict and strain in men (O'Neil, 1981b). (Reprinted by permission of the Personnel and Guidance Journal, *copyright 1981.)*

found that most college men experience some strain, especially regarding success, power, and competition issues, and regarding affectionate behavior between men (homophobia).

Other research supports the concepts of fear of femininity and gender-role strain for some males as a product of their intense socialization (Babl, 1979; Hartley, 1959; Pleck, 1981b). Masculine sex-typed males in particular may have strong fears of femininity (O'Neil et al., 1984). For example, in investigating the reactions of college men to a threat to their masculinity (information that American college males are becoming less masculine), Babl (1979) found that masculine-sex-typed males responded anxiously. They subsequently reported exaggerated levels of "masculinity" and antisocial behavior. In contrast, although androgynous males also reported anxiety, they responded by lowering their level of masculine endorsement and did not increase their endorsement of antisocial behavior. Sex-typed males, then, seem to adhere in a particularly rigid manner to their sex role.

There is some evidence that men may be becoming less behaviorally restricted than was once thought. O'Leary and Donoghue (1978) reviewed two studies that demonstrated that nonstereotyped males (those who had nontraditional personality traits and vocational interests or who advocated nontraditional behaviors) were not devalued by high school or college students. O'Leary and Donoghue suggest, however, that this may be so among adults only because childhood adherence to the male role was so strict. In other words, once "masculinity" is firmly established, then flexibility is allowed. These same authors do acknowledge that there are still limits on the latitudes of acceptable "masculine" behavior. For example, men are still punished for demonstrating incompetence and for failing (Feather & Simon, 1975; Fogel & Paludi, 1984; Larrance et al., 1979), for passivity and dependence (Costrich, Feinstein, Kidder, Maracek, & Pascale, 1975), and for sexual difficulties (Polyson, 1978).

How do different degrees of sex typing affect behaviors across a wide range of situations? Based on Sandra Bem's work, a number of researchers have suggested that androgynous people are the most adaptive, flexible, and ef-

fective of all sex-typed groupings. Although this simple conclusion has since been challenged, a closer examination of Bem's original research will be instructive.

Bem's Early Research. Sandra Bem and her colleagues have accumulated an impressive body of evidence demonstrating the effects of gender stereotypes on a wide variety of behaviors (1974, 1975a, 1975b, 1976, 1977; Bem & Lenney, 1976). Individuals who hold strongly to gender stereotypes—that is, those who rate themselves as strongly sex typed via an adjective check list (the Bem Sex-Role Inventory, or BSRI)—have been found to be markedly less flexible in their behaviors than are individuals who are less strongly sex typed. These latter individuals Bem termed *androgynous*.

In a sequence of studies, Bem and associates found that "masculine" males (those who checked more masculine than feminine characteristics on the BSRI) were highly capable of effective performance when it came to instrumental behaviors, such as independence in a conformity situation, assertiveness in a request situation. But when it came to expressive behaviors, they performed poorly. For example, they were less nurturant to a human baby, less playful with a kitten, and less empathic to a lonely student. "Feminine" females (those who checked more feminine than masculine characteristics on the BSRI), on the other hand, were the reverse—high in the expressive domain, except with the kitten, and low in the instrumental domain. Cross-sex-typed individuals (the 10% who scored much higher on the other-sex scale than on the same-sex one) showed the same pattern of behavioral restrictiveness as their other-sex partners; that is, "masculine" females and "feminine" males had the same behavioral pattern as "masculine" males and "feminine" females, respectively. It was only the androgynous individuals (those who possessed characteristics of both sexes in equal proportions), males and females, who were able to perform well in both domains. Thus, both androgynous males and androgynous females could be nurturant and empathic and independent and assertive. In the study with the kitten, in fact, androgynous individuals were more nurturant than "feminine" individuals, because the situation required some initiative, which "feminine" individuals were unable to take. Thus, androgynous individuals are the most flexible behaviorally and strongly sex-typed individuals, the most restricted.

The reason for this restrictiveness in strongly sex-typed individuals seems to be that, for them, engaging in cross-sex behavior is very uncomfortable and anxiety producing. Cross-sex behavior is thus actively resisted. Bem and Lenney (1976) found that sex-typed individuals were more likely than sex-reversed or androgynous individuals to prefer activities that are sex-appropriate and to resist those that are sex-inappropriate, even when those preferences incurred a cost to the individual in terms of loss of offered payment for engaging in sex-inappropriate tasks. For example, if a sex-typed male was asked to choose between being photographed preparing a baby bottle for 4¢ and oiling a hinge for 2¢, he would be more likely to choose the oiling task than would an androgynous or "feminine" male. Additionally, when sex-typed individuals did engage in cross-sex activity, they experienced discomfort and negative feelings about themselves. If the male subject in the above example did perform the bottle task, he said he felt more uncomfortable and negative doing so than did either the androgynous or "feminine" males.

These results extend findings in achievement behavior and fear-of-success studies to other types of behavior. Individuals, females and males, refrain from engaging in cross-sex activities or functions because of the consequences of so doing. This conclusion is further clarified by the concept of androgyny. It is primarily sex-typed individuals who appear concerned about the negative consequences of engaging in gender-inappropriate behaviors. Consequently, they are the ones who restrict their behavior accordingly. Androgynous individuals either do not expect such negative consequences or are not concerned about them. They seem the most balanced of all groups, with the most freedom and flexibility of behavior.

Current Findings. More recent investigations of the relationship between sex typing and behavioral flexibility have tempered somewhat the glowing reports about androgynous individuals. In the first place, there is some suggestion that androgynous men may differ from androgynous women in several ways (Flaherty & Dusek, 1980; Heilbrun, 1981, 1984; Wiggins & Holzmuller, 1978, 1981). For example, androgynous females may be more flexible and well-adjusted than androgynous males.

Another problem with Bem's conceptualizations involves the reason for less behavioral flexibility among sex-typed individuals than among androgynous individuals. In a conceptual replication of Bem and Lenney's (1976) study using the Personal Attributes Questionnaire (PAQ) instead of the BSRI, Helmreich and colleagues (1979) found a similar pattern of results but the relationships were much weaker than those found by Bem and Lenney. Androgynous individuals of both sexes had higher comfort ratings regarding performance of a variety of tasks, independent of the sex typing of the task, than did "feminine" and "undifferentiated" subjects. However, "masculine" individuals also had high comfort ratings, independent of type of task. The findings regarding "masculine" subjects somewhat contradict Bem and Lenney's (1976) hypothesis regarding why sex-typed individuals are behaviorally restricted. The different results, however, may be due to the different measures of sex typing used. Helmreich et al. (1979) explain their findings regarding comfort ratings in terms of differences in self-esteem among the sex-typing groups, rather than in terms of differences in sex typing per se.

Most disturbing to Bem's conclusions, however, are studies that do not find that androgynous individuals are always the most adaptive. For example, Jones, Chernovetz, and Hansson, (1978) found, after examining 16 specific behaviors in five different areas of psychological functioning, that people with strong instrumental ("masculine") traits showed the most adaptive behavior.

Thus, although androgyny is certainly not the least adaptive response mode, it is not clearly the most adaptive either, as Bem predicts. What this finding implies is that the instrumental behaviors that comprise the masculine sex role are vitally important for social rewards for both females and males. Similar conclusions were made with regard to self-esteem, self confidence, and achievement behavior. It must be noted, however, that Bem's concept of androgyny was meant to apply specifically to flexibility of expressive and instrumental behaviors. The study of Jones et al. (1978) extended Bem's predictions considerably by including such areas as attitudes and sexual identity. In the interpersonal domain, support for Bem's predictions has been impressive (Andersen & Bem, 1981; LaFrance & Carmen, 1980; Mills, 1983; Orlofsky & Stake, 1981; Senneker & Hendrick, 1983).

Locksley and Colten (1979) question the concept of androgyny on theoretical and methodological grounds, some of which were discussed in Chapter 1. Of relevance to the present discussion regarding behavioral flexibility is their contention that, because the world we live in makes distinctions on the basis of sex, in many situations it is more adaptive to be sex typed than to be androgynous. Indeed, these researchers conclude that the idea of being free entirely from the social effects of sex-related categorizations is impossible and that therefore androgyny is an arbitrary concept. Bem's (1979) response to this critique acknowledges that it is impossible to be free completely from sex-related social effects; however, individuals still differ in the extent to which they believe in sex differences and in their use of gender to code and process information. Indeed, as discussed in Chapter 7, Bem's more recent work (1981a, 1981b, 1982, 1983, 1984) has abandoned the focus on androgyny per se. Instead, her work now focuses on how gender is used as a cognitive schema. Androgynous individuals, for Bem, are relatively non-sex-typed individuals who use gender less often than do sex-typed persons in processing information about the world around them. Therefore the behavior of androgynous persons is less a function of the sex typing of a behavior or a situation than is the behavior of sex-typed persons. Other research supports this cognitive interpretation of sex typing (Bradbard & Endsley, 1983; Deaux & Major, 1977; Flaherty & Dusek, 1980; Tunnell, 1981).

Another important point is a developmental one. Almost all of these researchers have studied sex typing in college students. Yet, as was pointed out in Chapter 7, androgyny appears to be a developmental attainment, following a stage of sex typing. It appears logical, then, that many, if not most, college students are still in the process of achieving a stable sexual identity. Therefore, contradictory results at this life stage do not preclude clearer results with adults. Martha White (1979) argues this point well. She has shown that female nurse practitioners, median age 29, show strong differences as a function of sex typing. Women high in both agentic and communion competencies (measured by an original scale) had many advantages over those who were low in both competencies or who were competent in only one area. The high-androgynous-competency group were the most responsible, caring, competent, tolerant, self-controlled, and satisfied, to name just a few of the differentiating characteristics. Motowidlo (1982) found similar results with lower- to midlevel managers. Androgynous individuals (as measured by the BSRI) showed the most acceptance of nontraditional job change, support for persons in nontraditional jobs, and active listening to others. More research on adults is definitely needed.

In conclusion, then, the adaptibility of androgynous individuals and the comparability of androgynous males and females are still open subjects. It does appear clear, however, that certain instrumental qualities are extremely adaptive and that being strongly sex typed may limit one's behaviors in certain areas deemed appropriate for the other sex.

Summary. Because of their more intense socialization, boys appear to hold to the gender stereotypes even more rigidly than do girls. The cost of such sex typing is high. Bem demonstrated that many sex-typed males are markedly deficient in the expressive domain, being uninterested or unwilling even to play with a kitten. Furthermore, not only do males limit themselves from engaging in sex-inappropriate activities, they practically demand that others, both females and males, do likewise. Yet certain instrumental "masculine" qualities can be adaptive, especially in instrumental areas.

For many females, gender stereotypes have led to a negative self-image and to inhibitions about achieving in male-defined areas. For feminine sex-typed females in particular, the stereotypes appear to restrict their instrumental activities. Consequently, the behavior of feminine sex-typed females is sometimes less adaptive than that of masculine sex-typed males.

In general, across most interpersonal situations, androgynous individuals appear the most behaviorally flexible of all sex-typing groups. Behavioral restrictiveness, whatever the cause, does not aid one in developing the skills needed to lead a full life—that is, expressive and instrumental skills. Such restrictiveness for many sex-typed males and females affects their emotional and physical well-being as well.

Mental Health

In moving from the areas of self-concept and behavior to the area of mental health, it is again striking how strongly and how deeply the gender stereotypes affect individuals regarding their feelings of psychological well-being and their evaluation of the psychological well-being of others. Looking at the indexes of adjustment, anxiety, psychoses, hospitalization, depression, and drug and alcohol dependence, a common pattern emerges: both those individuals who feel they are not living up to their gender-appropriate stereotypes and those who hold to them most rigidly suffer from the greatest number of psychological problems. We will examine next three areas of mental health and their relation to sex typing—adjustment, mental illness, and depression.

Adjustment

Mental health is often viewed as proper adjustment. There is a strongly prevailing assumption that individuals will be "better off" if they conform to their gender stereotype (Bem, 1976). Thus, males who are doctors are considered, a priori, better "adjusted" than males who are nurses. The latter group, even if not considered disturbed, certainly would have their sexual identity questioned ("Is he 'gay'?"). This view can be classified as the traditional congruence model of mental health. Two other models of mental health have been

proposed as well: the masculinity model, which postulates that mental health is maximized when an individual possesses a high degree of instrumental "masculine" traits; and the androgyny model, which postulates that mental health is maximized when an individual incorporates a high degree of both instrumental "masculine" and expressive "feminine" traits. Research to date is fairly clear in not supporting the traditional congruence model of mental health, especially for females (Taylor & Hall, 1982; Whitley, 1983, 1984). Indeed, not only is good adjustment not positively related to sex-role conformity, it frequently is negatively related to sex-role conformity, especially for females. Support for the other two hypotheses is stronger, with more research supporting the masculinity model that the androgyny model, especially for males.

For females, the picture is relatively clear—the higher the "femininity" score, the poorer the adjustment—that is, the higher the anxiety, the lower the self-esteem, and the lower the social acceptance (Burchardt & Serbin, 1982; Frank, Towell & Huyck, 1985; Heiser & Gannon, 1984; LaTorre, Yu, Fortin, & Marrache, 1983; Olds & Shaver, 1980; Spence & Helmreich, 1978). Similarly, Bart (1972) found that it is the excessively "feminine" woman who encounters problems with middle-age transition. Particular aspects of the feminine stereotype (verbal passive-aggressiveness and excessive conformity) have been found to be related negatively to self-esteem (Spence, Helmreich, & Holahan, 1979). Furthermore, despite the traditional belief that women should not work outside the home, evidence has accumulated that career women are not worse off psychologically than home-oriented women (Rendely, Holmstrom, & Karp, 1984; Shehan, 1984). In some cases, career women may be even psychologically healthier and happier than noncareer women (Baruch, Barnett, & Rivers, 1983; Warr & Parry, 1982b).

The pattern of strong feminine sex typing going hand in hand with poor adjustment needs some clarification, however. Some research finds a weak relationship between "femininity" and measures of adjustment (DeGregorio & Carver, 1980; Silvern & Ryan, 1979; Whitley, 1984). Garnets and Pleck (1979) make a strong case for a sex-role-strain analysis of the relationship between sex-typed personality characteristics and psychological adjustment. Their point is that two variables are important: the amount of *discrepancy* between same-sex ideal and real self, and the amount of sex-role *salience*. It is only for those people for whom sex roles are important that a self-ideal discrepancy would cause stress. Thus, a sex-typed person for whom sex roles are salient is likely to experience role strain only if he or she desires to be androgynous. If the ideal is a sex-typed one, strain may not occur. Sex-role strain should be low, also, whenever sex-role salience is low.

One's choice of basic lifestyle is a critical factor in personal adjustment, as are situational factors. Hoffman and Fidell (1979) found that feminine-sex-typed women, although having lower self-esteem than androgynous and masculine-sex-typed women, did not differ significantly from the other groups on neuroticism. "Feminine" women also seemed adequately jadjusted, perhaps because their life choices (housework, no external employment, childcare responsibilities) were consistent with their sex type. Indeed, Hoffman and Fidell conclude that what is crucial for adjustment may be consistency between attitude and behavior, not attitude or sex typing per se. Thus, Schichman and Cooper (1984) found that people are satisfied with life to the extent to which they satisfy those aspects of living which they see as most important. Feminine-sex-typed persons appear to value socioemotional aspects, masculine-sex-typed persons appear to value instrumental aspects, and androgynous persons appear to value both the socioemotional and instrumental aspects of life. Furthermore, in some situations, for example college social life, "feminine" females may find more acceptance and suffer from fewer peer pressures than androgynous or "masculine" females (Kleinke & Hinrichs, 1983).

The relationship between masculine sex typing and adjustment has been relatively consistent of late. There has been an increasing body of literature that suggests that "masculine" instrumental traits are particularly likely to be associated with effective functioning. We have already seen that instrumental qualities are strongly associated with high self-esteem.

A great number of researchers have found that, for both sexes, high "masculinity" is strongly and positively correlated with high social competence and emotional well-being (Della Selva & Dusek, 1984; Frank, McLaughlin, & Crusco, 1984; Frank et al., 1984; Heiser & Gannon, 1984; Lubinski, Tellegen, & Butcher, 1981, 1983; Rendely et al., 1984; Taylor & Hall, 1982; Whitley, 1984; Zeldow et al., 1985). High masculinity score is negatively correlated with feelings of anxiety, depression, neuroticism, dissatisfaction with current life circumstances, achievement conflicts, and stress symptoms. "Feminine" expressive attributes also may contribute to high self-esteem and adjustment in both sexes, but these attributes are not as influential as the instrumental ones. Thus, androgynous and masculine-sex-typed individuals generally appear to be better adjusted than feminine-sex-typed and "undifferentiated" individuals.

Spence and colleagues (1979) caution, however, that not all components of the masculine stereotype are socially desirable. Such characteristics as arrogance, cynicism, and egocentrism are strongly and positively correlated with the occurrence of acting-out, sociopathic behaviors. For college women, competitiveness is associated with mental and physical health problems (Olds & Shaver, 1980). Indeed, both gender stereotypes, when examined in toto, have both positive and negative qualities, and neither by itself represent a well-adjusted individual (Williams & Best, 1982).

The androgyny model of mental health thus has received less support than the masculinity model of mental health. Although androgynous individuals do appear to be better adjusted (have higher self-esteem, fewer negative self-statements, higher levels of psychosocial development, and more stable, nonneurotic personalities) than feminine-sex-typed and "undifferentiated" individuals, such individuals are not necessarily better adjusted than masculine sex-typed individuals on all measures of adjustment (Burchardt & Serbin, 1982; Della Selva & Dusek, 1984; Hoffman & Fidell, 1979; Kimlicka, Cross, & Tarnai, 1983; Shaw, 1982; Tzuriel, 1984; Waterman & Whitbourne, 1980).

One exception to this pattern is a study

of professional middle-aged men (Downey, 1984). For them, androgyny was associated with higher self-perceived mental health than was masculine sex-typing. As discussed previously, androgyny for males and females may be somewhat different. Current research suggests that androgyny is a distinct asset for females (Burchardt & Serbin, 1982; Heilbrun, 1981, 1984; Shaw, 1982). Androgynous females have been found to be more likely than androgynous males to be competent socially, to have strong cognitive defenses, to have little tolerance for ambiguity, to blend expressive and instrumental behaviors, and to rate selves as adjusted and happy. Perhaps the combination of instrumental and expressive characteristics is more beneficial for females than males because instrumental traits are more socially valued than expressive traits. In this regard, "masculine" women have been found to be more extroverted and relatively free of symptom distress than other women in some studies (Frank et al., 1984, 1985; Jones et al., 1978). Males, whose traditional sex typing encompasses instrumental traits, may have less to gain from the addition of expressive traits, at least using traditional measures of adjustment. And indeed, "feminine" males report a relatively high level of symptom distress and neuroticism (Frank et al., 1984; Jones et al., 1978). It is interesting in this regard that a standard test of psychological adjustment, the California Personality Inventory, correlates significantly with "masculine" instrumental traits on eight scales, but not at all with expressive traits (Mills & Bohannon, 1983). This finding may be due to there being a stronger connection between instrumental traits and adjustment than between expressive traits and adjustment, or it may be due to a male-biased definition of adjustment and mental health. This latter possibility will be discussed further below.

There actually are two different models of androgyny in the research literature: androgyny as an additive construct, and androgyny as an interactive construct. As an additive construct, androgyny would simply be the sum of the separate effects of "masculine" instrumental and "feminine" expressive traits (Spence et al., 1975). As an interactive construct, androgyny would be more than the sum of its parts—

a unique psychological state (Bem, 1974). Research to date has provided stronger support for the additive model than the interactive model, although, as discussed above, this is due to the strong positive effect of the "masculinity" scale by itself (Hall & Taylor, 1985; Harrington & Andersen, 1981; Lubinski et al., 1981, 1983; Spence, 1983; Taylor & Hall, 1982; Zeldow et al., 1985).

There are other challenges to the use of androgyny as a new mental health norm (Garnets & Pleck, 1979; Hoffman & Fidell, 1979; A. Kaplan, 1979; Locksley & Colten, 1979; Logan & Kaschak, 1980; Olds & Shaver, 1980; Pleck, 1981b). Many situations involve different contingencies and norms for females and males. Just having high levels of instrumental and expressive characteristics does not mean that these characteristics will be integrated or adaptive.

Of all groups, the "undifferentiated" (those low on both "masculinity" and "femininity") appear to be the most poorly adjusted (Burchardt & Serbin, 1982; Downey, 1984; Hoffman & Fidell, 1979; Rendely et al., 1984; Shaw, 1982). They have the lowest self-esteem, the most external locus of control, and see themselves as less happy. They are also the most introverted and the most neurotic. Previous research that found "feminine" women to have the poorest adjustment may have inadvertently pooled "undifferentiated" women with those who are feminine sex typed. It is only in the past few years that general agreement has been reached regarding the importance of examining "undifferentiated" individuals separately from other groups (Bem, 1977; Spence et al., 1975).

Another problem with research in this area is the use of different scales to measure both sex typing and adjustment. Although the current scales do bear some relationship to each other, they are not interchangeable (Kelly & Worell, 1977; Spence & Helmreich, 1979b; Worell, 1978), nor are they clearly related to the earlier means of assessing sex typing. Furthermore, adjustment is a difficult term to define operationally. As Bryant and Veroff (1982) have demonstrated, there appear to be three related but separate factors involved in psychological well-being: happiness or unhappiness (positive evaluation), strain or lack of anxiety (negative evaluation), and personal adequacy or inadequacy (competence). The types of thoughts or activities that contribute to such feelings may differ as a function of an individual's sex as well as a function of social or historical circumstances. Thus, in a time period when attitudes toward sex roles are in flux, the relationships among sex typing, sex-role conformity, and psychological well-being also are likely to be unstable.

Until such time as a new mental health ideal is defined, however, we can sum up the current research relating sex typing to emotional adjustment. The safest conclusion that seems warranted is that instrumental "masculine" traits, whether by themselves or in conjunction with expressive "feminine" traits, appear to be associated most strongly with good adjustment; undifferentiated sex typing, with poor adjustment; and feminine sex typing, somewhere between the first and second groups. Thus, the belief that a high level of gender-appropriate traits facilitates a person's general psychological or social adjustment is not supported, at least for females. This is even more strikingly evident when more serious emotional problems are examined.

Mental Illness

In the last few years, there have been numerous books published examining the relationship between sex roles and psychopathology (Al-Issa, 1983; Franks & Rothblum, 1983; Gomberg & Franks, 1979; Widom, 1984a). Although mental disorders usually are multidetermined, reflecting various combinations of biological, psychological, and social factors, sex roles do appear to contribute to a number of disorders. One way they contribute is in the popular belief that women generally are more mentally disturbed than are men. Numerous studies using data from community surveys, first admissions to psychiatric hospitals, psychiatric care in general hospitals, psychiatric outpatient care, private outpatient psychiatric care, and psychiatric illnesses in the practice of general physicians have shown that from 1950 to 1975, more women than men were likely to be mental patients, to experience nervous breakdowns, to suffer from depression, nervousness, insomnia,

and nightmares, and to be in psychotherapy (Chesler, 1972; Gove, 1979, 1980; Gove & Tudor, 1977; Russo & Sobel, 1981). Although minority women are less likely than White women to suffer from depressive disorders, the finding of more female than male mental health users occurs across all ethnic groups. In college, females report more depression and anxiety than do males (Logan & Kaschak, 1980). Women are three times more likely than men to attempt suicide, although men are three times more likely than women to actually die from such attempts (Lester, 1984; Steffenmeier, 1984). These sex differences have been found among almost all subgroups in a population and across a variety of nations. The differences between suicide attempts and suicide completions are due almost entirely to the different methods used in suicide attempts by males and females. In the United States, males are more likely than females to use firearms whereas females are more likely than males to use pills.

However, a blanket statement that females are more mentally disturbed than males would be incorrect. It is only with regard to certain disorders and certain categories of females that the female incidence rate is higher than that of males. Table 9-2 summarizes the disorders in which sex differences in incidence have been found, based on the latest diagnostic system, the Diagnostic and Statistical Manual, 3rd edition (DSM-III), issued in 1980. As can be seen in this table, when disorders are examined across the life span, males actually suffer from more disorders than do females. Even among adults, there are a number of disorders more commonly found among men than among women—for example, certain personality disorders, alcoholism, and substance abuse disorders. These disorders often are considered forms of social deviance rather than "mental illness" per se. Possible reasons for this sex difference in incidence will be discussed below, along with another interesting finding— that marital status affects males and females differently with respect to emotional disorders.

When data on mental illness rates are broken down in terms of marital status (Gove, 1972; Rosenstein & Milazzo-Sayre, 1981; Walker, Bettes, Kain, & Harvey, 1985), an interesting pattern emerges (see Table 9-3 for a

Table 9-2

Mental Disorders That Occur More Frequently in One Sex

Male	Female

Childhood

Male	Female
1. Attention deficit disorder (10 times more frequent)	1. Elective mutism
2. Conduct disorder (excluding undersocialized, nonaggressive; range = 4:1–12:1)	
3. Overanxious	
4. Schizoid disorder in childhood	
5. Transient tic (3 times more frequent)	
6. Tourrette (3 times more frequent)	
7. Stuttering (4 times more frequent)	
8. Functional enuresis	
9. Functional encopresis	
10. Sleepwalking	
11. Sleep terrors	
12. Autism (3 times more frequent)	
13. Pervasive developmental disorder	
14. Specific developmental disorder (2 times more frequent)	

Adolescence and young adulthood

Male	Female
15. Schizoid disorder of adolescence	2. Anorexia (95% of cases are females)
	3. Bulimia
	4. Psychogenic amnesia
	5. Multiple personality

Adulthood

Male	Female
16. Multiple infarct dementia	6. Dementia arising in senium or presenium
17. Alcohol hallucinosis (4 times more frequent)	7. Major depressive episodes
18. Substance abuse disorder	8. Dysthymic disorder
19. Obsessive-compulsive disorder	9. Phobias
20. Transexual (2:1 to 8:1)	10. Anxiety neuroses
21. Paraphilias	11. Somatization disorder
22. Premature ejaculation	12. Globus hystericus (lump in throat)
23. Factitious disorder with psychological symptoms	13. Psychogenic pain
24. Factitious disorder with physical symtoms	14. Inhibited sex desire
25. Pathological gambling	15. Inhibited orgasm
26. Pyromania	16. Histrionic personality disorder
27. Intermittent explosive disorder	17. Borderline personality disorder
28. Paranoid personality disorder	18. Dependent personality disorder
29. Antisocial personality disorder	
30. Compulsive personality disorder	

Note. Ratios and percentages, where given, are reported in the DSM-III.
From "Sex Patterns in DSM III: Bias or Bias for Theory Development," by
R. Oakes, (letter to the editor), *American Psychologist, 39,* 1320–1322.
Copyright 1984 by the American Psychologist Association. Reprinted by
permission of the author.

Table 9-3
Rate of Residency in Mental Hospitals as a Function of Marital Status
(persons per 100,000), 1975

	Men	Women	Men/Women
Married	672.1	1101.6	0.61
Divorced	5318.8	4690.7	1.13
Widowed	1095.7	925.7	1.18
Never married	1937.5	1500.0	1.29

Adapted from Rosenstein and Milazzo-Sayre, 1981, Table 1.

typical pattern). The finding of greater mental disturbance in women than men is limited to married women compared to married men. When single (never married, divorced, widowed) individuals are compared together, it is the single male who is more likely to be disturbed. The pattern for suicide attempts and completions is similar. When single individuals are compared to married ones, it is single men who are most suicidal (Lester, 1984). It should be kept in mind that married people of both sexes, however, tend to have lower rates of mental illness than the unmarried (Walker et al., 1985). For the unmarried, Brody (1979) reports 1975 data from state and community psychiatric categories showing the rates of admission to mental institutions were highest for those separated and divorced, followed by those who were widowed and those who never married.

A number of explanations are possible for why married women appear to have higher rates of mental illness than married men, as well as for why the sexes differ in their pattern of incidence of mental disorders. The differences may be due to biological factors, different role definitions, sex biases in diagnosis, or differential role strain. Each explanation will be examined in turn.

Biology.   There is no support for the hypothesis that women may be biologically more susceptible to mental problems than men, since it is only married women who have higher rates of emotional disturbance than married men. Perhaps it is that the more biologically susceptible female and the less biologically susceptible male get married, while their "healthier" sisters and "sicker" brothers remain single either out of choice or because of inability to find a mate. Divorced and widowed individuals, then, having once been married, would be expected to have rates of mental illness similar* to their married counterparts. This again is not the case. Divorced and widowed women have lower rates of mental illness than divorced and widowed men. Thus, a biological explanation cannot account for the data on marital status.

Biological explanations are only slightly more useful in explaining the sex difference in incidence of mental disorders. In examining Table 9-2, we can infer that a number of problems more commonly found in males may have a biological component: attention deficit disorders, schizoid disorders in childhood, autism, developmental disorders, schizoid disorders of adolescence, multiple infarct dementia, alcoholism, and antisocial personality disorders. As discussed in Chapter 2, males appear more biologically susceptible than females from birth, and this factor may be involved in some of the childhood disorders mentioned above. Gove (1985) suggests that sex differences in physical strength, energy, and drive during adolescence and young adulthood may lead to differential rates of social deviancy. Biological factors also may play a role in major depressive episodes, more commonly found in women. This will be discussed further below. However, those disorders that have the strongest biological bases, schizophrenia and bipolar depression, are just those disorders in which a sex difference in incidence generally is not found, at least among adults. Whatever role biological factors play in the incidence of various mental disorders, they are unlikely to be sufficient to account for the differential pattern by sex.

Sex Roles. Another explanation for the mental health statistics centers on the definitions of male- and female-appropriate behavior—that is, the sex roles. Perhaps the sex roles make certain types of disorders more likely in one sex than the other. Perhaps more females than males act emotionally disturbed or seek treatment because it is more acceptable that they do so. Perhaps females are more likely to be diagnosed as emotionally disturbed because that is part of our stereotype of femininity. All these interpretations have received some support. Although they, too, fail to account for the data on marital status, they do shed some light on the sex difference in incidence of disorders.

The idea that females may have higher rates of mental illness than males because of their emotional expressiveness has received some support from Phillips and Segal (1969). They found that, when the number of physical and psychiatric illnesses were held constant, women were more likely than men to seek medical and psychiatric care. They argued that, in community studies, more women may appear mentally ill because it is more socially acceptable for them to talk about their psychological symptoms and to do something about them than it is for men. Other research supports the assertion that women may seek out health-care services more frequently than men do (Padesky & Hammen, 1981; Scarf, 1979). This pattern develops sometime around puberty, a time when female to male ratios of mental health problems start changing (Gove, 1979).

Although more women than men may seek treatment, this explanation alone cannot account for why females are diagnosed as more mentally disturbed, since such diagnoses presumably are based on more than self-reports. This approach also cannot account for the data on marital status, as it makes the same predictions as does the biological explanation. The data do not bear out either explanation; for example, divorced and widowed women are less likely than married women to seek help for emotional problems. Furthermore, research has indicated that when level of disorder is controlled for, there is no marked sex difference in

help-seeking behaviors (Gove & Tudor, 1977). Similarly, response bias has been ruled out as a satisfactory explanation for why women may report more symptoms (Clancy & Gove, 1974; Gove & Geerken, 1977).

However, as noted in the beginning of this section, a number of writers do think that the sex roles contribute to the sex differences in incidence of mental disorders (see Table 9-2). For example, the antisocial personality disorder, more commonly found among men than women, is characterized by aggressive and impulsive behaviors. Such behaviors are more integral to the male than the female sex role, as is pathological gambling, pyromania (fire setting), and intermittent explosive disorders (Spence et al., 1979). Similarly, although the incidence of female alcoholics and substance abusers has increased steadily since the mid-1940s with some leveling off in the 1970s, male alcoholics outnumber female alcoholics and substance abusers (Colten & Marsh, 1984; Gomberg, 1981, 1982, 1984). Again researchers suggest that sex roles play an important part in these rates, with alcohol use being more socially acceptable for males than females. Women may be more prone than men to exhibit their depression directly, whereas men may be more prone than women to cover their depression with alcohol and/or drug use (Weissman & Klerman, 1977; Williams & Spitzer, 1983). It is interesting that women are the major abusers of prescription drugs, such as Valium, although men predominate as abusers of other substances (Fidell, 1981; Gomberg, 1982; Verbrugge, 1982). Research has shown that two-thirds of the prescriptions for psychotropic drugs are written for women. Drug use may lead to abuse for some women due to its seeming encouragement by the medical profession, and due to components of the female sex role, such as dependency and low self-esteem.

Other disorders that are more common in women than men also seem to reflect aspects of the female sex role. Phobias and anxiety disorders may reflect, in part, the social encouragement of some fears in females and a greater willingness of females to admit to fears (Fodor, 1983; Wolfe, 1984). For example, if a female said, "Eek, a mouse!", she might receive a bemused but basically tolerant reaction. If a male said the same thing, he probably would be mocked quite intensely. It is also in keeping with certain aspects of the female sex role to be highly emotional and seductive (histrionic personality disorder), dependent (dependent personality disorder), inhibited sexually (inhibited sex desire, inhibited orgasm), and overly concerned with dieting and being thin (anorexia and bulimia) (Leon & Finn, 1984; Stock, 1984; Winstead, 1984). Depression is another disorder more common in women than men that may be linked to sex roles. This will be explored in more depth below.

To the extent that individuals have developed according to traditional sex roles, it does seem true that feminine-sex-typed individuals, especially females, are more prone to depression, anxiety, and low self-esteem than are masculine and androgynous sex-typed groups, as discussed previously (Burchardt & Serbin, 1982; Heiser & Gannon, 1984; La Torre et al., 1983; Tinsley, Sullivan-Guest, & McGuire, 1984). It should be remembered, though, that most research finds the "undifferentiated" group to be the most poorly adjusted, and such a group generally contains equal numbers of females and males. Thus, although gender-related personality traits may make some females more prone to certain psychological disorders, such a variable cannot account fully for the data on marital status, unless "undifferentiated" females are more likely, and "undifferentiated" males are less likely, to get and stay married than other sex-typing groups. There is no evidence that such is the case.

Another possibility related to sex roles is that more females may get diagnosed as emotionally disturbed because of the gender stereotypes. These findings can be grouped together as examples of sex bias in diagnosis.

Sex Bias. A closer look at how psychiatric diagnoses are made reveals a disturbing double standard of mental health operating in this country. Broverman and associates (1970), in their now classic study of 79 male and female psychologists, psychiatrists, and social workers, found that these mental health professionals made clear-cut distinctions between a healthy man and a healthy woman. The healthy woman, according to the subjects of the study, is more

emotional, more submissive, more concerned with her appearance, less independent, less aggressive, and less competitive than is the healthy man. Even more disturbing than this negative assessment of females, however, is the finding that the behavior and characteristics judged healthy for an adult, sex unspecified, were similar to those judged healthy for an adult male but not for an adult female. Thus, mental health workers saw women as having more negative and less healthy characteristics than a "typical" adult—that is, a man—a clear example of a male-centered bias.

More recent research suggests that much of this apparent sex bias in expressed attitudes of clinicians has disappeared, perhaps as a result of greater awareness of this issue, or of improved methodology (Davidson & Abramowitz, 1980; Franks, 1979; Phillips & Gilroy, 1985; Wise & Rafferty, 1982). Therapists today no longer say that the characteristics of a healthy female and a healthy male are very different from each other. There is a predominance of positive traits for both sexes. However, a number of studies still find that in practice, some psychotherapists (male and female) do stereotype according to gender to the disparagement of females (Abramowitz & Herrera, 1981; Brodsky & Hare-Mustin, 1980; Teri, 1982). Nontherapists have been found to hold a double standard of mental health as well, and to rate as maladjusted clients who do not conform to the gender stereotypes (Brooks-Gunn & Fisch, 1980; Costrich et al., 1975; Malchon & Penner, 1981; Tilby & Kalin, 1980; Zedlow, 1976). These findings, taken together, suggest that such stereotyping is a cultural standard. However, female therapists appear less likely than male therapists to use such a double standard of mental health, especially with regard to female clients (Abramowitz & Herrera, 1981; Davidson & Abramowitz, 1980; Garfinkle & Morin, 1978; Wright, Meadow, Abramowitz, & Davidson, 1980).

This double standard of mental health, paralleling as it does societal gender stereotypes, is probably a reflection of an "adjustment" standard of mental health. In other words, a woman is seen as healthy if she is more emotional and submissive because that is what society has termed acceptable for females. Using this approach, an independent, assertive woman might be labelled "deviant." Not only do clinicians holding this view foster conformity and restrict the choices open to women and men, but they also may foster emotional problems, because it has been shown that strong sex typing for women is more associated with emotional problems, not less so.

Chesler (1972) and others (Hare-Mustin, 1983; Tennov, 1975) go even further in their condemnation of such a view of mental health for women. These writers blame psychology and psychotherapists for directly tyrannizing and oppressing women into staying in their (second) place. According to Chesler, more women than men are in psychotherapy because psychotherapy is one of the two institutions socially approved for middle-class women; the other socially approved institution is marriage. Both institutions allow a woman to express and diffuse her feelings by experiencing them as a form of emotional illness. If a woman is married and her husband treats her well and provides for her (and for the children), then any feelings of dissatisfaction may be taken as a sign of some emotional problem on her part ("Why aren't you happy when you have everything a woman should want? There must be something wrong with you."). Both institutions also isolate women from each other and emphasize individual, rather than social, solutions to problems (the problem is in you, rather than in society or your husband). Both views are based on a woman's dependence on a strong male (in most cases) authority figure.

Even diagnostic categories may reflect a male bias. A number of writers (Hare-Mustin, 1983; M. Kaplan, 1983a, 1983b) argue that diagnostic systems, including the latest DSM-III, describe as disorders certain behavioral syndromes that are part of the "normal" female gender stereotype. For example, a woman who displays exaggerated emotions, irrational outbursts, overreactions to minor events, and vain, demanding, dependent, and helpless characteristics is likely to be classified as suffering from a histrionic personality disorder (formerly called *hysterical personality*). Thus, conforming to the female gender stereotype may lead to a psychiatric label whereas there is not label for those who conform to the male gender stereo-

type. It should be noted that *exaggerated* masculine characteristics might lead to a label, such as an antisocial or paranoid personality disorder. But in the case of females, the stereotypic traits need not be exaggerated to lead to a psychiatric label. Thus the diagnostic system may fail to distinguish between social deviance and true mental disorders, and therefore may lead to distorted patterns of incidence of mental disorders, such as found in Table 9-2. Although clinical diagnoses still can be useful when a problem has its roots in social factors (Williams & Spitzer, 1983), there is something wrong if socializing girls to conform to the female gender stereotype means they are being socialized into psychiatric categories.

Using this interpretation, it is no wonder that more females than males have higher rates of some emotional disturbances; they are more likely to be encouraged to develop unhealthy characteristics, to be diagnosed as disturbed even if they show "healthy adult" behaviors, and to fit into male-centered psychotherapy. Yet, although this explanation may account for the larger number of married women in psychotherapy and for some sex differences in incidence of disorders, it does not fully account for the other differences associated with marital status.

Role Conflict. Another explanation for the mental health statistics centers on the concept of role conflict. It is not that sex roles per se make males and females more susceptible to certain mental problems but that there is some conflict or strain in the roles males and females hold that promotes certain mental disorders.

In this view, women's role in modern industrial societies is seen as having a number of characteristics that produce stress. In the first place, most women until recently have been restricted to a single role—housewife—whereas men have had two roles—breadwinner and husband/father. This means men have had two potential sources of satisfaction, whereas women, for the most part, have had just one. If married women are employed, they may have the strain of holding down two jobs (inside and outside the home) and the strain of less satisfying jobs (less money, less prestige, fewer job openings, more career roadblocks, and so forth).

Employed married women have been found to have higher rates of alcohol consumption and problems than nonemployed married women and than employed single women (P. Johnson, 1982). Similarly, Frevert (1983) found that women who had graduated from college 25 years before and who had combined both family and employment roles tended to show patterns of high stress, low mental health, and low happiness, especially in the middle 15 years. Multiple roles can lead to work overload and inter-role conflict (Cooke & Rousseau, 1984; Gerson, 1985). Although performing two jobs may not lead to emotional problems, such stress may take its toll, emotionally or physically, over the years.

The critical variables here are choice, social support, commitment to the work role, and quality of employment (Baruch & Barnett, in press; Fisher, 1984). In Frevert's (1983) study, such variables were not measured. However, one can speculate that women in her sample received little social support because they graduated in the 1950s, a time when women were being urged to stay at home. Holahan and Gilbert (1979) found in their study of 51 employed mothers with equivalent levels of education (college graduates) that it was only those women who thought of their work as a job rather than as a career who experienced role conflict. The conflict arose between parent-self and spouse-self roles. Importantly, the support of a spouse was crucial in reducing such role conflict. Women who defined their work as a career reported no role conflicts. These women also tended to have more spouse support. Similarly, Black women, who generally expect to combine family life with employment, report relatively little role conflict (Malson, 1983). These women tend to have support networks and role models that may alleviate some of the stresses of multiple roles. (This is not to say that other stresses, such as low-status jobs, poverty, and discrimination, don't exist or affect Black women's mental health.)

Most studies find little difference between the mental health status of employed women and homemakers (Erdwins & Mellinger, 1984; Ferree, 1984; Rendely et al., 1984; Shehan, 1984). However, in a number of circumstances, paid employment has been found to be positively associated with a woman's psychological well-being—for example, among working-class women, among mothers with social support and with positive occupational attitudes, and among women with both families and high-prestige jobs (Baruch et al., 1983; Baruch & Barnett, in press; Horwitz, 1982; Warr & Parry, 1982a, 1982b). Many women appear to thrive on the challenges involved in juggling career and family lives. For example, Baruch et al. (1983) conducted interviews with 238 White women between the ages of 35 and 55, some of whom were single, single with children, married, or married with children. Half of the married women were homemakers. These researchers found that the employed women had higher levels of mastery (self-esteem and a sense of control) than the nonemployed women, and that a sense of mastery was vital for a woman's overall well-being. Interestingly, having children had no impact on well-being.

If a married woman does not work outside the home she may find her major instrumental activities, such as raising children and keeping house, to be frustrating and confusing, being often in conflict with her educational and intellectual attainments, having little prestige attached to them, and being virtually invisible. Selfless devotion to the needs of others may mean one's own needs are neglected (Marecek & Ballou, 1981). Bernard (1976a) suggests that the lack of emotional support from a husband (because of men's conditioning) and from female friends (because of social conditions mitigating against female-female bonds) has contributed to the apparent rise in female depression. In the Baruch et al. (1983) study, social supports were found to be very important to a woman's overall well-being, especially if she was a homemaker. A wife may also be under strain because of the unclear expectations for her future (husband may change jobs, transfer). This role strain is strongest for married women, hence their higher rates of emotional problems. Societal expectations may serve as another source of stress. Many people feel that a housewife should be happy because she's "out of the rat race" (Ferree, 1984). Conversely, and more recently, many others feel that housewives, especially middle-class ones, should really be employed. Perhaps as a result of these attitudes, housewives with liberal views toward sex roles appear to be more depressed than do housewives with traditional views (Kingery, 1985). Krause (1983) found that the more dissatisfied a housewife was with housework, and the more conflict there was with spouse over sex-role expectations, the higher the depressive symptom score of the woman.

If women's roles were clearer, were more highly valued, and demanded more time and skill, such strain should not occur. This was true more for women before World War II. Indeed, mental health statistics bear this out—more men than women were hospitalized for mental illness at that time (Gove & Tudor, 1973, 1977). It should be noted, however, as Dohrenwend and Dohrenwend (1976) point out, that the nature of psychiatric diagnosis has changed during that time. Since World War II, diagnoses have become broader and more inclusive, particularly regarding anxiety and depressive symptomatology. Hence, increasing rates of mental illness for women since World War II may reflect such methodological changes.

Related to this concept of differential role strain is a proposal by Bernard (1973) of a *shock theory of marriage* for women. When a woman enters into a conventional marriage, she undergoes a number of emotional shocks that could disturb her emotional well-being. She experiences conflict between attachment to her husband and attachment to her parents. She discovers her husband is not super strong, protective, and so forth. She is pressured to reshape her personality and behavior to meet her husband's wishes and needs. And she finds her husband values her domestic behaviors more than her affectional ones. Thus, marriage, for some women, appears to be an emotional hazard. This, of course, is not to say that marriage is a hazard for all women. Much depends on the woman and the marriage. It should be recalled that rates of emotional disturbance (and, as we shall see, physical disorders) are less for married individuals than for those who are unmarried. And many women handle role combinations without any role strain. Yet Bernard's thesis does account for the higher rates of mental disorders among married women than among married men, and is supported by other research. For example, some researchers have found that among hospitalized psychiatric patients, married women had the most severe symptoms whereas married men had the lowest

(Kirshner & Johnston, 1983; Walker et al., 1985). Furthermore, married women showed more symptoms than did formerly married women, suggesting that marriage may serve to exacerbate symptoms in women. Other research has shown that whereas the spouses of disturbed men tend to be supportive, spouses of disturbed women tend to be nonsupportive (Turkington, 1985; as reported in Walker et al., 1985).

The components of psychological well-being and life satisfaction are very similar for women and men, especially since the mid-1970s (Bryant & Veroff, 1982; Morgan, 1980). For both sexes, work satisfaction, marital/family satisfaction, and personal competence are very important. However, a national survey of more than 2000 adults found that whereas over one-third of the men expressed great satisfaction with life, only one-eighth of the women reported high satisfaction (Morgan, 1980). Borges, Levine, and Dutton (1984) also found less satisfaction with life among women than among men. This sex difference may reflect on the differences in the social roles for women and men. Whereas traditional male gender socialization is geared toward satisfying all three of the major components of life satisfaction, traditional female gender socialization is geared toward satisfying only one—the marital/family component. Thus women may experience unhappiness if they don't attain all three goals, and role strain if they do. Women today are expected to be both active and passive, and this conflicting pressure may lead to internal conflict (Davidson, 1981). Other research suggests that conflicts over appropriate sex-role behavior may lead to emotional problems, particularly alcohol abuse (S. Anderson, 1984; Gomberg, 1981, 1984; P. Johnson, 1982; Kleinke & Hinrichs, 1983; Rooney, Volpe, & Suziedelis, 1984).

Regardless of sex typing, research has shown that people who are relatively powerless have more symptoms of distress than people who are in powerful roles (Horwitz, 1982). Thus, women in general have higher levels of distress than men, with the exception of married women who are the chief breadwinners of their family, and married employed women without children. These two groups of women have some degree of power. The most distressed group of women are those who are unemployed and childless, perhaps because they are both powerless and deviant from sex-role expectations.

If mental health statistics are a product of the social system, it also can be predicted that those men who experience role conflict or strain or who are in relatively powerless positions should also have higher rates of emotional problems. For example, men whose wives are employed appear to become more anxious as the prestige of the wives' jobs increases (Fisher, 1984). There are numerous strains inherent in the male sex role, as described by Pleck (1976b, 1981b) and O'Neil (1981a, 1981b, 1982; O'Neil et al., 1984). (See Figure 9-1.) Because males are expected to devote themselves single-mindedly to achieving, single males are under more strain than single women and married males because they do not have anyone to take care of their other needs, both physical and emotional. Because of social inhibitions on males expressing their emotions, especially to other men, wives are often the only source of emotional relief for men. Thus, treatment outcome for alcoholic men is better if the man is married than if he is not (Cronkite & Moos, 1984). For alcoholic women, marital status is not related to treatment outcome. As a result of these role strains for men, there are higher rates of emotional disturbance in single men than in single women. The latter group has been trained to provide the basics of physical and emotional care for themselves. In recent years, the demands on men to be more emotionally expressive and involved in child-care and homemaking activities have increased. Such pressures may be responsible for more men seeking help for psychological distress than in the past (Bales, 1984; Goleman, 1984).

Because the major role for males centers on their working ability, in times of economic depression and high unemployment more men than women should experience problems. Statistics reported in Gove and Tudor (1973) bear this out, as do more recent reports of increases in male depression, suicide, sexual impotence, child abuse, and so on accompanying the high unemployment rates of the 1970s (Drummond, 1977). Unemployed men show significantly more signs of both psychological and physiological distress than do their employed male counterparts (Horwitz, 1982). One study (Brenner, 1973, 1979) found that, after looking at data from 750,000 New York State mental patients during a 127-year period, the only significant factor accounting for the rise and fall in admission to mental hospitals was employment. This negative effect of unemployment, supported by more recent studies, is true of women as well as men (P. Johnson, 1982; Kasl, 1979; Kasl & Cobb, 1979; Liem & Rayman, 1982; Warr & Parry, 1982b). Whether men are more affected than women by unemployment is debatable, however (Drummond, 1977; Horwitz, 1982). Retirement also may be stressful for women as well as for men (Herman, 1981). This may be because women's retirement often is involuntary, due to spouse's retirement or his failing health. These findings again point to the difficulty in dichotomizing the activities of the sexes and the consequences of these activities.

Role conflict and strain is a frequent occurrence among Black men in the United States. Most American Black men have internalized the cultural norms regarding "masculinity" (Cazenave, 1984), yet racism and economic exploitation have made it difficult, if not impossible, for most Black men to attain the cultural norm of achievement, success, power, and so on. Unemployment rates are much higher for Black males than for White males, and the gap in incomes between Black and White males has increased since the early 1970s (Cordes, 1985). In 1982, nearly 30% of all Black men between the ages of 20 and 64 were not employed, and about half weren't even in the labor force, having given up even looking for a job. Meanwhile, programs that support low- and moderate-income families have been cut drastically under President Reagan. Some consequences of these stresses are the strikingly high number of mental and physical health problems among Black males, as well as the disproportionately high incidence of social deviancy (Cordes, 1985; Gary, 1981). For example, in 1975, Black males had the highest admission rates as inpatients of any sex or racial group to state and community mental hospitals, and they were admitted at younger ages.

Using role conflict and role strain to explain emotional problems also helps explain certain age patterns as shown in Table 9-2. Adjustment pressures appear to be different for males and females at different ages. As was discussed previously, males experience the most intense socialization pressures during childhood and early adolescence, and it is then that males have higher rates of psychosis, learning problems, behavior problems, stuttering, and enuresis than females (Anastas & Reinharz, 1984; Eme, 1984). Girls experience their most intense socialization pressures during and after adolescence, and it is then that the statistical trends just mentioned start reversing themselves. By the end of the seventh grade in one study, girls attained greater neuroticism and alienation scores than did their male peers (La Torre et al., 1983). Girls begin receiving more diagnoses of anxiety and affective disorders after puberty than do males (Eme, 1979). The most striking disorders that affect females about nine times more frequently than males and that begin during adolescence are the eating disorders.

Both anorexia nervosa (self-starvation) and bulimia (the gorging-and-purging syndrome), which appear to be increasing in incidence since the mid-1970s, are thought to be the result of a combination of factors: low self-esteem; female adolescent conflicts regarding sexuality, independence, assertiveness, and peer acceptance; and a cultural obsession with female thinness (Basow & Schneck, 1984; Garfinkel & Garner, 1982; Leon & Finn, 1984; Wardle & Beinart, 1981). Research has shown that about three-fourths of college-age females are dissatisfied with their weight and desire to be thinner, more than half have used extreme forms of dieting, and about half admit to binging on food at least sometimes (Basow & Schneck, 1984; Halmi, Falk, & Schwartz, 1981). Sex typing affects these eating-related attitudes and behaviors as well. Femininity scale traits have been found to be positively correlated with restrictive dieting tendencies (Hawkins, Turell, & Jackson, 1983), and undifferentiated and feminine sex-typed college women tend to be the most dissatisfied with their bodies (Kimlicka et al., 1983). Males, in contrast, rarely suffer from eating disorders. However, they too may be dissatisfied with their bodies, and more anxious and less confident if they don't match the male muscular ideal (Tucker, 1982b, 1983b). Indeed, Tucker (1982a, 1983a) found that par-

ticipating in a weight-training program positively influenced self-concept in college men, regardless of their level of success.

It is important to note here that the problems for which males and females are referred to child guidance centers are different. Boys are most often referred for aggressive, antisocial, and competitive behaviors; girls, for personality problems, such as excessive fears, shyness, and feelings of inferiority (Anastas & Reinharz, 1984; Locksley & Douvan, 1979). These differences again parallel the stereotypes of males being more active, females more passive, illustrating the negative aspects of both gender stereotypes.

There are other age patterns as well. Although community surveys taken in the mid-1950s and the 1960s found that impairment rates rose regularly among successive age groups, being higher for women than for men at all ages, follow-ups done in the 1970s showed women in their 40s and 50s now were less impaired than in the past (Bird, 1979). In fact, their rates of impairment now were comparable to their male peers (around 8% to 9%) and were the lowest among all age groups. Surprisingly, new data on women in their 30s showed their impairment rate to be about 30%, the highest in the sample. This suggests that stress for this age group is higher now than ever before, perhaps as a function of changing role expectations and conflicts over motherhood and career ambitions. Middle-aged women may be past such conflicts, a hypothesis supported by other research as well (Baruch et al., 1983; Black & Hill, 1984). Indeed, cross-cultural research suggests that postmenopausal women actually are in their prime with regard to mental health and social influence (J. Brown, Kerns, et al., 1985). Troll and Turner (1979) report on significant sex differences in problems associated with aging but find that these differences do not favor either sex.

Thus, although role pressures and conflicts may be partially responsible for emotional problems, how the problems become manifest and how they are viewed by an observer are determined by what is socially acceptable for one's sex. And social acceptability is determined to a large extent by the gender stereotypes. Depression serves as a case in point.

Depression

Statistics show that the incidence of clinical depression is rising, affecting about one in every five Americans and affecting women two to six times as frequently as men (Scarf, 1979; Weissman & Klerman, 1977). This sex difference in incidence of depression does not appear to be related to a reluctance by men to report depressive symptoms (King & Buchwald, 1982). Depression is greatest among low-income women with young children, particularly those who are divorced or separated, or unemployed (Belle, 1982; Rothblum, 1983; Warr & Parry, 1982a). (The typical depressed person is a woman under age 35.) This can be viewed as a time when pressures (role, economic, social) on them are the strongest. Single women and married men are least likely to suffer from depression, and they also experience the least role strain. Women whose children have left home also are unlikely to suffer from depression, contrary to the myth that menopause and the *empty nest syndrome* are major producers of depression (Barnett & Baruch, 1978; Black & Hill, 1984; Radloff, 1980; Weissman & Klerman, 1977). Bart (1972) reported that it is only those women who defined themselves solely in terms of their maternal role ("the supermothers") who suffered from middle-aged depression.

Yet, the roots of depression are not just in social pressures but rather are in the female role itself. In this view, American society trains women to be susceptible to depression—for example, by encouraging them to feel helpless (Cox & Radloff, 1984; Dweck et al., 1978). It is this cognitive outlook that is directly related to depression, perhaps mediated by attributional style (Abramson, Seligman, & Teasdale, 1978). In particular, making external, unstable, and specific attributions in success situations appears to be associated with feelings of helplessness and with depression. As was discussed in the section on achievement, females are more likely than males to use such an attributional style, at least in some situations. However, it is important to note that depression may cause women to make these types of attributions rather than vice versa (Cochran & Hammen, 1985). Other criticisms of the attributional

model of depression exist as well (for example, Berndt, Berndt, & Kaiser, 1982; Jackson & Larrance, 1979). Still, it is likely that a feeling of helplessness may be particularly strong for married women, especially for those with young children, explaining their higher incidence of depression. Single women may be less indoctrinated with the helplessness stereotype than those who marry; widowed and divorced women may be less helpless than widowed men because women usually at least know how to care for themselves.

With regard to learned helplessness, it is interesting that Baucom and Danker-Brown (1979, 1984; Baucom, 1983) and others (Small, Gessner, & Ferguson, 1984) have found that feminine-sex-typed women appear to be particularly susceptible to some helplessness symptoms, especially in contexts defined as male-appropriate. High masculinity scores seem very important in order to resist the negative effects of helplessness. Similar results have been found with regard to depressed mood itself; that is, high masculinity scores are associated with low scores on various measures of depression (Burchardt & Serbin, 1982; Elpern & Karp, 1984; Feather, 1985; Golding & Singer, 1983; Tinsley et al., 1984; Whitley, 1984; Zeldow et al., 1985). Having high masculinity scale scores is particularly important for females high in femininity scale traits. High masculinity scores are related to self-esteem and to a strong belief in one's ability to control the environment. Such a belief in self-efficacy is important in resisting the negative effects of helplessness experiences and in avoiding depression. Because more males than females are masculine sex typed, the result may be a sex difference in the incidence of learned helplessness and depression.

Another explanation of the higher rates of female depression invokes the concept of *attachment bonding*. Weissman and Klerman (1977; Klerman, 1979) suggest that women, for reasons either biologically or socially based, are particularly sensitive to certain stressors related to disruption of intimate social relationships. Because modern industrial society is replete with disruptors of such relationships (moves, divorce, separation, diminution of family ties), women are more vulnerable to depression than are men. Supporting this hypothesis is the finding that women report more dependence than men; that is, women appear to be more concerned about rejection, abandonment, and managing anger, and to have more feelings of helplessness (Pidano & Tennen, 1985). Furthermore, women who derive their identity from their interpersonal relationships appear to have more depressive symptoms, especially when an important relationship ends, than do women with a more independent sense of self (Levitz-Jones & Orlofsky, in press; Warren & McEachren, 1985). Sex-role orientation also affects how men and women experience the loss of a relationship. For example, "masculine" males appear to be the least dependent of any sex-typed group on a romantic partner. It is not surprising then that the most common external trigger of depression for women, when one exists, is loss of a love bond (Scarf, 1979). For men, the relationship between depression and loss of a love bond is less strong, although it still exists.

In addition to learning helplessness as a part of learning the female role and to acquiring close attachments, females also are more likely than males to learn to use reflective defenses, that is, to turn anger and rage inward and to be self-critical. In contrast, males are more likely than females to turn these feelings outward and to be physically aggressive (Frank et al., 1984; Kleinke, Staneski, & Mason, 1982; Padesky & Hammen, 1981). These sex differences in the expression of feelings begin after puberty and appear to be learned (Webb & VanDevere, 1985). By college, men and women deal with depression in different ways. College women are more likely than men to cry, eat, smoke cigarettes, become irritable, lack confidence, and confront their feelings when depressed. College men are more likely than women to become aggressive, express somatic concerns, engage in sexual behaviors, and withdraw socially when depressed (Chino & Funabiki, 1984; Kleinke et al., 1982; Padesky & Hammen, 1981). Thus, statistics on emotional disturbance, reflecting an internal state, are higher for females. Statistics on drug and alcohol dependence, behavior problems, psychopathy, and crimes—more external indices—are higher for males (see Table 9-2). An interesting test of the hypothesis that depression is expressed directly by females but indirectly by males is a study of the Amish by Egeland and Hosteller (1983). The Amish are a very isolated group who eschew alcohol and the rest of the contemporary American lifestyle. They also have an extremely low crime rate. Among this group, affective disorders appeared to be equally distributed by gender. Thus, the frequently reported sex difference in the prevalence of depression may be more a difference of expression than of true incidence.

Summary

The findings regarding the effect of the gender stereotypes on mental health point in one direction—the more instrumental qualities an individual has (as in androgynous- and masculine-sex-typed persons), the better that person's psychological adjustment. One's marital status is also important. As a result of the gender stereotypes, more married women than married men and more single men than single women experience role strain and conflicts. Also as a result of the stereotypes, women are more likely than men to experience these strains as resulting from emotional, rather than social, problems, are more likely to talk about them, and are more likely to seek psychotherapeutic help. When they obtain help, women are more likely than men to be viewed as psychologically unhealthy as a result of a double standard of mental health, again based on the differential gender stereotypes. These factors explain the greater number of married women than married men who are diagnosed and treated as mentally ill and some of the sex differences in incidence of certain disorders. Once again, belief in the gender stereotypes bears the brunt of the blame.

Physical Health

As if the above consequences were not enough, gender stereotypes also affect one's physical health. More women than men suffer from psychophysiologic disorders and there are also sex differences in the incidence of specific disorders (Fisher & Greenberg, 1979; Gove, 1979; Seiden, 1979). Women are more likely than men to report headaches, throat and urinary problems, constipation, nervous stomach, weight difficulties, or hypertension. Men are more likely than women to report ulcers, asthma, stomach symptoms, and eye complaints. Some of these differences may involve sex differences in the reporting, not the incidence, of the symptoms.

Other statistics discussed in Chapter 2 show that males have a shorter life expectancy, contract more serious illnesses, and have more accidents than do females. Males also use and abuse alcohol and illicit narcotics more than do females. Many researchers and authors directly connect these statistics to the male sex role (Harrison, 1979; O'Neil, 1981a, 1981b, 1982; Pleck, 1976b, 1981b; Solomon & Levy, 1982; Waldron, 1983). Interestingly, when environment and lifestyle are held constant, such as for long-term psychiatric patients, there is a trend toward equalization of death rates between the sexes by specific cause of death (Craig & Lin, 1984). For example, the incidence of death from heart disease is similar for male and female patients whereas in the general population, this cause of death affects men nearly four times more frequently than it does women. This finding supports the hypothesis that lifestyle differences between the sexes, rather than differences in biological vulnerability, account for many of the sex differences in physical health.

Brannon (1976) has abstracted four themes of the stereotyped male role:

1. **No Sissy Stuff:** the need to be different from females.
2. **The Big Wheel:** the need to be superior to others.
3. **The Sturdy Oak:** the need to be self-reliant and independent.
4. **Give 'em Hell:** the need to be more powerful than others.

All four themes involve self-evaluation in terms of an external standard, and all four limit the expression of feelings. As discussed in the previous section, many aspects of the male sex role cause gender conflict and strain, as illustrated in Figure 9-1. One consequence of this strain is poor physical health. Men who are high in the instrumental/"masculine" scale traits alone tend to report lower levels of health

than men who are high in both instrumental and expressive traits (that is, androgynous men) (Downey, 1984).

Because many men's sole identity rests on their role as breadwinner, the stress is sometimes overwhelming when this role is threatened. A number of studies have found increased numbers of peptic ulcers, heart attacks, and strokes related to unemployment in middle-aged men (see Liem & Rayman, 1982). One study (Kasl & Cobb, 1979) found that 100 blue-collar male workers who were about to have their job terminated had significant increases in their cholesterol and norepinephrine levels and in their blood pressure in anticipation of their job loss. These changes continued for 24 months afterward. All of the above changes adversely affect the cardiovascular system and many of these men showed signs of coronary disease, dyspepsia, and hypertension. Women also experience adverse physiological effects from being unemployed, although the highest rates of illness appear to be for married men, perhaps because the stress of their unemployment is exacerbated by sex-role expectations (Horwitz, 1982; Liem & Rayman, 1982).

In addition, because many men tend to overestimate their abilities and because of the reality involved in competitive situations, they often do not win and achieve. Slobogin (1977) suggests that executive stress and/or the competition to get ahead may result in greater vulnerability for men. Yet, men have few acceptable ways of releasing feelings of inadequacy and frustration—"real" men do not show their emotions. Figure 9-2 gives an example of this. In fact, as Bem demonstrated, they may not even know *how* to release feelings. Jourard (1971) suggests that it is a male's typically low self-disclosure, lack of insight and empathy, incompetence at loving, and general dispirition that result in his earlier death. These factors certainly add to the stress arising from a male's life situation and make it difficult for some males to release the tension that builds up.

As described in the previous section, Black men in the United States may have particular problems living up to the male sex-role ideal of achievement and status. Not coincidentally, Black men are less healthy than White men: they are the most likely of any groups to die from injuries on the job, and they die at higher rates from heart disease, hypertension, cancer, strokes, cirrhosis of the liver, tuberculosis, diabetes, and lung diseases (Gary, 1981). Though poverty and poor medical care play major roles in these statistics, gender-related factors may play a role as well.

Even when men are ill, their stoic role may make it more difficult for them to seek help. Greenberg and Fisher (1977) found that anxiety

Figure 9-2

A "real" man never shows his feelings. (Reprinted by permission. © 1978 Newspaper Enterprise Association, Inc.)

about being passive is associated with resistance to becoming a patient. It is not surprising, then, that sixty percent of all medical appointments are made for females (Scarf, 1979). The fact that women go to physicians regularly regarding reproductive functions may inflate these statistics, however. Furthermore, the data on sex differences in medically related behaviors are somewhat contradictory. Fisher and Greenberg (1979) found negligible sex differences among college students in total symptom frequency, in delay in seeking medical consultation, and in the frequency with which medical treatment is obtained. Fisher and Greenberg also found no relationship between "masculinity-femininity" and the frequency with which physicians were consulted, although "masculinity-femininity" was related to the particular symptoms presented (Olds & Shaver, 1980). If men really are less likely than women to go to doctors with physical problems, minor illnesses may develop into major ones, accounting somewhat for the higher rates of serious physical problems in men than in women.

In looking more closely at the major causes of death (Table 2-1), we note that a number of them are directly attributable to certain behaviors, such as cigarette smoking, drinking, reckless driving, violence, and aggressive-competitive Type A or "coronary-prone" behavior. All these behaviors occur more in men than in women and all can be viewed as extreme forms of certain components of masculinity—risk-taking, competition, status, power, and violence. Harrison (1978) suggests that such behaviors may develop as compensation for the anxiety derived from sex-role expectations.

When employment or college status is similar, Type A personality traits do not occur more in men than in women (Blascovich et al., 1981; DeGregorio & Carver, 1980; Waldron, 1978). However, such traits are significantly related to masculinity scale traits and are unrelated to femininity scale traits (Blascovich et al., 1981; DeGregorio & Carver, 1980; Grimm & Yarnold, 1985). This pattern means that Type A personalities are most likely to be masculine or androgynous sex-typed. Type A behavioral traits appear to "fit" better with stereotypic masculine traits than with stereotypic feminine traits. People find a Type A male to be more

socially attractive than a Type A female (Faulkner, Holandsworth, & Thomas, 1983). There is other evidence that Type A traits for women may be associated with greater psychological distress than Type A traits for men, again because such traits and masculine traits may fit together better (Musante, MacDougall, Dembroski, & Van Horn, 1983).

Unfortunately, women seem to be joining men in some of these unhealthy behaviors, especially smoking and drinking habits. Consequently, their rates of physical problems, like lung cancer, heart attacks, and alcoholism are on the rise, as was cited in Chapter 2. Women in high-status occupations appear more likely to show the Type A behavioral pattern than the more relaxed Type B pattern (Greenglass, 1984a; K. Kelly & Houston, 1985; Waldron, 1978). One of the most frequently suggested reasons for the increasing percentage of women who smoke is that cigarette smoking may be a symbol of equality with men—"You've come a long way, baby." This would be a sad testimonial for equality indeed.

Interestingly, some writers have argued that there is, in fact, no increase in female death rates from stress-related diseases (see Ehrenreich, 1979), nor are women who are employed, as a group, more vulnerable to such stress-related ailments as heart disease. On the contrary, there is strong evidence that employed women actually have fewer physical ailments and fewer days in bed than housewives, especially if housewives have favorable attitudes toward employment (Horwitz, 1982; Verbrugge & Madans, 1985; Waldron & Herold, 1984). For example, analysis of a national health survey taken in 1977–1978 found that women who combine job and marriage tend to be healthier than women who are either unmarried or unemployed (Verbrugge & Madans, 1985). Furthermore, employed wives with children are just as healthy as those without children, suggesting that multiple roles are as potentially conducive to physical health as they are to mental health. The least healthy women were unemployed women with neither spouse nor children. Physical and emotional problems in employed women are associated with achievement conflicts and traditionally female jobs, such as clerical and sales work, especially for

Blacks (Ehrenreich, 1979). These problems are compounded when a boss is nonsupportive and the worker also has marital and family responsibilities. Employed Type A women who are married report greater tension and poorer physical health than comparable Type B women, perhaps because role conflicts are both more likely and more stressful for Type A than for Type B women (Greenglass, 1984a; K. Kelly & Houston, 1985). Type A women may try to be "superwomen." In general, employment by itself does not make women more vulnerable to health problems.

As with the data on emotional problems, an interesting interaction has been found between longevity and marital status. A number of researchers (Brody, 1979b; Kobrin & Hendershot, 1977) report that, although women outlive men by about eight years, the difference is much less for married men and women. In general, married individuals of both sexes live longer than single people, perhaps because close interpersonal ties are important for a sense of well-being. This seems particularly true for men. Gove (1973) found that single men were more likely than their female counterparts to die directly from prolonged diseases (tuberculosis and diabetes) and overt social acts (suicide, homicide, accidents) and to die indirectly from the use of socially approved "narcotics" (cirrhosis of the liver and lung cancer). Gove further found that, based on certain internal patterns within the data (the least vulnerable time for men is when young children are at home), a role explanation of these statistics is most likely.

Table 9-4 shows the percentage of higher mortality rates of single people compared to married persons of the same sex (Kobrin & Hendershot, 1977).

Unmarried men who live alone have the highest mortality rate, almost double that of their married counterparts. Unmarried males who head a family live the longest. A slightly different pattern emerges for unmarried females. Although they, too, benefit most from being family heads, women are much better off living alone than within a family in which they are not head. The explanation proposed suggests that social ties and status are both related to longevity, the former, perhaps, being most important. Women generally have social ties whether they live alone or not, but they lack status particularly when they live with a family without being its head ("doubly dependent"). Men have status whether they live alone or not (by virtue of their role), but they may lack social ties without a family. This study suggests that certain aspects of the gender stereotypes may indeed be "lethal" for certain women and men. Other research (Horwitz, 1982) finds a similar pattern for physiological symptoms: they are highest among individuals who are not the primary breadwinners, especially if the individuals are married men.

Another similarity with the data on emotional problems is the suggestion that doctors and other medical personnel may manifest a sex bias in treating their patients' physical complaints (Fidell, 1980, 1984; Wallston, DeVellis, & Wallston, 1983). For example, physicians and nurses tend to attribute symptoms presented by women to psychogenic rather than organic causes; the reverse is true for symptoms presented by men. Perhaps that is why doctors

Table 9-4
Percent Higher Mortality Rates of Single Persons Compared to Married Persons of the Same Sex

	Males	Females
Unmarried compared to married, family head	40%	19%
Unmarried compared to married, living with a family, not head	60%	100%
Unmarried compared to married, living alone	94%	27%

Based on a national cross-section of 20,000 individuals between 1966 and 1968 (Kobrin & Hendershot, 1977).

prescribe mood-modifying drugs at least twice as often for their female patients as for their male patients (Gomberg, 1982). However, a national survey of medical records for five physical complaints (fatigue, headache, dizziness, chest pain, and back pain) found little overall sex difference in the extent of medical workups, at least when other medical factors were controlled (Verbrugge & Steiner, 1984). Where sex differences in treatment exist, they typically reflected more workups for women than men. These results contrast with a smaller study done on the West Coast, which found that men received more extensive workups than women (Armitage, Schneiderman, & Bass, 1979). Whether sex bias exists in the extent of the workups given to female and male patients thus is open to question. However, there is other compelling evidence of both widespread sexism and racism in the U.S. health care industry which goes beyond the scope of this book (see Ehrenreich & English, 1978; Weaver & Garrett, 1983).

In sum, gender stereotypes appear to contribute, in part, to the higher rates in men than in women of serious physical problems. They also seem to account for differences in treatment for men and women.

Summary

The evidence shows that the gender stereotypes have a variety of negative consequences on the individual level, affecting one's self-concept, behavior, and mental and physical health. In regard to self-concept, it has been demonstrated that, for females, strong feminine sex typing is associated with low self-confidence and low expectations. For males, sex typing is associated with high expectations and low self-acceptance. For both sexes, instrumental "masculine" traits are positively associated with self-esteem. These differences in self-concept, combined with other aspects of the stereotypes, have direct consequences on one's behavior—feminine-sex-typed females perform poorly in "masculine" situations and activities requiring competition, independence, or assertiveness, all of which are abilities

needed to function effectively in an industrial, competitive society; masculine-sex-typed males perform poorly in "feminine" situations and activities requiring empathy, nurturance, or expressiveness, which are needed in relating effectively to other individuals. Thus, to the extent that an individual is strongly sex typed, she or he is restricted from living a full and rewarding life.

Of even greater importance is the effect of the stereotypes on one's mental and physical health. For both sexes, instrumental "masculine" traits are positively associated with psychological adjustment. Feminine-sex-typed and "undifferentiated" individuals tend to be more psychologically and socially maladjusted than "masculine" and androgynous individuals. Each sex also is more likely to develop certain disorders, partly as a function of sex-role socialization pressures. Married women in particular have the highest incidence of serious emotional problems, a consequence of the strain involved in their roles and the differing standards used to judge mental health in females and in males. Single males and unemployed males also show high rates of emotional disturbance, resulting from the strains of their roles. In addition, males in general are more likely than females to suffer from physical diseases and to die young, a possible result of the strains of their role-defined behaviors and of their limited means of tension release.

This picture of the consequences of gender stereotypes would be gloomy indeed if there also did not exist a model of a viable alternative. By examining those individuals who are not strongly sex typed—that is, the nearly one-third of Americans who are androgynous—a picture emerges of individuals who can function effectively in a variety of situations and who tend to be emotionally well adjusted. Thus, these people serve as a reminder of the alternatives to the stereotyping trap. By increasing the variety of behaviors allowed in male and female roles, there is also the likelihood of decreasing emotional tension and enhancing the personal growth for members of both sexes. And, although there may be problems involved in such a changeover, the results of so doing certainly seem worthwhile.

Recommended Reading

American Psychological Association Task Force on Sex Bias and Sex-Role Stereotyping in Psychotherapeutic Practice. Source materials for nonsexist therapy. *JSAS Catalog of Selected Documents in Psychology*, 1978, MS. 1685. Materials intended for use in the education and training of psychotherapists. Includes survey results.

Fee, E. (Ed.) (1983). *Women and health: The politics of sex and medicine*. Farmingdale, N.Y.: Baywood. A collection of 11 essays which examine the ways in which sexual divisions are reinforced in medical institutions, knowledge, and practice.

Pleck, J. H. (1981). *The myth of masculinity*. Cambridge, Mass.: MIT Press. A review of traditional assumptions about the male sex role and relevant research. A sex-role strain paradigm is offered.

Spence, J. T. (Ed.) (1983). *Achievement and achievement-motivation: Psychological and sociological approaches*. San Francisco: W. H. Freeman. Six well written articles summarizing research on a number of achievement-related topics.

Widom, C. S. (Ed.) (1984). *Sex roles and psychopathology*. New York: Plenum. An excellent collection of articles on how sex roles affect a variety of emotional disorders and their treatment.

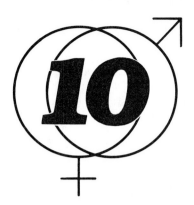

Relationship Consequences

A couple with their 5-year-old daughter visits some friends who have a 5-year-old son. As the parents become involved in conversation, the boy tells his parents that he and the girl will go upstairs to his bedroom and play. Although the girl's parents do not consider this statement noteworthy, the boy's father remarks with a sly smile "It won't be long before we'd think twice about letting them do that!"

This anecdote, modeled on a true story told by Sandra Bem, demonstrates that we have clear expectations regarding male-female relationships. Young children can have same- and other-sex friends. As children mature, however, we assume mixed-sex friendships will lead to sexual and/or romantic involvements. Such expectations are very much shaped by the gender stereotypes of our society.

In the previous chapter, the consequences to the individual of defining self in terms of gender stereotypes were examined. In many ways, the most negative consequences (lower self-confidence, higher incidence of some emotional disturbances, lower achievement) occurred predominantly in females, although males, as a group, certainly had their share of problems (for example, shorter life expectancy). In this chapter, the consequences for relationships of adherence to the stereotypes will be reviewed. It will become apparent that somewhat more negative consequences occur for males as a group than for females as a group, although, again, females also may suffer significantly.

This difference in area of most impairment (individual level for females, relationship level for males) parallels the differential emphasis on the appropriate sphere of activity for the sexes.

Females generally are expected to operate on a relationship, or *communal,* level and are encouraged to develop related skills—interpersonal sensitivity, empathy, emotional expressiveness, nurturance. These skills facilitate females' expected major role, that of mother. Females generally are not expected to be independent or assertive, and many females, in fact, have difficulty demonstrating these qualities. For males, the picture is reversed—they are expected to be agentic, independent, achievement oriented, and aggressive. These qualities facilitate the assumption of their expected major role, that of breadwinner. Males generally are not expected to be relationship oriented, except as it may further their individual goals, such as sexual achievement and professional advancement. Most males are not encouraged to develop relationship skills and are taught, instead, to hide their emotions. Indeed, research has found that men who disclose personal information are liked less than those who do not self-disclose (Chelune, 1976; Derlega & Chaikin, 1976). Such self-disclosing men may be considered poorly adjusted. In contrast, women who disclose themselves are liked more than those who do not self-disclose. Such women are likely to be considered well adjusted. Masking of emotion by males may facilitate competitive strivings, but it may also hinder the development of intimate relationships. Consequently, many men experience great difficulty in the area of relationships, which may be manifested in feelings of emptiness, isolation, and frustration.

Because of the mixed messages men receive about relationships (for example, "get close but not too close"), many men appear to perceive affiliative situations negatively (Mark & Alper, 1985). As discussed previously,

Pollak and Gilligan (1982, 1983) found that whereas more women than men perceive danger in achievement situations, more men than women perceive danger in affiliative situations. Furthermore, from national surveys conducted in 1957 and 1976, men appear to be decreasing in their affiliative motive whereas this motive for women has remained the same (Veroff et al., 1980). These same surveys found an increase among men in two power motives: motivation centered around fear of losing power, and motivation to have power over others. Taken together, these findings suggest that some men may perceive the changing roles of women as threatening their traditional power. To compensate, these men increase their need to control others and decrease their need for relationships, wherein they might see themselves as weak. Such a trend has disturbing implications since relationships are so vital to one's emotional and physical well-being, especially for men, as demonstrated in the last chapter.

For both sexes, the negative effects on relationships of believing in the gender stereotypes are far-reaching. In this chapter, the effects on friendships, love relationships, and parental relationships will be examined.

Friendships

The term *friendship* has been used to describe a variety of relationships, from those with casual acquaintances to those with colleagues to those with intimates. In this discussion, *friendship* refers to an intimate, personal, caring relationship with attributes such as reciprocity, mutual choice, trust, loyalty, and openness (Strommen, 1977). As was discussed in Chapter 4, males and females generally have different types of friendships—boys tend to have more numerous and less intimate relationships ("gangs"); girls tend to have a few close relationships and to use them more for interpersonal exploration (Bell, 1981; Fischer & Narus, 1981a; Hacker, 1981; Sharabany, Gershoni, & Hofman, 1981; P. Wright, 1982). This pattern is by no means universal, and a number of studies find same-sex friendships for males and females to be more similar than different, es-

pecially among college students (Caldwell & Peplau, 1982; Rose, 1985). Furthermore, individuals of both sexes choose friends who are similar to themselves. Kandel (1978) found in her study of nearly 2000 adolescents that both female and male friendships are characterized by similarity of sex, race, age, school grade, and certain behaviors, such as illicit drug taking. Similarity on personality characteristics is relatively unimportant during adolescence, although value similarity increases in importance during the college years, especially for women (Davidson & Duberman, 1982; Hill & Stull, 1981; Rywick, 1984).

Femininity scale traits appear to be strongly related to intimacy levels in both sexes. Thus "feminine" and androgynous individuals, when compared with "masculine" and "undifferentiated" individuals, tend to have more intimate relationships, more support from other people, and are less lonely (Berg & Peplau, 1982; Burda, Vaux, & Schill, 1984; Fischer & Narus, 1981a; Wheeler, Reis, & Nezlek, 1983; D. Williams, 1985). Thus, in contrast to research in the previous chapter which suggested that "masculine" instrumental traits are most facilitative of mental health and achievement, research on relationships suggest that "feminine" expressive traits are most facilitative. Again, being strong in both sets of traits may be optimal for the widest variety of situations and behaviors. With regard to friendships, women seem better off than do men.

An experimental study with 7- and 8-year olds (Foot, Chapman, & Smith, 1977) found that, for both sexes, friendships facilitated social responsiveness. Social responsiveness was defined as laughing, smiling, talking, looking at the companion, and touching. Children showed more expressive behaviors when watching a cartoon when paired with a friend than they did when they were paired with a stranger. Intimacy of the interactions was also varied by having the pair of children either sit close together (1 m apart) and draw pictures of each other (high-intimacy condition) or sit with a screen separating them (low-intimacy condition). Results showed that girls felt more comfortable (smiled more, laughed less) with a higher level of intimacy than did boys. Because the later development of love relationships is facilitated by the capacity for intimacy, which first develops in same-sex friendships (Strommen, 1977), these results may have serious implications. If some males are uncomfortable with intimacy and form less intimate friendships, this situation suggests negative consequences for their future love and marital relationships.

Although adolescence is a time in which friendships are most intense, adults, too, benefit from the support and enrichment of self that close friends can provide. Here, again, research suggests that male friendships may be less intimate than those of females (Aries & Johnson, 1983; S. Miller, 1983). Crawford (cited by Horn, 1978) studied 306 married couples in their 40s, 50s, and 60s. She found that many more women than men said they had a close friend. Of the women in the study, 63% specifically named someone of the same sex as their best friend. In contrast, 60% of the men named a married couple as their best friends. Furthermore, women defined friendships in terms of trust and confidentiality, whereas men emphasized companionship. Similar sex differences were found in a study of the friendship patterns of noninstitutionalized adults over 70 years old (Powers & Bultena, 1976). A closer look at the nature of female-female, male-male, and male-female friendships of all ages seems warranted.

Female-Female Friendships

As has been noted above, females as a group are more likely than males as a group to have close, intimate relationships. Female same-sex friendships have many positive qualities that are evident throughout the life span— for example, trust, loyalty, and attachment (Aries & Johnson, 1983; Burda, Vaux, & Schill, 1984; Caldwell & Peplau, 1982; Davidson & Duberman, 1982; Hacker, 1981; Wright, 1982). Women converse with each other frequently and in great depth about such intimate topics as personal and family matters. Among women who can be considered nonconventional (desirous of change and control over their lives, willing to take risks), same-sex friends are particularly close and important (Bell, 1981). Indeed, some research suggests that the end of a friendship is more painful for a woman than is the

end of a romantic relationship, unlike the situation for men (Pierce, Smith, & Akert, 1984). Such close friendships have been found to be therapeutic, in the sense of contributing to one's personal growth, support, or change (Davidson & Packard, 1981).

Yet there are many difficulties in female same-sex friendships, which vary with the individual's developmental stage. Bardwick (1979) describes the typical pattern of friendships between young girls as alternating between intimacy and repudiation. Most girls either experience or observe a close relationship between "best friends" that is broken by a third girl, only to have the triad reassemble in a different configuration shortly thereafter. This pattern may arise because more overt forms of aggression and dominance are not sanctioned for girls. Thus, covert aggression takes place. Such aggression can be even more potent than overt aggression. These experiences may lay the groundwork for girls to develop a core sense of mistrust of other females. This groundwork is established even before boys become the object of female-female competition.

During adolescence, female friendships are particularly intense, with great concern over sensitivity to others and mutual trust (Strommen, 1977). Friends are an important source of emotional support in personal crises. Female adolescents rank interpersonal relationships as third in importance, after identity and sexuality, as an area of concern. For males, autonomy ranks third in importance, the first two concerns being identical to those noted for girls.

Once dating begins, a change in friendship patterns frequently occurs. The capacity for closeness and intimacy developed in same-sex relationships begins to generalize to romantic relationships. Friendships become more neutral and playful and, in some cases, competitive. Since, traditionally, a female's identity has been determined by the status of the male to whom she is attached, for example, the high school football captain, girls may come to view other girls as competitors for the high-status males, thereby limiting friendships. Or they may view friendships with girls as unimportant, because no status accrues from such relationships. It is not uncommon for girls to break plans with their girlfriends if a "date" comes along. The girlfriend even is supposed to understand "the way it is." Candy and colleagues (1981), in their investigation of female friendships in women aged 14 through 80, found that friendships that enhanced status and power were greatest during teenage years and the twenties. After those years and through the fifties, these friendship functions decreased in importance. In contrast, the functions of intimacy and support remained the same throughout the life span. Yet, the most common reason for the breakup of female friendships in college is dating or marriage (Rose, 1983). For young men, the most common reason is physical separation.

Once married, if a woman is primarily a homemaker, she may have few opportunities to meet other women to form friendships. She therefore is likely to remain somewhat isolated. However, with the friends she has, married women tend to be particularly self-disclosing (Hacker, 1981). Keith Davis and Todd (1982) found that women tend to seek and maintain larger networks than do men, but this tendency gets restricted by such factors as responsibility for small children and not being in the paid labor force. Davis and Todd also found some differences in friendships as a function of race and age, with Black elderly having less satisfactory relationships than other groups, and Black women in their 20s having fewer friends than other groups. More research is needed regarding friendships among minority group members, because evidence exists that all women (as well as all Blacks) cannot justifiably be grouped together (A. Smith, 1983). Socioeconomic class is another factor that has been neglected, although it too appears important in terms of friendships. For example, working-class women tend to disclose more to their friends than do both lower- and upper-middle-class women (Hacker, 1981).

A further inhibiting factor in forming adult friendships is the generally deprecatory view that society has of women and that many women have accepted of each other. Many women believe that other women are gossipy, untrustworthy, and uninteresting. This view affects their interest in forming friendships with other women (Strommen, 1977). This depre-

catory view of women may be held particularly by those women who have achieved some measure of success in male-dominated fields. Although such women might be expected to help other women after succeeding in their own struggles against sexist practices and expectations, in the past, the reverse was more likely to be true. Women who achieved in male-dominated fields tended to identify with their male co-workers and superiors. Consequently, they tended to adopt the view that they have made it because they are different from most women. This attitude and the resulting behaviors have been termed the *Queen Bee syndrome* (Staines, Tavris, & Jayaratne, 1974).

If women manage to overcome the above obstacles, however, the resulting friendships tend to be deep and rewarding. Fortunately, since the rise of the feminist movement in the 1960s, increasing numbers of women have challenged the gender stereotypes and traditional patterns of relating to other women. Because more women have moved into male-dominated fields, there probably are fewer "Queen Bees." Through consciousness-raising groups, activities, meetings, and so on, women have learned to give and receive support from other women in meaningful ways.

Male-Male Friendships

Despite the popular image of the closeness of male "buddies," in the past ten years many male writers have acknowledged the poor quality of many male-male relationships (David & Brannon, 1976; R. Lewis, 1978; S. Miller, 1983; O'Neil, 1982; Pleck, 1981b). Although boys as a group do have some intimate friendships during adolescence, these friendships generally are concerned less with interpersonal intimacy and sensitivity than are those of girls (Reis et al., 1985; Strommen, 1977; D. Williams, 1985). The "gang" serves as a source of support in case of conflict with adults, rather than as a source of emotional support in personal crises. These generally superficial and often ritualized ways of relating extend into adulthood, when many friendships tend to focus on shared activities rather than on shared feelings (Aries & Johnson, 1983; Bell, 1981; Davidson & Duberman, 1982; Fischer & Narus, 1981a; Hacker, 1981; L.

Rubin, 1985; P. Wright, 1982). Indeed, intimate friendships appear to mean something different for men than for women (Caldwell & Peplau, 1982; Mark & Alper, 1985). As a result, many males do not receive maximum benefits from friendships—the relief of being able to release feelings with someone else and receive support, and the opportunity to broaden interests and perspective. Males do not appear to recognize affiliative behaviors in themselves or their male friends (Fitzpatrick & Bochner, 1981). In fact, many adult males never have had a close male friend or known what it means to share affection and concern with a male without fear of ridicule (H. Goldberg, 1976; Komarovsky, 1974).

As discussed above, being strong in "feminine" expressive traits is most conducive to intimate relationships. Such traits generally are not encouraged in males. However, most males do appear capable of intimacy. For example, certain situational cues (like being asked to have an intimate conversation with their best friend) will elicit conversations similar to those that take place between female best friends (Reis et al., 1985). Thus, the lower level of intimacy in many male-male friendships seems to be due to a reluctance to be intimate. This reluctance to be intimate with another male probably stems from the male gender stereotype as inculcated through socialization practices—the emphasis on independence and competition, suppression of feelings and self-disclosure, and an instilled fear of homosexuality. These barriers will be examined next.

Competition.   Most males are socialized early into believing that actions are more important than feelings and that they must compete in everything they do to "win" or come out on top. This intense male competition may pervade nearly every area of encounter among men, including sports, work, sex, and conversation. It makes intimate relationships among men most unlikely (Fasteau, 1974; Komarovsky, 1974; R. Lewis, 1978; O'Neil, 1982; Pleck, 1976a; Townsend, 1977). Using a questionnaire to measure gender-role conflict in men, O'Neil et al. (1984) found that more than half of their sample of college males found these issues of competition and success to be conflictual for

them. Because some males always are comparing themselves to other males, some relationships among men tend to be awkward and uncomfortable, sometimes marked by distrust and by an undercurrent of violence. It is difficult to be supportive toward people with whom one is competing.

Self-Disclosure.   An even more important factor than competitiveness in inhibiting male friendships is the strong message most boys receive to suppress feelings and, particularly, to suppress the *disclosure* of feelings. Thus, maxims such as "Big boys don't cry," "Keep a stiff upper lip," and "Take it like a man" all pressure boys to keep their feelings hidden. If boys do not hide their emotions, they are likely to suffer marked loss in prestige (such as when Edmund Muskie's public opinion ratings dropped after he shed a few tears during the 1972 Presidential primary), to be liked less, and to have difficulty assuming the competitive role society has set out for them. By sharing feelings, people become vulnerable. In a competitive atmosphere, this means that someone might take advantage of such vulnerability. According to male sex-role prescriptions, showing feelings is "weak" and must be avoided at all costs. Masculine-sex-typed males tend to be very low in self-disclosure to other males, although "masculinity" was not linked to males' self-disclosures to females (Winstead, Derlega, & Wong, 1984). Men from working-class backgrounds are particularly low in self-disclosure to other men, perhaps because they tend to be the most traditionally gender stereotyped (Hacker, 1981).

Males tend to be low in self-disclosure, beginning to cover up their feelings as early as age 4. Research has found, however, that the quality that most facilitates friendship formation is openness to others (Jourard, 1971; Strommen, 1977). Such openness may arise through willingness to reveal oneself (high self-disclosure) and/or through open-mindedness (low dogmatism). Males who have incorporated the stereotyped male sex-role expectations and are low in self-disclosure are at a marked disadvantage in forming close relationships with other men. Yet, ironically, it is only in close relationships that men get emotional support, unlike the situation for women, who receive support from many different types of relationships, such as those among colleagues (Wilson & Stokes, 1983). Low self-disclosure also explains why many male conversations tend to be monologues rather than give-and-take communications, since responding to another may reveal feelings (see Chapter 4). Another reason male conversations tend to be monologues may be because both of the men involved may try to dominate and interrupt the conversation.

Homophobia. Related to this fear of expressing feelings is an even more specific fear of expressing *positive* feelings toward other males—the fear of being thought a homosexual (*homophobia*). Imagine one man asking another to come over to his place just to talk, not to watch TV, go to a bar, or get together with other men or women. If the first time this happened, the man who was asked did not feel a little uncomfortable about possible implications, he would be unusual (Fasteau, 1974).

Homophobia occurs in both men and women, but is stronger and more commonly found in men (Lieblich & Friedman, 1985). For example, in the 1984 survey of American college freshmen, 58% of the men but only 38% of the women thought homosexual relations should be prohibited (Astin, 1985). This male homophobia is so pervasive that intimacy between males often is deliberately suppressed. Fathers stop kissing and hugging sons; boys stop touching each other except in ritualized ways (handshakes, shoulder slaps, and fanny patting in sports). A stigma is attached to anything vaguely feminine (Brannon, 1976; O'Neil, 1981a, 1981b, 1982). O'Neil et al. (1984) found that about three-fourths of their sample of college men were uncomfortable in situations where affectionate behavior between men was evident.

Male homophobia is not rational, since most beliefs about male homosexuals are false (Lehne, 1976; Morin & Garfinkle, 1978). For example, the majority of male homosexuals are not afraid of women, do not appear effeminate, are not limited to a few occupations, do not molest children, and are not psychologically abnormal or even unusual. Homophobia, then, is not a specifically sexual fear but rather a political one. It is related to a range of personality characteristics typical of prejudiced individuals: authoritarianism, conservative support of the status quo, and rigidity of sex roles. The best single predictor of homophobia is a belief in the traditional family ideology—a dominant father and a subservient mother. Individuals (male and female) with nontraditional sex-role behaviors, attitudes, and personality characteristics are least likely to hold negative attitudes toward homosexuals (Krulewitz & Nash, 1980; Lieblich & Friedman, 1985; Riddle & Sang, 1978). The real issue is the general maintenance by men of a society in which men control power through the regulation of sex roles. Homophobia serves this purpose by defining and reinforcing gender distinctions and the associated distribution of power. It keeps men within the boundaries of traditionally defined roles.

An experimental study by Karr (1978) exemplifies this social control factor. A group of college men were led to believe that one member of their group was homosexual. The labeled male was perceived by others in the group as being significantly less "masculine" and less preferred as a fellow participant in a future experiment than when the same individual had not been so labeled in a different group. Similar results were found by Krulewitz and Nash (1980). Furthermore, the man in the group responsible for labeling the targeted individual (both men actually were experimental confederates) was perceived as more "masculine" and more sociable when he did the labeling than when, in another group, he did not. These results suggest that men are reinforced for publicly identifying homosexual men and that men have good reason to fear being labeled "homosexual." The negative reactions to the labeled male and positive reactions to the labeler were even stronger when the subjects were homophobic men.

The price paid by men for conforming to male role expectations is great, since conforming to the male stereotype seriously impairs both same-sex and heterosexual relationships, causes severe anxiety, and narrows the range of legitimate male emotions, interests, and activities. In conjunction with this interpretation, Fasteau (1974) hypothesizes that the real function of all-male groups is to provide mutual assurance of masculinity, to make personal communication difficult, and to defuse any assumption of intensity of feelings. Homophobia must be eliminated before a change in sex roles can be brought about. Dispelling homophobia clearly is necessary before close male relationships can occur, since men high on homophobia have been found to be less intimate with their male friends than are less homophobic men (Devlin & Cowen, 1983).

Role Models. R. Lewis (1978) suggests a fourth barrier to the expression of emotional intimacy between men to be the lack of *role models* for such behaviors. We do not see many examples of affection giving between males, even between fathers and sons. This lack of warmth and affection by their fathers is a major complaint of men (Komarovsky, 1976; Salk, 1982), yet their sons are likely to repeat the process. That is, if a young boy grows up without seeing intimate emotions expressed between men, he most likely will inhibit his emotional expressiveness when he becomes an adult. Consequently, he will not be able to serve as a role model for such expressive behaviors for other young men. The pattern thus is likely to continue.

Male-Female Friendships

If male-male friendships are difficult to establish, male-female ones are even more so. By one estimate, only 18% of a representative sample of middle-class Americans reported a close friendship with a member of the other sex (J. D. Block, 1980); however, among college students in the 1980s, the percentages are higher (K. Davis, 1985).

The frequent sexual segregation of activities limits opportunities for meeting other-sex peers, and the perceived inequality in status between the sexes also makes other-sex friendships unlikely (Strommen, 1977). Sexual segregation begins in kindergarten, or before, and by second grade, children start trusting same-sex peers more than other-sex peers (Rotenberg, 1984). The stereotypes themselves play a large part in inhibiting such relationships. Both males and females tend to believe that members of the other sex are significantly dif-

ferent from themselves in attitudes, interests, and personal styles, even though actual sex differences in these areas are small and certainly are not found consistently (Borges, Levine, & Naylor, 1982; H. Freeman, 1979). Both women and men think the other sex demands conformity to the gender stereotypes, even though such demands tend to be minimal (L. Davidson, 1981). Furthermore, in some cases, boys' early socialization to reject anything vaguely feminine may lead to fear and hatred of females (Fasteau, 1974; O'Neil, 1982). Such feelings are unlikely to facilitate friendship formation between the sexes.

During adolescence, the emphasis by females on viewing males as potential mates and by males on viewing females as sex objects further mitigates against the development of male-female friendships (Chafetz, 1978; Townsend, 1977). Cross-sex friendships do appear to increase in frequency and intimacy during adolescence, with the transition occurring earlier for girls (seventh grade) than for boys (ninth grade) (Sharabany et al., 1981). However, men seem to be motivated primarily by sexual attraction in establishing such relationships, unlike women (Rose, 1985). Being married seems to inhibit the development of such friendships. Perhaps men have difficulty perceiving women in any way other than as sexual partners, or difficulty in expressing interest in any way other than the sexual. After all, men have difficulty relating directly to men as well.

In a laboratory experiment directly addressing these questions, Abbey (1982) found sex differences in people's perceptions of a five-minute unstructured conversation between a female and a male college student. Men tended to perceive both the man and the woman in the interaction as behaving in a more sexualized fashion than did women observers. In particular, men more often than women rated the female participant as being seductive or promiscuous. These results suggest that men are more likely than women to perceive the world in sexual terms. This may make for misperceptions of female friendliness as well as make the formation of male and female platonic relationships difficult.

As Figure 10-1 indicates, adherence to the gender stereotypes may make communication between the sexes difficult. Ickes and Barnes

Figure 10-1

How adherence to gender stereotypes can affect relationships between the sexes. (Copyright Bülbül, 1973. Reprinted by permission.)

(1978) studied this question by forming mixed-sex dyads of male and female undergraduates on the basis of their sex-role orientation as measured by the BSRI. The dyads were simply left in a room to await further instructions. The researchers found pronounced differences in the nature of the five-minute interactions that ensued. Specifically, the dyads composed of a sex-typed male and a sex-typed female showed significantly greater interpersonal incompatibility and stress than did dyads in which one or both members were androgynous. For example, sex-typed couples verbalized to each other less and had less positive feelings about the interaction than did other dyads. Ickes and Barnes account for these findings by assuming that sex-typed males and females adopt highly stereotyped and socially opposed sex roles in such unstructured situations, a hypothesis supported by Bem's gender schema theory (1981b, 1983; Andersen & Bem, 1981). The authors rule out the possibility that the sex-typed individuals

were more socially distant or less physically attractive than the non-sex-typed members of the other dyads. Differences in expressive control (masculine-sex-typed individuals controlling their emotional expressiveness more than feminine-sex-typed individuals) may compound the effects of the sex roles themselves in such situations. The result is that, in situations like the interaction described above, the stereotyped sex roles are dysfunctional in forming relationships. In actual practice, however, such effects may be somewhat mitigated by situational factors such as past history and external cues. For example, in more familiar and typical social situations, stereotyped male verbal dominance and stereotyped female verbal reticence may lead to positive feelings about an interaction. It has been found, however, that androgynous college women are more likely than sex-typed women to have a close male friend, so strict sex-typing indeed may inhibit cross-sex friendships (Lavine & Lombardo, 1984).

Another factor that may explain the findings of Ickes and Barnes is the perceived interpersonal attractiveness of sex-typed persons. A number of researchers have found that people, regardless of their sex type, consistently preferred, as friends, androgynous individuals of the other sex, rather than sex-typed individuals of the other sex. "Undifferentiated" individuals of the other sex were the least popular choice as friends, and were the least liked (Jackson, 1983; Jackson & Cash, 1985; Kulik & Harackiewicz, 1979; Major, Carnevale, & Deaux, 1981).

The frequently found difference in self-disclosure between the sexes also inhibits friendship formation. Although it appears that women are more likely than men to receive self-disclosures *from* men (Chafetz, 1978; Komarovsky, 1974; Olstad, 1975), communication is not necessarily two-way. Rather, females often provide a listening and support service ("ego boosting") for males without receiving any reciprocal service. Some males may not know how to listen or give support; others may not realize such behaviors are desired; and still others may not want to share the burden (Hacker, 1981; Pleck, 1976b).

It appears that females contribute emotional closeness and meaningfulness to an interaction, whether that interaction be with another female or male (Wheeler et al., 1983). Research on cross-sex friendships generally finds that for males, such relationships are similar to same-sex friendships in terms of acceptance, intimacy level, and companionship (Hacker, 1981; Rose, 1985). Indeed, because of the perception of males by males as unemotional and uninterested in relationships, females may be the only people to whom males can, or are willing to, self-disclose (Fitzpatrick & Bochner, 1981). In contrast, for females, cross-sex friendships tend to be less intimate and accepting than same-sex friendships. Women may trade acceptance for companionship and status in such relationships. It is no surprise, therefore, that men are more likely than women to be concerned about other-sex friendships and to nominate a member of the other sex as a close friend (K. Davis, 1985; Schneider & Coutts, 1985).

Cross-sex friendships frequently entail a great deal of role playing. Females are perceived as being dependent on the male friend, and males are perceived as being nurturant toward the female friend. Men tend to reveal mainly their strengths, and women their weaknesses, in cross-sex friendships. Such friendships do not match the relative spontaneity of same-sex friendships, probably due to the nature of our sex-role expectations (K. Davis, 1985; Fitzpatrick & Bochner, 1981; Hacker, 1981; Rose, 1985). Male-female friendships do occur, but society conspires against them. In fact, the very idea of platonic relationships between the sexes often is scoffed at, as the anecdote beginning this chapter implies. Instead, members of the two sexes are systematically steered into romantic relationships.

Romantic Relationships

If friendship formation is affected by gender stereotypes, the establishment of romantic relationships is affected by them even more. Dating, marriage, and sexual interactions all reflect society's messages about appropriate male-female behavior. Because sexual behavior was discussed in Chapter 5, only dating, marital, and other intimate relationships will be examined here.

Dating

On the average, dating begins shortly after puberty, at about age 14 for girls and age 15 for boys (Strommen, 1977). However, game-playing precursors to "real dating" may begin much earlier, as Figure 10-2 implies. With the beginning of dating begin many anxieties about sex role and sexual competence. For both sexes, many dating and romantic involvements serve instrumental purposes—peer acceptance and conformity to sex-role expectations—and not necessarily emotional ones. In fact, true intimacy often actually is discouraged between the sexes by the stereotypic emphasis on sexual achievement for males and by the stereotypic emphasis on attracting a mate for females. Being viewed as a status symbol by females may make some males feel superior, but it also

AMY. By Jack Tippit

"Don't pick it up, Denny. You'll be sorry!"

Figure 10-2

An early start on heterosexual game playing.
(Copyright 1983, reprinted courtesy Cowles
Syndicate, Inc. All rights reserved.)

may make them unduly attached to status-attaining activities such as athletics. Similarly, being viewed as a sexual object by males may make some females feel denigrated, but it also may cause some females to be overconcerned with their physical appearance. For both males and females, trusting the other sex would be difficult.

Intimacy also is discouraged by the highly ritualized nature of most dating situations and by the inequality in the dating relationship itself (Laws & Schwartz, 1977). Traditionally, males do the asking and initiating; females can only refuse or accept. Despite changing sex-role norms, men still initiate dates in the vast majority of instances, leading to the finding that more than one-third of college men experience dating anxiety in contrast to one-quarter of college women (Himadi, Arkowitz, Hinton, & Perl, 1980). Furthermore, women who do initiate dates are viewed less positively than are men who initiate dates (Green & Sandos, 1983).

The gender stereotypes themselves cause much strain in male-female romantic relationships. Both sexes believe that the other sex expects them to live up to the gender stereotypes (Braito, Dean, Powers, & Bruton, 1981; Crovitz & Steinmann, 1980; Davidson, 1981; D. Scher, 1984). Despite the fact that this belief

generally is wrong, especially on the part of males, the belief itself causes great strain as each person feels the pressure to conform to the impossible-to-attain standard. The strain may be greatest for women who now appear to feel pressured to be both passive and active at the same time. For all these reasons, L. Rubin (1983) refers to men and women together as "intimate strangers". The training of many males to avoid expressing emotions and to avoid empathy is an impediment to open communication.

Another factor affecting dating relationships is the traditional emphasis on *male dominance*, especially in intellectual matters. This "ideal" has been modified in recent years and the norm now is more one of equality and intellectual companionship (Komarovsky, 1973; Pleck, 1976a). One consequence of the fact that norms are changing is that females are less likely to hide their intellectual capabilities than they were previously (Komarovsky, 1973). However, nearly one-half of one sample of college women report having feigned intellectual inferiority on dates at least sometimes, in contrast to one-third of college men (Braito et al., 1981). Interestingly, men tend to overestimate and women to underestimate the percentage of members of the other sex who "play dumb." Furthermore, there are indications that many college-aged males actually are ambivalent in this regard. Because half of all college students are female, the likelihood of female intellectual equality and even superiority occurring in choosing a dating partner is high. Komarovsky (1973, 1976), in her study of male seniors at an Eastern Ivy League college, found that 30% of the men experienced some anxiety about not being intellectually superior to their dating partners. Of the 70% who expressed a desire for intellectual equality with their dating partners, most of the men in the study still felt their future wife should spend at least some of her life being a full-time homemaker, a role they held in low esteem. Olstad (1975) found similar results with a Midwestern college population. The ambivalence that college males have regarding their wife working outside the home can lead to conflict and frustration in marital relations if the spouse is truly equal or if the woman has other expectations.

Peplau and colleagues (Peplau, Rubin, & Hill, 1976, 1977), in their two-year study of 231 dating couples in Boston, found college men to be consistently more traditional than women regarding their preferred marriage option. (*Traditional* refers to the preference for the pattern of employed husband and nonemployed wife.) Table 10-1 presents the forced-choice response of Peplau et al.'s couples to a question about their marriage preference in 15 years. Although dual-career marriage is popular among a sizable number of students of both sexes, it is 17% more popular among women than men. And the traditional marriage with the wife not working is preferred by only 5% of the women but by 20% of the men. Such differences in preferences could cause problems in a marriage.

A 1979 national survey of high school seniors by Herzog, Bachman, and Johnston (1983) revealed a similar pattern of opinions, although the questions were not as personally relevant as for Peplau et al.'s sample. In the Herzog et al. study, the pattern of both marital partners working full time was opposed by 23% of the males but by only 10% of the females. Nearly three times as many females as males (40% to 15%) completely reject the traditional pattern of employed husband and nonemployed wife. Thus, although norms may be changing, they are changing more for females than for males (see also Allgeier, 1981; Rao & Rao, 1985).

Still, there is a trend toward greater acceptance of careers for married women in the 1980s than there was in the past. A nationwide survey conducted in 1978 found that three-quarters of Americans approved of employed wives, a direct turnaround from the results 40 years before. At that time, three-quarters of the population disapproved of a married woman earning money if she had a husband capable of supporting her (Yankelovich, 1981). Other research confirms the increasingly liberated view of the female role since the 1960s in terms of independence and assertiveness (for example, Crovitz & Steinmann, 1980). In the Herzog et al. (1983) national survey, most high school seniors accepted an employed wife, if she had no children. On college campuses as well, men view women who combine family and career (although not at the same time) as more attractive as a marriage partner than are traditional

Table 10-1

Fifteen-Year Plans of Dating Couples

	Males	Females
Single	6%	6%
Wife not working	20%	5%
Wife working part time	26%	24%
Wife working full time (dual career)	48%	65%

Adapted from Peplau, Rubin, & Hill, 1977.

homemakers (Hollender & Shafer, 1981; Michelini, Eisen, & Snodgrass, 1981). However, women who are primarily career-oriented or who plan to remain employed throughout the child-rearing years, are viewed as less attractive as a partner for marriage, especially by men with low self-esteem (Grube, Kleinhesselink, & Kearney, 1982; Hollender & Shafer, 1981). And women who desire success are expected to have a more difficult time in getting married than a non-success-oriented woman. It should be noted, that among Black college students, unlike among White college students, some research finds little discrepancy between women's and men's view of the ideal female role, which generally is more liberal than the view held by White males (Crovitz & Steinmann, 1980; Herzog et al., 1983). Thus, some ambivalence appears among some males regarding attitudes toward employed wives. Careers may be OK, indeed attractive for women, but only when these careers take second place to family needs. Not coincidentally, such a pattern is the most common one found among college women (Greenglass & Devins, 1982).

Another indication that more men than women have traditional expectations of their romantic partners is the finding that for mates, women prefer relatively androgynous men, but men, especially traditional ones, prefer relatively sex-typed women (Alperson & Friedman, 1983; Kulik & Harackiewicz, 1979; Orlofsky, 1982; Pursell, Banikiotes, & Sebastian, 1981; D. Scher, 1984). Interestingly, androgynous individuals have been found to be more loving (more aware of loving feelings, more willing to express feelings, more tolerant of faults) than either sex-typed or "undifferentiated" individuals (Coleman & Ganong, 1985). Non-sex-typed individuals also seem to be more satisfied with their relationships and less jealous than do sex-typed individuals (Hansen, 1985; Stephen & Harrison, 1985).

In the Peplau et al. (1976) study, dating couples overwhelmingly favored equality as the norm in their relationships in intellectual and other areas. Other studies confirm that equality in relationships is the current ideal (Herzog et al., 1983; "Views," 1983). This ideal contrasts strongly with reality, however—less than half the couples in Peplau et al.'s study actually felt there was equality in their particular relationship. When individuals perceived an imbalance of power, it was usually in the direction of male dominance.

Equality in a relationship is hard to achieve. A number of factors work against it: (1) belief in gender stereotypes (the more traditional, the more male power), (2) the relative involvement of one of the couple (the less the involvement, the greater the power), (3) the woman's educational career goals (the lower goals, the greater the male power), (4) male self-esteem (the lower the self-esteem, the greater the preference for traditional roles), and (5) sex typing (androgynous students prefer egalitarian relationships) (Grube & Kleinhesselink, 1982; Herzog et al., 1983; Hollender & Shafer, 1981; Peplau et al., 1976; Pursell et al., 1981; Sprecher, 1984).

In the Peplau et al. study (Hill, Peplau, & Rubin, 1981), neither sex-role attitude nor the amount of male dominance in the relationship was a good predictor of whether a couple would break up or remain together, however. What was most important was the sharing of attitudes and values, and each partner's subjective judgment of intimacy. When partners disagreed, the relationship generally was short-lived.

Similarity of ideology may not be important for all couples, however. Grush and Yehl (1979) found that sex and ideology interact when it comes to judgments of interpersonal attractiveness. Female college students with nontraditional attitudes toward sex roles in marriage had distinct preferences for partners who shared their ideology. Traditional college men also had a preference for partners with ideologies similar to theirs. Both groups rated similar other-sex individuals as more

likeable and as more desirable as dating and marital partners than they did other-sex individuals who had dissimilar views. For traditional women and nontraditional men, on the other hand, partner similarity was not important for ratings of likeability and desirability. The researchers suggest that this interaction between sex and traditionality is due to the possibility that nontraditional women and traditional men have irreconcilable differences that would make constant conflicts likely. In contrast, traditional women and nontraditional men are more likely to be adaptable to their partner's preferences.

What happens when the sexes do get romantically involved with each other? How do the gender stereotypes affect behaviors in romantic relationships?

Although women generally are thought of as emotional and likely to fall in love easily, research suggests that men tend to fall harder. Compared to women, men rate the *desire to fall in love* as a stronger motive in starting a relationship, they tend to fall in love more readily, they are less likely to end a relationship that appears ill-fated, and they are more upset when their relationship breaks up (Hill, Rubin, & Peplau, 1976; Pierce et al., 1984; Rubin, Peplau, & Hill, 1981). Indeed, women often are more disturbed when a friendship breaks up than when an intimate relationship breaks up. For men, the opposite occurs. It may be that, as a result of gender socialization, women become more adept at cognitively managing their feelings. Alternatively, because women traditionally have been so dependent on their mate for their own status and economic situation, they may need to be more practical and utilitarian than do men in choosing a mate. In contrast, men traditionally have been freer to "follow their fancy." Men place greater emphasis than do women on the physical characteristics of their prospective romantic partners (Deaux & Hanna, 1984). Perhaps with the economic liberation of women, women, too, will become freer to marry for love or become less likely to marry at all. The increased age of both sexes upon entering first marriages ("The Knot," 1985) may indicate that women no longer have to get married to survive in this culture. (In 1984, three-fourths of the men and more than one-half of the women under age 25 had never married; in 1970, the percentages were 55% and 36% for men and women, respectively.) It is also possible that the later age at which first marriages occur reflects the changing norms regarding premarital sex. People no longer have to get married just to get sex. The fact that most people eventually do get married may mean that at least some marriages currently are being based on more than practical necessity. If so, these marriages may be stronger and last longer than those already in existence. A closer look at marital and other intimate relationships is warranted.

Marriage and Other Intimate Relationships

From the dating situation, men and women often move into marriage. Such a progression is no longer inevitable, especially in recent years. More and more couples are deciding to live together without a marriage ceremony. By the Census Bureau's conservative estimates, 2 million mixed-sex couples were estimated to be living together in 1984, more than three times the number in 1970 and more than four times the number in 1960 ("The Knot," 1985). Those under age 25 account for most of the increase. More women also are deciding to remain unattached. Still, about 90% of the U.S. population will marry at some point in their lives, and some writers think that marriage is back "in style" (Kunerth, 1984; "Marriage," 1983). Such figures attest to the continued popularity of marriage or, at least, to the acceptance of the stereotype that a "normal" adult is a married one.

Traditionally, marriage has been viewed as one of two major goals of a female's life, the other being the bearing of children. Once the marriage goal is attained, a woman has been expected to give up all other interests and devote herself to satisfying her husband's needs and those of her future children. See Figure 10-3 for a tongue-in-cheek look at what a marriage proposal might really mean. Reinforced by marriage laws, customs, and beliefs, this sexist view of a happy marriage has remained the ideal until challenged by the women's liberation movement.

Marriage as a legal contract is based on a legal doctrine known as *coverture*. Although this doctrine has been modified in most states in the past 20 years, before 1960, this doctrine meant that, upon marriage, the wife loses her legal existence and is considered an extension of her husband's will and identity (Women in Transition, 1975). A wife takes on her husband's name and place of residence, gives up her right to accuse her husband of rape (he is legally entitled to her sexual services), and agrees to provide domestic services without financial compensation. The husband agrees to provide shelter, food, and clothing for his wife and children according to his ability. A wife has no legal right to any part of her husband's cash income or any say in how it is spent. Although each state has its own marriage laws and there has been an increasing trend to define marriage partners as equals, in many states the above legal elements still hold. For example, in most states, a wife cannot accuse her husband of rape, even if they are legally separated. Louisiana has a *head-and-master* law that allows a husband to sell the family home without his wife's consent and to cut off her credit even if she has her own salary. Few women or men, in contemplating marriage, consider these legal implications. If the relationship does not work out satisfactorily, however, these legalities may become extremely important.

In one type of analysis, marriage can be viewed as a bargaining situation—women trade domestic work and sex for financial support; men get their basic needs satisfied for a price (DeBeauvoir, 1953; Friedan, 1963). Few Americans think of marriage in these terms, however. In our culture, although it has not always been true and certainly is not true in many other cultures, romantic love is idealized as the basis for marriage. Some writers suggest that the current extremely high divorce rate (nearly one out of every two marriages ends in divorce) is due to the assumption that romantic love is necessary for a satisfactory marriage. Prince Charming will meet the Princess and they will live happily ever after. However, romantic love, with its strong sexual attraction and idealization of the partner, tends to fade over time. In contrast, companionate love, which involves deep attachment, caring, concern, and commitment,

Figure 10-3
What marriage might really mean. (From I'm
Training to Be Tall and Blonde, *by Nicole Hollander.*
Copyright 1979 by Nicole Hollander. Reprinted by
permission of St. Martin's Press, Inc.)

tends to endure (Coleman, 1984). These qualities often characterize intimate friendships. As
was noted above, the likelihood of such friendships forming between the sexes is small, and
males, in particular, prefer a different type of
woman for romance than for friendship. Yet,
tradition and the media have led people, especially women, to believe and expect that finding true love means happiness ever after. A
wife's general life happiness and overall well-
being are more dependent upon marital happiness than are her husband's, and women
consequently experience more dissatisfaction
with their marriages than do men (Donelson,
1977b). When the disillusionment comes, many
marriages do not survive.

If a couple has bought the romantic expectation of marriage and the traditional marital
roles that go with it, a number of consequences
are possible. If these expectations are not actualized, a couple might break up, they might
try to transcend the stereotypes and grow as
individuals and as a couple, or they might ignore the differences and work around them.
The last solution is the most common (Chafetz,
1978). However, when differences are ignored,
a wife may feel unfulfilled and try to get some
compensation from her husband via money,
material things, or vicarious achievements. In
turn, a husband may feel increasingly resentful
that his expectations have not been fulfilled,
and he may withdraw defensively from his
wife. From this sequence of events comes
the nagging-wife/withdrawn-husband pattern
of marital interaction that is the butt of so many
jokes and appears so often in the offices of
marriage counselors.

If the stereotypes are lived up to, the emotional cost for both sexes still may be great. A
woman financially and emotionally dependent

upon her husband can be an enormous burden. A fully stereotyped male usually is unable to satisfy his wife's emotional needs and may, in fact, find them threatening. A major complaint of married women is that their husband does not give them enough attention and affection (Cunningham, Braiker, & Kelley, 1982; L. Rubin, 1983). Noller (1980, 1981) found that couples with low marital adjustment tended to be ones in which the husband had trouble communicating effectively. In particular, he had difficulty sending clear messages to his wife, and decoding her messages accurately. As discussed in Chapter 4, males in general but especially "masculine" males, are poorer in communication skills than are women. In addition, the less similar two people's daily activities are, the more difficult is any form of communication between them. One person spending an entire day doing housework and child care usually is not a very stimulating or interesting partner for someone who spends the entire day working outside the home, as some househusbands have learned (for example, Roache, 1972).

John Antill (1983) and others (Schaupp, O'Connell, & Haupt, 1985) have come to an even stronger conclusion from their research: high femininity scale scores in both partners appear to be critically important in determining the happiness of the couple as well as each of its members. When both partners were either androgynous or "feminine," they rated themselves as happier than did couples in which at least one partner was low on femininity scale traits. Thus, as was found in male and female friendships, a "masculine" male and a "feminine" female do not appear to be the happiest couple, despite their conformity to sex-role norms. Blumstein and Schwartz (1983) similarly found that the man's ability to be tender and expressive was positively related to a couple's staying together.

Differences between wives and husbands in attitudes and expectancies about sex roles appear to be a critical factor in problem marriages (Nettles & Loevinger, 1983). In general, husbands tend to be more traditional than wives, and husbands in problem marriages tend to be the most traditional. Divorced women and divorced men tend to be even further apart in sex-role ideology than are married people,

suggesting that these differences may have contributed to their divorces (Finlay, Starnes, & Alvarez, 1985). Husbands with traditional attitudes as well as those with "masculine" personality traits and less than a college education tend to spend less time doing housework than less traditional men (Atkinson & Huston, 1984; Denmark, Shaw, & Ciali, 1985; L. Haas, 1981; Nyquist, Slivken, Spence, & Helmreich, 1985; Pursell, Banikiotes, & Sebastian, 1981). And who does the housework is an important factor in marital satisfaction, although it is more important to the wife than the husband (Cunningham et al., 1982; Madden, 1983; "Sharing," 1984). Interestingly, although the majority of husbands express support for the sharing of household responsibilities, only a minority of them do so ("Enlightened," 1980; Huber & Spitze, 1983).

Many writers argue that both people's expectations and the functions of marriage have changed in recent years (J. Bernard, 1981; Coleman, 1984; "Marriage," 1983). There is a new emphasis on an egalitarian relationship that provides love, companionship, and self-fulfillment. Concomitantly, men's traditional role as "the good provider" has changed. Indeed, Bernard (1981) argues that that role ended in the late 1970s, when men no longer automatically were considered to be the head of the household by the Census Bureau. Both Bernard (1981) and Ehrenreich (1983) suggest that men had been deserting that role long before the majority of wives were in the labor force in the late 1970s. Still, until recently, the role of the good provider was a clear expectation for most married men. Nowadays, expectations for married men are unclear and often contradictory, resulting in some role strain for both men and women (Goleman, 1984).

Actually, most marriages fall somewhere between traditional and egalitarian (Coleman, 1984; Huber & Spitze, 1983). As we have seen in the previous section, most young women want to combine employment with a family life. This is true of married women as well. Yet gender stereotypes, and particularly the attitudes of their mates, may hinder them from doing so. Fewer men than women want a marriage in which the wife combines family and paid work, although if these activities are done sequentially (for example, work for a while, take time off for raising a family, return to work), men tend to express positive attitudes.

Most marriages are *dual-earner marriages,* since two-thirds of all married women work outside the home (67% in 1981; "Two-income," 1984). Most such marriages still are conventional, however, because the wife's career usually is secondary to that of her husband and her primary interest is the family. It has been estimated that conventional dual-earner marriages outnumber *dual-career marriages* (in which both spouses are equally committed to their jobs and their families) by 10 to 1 (Parker, Peltier, & Wolleat, 1981). National surveys that find support for wives being employed also find that such support is mainly for conventional dual-earner wives. More than three-fourths of Americans think a woman should put her husband and children ahead of her career, and 55% think it is more important for a wife to help her husband's career than for her to have a career herself (Yankelovich, 1981). Employed wives are accepted mainly because two-income families have become an economic necessity for middle-class as well as blue-collar families ("Growth," 1983; "Two-income," 1984). Society still shows some discomfort with the idea of female employment, as depicted in Figure 10-4.

Given such social norms, it is not surprising that men's attitudes about employed wives are particularly influential in determining a wife's attempt to combine a career and a satisfying marriage. Indeed, such attitudes seem to determine the happiness of the marriage itself (Bailyn, 1970). In particular, marriages of career-oriented men to women who want to integrate career and family life are not very happy. This may be because no one is caring for home or family to either parent's satisfaction or because of competition between the partners. Research has found that having at least one partner who focuses attention on the relationship rather than on their work is important to a couple's satisfaction and commitment (Blumstein & Schwartz, 1983). Traditionally, that one partner has been the wife, although a comprehensive nationwide study of couples in the early 1980s in the United States found that that pattern no longer was the norm (Blumstein & Schwartz, 1983). In only 36% of the couples was the wife the sole emotional caretaker, in 39% the husband was, and in the remaining 25%, both partners were relationship-centered. Whether the wife is able to focus on her career seems to be partly a function of the husband's power orientation. A longitudinal study of 51 male college graduates (Winter, Stewart, & McClelland, 1977) found that the greater the

Figure 10-4 _____
The "dangers" that come from female employment.
(Copyright 1984, News America Syndicate. Reprinted by permission.)

male's power motivation, the lower the likelihood of his wife's working and/or the lower the level of his wife's career. The power-motivated man may choose a non-career-oriented wife, or he may use his power to suppress her career goals once married. In the latter case, the marriage itself may be adversely affected (Seidenberg, 1973).

In point of fact, mismatched marriages are unlikely to occur. Peplau and colleagues (1976, 1977) found in their longitudinal study of dating couples that couples mismatched regarding attitudes about dual-career marriages were nearly twice as likely as other couples (41% compared to 26%) to break up in the year following the initial testing. Such couples also were less satisfied with their relationships while they were together. Once married, couples who disagree over the division of labor and the woman's career interests also tend to be more unstable and more troubled (Blumstein & Schwartz, 1983; Nettles & Loevinger, 1983). Spouses who have similar attitudes toward sex roles tend to be more satisfied with their marriage than spouses with dissimilar attitudes (Cooper, Chassin, & Zeiss, 1985).

Women with a strong career interest may be less likely to marry. For example, women scientists, who may be viewed as having a strong professional commitment, have a much lower marriage rate than male scientists or female nonscientists (Cuca, 1976). Furthermore, married men appear to be more career-oriented than married women and than cohabiting men and women (Cunningham, et al., 1982; Kotkin, 1983). Marriage then may be an asset for career-oriented men but not for career-oriented women. Male career success does seem to be related to male career precedence, marriage, and the conventional allocation of household tasks. Perhaps that is one reason that mail-order Asian brides have become popular (Agus, 1984; Martinac, 1984). Such women are stereotyped as being more traditional, compliant, and subservient than are American women.

Dual-career marriages are difficult. The practical problems are many, especially if children are involved. And there is often the added pressure that arises from feeling that one is deviating from the social norm. The fact that there are more exceptions to, than examples of,

the norm does not much help. Yet many couples seem to be making such arrangements work, usually to the benefit of all involved. For example, Rotheram and Weiner (1983) find that androgynous dual-career couples report the highest personal satisfaction when compared to both nonandrogynous and nondual-career couples. Dual-career status does increase both personal and work stress, but it also increases relationship satisfaction. (For more information on dual-career couples, see: Aldous, 1982; Coleman, 1984; Haas, 1982; Pepitone-Rockwell, 1980; Skinner, 1980).

From a wide number of research studies, it now seems clear that the intellectual and psychological benefits in dual-earner couples seem to outweigh the disadvantages, particularly for wives (Coleman, 1984; Hornung & McCullough, 1981; "Sharing," 1984; Yogev, 1982, 1983). For women, choice is critically important. Women who are in the labor force out of choice tend to be happier than women who are compelled financially to be employed when they would prefer not to be. This explanation accounts for the finding that among lower socioeconomic families, marital happiness may be negatively related to the wife's employment, and more blue-collar than white-collar women would stay home if they could (Dowd, 1983; Yogev, 1982). Job satisfaction also is important. A wife who is happy in her job also tends to be happy in her marriage (Blumstein & Schwartz, 1983).

For husbands, the issue is less clear. Generally, husbands can accept their wive's employment as long as it does not threaten their own in terms of prestige, earnings, or psychological commitment (Pleck, 1978). However, if wives earn more than their husbands, or are in jobs with higher prestige, men frequently exhibit negative emotions, and a greater number of physical and mental health problems (Blumstein & Schwartz, 1983; Keith & Schafer, 1980; Ross, Mirowsky, & Huber, 1983; Rubenstein, 1982; Z. Rubin, 1983). Such men also are perceived as lower in social status by others (Richardson & Mahoney, 1981). As noted previously, for traditional men, and men with low self-esteem, even a wife who earns less than they do may be seen as a threat.

The problem lies primarily in traditional

gender stereotypes and traditional gender expectations. If men were not socialized to believe that males were, and should be, superior to females, men would not be so threatened by women's equality or their economic superiority. Interestingly, the association between an employed wife and low self-esteem among men was found among men in their 30s and 50s, but not among men in their 20s. Perhaps the younger generation of men has less traditional gender expectations regarding marriage, or is less likely to tie their feelings of self-worth to superiority over their wives. If this is true, it is a positive sign since the number of marriages in which the wife outearns the husband is increasing. Current estimates are that in 16% of all dual-earner couples in 1981, the wife earned more than the husband ("Two-Income," 1984). This may be the case especially among Blacks.

In general, benefits from marriage accrue primarily to men. As was discussed in Chapter 9 and above, marriage appears to benefit men more so than women physically, emotionally, and occupationally. The paradox here is that many men stereotypically view marriage as a trap, yet, statistically speaking, it does them a world of good, and they tend to remarry quickly if divorced or widowed (Bardwick, 1979; Bernard, 1973). Research (Brown & Fox, 1979) has shown that divorce appears to have more adverse consequences on the health of the divorced man than it does for the divorced woman. For many women, who stereotypically view marriage as their ultimate goal in life, marriage seems to be somewhat of a health hazard, at least according to statistics. A wife may experience more stress and strain in marriage than her husband, partly because she typically is the one expected to adapt to her husband's life and not vice versa, and partly because she typically receives little emotional support from him or anyone else. Employed wives, in particular, are under great strain, yet there is considerable evidence, presented in the last chapter, that employed wives do not show as severe an effect from marriage as do nonemployed wives. In a few studies, no difference between employed and nonemployed married women has been found. The critical variable may be what the individual woman's expectations are: if she expects to and/or wants to stay home, she is happier not being employed than being employed; however, if she expects to and/or wants to be employed, she is happier when she is in the labor force.

Ross and colleagues (1983) have found four types of marriages during this transitional period. In the Type I or traditional marriage, the wife is not employed by choice and she does all the housework and child care. This pattern is characteristic of about 25% of all marriages. The psychological benefits are high for both spouses, but more so for the husband. In Type II marriages, where the wife is employed by necessity rather than by choice but she still does all the housework and child care, distress is the highest for both spouses. Neither the wife's or the husband's expectations have been fulfilled, and he may feel like a failure. In Type III marriages, the wife is employed by choice but she still does most of the home duties. In such cases, distress for the wife is high, although lower than for Type II wives. For the husband, psychological benefits are as high as in the Type I marriage. In the Type IV or fully egalitarian marriage, both spouses are employed by choice and both share home duties. Distress ratings for both spouses are the lowest among all four groups.

Thus it is mainly in the most transitional marriages that the most distress appears. Other studies support the usefulness of such a taxonomy ("Marriages," 1983; Yogev, 1982). In the fully egalitarian marriage, the benefits for both spouses are the greatest. Although characteristic of only a minority of marriages (estimates range from 10% to 20%), such marriages appear to be on the rise (Kotkin, 1983; Rice, 1979).

In conclusion, adherence to the gender stereotypes may have negative consequences for marital satisfaction and stability, especially for women. A man's stereotypical lack of expressivity and lack of interpersonal sensitivity may put great strain on his marriage. His attachment to the traditional gender division of labor may put great strain on his wife and himself. Women's traditional subservient status and selflessness may put great strains on herself. A truly open, rewarding relationship is possible only among equals. Breaking away from the gender stereotypes thus is imperative.

Homosexual relationships offer a good

counterpoint to heterosexual relationships in this regard. Let us briefly examine this type of intimate relationship.

Homosexual Relationships.

Although the majority of Americans feel that homosexual relations are morally wrong, there is increasing acceptance of homosexuals as individuals (Yankelovich, 1981). Recent research that has examined homosexual relationships has even suggested that heterosexuals may be able to learn something from homosexual relationships. For example, homosexuals are more likely than heterosexuals to have egalitarian and dual-career relationships (Cardell, Finn, & Maracek, 1981; Peplau, 1981). Gay relationships more closely resemble "best friendships," with an added sexual and romantic component, than they resemble heterosexual marriages.

As discussed in Chapter 5, gender often exerts greater influence on a relationship than does sexual orientation. Compared to men, women tend to give greater importance to emotional expressiveness and personal compatibility, and are more self-disclosing, supportive, and sexually monogamous, whether in an intimate relationship with a woman or a man. Compared to women, men tend to be more interested in physical characteristics, more sexually active, engage in more casual sex, and are less self-disclosing, whether they are in an intimate relationship with a man or a woman (Blumstein & Schwartz, 1983; Deaux & Hanna, 1984; Kurdek & Schmitt, in press; Schullo & Alperson, 1984). Lesbians tend to be less sex-typed and engage in less role playing than do heterosexual couples or than gay men (Cardell et al., 1981; Kurdek & Schmitt, in press; Peplau, 1981). The latter finding may be due to the fact that gay men are less influenced by feminism than are lesbians. Equality appears to be particularly strongly valued among lesbians, and approximately 60% of such couples appear to be in an equal power relationship (Caldwell & Peplau 1984; Kurdek & Schmitt, in press; Peplau, 1981; Peplau, Cochran, Rook, & Padesky, 1978). Furthermore, among lesbians there is a clear association between power equality and relationship satisfaction. Such an association is less clear among heterosexuals, perhaps because of the traditional sex roles involved in such relationships (Peplau, 1979).

Although the stresses on homosexual couples differ somewhat from those on heterosexual couples, many aspects of their relationships are similar. For example, in their relationships, homosexuals and heterosexuals want both attachment and autonomy, are generally satisfied, and use similar power strategies (Falbo & Peplau, 1980; Peplau, 1981). In long-term relationships, both heterosexual and homosexual, partners tend to be matched in terms of expressive characteristics, although homosexual partners are the most similar to each other (Schullo & Alperson, 1984). From Blumstein and Schwartz's (1983) nationwide study of American couples, some interesting findings emerge. For all couples, conflicts over the way work intrudes into the relationship were often associated with the couple breaking up. Money conflicts occurred in all relationships, and the more equal the partners in controlling how the money was spent, the more peaceful the relationship. However, lesbians were more tolerant of economic self-sufficiency in their partner than were heterosexual males. Of all couples, male homosexuals tolerated outside sexual relations the best, perhaps because such activities were most likely to occur in those relationships.

Homosexual relationships, heterosexual intimate relationships, and friendships usually are voluntary relationships; that is, they are usually entered into intentionally and freely. But another powerful relationship that people have is not so intentional—that between parents and their children. Even if a child is planned, parents cannot predict exactly what characteristics their child will have, yet the relationship between a parent and a child may be the most profound relationship that either will ever have. And these relationships are strongly affected by gender stereotypes.

Parental Relationships

For both parents, the birth of a child involves great changes—changes much greater than those involved in marriage. The stressfulness of this period is reflected in the findings that child-free couples describe their lives in more positive terms than those with young children and that child-free women experience less stress than comparable women with children (Campbell, 1975).

Parent-child relationships have been undergoing marked changes in recent years, spurred by the women's liberation movement and resulting changes in gender stereotypic behavior, population growth, and control of contraception. More fathers are taking active roles in child care, and more mothers are in the labor force. Figure 10-5 shows the percentage (actual and projected) of married women from 1950 to 1990 holding outside employment with husband present.

In 1985, 62% of all mothers with school-aged children were employed, which was more than double the percentage in 1950. The number of mothers in the labor force with children under 6 years old has more than quadrupled in the same period of time (from 12% in 1950 to 52% in 1984). In 1984, 47% of all mothers with children one year old or younger were in the labor force as well. All together, about 60% of all mothers with children under 18 are now employed (Dubin, 1985; S. Rich, 1984, 1985). By 1990, only one in four married women is expected to be a full-time homemaker and mother (S. Rich, 1984).

Child-bearing patterns are changing (Bianchi & Spain, 1983; Hall, 1984). Women are having fewer children than ever before and are having them later in life. In 1959, the average American family had 3.7 children; in 1969, they had 2.6 children; and in 1984, they had 1.8 children, lower than the level reached during the Depression of the 1930s. Women today also are delaying childbearing. In 1982, 43% of women aged 20 to 24 who were, or had ever been married, were child-free; in 1950, the percentage of such women was 33%. Furthermore, first births to women over 30 have increased dramatically. Births to women in the 30–35 age group more than doubled between 1972 and 1982 ("More," 1984). Most of these women who delay childbearing are employed and tend to be in higher income brackets than those who give birth earlier. In addition, more women are deciding to remain child-free. In 1982, 14% of all women between ages 35 to 39 hadn't had children, up from 11% in 1976. Women in high status nontraditional jobs are particularly likely not to have children. In a 1984 Gallup poll of a nationwide representative group of female executives with the title of vice-president or higher, 52% were childless (Rogan,

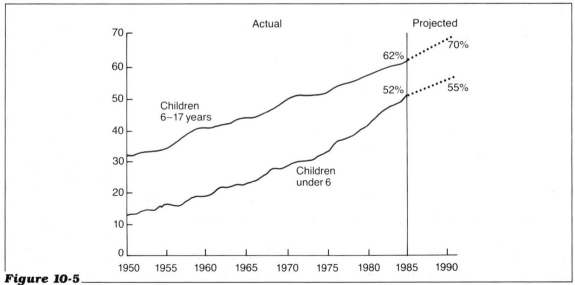

Figure 10-5
Percentage of mothers in the labor force, 1950–1990, projected. (From Dubin, 1985; S. Rich, 1984; Smith, 1979; U.S. Dept. of Labor, 1980.)

1984). Despite changes in childbearing, 92% of all women do have at least one child by the time they are 40 (Bianchi & Spain, 1983).

Some of the decline in the birth rate in the 1970s may have been due to a forced-choice situation for some women. Because most career patterns traditionally have ignored childbearing and child-care activities, women who have wanted both a career and a family may have felt forced to choose between the two. To some extent, the women's movement in the 1970s may have contributed to this conflict by emphasizing the importance of paid work, almost to the exclusion of family life. At the start of the 1980s, the movement began to focus on women's desire to have children, as well as on some ways in which family life and work could be integrated better (Friedan, 1981, 1983). As recent polls of high school and college students and of adults have shown, the vast majority of women today want and expect to combine jobs and family life (Dowd, 1983; Herzog et al., 1983; Komarovsky, 1982; Yankelovich, 1981).

Another major change with regard to parenting has been the dramatic increase in single-parent households. Such families nearly doubled in frequency from 1970 to 1982, from 12% to 22% of all American families ("One-parent," 1983). Ninety percent of these families are headed by a woman, and a disproportionate number of them are Black. In 1982, 41% of all Black families were headed by women with no husband present (Cordes, 1984a). The major cause of such families is divorce, but more and more women who are not married are having children, frequently by choice (Dullea, 1981; "Marriage," 1983).

Aside from changes in the size of the family, another type of change in parenting has been the increased interest in the quality of parent-child relationships. This interest has focused mainly on mother and/or daughter relationships, since most of the writers use a feminist perspective (Chodorow, 1978; Lynn, 1979; Stone, 1979; Trebilcot, 1984). The greatest emphasis has been on the special nature of the mother-daughter bond, with its inherent closeness and consequent challenge for separateness. Unfortunately, the special nature of mother-son and father-son relationships has been relatively neglected.

Gender stereotypes significantly affect parent-child relations but in different ways for mothers and for fathers. In fact, father-child relationships, by and large, have been ignored by most researchers—parental behavior has been assumed synonymous with maternal behavior. Therefore, both maternal and paternal relationships will be looked at separately in the following sections.

Mother-Child Relationships

"Why should a man marry a woman who refuses to be a mother to his children? He can get everything else he wants from women at a price much cheaper than marriage" (Schlafly, 1977, p. 51).

As Schlafly's quote illustrates, having children is usually viewed as a justification of female existence. Motherhood is chief among the requirements of female sex typing and has been considered a woman's major goal in life. Some writers (for example, Russo, 1976) go further and assert that, even more than a goal that one theoretically chooses, motherhood is a *mandate* that women are required to fulfill. According to this mandate, every woman should have at least two children and "raise them well"—that is, spend most of her time with them.

Motherhood Mandate. The Motherhood Mandate is transmitted in numerous ways. One means of transmittal is via restrictions on a woman's ability to control reproduction by limiting contraceptive information and availability of, and access to, abortions. Another way the mandate is transmitted is through the impact of gender socialization on the sexual behavior of young people. Although sex is emphasized in our culture, it is rarely connected with pregnancy. (Think of one case in the movies in which the man asks his sex partner if she is using contraception before they have sexual intercourse.) Hence come the skyrocketing rates of teenage pregnancies. One in every nine girls between the ages of 15 and 19 gets pregnant. Of these pregnant teenagers, 48% actually give birth, accounting for 15% of all live births in the United States in 1981 (Ventura, Taffel, & Mosher, 1985).

A third way the Motherhood Mandate gets conveyed is through the psychological restraints brought on by gender socialization.

Women who fear success in the business world may use family size as a form of achievement. White women with high fear of success have been found to produce larger families than those with low fear of success (Russo, 1976). Two other factors in the transmittal of the mandate are lack of alternative role models and the very real limitations of options.

The effects of such a mandate are quite serious for women. The responsibility of a child limits a mother's access to life options, such as higher education or work. This is especially true for young women who have children, which is particularly disturbing in the face of the soaring rate of teenage pregnancies. The Motherhood Mandate supports job discrimination against women because it maintains that women are likely to get pregnant and quit their jobs. It also produces role conflict in those women who also want careers, since society provides little support for employed mothers—few part-time jobs, few day-care centers.

It should be noted that it is not motherhood itself that is under attack here but rather the mandate that *all* women should experience motherhood. When motherhood becomes a choice, not a requirement, the quality of the mother-child relationship should improve, as should the happiness of individual women (Zaslow & Pedersen, 1981). Some changes already are occurring, as noted above—the birth rate is decreasing, more women are having fewer children at a later age, more women are deciding to remain child-free or have just one child, and more mothers are employed. These changes seem to be related to gender stereotypes.

Women who are traditionally sex-typed or who have traditional sex-role orientations tend to desire and have larger families than do non-sex-typed and nontraditional women (Gerson, 1980; Scott & Morgan, 1983). Traditional women also appear more personally interested in child rearing than more nontraditional women (Biaggio, Mohan, & Baldwin, 1985; Gerson, 1985). In one study of sexually active teenagers, those who got pregnant were found to be more traditional in sex-role orientation than the other young women (Ireson, 1984). Women who choose to remain child-free are even less traditional than other women with regard to their behavior, their attitudes, and their self-image (for example, they are more

concerned with achievement and equality, and tend to have higher educational levels and occupational status, and more egalitarian marriages) (Baber & Dreyer, in press; Bram, 1984; Yogev & Vierra, 1983).

The strength of the Motherhood Mandate can be seen in studies that find that women who are voluntarily child-free are viewed by others as misguided, maladjusted, or selfish despite the fact that research does not find such attributions to be accurate (Bram, 1983; Peterson, 1983; Ross & Kahan, 1983). In one study, college students actually refused to accept the fact that some couples did not want children (Ross & Kahan, 1983). Women more so than men see having children as necessary for a happy life. However, a study of women aged 60–75 did not find childless women to be more unhappy and dissatisfied with their lives than women with at least one child (Houser, Berkman, & Beckman, 1984).

Most women (92%) do become mothers, and, for most mothers, motherhood follows traditional lines prescribed by sex-role standards. Although many women always have expected to be mothers, many find with a jolt that mothering is learned, not innate. Many mothers undergo a difficult period of postpartum adjustment that is made more difficult by a mother's inability to share her feelings about motherhood (Bram, 1983; Feldman & Nash, 1984; Wilborn, 1978). Support for the mother is very important in facilitating her transition to motherhood (Power & Parke, 1984). Unfortunately, in a typical nuclear family, a mother may receive little support. Her husband may be unable or unwilling to give it, her own mother and other relatives may live at a distance, friends may not be that close, and societal supports, like day care, often are unavailable. Single mothers may receive even less social support than married mothers, although this typically is not the case in the Black community (Cordes, 1984a). However, female-headed one-parent families typically have to deal with the lack of economic support, since nearly half of all White, and nearly three-fourths of all Black, female-headed one-parent families live below the poverty level ("AFDC," 1984).

If a mother accepts the Motherhood Mandate and devotes all her time to nurturing her children and her husband, she is likely to lose touch with her own identity and needs and to live her life through others. She also is likely to lose touch with the world outside her domestic circle and have little intellectual stimulation. She is likely to spend a minimum of 80 hours a week in child-care and homemaking activities, plus being constantly "on call" for sick-care, entertaining, and so on (Polatnick, 1973–1974). Yet her activities generally are taken for granted by her family. As Figure 10-6 shows, homemakers typically are not even thought of as "working."

This pattern of activity produces a heavy burden on the nonemployed woman and on her family. Such mothers are more likely than others to interfere with their children's struggle for autonomy and privacy, to dominate their husbands and children, and to make their family feel guilty continually because they (the mothers) do "so much" (Ferguson, 1977; Hoffman, 1979; Wilborn, 1978). As was noted previously, a certain amount of pressure on the child toward independence, which is realistically timed, and moderate levels of maternal warmth and protectiveness, facilitate achievement behaviors in children. Thus, overprotective, overnurturing mothers may interfere with the development of achievement behaviors in their children.

Despite the strong belief that mothers should be home with their children, studies of other cultures have found that nowhere do mothers spend as much exclusive time with their children as do mid-20th century American mothers (Dally, 1983; Greenfield, 1981). In less complex societies, the job of mothering is shared by other members of an extended family, including husbands, or by institutional supports, such as day-care facilities and children's houses. More importantly, research has shown that it is not in the interest of either the mother or her children for the mother to be kept dependent and housebound. Bronfenbrenner (1974), after reviewing the literature on child development, concludes that "to function effectively as a parent, a mother must also have the opportunity of being a total person" (p. 4). The best arrangement for the development of a young child is one in which the mother is free to work outside the home part-time and in which the child is exposed to other caretakers, especially to the father (Dally, 1983; Hoffman, 1979).

The factors important for healthy infant and child development include consistent and sensitive care in a stable environment with physical and intellectual stimulation, love, and affection (Ainsworth, 1979; Scarr, 1984). While children need love and attention, they do not

Figure 10-6

When is work not thought of as work? When women do it in their home. (Copyright 1983, Universal Press Syndicate. Reprinted with permission. All rights reserved.)

need it constantly from their biological mothers. Children respond as well (or better) to multiple mothering, to paternal attachment, or to any other regular caretaker (Beit-Hallahmi & Rabin, 1977; Belsky & Sternberg, 1978; Greenfield, 1981; Rubenstein & Howes, 1979; Scarr, 1984). The fear that children will be harmed if mothers do not stay home is a myth that some argue is perpetuated by men because it serves their needs (someone takes care of all domestic responsibilities for them), because it eliminates women from competing with them in the labor force, and because it maintains their superior power in relation to women (Lowe & Hubbard, 1979; Polatnick, 1973–1974).

Employed Mothers. Perhaps one of the best-kept secrets from the American woman is that maternal employment is not harmful for children. In fact, it may be beneficial. As Figure 10-5 shows, more than 60% of all mothers with children aged 6 to 18 and more than 50% of all mothers with preschool children are in the labor force. Such findings are tremendously important in reducing the guilt working mothers often feel because of the Motherhood Mandate (Gilbert, Holahan, & Manning, 1981). Employed mothers often compensate for their absence by increasing the amount of direct interaction with the child when they are at home.

After surveying a broad range of studies (Colangelo, Rosenthal, & Dettmann, 1984; Dubin, 1985; Dunlop, 1981; Etaugh, 1980; Hoffman, 1979; Joy & Wise, 1983; Margolis, 1984; Rodman, Pratto, & Nelson, 1985; Rosenthal & Hansen, 1981; Scarr, 1984; Selkow, 1984), one must conclude that there is absolutely no evidence that children of employed mothers are neglected or affected adversely on the whole. Most studies find little difference between children of employed mothers and children of nonemployed mothers. For example, both sets of children form similar interpersonal attachments. When differences are found, they tend to favor children of employed mothers. These children, compared to children of full-time housewives, tend to receive more independence training, have generally higher career goals and somewhat higher achievement motivation, tend to have less traditional conceptions of the sex roles and a more positive evaluation of female competence. These results are particularly true for daughters, perhaps because employed mothers present a positive model of female achievement and because girls, under traditional child rearing, usually do not receive independence training. Sons of middle-class employed mothers do not fare quite as well as do daughters in a few studies involving academic performance, although this finding has not been a consistent one. A more consistent finding is that middle-class sons of employed mothers tend to be less stereotyped in their conceptions of sex roles and to be better adjusted socially than middle-class sons of nonemployed mothers. Sons of working-class employed mothers appear to do as well as their sisters in terms of cognitive ability and social adjustment, although the sons tend to be somewhat stereotyped regarding sex roles. Thus the guilt many employed mothers feel is unwarranted and may even be counterproductive (Ogintz, 1983). Mothers with positive attitudes toward their multiple roles are likely to have better-adjusted children than are mothers with less positive attitudes (Etaugh, 1980).

Most child-care experts now agree that as long as the children get good daycare and plenty of attention from their parents when they are home, the children will be fine (for example, Scarr, 1984). Public opinion, however, has lagged behind. A nationwide poll taken in November 1983 by *The New York Times* (Dowd, 1983) indicates that more than one-third of those interviewed (40% of the men, 31% of the women) believed employed women were worse mothers than those who devote all their time to the home. As Figure 10-7 shows, many (one out of four) employed women felt the same way. No wonder mothers who are engaged in outside employment often feel concerned about whether they are doing the right thing—one out of three Americans feels they are poor mothers! If a woman has a preschool child, attitudes toward her employment become even more negative. The majority of people, especially of men, think such mothers should not be employed (Herzog et al., 1983; "Views," 1983). Women tend to be a little more flexible than men in this regard, since the majority of women include part-time employment as an option for mothers with preschool children as well.

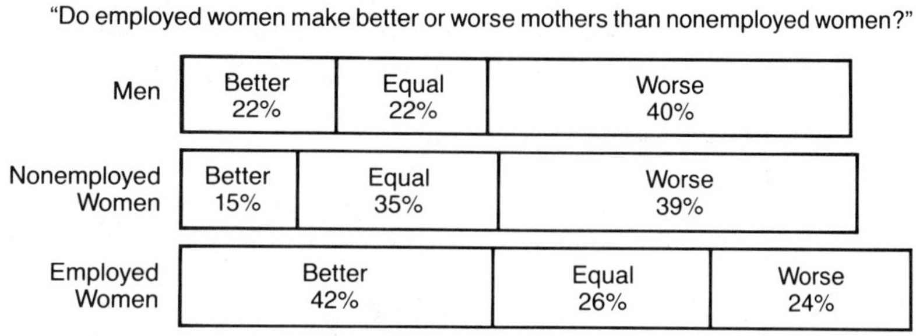

"Do employed women make better or worse mothers than nonemployed women?"

Men	Better 22%	Equal 22%	Worse 40%
Nonemployed Women	Better 15%	Equal 35%	Worse 39%
Employed Women	Better 42%	Equal 26%	Worse 24%

Figure 10-7

Opinions on mothers and wives who hold outside employment. (Adapted from Dowd, 1983. Poll taken by New York Times, *November 1983.)*

Such negative attitudes about employed mothers are particularly unfortunate, because most mothers are employed. A somewhat optimistic note is the finding that about 50% fewer women in 1983 thought employed mothers made poorer mothers than did in 1970. Perhaps, then, some change is occurring.

The effect of maternal employment on the mother also is important. Numerous studies have found that employed mothers tend to have higher morale, higher self-esteem, stronger feelings of competence, and fewer feelings of loneliness or of being unattractive than nonemployed mothers. Employed mothers also tend to see child rearing more in terms of self-fulfillment than self-sacrifice (Dunlop, 1981; Ferree, 1976; Fisher, 1984; Hoffman, 1979). This increased happiness and self-esteem in employed mothers compared to nonemployed mothers is particularly true after a woman's children start school. When children are preschool, women may experience more conflicts about being employed since public opinion is very clear and very strong that mothers of young children should stay home with them. Furthermore, finding good child care is a considerable problem (Dunlop, 1981; Ogintz, 1983; Scarr, 1984). Yet a number of studies find that multiple role involvement for mothers of preschoolers does not necessarily diminish a woman's well-being. This is especially true the stronger the woman's commitment to work (Barnett, 1982; Ritter, 1984). Indeed for most

women and men, combining work and family life leads to greater general satisfaction than either work or family alone (Baruch & Barnett, in press; Baruch et al., 1983; Bersoff & Crosby, 1984; Gump, 1980; Malson, 1983; Ritter, 1984; Veroff et al., 1980).

Family-cycle phase appears important in terms of a woman's personal development and feelings of satisfaction (Reinke et al., 1985). As child-bearing demands decrease, personal and life satisfactions appear to increase. Once women reach midlife, employment seems to be a strong psychological advantage, as discussed in the previous chapter (for example, Baruch et al., 1983).

Employment does produce a considerable amount of strain for most mothers, whether employment is a necessity or a personal desire. Two important variables in the amount of strain experienced by employed mothers are work commitment and social support (Barnett, 1982; Cooke & Rousseau, 1984; Dunlop, 1981; Holahan & Gilbert, 1979; Houseknecht & Macke, 1981; Power & Parke, 1984; Rogan, 1984). Employed mothers with a strong commitment to their work and those who receive support from their husbands and others tend to report less role conflict and strain. Employed mothers without social support, especially from husbands, who also have little work commitment tend to experience the most conflict and strain.

For nearly all employed mothers, the major source of stress is *role overload*. Employed mothers, unlike employed fathers, still assume primary responsibility for housework and child care (Cook, 1981; Crosby, 1982; Lein, 1982; Nyquist et al., 1985; Pleck, 1981a; Rogan, 1984; Yogev, 1982). Thus employed mothers tend to have three full-time jobs. In egalitarian relationships, where the ideal is a complete sharing of all tasks, men do more housework than in traditional families. However, women still do most of the family work. For example, in one study of 545 families ("Study," 1982), nonemployed women were found to spend about five hours a day on housework and two and a half hours per day on child care; mothers employed part-time spent about four and a half hours per day on housework and nearly two hours per day on child care; mothers employed full-time spent over two hours per day on housework and over one hour per day on child care. In contrast, husbands of both nonemployed women and women working part-time spent about three quarters of an hour per day on housework; if their wife was employed full-time, they spent nearly one hour per day on housework. But in all families, child care took up only 22 minutes of father's time regardless of their wive's work status.

Other research (Pleck, 1981a) suggests that men are increasing the time they spend in child care, especially when their wives are employed. Furthermore, the better educated the husband and the higher the wife's earnings, the more likely it is that the husband will "help out" with the housework (Haney, 1984; Hiller, 1984). Due primarily to the decrease in the amount of time employed mothers spend on family tasks, some writers suggest that the time expenditure of men and women in dual-earner marriages is becoming more similar (Huber & Spitze, 1983; Pleck, 1981a). Certainly, people's attitudes are becoming more supportive of couples sharing housework and child care (Herzog et al., 1983; Pleck, 1981a). Yet most people, including women, feel housework and child care are primarily a woman's responsibility. For example, in Herzog et al.'s (1983) national survey of high school seniors, women with preschool children were expected to stay home and men with preschool children were expected to work full-time, despite the fact that the majority of seniors endorsed equal sharing of child care. Further-

more, the myth of "Supermom" abounds, encouraged by media reports of the exceptional woman who appears to have (and do) it all: a rewarding professional career, a close relationship with her children and participation in child-related activities such as the PTA and Girl Scouts, a sexy and romantic relationship with her husband, time for physical fitness activities, and a spotless home. Although this ideal is impossible to live up to, many women try, despite the toll on their physical and emotional health. For example, most employed mothers are always tired (Lein, 1982).

How do employed mothers handle such a load of responsibilities? A variety of coping strategies may be used (Dunlop, 1981; Gray, 1983; Harrison & Minor, 1983; Ogintz, 1983; "Study," 1982). Employed mothers may (1) look primarily at the benefits of combining career and family, (2) decide in advance which role to emphasize (almost always the family) in case of conflicting demands, (3) compartmentalize the two roles as much as possible, (4) reduce standards within certain roles (like housekeeping), (5) get help from within and/or outside of family, (6) carefully schedule their time, (7) cut back on sleep and personal time, or (8) compromise their career to fit into family commitments. The compromised career is a frequent solution and accounts for the fact that many women are underemployed, underpaid, and undercommitted. The majority of traditionally female jobs, such as teaching and secretarial work, are least in conflict with a primary commitment to home and family. About 30% of all employed mothers are employed part-time (S. Rich, 1985). Unfortunately, such compromising also reinforces the stereotype that women are not really serious about their work. Because of the strains involved in full commitment to both motherhood and a career, increasing numbers of professional women are choosing to remain child-free (Rogan, 1984; Yogev & Vierra, 1983). Others are trying innovations like job sharing (one job is split between both spouses), or working different shifts (Arkin & Dobrofsky, 1978a; Dullea, 1983).

It should be noted, however, that for some women, activities associated with child care and homemaking are truly productive and satisfying. Such activities seem to engage their interests and talents, at least for part of their lives (Baruch et al., 1983). However, for other women, the lack of economically productive work is associated with problems of self-esteem, dignity, and life satisfaction. As noted previously, a critical factor in determining life satisfaction is doing what one finds most rewarding. Thus choice of lifestyle is critical. Even in terms of the division of labor within the family, if a woman is satisfied with her husband's contribution, regardless of how much it is, both she and her family tend to be happy (Pleck, 1981a).

If a mother stays home for a number of years while her children are young, it often is difficult for her to enter the labor force in her late 30s (or later) and still achieve a significant degree of success. She may never have acquired job-related skills and therefore must settle for very low-level jobs. Her training may be outdated. She may be without the crucial informal contacts for professional success. She may have lost self-confidence through years of subverting her needs to those of her family. She may have lost her ambition. Yet, despite these inhibiting factors, increasing numbers of middle-aged women are joining the labor force. In March 1985, 74% of women aged 35–44 were in the labor force, compared to 59% in 1977 and 50% in 1970 (U.S. Dept. of Labor, 1976b, 1977a, 1985). Older women also are returning to school. The number of women over age 24 attending college in 1983 was two and a half million, more than one-third of all women attending college (U.S. Bureau of the Census, 1983). These numbers reflect women's growing recognition of the rewards of outside employment and the realities of our economic system and of our 50% divorce rate.

Change. Attitudes toward, and theories about, motherhood are changing (see Margolis, 1984; Trebilcot, 1984). Most women no longer think motherhood is the only important thing a woman can do in her life (Heffner, 1983; Merriam & Hyer, 1984). Indeed, most women value both a career and a family life and intend to combine the two. For example, in *The New York Times* Nov. 1983 poll (Dowd, 1983), only 26% of the women surveyed thought that being a mother was one of the most enjoyable things about being a woman today; twice that per-

centage was found in 1970. Indeed, in 1983, 26% also thought that jobs and careers were among the most enjoyable things about being a woman today. In 1970, that percentage was only 9%. And being a homemaker was chosen by only 8% of the women in 1983 in contrast to 43% of the women in 1970.

More than consciousness raising is needed, however, to ameliorate some of the negative effects of the Motherhood Mandate. The negative effects of motherhood for both mothers and children probably will continue unless a number of changes occur. Fathers need to be more willing to share household and child-care functions. Society and employers need to provide some supports for employed mothers— daycare centers, good part-time jobs, flexible-hour jobs, paternity leave, equitable tax deductions. The Motherhood Mandate needs to be eliminated. These suggested changes would go a long way toward making motherhood predominantly rewarding—a choice, not an obligation; an opportunity for growth, not a burden.

From another perspective, of course, it can be argued that, rather than adjust the lives of women to the Establishment, it might be more appropriate to adjust the Establishment to the lives of women (Bernard, 1971; Friedan, 1981). That is, the concept of a career itself is a "masculine" concept, entailing full devotion to a job at the price of other interests. Perhaps the goal should be to reduce the emphasis on having a career for everyone, males especially, and to encourage more interpersonal activities (including child care) for both sexes. Such a change would liberate men as well as women. Many men, in fact, are finding the strains of ambition and the breadwinner role to be excessive. These men are finding alternatives, including more time in their family relationships. And some employers are establishing on-site childcare, paternity leaves, flextime, job sharing, and so on, in order to accommodate workers with children.

The problem with motherhood is not that it is a worthless activity. It can be argued quite convincingly that such activity is the most important thing anyone can do, if it is done well, because society's future depends on it. Rather, the problem is that motherhood is held in such low esteem by everyone, including many women, and that the strains involved in being a mother are magnified by the lack of alternatives and supports for women in that role. As the Motherhood Mandate recedes, as institutional supports increase, and as people speak of parental, not specifically maternal, behavior, we can expect to find happier and better adjusted parents and children.

Father-Child Relationships

Although there is no mandate for fatherhood comparable to that of motherhood, gender stereotypes still strongly affect father-child relationships. The belief in a maternal "instinct" has been so strong that little research has been done directly on paternal relationships. Yet evidence has accumulated indicating the importance of paternal relationships to both children and fathers. Future fathers in equally high proportion to future mothers report strong desires for children and anticipate their children being important in their life. For example, in 1984, more than two-thirds of both male and female college freshmen rated raising a family either as "essential" or "highly important" to them (Astin, 1985). In a national survey taken in 1976, having children as well as enjoyable work figured strongly in both men's and women's overall sense of well-being (Bryant & Veroff, 1982). The importance of parenthood for men in 1976 was a big change from 1957, when the parenting role had less importance. Yet, most people also believe children are more important to women in general than to men and that women want children to fulfill a basic need or purpose in life. Thus, many men consider their desire for children unusual, even though it is not. Furthermore, in a 1984 survey, nearly twice as many male as female freshmen thought women's activities should be confined to the home (30% to 15.5%; Astin, 1985). Thus, although men may want families, many still see women as the primary caretakers.

There appears to be much conflict regarding men's desire for children. Whereas most women see children as adding to a person's life satisfaction, many men see children as lowering a person's satisfaction (Ross & Kahan, 1983). Many men experience doubts about their ability to be closely involved with their children

(Goleman, 1984). As a result, many men experience ambivalence about making a decision to have, or not have, a child (Baber & Dreyer, in press).

Immediately after their child is born, fathers often become completely engrossed in their child, showing immediate, strong affective responses (Collins, 1979; Greenberg & Morris, 1974; Parke & Sawin, 1977). This is especially true if fathers are allowed to interact with the baby immediately after birth. Early contact with infants may be as important for the development of father-child bonds as it is for the development of mother-child bonds (Lamb, 1981a; Parke & O'Leary, 1976; Parke & Tinsley, 1981). Traditionally, however, a father is not encouraged, or even allowed, in some hospitals, to see his newborn. His interaction with his child soon wanes, and both are deprived of continuing, meaningful intimacy. When fathers do interact, they tend to be more attentive and physically playful than mothers but are less active in feeding and caretaking activities (Bronstein, 1984a; Collins, 1979; Lamb, 1981a; Parke, 1981; Parke & Sawin, 1977; Parke & Tinsley, 1981). Nonetheless, when fathers do undertake these traditionally female tasks of child care, they do very well. Recent findings suggest that fathers are more likely to do these tasks if they are specifically instructed in these aspects of child care and if the child is a boy (Parke, 1981; Parke & Tinsley, 1981). In fact, regardless of instruction, fathers are more likely to touch and vocalize to first-born sons than to first-born daughters or to later-born children (Collins, 1979).

Cross-cultural studies of the time mothers and fathers spend in child care indicate that nowhere do fathers spend more time with children than do mothers (Lamb & Sagi, 1983; Mackey, 1985; Stone, 1979). American fathers may not be the worst in this regard, but neither are they the best. For example, fathers from Eastern European countries seem to spend more time with their children than do Western fathers. A 1982 survey previously cited found that the average American father spends 22 minutes a day with his children ("Study," 1982). Not surprisingly, a 1977 Gallup Youth Survey found that three times more teenagers of both sexes reported getting along better with their mother than with their father (twice as many boys; more than three times as many girls). Only 18% thought their relationship with their father was better; one-third thought their relationships with both parents were the same. This is a sad commentary on the father-child relationship, especially in light of the studies, reviewed in Chapter 7, that fathers are important figures in the lives of their children from infancy on.

A number of factors account for the generally inadequate father-child relationship typically found. Among them are belief in the motherhood myth, the existence of strong sex typing, the power differences between the sexes, and the traditional pattern of divorce and custody arrangements.

Motherhood Myth. The Motherhood Myth states that only mothers can establish an intimate relationship with their children because of the maternal "instinct." As was discussed in Chapter 4, there is no such thing as a maternal instinct. Nurturing behavior is learned, and fathers are equally capable of acquiring such behaviors, especially if they have early contact with the child. In addition, although mothers are biologically equipped to bear and nurse children, there is no biologically decreed responsibility to rear and care for them (just as there is no biological prerequisite for doing housework, often seen as part of a mother's "natural" work). In fact, Harlow (1958) found with his studies of monkeys that the critical aspect of mothering is not the provision of food but the provision of warm, comforting physical contact. Fathers are equally as capable as mothers of providing this.

Yet the father role for males is usually consistently ignored during a boy's socialization or is specifically deemphasized. Boys generally do not have any early experience with parental behaviors, such as dolls and babysitting (Chafetz, 1978; Fasteau, 1974; Fein, 1974). They often see in their own homes and in the media that fatherhood is either irrelevant or very narrow. They usually are taught that fatherhood is only a minor part of the masculine role, that achieving comes first. Because of this lack of role models for involved fatherhood, many men who want to be more involved with their own children feel insecure. In addition, there is no

clear role for fathers. They used to be the benevolent disciplinarians and mentors ("Father knows best"), but such a role is no longer viable in our current egalitarian family ideal. As a result, fathers often feel like outsiders, not knowing what role to play, often opting simply to avoid the situation completely. Some research suggests that a father's adaptation to the birth of a child is improved if the father makes a decision to assume either the traditional or the involved father role, rather than vacillating between them (Pedersen, 1980; Zaslow & Pedersen, 1981).

In many families, women actually may discourage their husbands from becoming involved in child care, probably because child care has been the one area in which women have been allowed to feel competent (Cordes, 1983b). In one study (Palkovitz, 1984), the single best predictor of a father's interaction with his infant was his wife's attitude toward paternal involvement. As more women challenge the Motherhood Mandate for themselves, more women are welcoming men's participation in child care. Husbands of wives with a nontraditional sex-role ideology, as well as husbands of employed wives, tend to participate more in child care than do other men (Baruch & Barnett, 1981; Nyquist et al., 1985). Furthermore, programs are being instituted both in schools and in communities that deliberately encourage and instruct males in how to care for babies and young children (for example, Lovenheim, 1981; Phillips, 1981).

Sex Typing. A major obstacle in father-child relationships is the masculine personality itself. Men who are uncomfortable with expressing their emotions may be inhibited from establishing closeness and intimacy with their children. As illustrated in Figure 10-8, men may feel uncomfortable being seen in a silly or less-than-authoritative role. Small children cannot be dealt with using reason alone, and they need more direct expressions of affection than roughhousing, slaps on the back, or material rewards. In addition, the pressure of the male sex role to achieve concrete things (money, status, top grades, and so on) makes it difficult for many men to appreciate the much subtler rewards of feelings and relationships. Consequently, if fa-

Figure 10-8

Can masculine men be effective fathers? (Copyright 1980 by Universal Press Syndicate. Reprinted with permission. All rights reserved.)

thers do spend any time with their children, which is often difficult if they are the primary breadwinner, they may displace their achievement strivings onto their children and engage in competition with them. Relationships between fathers and sons, in particular, may be very competitive and conflicted (Z. Rubin, 1982a; Yablonsky, 1982). Some fathers also may make their children feel they must earn their father's love in mechanical ways (Chafetz, 1978; Fasteau, 1974; Pleck & Sawyer, 1974). As a result, paternal relationships tend not to be close, as the Gallup Youth Survey noted above illustrates. Perhaps the most common complaint voiced by grown sons is that they wish they could have been closer to their fathers (Komarovsky, 1976; Z. Rubin, 1982a; Yablonsky, 1982).

Men who have a nontraditional sex-role ideology and who don't think of themselves as strongly "masculine" tend to participate more in child care than do other men (Baruch & Barnett, 1981; Nyquist et al., 1985). In one study, androgynous fathers were more involved with their infant child than any other sex-typing group (Palkovitz, 1984). Men who participate in child care tend to be more nurturant than other men (B. Carlson, 1984), perhaps because nurturance in men leads to greater participation, or because greater participation leads to increased nurturance. There is evidence for both sequences.

Power Differences. Another reason that men, as a group, do not rear children may be that it is to their advantage, in a power sense, not to be the caretakers. Polatnick (1973–1974) analyzes the advantages of avoiding child-rearing responsibilities and the advantages of breadwinning responsibilities. Full-time child rearing limits the opportunities one has to engage in other activities, whereas the breadwinning role earns money, status, and power in society as well as in the family. Consequently, many men have an interest in defining child rearing as exclusively a woman's role—it limits women's occupational activities and thus their competition, and it enables men to have children without limiting their own occupational activities. As Wetzsteon (1977) has noted, "The real difficulty men have in becoming feminists . . . lies in the fact that American capitalism . . . still gives a strong competitive edge to men with traditional masculine values" (p. 59). Having a wife who cares for home and children is a strong advantage to men in the professional and business worlds. Although it is true that breadwinners must shoulder the financial burden involved in raising children, many men at least have the possibility of selecting work suited to their interests, and they can take time off from such work. In contrast, many women are arbitrarily assigned to child rearing on a 24-hour-a-day, 365-day-a-year basis.

The pressure on men to remain in their traditional dominant breadwinner role is intense. Indeed, men are more likely than women to see marital, parental, and work roles as conflicting (Richardson & Alpert, 1980). Men who do increase their involvement in family life often feel enormous competing pressures from their job, and censure from their peers (D. Bell, 1983; Berger, 1979). Such censure and pressure are far from imaginary. In Herzog et al.'s (1983) national survey of high school seniors, the researchers found marked rigidity regarding expectations of men. Although there was a preference for shared child-care responsibilities between wife and husband, anything less than full-time employment for the husband was frowned upon. In contrast, anything more than part-time employment for a mother was frowned upon. Thus father's involvement with children could hardly be fully equal. Even students who have liberal or neutral attitudes toward the mother role tend to have traditional attitudes toward the father role (Rao & Rao, 1985). The job market as well does not support child-care responsibilities by fathers. Paternity leaves are uncommon (the Ford Foundation in 1982 was one of the first to offer such leaves in the United States) and usually short. Furthermore, most traditional male jobs do not consider men's family responsibilities (Bohen & Viveros-Long, 1981; Cowan & Cowan, 1983). Men may be penalized even more than women for taking time off or refusing additional job responsibilities for the sake of the children. In a somewhat different vein, Mackey (1985) notes that across all cultures men have been assigned the role of soldier/warrior. Because this role is incompatible with the role of primary caretaker of children, men have been socialized to avoid internalizing the latter role. Mackey argues, however, that the actual behaviors of men toward children still can be, and in fact are, nurturant.

Although there are many disadvantages to full-time child rearing, these disadvantages could be alleviated by changed societal conceptions of the parent role and by the sharing of responsibilities among both parents and society. Many fathers now are beginning to find the rewards of child rearing from which they previously have been excluded (and have excluded themselves). The joys of nurturance and the pleasures of exchanging love with children are allowing some fathers to get in touch with the emotional aspects of themselves that they previously had shut off (D. Bell, 1983; Fasteau, 1974; Fein, 1974, 1978; Yablonsky, 1982). The emotional rewards are high—emotional honesty, simplicity, and directness—and many fathers are deciding that they want to be more involved with their children, even if that means changing their career plans and/or their ambitions.

The *emergent* perspective on fathering (Fein, 1978), one that characterizes current research, is based on the premise that men have the capacity to be effective nurturers of their children and that such behaviors would be beneficial to both children and parents. This perspective contrasts with the traditional one of the aloof and distant father. It also contrasts with the "modern" perspective of the 1960s, which concentrated on certain child-outcome variables, such as gender development, but ignored the positive effects of parenting on fathers and ignored men's capabilities in this area.

Increasing numbers of fathers are participating in childbirth classes and the birth process itself and are finding it rewarding. More men are sharing child-care responsibilities with their wives, using a variety of patterns—househusband, two part-time jobs, morning-evening shifts, weekly shifts, dual careers, and more. The amount of time fathers spend in child care has increased, with some studies finding a 30% increase since 1967 in child care by men (Goleman, 1984; Pedersen, 1980; Pogrebin, 1982a). Recent research in fact suggests that on weekends, fathers spend an equal or greater amount of time with their children than do mothers (Booth & Edwards, 1980; Ziegler, 1983). More men are becoming involved in early childhood activities as child-care workers, elementary and nursery school teachers, and so on. But the numbers participating in these child-care activities, in general, are still small. And the numbers of men participating in the truly critical aspect of parenting—the sense of emotional responsibility—are smaller still (Collins, 1979; McBride & Black, 1984).

Divorce. There is still another factor that has contributed to the difficulties of the father-child relationship: the typical pattern of child custody has been to award custody of children to the mother if a couple divorces. This custom is, of course, both a result and a cause of distance in father-child relationships. The awarding of children to the mother has been a result of the 20th century's emphasis on maternal care of children and the diminution of the father's role in child rearing. Before the 20th century, children were considered property, and as such belonged to the male head of household. However, because nowadays children in Western society are generally considered to "belong" to the mother, fathers often keep their distance from their offspring.

It is an indication of changing father-child relationships that increasing numbers of divorced fathers are requesting and, in many cases, obtaining custody of their children after divorce. Other fathers are getting joint custody in some kind of cooperative, co-parenting arrangement. In a society in which two out of every five children born in this decade will spend part of their childhood in a single-parent household, it is becoming more and more a possibility that that household will be the father's ("Custody," 1980; Meredith, 1985). In 1982, about 20% of all American households were single-parent families ("One-parent," 1983). More than 90% of these one-parent units were female headed. Yet, more than one million children under 18 lived with their fathers, and at least an equal number shared their fathers through joint custody (Meredith, 1985; Roman & Haddad, 1978). Between 1970 and 1984, the number of children under 18 residing with their fathers alone increased by 127%. This number is likely to increase as courts begin reflecting society's changing attitudes toward the male role. For example, *Kramer vs. Kramer,* a movie about a father's awakening to parenthood was released in 1979, and received an Academy Award as the best movie of the year.

Many divorce lawyers and judges still are reluctant to recommend and grant custody to fathers for two reasons: (1) the stereotyped belief that mothers are "naturally" the better parent, and (2) the more than a century of mother-oriented custodial rules and traditions. Yet, changes have begun. Part of the pressure has come from men's rights organizations, which have active memberships in more than 30 states, and from the National Congress for Men, organized in 1981 by men who wanted to reform divorce settlements (Astrachan, 1984; Silver & Silver, 1981). Another pocket of pressure has come from men who have come to terms with their own nurturing capabilities and with what they view as the best interest of their children. With increasing numbers of mothers pursuing careers, women are not automatically considered the best parent. In 1980, California was the first state to enact a joint-custody law in which preference is given to such arrangements.

A key factor in determining whether a father will seek custody of his children is not his sex-role orientation, but his own experiences with his family when he was a child. Gersick (in Albin, 1977) found that male custody seekers described their childhood family experience in terms of distance from their fathers, along with ambivalent but intense relationships with their mothers. They may thus be trying to make up for the lack of closeness they experienced with their own father in their relationship with their children. In any case, fathers awarded custody were similar to divorced mothers in coping patterns and adjustment (Greif, 1985; Meredith, 1985). They had little difficulty managing the care of their children and fared much better psychologically than did divorced fathers without custody. Of course, fathers who seek child custody may be quite different, as a group, from fathers who do not seek custody. Many of these fathers who sought custody became more sensitive and expressive and did not experience the marked depression and feelings of incompetence characteristic of other groups of divorced fathers (Hetherington, Cox, & Cox, 1977; Meredith, 1985; Moreland, 1983).

Divorced fathers not given custody often withdraw from their children as a function of the strain of dealing with their ex-wives, geographical distance, financial status, their own discomfort or pain in relating to their children, and/or the nature of the marriage itself (Brown

& Fox, 1979; Hetherington et al., 1977; Meredith, 1985; Silver & Silver, 1981). If fathers have little contact with their children before the divorce, they are less likely to have contact with them afterward than are fathers who had much contact with them prior to the divorce. Such limited contact is especially true in working-class families. Yet, many fathers spend more time or have qualitatively more meaningful interactions with their children after the divorce than they had previously. Often such parent-child experiences lead to personal change for the father. Many fathers report increased personal growth, more expressiveness, greater sensitivity to others, and less concern about work as a consequence of their parenting involvement (Greif, 1985; Meredith, 1985; Moreland, 1983). Such changes suggest some of the rewards men are likely to obtain from increased parenting.

In examining the effects of divorce on children, more researchers are beginning to acknowledge that single-parent families are an alternative to two-parent families and that they are not necessarily pathological (Lynn, 1979; Meredith, 1985). When divorce produces negative outcomes in a child, such as insecurity, depression, and poor academic performance, the cause is likely to be unclear communication between parents and the child, or the guilt a child may feel in missing the absent parent (Albin, 1977; Biller, 1981a). The negative consequences are not necessarily the result of the divorce per se.

Continued relations with fathers are important to children. Numerous studies have found that a child's adjustment to parental divorce is a function of the frequency of the child's contact with the noncustodial parent, usually the father, as well as of the relationship between the ex-spouses (Hess & Camara, 1979; Moreland, 1983; Wallerstein & Kelly, 1980). Furthermore, sons in particular appear to suffer from lack of contact with their father, and may do better living with him than with their mother (Franke, 1983; Hetherington, Cox, & Cox, 1979; Santrock & Warshak, 1979). Indeed, people who have been deprived of a relationship with their father are overrepresented among individuals with psychological problems (Biller, 1981a). Of course, the father relationship is

more likely to be the one children are deprived of given custody patterns and men's sex-role socialization. Thus, despite the Motherhood Myth and judicial custom, fathers are important to their children too. An examination of families practicing joint custody (Roman & Haddad, 1978; Rosenthal & Keshet, 1981) indicates that the children involved are thriving, not just "adjusting." Contrary to popular opinion, children in such families are not "torn" between two parents. Although such arrangements may necessitate a great deal of planning and negotiation, they certainly seem a viable alternative, if desired, to a battle of custody.

In sum, many fathers are beginning to realize how much they have missed by not sharing child-care responsibilities. The lessons learned in parenting—relating to someone weaker and dependent in a socially responsive way—may carry over into men's relations with the rest of the world and may lead to a more caring, humane society. At the very least, greater involvement in child care would permit men to both work and love, to touch the parts of their emotional lives they have kept hidden. And because men would be *sharing* child-care responsibilities, it would free more women to develop their competencies in other areas. The end result may be the development of more fully functioning individuals—mothers, fathers, and children.

Summary

In this chapter, the effects of the gender stereotypes on relationships have been examined. As friends, males as a group tend to have a large number of casual relationships with other males. Females as a group tend to have intimate relationships with a few females. (These and all differences noted for males and females are group differences and are not necessarily true of all individuals of the group.) The superficiality of many male friendships is due to the emphasis of the male role on competition, suppression of emotions, fear of homosexuality, and the lack of adequate role models. Male-female friendships are also difficult to form because of the behaviors associated with sex roles themselves and because of the difficulty males have in establishing any form of intimate relationship.

Romantic relationships also show the effects of the gender stereotypes. Dating relationships often are characterized by much game playing and manipulation. Although equality in relationships has become more the norm among college students, in practice there is still ambivalence on the part of many males. Despite prevailing opinion, males as a group tend to be more emotionally involved in such relationships than do females. Once married, men generally flourish, but many women experience great strain. Employed wives generally are as satisfied or more satisfied than homemakers. Homosexual relationships tend to be more egalitarian than heterosexual relationships.

Parental relationships suffer from adherence to gender stereotypes as well. Sex-role expectations force women to believe they should be mothers and stay home with their children. The same expectations neglect the important role fathers play with their children. If women live up to the Motherhood Mandate,

they may feel frustrated and take out their feelings on their families. If they are employed, they are generally happy but tend to feel guilty, despite there being no evidence of any negative effect of maternal employment on children. Paternal relationships have been ignored because of men's lack of training, the characteristics of the stereotyped masculine personality, and the career disadvantages of parenting. However, this pattern appears to be changing.

Thus, nearly all relationships, particularly men's, suffer from adherence to the gender stereotypes. Men and women both would benefit if they could develop the emotional and agentic parts of their personalities. Such an androgynous development would facilitate all the relationships of women and men.

More than the stereotypes need to be changed in order to liberate males and females in their relationships, however. Societal support in the form of job flexibility, child-care facilities, and changed institutional practices are also needed. These will be examined in succeeding chapters.

Recommended Reading

Aldous, J. (Ed.). (1982). *Two paychecks: Life in dual-career families*. Beverly Hills, Calif.: Sage. A collection of research articles on dual-career families that describe the various ways participants structure their time and priorities.

Ehrenreich, B. (1983). *The hearts of men: American dreams and the flight from commitment*. Garden City, N.Y.: Anchor. A fascinating and provocative analysis of the reasons underlying the demise of the male breadwinner role and the loosening of marital bonds.

Lamb, M. C., & Sagi, A. (Eds.). (1983). *Fatherhood and family policy*. Hillside, N.J.: Lawrence Erlbaum

Associates. A systematic review of the research on the impact of fathers on family members plus a section on alternative policies that would permit fathers to increase their involvement in child care.

Safilios-Rothschild, C. (Ed.) (1981). Relationships. *Psychology of Women Quarterly, 5* (Whole No. 3). A special issue of the journal, devoted to recent research on relationships, particularly friendships.

Scarr, S. (1984). *Mother Care/Other Care*. New York: Basic. A review of child development and child-care options, especially written for employed parents of young children. Critiques the myths surrounding motherhood.

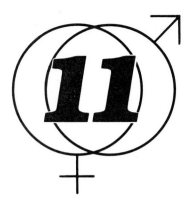

11 Societal Consequences: Prejudice and Work

As discussed in the last two chapters, gender stereotypes seriously affect nearly all aspects of personal and interpersonal functioning. The stereotypes also affect our interactions with society at large. As shown in Table 11-1, one effect is on paychecks. Women consistently earn less than men and the salary gap has remained relatively the same for the last 30 years. For every dollar earned by a man, a woman earns about 60¢. These salary figures are examples of two major social areas affected by the gender stereotypes—interpersonal prejudice and the world of work. Figure 11-1 gives a "humorous" look at how these two areas overlap. However, this overlap does not account for all the data on work force sex differences and for that reason we will deal separately with the areas of prejudice and work.

Because societal effects are so pervasive, this book can, of necessity, only examine a few areas. This chapter will focus on prejudice and work; the next, on power and aggression.

Table 11-1
The Wage Gap, 1955–1984: Women's Median Full-Time Earnings as a Percentage of Men's

Year	For Every Dollar a Man Earns, a Woman Earns
1955	63.9¢
1960	60.8¢
1965	60.0¢
1970	59.4¢
1975	58.8¢
1980	60.2¢
1984	64.8¢

Source: U.S. Department of Labor (1975, 1983, 1985).

Prejudice

Numerous studies and personal experiences have documented that men and women are prejudiced against women solely on the basis of their gender. In Philip Goldberg's (1968) classic study, female college students were asked to evaluate journal articles for their value, persuasiveness, and profundity. They also evaluated the authors for their writing style, professional competence, status, and ability to persuade the reader. The articles were from predominantly "masculine" fields (such as law and city planning), predominantly "feminine" fields (elementary school teaching and dietetics), and "neutral" ones (linguistics and art history). They differed only in that the author was presented as male in half of the articles and as female in the other half. The results showed that college women consistently found an article more valuable and its author more competent when the article bore a male rather than a female name. These differences in evaluation as a function of author sex were significant only in the traditionally masculine fields and the "neutral" field of linguistics. The importance of the sex typing of the field has been overlooked frequently by later researchers.

Further study of this phenomenon, using different procedures, has lent clarification to Goldberg's findings. The important variables in demonstrations of prejudicial attitudes toward one sex appear to be: (1) the gender appropriateness of the behavior or person being rated; and (2) rater characteristics, including sex typing, sex-role attitudes, age, and sex. From the vast amount of research in this area since 1968, it is clear that prejudice still exists in both men and women, but it usually exists in interaction with situational factors, and more often in

Figure 11-1

Example of how gender stereotypes affect us on a societal level: prejudice against women and salary inequities. (Copyright 1977 by G. B. Trudeau/ distributed by Universal Press Syndicate. All rights reserved.)

subtle, as opposed to obvious, ways. Let's examine some of the recent research in more detail (also see Wallston & O'Leary, 1981). Unfortunately, although Black women appear to suffer from both racism and sexism, little research has examined the dynamics involved in their particular situation (Reid, 1984).

Gender Appropriateness

Prejudice against women is most likely to occur toward those women who are seen as violating gender stereotypes. Under some conditions, bias has been found against women who aspire to status or power equal to that of men, as in fields or behaviors typically associated with men (Basow & Silberg, in press; Cann & Garnett, 1984; Etaugh & Kasley, 1981; Etaugh & Riley, 1983; Lenney, Mitchell, & Browning, 1983; Paludi & Bauer, 1983; Toder, 1980; Ward, 1981). For example, Basow and Silberg (in press) found that female professors in comparison to male professors were negatively evaluated by their students on a number of dimensions, as illustrated in Figure 11-2. However, as Kaschak (1978) also had found using written descriptions of teachers, it is mainly male students who devalue female professors.

Compared to female students, male students see female professors as being less scholarly, less organized, less dynamic, and less capable in group interactions with the class. Female students also see female professors as less dynamic and less involved with students individually than are male professors, but generally female students make fewer distinctions between professors on the basis of gender. Because college teaching still is regarded as a male profession (more than 70% of college professors were male in 1985), female professors may be stigmatized.

Interestingly, a second study by Kaschak (1981a) using written descriptions found different results when the professors were described as award-winning teachers. Under this condition, some of the sex bias disappeared. Male and female professors were seen as equally excellent and male and female students were equally desirous of enrolling in their courses. Yet all evaluations were not equal. Female and male professors were seen as achieving their award-winning status in different and stereotypic ways: female professors in traditionally "feminine" fields were rated as more concerned and likeable than male professors in those fields. Male professors in all fields were rated as more powerful and effective than female

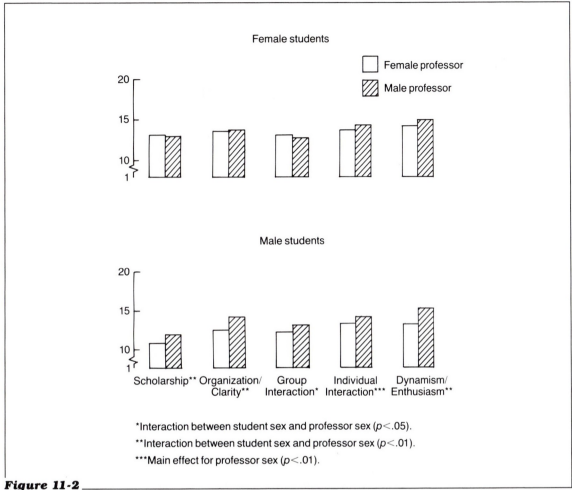

Figure 11-2

Mean ratings of female and male college professors by female and male students. (Adapted from Basow & Silberg, in press.)

professors. Again we see an affective/instrumental split in attributing success to females and males. One implication of this study and others (Isaacs, 1981; Starer & Denmark, 1974; Taynor & Deaux, 1973) is that when female accomplishments are "legitimized" through awards or high status, prejudice against females is minimized.

In fact, in some situations where women behave in a nonstereotypical but laudable or superior manner, they may be evaluated even higher than men in the same situations. Such results have been found by numerous researchers (Abramson, Goldberg, Greenberg, & Abramson, 1977; Basow & Howe, 1982; Etaugh & Stern, 1984; Gruber & Gaebelein, 1979; Taynor & Deaux, 1975). For example, Taynor and Deaux (1973) found that a woman who behaved in an exemplary manner in a civic emergency was perceived as being more deserving of a reward, as performing better, and as trying harder than a man. Abramson and colleagues (1977) have termed this pattern of results the *talking platypus phenomenon.* That is, when an individual achieves an unanticipated level of success, the achievement becomes magnified because "After all, it matters little what the platypus says, the wonder is that it can say anything at all" (p. 123).

Although prejudice in evaluations may be minimized for successful individuals, differential sexist attributions regarding the reasons for success may remain. Indeed, given the current social climate where overt prejudice no longer is socially acceptable, prejudice is more likely to be seen indirectly in terms of attributions made rather than directly in terms of differential evaluations (Bond, 1981; Deaux & Emswiller, 1974; Galper & Luck, 1980; Lips & Myers, 1980; Post, 1981; Smith, Whitehead, & Sussman, 1984). In sum, because people are expected to conform to the gender stereotypes, when they don't, they may be negatively evaluated. And, more to the point, most people, whether males or females, are not award winners or superior performers. Sexist prejudice against these "everyday" people is still prevalent.

With respect to jobs or articles on subjects that are traditionally "neutral" or "female related," some studies have found that females are judged to be equal or better than males, at least by female critics (Etaugh & Riley, 1983; Gross & Geffner, 1980; Isaacs, 1981). This latter finding suggests that discrimination can work both ways. For example, in one study (Basow & Howe, 1979b), female college students found a non-sex-typed career that was presented and explained by a female to be more interesting and of more importance than the identical career presented in the identical way by a male. There were no differences in the ratings on competence required, status and prestige, or salary. Thus some prejudice against women may be abating, at least in non-sex-typed fields (Etaugh & Foresman, 1983).

As suggested above, prejudice may operate against men who violate gender stereotypes. Studies have found that males who talk about their emotional problems, who are passive in group discussions, or who express sexual concerns are liked much less and are viewed as more in need of professional help than are females who do so (for example, Costrich et al., 1975; Polyson 1978). In fact, prejudice against males may be even greater than prejudice against females when one's behavior is con-

sidered gender-inappropriate. For example, data cited in Chapter 9 about female and male achievement behavior indicate that males who succeed in gender-inappropriate activities more often have negative consequences predicted for them (by both females and males) than do females who succeed in gender-inappropriate activities.

Similarly, men who are in gender-inappropriate occupations are generally perceived less favorably than are women who are in either gender-appropriate or gender-inappropriate occupations, at least by male and female undergraduates (Shinar, 1978). In gender-inappropriate occupations, men are perceived as significantly less likeable, less well adjusted, and less physically attractive than are women in gender-inappropriate occupations. These men are also perceived as being even less active and having even fewer leadership attributes than are women in the same occupations. Shinar explains these findings by suggesting that the emergence of women's liberation has resulted in increasing acceptance of women in formerly "male" occupations. The lack of a parallel men's movement, however, has left man with less social sanction for crossing gender boundaries. Alternatively, the results may be explained by the differential evaluation of "masculinity" and "femininity." Since male-related things have high value, women who begin doing them benefit from the positive assessment. In contrast, since female-related things have low value, men who do them are rated even more negatively than women, since there is no "acceptable" reason for them to want such a change. We saw a similar process at work in the differential reactions people have toward male and female homosexuality (Chapter 5).

Because of these differences in how male and female violators of sex-role norms are perceived, the pressures on women and men who take on nontraditional jobs are different. Schreiber (1979), in a study of 50 such employees, found that the nontraditional women wanted to be regarded as like the men with whom they worked, but the nontraditional men wanted to be viewed as different from and superior to their female co-workers.

Other research supports the hypothesis that women and men are evaluated differently. For example, competent men appear to be perceived more positively than are competent women, but males of low competence generally are rated lower than females of low competence (Brown & Geis, 1984; Deutsch & Leong, 1983; Etaugh & Foresman, 1983; Etaugh & Riley, 1983; Larrance et al., 1979; Rhue, Lynn, & Garske, 1984). Again, conformity to sex-role expectations may explain these findings. Males are expected to be more competent than females, at least in a wider variety of situations. When men conform to role expectations by being competent and in control of their emotional lives, they benefit by being perceived favorably. When they do not conform to these expectations, they receive even lower ratings than females. The situational component is important, however. In some situations (for example, cooperative conditions), competent females may be evaluated more positively than competent males (Deutsch & Leong, 1983).

Whereas competence is a quality seen as more appropriate for males than females, physical attractiveness is a quality that is seen as more appropriate for females than males. Thus, women who don't conform to the level of physical attractiveness expected of them frequently may be described more negatively than similarly unattractive males (Bar-Tal & Saxe, 1976; Cash, Gillen, & Burns, 1977; Wallston & O'Leary, 1981). Furthermore, physical attractiveness appears to interact with other factors to yield complex effects. For example, a physically attractive female in a "masculine" field, such as most executive positions, may be downgraded compared to her less attractive colleague or compared to how she would be evaluated in a "feminine" field (Cash & Trimer, 1984; Dullea, 1985; Heilman & Stopeck, 1985). This effect may be stronger for male than female raters (Holahan & Stephan, 1981).

There are many complex social and situational factors that interact with each other to determine how one evaluates a woman or a man. For example, besides those factors already mentioned, there are factors such as the marital status of the target person (Etaugh & Kasley, 1981; Etaugh & Riley, 1983; Etaugh & Stern, 1984), the sex-typed characteristics of the target person (Basow & Distenfeld, 1985; Basow & Howe, 1982; Jackson & Cash, 1985;

Major, Carnevale, & Deaux, 1981; Stoppard & Kalin, 1983; Wiley & Eskilson, 1985), and whether the ratings are done in same-sex or mixed-sex groups (Etaugh, Houtler, & Ptasnik, 1984; Toder, 1980). Also of importance are characteristics of the rater. We will briefly examine these qualities in the next section.

Rater Characteristics

Among the characteristics of the rater that influence her or his evaluation are the rater's sex, gender conformity, and age. Although Goldberg's (1968) initial research suggested that women are prejudiced against women, more recent work suggests that it is primarily men who evidence prejudice against women (Basow & Silberg, in press; Etaugh & Kasley, 1981; Gross & Geffner, 1980; Isaacs, 1981; Kaschak, 1978; Paludi & Strayer, 1985; Ward, 1981). This sex bias on the part of males may be because men are more traditional in their attitudes toward gender stereotypes than are women, or because the current emphasis on women's rights is causing a backlash. Both interpretations have some support. It is important to point out that not all research shows sex bias on the part of males (see, for example, Deutsch & Leong, 1983; Lenney, Mitchell, & Browning, 1983).

Sex-role attitudes may affect such perceptions. It is predominantly males with traditional attitudes toward women who downrate competent women (Holahan & Stephan, 1981; Kahn, 1981; Spence & Helmreich, 1972). In general, ratings of competent women by college students are a complex function of the rater's sex and sex typing, the ratee's description, and the specific attributes rated.

Among noncollege students, more prejudice against women is found than among college students (Gross & Geffner, 1980). This is especially true of people over the age of 40. The fact that most research uses college students may obscure the true prevalence of such attitudes. College students may truly be less sexist than noncollege students, or they may be participants in a subculture in which the expression of such attitudes is not socially desirable. There is evidence for both possibilities. For example, Etaugh & Spandikow (1981) found that both female and male college students tend to become more liberal in their attitudes toward women over a two-year period. Given the relative sophistication of college students with regard to sex-role ideology, less transparent research designs are needed (Beattie & Diehl, 1979; Galper & Luck, 1980; Madden, 1981).

Even children show this sex bias. As mentioned in previous chapters, boys show much more negativity toward traditionally female-related qualities and activities than do girls toward male-related qualities and activities. Connor and Serbin (1978) conducted a study of fourth-, sixth-, and eighth-graders' reactions to male and female story characters. In this study, the stories were identical except for the sex of the main character. Thus there were four stories—a boy or girl engaged in either boy-related or girl-related activities. Both girls and boys preferred to be the male character and to do the things the male character did when the story's main character was male. What girls did, regardless of its sex typing, appeared to have less intrinsic value than what boys did. Furthermore, boys' negativism toward stories about girls and girl-related activities was stronger than girls' and increased with age.

Children younger than the fourth-graders used by Connor and Serbin also demonstrate prejudicial attitudes. For example, Cann and colleagues (Cann & Haight, 1983; Cann & Garnett, 1984) found that children aged 5½ to 9 rated gender-appropriate jobholders as more competent than gender-inappropriate jobholders. It was encouraging, however, that people in gender-inappropriate jobs were not viewed as incompetent, only as less competent than their more gender-appropriate counterparts. Adherence to the stereotypes increased with age, although same-sex preference also was evident.

In summary, much of the sex bias demonstrated in research and in real life appears to operate unconsciously (Brown & Geis, 1984) and increasingly in subtle ways. Evaluations of individuals on the basis of their gender are affected by a variety of situational and personal factors. For example, a female achieving in a neutral or feminine-sex-typed field or occupation may be viewed quite positively. Still, to the extent that an irrelevant variable such as gender enters into any evaluation of an individual, it is unfair. Furthermore, most achievement situations are sex typed as masculine. In these, prejudice seems to operate against women. The consequences of such prejudice can be seen in educational settings and media portrayals of the sexes (see Chapter 8), in the treatment of children by parents and others (see Chapter 7), and in the worlds of work, politics, and law. These last two areas will be discussed in Chapter 12. It is to the world of work that we now turn.

Work

Volumes of data have been accumulated regarding women and men in the labor force. Because of the wealth of data, only a cursory survey will be attempted here. The interested reader is encouraged to read Berch (1982), Fox and Hesse-Biber (1984), and the additional sources cited within this chapter for more detail.

In general, women in the labor force have been underemployed, underpaid, and discriminated against. Figure 11-3 gives a simplified view of how the gender stereotypes influence our work lives. Occupational tracking and salary inequities are just two of the major consequences.

In this section we will review the data on participation rates, salaries, barriers to equal employment opportunities, and men's role in the work force.

Participation Rates

As Figure 11-4 indicates, the participation of women in the labor force has been steadily increasing since 1950, whereas participation by men has been slowly declining. More than half of all women (55%) currently are in the labor force, compared to about three-quarters (77%) of all men (U.S. Dept. of Labor, 1985). The participation of women is expected to continue to increase through 1990 to nearly 60%. The greatest increase in labor force participation has been by women between 25 and 34 years of age. Between 1970 and 1984, their participation rate advanced nearly 30 percentage points, from 45% to 73%. These are the women

Figure 11-3
For this you went to college? One example of how the gender stereotypes influence our work lives. (Copyright 1973, Bülbül. Reprinted with permission.)

who historically remained at home to rear children.

Despite the strong belief that a breadwinning husband, homemaking wife, and at least one child constitute the typical family in the United States, only 15.9% of all households actually conformed to this pattern in 1976 (U.S. Bureau of the Census, 1977). A more common pattern (18.5%) is one where both father and mother are wage earners.[1] Only 7% of all husband-wife families conform to the stereotypic employed husband, nonemployed wife, and two children pattern. More than half of all mothers (about 62%) and wives (54%) are in the labor force (U.S. Dept. of Labor, 1985). Of all single women (either never married or presently sep-

arated, divorced, or widowed), more than three out of five (61.4%) were employed in 1984.

In 1985, more than two-fifths of the labor force (44%) was composed of women. More than nine out of every ten women work for pay at some point during their lives. Given the large participation of women in the labor force, relatively little preparation is given them for later employment.

The reasons for the increasing participation of women in the labor force are numerous. Among them are economic necessity, rising educational attainments, changing demographic trends, and changing employment needs.

Economic Necessity. Like men, most women are employed out of economic necessity. In March 1985, nearly half (45%) of all employed women were single, separated, divorced, or widowed. Nearly another 20% had husbands earning equal to or less than a poverty-level salary (U.S. Dept. of Labor, 1985).

---

[1]Most households comprise married couples without children (30.5%) or single persons (20.6%) (U.S. Bureau of the Census, 1977).

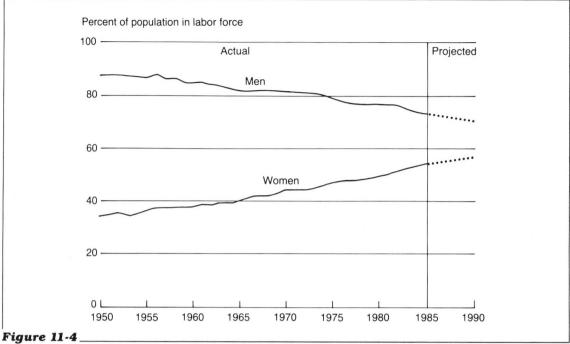

Figure 11-4 _____

*Labor force participation rates of women and men,
annual averages, 1950–1985, and projected rates for
1990. (From the U.S. Dept. of Labor, 1977b; 1985.)*

High unemployment, high inflation, and changing notions of what constitutes a decent standard of living all contribute to the need for married women (and men) to work for pay. Because of inflation alone, many families now need two paychecks simply to maintain their former standard of living.

Many people think that most divorced women are financially secure because of alimony. However, less than 15% of all divorced women even are awarded alimony, and fewer than half of these receive regular payments (Weitzman, 1985). Divorced women and their children suffer an immediate 73% drop in their standard of living whereas their ex-husband's standard of living increases 42% in the first year after divorce. Only 60% of single mothers are awarded child support by the courts, and fewer than half of these mothers collect the full amount ("One-parent," 1983; "Study: Many," 1983).

In 1982, a record 9.7 million families (one out of six) were headed by women. This is nearly double the number of female-headed families that existed in 1972 (U.S. Dept. of Labor, 1983). Three-fifths of these women were in the labor force, but about one out of every three of these families was living in poverty in 1981. Among White female-headed families, the rate was 27%. Among Black and Hispanic female-headed families, the rate was 53% ("Poverty," 1983). The comparable rate for families headed by men only is 1 out of 18, and for married-couple families, 1 out of 16 (U.S. Dept. of Labor, 1983).

Rising Educational Attainments. Another reason more women are working is that more women are obtaining college and advanced degrees, giving them access to jobs for which they were previously unqualified. Table 11-2 illustrates this trend. More than half of all bachelor's and master's degrees now are awarded to women. On the highest educational levels, the increased percentage of women has been dramatic. Women received only 3.5% of

Table 11-2

Percent of Educational Degrees Awarded to Women in 1965, 1971, 1977, 1983, and (Projected) 1986

	1964–1965	1970–1971	1976–1977	1982–1983	1985–1986 (projected)
B.A.'s	42.4	43.4	45.7	50.3	50.3
M.A.'s	33.8	40.1	47.0	50.8	52.7
Ph.D.'s	10.8	14.2	24.0	32.1	36.8
First Professional (e.g., law, M.D.)	3.5	6.3	18.6	27.5	31.7

From the National Center for Education Statistics, 1985.

first-professional degrees in 1965 but are expected to receive 31.7% of them in 1986. Women in 1986 are expected to receive more than one-third of all Ph.D.'s compared to only 10.8% in 1965.

Postsecondary education increases the likelihood of women being in the labor force. In all income brackets, wives who had completed college were more likely to be employed and have positive attitudes toward employment than were wives with less education (Houser & Beckman, 1980; U.S. Dept. of Labor, 1980). Also, because college-educated women are more likely to have been employed for a longer period of time both before marriage and before childbearing, they are accustomed to employment outside the home and therefore less likely to drop out of the paid labor force (Van Dusen & Sheldon, 1976).

Changing Demographic Trends.
Women's marital and family status is changing and these changes affect their participation in the labor force. As discussed in the previous chapter, young persons in the 1980s are remaining single longer than in previous decades. The number of women in their early 20s who have not married rose from 36% in 1970 to 54% by 1980 (Bianchi & Spain, 1983). Too, families are decreasing in size and are being started at later ages than was true in previous decades. Consequently, more women are experiencing longer periods of time during which they may advance their careers. In 1983, the average American woman could expect to spend 26 years of her life in the work force,

compared with 37 years for men (U.S. Dept. of Labor, 1983).

Changing Employment Needs. Another factor contributing to women's entry into the paid labor force has been the growth of those industries that have primarily employed women. The post-World War II baby boom created the need for more services—educational, medical, governmental, and recreational. These services, especially the professional ones, have been traditional employers of women. Consequently, the demand for female workers has increased significantly since the 1940s. For example, in 1950, 62% of all clerical workers and 45% of all service workers (other than household workers) were women. In March 1985, the numbers were 84% and 60%, respectively (U.S. Dept. of Labor, 1985). Between 1972 and 1985, the number of women working in clerical and professional occupations (mainly teaching and nursing) rose by more than 50% to more than half of all employed women. A substantial increase also occurred in the service occupations which accounted for 18% of all employed women in 1985. The labor demand for women should intensify in the future, because women outnumber men in the population by 7 million, population expansion has been halted, and the participation rate of males in the labor force has been declining due to earlier retirement.

Other Factors. Another factor that may contribute to the increasing participation of women in the labor force is diminishing social prejudice against the idea of women working outside of the home. As discussed in the previous chapter, the majority of adult Americans, and the vast majority of college students, support the idea of married women being in the labor force. New legislation promoting equality in employment and education, and advances in household technologies, have also aided women's entry into the world of paid work.

It should be noted that the reasons women are employed are virtually identical to the reasons men are employed: economic necessity, work as part of their identity, a desire for achievement, and the satisfaction from meaningful, rewarded activity (Renwick & Lawler, 1978; Thom, 1984).

Women's compensation for employment, however, has consistently been below that of men. Salary inequities between the sexes are as pervasive as they are long-standing.

Salary

What is a woman worth? In terms of employment compensation, only about two-thirds of the worth of a man (see Table 11-1). When part-time workers are included, the average earned income of women in 1980 was only one-half that of men ("Men," 1984). Even though more women are employed and most are employed out of economic necessity, the salary differential between men's median income and that of women has fluctuated around the 60% mark for the last 30 years. Women belonging to minority groups are especially at a disadvantage. In 1984, Black women employed full-time earned only 60% of the salary earned by White men, and 80% of that earned by Black men (U.S. Dept. of Labor, 1985). For Hispanic women, the situation is even worse: employed full-time Hispanic women earned only 55% of the salary earned by White men, and 77% of the salary earned by Hispanic men.

Table 11-3 shows the salary differential for several occupational groups in 1984. The salary differential is greatest for sales and craft workers and least for farmers and mechanics. A number of factors contribute to this salary differential. One is occupational segregation. Women are concentrated in low-paying jobs. Another factor is the increased numbers of women in the labor force in entry-level positions. A third factor is the differences in education and training between the sexes that direct women into lower-paying jobs. A fourth factor is the greater likelihood of women taking time out for childcare activities. Men also are three times more likely than women to work

Table 11-3

Median Weekly Earnings of Full-Time Wage and Salary Workers by Sex, Occupation, and Industry Group, 1984

Occupation and Industry Group	Usual Weekly Earnings		Women's Earnings as Percent of Men's
	Women	Men	
Farm, forestry, fishing	177	205	86
Mechanics	340	399	85
Nonfarm laborers	207	258	80
Professional	394	534	74
Transportation operators	253	354	71
Technical	312	451	69
Service	180	259	69
Clerical	257	380	68
Managerial	358	568	63
Machine operators	208	331	63
Craft	246	406	61
Sales	212	403	53

From U.S. Dept. of Labor, 1985.

overtime and earn extra income (U.S. Dept. of Labor, 1976a). Yet even these factors do not sufficiently account for the large difference in salaries. A major longitudinal study of a nationally representative sample of American families has found that two-thirds of the wage gap between White men and White women, and three-quarters of the gap between White men and Black women cannot be accounted for by sex differences in skills, work participation, or labor-force attachment (Corcoran, Duncan, & Hill, 1984). The major factor explaining the salary differential appears to be direct and indirect discrimination.

These factors all serve as barriers to equal female income achievement in the labor force. All these factors affect female occupational achievement in ways other than monetary reward as well. A closer look at some of these barriers, both internal and external, will illustrate the complexity of the problem. Of the barriers, the external ones are most important and most serious, yet people often deliberately ignore them to focus on internal ones. It is easier to "blame the victim" than to institute social change, and psychologists have been as responsible as anyone else for this misdirected emphasis. Therefore, after briefly noting some of the internal barriers, we will focus at length on some of the external ones.

Internal Barriers to Female Achievement

There are many internal barriers to female achievement—a traditional female life plan, sex-typing and sex-role attitudes, fear of success, and attribution patterns. These were discussed in previous chapters. Of them all, the most critical internalized factor barring women from achievement is the different *life plans* for the sexes to which children are socialized. Despite the facts that nine out of every ten women will work in the paid labor force at some point in their lives, many women are employed their entire adult lives, and more than three out of five mothers are employed, most girls grow up unprepared psychologically and professionally to assume a career. Traditionally, girls grow up expecting to be mothers; boys grow up expect-

ing to have careers. Although today more young women than ever before plan on being employed, their careers come second to their families (see Chapter 10), and their job aspirations most often concentrate on traditionally "female" jobs such as nursing and education (Zuckerman, 1981; Zuckerman & Sayre, 1982). These fields have low status and low salaries. This preference for traditional "female" jobs by females is particularly interesting since girls (more so than boys) increasingly tend to rate most jobs as suitable for both males and females (Archer, 1984; Franken, 1983; Hensley & Borges, 1981; Mellon, Crano, & Schmitt, 1982; Umstot, 1980; Zuckerman & Sayre, 1982). But, when it comes to their own choice of career, females still predominantly choose traditional jobs. In a six-year longitudinal study of women, Harmon (1981) found that the occupations considered became more traditional in sex type and lower in socioeconomic status over time. Sex-typed job choice is even more typical of men than of women. In one major Rand Corporation study of more than 13,000 adolescents, three out of four males chose traditionally male jobs whereas only 47% of the females picked traditionally female jobs (Parachini, 1985).

Sex typing and *sex-role attitudes* also affect career planning. Among adolescents and college students, feminine sex typing is associated with choice of female-dominated majors and occupations (Greenglass & Devins, 1982; Harren, Kass, Tinsley, & Moreland, 1978, 1979; Komarovsky, 1982; Young, 1984; Zuckerman, 1981). Feminine sex typing also appears to be associated with lower career achievement (Wong et al., 1985). A liberal attitude toward women is associated with career salience and with more male-dominated majors and occupations, among Blacks as well as Whites (Burlew, 1982). Liberal attitudes toward women's roles also are related to the number of hours employed mothers worked each week (Krogh, 1985). The causal sequence here is not clear, however. Sex-role attitudes and sex typing seem to lead some individuals to choose certain career paths, whereas for others, the choice of a career itself leads to certain attitudes and attributions. For example, women in atypical careers such as in law and medicine were found to score higher on instrumental/agentic traits than did women in more typical careers (Lemkau, 1983; Williams & McCullers, 1983). Canter (1979) suggests that sex-role conceptions play a central role in career aspirations and mediate the effects of all other career-related variables.

A related internal barrier to equal employment possibilities is the attitude of females regarding helping others. National surveys of college and high school students consistently show that females are more concerned than are males with helping others, and are less concerned than are males with money, prestige, or status factors in their career decisions (Astin, 1985; Block, Denker, and Tittle, 1981). For example, of all American freshmen in 1984, 70% of the females compared with 53% of the males considered it essential or very important to help others who are in difficulty. Being very well-off financially was considered essential or very important to 76% of the males and 67% of the females. Thus, women may be more motivated than men to pursue jobs in the service sector, which typically are low-status and low-paying jobs, whereas men may be more motivated than women to pursue a job for its practical advantages, such as pay and fringe benefits.

Another internal barrier to female achievement is the *anxiety* ("fear of success") some women have with regard to achieving in male-related activities. Because most jobs are male dominated and having a primary career focus is itself seen as masculine, many women steer away from such fields and such a focus.

Women's typical *attribution pattern* also may serve as a barrier to occupational achievement. By attributing their successes to luck rather than skill, women's level of aspiration remains low. A 1978 survey of women at six of the country's most prestigious colleges found that women underestimate their academic ability by overpreparing for exams and they under-aspire in their career goals ("College Women," 1978). Therefore, many women never establish any occupational life plan or prepare themselves for a career. When they do enter the labor force, it is usually at low-level jobs. Even among women who serve on national boards of directors of major U.S. corporations (a small but growing number), "luck" is the reason they

cite most often to explain their success (mesrud, 1979). Similar results were obtained in Deaux's (1979) study of female and male first-level managers. The men were significantly more likely to attribute their success to their ability than were the women. And, perhaps they are right. Larwood and Gattiker (1984) found that top positions in 17 major corporations were predictable for men on the basis of their earlier positions or successes. In contrast, for older women, no important paths predicted their attainment of top positions, suggesting the operation of chance.

Women also have lower work-related *expectations* than do men, especially than do White men (Gurin, 1981). For example, fewer women than men expect and plan for promotions, salary rises, and so on. This may lead to a self-fulfilling prophecy, since low expectations may lead women to make fewer work changes and therefore to have fewer advancement possibilities. Furthermore, female employees also expect more negative reactions to their performance and abilities than do men (Heilman & Kram, 1983). Although this expectation may be accurate in some cases, such a pervasive belief may become self-fulfilling.

External Barriers to Female Achievement

Of greater importance than any internal barrier, however, are the many external barriers to female achievement in the labor force. These are both social, as in socialization and discrimination, and institutional, as in occupational segregation, restricted access to education, business, and the professions, and trade unions and laws.

Socialization. Primary among the social factors are those associated with socialization. As discussed in Chapter 8, the media, school environment, and vocational and counseling programs traditionally have ignored the concept of female employment and, instead, have promulgated the "feminine mystique"—that complex of beliefs and attitudes assuming that women's primary focus should be domestic. Whereas males always had to choose their careers, traditionally most White females first

...ser to have a career at all. ...erally have expected to be ...orkers and homemakers (Mal- ...expectation that is becoming ...among White females as well.

...ecisions for all individuals are af-...variety of factors (see Canter, 1979; Danzi..., 1983; Marini, 1978; O'Neil et al., 1980; E. Smith, 1982; Tittle, 1981, for more detail). Among the important factors are:

1. Parental encouragement, particularly by fathers, particularly for girls.
2. Role models of successful women, especially mothers and college professors (Basow & Howe, 1980; Burlew, 1982; Gilbert, Gallessich, & Evans, 1983; Gilbert 1985; Goldstein, 1979; Greene, Sullivan, & Beyard-Tyler, 1982; Lemkau, 1983; Selkow, 1984; Simpson 1984; Zuckerman, 1981). This is especially important for nontraditional careers. A study of nearly 13,000 young women found that if a girl's mother worked in a blue-collar field, the daughter had an 8% greater chance of selecting a nontraditional job for herself than if her mother worked in a traditional job (Parachini, 1985).
3. Expectations of women held by others. Greenstein, Miller, and Weldon (1979) found this factor to be a better predictor of college women's occupational choice than the women's own attitudes toward work or toward achieving women. This may be especially important for Black females (Simpson, 1984). Men's expectations, in particular, may influence females (Canter, 1979; Lemkau, 1983). For example, college women who perceive traditional sex-role expectations in their male friends expect more negative outcomes from success and have lower career aspirations than do women who do not perceive such expectations in their male friends.
4. Number of siblings. The more siblings, the lower the career and educational aspirations, particularly for boys.
5. Supportive peer group, male and female. Especially important for nontraditional career choices (Holahan, 1979).
6. Social class. There is greater sex typing of occupational aspirations among lower-middle-class children than among middle- and upper-middle-class children (Franken, 1983). Careers are more an ideal of middle- and upper-class women, although lower-middle-class women are the ones most apt to be in the labor force. However, socioeconomic background is a stronger indication of a boy's educational and occupational aspirations than it is of a girl's (see also Harmon, 1981).
7. Academic ability and academic performance. Academic strengths are more strongly related to boys' educational and occupational aspirations than to girls' (Danziger, 1983).
8. Dating behavior. An orientation toward activities leading to early marriage are negatively related to girls' educational and occupational aspirations.
9. Residence. Those women more likely to work outside the home come from urban as opposed to rural settings, and from the Northeast and Far West as opposed to the South. Young men in the South tend to have higher occupational aspirations than other men.
10. Religion. Religious attendance is positively related to higher aspirations for boys, but not for girls. For both sexes, denominational discrimination against women is related to traditional career choices (Rhodes, 1983). For males only, being Jewish is strongly correlated with prestige of occupational aspiration.
11. Supply of and demand for jobs. In World War II, when the demand for the labor was high and the supply low, 38% of all U.S. women were in the labor force, compared to 29% and 34% for the nonwar years of 1940 and 1950, respectively. The current increasing number of service sector jobs traditionally employing women has presented a similar picture of high demand and low labor supply.
12. Availability of solutions to the real problems of dual-career marriages and of combining motherhood and a career (Berger, Wallston, Foster, & Wright, 1977; Best, 1981; Rogan, 1984; Simpson, 1984). Women's participation in the work force tends to be broken. Many drop out for a few years to rear children, then reenter the work force either full- or part-time. About 25% of all female workers work part-time (U.S. Dept. of Labor, 1985). Women with children are more likely to work part-time (about 30% of them do). Such women also tend to limit their professional involvement (Samuelson, 1983). For example,

such women are three times less likely to work overtime or to engage in extraprofessional activities than are men or women without children (U.S. Dept. of Labor, 1976a). Furthermore, many women may experience geographic constraints on their career opportunities. In two-career families, the woman is usually the one to accommodate her own job location to her husband's job location. This factor of geographic constraint has been found to be a major one in explaining the status difference between men and women in academia (Marwell, Rosenfeld, & Spilerman, 1979; see Macauley, 1979, for a response).

These patterns handicap women in occupational achieving. Because of geographic constraints and child-care demands, some competent women may be underemployed or even unemployed. The jobs currently available for part-time workers are usually limited to low-paying, low-skilled jobs. Limitations on the time available to women for professional involvement can seriously limit professional advancement. If more professional jobs were available on a part-time basis, if more jobs had flexible hours, and if more women postponed child rearing until their 30s, more women could achieve occupationally. Having daycare centers, after-school care, child care, and household help available and reasonably priced would also help, as would greater cooperation by husbands in housework and child-care activities and in employment flexibility.

Discrimination. Of general societal factors, perhaps the most dramatic is outright discrimination against women. As discussed at the beginning of this chapter, many men and women believe that men are more competent and more interesting and their contributions more valuable than those of equally qualified females. Fidell (1976) found that psychology department chairpersons (all male) tended to place male applicants in higher positions than similarly qualified female applicants. (Written profiles were used with only the names and pronouns changed.) Likewise, Firth (1982) found that when job application letters were sent in for an advertised opening in accounting, men were more likely to pass the initial screen-

ing than were women, even though all had identical qualifications and work experience. The unemployment rates also show the effects of discrimination, women's rates being higher than men's for all classifications of workers (6.6% and 6.3%, respectively, in July 1985—Yost, 1985).

However, at least one study by Cole (1979) reports that there is little discrimination in the upper levels of American science, except in the area of promotions. Cole's study has been strongly attacked by other researchers on the basis of sample size and data interpretation. Promotions, of course, are important and strongly linked to salary and status. Other research also suggests that male employees receive more and bigger promotions than do female employees (Gupta, Jenkins, and Beehr, 1983; "You've Come," 1984). In general, bias against females is evident in a wide variety of employment evaluations (also Bronstein, 1984b; Frasher, Frasher, & Wims, 1982). It is important to note, however, that in ratings of managerial job performance, some field studies find very little bias (for example, Peters, O'Connor, Weekley, Pooyan, Frank, & Evenkrantz, 1984).

Certain factors affect the likelihood of discrimination occurring: for example, clear evaluation criterion can minimize discrimination (Lenney, Mitchell, & Browning, 1983; Martinko & Gardner 1983; Siegfried, 1982). Conversely, the more ambiguous the job or evaluation criteria, the more likely it is that stereotypical evaluations will occur (Clayton, Baird, & Levinson, 1984; Dobbins, Stuart, Pence, & Sgro, 1985; Gerdes & Garber, 1983). More discrimination appears against applicants for gender-incongruent jobs, especially women applicants (Gerdes & Kelman, 1981; Landy & Farr, 1980; Martinko & Gardner, 1983), especially by individuals who endorse traditional gender stereotypes (Motowidlo, 1982; Sharp & Post, 1980). However, if raters learn about women who are successful in a nontraditional occupation similar to the one for which they are evaluating a woman applicant, the raters are less likely to devalue the female applicant vis-à-vis the male applicant (Heilman & Martell, 1986). Minority women, lesbians, women with children, and older women are especially likely to be discriminated against (Firth, 1982; Levine & Leonard, 1984; Woody & Malson, 1984).

As noted above, the major index of discrimination is the salary differential between women and men. In 1983, female college graduates earned less than male high school dropouts and only 62% of the salary earned by male college graduates ("Devaluation," 1983; U.S. Dept. of Labor, 1983). Even when female and male workers are matched for skill, education, tenure on the job, and so on, the salary gap still remains (Crosby, 1982; "Despite," 1982; Linscott, 1984). For example, a study of 90 MBA graduates found that after 10 years in the job market, men earned an average of 20% more than their female counterparts (reported by Linscott, 1984). Because background, credentials, job motivation, and beginning salaries were similar, and because the salary gap held for married women and mothers as well as for single women, the main explanatory variable appears to be discrimination.

Some discrimination is subtle. For example, research in letters of recommendation written for students applying to graduate school show that referees describe same-sex applicants more positively than they do other-sex applicants (Stake, Walker, & Speno, 1981). Because most college faculty members are male, the net result may be relatively poorer letters for female applicants. When people write letters for academicians applying for a job, their way of referring to the applicant appears to vary by sex of applicant (Cowan & Kasen, 1984). Recommenders make more frequent use of titles for females, and more frequent use of first names for males. What this means seems to depend upon the gender of the recommender. Male letter writers use first names for males to imply liking and knowledge, so their use of titles for females may imply distance. Female letter writers, on the other hand, use titles for both males and females to indicate respect. Again, because most letter writers are males, the end result is that male applicants may benefit from a certain same-sex solidarity.

Another subtle way discrimination operates is through differential attributions for performance. As discussed in Chapter 9, external attributions for success are more likely to be applied to women than to men. For example,

in relation to the question, "Why did Mary get this promotion?" people are likely to respond because she (a) is a woman, (b) is pretty, (c) sleeps with the boss, (d) is lucky. Why did John get the promotion? Because he's capable and deserved it. White males, in particular, are more likely to have success attributed to ability than are Black males and than are White or Black females (Yarkin, Town, & Wallston, 1982). Attributional patterns may be qualified by the sex typing of the job, the gender of the person making the attributions, and other contextual factors (Garland, Hale, & Burnson, 1982; Haccoun & Stacy, 1980; Lips & Myers, 1980).

Awareness of sex discrimination has increased since the early 1970s, and today, a majority of the adult public believes that women are discriminated against in the labor force (Thom, 1984). Of employed women, nearly half say they personally have been discriminated against in the workplace (Dowd, 1983). However many women still are not aware of sex discrimination. For example, among academic women in predominantly male departments, approximately 30% are aware of little sex discrimination. These same women attribute male-female status discrepancies to the individual woman, rather than to the system (Young, MacKenzie, & Sherif, 1980). Indeed, such attitudes on the part of academic women have been linked to their success with regard to obtaining tenure (M. Miller, 1985). That is, academic women who had low awareness of sex discrimination and who saw the university as a meritocracy where ability and performance would be rewarded were more likely to obtain tenure than were women who were more aware of sex bias issues. Interestingly, women who were denied tenure were as achievement oriented and as productive as women who achieved tenure.

Many women who have a male supervisor or who work on a male-sex-typed task expect to be discriminated against (Calder & Ross, 1977). Other research suggests that some women accept sex discrimination as a condition of employment. In fact, they also feel such discrimination is "socially appropriate"—that is, that a man should earn more than a woman. This is a sad commentary on the internalization of the gender stereotypes. Perhaps for this reason, even women who are victims of sex discrimination, by and large, still feel contented with their own jobs (Crosby, 1982). Because women generally compare themselves to other women in deciding how good their own job is, they may not notice or feel affected by the fact that their male colleagues earn much more than they do.

Because of socialization, women may see a different relationship between work and money than do men (Chesler & Goodman, 1976). Where men see paid work as being central to their identity, many women see paid work as tangential to their major socioemotional role. (Some of these differences regarding the meaning of work and achievement were discussed in Chapter 9.) Support for this contention comes from research on self-pay behavior conducted by Messé, Major, and others (Callahan-Levy & Messé, 1979; Major & Adams, 1983, 1984; Major, McFarlin, & Gagnon, 1984; Messé & Watts, 1980; Watts, Messé, & Vallacher, 1982).

Females from first grade through college paid themselves less for work performed than did males. They also paid themselves less than other people (males and females) paid them. Females were less certain than males of the connection between their work and monetary pay and consequently relied more on external cues than did males. Females also felt less comfortable about paying themselves than did males. However the more "masculine" the occupational orientation of these females (that is, the greater the number of male-dominated occupations preferred), and the more agentic the characteristics they possessed, the more their allocation pattern resembled that of the males. Perhaps, then, as women become more androgynous and move out of "female" occupations, they will be less willing to tolerate economic discrimination directed against themselves.

Much of this discrimination is due to a variety of myths people hold regarding women workers:

Myth 1. Women work just for "pin money." *Fact:* As discussed above, most women work out of economic necessity.

Myth 2. Women don't really want to work or to have a "career." *Fact:* Most studies have found that the majority of women still would work even if they did not have to. The one exception is blue-collar women, half of whom would choose to stay home if they could (Dowd, 1983). Women and men are equally concerned about getting ahead when they have a realistic chance of being promoted, and are equally concerned that work be self-actualizing (Kanter 1977; Renwick & Lawler, 1978; Yankelovich, 1981). A study of 123 workers (Rosenbach, Dailey, & Morgan, 1979) found that when organizational job level was held constant, female and male workers viewed job dimensions and work outcomes in similar ways. Furthermore, men and women require similar job characteristics to be satisfied in their jobs (Pines & Kafry, 1981; Voydanoff, 1980).

Myth 3. Women are less reliable employees. *Fact:* Although the sex difference in absence because of illness is small, most reports do indicate that women are more likely than men to be absent from work—5.1 days a year for women, 4.8 days a year for men (U.S. Bureau of the Census, 1977; U.S. Dept. of Labor 1977b). Women are out more often for shorter periods of time on account of acute illnesses; men are out for longer periods of time because of chronic illnesses. These official causes for sick leave may be misleading. A recent study of personnel sick-leave records and self-reports found that women were more likely to be absent due to child-care activities and to officially report these activities as personal illnesses than were men (Englander-Golden & Barton, 1983). Women and men without children did not differ significantly in sick-leave hours.

Myth 4. Women have a higher job turnover rate than men and thus their training and education often are wasted. *Fact:* Although some studies show that turnover rates are higher for women than for men, when skill level, education level, age of worker, and length of service are controlled variables, there is no significant difference between the sexes in job turnover (U.S. Dept. of Labor, 1975). For example, a recent longitudinal study undertaken by the Rand Corporation of nearly 13,000 women found that for women working in primarily blue-collar jobs traditionally held by men, there is virtually no difference in turnover rates (Parachini, 1985). However, a 1978 survey of 321 U.S. graduate departments of psychology

(Stapp, 1979) found that women and minority faculty members were more likely to leave their university before a tenure decision was made than were White male faculty members. The reasons for such early leavetaking by women are unclear. The women may receive better job offers elsewhere, may be discouraged by their departments from remaining, or may have conflicting career demands from a two-career household.

In a variety of professions, women have been found to be as committed to their jobs as are their male peers, although women's commitment to the organizations that employ them tends to be less than men's commitment (Graddick & Farr, 1983). The reasons for this difference in organizational commitment appear to be that women feel more unfairly treated than do men by their organization, and women experience more role conflicts between home and work commitments than do men.

It is true that the average female's work life is 11 years shorter than the average male's, because most women do take some time off for child rearing (U.S. Dept. of Labor, 1983). Yet, one-tenth of all women never marry and they average a 2-year longer work life than the male average because women live longer; one-tenth more marry but don't have children, and they average a 35-year work life. Of those who do marry and have children, most still work for between 24 and 28 years. Thus, job training and preparation are not "wasted." If daycare were more available, even more mothers would be employed. Furthermore, childbearing appears to have no negative effects on work productivity, at least among female professionals (Pyke & Kahill, 1983).

Myth 5. Women have different aptitudes than do men and therefore should stick to "women's jobs." *Fact:* There are very few group differences between males and females in aptitudes, intelligence, or behavior, and what differences exist are not all-or-none (for example, some females are better at mathematics than some males). In addition, most jobs are genderless—tradition and status, not aptitudes, have labeled jobs as more appropriate for one sex than another. For example, it is commonly believed that women have greater manual dexterity than do men, a belief used to justify employing women in low-paying jobs like typing and making electronics components (Messing, 1982). However, great manual dexterity also is required in surgery and mechanics, yet these jobs are nearly exclusively male ones.

Myth 6. Women take jobs away from men. *Fact:* Women and men traditionally have not competed for the same jobs (for example, jobs as a secretary or a nurse). The reason that nearly two-thirds of the displaced workers in the early 1980s are men is because the manufacturing field, which predominantly employs men, is shrinking. In contrast, the service industry, which predominantly employs women, is expanding (Serrin, 1984b). Yet men are reluctant to move into "women's jobs." Because women make up more than 40% of the work force, if they all quit, the economy would collapse. However, as more women enter the work force and apply for nontraditional jobs, they will be competing with men (Hacker, 1984). In times of high unemployment it may, in fact, be true that some women will take some jobs away from men. In a society that prides itself on equal opportunity, this situation will have to be accepted.

Myth 7. Mixing the sexes in the work environment disrupts concentration. *Fact.* Initially, mixed-sex groups may be more self-conscious than single-sex groups, but they tend to adjust with time (Aries, 1977; Kanter, 1977). Recent research suggests that both sexes may be better motivated in mixed-sex groups than in same-sex groups or than individually (Kerr & Sullaway, 1983). Women may suffer more than men in a mixed-sex group, especially if the women are greatly outnumbered. Studies of "token women" show that such individuals have a hard time being accepted as full members of the work group and feel isolated and invisible (Hennig & Jardim, 1977; Kanter, 1977; Kanter & Stein, 1980). When one sex is in the minority in a group, sex-role issues seem to become more salient (Hans & Eisenberg, 1985). Even when men and women are equal in number in a mixed group, women tend to be less assertive, less competitive, and perceived as less competent than are the men (Bunker, Forcey, Wilderom, & Elgie, 1984; Wood & Karten, 1984). Given training and time, increased numbers of women in mixed-sex groups, and institutional supports, such problems should be reduced.

Myth 8. Women cannot handle positions of power and men would not want to work under them. *Fact:* A few studies (Arkkelin & Simmons, 1985; Inderlied & Powell, 1979; Massengill & DiMarco, 1979; Powell & Butterfield, 1984) have shown that individuals do prefer a "masculine" manager but this refers to sex-role identity, not to actual sex. Thus, masculine-sex-typed female managers were preferred over feminine-sex-typed managers. Poor managers appear to be individuals low in both masculine and feminine-sex-typed characteristics. Interestingly, the majority of business school graduates, male and female, are masculine-sex-typed.

Much field research has demonstrated that sex does not strongly affect leadership style or ability, although it may affect co-workers' expectations and perceptions of the leader (Arnett, Higgins, & Priem, 1980; Bartol & Wortman, 1979; S. Brown, 1979; Geis et al., 1985; Kanter, 1977; Liden, 1985; Rice, Instone, & Adams, 1984; Stitt, Schmidt, Price, & Kipnis, 1983). For example, in a study of people's nonverbal reactions to female and male leaders, Butler & Geis (1985) found that group members generally looked pleased in response to a male leader's contributions. In contrast, group members generally looked displeased in response to a female leader's contributions. Because the male and female leaders were following the same script, their actual behaviors did not differ. However, because group members reacted to these behaviors differently on the basis of leader sex, an evaluator would interpret the negative reactions to the female leader as somehow her fault and see her as a less effective leader. This indeed has been found to be the case (Brown & Geis, 1984).

In general, however, people usually are equally satisfied with male and female leaders, and female supervisors usually are evaluated favorably, especially by female subordinates (Feild & Caldwell, 1979; Kanter, 1977; Terborg & Shingledecker, 1983). (See Figure 11-5 for a "humorous" glimpse as to how this may be perceived by others.) It does appear to be true that men are more likely than women to assume leadership in unstructured situations and to be influential (Bunker et al., 1984; Instone, Major, & Bunker, 1983; Liden, 1985; Rhue et al., 1984; Stitt et al., 1983). These findings are most likely due to sex-role expectations and differences in sex-role socialization. Men are expected to be leaders, and therefore are more likely to be perceived as leaders (Geis et al., 1985). Furthermore, men's higher status in general

Figure 11-5

Female managers generally receive positive evaluations from their employees. (Copyright 1984, News America Syndicate. Reprinted by permission.)

may make them more influential, especially to individuals with traditional attitudes toward women.

Leaders are most often someone with power. Unfortunately, women supervisors and managers sometimes are given less power than men supervisors and managers. This situational factor may affect subordinate's perception of women managers as well as affect the managers' behavior (Liden, 1985; Riger & Galligan, 1980). If someone is given a supervisory position without real system power, he or she may become petty and punitive (Kanter, 1976). Hence the image of the "bitchy boss," although this effect is true for both females and males. Because women have so rarely been given legitimate power (power that comes from occupying a particular role), they may need some time to adjust to it and learn how to use it effectively. Subordinates also may need time to adapt, since some research suggests that challenging a female authority figure is seen as more legitimate than challenging a male authority figure (Sterling & Owen, 1982). However, other research finds equal compliance to female and male leaders (Geffner & Gross, 1984; Son & Schmitt, 1983). As more women move into positions of leadership and power and more programs develop to ease their adaptation, more adjustment will occur.

Myth 9. Women have come a long way already. *Fact:* Women's relative status has been declining or remaining the same in recent years. The salary differential has hovered around 60% for the last 30 years. Only in 1984 did the wage gap decrease slightly from its previous record in 1955 (see Table 11-1). The percentage of doctorates in science awarded to women is just now matching the rate during the 1920s (nearly 30%) (J. Brown, Aldrich, & Hall, 1978). The all-time low was during the 1950s when fewer than 15% of all such degrees were awarded to women. Furthermore, women's unemployment rate has always been higher than men's even among Ph.D.s. Occupational segregation remains strong and shows little sign of decreasing much further since the fastest growing jobs are in the female-dominated service sector.

These nine myths all serve to perpetuate job discrimination against women. When com-bined with *institutional barriers,* their effect is overwhelmingly negative on the career aspirations of women.

There are a number of institutional barriers to women's career aspirations, most reflecting a lack of understanding of and/or a lack of consideration for women's unique *career patterns.* That is, institutions do not take into account that most women have children for whom they are primarily responsible and thus women may need or want to take some time out from full-time careers for child rearing or to work or go to school part-time. By having only one career pattern in mind—full-time, uninterrupted work—institutions shut many women out of many jobs.

The primary institutional barrier is the sex typing of occupations. If women are steered into and hired for jobs in only a few low-paying, low-status job fields, it is no wonder that there is where most end up. It has been estimated that 35% of the earnings gap is due to job segregation (Kassell, 1984).

Occupational Segregation. Figure 11-6 illustrates the occupational distribution of women in the labor force in 1984. The demand for female workers is restricted to a small number of sexually segregated occupations. The principal employer of women in 1984 is the service industry, as it was in 1970. As Figure 11-6 shows, women are particularly underrepresented as mechanics, transportation workers, farmers, and craft workers, and are overrepresented as service workers, retail sales workers, teachers, clerical workers, and private household workers. Of the 500 occupations listed by the U.S. Census Bureau, women primarily are concentrated in the 22 lowest-paid job classifications ("That's," 1985). A comprehensive study of pay equity has found that the more an occupation is dominated by women, the less it pays (Hartmann & Treiman, 1981).

Thus, there are really two labor markets—one male, one female—and the two groups rarely compete for the same jobs (Oppenheimer, 1975). Nine out of ten workers have co-workers of the same sex (Kassell, 1984). Segregation of jobs by sex is even more severe than segregation of jobs by race (Blau, 1975; National Science Foundation, 1984; Reskin, 1984). Black women are segregated into even fewer industries than White women or than Black or White men (Kassell, 1984). More than 70% of Black women are in the nonprofit sector, such as hospitals.

Not only are many women limited in terms of which jobs they may hold, but even within the same occupations men and women are often assigned different tasks. Females are usually assigned the lowest-paying ones. For example, most female sales workers sell items costing under $70, whereas most male sales workers sell items costing over $100. Thus, males make more money in commissions and, as a result, earn two and one-half times what female sales workers earn (Blau, 1975). Even in high-status

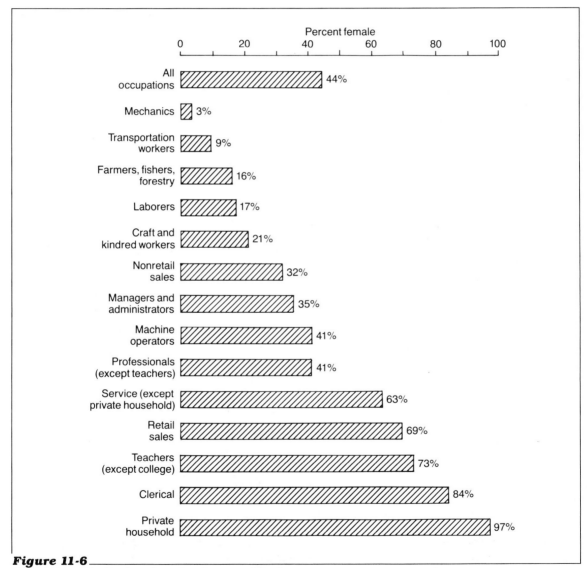

Figure 11-6

Occupational distribution of employed women, March 1985. (From U.S. Department of Labor, 1985.)

occupations, such as medicine, men are more likely than women to be administrators, a powerful position, whereas women tend to be overrepresented in the relatively low-status position of teachers (Sherman & Rosenblatt, 1984).

This pattern of males holding the highest-paid and highest-status jobs is found in other societies as well. For all occupations in all societies, as the salary and status of an occupation increase, the proportion of women in that occupation decreases (Feldberg, 1984; Jacobs & Powell, 1985). In fact, as discussed in Chapter 6, the status of an occupation can be manipulated by varying the proportion of women in it—the more women, the lower the status.

Organizational practices and structures are among the principal sources of gender inequality (Baron & Brelby, 1985). For example, compared to men, women are offered different jobs, and are less likely to be recommended for job changes and advancement.

Underlying the sex labeling of jobs are factors that have traditionally influenced female participation in the labor force but that no longer are valid for many female workers. Most traditional "women's jobs" do not require long-term commitment. The hours are flexible, the jobs exist all over the country, and the jobs do not necessitate employer investment in training. Hence, women can drop in and out of these jobs according to family needs and personal desires. These jobs are also viewed as an extension of "natural female functions"—nurturing, servicing others, housework, and so on (Van Dusen & Sheldon, 1976). The fact that women are limited to a few jobs and may have limited mobility (they traditionally have lived where their husbands are employed) means that many constitute a reserve pool of qualified women outside the paid labor market (Blau, 1975). This, in turn, allows salaries to be kept low.

Since the 1960s there appears to be a slight decrease in occupational segregation and a slight increase in social acceptance of nontraditional career choices (Lifschitz, 1983; Reskin, 1984). Still, most people choose traditional careers, and the small decrease in job segregation from 1960 to 1980 was due to the increase in less sex-segregated occupations, such as computer specialties, and to an increase in the number of women in a few managerial jobs (Rytina & Bianchi, 1984).

Because the majority of emerging jobs are in heavily segregated, mostly female-dominated occupations, only small declines in occupational segregation are predicted through 1990 ("That's," 1985). Few men have moved into "female" occupations, but when they do, the salary and status of the occupations increase. For example, the number of male secretaries increased from 60,000 in 1972 to 75,000 in 1980. Their average yearly salary was 62% more than women's yearly salary (Doudna, 1981). Male home economists, only 1% of all home economists in 1983, earned 54% more than their female counterparts (Townsley, Scruggs, Callsen, & Warde, 1984).

High technology, rather than helping women to break free of their traditional low-salary jobs, actually has worked to enmesh women there. Women perform most of the low-skilled hi-tech labor, and receive even lower salaries than men in the same positions (Stanley, 1983). Indeed, many hi-tech companies locate assembly plants in areas where the pool of women workers is high, for example, along Mexico's border (Nash & Fernandez-Kelly, 1983; Rytina & Bianchi, 1984).

Access to Education. Occupational segregation is just one institutional factor of the many that act as barriers to female achievement in the labor force. Another is access to education.

The lack of equal access to higher education seriously handicaps many women in their career plans (J. Brown et al., 1978). As discussed in Chapter 8, there are stricter admission policies, less financial aid, active discouragement or disregard of women's career aspirations by some counselors and faculty, inflexible residence and full-time study requirements, lack of maternity and paternity leaves, and lack of child-care facilities. There are also few female faculty members as role models, especially in higher ranks (only 10% of full professors were female in 1983–1984). Although the number of women in higher education has been increasing (see Table 11-2), women received less than 40% of the doctorates and less than one-third of first professional degrees awarded in 1986.

Many people consider education to be the key factor in women's career advancement (for example, Brooks, 1983). However, the chance of obtaining a job commensurate with her advanced training may discourage a woman from pursuing further education. Solomon (1978) found that the inability of many female Ph.D. psychologists to obtain jobs as good as those of men was a prime factor in dissuading women from pursuing a career in psychology. Thus restricted access to business and professional opportunities may limit female educational achievement.

Access to Business and Professions.

In the professions and business, a number of characteristics serve as barriers to women (J. Brown et al., 1978; Gilkes, 1982; Hennig & Jardim, 1977; Kanter, 1977; Riger & Galligan, 1980). Having a female *role model* has been found to be particularly important for women, especially with regard to integrating work and family lives (Basow & Howe, 1980; Erkut & Mokros, 1983; Gilbert et al., 1983). In this regard, the dearth of information on women of achievement has had a particularly negative effect on women. Fortunately, this gap in our knowledge now is being corrected with new information on many of our foremothers (for example, O'Connell & Russo, 1983).

Having a sponsor or *mentor*, someone who takes you under his or her wing, has been found to be important for professional aspirations and advancement (Pressler & Blanchard, 1984; Project on the Status and Education of Women, 1983; Young et al., 1980). Yet, there are few women in high enough positions to serve as mentors, and men often are reluctant to assume that role with women. In sex-typed male occupations (that is, most professions, such as science, engineering, medicine, mathematics, and law), women frequently are excluded from "socialization into a profession" by not being "adopted" by a sponsor or mentor. For example, a study of 627 graduate students in departments of science, engineering, and medicine at Stanford University found that the male students had greater access than the female students to informal interaction with their advisors outside the adviser-advisee relationship ("Graduate," 1985). Women graduate students also appeared less certain of their advisors' support then did men graduate students. The result may be a discouraging one for women trying to move into male-dominated fields.

The *colleague* system also is important for professional advancement. Women tend not to become as involved as men in the system, since women's contributions and performances are less visible, partly because of discrimination. Women tend to be cited in professional publications less frequently than are men, which may contribute to their work being under-recognized and undersupported (Helmreich, Spence, Beane, Lucker, & Matthews, 1980; Miller & Zeitz, 1978; Persell, 1983). Women also are more likely than men to be given leadership positions without real power. Women belong to fewer professional organizations, limit their own professional interactions, and generally put in fewer hours (often because they have family responsibilities). In addition, women usually are excluded (and exclude themselves) from informal channels of communication, like lunches, in which they may stand out and feel uncomfortable. A number of private clubs, such as the Bohemian Club in California, actually exclude women. Yet, these are places where major career contacts are made and strengthened (Domhoff, 1981; "Starting," 1983).

To counteract the "old boy network," scores of new professional women's groups have begun in the last fifteen years—for example, the Women's Forum, Women in Business, and the Association for Women in Psychology (Nemy, 1979). Most of these groups were formed deliberately "to make the buddy system work for women." Women are even forming their own clubs ("Starting," 1983).

There also is the issue of *sexual harassment* and sexual intimacy, to which women are particularly vulnerable. Numerous studies since the late 1970s have documented that between 25–50% of women students and 30–50% of women employees have experienced some form of sexual harassment (Dziech & Weiner, 1984; Gutek & Nakamura, 1980; Maihoff & Forrest, 1982; McCain, 1983; U.S. Merit Systems, 1981). Although men sometimes are sexually harassed as well (about 10–15% of men report harassment), the most common pattern is a man harassing a woman. Such harassment can result in stress, lowered self-esteem, poor performance, and damaged careers. It can also keep women out of traditionally "male" jobs, which sometimes is its intent. Such behavior is illegal because it is a form of sex discrimination, but many victims are not aware of this fact or of the formal remedies available to them. Furthermore, sexual harassment often is difficult to prove since many people don't understand what constitutes harassment (see Brewer & Berk, 1982; MacKinnon, 1979).

The intent of sexual harassment often is to demonstrate power and/or privilege rather than sexual interest or desire, although sexual contact may occur. Indeed, one nationwide survey of clinical psychologists in 1978 (Pope, Levenson, & Schover, 1979) found that when the respondents were students, 16.5% of the women and 3% of the men reported that they had had sexual contact with their educators. A striking finding was that, of the female respondents who graduated in the last six years, 25% had had such sexual contact. As psychology educators, 19% of the men—compared with 8% of the women—reported sexual contact with their students. Other research has found that some men may try to use their power to get sexual favors, to test the woman, or simply to enact sex rituals because it is their most familiar mode of interacting with women (Bunker & Seashore, 1977; Hennig & Jardim, 1977). Many women are thus put in awkward positions, face a risk to their job and to a superior's good will, and have the focus shifted from their job ability to their physical attributes. Similar negative effects appear to be true for some men.

Lack of adequate *child-care* options and infant-care leaves seriously handicaps women from pursuing business and professional careers (Catalyst, 1983; Cordes, 1983a; Ogintz, 1983; Rogan, 1984; Zigler & Muenchow, 1983). Although inadequate child care is a serious problem for all employed mothers, professional women frequently have longer working hours, fewer part-time options, and a work environment less supportive of family responsibilities. Furthermore, career interruptions can be damaging for professional women in terms of future advancement and pay. It has been estimated that an absence of two years results in a permanent 10% decline in pay (Samuelson, 1983). This problem also affects some employed fathers, but because child-care responsibilities still fall predominantly on the mother, it is a more common problem for women than men. Indeed, family responsibilities are often used

against women, such that employers view female workers as less serious and are more reluctant to select a woman for a job requiring travel (Frasher et al., 1982). A more logical solution is to provide greater flexibility in work schedules for all employees (Best, 1981; Greenglass, 1984b). Overall, women must learn the informal rules of business and professional behavior with which most men are brought up (See Chapter 8 on the importance of sports and teamwork for success in business.)

There are some factors that can help professional women (Catalyst, 1983; Larwood & Kaplan, 1980; Lenney, Mitchell, & Browning, 1983; Riger & Galligan, 1980; Siegfried, 1982; Smith & Grenier, 1982). Among them are part-time training and work opportunities, flexibility of role playing, and awareness on the part of male colleagues of women's particular problems. Training managers in nondiscriminatory procedures and punishing those who discriminate against women are important. Structuring the work situation also aids women. Women benefit by formality in the professional context, clear job requirements, defined standards of performance, and supervision of the professional interaction. Professional women also fare better as a function of the length of their career and professional relationships, and as a function of the rank of their institution. A major aid to such women is active support by men with power and by female peers.

Trade Unions. Trade unions often pose another barrier to female occupational aspirations (Berch, 1982; Falk, 1975). In 1984, fewer than 15% of all women workers belonged to a labor union (Serrin, 1984a). Occupations dominated by women usually are not unionized (household workers, nurses, secretaries), although some attempt currently is being made toward unionization. Traditionally, women have shied away from union organizing because they tended not to define themselves as "workers," they often worked in isolation from other women (as in a home, or a small office), and they generally lacked self-confidence and assertiveness. In most cases, unions did not welcome women either. It has been difficult for women to get into some unions, and especially into apprenticeship programs in which a sponsor is needed and sons of union members are preferred. In addition, women frequently are discriminated against in seniority systems and underrepresented in union leadership.

Union membership is valuable. The salary differential between the sexes is much less for union workers than it is for nonunion workers (Levitin et al., 1973). Recent successful contract bargaining by unions composed of women office workers also has highlighted the advantages of unionization for women (Serrin, 1984a; "Union," 1981). Clerical workers represented by unions earned 30% more than nonunionized clerical workers in 1980.

Laws. Legally, women face barriers also, although the 1972 amendments to the Civil Rights Act of 1954 and the Equal Pay Act of 1963 make job and salary discrimination illegal. Complaints often take years to be resolved, and many employees simply do not bother. After the Reagan administration took office in 1980, enforcement of these laws has been markedly curtailed. For example, the number of cases filed by the Equal Employment Opportunity Commission (EEOC) involving sex discrimination in employment dropped more than 70% between 1981 and 1983 (Kennelly, 1984). EEOC's emphasis has shifted away from the more far-reaching class-action lawsuits and toward more individualized cases of bias (Evans & Fields, 1985). This change in emphasis may make large employers less concerned about discriminating on the basis of sex. As noted in Chapter 8, another change in laws that affects women's career opportunities is the Supreme Court–mandated narrow interpretation of Title IX of the Civil Rights Act, which forbids denial of educational opportunities based on sex.

Changes in the law in the last 20 years have certainly helped, although more change still is needed. Furthermore, when employers are warned about illegal discrimination, more bias in favor of male applicants sometimes occurs (Siegfried, 1982). The federal minimum wage law still does not apply to household workers, 97% of whom are women. Part-time workers, most of whom are women, also are denied major benefits from employers. The 1978 Pregnancy Disability Bill finally made discrimination on the basis of pregnancy illegal. Previously it was common practice to exempt pregnancy-related disability from coverage under temporary disability or health benefit programs while allowing men to get benefits for vasectomies and hair transplants. In fact, such exemptions had been ruled legal under the 1976 *Gilbert* versus *General Electric* decision by the U.S. Supreme Court. Even the new law, however, has its limitations. It applies only to those employers covered by the federal antidiscrimination law in Title VII of the Civil Rights Act and to those employers who provide disability benefits. Most employers do not provide such benefits and pregnancy is not covered for most women ("Study finds," 1983). This can be a serious handicap for women who cannot afford to take time off from their job without monetary compensation. Most importantly, there still is no federal Equal Rights Amendment.

A recent legal development is the argument for a "*comparable worth*" interpretation of the Title VII provision of the 1964 Civil Rights Act. In 1983, a federal court ordered the state of Washington to raise the wages of 15,500 state employees in predominantly "female" job classifications because these employees, mainly women, earned less than employees, mainly men, in male-dominated jobs requiring equivalent skill, effort, and responsibility (*AFSCME* v. *State of Washington*). For example, dog pound attendants, who are mostly male, earn more than child-care attendants, who are mostly female. Although that court order later was overturned, the issue has resurfaced in numerous courts across the country (for more information, see Feldberg, 1984; Ferraro, 1984; Gold, 1983; Remick, 1984). At issue is the traditional "supply and demand" argument for determining wages versus the principle of equal pay for comparable work. If the "comparable worth" position is established, it would lead to questioning the market basis of all wages. This questioning might lead to a reevaluation of all the work women do, both inside and outside the home, which in turn might challenge the gender hierarchy in society (Feldberg, 1984). In this context, "comparable worth" is a radical concept indeed.

Until now, we have mainly been examining women's role in the labor force. As has been shown, the gender stereotypes markedly affect what kinds of jobs a woman might have as well as the salary she might earn. But the stereotypes also affect men's role in the labor force. And, contrary to prevailing opinion, not all effects are beneficial. We now will examine some of these effects.

Men and the Labor Force

Whereas many women have had to struggle to enter the labor force, such participation usually is required of men by virtue of the male sex role. A woman's identity traditionally has been defined by her relationships; a man's, primarily by his job. As Pleck and Sawyer (1974) note, "work is the institution that most defines the majority of males" (p. 94). Although work can provide a sense of satisfaction and self-worth and is usually necessary for satisfying one's material needs, the overexaggeration of the work role for men has as serious consequences for them as does the overexaggeration of the homemaker role for women.

In the first place, as was discussed in Chapters 9 and 10, the emphasis on most males to participate in the work force encourages males to develop a high achievement and competitive orientation. Success and status become the bedrock of the male sex role, and "masculinity" is often measured by the amount of money a man earns or by his material possessions (David & Brannon, 1976; Doyle, 1983; O'Neil, 1981b). This goal orientation and competition often obliterate other rewards of working, such as mastery of a skill. They also may lead to finding substitute ways of gaining status—one-upmanship, athletic prowess, emphasis on sexual performance—especially if one's job is not intrinsically rewarding (Fasteau, 1974; Tolson, 1977). Such intense competition and stress to achieve also may make many men more vulnerable to stress-related diseases.

As a result of such an achievement and competitive focus, some men's relationships may suffer. As was discussed in Chapter 10, because they are usually trained to develop these qualities and neglect their emotional side, it is difficult for many men to trust other men and form close relationships with them, with women, and especially with their children. When work becomes a primary focus in one's

life, other things and people are excluded. Many jobs actually require such exclusion. Men often are expected to work overtime, to put in many hours in work-related activities (for example, cocktail parties, golf), to travel, and so forth. Research has shown the business executive and the blue-collar worker to be particularly caught in the masculine stereotype, the former because he believes he can "make it" (Bartolome, 1972; Maccoby, 1976); the latter, because he realizes he cannot (Cazenave, 1984; Tolson, 1977). In any case, many families rarely see their "breadwinner," causing serious damage to the marital and the parent-child relationships.

In addition, when an individual's identity is defined solely by one thing, when that one thing ends, emotional problems may result. Thus women who are identified solely as mothers may experience marked depression and marked loss of self-esteem when their children leave home. Similarly, many men who are unemployed or retired also may experience marked depression and loss of self-esteem, often leading to alcoholism, suicide, heart attacks, and other ailments (see Chapter 9). Black men, who have the highest unemployment rates, may suffer the most severe consequences (Cordes, 1985). Unemployment among men is increasingly due to a decrease in jobs traditionally held by men, such as in manufacturing, and due to increased competition with women for other traditionally "male" jobs (Hacker 1984; Serrin, 1984b). Ironically, most new jobs are in the service or clerical sector and are regarded as "women's work." Most men, given their socialization experiences plus the low salaries attached to such jobs, won't apply for such positions.

As many women have rejected their sex typing, many men, especially the younger ones, also are doing so. Both as a result of the questioning of sex roles prompted by the women's movement and the fact that most paid work no longer provides the sense of self-worth that it is supposed to, many men are also beginning to question the responsibility and expectations placed on them (Doyle, 1983; Friedan, 1981; Tolson 1977; Voydanoff, 1984). Like women, many men want more options and more satisfaction. Some retire early. Others drop out of the work force because of health problems, lack of education, or because they are economically able to do so. Still others are becoming less willing to transfer from one location to another. Many men now show a preference for shorter or more flexible work hours, and some are increasing their participation in household maintenance and child-care functions (for example, Winnett & Neale, 1980). Many men also are rejecting the whole notion of a career as being the sole means of male identity. They want a richer, fuller life, one that makes use of their full range of human potentialities. Instead of adjusting to the "Establishment," many are expecting the Establishment to become more androgynous and to adjust to them (Bernard, 1971).

Some organizations are, in fact, changing (Kanter, 1983; Peters & Waterman, 1982). Many jobs now require more emphasis on human relations and less on simple hierarchical relationships. In some cases, competition is becoming less important and, in fact, dysfunctional. Authority and obedience are no longer always the foundation of an organization. Many modern businesses are requiring nonstereotyped, multifaceted functioning for maximum effectiveness. Androgyny as an ideal for occupational and individual functioning is supplanting the traditional ideology of strictly sex-typed functioning in a number of places.

In sum, women are a vital part of the work force, yet their importance often is not acknowledged, materially or otherwise. They often are discriminated against, steered into a few low-paying, low-status job fields, and barred from advancement and alternatives. Yet change is occurring and women are continuing to enter the labor force in record numbers, currently constituting 44% of all workers.

Men also often are steered into certain jobs, but their choice of jobs tends to be broader and their pay and status higher. Many suffer from the pressure of them to achieve, to be "a success," and some men are rejecting their stereotyped identity as "breadwinner" for a more human one. Recent trends to decrease occupational sex typing and to temper the "work ethic" will help humanize both the work world and the workers.

Change is needed in five major areas in order to allow women full entry into the labor force: (1) Vigorous new measures are needed to reduce unemployment, such as flextime opportunities (whereby individuals work 40 hours a week but not necessarily from 9 to 5) and job-sharing. New measures are also needed to press for compliance with laws that prohibit discrimination against women, increase the advance of women (such as by vigorous recruitment and training), and build in recognition of parental child-rearing responsibilities (such as by leave policies, child-care facilities). (2) A comprehensive family support system is needed with adequate daycare and after-school care arrangements for all who need them. (3) Continuing attack on sex discrimination and sexist practices in education must be made. (4) Traditional assumptions of female dependence will have to disappear. (5) Greater flexibility in the traditional life-cycle patterns is needed, allowing males and females to alternate periods of study, employment, and work in the home. All these changes entail a reordering of American priorities with greater choice for the individual and improved quality of life in contrast to the traditional concern for productivity. Whether or not we, as a society, will embrace this new goal remains to be seen.

Summary

In this chapter we have reviewed some of the societal consequences of the gender stereotypes. One of the most basic is the widespread prejudice against women on the part of both males and females. This prejudice is particularly manifested in the world of work, where women as a group are underpaid and are channeled into only a few, low-status positions. The barriers against women achieving in the area of employment are both internal, as a result of sex-role socialization, and external, in the form of societal and institutional obstacles.

Men, too, may be penalized by their sex role in the world of work. They stereotypically are expected to be aggressive, competitive breadwinners and are defined predominantly by their job. This role restricts the development of men's full human potential and may affect their relationship with others and their own health.

The gender stereotypes have other societal consequences as well, particularly in the areas of power and aggression. These areas will be explored in the next chapter.

Recommended Reading

Fox, M. F., & Hesse-Biber, S. (1984). *Women at work.* Palo Alto, Calif.: Mayfield. A comprehensive look at women in the labor force, and the impact of economic, legal, social, educational, and political factors.

Gold, M. E. (1983). *A dialogue on comparable worth.* Ithaca, N.Y.: ILR Press. A concise book summarizing the arguments and facts for and against the issue of comparable worth.

Hennig, M., & Jardim, A. *The managerial woman.* New York: Doubleday, 1977. Interviews with and analysis of the women who have "made it" into management: how to get and stay there.

U.S. Department of Labor, Bureau of Labor Statistics, U.S. Government Printing Office. Monthly and yearly compilation of employment and earnings statistics, broken down by numerous factors.

Wallston, B. S., & O'Leary, V. (1981). Sex makes a difference: Differential perceptions of women and men. In L. Wheeler (Ed.), *Review of personality and social psychology,* Vol. 2 (pp. 9–41). Beverly Hills, Calif.: Sage. A good review article summarizing current research on the ways in which men and women are perceived differently.

Societal Consequences: Power and Aggression

Gender stereotypes affect society on a structural level. That is, gender stereotypes are built into the very structure and fabric of our society and into virtually all societies. In the previous chapter, we saw how gender stereotypes operate in our society on a specific, tangible level, as in discrimination and employment patterns. In this chapter, we will examine how gender stereotypes operate in our society on a more abstract and global level, as in the use of power and aggression.

Power

In terms of power in American society (the ability to influence another, to get done what you want to get done), women are generally at a marked disadvantage. This is true personally, economically, politically, legally, and militarily. Power in America is predominantly in the hands of the "White male club," from which women and minorities traditionally and deliberately have been excluded. Table 12-1 shows evidence of this club. In every public office, particularly the most powerful, men predominate. This is true around the world (Leghorn & Parker, 1981; Sciolino, 1985). Patriarchy prevails, as does women's relative powerlessness (MacKinnon, 1982; Millet, 1970). The world mean for the proportion of female to male administrators is only about 10%.

Power is important because, as a number of writers have noted (for example, Blumberg, 1979; Kahn 1984), it is differential power that underlies all inequality. Therefore, it will be instructive to examine the five forms of power (personal, economic, political, legal, and military) and the sexes' relationship to them in more detail.

Table 12-1

Men Run America, 1979 and 1984
(Percentage of Men)

	1979	1984
U.S. population	48.7	48.6
U.S. Senate	99	98
U.S. House	96	94
U.S. Supreme Court	100	99
Federal judges	95	93
Governors	96	98
State representatives	89	86
State senators	95	94
Statewide elective offices	89	87
County governing boards	97	92
Mayors and councilors	92	89
School board members	75	72

Data compiled by the Center for American Women in Politics.

Personal Power

Goodchilds (1979) discusses three different aspects of personal power—the ability to get one's way, the ability to get along with others, and the ability to get things done. Traditionally, men have been associated with getting one's way, and this aspect has been the most emphasized of the three. Getting along with others is an aspect of power traditionally associated with women, and this aspect has been viewed as conflicting with the first. Men and women perceive the sexes as handling power differently, even if they don't. Goodchilds' point is that we should be concerned about the third aspect of power, getting things done. Power should be conceived in terms of accomplishments, rather than relationships. In this way, conflict between "masculine" and "feminine" power styles would be reduced and such distinctions, in fact, might be irrelevant.

In general, personal power (the ability to get a person to do something) can be viewed as having six different uses: reward power (influence through the use of rewards), coercive power (influence through use of punishments), referent power (influence through being looked up to), expert power (influence through superior skills or knowledge), legitimate power (influence due to role definition, such as in an elected office), and information power (influence through persuasion and information). In all areas, men possess more power than do women (Kahn, 1984).

When interpersonal relationships are examined, women have been found traditionally to use indirect, emotional, helpless strategies to get their way. Although somewhat successful in the short run (for example, Weimann, 1985), these strategies tend to be markedly ineffective in the long run (P. Johnson & Goodchilds, 1976). Futhermore, the use of such strategies decreases the user's self-esteem and increases others' personal dislike. Ironically, when women use more direct messages that rely on their expertise, they tend to be rated as more aggressive than men who use such messages.

These findings have obvious implications for women in positions of legitimate power such as in management, in the military, and in politics. In an organizational setting, women appear to make fewer attempts to exert influence and to use fewer rewarding and more coercive strategies than did men (Instone et al., 1983). This pattern was related to women's lower levels of self-confidence. Another pattern of women in management is to be more accessible to subordinates than are men in similar positions (Josefowitz, 1980). This too may be related to women's lower levels of self-confidence and perhaps their greater "need to be liked." Conversely, this pattern may be related to men's greater need for hierarchical distinctions and interpersonal distance. As mentioned in the previous chapter, women in power tend to be seen as less legitimate than men in power. This perception may undercut women's ability to get things done. However, when expertise is clearly established (that is, when women have expert

and information power), people will comply with women as well as with men (Dobbins et al., 1985; Son & Schmitt, 1983).

Within a romantic relationship, clear-cut sex differences in power strategies are less likely to occur. The major finding from a number of studies by Falbo and colleagues (Falbo, 1982; Falbo & Peplau, 1980; Peplau et al., 1976) is that people who preferred and perceived themselves as having more power than their partner were most likely to use bilateral and direct strategies to get their way, such as by bargaining or by reasoning. Such people are most likely to be heterosexual males, and masculine-sex-typed people. People with less power in a relationship were more likely to use indirect and unilateral strategies, such as growing silent or leaving the room. Such people are most likely to be heterosexual women and "feminine" individuals. In homosexual relationships and in friendships, both of which tend to be relatively egalitarian, people are more likely to use bilateral strategies (Cowan et al., 1984; Madden, Brownstein, & Marshall, 1985). Thus strategy differences appear to stem from differences in power.

In most relationships, men are viewed as dominant, and this certainly is true in traditional marital relationships. Most husbands obtain power in marriage not because of individual resources or personal competence but simply because they are male (Gillespie, 1971; Kahn, 1984). Indeed, men often define themselves in terms of the power they exert over others, particularly over women. For a wife to gain even a little power, she usually must obtain it from external sources—she must be employed, have an education superior to her husband's, or participate in organizations more than he. As discussed previously, access to these sources of power traditionally has been blocked for women.

Times are changing somewhat. In 1980, the U.S. Census Bureau announced that it would no longer view husbands as the only legitimate head of a household. The Bureau now interviews the owner or renter of the house or, failing such a person, any adult household member. Furthermore, a national survey of adults taken in 1976 found that, compared with a similar survey in 1957, women have increased their motive for power, defined as fear of weakness (Veroff et al., 1980). Of course, men have increased their power motive as well. The result is that men still have a stronger need for power than do women. This pattern may change when women actually obtain legitimate power. For example, women managers demonstrate a higher need for socialized power than do men (Chusmir & Parker, 1984). Socialized power is the kind of power used to facilitate institutional as opposed to personal advancement and is preferred in managers.

The fact that economic power generally translates into family power should not be surprising given the fact that traditional marriages have been based on female financial dependence. The more money a woman brings in, the more power in the family she tends to have and the more egalitarian the marriage arrangement tends to become. Interestingly, the more money a woman brings in, the more likely it is that the couple will divorce. Because a woman generally does not earn as much as her husband, the husband's dominance still is somewhat assured. This fact may work directly or indirectly to keep the salary differential wide. It should be recalled from Chapter 6 that, throughout history and across cultures, the more women work in the main productive activity of a society, the greater their societal status. Although productive labor does not lead women directly to freedom and equality, it can lead them to economic power, which, in turn, seems to be the strongest influence on women's relative equality and freedom. Such power can aid women in controlling their personal destiny—marriage, divorce, sex, children, free movement, education, and household power (Blumberg, 1977, 1979; Youssef & Hartley, 1979).

Economic Power

Even though more women are in the work force than ever before, they are still predominantly in the low-salary, low-status jobs. Very few women are in the upper ranks of corporate management in the United States. In 1984, women held approximately 2% of the top management posts in major U.S. corporations, and fewer than 3% of the seats on the boards of the country's top 1300 public companies ("You've,"

1984). They have made little headway in the hierarchies of heavy industry, insurance, many high-technology fields, and retailing. The reasons for the slow pace of women's progress have been attributed to the ambivalent attitudes of many male managers, a reluctance to take a chance and relax requirements for extensive experience, and the need for women to prove their competence repeatedly. Women have made significant progress in moving into middle-management positions, constituting about 25% of all such positions in 1984, but the move up from there appears slow-going. It is in these high-level promotions that subjective impressions of compatibility play a major role. Most chief executives are men, and they appear to feel more comfortable dealing with other men.

Poverty has become a women's issue (Kamerman, 1984; Scott, 1984; Smith, 1984; Stallard, Ehrenreich, & Sklar, 1983). Nearly two-thirds of the people over 17 years of age who are living below the poverty line are women. The most affected are Black women, single mothers, and women over 65. The reasons for the increase in female poverty levels are complex but three factors are important: low salaries, increased longevity, and single parenthood.

As discussed in the previous chapter, women earn about three-fifths of what men earn. Minority women earn even less. Three out of five employed Black women earn incomes below the poverty level (Woody & Malson, 1984). Most available new jobs offer workers little chance to climb out of poverty because such jobs are in the low-paying service sector. Furthermore, women, who have a disproportionate share of unemployment, have been underrepresented among recipients of unemployment benefits and services (Pearce, 1985). This underrepresentation is due to the greater likelihood of female employees to work part-time, at temporary jobs, and at jobs not covered by unemployment insurance (such as waitressing). Women also have been hurt by the presumption that married women are not committed to working, and therefore are not entitled to unemployment benefits.

Age also is a factor in women's poverty. Women live longer than men and 18% of all elderly women have incomes below poverty level ("Social," 1985). Minority women have the highest poverty rate: 42% of all elderly Black women and 31% of all elderly Hispanic women live in poverty. The poverty of elderly women is a result of their spending most of their lives as homemakers or in low-paying jobs with few benefits. As a result, they rarely have pensions of their own, and only 10% receive pension benefits from their husbands' plans if they outlive him, as 85% of married women do. Social Security income helps these women only slightly. Half of the 8.4 million single elderly women receiving benefits live at or near the poverty level.

Perhaps the most important factor in the increased poverty of women is the increased number of families headed by women. More than two out of five (43%) of all Black families and 13% of all White families are headed by women (Norton, 1985). These rates are nearly double what they were in 1970. In 1981, more than one out of every three families (including half of all families headed by a Black or Hispanic woman) maintained by a woman was in poverty, compared with one out of 16 married-couple families (U.S. Department of Labor, 1983). Single-parent female-headed families constituted almost half of all poor families in the United States in 1982 (Kamerman, 1984). The National Advisory Council on Economic Opportunity predicts that by the year 2000,

the entire poverty population will be women and children living in female-headed households.

Figure 12-1 gives one example of how the issue of poverty for women is ignored. Because of this insensitivity to women, public policy issues generally affect women adversely. For example, since President Reagan took office in 1981, the number of people living in poverty has risen from 11.7% to 15%, and most of these people are women. Cuts in income security programs (for example, food stamps and child nutrition programs) and all human resource programs (for example, Medicaid) have the greatest impact on households with incomes of less than $10,000 (Eisenstein, 1984; "Inequality," 1984). Furthermore, the massive transfer of government funds from the civilian economic sector, where 99% of employed women work, to military production also affects women negatively.

The consequences of male dominance of the economy are manifest not only in the power men exert but also in the way the economy, especially business, is run. The way business is run, in turn, affects all members of the society, workers and nonworkers alike. Because business executives succeed based on their ability to make decisions that maximize corporate profit, and because such executives usually epitomize the rational, nonemotional, insensi-

Figure 12-1 _____

How to maintain the image of America as the land of good and plenty: Ignore the lives of women and other people without power. (Copyright 1982 by Field Enterprises, Inc. Reprinted with permission.)

tive, competitive male, these decisions often are contrary to human needs (MacKinnon, 1982; Pleck & Sawyer, 1974; Tolson, 1977). Thus, we live in a country of enormous wealth, natural resources, and productivity, yet many children suffer from malnutrition, our air and water have become increasingly polluted, and our safety standards for motor vehicles and consumer products are low. The hierarchy that is dominant in the business world (as well as in the political and military worlds) implies control of many by a few. This hierarchical structure then becomes the primary mode in which many men operate—being dominated and oppressed at work and going home to dominate their wives and children. Institutions may use and perpetuate the masculine stereotype because it serves their purpose. Through the emphasis on getting ahead and "staying cool," many men fit right into institutions "whose function is not to increase general human welfare but to enhance the profit, power and prestige of the few who control them" (Pleck & Sawyer, 1974, pp. 126–127).

The fact that many women are now trying to enter these bastions of male power may mean that they will need to adopt similar ways of dealing with situations—competitively, hierarchically, and unfeelingly. Whether this is a desirable state of affairs is, of course, a value judgment. It is the opinion of the author that the integration of instrumental and expressive qualities should be an ideal of institutional as well as individual functioning, that the masculine stereotype of achievement should be used in conjunction with the feminine stereotype of concern for people. Some companies are beginning to realize such a shift is necessary, and are focusing on skills traditionally encouraged in most women—their talent for teamwork, their tenacity, and their human relations skills (Kanter, 1983). Society will certainly benefit as a result. Thus humanization of institutions is as much a goal of the women's liberation movement as is human liberation.

Political Power

Salaries, a small part of economic power, are an even smaller part of political power. But political power can and does influence salaries and the work situation in general. And, politically, women have consistently had negligible power. Women won the right to vote in the United States in 1920 and currently make up 53% of the nation's registered voters. Yet they have never used this voting power to their advantage—for example, by voting as a bloc (Bernard, 1979b; Perlez, 1984). Although women currently (beginning in 1980) vote with the same frequency as do men (education is the most important factor in voter participation), they are underrepresented in the party hierarchies and in elected and appointed offices. They are, however, overrepresented in volunteer (unpaid and nonpowerful) positions.

On the political party level, women have served as indispensable volunteers, but rarely in positions of responsibility or decision making. Few of the top jobs of the 1984 major presidential campaign were held by women. Since 1972, more women have served as party delegates at the Democratic conventions than ever before. For the 1980 convention, Democrats required that half their delegates be women. Republicans have aimed for similar representation, but reached only 29% in 1980 and 44% in 1984. Although delegates are visible and this is certainly an improvement, these are not the most powerful party positions.

Women still occupy less than 10% of all elected offices in the United States, with Black women representing less than 1% of all elected officeholders (Center for the American Woman and Politics, 1984). Women officeholders tend to be concentrated in a few offices at the state and local level (see Table 12-1). At these lower levels, there have been impressive gains. By 1985, the number of women who had been elected to state legislatures had increased more than three times what it had been in 1969 (from 305, or 4.1%, to 1096, or 14.7%). Even more gains have been made in local government, but primarily in positions traditionally reserved for women, such as on library boards or in part-time, poorly paid elective offices. Few women are state governors (2 out of 50 in 1985), mainly because women are more readily accepted as a representative than as a leader.

On a federal level, the number of women in Congress is still minimal, as shown in Table 12-2. During the last 30 years, the proportion

Table 12-2
Number of Women in Congress, 1947–1986

Congress	Year	Senate	House	Total
80th	1947–1948	0	8	8
81st	1949–1950	1	9	10
82nd	1951–1952	1	10	11
83rd	1953–1954	2	11	13
84th	1955–1956	1	16	17
85th	1957–1958	1	15	16
86th	1959–1960	1	16	17
87th	1961–1962	2	17	19
88th	1963–1964	2	11	13
89th	1965–1966	2	10	12
90th	1967–1968	1	11	12
91st	1969–1970	1	10	11
92nd	1971–1972	1	12[a]	13
93rd	1973–1974	0	16[b]	16
94th	1975–1976	0	19	19
95th	1977–1978	2[c]	18	20
96th	1979–1980	1	16	17
97th	1981–1982	2	19	21
98th	1983–1984	2	22[d]	24
99th	1985–1986	2	23[e]	25

[a]Charlotte Reid left Congress to accept a presidential appointment.
[b]Lindy Boggs and Cardiff Collins were elected in special elections in 1973 to succeed
their late husbands.
[c]Muriel Humphrey and Maryon Allen were appointed in 1978 to succeed their late
husbands.
[d]Sala Burton was elected to fill seat vacated by death of her husband in 1984.
[e]Cathy Long was elected to fill seat vacated by death of her husband in 1985.

of women in Congress has fluctuated between 2% and 3%. In the 99th Congress, representation by women has reached the all-time high of 5%. Representation in the Senate has been strikingly low. There have never been more than two women in the Senate at any one time. Since Jeannette Rankin was first elected to the House of Representatives in 1917, women's representation there has increased, although with fluctuations. For minority women, the situation is far from encouraging. Shirley Chisholm, in 1968, was the first Black woman to serve in Congress. Since that time, only four other Black women and one Asian-American woman have served in the House, none in the Senate. In the 1985–1986 Congress, there were 24 women in the House, 2 of whom were Black. Few women who have served in Congress have been able to build up enough seniority to be powerful, and none has been elected to any of the party leadership roles.

In other positions on the federal level, women also have little power. By 1984, Reagan had appointed only 86 women to full-time administrative posts requiring Senate confirmation compared to Carter's 98 women in the same time period. Indeed, Reagan is the first president in over a decade who has failed to appoint more women to top level positions than his immediate predecessor. In the Carter administration, women's representation was about 18%; Ford's record was 14%. Again, women's representation mainly has been at the lower levels, although Carter did appoint three women cabinet officers. Interestingly, in federal agencies headed by women, nearly 50% of the appointed positions have been filled by women. Such appointments suggest that qualified women are available. Certain appointive posts have rarely been held by a woman, most noticeably in the judiciary, although Reagan did appoint the first woman to the Supreme Court—Sandra Day O'Connor—in 1981. Among nations, the United States still has one of the worst records for the holding by women of national public office (N. Lynn, 1975).

Barriers to Women in Politics. The barriers to women in politics are numerous and are similar to those present for women in the work force. One set of barriers arises from *gender socialization*. Many women and men still think politics is "masculine" and are concerned that political participation would somehow "coarsen" women (Bernard, 1979b). Consequently, women have a difficult time developing the self-confidence needed to run for public office. They also tend to believe that family responsibilities should come first. Women in politics do not appear to be less politically ambitious than men at the local level (Merritt, 1982). However, politically ambitious women do appear to have a special approach to office, one that emphasizes public service rather than power brokerage or personal career advantages.

The major barriers against women's participation in politics are external; for example *prejudice* and *discrimination* against female candidates. In 1970, the Gallup Poll found that 13% of men and women would not vote for a qualified woman for Congress (N. Lynn, 1975). In 1983, 10% still said that they would not vote for a woman "under any circumstances" (Sloane, 1983). Although clear-cut sex discrimination in people's conscious responses has decreased, there is evidence that sex bias still operates in election decisions. A 1984 study of 200 selected registered voters by Yankelovich, Skelly, & White, Inc. found that although three-fourths of the sample said that the sex of a hypothetical gubernatorial candidate would not affect their vote, they still were highly influenced by traditional gender stereotypes (Basler, 1984). Overall, people tended to vote for men. Only when women clearly were more qualified than men did people vote for women. The stereotypes were strongest among men, older voters, the less educated, and those in lower income groups.

Preconceptions about female candidates, such as "she can't take time away from her family," "she's too emotionally unstable due to her menstrual cycle," "she can't make tough decisions," and so on, serve as barriers. About one-third of the electorate think men are "better suited emotionally" for politics than are women ("U.S.," 1983). Such opinions turn into votes. In a 1984 study of five congressional races between a man and a woman, 40% of those surveyed said the men could handle the emotional demands of public life while 27% said the women were prepared to do so ("Poll," 1985). Similarly, the men were seen as better able to handle a crisis than were the women. However, some stereotypes may work to the advantage of women candidates. For example, in the same study, the women were rated higher than the men in personal integrity, strong convictions, and compassion for the needy. Women also were viewed as more likely to work hard. Yet, four out of five of the men won in the actual elections.

In practice, women candidates are subject to closer scrutiny than the familiar White, male candidate. In particular, women's age, height, weight, clothing, and physical attractiveness play a big role in how seriously she is taken as a candidate (Mandel, 1981). For example, during the 1984 Presidential campaign, Democratic vice-presidential candidate Geraldine Ferraro was scrutinized endlessly with regard to how she wore her hair, where she got her clothes, and so on. Such topics were ignored in discussions of her male rival. Ironically, of course, there is never a "right way" for a woman candidate to be since she will never be male. She is either too young or too old, too shrill or too quiet, too fat or too thin, and so on.

Jobs women hold often make office seeking difficult. Family responsibilities, a major obstacle, have traditionally fallen on women. Most women who have been elected to office are older and they are usually widowed or divorced (N. Lynn, 1975). Women also have a great deal of trouble raising *funds*. They suffer from a loser's image and frequently shoulder the burden of mistakes and reputations built by other women in public life. In addition, *political clubs* and social activities usually exclude women formally and informally (the "smoke-filled back rooms"). Party leaders may force women into a no-win position by encouraging them when a nomination seems worthless and ignoring them when it looks valuable. Yet more and more women have been running for office. In the 1984 elections, there was a record number of women candidates, including the first woman vice-presidential candidate.

Even when a woman has some political power, she may not be able to wield it as effectively as a man in the same situation because of gender stereotypes. Female politicians may be reproached for assuming male prerogatives (Abzug, 1984; Jaquette, 1974). Outspoken women, in particular, may be negatively evaluated, especially by women (Mandel, 1981). An interesting example of the difficulties facing women in politics occurred in February 1979 when Queen Elizabeth II of England visited the Persian Gulf countries. In order to be received by her Moslem male hosts and be accorded the honors generally bestowed upon a visiting chief of state, Queen Elizabeth had to become an "honorary man" and cover herself with veils and wrist-to-ankle clothes. Women in most of these countries generally are not even allowed to speak in front of men.

The outlook is improving, however, and the traditional attitudes and barriers to women's involvement in politics can be broken down. A 1983 poll by the National Opinion Research Center found that 86.5% of their sample said they were willing to vote for a woman for president, up from 74% found in 1972, and 54% in 1969 (N. Lynn, 1975; "U.S.," 1983). However, not all recent polls have been so optimistic. A 1983 public opinion poll conducted by *The Washington Post* and *ABC News* found that only 68% of the respondents said they would vote for a woman candidate for president, in contrast to 77% who said they would vote for a Black candidate and 79% for a Jewish candidate for president (Sussman, 1983). Once again, the most negative attitudes have come from older, less educated, and lower-income individuals. Still, most people now say the sex of the candidate does not make a difference (Basler, 1984; Sloane 1983) and this was true in the 1984 presidential election as well. Exit-poll interviews found that most voters said that the presence of a female vice-presidential candidate

was not an important factor in their voting. Unfortunately, for those for whom it was a factor, it was more likely to be a negative than a positive one. Furthermore, as the 1984 Yankelovich study revealed (Basler, 1984), sex bias can operate on more subtle and unconscious levels than is evident by expressed attitudes.

The Gender Gap. Much has been made of the "gender gap" since the 1980 presidential election when it was first observed in voting patterns. This term refers to the greater percentage of males, particularly White males, who voted for President Reagan, than females. Men backed Reagan by a 54–37% edge in the 1980 election, whereas women split their votes 46–45% (Abzug, 1984). Among Blacks, only 23% of the men supported Reagan, still greater than the 16% of Black women who supported Reagan. In national surveys taken in 1981, 1982, and 1983, White men consistently gave Reagan higher marks than did women (Abzug, 1984; Carroll, 1984b; Raines, 1983; Smeal, 1984). And, in the 1984 elections, although the majority of both sexes voted for Reagan, a gender gap still was evident. Men favored Reagan over Mondale by 63–36% whereas women went for Reagan by 56–44% (Beck, 1984). In close races, women frequently made the difference and elected Democrats (Houghton, 1984).

This consistent 7 to 8 percentage point "gender gap" has been attributed to a variety of causes. Carroll (1984b) evaluates four competing explanations for the gender gap, but concludes that none individually can fully account for the differences in the way men and women vote. The economic self-interest explanation links the gender gap to differences in socioeconomic status. As already has been discussed, women occupy a more disadvantaged economic position than do men, and Reagan's policies have had a disparate negative impact on the poorer segments of our society. But women at higher income levels also were less likely to vote for Reagan in both 1980 and 1984 (Dowd, 1984), so this explanation is not sufficient. The second explanation, based on economic vulnerability, suggests that all women are economically vulnerable even if they are not currently in low-income groups. Thus, women should find Reagan's policies more threatening to their economic well-being than do men. Although this hypothesis has some support, many of the women who claim to have benefited from Reagan's policies and who expect to continue to do so still are less likely to vote for him. A third explanation is the nurturance argument, which suggests that because women are socialized to be more compassionate than are men, they find many of Reagan's policies to be objectionable—in particular, his tough foreign policy posture and his cuts in social programs aimed at the disadvantaged (Baxter & Lansing, 1983). Again, there is some support for this argument, because women are more likely to object to Reagan's stance on these topics than are men (Stanwick & Kleeman, 1983). Still, the size of the gender gap varies across demographic groups, which suggests that the gap is not a purely gender-related phenomenon. For example, there is a smaller gender gap among single voters than married voters, and among voters over age 45 than among voters between ages 25 and 44 (Dowd, 1984). The fourth explanation attributes the gender gap to the feminist movement, and the resultant difference in perspectives or interests between women and men (Abzug, 1984). As in the previous explanation, there is some support for positing differences in perspectives between women and men. For example, women are more likely than men to support the Equal Rights Amendment, and less likely to support capital punishment. Among those who agree with basic tenets of feminist ideology, the gender gap was minimal. Still, some women who do not express feminist beliefs are also less likely to vote for Reagan.

Carroll (1984b) suggests integrating these four explanations of the gender gap into one emphasizing women's autonomy from men. Women increasingly are becoming both economically and psychologically independent from men; for example, they are more likely than men to favor egalitarian relationships. It is these women, those who are both psychologically and economically autonomous from men (for example, single women and employed women) who were least likely to support Reagan in 1980 and 1984 (also Dowd, 1984). Carroll concludes that these trends toward increasing autonomy indicate that patriarchy is

starting to break down. In light of Reagan's reelection in 1984, others might be less sanguine about the impending demise of male dominance in our political system.

With increased numbers of women in the labor force and in higher education, their political activity also should increase. More women than ever before are running for office and this means they are gaining valuable political experience for future races as well as serving as role models for other women. Nearly two-thirds of women in Congress came from elected offices at the local and state levels ("Women hold," 1981). Two national groups have been organized to help women raise funds—the National Women's Political Caucus and the Women's Campaign Fund. In 1983, both the Democrats and the Republicans held conferences across the country for female party activists to offer policy information and urge them to run for office in 1984 (Klemesrud, 1983). These factors combined may help women attain some measure of political power.

Since the "gender gap" first was noted in 1980, women appear to be gaining power during election campaigns as an important interest group. Many view the selection of a female vice-president by the Democratic party in 1984 as a response to this gender gap. It remains to be seen whether the Republican landslide in the election will be blamed on women and used as an excuse to resume ignoring them. Despite all hopes to the contrary (for example, Abzug, 1984; Smeal, 1984), women still do not vote as a self-conscious interest group, although they are more likely to vote for women and women's issues than ever before. For example, a 1984 national Louis Harris and Associates poll (Steinem, 1984) found that when asked if they would vote for an equally qualified female over a male candidate for Congress, 46% of Black women and 42% of White women said they would, in contrast to 22% of Black men and 17% of White men.

Consequences. The consequences of male dominance of the political system are far-reaching. The stereotypic male preoccupations with power and status and the need to prove masculinity by being "tough" and unemotional have had tremendous impact on both domestic and foreign policy. George Romney (1968 presidential primary candidate), Edmund Muskie (1972 presidential primary candidate), and Thomas Eagleton (1972 first-choice running mate of McGovern) each had their political careers seriously damaged after an admission of "weakness"—having been "brainwashed," tearfully upset over slander, or having had previous treatment for emotional problems, respectively (Farrell, 1974).

A number of writers (Doyle, 1983; Farrell, 1974; Fasteau, 1974; Steinem, 1972; Stone, 1974) have argued persuasively that the United States' reactions to the Cuban missile crisis and, particularly, the Vietnam war, were significantly colored by the needs of Presidents Kennedy, Johnson, and Nixon to prove their "toughness." As I. F. Stone (1974) notes, "The first rule of this small boy statecraft is that the leader of a gang, like the leader of a tribe, horde, or nation, dare not appear 'chicken' " (p. 131). Not only must a leader prove his toughness to other leaders but he must be at least as tough as his predecessors. Thus President Johnson was concerned that he would be thought "less of a man" than Kennedy if he did not follow through with Vietnam. Nixon was particularly obsessed with "winning," "saving face," and being "tough," as the Pentagon papers and the White House tapes all too clearly show. The "cult of toughness" during the Vietnam years extended to political advisors as well, whom some considered intellectuals and unmasculine (Fasteau, 1974). From this perspective, some advisors might have had a double reason to prove their masculinity.

All this is not to say that standing firm, threatening, or using force is never valid. Clearly, certain situations require such responses, as President Carter learned during the Iranian and Afghanistan crises of 1979 and 1980. What is being questioned is the use of such responses to satisfy a psychological or political need, rather than as a clearly thought out and appropriate humanitarian foreign policy. A study of State Department staff and policy disagreements between U.S. presidents and secretaries of states between 1898 and 1975 revealed a connection between aggressive "masculine" traits and hard-line foreign policy (Etheredge, 1978). A specific example of how the masculine sex role may influence foreign policy can be found in the Pentagon papers. They revealed that in March 1965, the U.S. aims in South Vietnam were only 20% to keep South Vietnam out of Chinese hands, only 10% to allow the South Vietnamese a freer, better way of life, but 70% to avoid a "humiliating defeat" (in Fasteau, 1974). More recently (July 1985), Congress adopted an extremely tough-minded foreign aid bill, amid dozens of references to Rambo, a movie hero who single-handedly rescues American prisoners in Vietnam (Roberts, 1985). As one legislator described it, "the mood is machismo."

Many people view President Reagan's popularity as due to his "macho" image (for example, Friedman, 1983; Z. Rubin, 1982b). Although most political analysts have concentrated on the question of why women did not vote for Reagan in as great strength as did men, the more accurate question is why Reagan was so popular among White males. (The first question is an example of using the male as the norm. In fact, because most men and women are registered Democrats, it is really men's voting patterns in the last two presidential elections that were the anomaly.) As Reagan's 1984 campaign director said, "Ronald Reagan is a man's man. He is a leader. He is providing direction, whether you agree with the direction or not. He's not afraid of taking action, decisive action. And that appeals to men." (Friedman, 1983). In a 1983 poll, half of the women surveyed feared Reagan's policies would get us into war; only 36% of the men felt that way (Friedman, 1983). Black and Jewish women overwhelmingly opposed the president because they felt that Reagan lacks compassion and would too easily use military force (Perlez, 1984). Much of the 1984 presidential campaign rhetoric hinged on who would be the "strongest" and "toughest" leader—Reagan or Mondale. Reagan, with his strong, tough but sincere, cowboy image, prevailed, especially for White males.

As is true with business institutions, if women want to achieve positions of political power, they often must prove themselves even "tougher" than men. Yet women, for the most part, are not obsessed with proving their strength, saving face, or prestige. Polls consistently show women to be generally against specific wars and against military solutions to international problems. For example, the only person to vote against World War I in Congress was the first woman to serve in Congress, Jeannette Rankin. And about 5% more women than men thought U.S. entry into World War I was a mistake. Indeed, women have been less likely than men to support all issues having to do with the military or violence, such as defense spending and capital punishment (Baxter & Lansing, 1983; Steinem, 1984). In contrast, women tend to show greater support than do men for issues having to do with equality, as well as those related to greater health, education, and domestic spending.

Women politicians apparently reflect these views when they vote. Studies of the voting patterns of women in Congress from 1917 through 1976 show them to be more humanistic and altruistic than are men (see Bernard, 1979b). Since 1977, the Center for the American Woman and Politics has profiled male and female officeholders (Stanwick & Kleeman, 1983). Results of their surveys show that women, regardless of whether they described themselves as conservative, moderate, or liberal, were more likely than men to take feminist positions on women's issues, such as ratification of the Equal Rights Amendment, opposition to curbs on abortion, government support for child care, and social security for homemakers. Women politicians also differed from men politicians on attitudes toward military strength, nuclear power plants, and capital punishment, with women less likely to favor these issues than were men. The gender gap on all issues was greater among those elected to higher levels of office. At all levels, Black women holding elective office were the most liberal. Thus women politicians as a group do seem to be different from men politicians as a group, more humanitarian and public-service oriented (also Carroll, 1984a; Merritt, 1982).

Women are not biologically more humane than men, but many learn to be so due to gender socialization. Yet political institutions, by their very structure, tend to operate on "masculine" aggressive, nonhumanitarian, competitive principles, and women who "make it" to the top often have adopted those values.

To expect more humane politics just because women are in power is a sexist as well as a false notion, as Indira Gandhi in India and Margaret Thatcher in England have demonstrated. The "system" itself must change and become more concerned with human values. Again, an androgynous political system seems most beneficial to individuals, the country, and even the world.

Legal Power

Few women serve in the judiciary of the United States, especially in the higher courts, and few serve in the political offices responsible for making and enforcing laws. Only one woman has served on the U.S. Supreme Court, and she was appointed only in 1981. Judicial appointments are particularly important because such judges can strike down laws as unconstitutional and can order the executive branch to perform specified actions. During the Carter administration, some progress was made in increasing female representation in the judiciary. More women were appointed as judges during that administration than during all previous administrations combined. For example, President Carter named 41 women, or 16% of his 259 appointments, to life-time federal judgeships (Pear, 1983). In contrast, only 8% of President Reagan's 165 federal judicial appointees during his first term of office were women ("Reagan judges," 1985).

In 1980, women constituted only 17% of all judgeships in the United States, up from 6% in 1970 (Schmid, 1984). Although every state now has at least one woman in its judiciary system, most of these are justices of the peace or otherwise serve on courts of limited jurisdiction. A factor contributing to Carter's impressive record on judicial appointments was the 1978 Omnibus Judgeship Act, which created 152 new federal judgeships. Of those appointed to these positions, 20% were women (Ness, 1980). These seats now are filled, and given President Reagan's track record to date, it is unlikely that women will increase their representation in the courts in the near future. Reviews of the judiciary nominating and selection process reveal that the process is slow, discriminatory, and generally indicative of "politics as usual" (that is, federal judgeships being used as political patronage) (Ness, 1980; Tolchin, 1979). Thus, women currently have very little legal power and are unlikely to make significant gains in the near future.

Women are, however, becoming lawyers in increasing numbers. In 1982, 16% of all lawyers were women, a fourfold increase over 1972 ("Change," 1985). And more are on their way, because more than one-third of those entering law school now are women. These numbers represent a tremendous change since 1873, when U.S. Supreme Court Justice Bradley allowed Illinois to bar Myra Bradwell from practicing law because women "naturally" belonged in the domestic sphere (Agate & Meacham, 1977). Because law is the route to power, particularly political power (one-third of President Carter's female appointees were lawyers), we can expect to see some changes in male dominance of this area in the future (Lipson, 1977).

Partly as a result of male dominance of the legal system and partly due to gender stereotypes themselves, women are frequently at a marked disadvantage under the law. Unfair treatment still exists despite significant changes in the laws and their enforcement over the past 15 years toward the reduction of discrimination against women in employment, salaries, education, family planning, and credit (for example, the Pregnancy Disability Bill of 1978; the Equal Employment Opportunity Act of 1972; the Equal Pay Act of 1963 as amended by the Education Amendments of 1972; Title IX of the Education Amendments of 1972 as amended by the Bayh Amendment of 1974 and the Education Amendments of 1976; and the Equal Credit Opportunity Act of 1975). These are statutory laws, however; judicial decisions (common law) are made by legislators and judges, who are usually men, some of whom may not be able to transcend their own socialized belief that women and men are meant to have distinct and different roles in life.

There are many ways in which gender stereotypes or attitudes can affect the types of laws made and enforced. For example, The Task Force on Women in the Courts in New Jersey found that women were treated unequally both as lawyers and in judges' decisions

(Hanley, 1983). For example, judges appeared to give less credibility to lawyers, witnesses, experts, and probation officers who were women than to their male counterparts. Judicial decisions have become increasingly important in setting policy since 1980. Reagan's Justice Department succeeded in narrowing Title IX protections against sex discrimination in education (*Grove City College* v. *Bell,* 1984; Nicholson, 1984) and argued against affirmative action and comparable worth legislation. In 1980, the Supreme Court upheld the Hyde Amendment, which severely restricts funding of medically necessary abortions under the Medicaid program. The result is to make it extremely difficult for poor women to obtain abortions.

Even when nondiscriminatory laws are on the books, enforcement can be curtailed by restricting necessary funding. Thus, Reagan's cuts in funds for the Equal Employment Opportunity Commission have hampered their prosecution of discrimination cases. The number of cases filed by the Commission involving sex discrimination in employment dropped more than 70% between 1981 and 1983 (Kennelly, 1984). Before Congress passed the child-support bill in 1984 which toughened procedures for collecting court-ordered child-support payments, less than half the women who were supposed to receive such payments actually received them in full (Roberts, 1984).

Until 1971, sex was always held to be a difference that warranted different legal treatment (Agate & Meachman, 1977). In the case *Reed* v. *Reed,* a woman was prevented from becoming a bartender due to a state law excluding women from that occupation. The Supreme Court, for the first time, held a state statute to be unconstitutional because it discriminated against women. However, in 1974, the Supreme Court upheld a Florida law (*Kahn* v. *Shevin*) which granted widows a property tax exemption but did not extend the benefit to widowers (Agate & Meacham, 1977). In 1976, the Supreme Court's *Gilbert* v. *General Electric* decision allowed employers to exempt pregnancy-related disability from coverage under temporary disability or health benefit programs while allowing vasectomies and hair transplants to be covered. (The 1978 Pregnancy Disability Bill has changed the law for certain employers.)

Thus, sex still has not been given the status of a suspect classification (as has race). Discriminatory laws still abound.

In property law especially, women are discriminated against. Only eight states have community property laws that theoretically recognize the contribution of housework to a marriage and consider that each spouse owns half of the earnings of the couple. In the 42 other states, the husband has sole control over his earnings and the right to support his wife in the manner *he* chooses. In several states (Alabama, Florida, Indiana, North Carolina), a wife cannot even sell her own property without her husband's consent.

Social Security laws also discriminate against women (Burkhauser & Holden, 1982). Especially disadvantaged are those women who take time out of the labor force to rear children, a job that offers no retirement benefits. Displaced homemakers (those who are widowed, divorced, or separated) who have no other options for their own support must fend for themselves. If eligible, they may elect to take Social Security benefits early, at age 60 instead of 65, but must do so at a lower rate. Some homemakers do not qualify at all—women married less than 10 years are not entitled to any of their former husband's benefits. (Before 1979, the law required 20 years of marriage before benefits could be collected.) The Retirement Equity Act, passed in 1984, will begin to make pension plans fairer to women, but many military ex-wives still are unprotected. Employed women, if their husbands also pay into the system, generally receive no benefit for their own contributions because their salary was usually less than their husband's. And, of course, because women earn less than men, fewer women receive maximum benefits. The plight of many elderly women is tragic. As noted previously, half of all single female elderly Social Security recipients live at or below poverty level, Black women being the most disadvantaged. Amendments and new laws to alleviate these inequities have been proposed each year (for example, the Householders Benefit Act; the Displaced Homemakers Act), but have yet to be passed by a predominantly male Congress.

There are other laws that discriminate on the basis of sex. For instance, in many states it is illegal for males to use obscene language in the presence of females and children. In some states, statutory rape is possible only for males. (The Supreme Court upheld one such law in 1981.) Women are allowed to marry younger than are males in most states. A woman is generally assumed to be the person best qualified to care for her children and the husband to be the person best qualified to financially support them. Unwed fathers have no rights in many states. Only men have to register for the draft. Some "protective" labor laws in some states still establish a maximum number of hours a woman may work. As can be seen from this sampling, men, as well as women, are often discriminated against by law (see Hayman, 1976).

The Equal Rights Amendment, introduced into every Congress between 1923 and 1972 until it passed, would equalize men's and women's rights in almost all instances. The amendment provides that "equality of rights under the law shall not be denied or abridged by the United States or by any State on account of sex." It would finally eliminate legislative inertia that keeps discriminatory laws on the books. It would provide clear constitutional recognition of equal rights and responsibilities for men and women. And it would serve as a clear statement of the nation's moral and legal commitment to full sexual equality. Although seemingly clear-cut and favored by a majority of the populace (64% of women and 56% of men; Toth, 1984) the amendment fell three states short of being ratified by its extended deadline of June 30, 1982. It has yet to be successfully passed in Congress again. It even was removed from the Republican platform in 1980, where it had been for 40 years.

Military Power

Women traditionally have been excluded from gaining military power. They have not been subject to the draft in the United States, and it has only been since the draft ended in 1972 that women have entered the services in significant numbers. They now constitute nearly 10% of all military personnel, nearly five times the 2% cap previously mandated by law (E.

Fein, 1985). Because of the present volunteer nature of U.S. military service, a decrease in the number of available males due to the lower birth rate, and competition from the civilian job market, the armed forces have had a difficult time filling their quotas with males. Thus they have been taking in more females, but discriminatory regulations and practices abound.

By federal statute, women are prohibited from combat duty and from jobs that are labeled combat-related in the U.S. Navy, Marines, and Air Force. In practice, this means that women are excluded from 73% of military positions, even though only 43% are designated as combat or combat-support positions ("The Registration," 1980). Additional positions are reserved for men to facilitate rotation of positions and to provide career opportunities for men. Lack of acceptable housing also disqualifies women from many overseas positions. The fact that women are barred from serving in combat makes them exempt from the 1980 law requiring registration for the draft, at least according to a 1981 Supreme Court decision— this, despite the fact that in the last draft, less than 1% of the men eligible were inducted and subsequently assigned to a combat unit ("The Registration," 1980).

Women in the military have to face an environment oftentimes overtly hostile to them (Cheatham, 1984; "The Registration," 1980; Rustad, 1982; Schroeder, 1982; Yoder, 1983). Clothes and equipment generally are not designed for most women and short-statured men; standards of performance do not take women's different strengths into account (for example, leg as opposed to upper-body strength); family and social services are poor; and sexual harassment abounds. The frequency of vulgar and obscene language directed at women is significantly correlated with women's ratings of their own job dissatisfaction (Woelfel & Savell, 1981).

In all branches of the service, as in civilian life, women are restricted to the less prestigious, lower-paying jobs. Approximately 83% of enlisted women are in the four lowest pay grades as compared to 68% of men ("The Registration," 1980). The four highest pay grades hold 23% of enlisted men and only 3% of enlisted women. As in civilian life also, women seem to prefer traditional specialties, such as those in offices and hospitals and in communications.

It is difficult to break free of traditional roles, although there is evidence that some change is occurring. From 1973 to 1975, the percentage of enlisted female soldiers in traditional jobs declined by 14% while the percentage in nontraditional jobs rose by 11% (Savell, Woelfel, Collins, & Bentler, 1979). The trend has continued (Woelfel, 1981). From 1975 to 1978 the percentage of army women in traditional jobs decreased another 17% to 57%. During the same time period, the percentage of army women in nontraditional jobs has risen another 8% to 20%, with maintenance remaining the most popular nontraditional category. The Army's Reserve Officers Training Program (ROTC) first admitted women in the 1973–1974 academic year. In the 1978–1979 academic year, women made up 25% of the total enrollment (Card & Farrell, 1983). The service academies opened their doors to women in 1976 after being ordered to do so by federal legislation. By the end of 1985, more than 1500 women had gone through the service academies (E. Fein, 1985).

In 1977, the armed forces adopted a recommendation by the Brookings Institute to move toward less restrictive personnel policies so that more women could enter the services. The Brookings report recommended that women constitute 22% of the forces; the Pentagon's final goal was 12.5%. This goal could be met even if women still were excluded from front-line combat jobs. However, that five-year plan was scrapped after the Reagan administration took over and after a slumping economy made it possible to enlist enough men.

There is no rational basis for denying women an equal role in the military. Studies have shown that women as soldiers prove less expensive than men and have a rate of lost time for illnesses and absenteeism (including time lost for pregnancy) only half that of men ("The Registration," 1980; Schroeder, 1982). They learn fast, perform well, and stay in service longer and have lower disciplinary rates than many male volunteers. Studies of women army recruits given regular male basic training and extended field exercises have found little difference in relative performance when these women were compared to an equal number of men, using scientifically based standards ("The Registration," 1980). Most women at the service academies are doing well, although attrition rates are higher for females than males (Card & Farrell, 1983), and males still are more likely than females to be perceived as leaders, at least when traditional agentic criteria are used (for example, athletic/physical ability) (J. Adams, 1984; Rice, Yoder, Adams, Priest, & Prince, 1984; Woelfel, 1981). Within the military, the majority of men and women now favor the concept of assigning women to traditionally male jobs, including assignments to combat units or aboard naval vessels (Savell et al., 1979).

However, 56% of military respondents do not think women would make as good front-line soldiers as men (Woelfel, 1981) and if women were assigned to combat units, about half of military respondents think the army would be less effective. The majority of the American public also thinks that women should not be assigned to combat roles (E. Fein, 1985).

Some people feel that having women in the military who are not prepared for combat is "a can of worms" (Revell, 1976). Others are concerned about what would happen if women *were* prepared for combat. Gilder (1979) argues that "the hard evidence is overwhelming that men are more aggressive, competitive, risk-taking, indeed more combative, than women" (p. 44). Greater aggressiveness and physical strength are seen as imperative in a combat situation. Furthermore, such writers hold that every society must protect its women for its own survival. Societies do this by ensuring that male physical strength and aggressiveness are not directed against women. Thus, if women are allowed to engage in combat, the result may be "nothing more nor less than a move toward barbarism" (Gilder, 1979, p. 46).

It is important to note that only 10% to 15% of our defensive force consists of front-line troops. Technology has displaced brute strength in conventional combat situations. And if women were eligible for combat service, it is most likely that only women with the same minimum skills as men would be allowed in a combat situation. The "brute strength" argument against women is further diminished by recognizing the fact that most Asian men are smaller than American women, yet size was no apparent disadvantage for Asian fighters in the Korean and Vietnam wars.

The critical issue seems to be whether to allow women to be killed in war time. To date, neither Congress nor the Supreme Court are ready to put women into military combat. It is indeed a terrible thing to have to decide whose life to risk, but if defending one's country is a duty of citizenship and women and men are supposedly equal citizens, it is difficult for many people to justify sparing one sex over the other as a general rule ("The Registration," 1980). The feminist community itself is split over this issue (Goldman, 1982; Steinem, 1984; Stiehm, 1983). Many argue that feminism should mean nonviolence and that war is a masculine "game," in which women should play no role, especially because women have little to no policy-making power (McAllister, 1982). Others argue that women already live in a war zone in their own country, vulnerable to rape, intimidation, and brainwashing. Therefore, "real" combat should pose little additional threat. Furthermore, exempting women from combat perpetuates the stereotype that women need protection and are not as capable as are men ("The Registration," 1980).

One consequence of current military policy is that men do risk their lives as combat troops during war and women do not. The military has been viewed by some writers as the last bastion of masculinity, where men can prove their "toughness" physically through aggressiveness, risk taking, and violence (Arkin & Dobrofsky, 1976; Pleck & Sawyer, 1974). And the military has fostered this image of masculinity in order to train men to kill and to risk their lives. "Be a real man," the ads say. The U.S. Marines want "men at their best." This masculine image of the military may account for some of the marked resistance against allowing women to participate equally.

One of the consequences of "macho" military training is that military men often engage in unnecessary violence and wanton acts of killing and destruction. Seymour Hersh (1970) analyzed the My Lai massacre in Vietnam as a predictable outcome of military exaggerations of the male gender stereotypes. These occur in every war by every army, and gender stereotypes may have much to do with it.

The effect of women on the military remains to be seen. Because so much training goes into the making of a soldier, it seems clear that women recruits can be trained to be equally as cold, aggressive, and deadly as male recruits. A study of West Point cadets during the first three years of coeducation found few personality differences between the men and women (J. Adams, 1984). Both groups were strong in agentic characteristics (for example, competitiveness, independence), potential for leadership, and motivation to achieve. Nearly half of the women do not see themselves as having children in the future, compared to less than 20% of the men. Another study found senior cadets to be more agentic than freshmen, suggesting that military training may have a "masculinizing" effect (Apao, 1982). Given the tendency, because of socialization, for more women than men to be against war in general, and to be humanistic, it is possible that not many women will desire such a role. There is some evidence that female ROTC cadets have less accurate knowledge about ROTC and the army than do male cadets (Card & Farrell, 1983). This may account for the higher attrition rates of women in some aspects of the military. But it only seems fair to let those who do desire that role to have access to it. An important point is the fact that in peacetime, the military is a job with excellent educational and training opportunities, excellent fringe benefits, and good chance for advancement. It is the kind of job from which women have traditionally been barred. In addition, all individuals who have served in the military—in the past, predominantly men—receive five points' preference on federal Civil Service exams. In some states (for example, Massachusetts) veterans receive an absolute preference. This procedure was upheld by the Supreme Court in 1979. Historically, veteran's preference points have hurt women's job chances. Consequently, although women make up 41% of those who pass the Civil Service Professional and Administrative Career Exam, they are only 27% of those who

are hired ("Veterans," 1978). Allowing women full equality in the military will go a long way toward allowing them an equal role in society. It will also alleviate the burden now placed on men.

Aggression and Violence

Inherent in the above discussion regarding military activities is a questioning of the commonly held belief that because men are "naturally" more aggressive, they should, of course, be the soldiers and fighters. Although males, in general, do seem to have a greater predisposition toward aggression, aggressive behavior is definitely learned and is responsive to a wide range of situational conditions. In our culture, far more than in most others, male aggressiveness appears to be viewed ambivalently. While violence and its social effects (crime, rapes, wars) are overtly condemned, aggression and violence are covertly glorified in the media (films, books, and especially, TV) and in daily interactions (Millet, 1970). For example, an advertising campaign for a Rolling Stones record album entitled "Black and Blue" showed a scantily clad, bound and beaten female saying, "I'm 'Black and Blue' from the Rolling Stones and I love it."

Aggressiveness and violence are definite parts of the "masculine mystique" in America, and probably Western society as a whole. As discussed in Chapter 4, males with traditional attitudes toward women have been found to be more aggressive than males with non-traditional attitudes toward women. These attitudes were not related to female aggressiveness. Boys generally are encouraged to "fight for their rights." Those who avoid fights are considered "sissies"—something feminine and, by implication, inferior (David & Brannon, 1976). One way to "prove" one's masculinity is by some form of aggression or act of daring. This may manifest itself in criminal activity, aggression against women and children, risk-taking acts, obsession with sports, and war.

Crime

Most crimes are committed by men between the ages of 13 and 24, mostly poor. Not only do males commit more offenses than do females, but male offenses are generally more serious and violent than female offenses (Gove, 1985; Warren, 1981). This is true among juveniles as well as among adults.

In this section, criminal activity for the two sexes will be examined only as a function of the gender stereotypes. The crime of rape will receive special attention because it is so closely associated with the themes of this chapter—power and aggression.

Men and Crime.   Criminal behavior is often a way for a young man to prove his masculinity at a time when such proof is important—that is, during adolescence and young adulthood. That age period also is the time when the male's physical strength and energy are at their peak (Gove, 1985). If the conventional status rewards of a society (money, good job, athletic success) are not available to some young men, they may try to maintain a "masculine" image by being considered aggressive and violent. The problem of youth gangs and their violence is a direct function of the fact that many members of gangs are cut off from the mainstream status system due to age, class, or race. For example, in 1985, 39% of Black teenagers were unemployed, two and a half times the number of unemployed White teenagers (Norton, 1985). Their status may become based on public aggressiveness and their willingness to fight (Cordes, 1985; David & Brannon, 1976; Short & Strodtbeck, 1976; Tolson, 1977).

Although the rate of reported crime in the United States has continued to drop since 1977, violent crime has increased. The sharpest rise has been in the category of forcible rape, which rose 38% between 1976 and 1980 (Federal Bureau of Investigation, 1981). A closer examination of this particular crime appears warranted. It has been estimated that about one woman in four will be a rape victim during the course of her lifetime, and nearly one out of two women will be a victim of rape or attempted rape (A. Johnson, 1980; Russell & Howell, 1983).

Rape.   Rape is a crime that can be viewed as being directly related to sex roles (see Brownmiller, 1975, and Sanday, 1981b, for excellent

discussions of this subject). As Fasteau (1974) notes, violence, to some degree, is equated with both masculinity and sexuality in America. The words we use for sex demonstrate this connection with violence: sexual "conquest," "screw," "bang," and so forth. Such an equation makes rape the "perfect" combination to prove masculinity: it is aggressive, it is sexual, and it involves dominance over and denigration of a woman (Briere, Corne, Runtz, & Malamuth, 1984; Brownmiller, 1975; Griffin, 1975).

The masculine stereotype, the sexual double standard in which women supposedly want to be dominated and have no sexual feelings themselves, and the traditional female role (helpless, passive, dependent), all help serve to make rape part of traditional male-female relationships in a patriarchal society. In male-dominated cultures with interpersonal violence and separation of the sexes—such as the United States—rape appears to be innate (Sanday, 1981b). In cultures where women are respected and "feminine" qualities such as nurturance are valued, rape rarely occurs.

A series of studies by Feshbach, Malamuth, and others elucidates the connections among sex, aggression, and violence toward women (Briere et al., 1984; Briere & Malamuth, 1983; Donnerstein, 1982; Malamuth, 1981, 1983; Malamuth & Donnerstein, 1984; Malamuth, Feshbach, & Jaffe, 1977; Malamuth, Haber, & Feshbach, 1980; Malamuth, Heim, & Feshbach, 1980). Sex and aggression seem to be reciprocally related for American men and women in that loosening inhibitions in one area also loosens inhibitions in the other. However, when aggression is extreme (that is, painful and violent) and is connected to sexual activity (as in forcible rape), the direct relationship no longer holds, at least for most women and some men. In one study, male and female college students were presented with stories of a rape containing either high or low pain cues and either a positive or negative victim reaction. For women, high pain cues resulted in low sexual arousal regardless of depicted outcome. In contrast, for men, high pain cues were associated with sexual arousal when the outcome was depicted as pleasurable, the typical pornographic rape-story outcome. Positive-outcome aggressive pornography films also were likely to lead to aggression against women in a laboratory setting (Donnerstein & Berkowitz, 1981). Thus, sex and violence may be more closely connected to the male sex role than usually is admitted.

Other research supports the hypothesis that aggression, dominance, and misogyny serve as sexual stimuli for a majority of males. For example, three-quarters of college men find rape scenes sexually arousing (Briere et al., 1984), and most college men have fantasies of forced sex and domination (Greendlinger & Byrne, in press). Those men who were most aroused or most likely to fantasize about forced sex were most likely to use or to have used force in sexual interaction with a woman. Furthermore, college men who score high on scales measuring sexual arousal to rape and attitudes facilitating violence were most likely to aggress against a female in a nonsexual way in a laboratory situation (Malamuth, 1983). So were college men who were exposed to highly erotic films (Donnerstein & Hallam, 1978). Thus, there appears to be a reciprocal relationship between sexual arousal and aggression for men: the more aggressive the stimuli, the more the sexual arousal.

There is a great deal of research suggesting that aggressive images of women in pornography (the most prevalent kind) are strongly related to aggression against women in real life (Donnerstein, 1980, 1982; Donnerstein & Berkowitz, 1981; Silbert & Pines, 1984). For example, even nonangered male college students showed an increase in aggression using electric shock toward a female in a lab setting after viewing aggressive-erotic films. Such films increased levels of aggression toward men, too, but not as much. Furthermore, there is a strong relationship between exposure to aggressive pornography and arousability to rape scenes, acceptance of rape myths, and self-reported likelihood to commit rape (Briere et al., 1984; Donnerstein, 1982). Repeated exposure to violent pornography results in reduced negative reactions (such as anxiety and depression) to the material and to reduced sensitivity to female victims of violence in other contexts (Linz, Donnerstein, & Penrod, 1984).

These results and others have fueled an intense debate about whether pornography should be made illegal (Blakely, 1985; Dworkin, 1981; Ferguson et al., 1984; Griffin, 1981; Vance, 1984). It has been argued by some that pornography infringes on the civil rights of women. In Minneapolis in 1983, a proposal by Catharine MacKinnon and Andrea Dworkin was adopted to amend the city's civil rights ordinance to make pornography a form of sex discrimination. Although later vetoed by the mayor, similar antipornography legislation has appeared in numerous cities across the country. However, other feminists (for example, the Feminist Anti-Censorship Taskforce) argue that any form of censorship is dangerous and likely to be ineffective. They recommend educational measures instead. Whatever one thinks of such legislation, there seems to be a clear relationship for many men between sex and violence against women.

In the Feshbach and Malamuth studies, it is striking to note that both sexes estimated that nearly half of all men would engage in acts of sexual violence if assured they would not be caught (Malamuth et al., 1980) (see Table 12-3). Both sexes also estimated that a substantial percentage of women (about 30%) would enjoy being victimized if no one knew. However, when asked to estimate their own reactions to such situations, very few women believed they themselves would derive pleasure from such an experience. In contrast, more than half of the males indicated some likelihood that they would engage in such behaviors under the circumstances described. When replicated with more males from various parts of North America, the likelihood of raping averaged about 35% (Malamuth, 1981). That is, at least one out of every three males indicate some possibility that he would rape a woman under some conditions. In other studies, however, nearly 60% of the males indicated some likelihood (Briere et al., 1984; Briere & Malamuth, 1983). This self-reported tendency was correlated with greater acceptance of rape myths (for example, agreeing that women enjoy being raped), greater incidence of forced sex fantasies, and relatively high sexual arousal to rape depictions (Briere & Malamuth, 1983; Greendlinger & Byrne, in press; Koss, Leonard, Beezley, & Oros, 1985; Malamuth, 1981). A similar pattern was found among convicted

Table 12-3

Estimating the Likelihood of Rape

	Projections		Self-Report (percent indicating at least some likelihood)
	Males	Females	
Percent of men likely to commit rape if they would not be caught	45	42	51
Percent of women likely to enjoy rape if no one would know	32	27	2

Adapted from Malamuth, Haber, & Feshbach, 1980.

rapists. Furthermore, college males with a high proclivity toward rape were also more likely to aggress against women in a laboratory setting (Malamuth, 1981). These findings support the interpretation of rape as a part of the traditional masculine sex role and traditional attitudes toward women (Brownmiller, 1975; Burt, 1980; Feild, 1978; Marolla & Scully, 1979; Russell, 1984). There appears to be a continuum of sexual aggression against women ranging from no aggression, to coerced intercourse, to likelihood of forced intercourse, to actual forced intercourse (Briere et al., 1984; Briere & Malamuth, 1983).

The myths that have been perpetuated about rape illustrate masculine prejudice and are most likely to be believed by older, less educated people, and those high in gender stereotyping, adversarial sexual beliefs (for example, the belief that sexual relationships are fundamentally exploitative), and acceptance of interpersonal violence as a legitimate way to gain compliance (Burt, 1980).

Myth 1. Women provoke rape by their appearance or actions. *Fact:* As many as 90% of rapes are premeditated—for example, a decision is made to rape the next unaccompanied female who enters an elevator. Thus, what a victim does or wears cannot be considered relevant. In fact, less than 4% of all rapes are provoked by the victim (Griffin, 1975; Lester, 1976).

Myth 2. Rape is a sex crime committed by sexually abnormal males. *Fact:* Men who commit rape are psychologically indistinguishable from other men in terms of general personality factors (Koss et al., 1985; Lester, 1976; Marolla

& Scully, 1979). A man's responses to questions about his sexuality, such as the adequacy of his sex life and the importance of sex, do not predict a man's self-reported likelihood to rape or to use sexual force (Briere & Malamuth, 1983). Rape is a crime of violence, a form of assault, not a crime of passion.

Myth 3. Many reports of rape are unfounded. *Fact:* Fewer than 10% of rape complaints are unfounded, about the same as for other violent crimes. In some areas, the percentage of false reports may be as low as 2% (Lester, 1976). Unfortunately, a 1985 case where a woman recanted her testimony against a man convicted of raping her six years earlier will probably strengthen this myth.

Myth 4. Most rapes are committed by strangers in dark alleys. *Fact:* Most rapes are committed by someone known to the victim, and half of all rapes occur in the victim's home (Amir, 1971; Russell, 1984). However, acquaintance rapes are least likely to be reported because they are least likely to be taken seriously by the police, medical personnel, and the courts (Check & Malamuth, 1983; L'Armand & Pepitone, 1982).

Myth 5. Rape has no lasting effects. *Fact:* Nearly all victims suffer severe aftereffects, both emotionally and in their relationships with others. Even one year after the rape, victims were more anxious, fearful, suspicious, and confused than matched nonvictims (Burgess & Holmstrom, 1979; Kilpatrick, Resick, & Veronen, 1981; Scheppele & Bart, 1983).

Myth 6. Most rapes are performed by Black men on White women. This myth reflects both sexism and racism—the White woman viewed as valuable property of the White man. *Fact:* Over 90% of reported rapes are *intra*racial, with Black women being the most vulnerable victims (Amir, 1971; Lester, 1976).

The preposterousness of such myths is illustrated in the following story using a robbery as an analogy for rape.

> *A man was testifying regarding his having been robbed while walking down a street.*
>
> *Prosecutor:* Can you tell the jury what time the alleged crime occurred?
> *Victim:* About 11:30 P.M.
> *Prosecutor:* And what exactly were you doing?
> *Victim:* Just walking down the street.
> *Prosecutor:* Alone?
> *Victim:* Yes.
> *Prosecutor:* And what were you wearing?
> *Victim:* Oh, a three-piece suit.
> *Prosecutor:* An expensive suit?
> *Victim:* Well, I do like to dress well.
> *Prosecutor:* Let me ask you this. Have you ever given money away?
> *Victim:* Why, of course . . .
> *Prosecutor:* In fact, Mr. D., you have quite a reputation for philanthropy. So here you are, a well-dressed man, with a history of giving money away, walking alone late at night, practically advertising yourself as a mark. Why, if we didn't know better, Mr. D., we might even say that you were asking for it!

Because of these myths, rape victims often are treated insensitively and antagonistically by the police, medical personnel, and the courts (see Holmstrom & Burgess, 1981). Most research studies have found that male respondents consistently respond less positively and empathically toward a female rape victim than do females, although situational and personal factors can strongly affect people's perceptions of the victim and the case (Acock & Ireland, 1983; Check & Malamuth, 1983; Deitz, Littman, & Bentley, 1984; Howard, 1984; Jacobson & Popovick, 1983; Krulewitz, 1981; L'Armand & Pepitone, 1982; Villemur & Hyde, 1983). For example, victim age, attractiveness, and sexual

history, defendant age and attractiveness, degree of victim resistance, sex of defense attorney, and sex-role attitudes of the observer all appear to affect the degree to which people believe the victim, and attribute responsibility for the crime to her or to her assailant. Exposure to depictions of women as sex objects and to pictures of aggression (Wyer, Bodenhausen, & Gorman, 1985) also affect people's perception of the victim and the case. It is important to recall that most police, doctors, and judges are men and this fact may affect their treatment of rape victims. For example, in a June 1977 rape trial in Wisconsin, a judge released a convicted 15-year-old boy remarking that he had reacted only "normally" in a community known to be "permissive." In that situation, the community mobilized and successfully sought to repeal the judge. Such consequences are not frequent. In the same state in 1981, another judge called a five-year old female victim of sexual assault by a 24-year-old man "an unusually sexually permissive young lady" ("Judge," 1982).

Only one complaint of rape in four results in an arrest, and only one in 60 ends with a conviction, according to a two-year research project by the Law Enforcement Assistance Administration (LEAA) released in August 1978 ("New," 1978). Consequently, prosecutors often are reluctant to pursue rape cases since a low percentage of convictions is "not good for one's career." Due to judicial treatment and the fact that courts frequently do not make convictions, many women fail to report the crime in order to spare themselves additional trauma. Russell (1984) estimates that only one in ten rape or rape attempts is ever reported.

Reporting the crime may itself be traumatic because of treatment by the police. Field research and personal reports have indicated that police officers often treat the victim as if she were the guilty party. In fact, Feild (1978) and Holmstrom & Burgess (1981) found that the attitudes of police officers toward rape did not differ from those of convicted rapists on four out of seven dimensions. As a consequence of all this, the LEAA estimates that four out of five rapes never even are reported. Minority women are least likely to report rape although they tend to be the most frequent victims

(Feldman-Summers & Ashworth, 1981). Their reluctance may be due to the fact that minority women are least likely to be believed.

Because nearly half of all women will be a victim of an attempted or actual rape at some point in their lives, the fear of rape serves as an important form of social control (Griffin, 1979; Riger & Gordon, 1981). This fear keeps women passive and dependent, especially on men. This fear also keeps women at home, especially at night. Brownmiller (1975) argues that rape thus serves as "a conscious process of intimidation by which *all* men keep *all* women in a state of fear" (p. 15). Avoidance strategies traditionally recommended for females (don't go out at night, don't anger your assailant) reinforce this type of social control and have been demonstrably ineffective (Bart & O'Brien, 1984); much more effective in avoiding rape are multiple strategies, especially those combining yelling and using physical force. Even some fashion designers and advertisers exert a form of social control over women by encouraging clothing (such as tight skirts and high heels) that suggests sexuality but that limits a woman's ability to escape or defend herself from attack. Designer Karl Lagerfeld, in showing his 1984 spring collection, said his new designs were "shaped to be raped" (L. Anderson, 1984).

Laws against rape originated to protect the rights of males, not the rights of women (Brownmiller, 1975; Griffin, 1975, 1979). Because a woman was viewed as her father's property, to be bartered in marriage, virginity was important to ensure exclusive "ownership" for the prospective husband—hence, the assumption that raping a virgin is more serious than raping a nonvirgin because the virgin is more highly valued by men. For example, in Florida in 1983, a 36-year-old man who had consensual sex with a 12-year-old girl was convicted of a misdemeanor rather than a felony, because the girl was not a virgin (Volsky, 1983). After marriage, a woman "belongs" to her husband, and this is the reason a man cannot be accused of raping his wife in most states—she already is his "property." People with traditional sex-role attitudes, especially those who are most religious (in terms of Judeo-Christian religions) are least likely to disapprove of forced marital intercourse (Jeffords, 1984).

Given the way sexual behavior fits into a culture that encourages male dominance, recent revelations of male sexual abuse of children perhaps should not be surprising (Herman & Hirschman, 1981; Rush, 1980; Russell, 1984; Silver, Boon, & Stones, 1983; Timnick, 1985). It has been estimated that between one-quarter to two-thirds of all women have been victims of sexual abuse as children. Father-daughter incest in particular is much more common than previously thought, although apparently not new. Freud, for example, in the late 19th century, was aware of many reports of female children abused by their fathers or other family members, but chose to disbelieve his women patients. Father-daughter incest is most likely to occur in highly patriarchal families, and the effects on the daughter are devastating and long-lasting.

The publicity over incest and sexist notions regarding rape has begun to bring a change in some people's attitudes, especially those of women. But another crime, also an extension of the glorification of aggression, violence, and dominance of the male sex role, is misunderstood and devalued—wife beating.

Wife Beating. It has been estimated that the incidence of battered wives ranges from 4% to 40% of all wives (Resick, 1983). It is difficult to get precise estimates of the number of women affected because most cases are not reported to the police. (See Moore, 1979; Walker, 1979, 1984, for more thorough accounts of this crime.)

Whether the incidence of such assaults is increasing or whether just the reporting of them is, the numbers are startling and serious. Many women's groups currently are trying to set up shelters for battered wives and are pressuring the police and the courts to be more responsive to their problems. Researchers are beginning to probe the reasons for both the behavior of the husband and that of the wife (see Bayes, 1981; Resick, 1983, for recent findings). In general, gender stereotypes and expectations, marital roles, traditional attribution patterns, and situational factors appear to have much to do with the problem.

The crimes discussed so far have been committed by men. However, gender stereotypes, in relation to criminal behavior, can affect women as well.

Women and Crime. While most crimes are committed by males, the rate of female crime appears to be increasing rapidly. Between 1960 and 1975, arrests increased over 100% for women but only 23% for men. The highest arrest rates were for juvenile females (Sarri, 1979; Mann, 1984; Widom, 1978). Since the mid-1970s, the relative increase in arrest rates of women has been quite modest (Gove, 1985). The crimes that increased the most for females were embezzlement, larceny, forgery, and fraud—all property crimes. Even more so than her male counterpart, the female criminal usually is interested more in improving her financial circumstances than in violence (Adler, 1975, 1981). Women no longer are limiting themselves to the so-called feminine crimes of shoplifting and prostitution.

Although some people have tried to blame the rise in female crime directly on the women's movement, studies of female offenders show that they generally have traditional sex-role views, sometimes more so than females of comparable age and socioeconomic level (Widom, 1978, 1979, 1984b). In addition, female offenders do not differ from nonoffenders in terms of sex-typed characteristics, nor are their crimes an assertion of equal rights. In fact, some female criminals may be operating to gain male approval or operating in auxiliary roles (Weisheit, 1984). Still, the trend toward more equality for males and females may underlie some of these statistics. As more women seek and obtain jobs, they probably experience stresses and frustrations similar to those that men experience. Some women, therefore, may attempt similar solutions. For example, with more women working in banks, embezzlement by women becomes more possible. [However, it should be noted that the majority of crimes by women do not fall into the white-collar category (Widom, 1978).] Even old frustrations may be alleviated in new ways (that is, by crime) as women stop blaming themselves for their situation and start blaming society, as many men have done. And guns, more prevalent than ever in crimes, are a great equalizer of strength. Adler (1975), an expert on female crime, predicts that "as the social status of women approaches that of men, so . . . will the frequency and nature of their crimes" (p. 42). The most promising explanation for female crime is likely to be multifaceted, including both individual, situational, and societal factors (Weisheit, 1984; Widom, 1984a).

Yet, crimes by males, especially violent crime, still greatly exceed that by females, and do so around the world (Adler, 1981). Some writers (Mann, 1984; Sarri, 1979; Weisheit, 1984) question whether there has been a true increase in crimes committed by females at all, especially because differences in the sizes of the cohorts being compared rarely have been controlled for. Reporting practices also have become more formal, and police are less willing to release women for minor offenses than before. The most frequent offenses for which women are brought into court are drunk driving, disorderly conduct, illegal lotteries, prostitution, and narcotics violations. Thus, it may be that women are turning to alcohol and drugs more than even property crime as a way to deal with their frustrations. Certainly the incidence of female alcoholism has skyrocketed in recent years (see Chapter 9).

One difficulty in evaluating criminal statistics correctly is that so many biases operate in the penal and judicial systems. In general, adult women traditionally are less likely to be arrested and often are treated more leniently by the courts than are their male counterparts, part of a paternalistic pattern of discrimination (Sarri, 1979; Warren, 1981; Weisberg, 1982; Widom, 1978). However, they are more likely to be picked up for certain offenses than are their male counterparts—for example, prostitution. This differential treatment by sex is even more the case with adolescents. Female adolescents generally are dealt with more punitively by the criminal justice system than are male youths. For example, nearly 75% of underage females arrested, as opposed to fewer than 30% of the boys, are charged with a noncriminal "status offense" such as promiscuity, running away from home, or "bad behavior" (Mann, 1984; Milton, Pierce, & Lyons, 1977). Such girls also are more likely to be detained and held longer than boys accused of criminal offenses. Until recently, in some states, women who were 18 were treated as minors while their male peers were tried as adults. Another disparity is that in some jurisdictions some crimes, especially sex-related ones (for example, statutory rape and homosexuality), are exclusively male offenses.

In sum, crime statistics are frequently influenced by the gender stereotypes. Many crimes, especially those committed by men (by far the majority of crimes), can be viewed as an extension of the masculine mystique of violence and aggression.

Sports. Another area in which the male mystique of violence and aggression can be seen is in sports. Although defined as "good clean fun," many sports (the contact ones—football, hockey, boxing, wrestling, basketball, soccer) involve often serious and violent confrontations. The frequent injuries to the participating athletes demonstrate the violent nature of these sports. The greater the danger of injury and the more combative the activities, the more the sport and its players are likely to be viewed as "masculine" (David & Brannon, 1976; Farrell, 1974; Fasteau, 1974). Sports such as golf or swimming, which are neither combative nor extremely competitive, generally do not earn the "masculine" label. Perhaps not coincidentally, there is considerable evidence that athletes in the contact, "masculine" sports, tend to be more violent in their attitudes and behaviors than are comparable groups of nonathletes, or than athletes in noncontact sports, at least on college campuses (J. Brown, 1982; J. Brown & Davies, 1978).

Watching contact sports may give vicarious satisfaction of aggressive impulses and affirm one's masculinity (Fasteau, 1974; Tuohy, 1985). The increasing popularity of watching such sports relative to watching noncontact sports suggests that there may be fewer outlets for aggressive impulses than there were previously. Physical strength can no longer be taken as the measure of manhood in the modern world. Yet many men still are learning aggressive behaviors as part of their sex role. Sports, being one of the few areas where strength still counts, may be one of the few remaining socially acceptable outlets for aggression. So aggression in sports may continue, and some players may endure physical pain and injury to prove they are "men." Aggression among sports fans also may occur, as evidenced in the bloody 1985 riot by British soccer fans in Belgium (Tuohy, 1985).

As was discussed in Chapter 8, one result of this connection between sports and aggression may be that many young boys (and girls) develop a distorted view of sports and athletics (Pleck, 1976b). Rather than viewing athletics as a way to develop and enjoy one's body and have fun, athletics may become equated with combat and aggression. As a result, some adolescents may reject athletic activity completely and may lose touch with their bodies as well. The recent interest in physical fitness for females and males, such as in jogging and aerobics, may reflect a move away from the equating of sports with aggression and toward a more balanced view of physical activities.

War

In many ways, war may be viewed as similar to violent athletic contests (Fasteau, 1974). In both situations, one side is pitted against the other, both trying to win. In both, the allowable level of violence is not always clear or clearly adhered to. Some writers (Fasteau, 1974; Gilder, 1979) view the military, and contact sports as well, as the last bastion of "masculinity"—where some men can act out, to the utmost, the aggressive, competitive, unfeeling sex role they have been socialized into. This may explain, in part, the strong resistance to allowing women to join in these particular activities.

Throughout most of history, militarism and "masculinity" have been strongly linked, whereas nonviolence and pacifism have been linked with "femininity" (Cambridge Women's Peace Collective, 1984). [Militarism is the view that all problems can be solved by force; patriarchy (male dominance) spawns militarism, with nuclear weaponry as a direct by-product (Feminism & Nonviolence Study Group, 1983).] The current concern over nuclear war has fueled a strong international peace movement dominated by women (Cambridge Women's Peace Collective, 1984; McAllister, 1982). For example, women in Seneca Falls, New York; Greenham Common, England; and Comiso, Sicily, have created women-only peace camps near military sites to protest what they perceive as a threat to peace and to human lives.

However, there is much controversy among feminists as to whether the simple equation of men with war and women with peace is wise, or indeed accurate (see Stiehm, 1983; Feminism & Nonviolence Study Group, 1983). Is it more consonant with feminism for women to resist becoming warriors or to refuse to be excluded from the military? Should war and peace issues take precedence over other feminist concerns? Should women involved in Third-World wars of liberation be looked at positively or negatively? The issues of war and peace are complex and important, yet their association with gender concerns makes understanding and resolving these issues even more difficult.

Summary

This chapter has examined two global consequences of the gender stereotypes. In a variety of areas, women consistently have little power. Although they may have some personal power in a relationship, even there males tend to dominate. Institutionally, power remains in the hands of White males—economically, politically, legally, and militarily. Although women are gaining in the employment area, their progress in the power area is extraordinarily slow and difficult. Women's lack of power means men virtually run our society. Consequently, society generally functions using the standards of the male gender stereotype: competition, achievement, aggression, hierarchical relationships, and insensitivity to feelings. Thus, our society, in general, has been run for profit and the good of a few, those at the top of the status hierarchy, rather than for the benefit of the many.

Major aspects of the male sex role that are strongly emphasized by our society are aggression and "toughness." This emphasis may be associated with crime rates, especially violent, aggressive crimes by males (often teenagers) who may be "proving" their masculinity. The values of the male sex role also indirectly may foster the crimes of rape and wife beating, both on the rise. Greater equality for males and females in the general society seems to be related to a rise in crime by females, which has become more similar in some respects to crime by males. But crime by males still is far more frequent. The "masculine" emphasis on violence and aggression also is evident in the traditional "masculine" sports and in war—two areas compatible with the "male mystique." Changes here may mean less emphasis on contact sports compared to noncontact sports, fewer injuries, and perhaps less chance of war or fewer acts of meaningless violence in a war.

Recommended Reading

Abzug, B., with Kelber, M. (1984). *Gender gap: Bella Abzug's guide to political power for American women.* Boston: Houghton Mifflin. A fascinating discussion not only of the issues on which men and women tend to differ, but of the role of women in politics in the last 15 years.

Brownmiller, S. (1975). *Against our will: Men, women and rape.* New York: Simon & Schuster. A powerful feminist analysis of rape as a "natural" product of our gender stereotypes.

Dworkin, A. (1981). *Pornography: Men possessing women.* New York: Perigee/Putnam. This hard-hitting book presents the case that pornography is dangerous to women.

Scott, H. (1984). *Working your way to the bottom: The feminization of poverty.* Boston: Routledge Kegan Paul. A short well-written book describing how and why women everywhere are becoming a growing share of the poor.

Stiehm, J. (Ed.) (1983). *Women and men's wars.* Oxford: Pergamon. An excellent collection of essays exploring the issues of whether women should become warriors, or resist war.

Walker, L. E. (1979). *The battered woman.* New York: Harper & Row. Presents a social learning theory framework for understanding the battered woman and her situation. Includes an impressionistic study of 120 battered women.

Part 4: Summary

In the preceding four chapters, the effects of gender stereotypes on individuals and their relationships and on society in general have been examined. The evidence is persuasive that the stereotypes negatively affect nearly all aspects of human and societal functioning for men as well as women.

On a personal level, many women experience a negative self-concept, particularly low self-confidence and self-blame for failures, constricted achievement behavior and fear of success in masculine-defined activities, and serious problems in adjustment and mental health, particularly depression. Many men suffer from physical health problems as well as from overconfidence and fear of success in feminine-defined activities. Both sexes, if strongly sex typed, suffer from behavioral constriction and inflexibilty, especially those who are feminine sex typed. All these consequences can be traced to the gender stereotypes.

On a relationship level, both sexes experience difficulty in forming close relationships with members of the same sex and of the other sex. This is especially true for males, and may account for the sometimes superficial quality of their relationships with friends, lovers, spouses, and children. Women, who more often are trained for and steered into interpersonal relationships, frequently experience marked disappointment in their relationships with men, and marriage often is a great stress for them. Because of the Motherhood Mandate, many women become trapped in that role. Negative effects then may occur for the woman, her husband, and the children.

Fathers may become trapped in the breadwinner role, resulting in minimal interactions with their children and negative effects on the entire family.

On a societal level, the gender stereotypes have led to marked prejudice against women by both men and women; underutilization and discrimination against women in the world of work in terms of hiring, status, and salary; a dramatic lack of power by women vis-à-vis men in the areas of economics, politics, law, and military affairs; and high rates of male aggression and violence as revealed in crime rates, sports, and war.

The effects of these stereotypes may be seen in the priorities of American society—profit, concrete rewards, competitiveness, dominance, unemotional functioning, aggression—that is, the masculine stereotype. This is in contrast to a society in which human life and human qualities are valued above profits, a less hierarchical and authoritarian mode of operation, greater concern with the quality of life, cooperative efforts—that is, the feminine stereotype. Evidence was presented to argue that androgynous functioning, the incorporation of positive masculine and feminine stereotyped characteristics—the agentic with the expressive, as in an action-oriented concern about the environment—would improve not only individual functioning and adjustment but societal functioning as well.

The next section will explore the implications of such changes and ways to achieve them. Problems that might arise also will be discussed.

Part 5
Alternatives to Gender Stereotypes

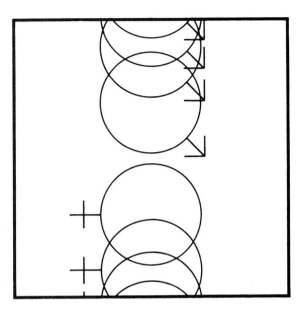

In the preceding chapters, the traditional gender stereotypes, their underpinnings, origins, and consequences have been examined in some detail. A study of the material leads to the conclusion that such stereotypes have little basis in facts and, in today's world, are dysfunctional for individuals, their relationships, and society in general. This section will address itself to some alternatives to rigid sex typing, ways to achieve such changes, and the implications of such changes for our society.

13 Beyond Sex Roles and Gender Stereotypes

Instead of a society where females attempt to be "feminine" (nurturant, emotional, intuitive) and fear being called "mannish," and males attempt to be "masculine" (aggressive, logical, strong) and fear being called "effeminate," imagine a society where each individual can develop in her or his own unique way. This chapter will examine how to transcend sex roles and gender stereotypes. Models and modes of change, problems, and some of the implications for individuals, society, and institutions will be considered.

Goals

Moving beyond sex roles and gender stereotypes is an enormous and difficult endeavor. The first difficulty is having some idea of what we are changing to, or toward. The clearest goal of change presented to date is the concept of androgyny, as discussed throughout the book. But many writers argue that we must move beyond androgyny as well as traditional sex roles; that is, we must transcend sex roles entirely. Before discussing this idea, we will summarize briefly the concept of androgyny as a goal, and why many feel that that goal is insufficient.

Androgyny

As described by Bem (1976) and refined by A. Kaplan (1979; Kaplan & Bean, 1976), androgyny refers to flexibility of sex role, the integration of strong "masculine" (agentic) and "feminine" (expressive) traits in unique ways, influenced by individual differences across situations and over the span of one's life. Individuals who alternate between "masculine" and "feminine" behavior in inflexible ways are not

androgynous, according to our definition. Thus a woman who is always very competitive and aggressive at work but very passive and dependent at home (or vice versa) and who is unable to adjust her behavior to what the situation requires is neither integrated nor flexible and is therefore not androgynous. Uniqueness refers to the fact that because androgynous individuals would no longer be restricted by stereotyped behavior, it is impossible to predict their behavior across situations. For example, an individual may be nurturant in one situation, assertive in another, sensitive in a third, and rational in a fourth. Thus, each individual will have the opportunity to develop his or her potential to its fullest, without the restriction that only gender-appropriate behaviors be allowed.

Still, the concept of androgyny has many problems, as discussed in Chapter 1 and throughout the book. Let us briefly examine them again.

Problems. Methodological problems were discussed in Chapter 1. Different androgyny scales apparently are measuring different things, yet all use the same terminology.

For our current purposes, a bigger problem is definitional. As Trebilcot (1977) argues, androgyny can mean two things: (1) *monoandrogynism,* where both "feminine" and "masculine" characteristics exist together in every individual; and (2) *polyandrogynism,* whereby people could develop any set or sets of traits at all, regardless of their biological sex. Most psychologists when using the term *androgyny* are referring to the first definition, *monoandrogynism.* Indeed, that is how androgyny is defined operationally, as in the Bem Sex-Role Inventory. As a number of writers have argued, however, the concept of monoandrogynism may become as restrictive as traditional sex roles if everyone *must* develop both agentic and expressive characteristics. In this sense, polyandrogynism, or sex role transcendence, allows individuals greater freedom.

Another problem with the psychological concept of androgyny is that it is based on defining two distinct sets of personality characteristics, one called "masculine," the other "feminine." In this sense, androgyny as a concept has a built-in obsolescence (Bem, 1979; Locksley & Colton, 1979). If people stop adhering to such characteristics, and if the two gender stereotypes become modified and less distinct from each other, androgyny in its current sense no longer would be meaningful. This problem can be circumvented by speaking of agentic and expressive attributes, instead of sex-role attributes, as Spence and Helmreich (1979a, 1980) suggest. Thus, androgyny could mean a flexible integration of agentic and expressive qualities; sex typing of these qualities could be ignored.

Furthermore, we simply do not know enough about androgynous individuals to assert that androgyny is always superior to sex typing. Related to this problem are the findings discussed in Chapter 9 indicating that high "masculinity" scores, as measured by the Bem Sex-Role Inventory and the Personal Attributes Questionnaire, may be related more to effective personal functioning and self-esteem than high androgyny scores per se (for example, Taylor & Hall, 1982). These findings reinforce the view that there are serious hazards in using androgyny as a new criterion of mental health. What we need is to define healthy human functioning independent of gender-related characteristics (Olds & Shaver, 1980; Vogel, 1979). That is, we need to construct an ideal of adult behavior without reliance on traditional concepts of "femininity" and "masculinity." We need also to pay more attention to situational factors, because different traits are used in different situations (Uleman & Weston, 1984). We need to determine those situations in which androgyny is more functional than sex typing, those in which sex typing is more functional than androgyny, and those in which sex typing per se is irrelevant (Lenney, 1979b; Locksley & Colton, 1979).

A fourth difficulty with the concept of androgyny is that it does not, in fact, eliminate sex differences. Males and females can be androgynous in different ways—that is, by having different combinations of agentic and expressive qualities. For example, males may be androgynous by being strongly athletic, aggressive, dominant, warm, affectionate, and unpredictable. Females may be androgynous by being strongly self-reliant, assertive, ambitious, compassionate, soft-spoken, and loving of children. (These are hypothetical combinations.) Although there have been some suggestions that androgynous females and males may differ from each other behaviorally (Jones et al., 1978; Wiggins & Holzmuller, 1978), studies have not examined yet whether there are different components of androgyny in females and males. One study that examined this question by separately factor analyzing the response of male and female graduate students to the BSRI did find different factor structures for the sexes (Pedhazur & Tetenbaum, 1979). To the extent that the sexes still might be socialized into developing different attributes as a function of their sex, androgyny itself would not eliminate that problem.

Alexandra Kaplan (1979) proposes that there really are two stages of androgyny. The first is the *dualistic* stage where "masculine" and "feminine" characteristics coexist but are not necessarily integrated. The second, more advanced level, is the *hybrid* stage where each group of characteristics truly becomes integrated and tempered by the other. Indeed, in this advanced stage, speaking of androgyny at all would be misleading since such a term implies two differing sets of gender-related characteristics. As Garnets and Pleck (1979) suggest, we need to go beyond merely broadening the sex-role norms. Rather, we need to transcend the norms themselves and help make sex roles less salient.

Transcendence

In the transcendence model, personality traits would be divorced from biological sex. Trebilcot (1977) called this model *polyandrogynism*. When transcendence occurs, people can be just people—individuals in their own right, accepted and evaluated on their own terms. Bem's (1979; 1981b; 1984) most recent writing also reflects this point of view. Non-sex-typed persons are thought to use gender distinctions less frequently than sex-typed persons in perceiving and structuring their environment. Whereas a sex-typed person might describe a social situation by first noting the number or proportion of males and females present, a non-sex-typed individual might describe the same situation without making any note of gender facts.

When sex roles and stereotypes are transcended, each individual will be different from others, because each individual has different capabilities and interests. Conceptions of a completely unisexual society with no sex differences (for example, Winick, 1968) are not models of androgyny and, as we'll see in the next paragraph, they are more scare tactics than they are realistic alternatives.

Winick suggests that without gender stereotypes, a society of neuters would develop, with males and females indistinguishable from each other in behavior and appearance. According to him, a likely consequence of such a society would be the lack of sexual attraction between the sexes and the eventual extinction of the species. Besides the obviously alarmist conjecturing involved (sexual attraction is learned and is not contingent on certain hair styles or behavior), without gender stereotypes society would not be "neuter" or regulated in its conformity at all. Individual differences abound and are much greater than sex differences for nearly all measurable behaviors and attributes. Such differences would remain, but the negative consequences now experienced by individuals who do not conform to current sex-role norms would be eliminated.

Implicit in this definition of androgyny is the concept of transcending traditional sex-role polarities to reach a new level of synthesis. Transcendence is not just a question of combining what have been considered opposite qualities, but is rather a third dimension. There appear to be at least three stages in reaching sex-role transcendence, as discussed in Chapter 7 (Parsons & Bryan, 1978; Rebecca, Hefner, & Olenshansky, 1976). First is the stage of the thesis or initial proposition. This first stage represents an undifferentiated conception of sex roles. Such a conception exists in preschool children who have not yet learned the sex dichotomy. From this stage stems the antithesis, the opposite of the initial proposition. Stage II is a polarized either/or conception of sex roles. Here, males and females are seen as opposite and distinct from each other in nearly all behaviors. This stage is cognitively necessary in order for a young child to organize her or his world. Everything is classified absolutely into black/white; good/bad; masculine/feminine; and so on. But the antithesis too is one-sided and generates its own countervailing force. The third stage thus combines or synthesizes these propositions into a new and more balanced whole. Stage III involves first a transition to androgyny and then a transcendence of sex roles. Here, an individual is able to move and behave freely and adaptively as a function of the situation. In this stage, a person might act tenderly with a child, forcefully with subordinates, and sympathetically with a friend. The world, in this stage, is not divided into polarities of "masculinity" and "femininity." Rather, it is composed of unique individuals with different aptitudes and potentials.

A majority of individuals and institutions of the Western world appear to be fixed at the Stage II level of polarities. Yet Stage III functioning is possible, although probably not before late adolescence. It evolves over a long period of time, is facilitated by societal supports, and is a dynamic, not a final, process. Given present socialization practices, differentiation of "masculine" and "feminine" might well be a precondition of the integration of the two (M. White, 1979). Furthermore, from the middle twenties on, males score increasingly "feminine" on traditional "masculinity-femininity" scales (Constantinople, 1973; Fischer & Narus, 1981b). Middle-aged people, especially, admit to and display traits usually considered appropriate only for the other sex (Neugarten & Gutmann, 1968; Sheehy, 1976). In fact, such an integration is considered part of the healthy adult by some personality theorists, such as Erikson (1963), Jung (1956), and Maslow (1962).

Thus, the major thrust of change should be on transcending gender stereotypes. Androgyny simply is one way that may be done, at least in this transitional period. It certainly is not the only nor necessarily the best way and it may not be the endpoint of change.

With these cautions in mind, we now will examine three different ways of conceptualizing social change.

Models of Social Change

There are three basic models that can be used in conceptualizing social change for equality between the sexes (the meaning of the term *feminism*): liberal feminism, socialist feminism, and radical feminism.

We will discuss each in turn, starting with the most conservative (see M. Andersen, 1983; Deckard, 1983; Donovan, 1985; Jaggar & Struhl, 1978, for more details).

Liberal Feminism

In liberal feminism, the stress is on equality of opportunity between the sexes. There is no critique of societal inequalities, such as between social classes, or between races. The goal is to obtain for women economic, political, and social rights equal to those of men within the existing system. Sex roles are seen as inhibiting both women and men, although "innate" differences between the sexes may exist. Because the roots of women's oppression are seen in terms of sexist discrimination, actions that stem from this model are aimed at changing the institutional and organizational levels of society where inequities occur.

This model dates back to 1792 with Mary Wollstonecraft's essay "A Vindication on the Rights of Women." Current feminists, such as Betty Friedan and Gloria Steinem, magazines like *Ms.*, and organizations like the National Organization for Women, work within this model of social change. Their actions are directed at changing laws (for example, passing the Equal Rights Amendment), and equalizing educational and employment opportunities. Because a central emphasis of this model is that a person's abilities are learned through socialization, a relearning of traditional sex-role attitudes and behaviors must occur before egalitarian gender relations are possible. This model

is the mainstream feminist perspective, and its adherents tend to be middle-class and upper-middle-class professional and career women. Some men also are involved. This model has the most widespread appeal of the three, since it reflects Western cultural values of individualism and personal achievement.

This model is sometimes referred to as an *assimilation* model, in which women are encouraged to assume the lifestyle and characteristics of the mainstream male culture. The assumption underlying this model creates problems. Institutions run by "masculine" values (that is, most institutions) are goal- (that is, profit-) oriented, competitive, aggressive, and insensitive to human values. Furthermore, women are unlikely to be assimilated into high-paying jobs where competition with men would be the strongest. Because many higher positions require an unpaid wife to fulfill social obligations and take care of domestic functioning, women would still be at a disadvantage even if they obtained such positions. Adjusting women's lives to the standards of the Establishment (Bernard, 1971) would do little to alleviate the negative consequences of such institutional practices. Women would just learn to be as competitive, aggressive, and insensitive as are many men (Bernard, 1974). Because the uninterrupted work pattern would continue to be the norm, women and men interested in child-rearing would continue to be at a disadvantage. Furthermore, class and race distinctions are ignored in this model.

Socialist Feminism

Socialist feminism is based on, but goes beyond, the traditional Marxist view of society. It arose in the 1970s as a result of feminists' dissatisfaction with the traditional Marxist perspective on women and the family (see Chapter 6; also Eisenstein, 1979; Hartmann, 1976; MacKinnon, 1982; Mitchell, 1971). In contrast to liberal feminism, this model emphasizes the necessity of changing our economic system as a precondition for the establishment of gender equality. Economic oppression and sexist oppression both are seen as fundamental and as reinforcing of each other. A few wealthy White men exploit the working class and all men exploit women, because women earn less than men in the marketplace and their labor at home receives no pay at all.

Because of their emphasis on cultural institutions, like the family, within a class society, socialist feminists emphasize the distinct problems faced by women in different classes and from different racial groups. For example, the issue of birth control is different for working-class and Third-World women than it is for White upper-middle-class women. Liberal feminists ignore these distinctions and have concentrated on obtaining the right to safe and legal abortions for all women. But Third-World and working-class women also must face the problems of compulsory sterilization, and the right to conceive and bear children free from poverty and discrimination. Most of the people involved in socialist feminism are students and workers from the working class and middle class, and women from such traditional New Left groups as the civil rights movement.

Most of the activities of socialist feminists are aimed at educating people about the relationship between women's oppression and economic class oppression. Women are organized around these economic issues as well as around health-care and child-care issues. Men's sexist attitudes are seen as stemming from the capitalist economic system. Therefore, the system itself must be changed.

Radical Feminism

Whereas socialist feminism emphasizes the importance of both economic and sexist oppression, radical feminists argue that men's oppression of women is primary, and serves as the model for all other oppression (for example, economic and racial oppression). Because it is a newer ideology, radical feminism is less fully developed than socialist feminism and there are a number of different perspectives. All agree, however, that women's oppression was the first oppression historically, that it exists in virtually all societies, and that it will not be eliminated solely by social changes, such as by the abolition of a class society.

There is a disagreement among radical feminists as to the root causes of women's oppression. Some argue it rests in women's child-bearing capacities and women's resultant physical dependence on men (for example,

Firestone, 1970). Thus the full liberation of women may depend upon extrauterine production of children, a possibility that is becoming increasingly feasible. Other radical feminists (for example, G. Rubin, 1975) emphasize the importance of kinship systems that were set up to control women's sexuality and reproductive processes. As a result, offspring became products, and women were bartered and exchanged. (See Chapter 6 for further hypotheses of the origins of patriarchy.)

The goal of radical feminism is to abolish class and sex distinctions, and create a new culture based on a more balanced synthesis of male and female modes of power. To end women's oppression by men, women-centered systems and beliefs must be established. Thus change is sought on all levels, both personal and institutional. The goals of radical feminism can be accomplished through grassroots organizations and by building an alternative culture. Some radical feminists argue that in order to fight sexism fully, women must become lesbians (Bunch, 1975; Daly, 1978). Only in that way, where women have attachments to other women and not to men, could a woman-identified world be created. In this context, the personal is seen as political. Proponents of radical feminism tend to be middle-class women from the New Left, and those never before involved in politics.

In both socialist and radical feminism, society must change. It is not sufficient to encourage women to adapt their lives to the Establishment, as some feel liberal feminists have done. Rather, the Establishment itself must be changed, and adapted to the lives of women. Socialist and radical feminism differ as to how to achieve this new society. Socialist feminists view the overthrow of capitalism as primary, but it should be done with the active involvement of committed socialist feminists. This will ensure the demise of sexism. Radical feminists, on the other hand, believe that overthrowing patriarchy is primary in order to destroy sexism. For them, overthrowing patriarchy will result in the institution of socialism. There is some empirical support for this linkage of socialism with a reduction in sexism. For example, Block (1973), in examining gender stereotypes across six cultures (Norway, Sweden, Denmark, Finland, England, and the

United States), found that the countries with the longest and most well-established commitment to social welfare (Sweden and Denmark) were also the countries with fewest sex differences. (Sweden will be discussed further below.) However, recent writings about the People's Republic of China (Andors, 1983; Stacey, 1983) and the Soviet Union (Lapidus, 1982; Mamonova, 1984) suggest that Marxist models do not lead inevitably to gender equality.

If we integrate radical and socialist feminism, we come to view sexism as a result of a number of factors: the division of labor according to gender, the emergence of class systems, the formation of patriarchal relations, and the social organization of the family. We are forced to look not only at gender oppression, but at race and class oppression as well. Integrating the two models and examining sexism as it interacts with race and class factors appears to be the current trend in the development of feminist theory (M. Andersen, 1983; Donovan, 1983).

Both socialist and radical feminism partly grew out of the dissatisfaction of many New Left women in the late 1960s, who became dissatisfied with the sexist and patronizing behavior of their male colleagues in what they had thought was a joint struggle against the Vietnam War and for civil rights for Blacks. A historical look at what is loosely called "the women's liberation movement" will help throw light on the development of these three models of change. Although the cry for women's liberation has been at the heart of the movement, it is important to recognize that what is really being proposed is human liberation: freeing both women and men from the restrictiveness of their sex roles so that each individual can realize her/his full human potential. The men's liberation movement, begun in the early 1970s, reflects this broader perspective.

Liberation Movements

Women's Liberation

In the United States, the movement to grant women legal rights began in the early 1820s, and, for a time, was tied to the abolitionist movement (see Deckard, 1983, for an excellent history of the women's movement). After the Fourteenth and Fifteenth amendments were introduced in Congress in 1866, women felt betrayed. They had expected equality for both Blacks and women, but these amendments only granted all male citizens the right to vote. In fact, these amendments introduced the word *male* into the Constitution for the first time. In response, feminists like Susan B. Anthony and Elizabeth Cady Stanton formed organizations to guarantee women equal rights. From the beginning of the 20th century to 1920, the women's rights movement gained momentum and culminated in the passage of the Nineteenth amendment, guaranteeing women's right to vote. Because of the single goal of most groups, however, after this goal was achieved, most of the women's groups disappeared. The Equal Rights Amendment was successfully introduced into Congress in 1923 but not passed, and the women's liberation movement became dormant for about 40 years. Still, there was a steady influx of women into the labor force between 1920 and 1940, increasing dramatically during World War II.

After World War II many women who had been urged to join the labor force during the war were urged to leave to make room for the returning male soldiers. Of course, many others willingly quit to have families. During the 1950s, the "feminine mystique" was promoted (Friedan, 1963): women should be mothers, housewives, and consumers, roles very profitable to an industrialized capitalistic society changing over from peak wartime production to peacetime production. During the early 1960s, society itself began to change: the "baby-boom" children rediscovered a social conscience and became active in civil rights, the New Left, and the antiwar movement. Some males began rejecting the masculine mystique and the goals of blind patriotism and productivity. Some also began rediscovering sensuality and emotionality. Hence, the occurrence of "hippies," draft resistance, and concern about ecology. On another level, career women also were becoming mobilized. In 1961, the federal Commission on the Status of Women was formed and documented women's second-class status. State commissions followed, and the federal Equal Employment Opportunity Commission (EEOC) was established on the basis of, among other things, complaints of discrimination.

Two forces—younger New Left women and older career women—became welded together into a movement in the late 1960s as a result of a series of crises (J. Freeman, 1975). Their orientations and values, however, remained different. The older group became dissatisfied with the refusal of EEOC to take "sex discrimination" complaints seriously and they formed their own political and professional organizations. The National Organization for Women (NOW) was founded in 1966 by Betty Friedan, followed by the Women's Equity Action League, Federally Employed Women, and many professional women's caucuses.

At the same time, women from New Left and civil rights organizations became dissatisfied with the traditional roles they were being forced to take in the movements (making coffee, typing, and so forth). They spontaneously formed their own groups in 1967 and 1968, focusing on personal revolution through grass-roots organizing and consciousness-raising groups.

These two groups remained separate, the older branch functioning as a pressure group, focusing on political, legal, and economic changes. This movement developed into what we have termed *liberal feminism*. The younger branch focused on consciousness raising and individual changes and, later, institutional changes. This younger branch divided itself into two groups, socialist feminists and radical feminists. Despite their differences, all groups agreed on two theoretical concerns: criticism of the gender-stereotyped division in our society, and the view that sexism exists as institutionalized discrimination, sometimes beyond conscious awareness. The two core concepts of sexism are that men are more important than women and that women exist to please and serve men (Freeman, 1975). The goal of the women's movement, then, is to eradicate sexism and replace it with the concepts of equality and liberation. The former means that the sexes are equal and therefore differential sex roles must go; the latter means that the sex roles themselves must be changed since they are restric-tive. Thus, the goal of the women's movement is really human liberation.

The women's movement in the 1980s is quite fragmented, but alive and well, albeit in different forms (see Ferree & Hess, 1985). Rather than a single movement, there are a variety of groups operating to eliminate sexism in different ways. As we have seen, there are at least three different models of feminism— liberal feminism, socialist feminism, and radical feminism. Each model attacks sexism from a different perspective. And there are subgroups as well—lesbian feminists, Third-World feminists, and so on. People have been claiming the demise of the "women's liberation movement" for years (for example, Dixon, 1983), especially since the defeat of the Equal Rights Amendment in 1982. But the movement has not died; rather it has evolved in two directions. One is toward socialist and radical feminism, giving more attention than does liberal feminism to structural, class, and race issues. The second direction has been to become absorbed into mainstream thought. For example, in 1972, 47% of the U.S. public agreed that women should have an equal role with men in running business, industry, and government; by 1980, 58% agreed (Deckard, 1983). The change in ideology has been greatest among women. For example, in 1970, 40% of women favored efforts to strengthen women's status in society; in 1980, 64% of the women were in favor (Deckard, 1983). Indeed, 57% of a nationwide sample of American women in 1984 believe that the women's movement "has just begun" (Steinem, 1984). Of course, liberal feminists still exist and are working on a number of different fronts in the 1980s: (1) the way women are portrayed in the media, (2) equal opportunity in employment and education, (3) child care, (4) the position of the homemaker, (5) woman's right to control her own body, (6) violence against women, and (7) the Equal Rights Amendment.

Men's Liberation

As a result of the changes women were making and the questions they were asking, and also as a result of the inherent strain of the male role, many men began reevaluating their roles and raising their own consciousness. To this end, the men's liberation movement arose in the early 1970s and has been slowly growing, especially in urban areas (Astrachan, 1984; Berkeley Men's Center, 1974; David & Brannon, 1976; Doyle, 1983; Sawyer, 1970; Tolson, 1977). The focus is on the changes men want in their lives and how best to achieve them. The men's movement generally has not been driven by a passion to change the system because most men derive too much benefit from the existing social, political, and economic systems (Astrachan, 1984; Doyle, 1983). Instead, the men's movement has tried to give men a forum in which to air and discuss their confusions and distress, as well as to gain other men's support in personal and social areas (Gross, Smith, & Wallston, in press). So far, the most common activity of this movement has been consciousness-raising (CR) groups, and many of the men in them do not consider themselves part of a "movement." The main concerns have been the stresses caused by women's changes, relationships with other men, and the male sex role itself (Astrachan, 1984; Gross et al., in press).

Although the men's movement does not yet qualify as a full-fledged social movement (Doyle, 1983), it is moving in that direction. Currently, there are two main wings: the profeminist group, and the divorce reformers (Astrachan, 1984). The profeminists, who organized the first men's CR groups in 1970, focus on personal growth, new experiences with other men, and support of the women's movement. In 1975, the first National Conference on Men and Masculinity was held, which has become an annual event. These conferences combine the personal with the political via workshops and plenary sessions. In 1983, profeminist men formed the National Organization for Changing Men. In 1984, it had close to 1000 members in more than 40 states. Its goals are to transcend the traditional male sex role, to support women's struggle for equality, and to support gay rights and fight homophobia.

Divorce reformers are a second wing of the men's movement, joined by a group of men Astrachan (1984) calls the "no-guilt" group. The divorce reformers joined together in the early 1970s in outrage at the impact of their divorce settlements. Divorce and child custody were two of the few areas in which women sometimes had a real advantage over men, although the men tended either to ignore statistics that showed how few actually pay alimony or child support, or to oppose legislation to enforce payment. At first, these men formed local organizations, like Fathers United for Equal Rights. In 1981, they formed their own national organization, the National Congress for Men. Concern about legal issues dominate, but many of the men are recognizing a common bond as well. The "no-guilt" group developed around the philosophy that men have no reason to feel guilty in their relationships with women. It emphasizes men's angers and fears, and the feeling that men as well as women are victims of sex roles—and of feminist-inspired social changes (H. Goldberg, 1976). These men at first organized into regional chapters, called Free Men. Later, many of these men joined the National Congress for Men. In 1984, membership in the Congress was estimated to be between 5,000 and 10,000 including local component organizations.

Although the men's movement still is small, it is growing. Since the mid-1970s, the number of books, newsletters (for example, "M.— Gentle Men for Gender Justice"), magazine articles, research articles, and men's studies courses (there even is a " 'Men's Studies' Newsletter") have increased dramatically (see Astrachan, 1984, for more information). For example, in 1978, a nonprofit organization called the Society for the Study of Male Psychology and Physiology was started by a group of faculty members at Bowling Green State University. At least one study has suggested that changes for women have reached a plateau and it now is men who are becoming more androgynous (Heilbrun & Schwartz, 1982).

Human Liberation

Both men's and women's liberation movements appear to be expanding slowly and infiltrating our cultural consciousness. Studies have found a decrease in traditional attitudes toward women since the early and mid-1970s (Helmreich, Spence, & Gibson, 1982; McBroom, 1984). Women have changed more than men, and younger people are changing more than older people. Level of education also predicts less traditional attitudes, although change has occurred across both class and race lines. For example, working-class women, although not strongly committed to the women's movement, generally are tolerant and sympathetic rather than hostile toward it (Ferree, 1983). Whereas 15 years ago women who wanted both to work outside the home and to have a family might have their mothering abilities questioned, this is much less true today. Indeed, the goal of combining employment and family life has become the norm for most young women. Similarly, 15 years ago, few men could talk about cooking, doing the laundry, or child care without having their masculinity questioned; this too is much less true today.

Betty Friedan (1981, 1985) argues that the second stage of feminism must include men. Men must be helped to overcome the "masculine mystique" created by the polarization of the sexes. Only when this barrier is overcome, will men be able to unite with women. She sees the needs of both sexes converging as they try to live together and raise children in dual-career marriages. Men and women need to work out the trade-offs at work and at home. Friedan's message is strongly within the liberal feminist tradition and, as such, it neglects structural changes in society. Still, it is a message that appeals to a large number of people today. After all, feminism does not mean dominance by women, but the equality of women's political and social rights with those of men. As argued throughout this book, such equality and liberation will be beneficial to all members of society.

How does change come about? How can we help move individuals and society beyond sex roles and gender stereotypes? The following section suggests some alternatives.

Modes of Change

Change needs to occur on individual, social, and institutional levels. No one tactic or orientation will accomplish the entire task. People choose their tactics based on personal preferences and their diagnoses of the problem. Their approach will be influenced by whether they view women's oppression as due, for example,

to gender socialization, value differences between masculine and feminine culture, the power inequality between women and men, or capitalism itself, with its view that women are property and cheap labor (Polk, 1976).

Personal Level

Regardless of perspective, self-change is an important part of any alteration in the social order. Ways to achieve such changes are numerous and include consciousness-raising groups, personal psychotherapy, experiential groups, general education, explicit training, and experimenting with new behaviors. Each of these ways is discussed below.

Consciousness-Raising Groups. Perhaps the most prevalent and valuable contribution of the women's movement has been the consciousness-raising (CR) group as a way to achieve personal and social change. CR groups generally consist of 7 to 15 same-sex individuals who meet together, usually weekly, to focus on members' common values, attitudes, and experiences. Many personal problems are seen as having a social cause and a political solution. Through sharing of experiences, members increase their awareness of gender stereotypes and their consequences, receive support, explore new ways of behaving and relating, and learn to trust and respect other members of their sex (J. Freeman, 1975; Kravetz, 1978; Nassi & Abramowitz, 1978; N. Rosenthal, 1984).

A key aspect of CR groups is the alteration of traditional (that is, masculine) hierarchical leadership norms. Most groups are run democratically with no fixed leader and each member is regarded as an expert. This new norm applies to the women's liberation movement itself and partially explains why many observers view the movement as disorganized and fragmented. With no recognizable leader or spokesperson, the media have a difficult time focusing on an organization—the male norm expectation here is evident.

Research has documented many changes that appear to occur as a result of CR groups: an altered world view and greater understanding of social, political, and economic factors; a clearer sense of identity and job-career orientation; a greater sense of self-acceptance and higher self-esteem and self-confidence; more egalitarian relationships with other-sex members and increased trust and respect for same-sex members; and a feeling of group solidarity (Astrachan, 1984; Farrell, 1974; J. Freeman, 1975; Kravetz, 1978; Lieberman, Solow, Bond, & Reibstein, 1979). The strongest findings have been with regard to the development of pro-feminist attitudes. The most equivocal data have been with regard to the promotion of self-esteem and personal growth. Although self-reports verify such psychological changes, results from various psychometric measures have been conflicting and few in number (Nassi & Abramowitz, 1978). All researchers agree, however, that CR groups are potent vehicles for resocialization. For men, especially, CR groups appear to be extremely powerful. By their egalitarian structure and their concern with talking about feelings and doubts, these groups challenge male gender stereotypes. For this reason, men's CR groups are more difficult to start and to continue than women's CR groups, but the experience itself often is profound (Farrell, 1974; Gross et al., in press; Pleck & Sawyer, 1974; Tolson, 1977; Weiss, 1974). However, men may find it easier to open up and explore sex-role issues via structured group programming rather than the unstructured CR group (Croteau & Burda, 1983).

A question arises as to whether these changes are brought about by CR groups themselves or because only certain predisposed individuals join such groups. The answer seems to be, both. Studies of individuals who joined women's CR groups in the late 1960s showed that members—when compared with nonmembers of similar ages, education levels, and socioeconomic levels—were more active, independent, creative, and achievement-oriented, as measured by questionnaires. More members than nonmembers had strong mothers from whom they were often estranged during adolescence. Members as a group also were less authoritarian than nonmembers, were more tolerant of ambiguity, and felt more control over their environment as measured by standardized tests (Joesting, 1971; Pawlicki & Almquist, 1973).

The goals and composition of CR groups during the 1970s seem somewhat different from those described for CR groups in the 1960s. Personal change and support have been emphasized more in the recent groups, and most women who joined the 1970s groups were already members of the women's movement (Kravetz, 1978; Kravetz, Marecek, & Finn, 1983; Lieberman et al., 1979; N. Rosenthal, 1984). Those using the groups as a form of psychological self-help were likely to be housewives, women with children, and women with higher levels of symptoms. In contrast, those who joined groups to strengthen their own feminist consciousness were more likely to be employed women and students, women without children, and women with fewer symptoms. Yet in nearly every case studied, involvement in the groups intensified the individual's ideological commitment and also produced real personal change. For example, in a before-and-after study conducted in 1976, Weitz (1982) found that participants increased their self-esteem and reduced feelings of depression, perhaps because they increased their sense of control, and learned to externalize their attributions of blame.

Friedan (1985) has suggested that what the women's movement of the 1980s needs is a new round of consciousness raising for the women brought up to believe that they could "have it all." Such women need to see that their failure to have it all is not a personal failure, but rather a societal one. It is impossible for women to have it all when careers and child care still are organized around male patterns. CR groups can help women free themselves from the double burden of guilt and isolation that the belief in "Superwoman" engenders.

Psychotherapy. A second and more traditional way of achieving personal change has been through psychotherapy. Despite popular misconception, psychotherapy is not reserved for individuals who are severely emotionally disturbed. Rather, it is a way to increase self-awareness and effect behavioral and emotional changes. This method is likely to be beneficial to most people since most of us can benefit from learning more about ourselves and our behaviors. But, as was discussed in Chapter 9, traditional psychotherapy may discriminate against women in a number of ways. It may incorporate a double standard of mental health. It may "blame the victim" by looking for personal solutions to social problems. And it may reinforce powerlessness by the hierarchical nature of the therapist/client relationship itself. Awareness of these problems has brought changes in therapeutic techniques and has given rise to a new approach, feminist or nonsexist therapy (Brodsky, 1980; Brodsky et al., 1978; A. Kaplan, 1979; Kaschak, 1981b; Robbins & Siegel, 1983; Rosewater & Walker, 1985).

In feminist therapy, anger and dependence are dealt with, gender stereotypes are discussed, and traditional assumptions regarding appropriate behavior are discarded. Clients are helped to appreciate the social/political context of their behavior, and self-nurturance is encouraged. The therapist-client relationship is nonauthoritarian and the therapist serves as a model of androgyny. Feminist therapy also can be applied to couple and family counseling, and to counseling with nontraditional clients (Hare-Mustin, 1978; Robbins & Siegel, 1983; Rosewater & Walker, 1985). Although there are many variations of feminist therapy, they all have in common the recognition that the social context is an important determinant of human behavior, and that sex roles and statuses prescribed by society are disadvantageous to both sexes, but especially to women. Feminist therapists in particular have become very involved with victims of sexual assault and family violence (Brodsky, 1980).

Because feminism refers to equality between the sexes, men as well as women can be feminist therapists or clients of feminist therapists. Some people (for example, Chesler, 1971) do argue that only women should be therapists for other women because the therapist's role as a model can be one of the most powerful aspects of therapy. Orlinsky and Howard (1976) found that of 118 women receiving outpatient psychotherapy, those being treated by men were more uncomfortable and self-critical and felt they were getting less encouragement than did women with female therapists. This was especially true of single women 18 to 28 years old. Brodsky (1980), summarizing research, con-

cludes that women who are young, single, and/or uncertain in their relationships with men, should probably see a female therapist. Yet a woman is not a better therapist simply by virtue of her sex. Counselors' reactions to female clients vary according to client age, problem type, and counselor sex (Hill, Tanney, Leonard, & Reiss, 1977). The key seems to be sensitivity and awareness of issues particularly relevant to women. Certainly men can become aware and sensitive. It may be, however, at this point in time, that feminist female therapists have more to offer other women than do feminist male therapists, who perhaps would be better working with men.

The question of using psychotherapy for males who are trying to adopt nontraditional sex roles only recently has received some consideration (Bear, Berger, & Wright, 1979; O'Neil, 1981a, 1982; Scher, 1981; Solomon & Levy, 1982). These writers have argued that counseling practitioners need to assess, conceptualize, and intervene in gender-role conflicts of clients. In particular, counselors can help men examine the degree that gender-role conflicts limit their interpersonal, physical, and emotional lives. Problems with psychotherapy could arise from the fact that many therapists may not be sensitive to the negative effects of the gender stereotypes on males, some therapists may have difficulty accepting non-sex-typed behavior in men, and different psychotherapeutic techniques may be needed with men than are needed with women. For example, groups may be particularly important for men to break down the barriers to self-disclosure built up by traditional male socialization (Croteau & Burda, 1983; Heppner, 1981).

Feminist psychotherapists have been concerned about some of the problems discussed earlier in this chapter related to using androgyny as a standard of mental health. One concern focuses on the importance of helping clients deal with the problems an androgynous sex-role orientation in a sex-typed society might involve (Franks, 1979; Kelly & Worell, 1977; Kenworthy, 1979). Another problem is helping clients move beyond the first stage of androgyny to a level of true integration and sex-role transcendence (Garnets & Pleck, 1979; A. Kaplan, 1979). Having begun as a grassroots movement during the 1970s, feminist therapy is now a legitimate school of thought (Kaschak, 1981b). As such, it continues to evolve and to influence more traditional forms of therapy such that, even if a therapy is not explicitly "feminist" it still may be nonsexist.

Experiential Groups.   A third vehicle for personal change is experiential groups or T-groups ("Training groups"). These groups have been particularly helpful in opening men up to their feelings and in improving their listening skills and interpersonal sensitivity. For this reason, some businesses have instituted such programs to improve the effectiveness of their staff. Interestingly, it is in precisely these areas that most women already are competent due to gender socialization. Putting more women who are otherwise qualified in influential positions also might achieve the business objectives, although anything that helps men increase their interpersonal sensitivity should be encouraged.

Robert Lewis (1978) reports that an increasing number of men have been attending his intimacy workshops conducted at men's conferences around the United States and Canada since 1975. These workshops focus on developing self-disclosure communication skills and the ability to extend affection. Other groups, especially those on college campuses, are more structured, aimed at helping men become more aware of their sex-role conditioning and its effects on their lives. These groups also help men learning how to live free from traditional masculine roles (Croteau & Burda, 1983).

Education.   Education, both general and specific, is a fourth way to promote individual change. Women's studies, men's studies, courses on sex roles, the psychology of women, and so on have proliferated in the last fifteen years on the college and, in a few cases, the high school level. The American Psychological Association (APA) officially accepted the psychology of women as a legitimate field of study by establishing a separate Association division in 1973. By 1979, this division had nearly 2000 female and male members and published its own journal. That work in the field is growing is indicated by the increasing number of papers presented at meetings, and in books, journal articles, and dissertations (Denmark, 1977). The National Women's Studies Association was founded in 1976, and in 1984 there were more than 20,000 women's studies courses being taught and more than 500 women's studies programs (see M. Johnson, 1982b, for more information on the psychology of women, and Bowles & Duelli-Klein, 1983, for more information on women's studies). Black women's studies (see Hull, Scott, & Smith, 1982) and lesbian studies (Cruikshank, 1982) are two offshoots of these developments.

Men's studies also has developed as a field (see Yoshihashi, 1984). Starting in 1972, a men's studies newsletter has been published semiannually by the Men's Studies Task Group of the National Organization for Changing Men. In 1975, the University of Southern California established a division for the Study of Women and Men in Society, followed by the first professorship in men's studies in 1984. In 1978, a task force on the male sex role and the psychology of women was formed, and a new APA division was proposed, the Division of the Psychology and Physiology of Men.

The general focus of all these educational endeavors is to encourage people to challenge traditional gender stereotypes and assumptions and to consider seriously the consequences of such sex typing. Research on the effects of women's studies and psychology of women courses suggests that the effects duplicate some of the results of CR groups; that is, after such courses women tend to feel better about themselves and about other women, become less traditional in their sex-role attitudes, and sometimes change their future plans (Brush, Gold, & White, 1983; Howe, 1985; M. Johnson, 1982a; Kahn & Richardson, 1983; Steiger, 1981; Vedovato & Vaughter, 1980; Zuckerman, 1983). Even 3- to 5-year-olds have been found to decrease their own gender stereotyping after being exposed to a nonsexist curriculum (Koblinsky & Sugawara, 1984). Not all studies have found such changes, however, and the effects of such courses on men are not clear.

Explicit Training.   A fifth method of achieving personal change is through explicit training. For example, some women might benefit from explicit training in problem solving (Sherman, 1976), mathematics (Tobias, 1978), career planning (O'Neil, Ohlde, Barke, Prosser-Gelwick, & Garfield, 1980), management and leadership skills (Hennig & Jardim, 1977), and self-defense (Kidder, Boell, & Moyer, 1983). Some men could benefit from training in sensitivity to women's concerns. For example, workshops designed to retrain men's perceptions of pornography have met with some success (Astrachan, 1984). Both sexes may need training in assertiveness (Alberti & Emmons, 1978). In assertiveness training, individuals are taught to discriminate among passive responses (letting others violate your rights, particularly common among women), aggressive responses (infringing upon the rights of others, particularly common among men), and assertive responses (respecting your own rights and those of others). Through role playing and homework assignments, stereotypic sex-role behaviors can be changed. A six-week group treatment program incorporating principles of both assertiveness training and consciousness raising was found to increase the assertiveness and androgyny and masculinity scores of participating feminine-sex-typed college women when these women were compared one year after participation with a matched control group who had been placed on a waiting list (Gulanick, Howard, & Moreland, 1979). Another study (Lewittes & Bem, 1983) found that undergraduate women who received three sessions of behavioral training in assertiveness later increased their participation in mixed-sex discussion groups when compared with control groups of women. It would be interesting to assess the consequences of similar programs on males.

Changing Behavior. A sixth way of achieving individual attitude change is through focusing on changing behaviors. As was discussed in Chapter 10, increasing numbers of men are trying out the role of househusband and are learning much about themselves in the process. In Chapter 11 we saw that women executives are learning how to deal with situations they had never before encountered and many wind up reevaluating previously held beliefs. Other changes are occurring on a smaller, more personal scale—a wife going

out to work, a husband doing the laundry, a woman asking a man for a date, a man refusing a sexual overture, and so on. Because behaviors and attitudes interact, such behavioral changes often increase the individual's level of awareness.

All these changes, by their very nature, occur on the individual level and thus touch only one part of the problem. They often are slow and limited to a few, highly motivated people. In addition, individual change itself is not always linear. As Kaplan and Bean (1976) suggest, we seem to follow the pendulum principle: at the beginning, there may be a move from one extreme to another, as in a move from passive to aggressive behavior. With time, however, modifications are made and a middle ground is gradually attained, as in the development of assertive behavior. Such a middle position is never static however; an external force is able to start the swing again at any time. The point to remember is that in order to reject an old, extreme behavior or attitude, a new, equally extreme behavior or attitude may temporarily be needed. It's the dialectical process again: first the thesis, then the antithesis, and finally, the synthesis. Although this process may be difficult for those dealing with someone at the time of antithesis, knowledge of its necessity and temporary nature might help.

Social Level

Changes in individual consciousness only go so far. To be effective, individuals must join together to urge changes at social and institutional levels. On a social level, changes are needed in our basic ideology, socialization practices, and relationships with others.

Ideology. The liberation movements have gone a long way toward changing the ideology of our culture. Equality and freedom of choice are becoming more the norm in personal relationships and individual functioning, although they are not always practiced. Standards of mental health, intelligence, creativity, achievement, and child rearing are all changing in a non-sex-typed direction although progress is slow and by no means continuous. Such changes are imperative, however, especially for succeeding generations. Interestingly, even though women tend to have more egalitarian values than do men, and an increasing awareness of the disparities in status between men and women, women generally do not have a group consciousness, that is a sense of identification with other women ("Group," 1982). Without such a sense of identification, which other minority groups such as Blacks and the elderly have, organizing and acting together to bring about change could be very difficult. Some indication of this was the 1984 presidential election, where the majority of women voted for President Reagan even though they recognized his policies were damaging to the status of women.

Socialization.   Because we learn our sex roles through socialization, radical changes need to be made in this area. Parents need to be made aware of the potentially maladaptive consequences of rigid sex typing. Child-rearing practices deliberately need to foster non-sex-typed functioning, such as by encouraging independence in girls and emotional sensitivity and expressiveness in boys (see Pogrebin, 1981, for some suggestions). Parents also need to try to raise their children without a schema for gender, as advocated by Sandra Bem (1983, 1984) and discussed in Chapter 7. This means deemphasizing the importance of gender in children's lives, including toys, games, clothes, and colors. Because males very likely would continue to display higher levels of aggression due to hormonal differences, they may need greater reinforcement of gentleness than girls (Gullahorn, 1977b). Language needs to become less discriminatory (for example, *Ms.* and *Mr.,* not *Miss, Mrs.,* and *Mr.*) and more egalitarian (for example, chair*person,* not chair*man*).

The media need to give a more accurate and liberated picture of the roles available for women and men. To these ends, pressure groups have formed that are having some effect. For example, Women on Words and Images, an outgrowth of the Princeton NOW chapter, studied sex typing in children's books. Their recommendations have begun to be incorporated by publishers and adopted by school systems (see Chapter 8). Women Against Violence Against Women, an activist organization based in Los Angeles, has protested media violence against women by joining with various NOW chapters in 1977 and instituting boycotts against socially irresponsible record companies. Companies that use images of violence against women as an advertising gimmick are targeted. There are groups against pornography (for example, Women Against Pornography) and groups concerned about television images (for example, Action for Children's Television).

Changing sex typing in schools also is imperative. As was discussed in Chapter 8, present school practices and organization, textbooks, curricula, and counseling all perpetuate sex typing. Laws banning any form of sex discrimination in any educational institution receiving public funds could help remedy the situation, but the laws have been narrowly interpreted, and enforcement is weak (see Chapters 8 and 11). Additionally, the changing of regulations does not necessarily change attitudes or behavior. As Guttentag and Bray (1977) found when they tried to institute curriculum changes to counteract sexism in kindergarten, fifth, and ninth grades, the teachers' own attitudes and the age and sex of the children were the most important factors: teachers who cared about the issue of sexism could change the attitudes of their students, and kindergarteners and females were especially affected by the six-week program. Thus, change *can* be effected in the schools, but it also can be thwarted by teachers' attitudes and practices. Perhaps specific training in sexism for our nation's teachers is needed (as well as training in racism, which many schools already have instituted). As a result of the Women's Equity Act of 1974, many resource materials for teachers of all grades have been developed (see S. Klein, 1985). However, many of these federally funded programs have been targeted for extinction by the Reagan administration. Parents' groups might be particularly effective in monitoring teacher behavior and school compliance with federal regulations (see the checklist put out by the Council on Interracial Books for Children, 1977). On the college and university level, the Project on the Status and Education of Women of the Association of American Colleges has a number of resource materials to help monitor and decrease sexism in higher education.

Relationships. It is very important that sex-role changes be applied to relationships, however difficult such applications may be. Safilios-Rothschild (1979) argues that social change in the United States must occur on both relationship and institutional levels and must involve *conflict confrontations* between the sexes. Such conflicts already have been occurring on the institutional level and they are needed in order to move beyond the status quo and break out of paternalistic structures. Conflict confrontations also are needed on a more personal level in order to prevent the substitution of subtle, informal discrimination for structural, institutional discrimination. It is in relationships that have a strong degree of affective and esteem feelings (such as friendships, love, and marital relationships) that such confrontations can lead to personal change and eventually to a gradual diminution of interpersonal conflict.

Jean Baker Miller (in Gordon, 1985), in discussing the psychology of the future, argues that women should work with men to restructure relationships so that men's supportive and generative qualities can be enhanced. Women should no longer bear responsibility for all the emotional work in a relationship, and men should no longer bear responsibility for all the decision making in a relationship.

Even in less personal relationships, confrontation can restructure roles. For example, exposure to overt sexist statements and actions has been found to raise the consciousness, and lead to less traditional sex-role attitudes, of other group members (Dworkin & Dworkin, 1983).

Alternative Lifestyles. A fourth way to effect change on the social level might be to provide for living situations other than the nuclear family. In a nuclear family, a strict division of labor often is encouraged and family members often feel isolated. Popularization of communes, living complexes with communal cooking and child-care arrangements, increased acceptance of single women living alone, unmarried couples living together, and single-parent families, all represent ways of providing more alternatives for more people and they facilitate breaking away from traditional sex-typed behaviors and patterns. (See Macklin, 1980; Pogrebin, 1983, for general discussions of alternatives.) However, recent research on communes in America suggest that such a lifestyle, although resulting in less competitive, hostile, and independent behaviors among its members than among noncommune peers, nevertheless frequently maintains traditional roles and statuses for women and men (Minturn, 1984; Wagner, 1982).

Institutional Level

Even though change has been progressing on the individual level and some change is beginning on the social level, the institutional level has been markedly resistant to change—although many confrontations have occurred. This level represents "the incorporation of ideology into legally required or generally expected actions" (Kaplan & Bean, 1976, p. 386). Laws, organization of work and family, direct action, and alternative institutions come under this heading and will be examined in succeeding paragraphs. The master variable on the institutional level is *power.* As was discussed previously, power in our society rests predominantly in White male hands; significant change is impossible without a reallocation of society's resources, including power. This is difficult because those in control of societal power administer it in ways that work to their continuing advantage and privilege (see Boneparth, 1982; Lipman-Blumen & Bernard, 1979, for an excellent collection of articles on the interface between sex roles and social policy). Many feminists now view electoral politics as the key to changing the power structure (for example, Katzenstein, 1984). However, even when laws change, socialized beliefs take time to follow.

Laws. There has been a tentative thrust toward enacting legislation prohibiting discrimination on the basis of sex. Yet, despite Affirmative Action guidelines, Title IX of the Higher Education Act of 1972, and other legislation, enforcement still is a problem. "Reverse discrimination" suits are increasing, especially since the 1978 *Bakke* decision. As discussed in the previous two chapters, since 1980 the Equal Employment Opportunity Commission has had its funds and staff cut, is behind in hearing sex discrimination cases, and actual prosecution has been minimal. (See Figure 13-1 for an example of grounds for a successful lawsuit.) Many requirements of existing legislation are neither comprehensive nor mandatory, and some regulatory agencies still do not enforce the legal statutes already on the books.

Perhaps most discouraging have been the failure to ratify the Equal Rights Amendment (ERA) and the equivocation regarding abortion. The ERA, proposed yearly since 1923, finally was passed by Congress in 1972. It required ratification by 38 states to become law. It fell three states short of ratification despite an extended deadline. It has been reintroduced in Congress yearly, but has yet to be passed again.

The amendment states that "Equality of rights under the law shall not be denied or abridged by the United States or any State on account of sex." It also gives Congress the power to pass appropriate legislation to enforce its provisions. The amendment calls for nothing less than equal sharing by all citizens of those rights, freedoms, privileges, and responsibilities already spelled out by the U.S. Constitution and our laws. Society would not be drastically changed, since some states (12) already have their own Equal Rights Amendments, and many laws that prohibit discrimination already exist. Passage of the ERA would make such laws uniform, stop the piecemeal approach to enforcement, express a further commitment to equality, and provide a clear basis that all discrimination, even "benign," is unconstitutional. President Reagan's administration has shown that without an ERA, federal statutes can be repealed or effectively voided by a president who doesn't enforce or who narrows the scope of the law (Honegger, 1983).

Despite its seeming reiteration of the American value that all "men" are created equal and the fact that 64% of American women and 58% of men in a nationwide poll in 1984 favor it (Thom, 1984), passage of an ERA is by no means assured, for four main reasons.

1. Many of those in opposition to the ERA have been organized effectively and supported by big business (Feinsilber, 1982). The anti-ERA movement consists of both men and women and is shaped and directed nationally by Phyllis Schlafly. Funding and support come predominantly from such politically conservative organizations as the Conservative Caucus, the John Birch Society, the American Conservative Union, and fundamentalist and Mormon churches (Komisar, 1977). Indeed, some argue that Schafly has been used as a front for right-wing organizing (Packwood, 1983).

2. Pro-ERA groups are not a homogeneous movement but are a number of diverse ideological groups that cut across party and class lines. Until 1977, they did not present a unified approach. However, in that year, NOW spearheaded an economic boycott of states that had not ratified the ERA that cost the targeted states millions of dollars in lost convention and travel business, and served to educate the public. The feminist movement did not pay as much attention as it should have to translating public support into legislative endorsement (Katzenstein, 1984). They started too late (1982) to elect women and men who were committed to equality. Next time around, NOW will seek to "create an independent third political force" (Feinsilber, 1982).

3. The states that did not ratify (mostly Deep

Reporting on the Chase Manhattan Bank $2 million job-bias settlement with female workers, *The Wall Street Journal* (11/3/78) wrote: "One named plaintiff, Irene LoRe, said she applied for a job as a credit manager with Chase in 1972 under the name I. S. LoRe. When her application went unanswered for several weeks, she filed a second, identical resume. She said she subsequently received two replies—one addressed to Mr. I. S. LoRe and one addressed to Miss I. S. LoRe. 'The one addressed to Mr. LoRe said I had a wonderful background, please call for an interview,' she said, 'The one addressed to Miss LoRe said I had a good background, but no positions are available.' "

Figure 13-1_____
Grounds for a successful lawsuit

South and Sun Belt states) have a politically conservative tradition. Despite findings from opinion polls that a majority of voters in these states have continued to favor passage of ERA, the legislators (mainly White males) have continued to vote it down.

4. Some of the issues involved, such as the draft for women and the support obligation of marital partners, are highly emotional. People's fears can be, and have been, appealed to and manipulated. Certain myths that play upon people's fears have been promulgated, apparently deliberately (Feinsilber, 1982; Packwood, 1983).

Some of the myths surrounding the ERA are the following. Figure 13-2 is a tongue-in-cheek depiction of one myth.

Myth 1. The ERA would not require a husband to support his wife and would require a wife to provide "half the income." *Fact:* What the amendment actually would require would be contributions by both members of the marriage to the marriage, but this contribution may be monetary or in terms of services. Thus, a wife who stays home and cares for house and children would be seen as making as equal a contribution to the marriage as is a husband who earns money. Thus a wife's status would increase, not decrease. This equal contribution requirement already exists in states with community property laws. Financial support would be required from the spouse able to give it to the spouse who needs it. In most cases this would be from the husband to the wife. In some

Figure 13-2

The "threat" of the ERA. (From I'm in Training to Be Tall and Blonde, *by Nicole Hollander. Copyright 1979 by Nicole Hollander. Reprinted by permission of St. Martin's Press, Inc.)*

divorce cases, husbands might receive alimony. This already is the case in some states. The U.S. Supreme Court in 1979 found that Alabama's law providing for alimony only for wives in unconstitutional (*Orr* v. *Orr*). Similar sexist laws still exist in a number of other states. Child custody would be awarded according to the best interests of the child, which is the current court practice.

Myth 2. The ERA would mean that having bathrooms and living quarters, such as in dormitories, segregated by sex would be illegal. *Fact:* This is blatantly false. The ERA deals only with public legal relationships. The constitutional right to privacy protects private behaviors such as elimination and sleeping. Even in the legal area, sex classification based on physical or functional differences would continue.

Myth 3. Women would be drafted and assigned to combat duty. *Fact:* Young women would be subject to any military draft but would not be required to perform military duties for which they were not qualified. Congress already has the power to draft women and to exempt people because of family responsibilities.

Myth 4. Husbands will have to pay Social Security taxes twice, once on their own earnings and again on the value of their wives' services as homemakers. *Fact:* This charge has no foundation. The ERA would have no impact on the establishment of Social Security benefits for homemaking activities. The concept of homemaker credit, an excellent idea, would require enactment of a separate law.

Myth 5. ERA is anti-male. *Fact:* The ERA guarantees equality for both sexes. Laws that discriminate against men (for example, alimony and child-custody laws) would also be eliminated. Interestingly, as columnist Ellen Goodman (1979) noted, following the Supreme Court's 1979 decision ruling that alimony is not for women only, it was the *anti*-ERA forces who came across as anti-male. They are the ones who protested against extending equal parenthood and alimony rights to men, demonstrating a deep-seated reluctance to "let men off the hook."

Other myths abound regarding the ERA and, in some cases, have been fostered by anti-ERA groups. Because of their sensationalism, they receive press coverage and stick in people's minds despite factual refutations. As a result of these factors, the passage of an ERA is uncertain. In 1980, the Republican party reversed its 40-year support for the ERA, and President Reagan has been quite vehement in his anti-ERA stance. Despite his 1980 campaign pledge to work within the current system to eliminate discriminatory laws, he has not done so (Honegger, 1983). Indeed, he has reduced enforcement of many existing antidiscrimination laws and narrowed the interpretation of others. Current estimates are that it will take another 10 to 25 years to get an ERA into the Constitution (Feinsilber, 1982).

Another legal battle has centered on *abortion*. In July 1977, Congress passed an amendment that prevented Medicaid funds from being used for abortions. This, in effect, denies low-income women the right to a legal and safe abortion, despite the 1973 U.S. Supreme Court ruling that restrictions on abortions are unconstitutional. "Right-to-life" groups still are pressuring Congress to ban legal abortions through a constitutional amendment, and, since 1984, an increasing number of "right-to-lifers" have been bombing abortion clinics to try to put a halt to their activities. President Reagan has actively supported restrictive antichoice family planning measures, including those that would ban the IUD and various forms of the pill, as well as abortion. In both the 1980 and 1984 Republican platform were planks requiring that all Republican appointees to the Supreme Court be antichoice. This, despite the fact that national surveys show that a majority of both sexes oppose a constitutional ban on abortion (from 60–65%; Thom, 1984).

The right of women to control their own bodies is an integral part of the women's movement. The issue is a complex one, involving religious, philosophic, political, economic, and other factors. Being against abortion does not necessarily mean being against women. However, a distinction needs to be made between a personal decision and a legal option. Although someone may be personally against abortions, he or she still can support a woman's legal right to choose. Without such a legal right, some women would be forced to find "home remedies" or have unsafe illegal abortions. Other women would be forced to bear unwanted children who, studies indicate, are twice as likely as wanted children to end up abused, delinquent, on welfare, or with serious emotional problems (for example, David & Baldwin, 1979). Furthermore, unwanted pregnancies would force some women to abandon their jobs or education and/or enter pregnancy-related marriages that might have little chance of success.

Legal action is needed in at least eight areas to guarantee equal rights and opportunities to all. (1) Support of the ERA is imperative. (2) Legislation to assure equal opportunity in employment and salaries must be supported. This involves the effective enforcement of all laws, recognition of the necessity of affirmative action programs, and close monitoring of the 1976 Vocational Education Act. It also involves the passage of displaced homemakers legislation and legislation increasing part-time and flex-time work opportunities. Legislation is needed to reduce veterans' preference, and to expand the opportunities and benefits of women in the military. (3) Legislation is needed to assure economic equity, especially for married couples. This involves the reform of Social Security regulations and federal and military pensions to give both spouses equity and benefits. Appropriation of adequate funds is needed to enforce the Equal Credit Opportunity Act. Legislation barring sex discrimination in insurance and pension coverage must be passed. Divorce settlements must take account of a woman's nonmonetary investments in her husband's career potential. (4) Reproductive freedom must be guaranteed, and a national policy on child care, with accompanying legislation, must be developed. (5) Full attainment of sex equity in education must be achieved. The scope of Title IX needs to be broadened, and the amendment needs to be enforced. Math/science equity legislation also needs to be passed. (6) Guarantees for women's health care must be obtained. Any national health insurance legislation must provide adequate and equitable coverage for women. Development and enforcement of health and safety standards also are needed. (7) Welfare reform is important, including opportunities for nonstereo-

typed job training and child care and family-planning services. (8) Tax reform is needed to ensure that families with two wage earners would not be penalized.

In sum, with equal treatment under the law, protection from discrimination based on sex, and the right to physical self-determination, political and economic power for women as a class should increase.

Organization of Work and Family. In contrast to changing laws, a second way to effect institutional change is by changing our way of compartmentalizing work and family functions. For an egalitarian society, women need to be truly integrated into the occupational world and men need to be truly integrated into the domestic sphere. Although a number of nations have attempted the former, very few have attempted the latter. The result has been that everywhere in industrialized societies, many women must bear the burden of two jobs—one in the work force and one at home (Bernard, 1979a; Sciolino, 1985). This lack of inclusion of men in domestic and child-care responsibilities, and the work overload for employed women partially account for the redifferentiation of sex roles occurring on many an Israeli kibbutz, contrary to the inhabitants' professed ideology (Beit-Hallahmi & Rabin, 1977; Blumberg, 1977; Nardi, 1981; Snarey, Friedman, & Blasi, 1985). Even in socialist countries, such as the Soviet Union and the People's Republic of China, whose founding ideals included gender equality, women must work a "double day"—first outside, then inside the home. This "double-day" pattern is one reason those countries have failed to achieve true gender equality, even though in both countries 90% of the women are employed (see Lapidus, 1982; Mamonova, 1984, for information on the U.S.S.R., and Andors, 1983, Stacey, 1983, for information on the People's Republic).

When both men and women share domestic as well as subsistence activities, sex roles tend to be relatively egalitarian, since men develop a more communal orientation and no longer can be paternalistic and distant (Gullahorn, 1977a). This can be seen in primitive hunting and gathering and horticultural societies (see Chapter 6) and currently in Sweden, "the only example to date of a comprehensive, long-range policy for increasing women's and men's active participation in both parenthood and gainful employment" (Gullahorn, 1977a, p. 278).

While Swedish society in practice is not completely egalitarian, Sweden has come further than any other country in egalitarian ideology and national policy except China (Baude, 1979; Haavio-Mannila, 1975; Pogrebin, 1982b; Safilios-Rothschild, 1975, 1979). Perhaps the most important aspect of the Swedish model is that the government has strongly emphasized *men's* role changes. To accomplish this, the Swedes have reformed textbooks, changed school curricula, and developed non-sexist parent education. Nearly all boys learn homemaking and child-care skills, and preference usually is given to male applicants for preschool teacher training. The government has offered a system of incentives to employers to combat traditional sex typing of occupations, provided occupational counseling, grants-in-aid for education, and training for women, and taken care of child-care costs. Either mother or father can take child-care leave or child-sickness leave, or work part-time and receive the child-care allowance paid to parents of children under 16. Each adult is considered economically independent and pays individual income taxes. Yet, true equality has lagged behind national policy. For example, more than 72% of all women are wage earners, yet they earn about 10% less than men do, mostly work in sex-segregated low-status jobs, and are still responsible for household and child-care tasks. Only 12% of all fathers utilize child-care leave, and only one-third take time off to nurse a sick child. Still, even these percentages are much higher than in the United States.

Some elements of the Swedish model can be incorporated here. Our country needs a national policy, not just piecemeal efforts toward equality. Important changes would be increasing child-care options, such as leaves of absence for either parent and community-controlled daycare centers (Catalyst, 1983; Chavkin, 1984; Cordes, 1983a; Lamb & Sagi, 1983; "Study Finds," 1983; Zigler & Muenchow, 1983). Some progress has been made in this regard (for example, about one-third of the top corporations in America extend parental leaves to men), but there is still a long way to

go. The United States is alone among the industrialized nations of the world in not guaranteeing compensation to employed women at the time of childbirth. One hundred seventeen countries, industrialized *and* developing, guarantee work leave to women at the time of delivery and payment to replace wages. Job, seniority, and pension plans also are protected. In the United States, less than 40% of employed women are entitled to paid disability leave of six weeks or more when they give birth, and paid child-care leaves for employed men are extremely rare. High-quality child daycare is expensive, if it is available at all, yet the majority of children under age five have employed mothers, as well as employed fathers. (See Figure 13-3 for one way to get more daycare centers.) Alternative work schedules also need to become more available, such as opportunities for part-time work, flextime, job sharing, and the four-day "compressed" work week (Friedan, 1981; Winnett & Neale, 1980). Most importantly, there must be an emphasis on changing men's roles as well as women's roles. Such changes would help in creating an egalitarian society. (See Voydannoff, 1984, for a closer look at ways in which work and family roles can be changed.)

Direct Action.   While legal action is one of the most powerful tactics to employ in trying to change male dominance of institutions, other tactics also can be effective, such as direct action and conflict confrontations (Polk, 1976; Safilios-Rothschild, 1979). Through a variety of actions, women increasingly not only are being heard but heeded. Some organizations, like Women Against Violence Against Women and NOW, are engaging in sit-ins and economic boycotts against products, companies, and states that disparage or discriminate against women. Other women have utilized moral pressure by publicizing reports of sex discrimination or sex typing. Still others are organizing and unionizing groups of secretaries, nurses, and household workers. Women often need help in learning such tactics, and skill building is an important part of many feminist projects (Polk, 1976).

Some feminists (for example, Friedan, 1985; Safilios-Rothschild, 1979) urge women to become actively involved in crucial issues and

Figure 13-3

*How to accomplish change in the structure of work
and family relationships: get men to bear children.
(Copyright, 1982 by Field Enterprises, Inc. Reprinted
with permission.)*

protest movements other than those specifically related to women in order to achieve maximum sex-role change. Because some changes are occurring on the personal and social levels, confrontations on an institutional level are currently being eroded. By joining with other groups and issues, confrontations can continue. This may speed up the acceptance of nonsexist legislation and social policies as well.

Alternative Institutions. A fourth approach to accomplishing institutional change is by building alternative institutions (Polk, 1976). The women's movement itself represents an alternative to masculine hierarchical authoritarian organizations, and many groups have begun to use the nonhierarchical model—feminist therapy, Association for Women in Psychology, women's studies courses, and so forth. Numerous self-help organizations have challenged the traditional male monopoly of medical, legal, and psychotherapeutic information, and have helped large numbers of people whom the professional institutions had turned off, put down, and overcharged (Polk, 1976). Collective living situations, as discussed under Alternative Lifestyles, also provide couples and single individuals with an alternative to the nuclear family. Such an alternative may facilitate sex-role change if the group makes that a conscious goal.

Problems

The difficulties of instituting such a total change in society are enormous. There is the problem of integrating changes occurring on three levels, and there are also the problems posed by minority groups and the general resistance to change.

Integration of Changes

Unless changes occur on all levels—personal (attitudes), societal (ideology), and institutional (power)—the likelihood of achieving a truly egalitarian society where each individual can develop according to his or her potential and society itself can be run in an effective and humanistic way is small. Legislation without comparable changes in people's attitudes will raise unrealistic hopes and increase resentments. Changes in attitudes without changes in socialization forces and institutions will lead to frustration and hostility. As social psychologists and sociologists have learned, the relationship between attitudes and behavior change is complex (see Bernard, 1976b). Changing behaviors sometimes can lead to changes in attitudes and of the social norm. For example, female premarital virginity no longer is the norm it once was. It is also possible that the norm may change and behavior will follow. For example, equality in relationships now is the norm and behavior is slowly changing. On the other hand, the norm may change and behavior may not follow. For example, the Civil Rights Bill of 1964 legislated racial and sexual equality but equality has yet to be achieved. Or behavior may change but the norm may not. For example, most mothers work outside the home, but the norm is that they do not. Clearly, the relation is a complex one and difficult to predict. Time and persistence are undoubtedly crucial variables.

Further evidence of problems that occur when the three levels of change are not integrated currently can be seen in communist countries, especially those of eastern Europe (Jancar, 1979; Scott, 1979). In their initial stages of development, communist societies generally facilitate progress toward sexual equality, especially when such countries first are moving toward industrialization. Labor is scarce at that time, and women are needed in the labor force. Their participation thus is encouraged through emphasis on equality. But once such advances begin to pose a threat to the male political hierarchy or to lead to greatly reduced fertility, sexist policies reappear. Change never really had taken place on the individual or relationship level. Incorporating women into the work force had meant only that women were called on to perform two roles while men still performed one. When other policy matters became more important, the interest in "equality" abated.

Integration of changes also is important to avoid the "superwoman effect." With changing sex-role ideologies, many women now feel they can, and should, do everything—have a stimulating career, establish intimate relationships, rear children, engage in recreational activities, and so on. Without social support from family and friends—and institutional support, such as child-care assistance and flexible work schedules—many women find themselves subject to seemingly endless demands for their time and energies.

Minority Groups

Problems also arise in trying to reach all segments of society. Most of the research and literature reported in this book have been on White, middle-class, usually college-educated individuals, primarily because this is the group that most researchers and writers have studied. Yet this sample is clearly only one part of the whole population, and other groups have somewhat different definitions of, problems with, and reactions to gender stereotypes. For example, Black women particularly have been denigrated by White society. They traditionally have been cast into the stereotyped image of "non-feminist"—not interested in equality between women and men—"deprecated sex object," or "loser," or else they simply have been ignored (King, 1973).

Where White women suffer the effects of sexism, Third World women suffer from sexism and also from racism, and often from poverty as well. More than one out of four Black and Hispanic children were poor in 1981 ("Poverty," 1983). For female-headed families, who are disproportionately Black and Hispanic, the poverty rates are striking. Whereas for White, female-headed families, the poverty rate was 27%, for Black and Hispanic female-headed families, it was 53%. As discussed in Chapter 11, this high rate of poverty among Black and Hispanic female-headed households is due in part to the very low wages earned by minority women. Minority, as well as White, women earn less than minority and White men; within this hierarchy, White men earn the most and Hispanic women earn the least. Because of this dual, sometimes triple, oppression, many minority women have had difficulty identifying with the women's movement, which has been primarily a product of the White middle class.

As discussed previously in this chapter, the women's movement as it developed in the 1960s and early 1970s completely neglected the special concerns of minority women. Many minority women have written eloquently on this issue (Hemmons, 1980; Hooks, 1984; D. Lewis, 1977; Lorde, 1984; Moraga & Anzaldua, 1981; B. Smith, 1982). Both socialist feminism and radical feminism arose, in part, to address this important omission of race from liberal feminism. Liberal feminism assumed that sexism was the same for all cultural and ethnic groups, and that by removing the barriers of sex discrimination, all groups would move into the system and become assimilated with the dominant (White male) culture. But sexism is not the same for all cultural and ethnic groups, and racial inequality can exist even when sexual inequality doesn't, as within the women's movement itself.

Socialist feminism analyzes race issues within the context of class and gender, but still does not fully examine cultural differences (M. Andersen, 1983). Radical feminists, too, assume that class and race oppression are just extensions of patriarchal domination (Daly, 1978). However, in assuming that patriarchy is the cause of women's oppression, radical feminism divides minority women and men. It also takes the experience of White American women as the universal social experience (M. Andersen, 1983). It is imperative that a feminist theory develops that can describe and explain the experience of *all* women. Minority women are taking the lead in this effort (for example, Hooks, 1984; Hull, Scott, & Smith, 1982; Moraga & Anzaldua, 1981; B. Smith, 1983), but all women need to confront the issue of race in their personal and collective lives.

Blacks, Asians, Hispanics, and Native Americans each have a unique cultural background and a unique position vis-à-vis the dominant White male culture (Hull et al., 1982; Mirande & Enriquez, 1980; Moraga & Anzaldua, 1981; Murray, 1981; Murray & Scott, 1982; Roders-Rose, 1980; Senour, 1981; A. Smith & Stewart, 1983; B. Smith, 1983; True, 1981; Witt, 1981). Yet, despite ethnic group differences, certain similarities emerge among Third-World women. As a group, they are a minority in a White culture. They tend to hold the lowest-status, lowest-paying jobs. They generally have been made to feel inadequate as women regarding their physical appearance and behavior. They may have difficulty establishing their own identity. And they often disagree with the (White) women's movement on a number of issues. They are likely to define racial oppression as the top priority item rather than sexual oppression. They are also likely to favor the traditional structure of the family and to be against birth control and abortion, which may be viewed by them as genocidal and racist and are particular problems for Catholic Chicanas.

Certain similarities also exist among Third-World and White women, and minority group membership and feminism need not be antithetical (Reid, 1984). Indeed, Black women appear more liberated than White women in their attitudes toward sexism. For example, in a national Louis Harris poll taken in 1984 and pictured in Table 13-1, Black women appeared more aware of sex discrimination, and more supportive of women's rights than did White women (Thom, 1984). In contrast, Black men appeared similar to or more conservative than White men, except on questions of equal rights.

Sexism is a part of all cultures, particularly those from which Third-World women come. The sexual double standard exists in all cultures, and their employment and educational opportunities are limited by sex as well as by race. Above all, the oppression of all women, especially Third-World women, is intimately tied to maintaining the political and economic equilibrium of our society. Increasingly, Third-World women and men are viewing sex roles as part of a "sick" White society that they do not want to imitate, and they are rejecting the current assimilation model. Blacks, for example, already have role integration to a certain degree since circumstances have required Black women to work and be strong (Wallace, 1979). As a result of their heritage, Black women have found ways of coping and surviving that could be helpful to other women (Lykes, 1983; Reid, 1984). It is hoped that the current trend in the women's movement to acknowledge and learn from the differences that exist among women will continue and coalesce into a stronger and more united front. True liberation means respect for all individuals, and an acceptance of diversity. The recent development in the feminist movement to examine issues relevant to women all over the world is a step in the right direction. (See R. Morgan, 1984, for an introduction to global or planetary feminism.)

The socialist feminist and radical feminist models of society that have been proposed would mean respect for and tolerance of racial and ethnic diversity as well as of sexual diversity, would change the values of the dominant society so that it no longer would reflect only White male values, and would involve equality for all citizens.

Table 13-1
Results of a Louis Harris and Associates poll in March 1984. Taken from Thom, 1984, p. 59. Copyright 1984, Ms. *magazine; used with permission.*

Views of Discrimination: Black Women in the Lead				
	Black Women	White Women	Black Men	White Men
Women often do not receive the same pay as men for doing exactly the same job	79%	74%	59%	64%
Women often have much more trouble than men in getting credit, bank loans, and mortgages	74	63	56	57
Women are often discriminated against in being promoted for supervisory and executive jobs	75	62	55	55
Women often receive lower pensions or pay more on annuities than men doing the same work	62	44	40	40
Women often do not receive the same pay as men for doing comparable jobs with similar skill and training	82	71	56	64
Women are discriminated against in being able to earn enough to support themselves independently	74	56	45	50
Favor the Equal Rights Amendment	71	63	58	55
Believe ERA will pass	68	62	78	54
It is very important that women's rights be strengthened	76	55	57	44
Would vote for woman for Congress if man and woman equally qualified	46	42	22	17
Favor woman for vice–president in 1984	68	69	66	72

Resistance

A third major problem in instituting change is the resistance of many men and women and of institutions. Some resistance may stem from a general fear of the unknown, and some from confusion about the sexual and nonsexual aspects of gender roles. Because men typically have been the dominant sex with most of the power, it will be much more difficult for them to give some up than it will be for those without power to acquire some (David & Brannon, 1976; Doyle, 1983; Kahn, 1984). This especially will be true as long as power remains the criterion by which status is determined. Secondly, as children, most males defined themselves by avoiding anything even vaguely feminine. To now alter their self-definition to include "feminine" behavior may mean a perceived loss of status and self-esteem for some men. Thirdly, the unemotional nature of the male sex role

mitigates against some men recognizing problems they may have as a result of their sex role, and certainly mitigates against their expressing such problems.

Arnold Kahn (1984) hypothesizes that because power is such an integral part of masculine self-esteem, all men will have difficulty handing power over to women. Some men, with the least diversified power base, will experience power loss most keenly, and will attempt to regain power with the only power base they have left—coercive power. (See Chapter 12 for a discussion of the different bases of power.) Thus, the apparent increase in rape, spouse abuse, and child abuse by men in recent years may be one indication of this type of male resistance. For men with more diversified bases of power, such as expert, reward, informational, or legitimate power, the reaction likely will be more subtle. Their resistance may appear in hiring and promotion decisions, in decisions concerning how women are portrayed in the media, and so on. For those men who intellectually believe in equal rights, behavioral change is more possible, but probably only after learning how to act differently. In two representative national surveys of adults done in 1957 and 1976, Veroff and colleagues (1980) found that men's power motives (fear of weakness and desire for influence over others) have increased since the 1950s. This quest for power over others seems to make it difficult to establish affiliative concerns as well. Thus as women have been gaining more rights in American society, men have become more concerned with power. Certainly the 1980s have seen increased male resistance to women's fight for equality: the ERA has been defeated the right of women to control their own bodies is threatened; women's advances in politics and business have slowed; and "profamily" campaigns are trying to put women back in the homemaker role.

Yet, as we have seen throughout this book, negative consequences of the male sex role are numerous and are becoming increasingly recognized, especially by men involved in alternative lifestyles. Increasing numbers of men are rejecting the quest for status and success. They are striving to reduce their competitiveness and increase their sensitivity to themselves and others (Friedan, 1981). Major stimuli for change have been the recent changes in women's definitions of themselves and their place in society as well as the restrictiveness some men have felt regarding acceptable behavior. Although some men have felt threatened and have become entrenched further in traditional roles, men's liberation has been spreading.

Warren Farrell (1974) describes 21 ways in which women's liberation could function as men's liberation. Essentially, Farrell notes that if a man were no longer the primary breadwinner, he probably would experience less fear about losing his job and probably would feel greater freedom to choose an interesting, low-paying one over an unfulfilling, high-paying one. He might feel less need to compete and less pressure to be the sole source of his partner's happiness. He might be able to devote more time to his children, to the pursuit of nonvocational goals, and to alternative household arrangements. His relationships might be based more on feelings than on security. Sexual interest might increase, and his relationships probably would be more rewarding. Men most likely would experience a reduction of anxiety about their sex role and about homosexuality, an increase in autonomy and intellectual achievement, and might develop a new set of values that accompany true listening and a more balanced ego. Poor men would benefit from the additional income of an employed wife and from "homemaker payments," if needed. Men also would become free of many legal burdens that currently fall on them.

There have been signs that American men as a group have been becoming more sensitive and less macho (Ehrenreich, 1984; Franklin, 1984; H. Goldberg, 1980, 1983), especially when compared to the 1950s. But many feminists now are concerned that in becoming more sensitive, men also are becoming more narcissistic, more class-conscious, and more avoidant of making commitments—to friends, family, and society. A truly feminist goal would include equality among men and women as well as between them, and the ability to make and keep relationships. That goal is still to be realized.

Of course, men are not the only group resistant to sex-role change; many women are resistant as well. Some of the backlash can be seen in books like Marabel Morgan's (1975) *Total Woman,* and Helen Andelin's (1975), *Fascinating Womanhood,* where women are encouraged to use their "feminine wiles" to get what they want out of "their man." Women's resistance may stem partly from misunderstanding the goals of the liberation movements. This misunderstanding is perpetuated by myths, such as those about the ERA. Women's resistance also may stem from a resistance to any change and from women's own prejudice against women (see Chapter 11). Many women have accepted male sex-role standards as the norm and as the way it "should" be. Some women may have religious or philosophical reasons for preferring present sex-role standards. For example, many women (and men) feel it is God's law for women to be inferior to and dependent upon men. Antifeminists have argued that men must be made to support their wife and children (Ehrenreich, 1983). Thus, most of Schlafly's anti-ERA campaign played on the dependent homemaker's sense of vulnerability that she might lose her husband's economic support. Nonemployed working-class women without a college education tend to hold the most traditional attitudes toward women (Houser & Beckman, 1980), but only a minority are overtly hostile to the women's movement (Ferree, 1983). Those who are hostile tend to confuse the movement with uninhibited sexuality, or to be committed to the idea of separate-but-equal spheres of activity and association.

Greater publicity about the social, political, and economic factors involved in the current role of women and more accurate portrayals of the women's movement and its goals by the media may change the views of some of these women. A direct effort may be needed to reach women feeling alienated from the women's movement because they cannot identify with some of the extreme positions taken. Some writers (for example, Friedan, 1981) view the women's movement as entering a new stage with its new concern about the family. Such a concern may appeal to many of the men and women who previously had felt alienated from the women's movement.

Institutional resistance has been more difficult to overcome. Part of the problem involves the inertia of institutions in general to respond to any type of change. Another part of the problem involves the paternalistic nature of institutional discrimination against women. This form of discrimination encourages women to maintain their dependence on men and fragments the position of women as a group while strengthening the position of men as a group (Safilios-Rothschild, 1979). A third part of the problem involves the lack of a clear image of what a more sex-egalitarian future society would look like (Boulding, 1979). This unknown is frightening since it may involve undesirable as well as desirable changes and certainly would involve a redistribution of power. It thus is interesting to consider what such a future society might be like if sex-role changes did become real. We turn now to such speculations.

Implications

If the changes considered above come to pass, their effect on our society, as we have discussed previously, would occur on three levels—the personal, the social, and the institutional. Figure 13-4 gives a satiric view of one possible future.

Personal

Although non-sex-typed males and females probably would not be differentiable by activities, interests, or personality patterns, they still would maintain their separate sex identities. Sex identity is basically one's sense of maleness or femaleness (see Chapter 2). It involves appreciating and valuing one's genitals and, later, one's secondary sex characteristics and their potentialities. It has little intrinsic connection to sex roles. Although some writers (for example, Winick, 1968) have predicted that the perpetuation of the species might be threatened by eliminating stereotyped sex roles, further consideration of the question shows this prediction to be unfounded. On the contrary, sexual experiences should be more gratifying than they are presently since good sex requires openness, trust, vulnerability, assertiveness, and activity—all part of an androgynous individual but only partially represented in sex-typed individuals (see Chapter 5). The sexual double standard should no longer exist.

Many people have expressed a concern that increased androgyny will result in increased homosexuality. Many of these individuals fail to distinguish between sex role and sexuality. Additionally, this fear often demonstrates homophobia (see Chapter 10). Yet there may be some basis to such a concern, because as inability to express feelings to same-sex members decreases, particularly for males, some homosexual experimentation might increase. However, the number of persons who are exclusively homosexual should decrease because an either/or choice no longer would be necessary, the male and female sex roles being sufficiently flexible to incorporate both homosexual and heterosexual behavior.

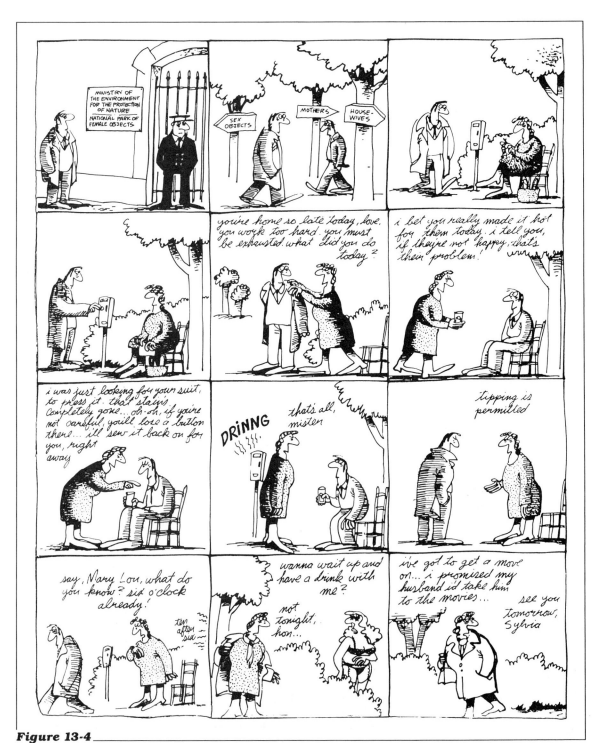

Figure 13-4

A glimpse of the future? (Copyright 1978 by National Lampoon, Inc. Reprinted by permission.)

The institution of marriage probably would change. Since women no longer would need to look for economic security in a mate, both men and women could choose mates on the basis of companionability, understanding, tenderness, physical attractiveness, or sexual ability. Because a woman would no longer have to marry to fulfill herself, there might be fewer marriages and they probably would occur at a later age—a trend that has already begun. The resulting marriages, however, might be stronger, more emotionally satisfying, and less likely to end in divorce because they would be based on free choice, not economic survival. Because marriage would be an equal partnership, wives would be less like parasites and husbands would be less like exploiters (see Chapter 10).

In reply to those who argue that such equality would destroy the family, it is hard to imagine a more destructive situation than currently exists. About half of all couples now marrying will eventually divorce. In the past, the family provided a legitimate outlet for sexual activity and served as a shelter for dependent offspring. It was a unit of production and a source of status, identity, and personal worth. None of these functions is currently the exclusive province of the family. As marriage becomes more an emotional bond, families will assume a new purpose; they will become a refuge from an intensely complex and frustrating world.

Because marriages might come later and divorces no longer would be viewed as a sign of failure, there would be more single people in the population at a given time than currently exist. Thus there should be an increase in single-person households, a trend already begun, and in alternative living situations such as single parents and communes. These alternatives probably no longer would be considered deviant.

The effects on children of alternative family structures probably would differ very little from the effects of traditional family structures. A study by Jerome Cohen (cited in "Alternative," 1977) found that children of single mothers (preplanned) and of couples living in a communal setting and in social contract marriages differed very little in terms of behavior and emotional adjustment from those brought up in standard two-parent marriages.

This was predominantly because child-rearing practices differed very little. In an egalitarian society, parents probably would serve as non-sex-typed models, sharing responsibility for work and family. Through their own example and their own values, such parents should produce non-sex-typed children (see Chapters 7 and 10). "The feminist prescription . . . is not that the individual be androgynous, but that the society be gender-aschematic" (Bem, 1984, p. 63). In a gender-aschematic society, females most likely would be less frustrated, and maybe mentally healthier—better adjusted, with higher self-esteem. Males probably would be under less strain and maybe physically healthier. Other negative consequences of gender stereotypes discussed in Chapters 9 and 10 also should be eliminated, leading to better feelings about oneself and better relationships with same- and other-sex individuals and with children.

Social

On a social level, the work situation probably would show the most changes. More women would be in the labor force and perhaps fewer men. Job competition would mean that the best person would be in any specified position. Greater job flexibility would mean that both women and men would be freer to quit, take leaves, work part-time, and make career changes. There might be more emphasis on psychic as opposed to financial rewards.

If a parent decided to stay home, she or he might receive a percent of the spouse's pay and be entitled to pension fund and/or Social Security benefits and a job training allowance if divorced. An adequate program of government income support is essential for people who cannot enter the labor market, either because they have to care for young children, or because they cannot find jobs (Ehrenreich, 1983; Kamerman, 1984). Job training programs must be available to teach women not only practical job skills but attitudes of assertiveness and independence.

A man's mobility would be affected by his wife's job and ambitions, a situation that currently exists in reverse for many married women. It even might be viewed as a form of downward mobility to have a nonemployed wife. Women, in the same numbers as men, would probably take over and run the family business or follow in the profession of their physician, lawyer, or dentist father or mother.

Sex-typing of occupations would be vastly reduced and although a 50–50 sex composition probably would not occur in all jobs, motivation and talent not being equally distributed, the status and salary differences between jobs in which women primarily work and those in which men do should be eliminated. All workers should be able to earn a living wage and receive equal pay for comparable jobs.

Given that people's life spans are increasing, if more people entered the labor force they probably could not all work 40-hour weeks until age 70. This means that there might be more leisure time for all. More activities and hobbies could be pursued by women and men. Such people may fill the gap left by women who used to be available for traditional community voluntary activities. Since a man's identity would no longer be based solely on his role as worker and breadwinner, much of the emotional and physical stress now experienced by men who retire or who are laid off would be reduced or eliminated.

Child care would be restructured. More day and after-school care would be available, sponsored by government, business, or the community. More job flexibility would be possible— shorter hours, flexible hours, shared jobs, and equal leave policies. Housework might become professionalized and greater status (pay and benefits) for child care might be given. Major alterations in life-cycle stages, such as alternate periods of study, employment, and work in the home, probably also would occur. (See Best, 1981, for a discussion of how changing sex roles affect worklife flexibility.)

It might be argued that many of the possible changes depend on society being affluent. However, even in economically depressed times, non-sex-stereotyped functioning still should lead to change. Although employment might be difficult to obtain, layoffs and limited hiring practices should affect both sexes equally. Child care still could be shared by parents and helped by institutional support. Housework too could be shared, since one sex is not more likely than the other to be employed outside the home.

Institutional

In an egalitarian society, industry as well as politics might become more humane and socially oriented. There should be a move away from power, competition, and dominance, and toward democracy and group decision making. More women would be in managerial and top political posts and in other positions of power. Such restructuring of society might lead to more humane domestic and foreign politics. (See "If women," 1985.) For example, our support of corrupt inhumane foreign dictatorships for economic reasons might be reduced. Health care might improve, malnutrition and poverty-related illnesses should decrease, ecological implications of policies should be weighed more strongly, and inhumane work practices should be reduced. In the last few years, feminists have written extensively about science and technology (for example, Bleier, 1984; Keller, 1982, 1985; Pfafflin, 1984; Rothschild, 1983). In particular, these writers have argued that tradiional science and technology need to be infused with a feminist perspective so that their products will be respectful of human life and human dignity.

If violence became less tied to the masculine sex role, we would expect less violent behavior by men as manifested in violent crimes and wartime atrocities. As the peace movements of the 1980s suggest, a society that incorporates egalitarian values might be more inclined to nonviolence than violence, and to settling conflicts peaceably, rather than forcefully. A society structured around egalitarian values would probably be one in which the incidence of crimes against women, especially sexual abuse, would be greatly reduced. Indeed all crimes based on dominance and power, such as rape, incest, and child abuse, should be lessened. Violent pornography should find no market and therefore would disappear. Sexist advertising and other forms of media also should be eliminated. We might also expect to find more interest in nonviolent sports (see Chapter 11).

In an egalitarian society, ethnic and racial diversity would be acknowledged and embraced, rather than stigmatized and punished. Without patriarchy as a model, the need for one group to dominate another group should be diminished. An egalitarian society will not come about automatically, even if people become less sex-typed individually. Institutions run on a different dynamic than do individuals and a concerted, deliberate, and persistent effort would be needed before social change became a reality.

Summary

In this chapter, a review of alternatives to gender stereotyping has been made. Transcendence of sex roles presents a desirable goal: a maximization of individual potential and a flexible integration of agentic and expressive behaviors where possible. Individual differences still would exist; it is their differential evaluation that would be altered. Moving toward non-sex-typed functioning on an individual as well as a societal level implies the use of a socialist feminist or radical feminist model of social change. In these models, individual and cultural differences are recognized and appreciated and society itself must change to accommodate them. This means institutional as well as individual change.

Because gender stereotypes have implications for all levels of functioning—personal, social, and institutional—change will be required on all levels before real change can occur on any one. The liberation movements have created and reflected the impetus for change and have begun the process. On a personal level, consciousness-raising groups, psychotherapy, experiential groups, education, and alterations in behavior all can lead to change. Changes in ideology, socialization practices, and attitudes toward alternate lifestyles can lead to change on the social level. Changes in the law, organization of work and family, direct action, and alternative institutions can lead to changes on an institutional level. Such changes will not come easily. Firstly, there needs to be an integration of the changes occurring on the three levels, institutional change being the most difficult to achieve. Secondly, minority groups and their special needs need to be specifically addressed. Thirdly, resistance by both women and men needs to be expected and handled constructively.

If such changes occur, and our society and the individuals it contains become less sex-typed and more egalitarian, the ramifications will be widespread, occurring on personal, social, and institutional levels. Some changes already have begun; others will be more difficult to implement. The future, however, is open. What is at stake is no less than the happiness and effectiveness of our entire country. Eliminating gender stereotypes does not mean simply liberating women but liberating men and our society as well. What we have been talking about is allowing people to be more fully human and creating a society that will reflect that humanity. Surely that is a goal worth striving for.

Recommended Reading

Deckard, B. S. (1983). *The women's movement: Political, socioeconomic, and psychological issues.* New York: Harper & Row. Thorough review of the women's movement to date, as well as a compact discussion of feminist theories and issues of particular relevance to women.

Kaschak, E. (1981b). Feminist psychotherapy: The first decade. In S. Cox (Ed.), *Female psychology: The emerging self,* 2nd ed. (pp. 387–401). New York: St. Martin's. A brief but excellent summary of the development of feminist psychotherapy.

Men's Studies Newsletter. Published semiannually by the Men's Studies Task Group of the National Organization for Changing Men. (Available from Harry Brod, Editor, SWMS-THH 331M, University of Southern California, Los Angeles, Calif. 90089-4352). Publishes items of interest to those concerned with research and teaching in the areas of men's studies and the antisexist men's movement.

Moraga, C., & Anzaldua, G. (Eds.) (1981). *This bridge called my back: Writings by radical women of color.* Watertown, Mass.: Persephone Press. An exciting interdisciplinary blend of stories, poems, and articles illustrating the perspective of minority women.

Voydanoff, P. (Ed.) (1984). *Work and family: Changing roles of men and women.* Palo Alto, Calif.: Mayfield. A collection of 24 articles on the interface between work and family roles for women and men. Includes discussion of relevant social policy issues.

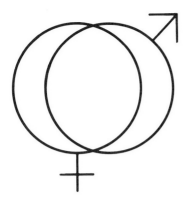

References

Abbey, A. (1982). Sex differences in attributions for friendly behavior: Do males misperceive females' friendliness? *Journal of Personality and Social Psychology, 42,* 830–838.

Abramowitz, S. J., & Herrera, H. R. (1981). On controlling for patient psychopathology in naturalistic studies of sex bias: A methodological demonstration. *Journal of Consulting and Clinical Psychology, 49,* 597–603.

Abramson, L. Y., Seligman, M. E. P., & Teasdale, J. D. (1978). Learned helplessness in humans: Critique and reformulation. *Journal of Abnormal Psychology, 87,* 49–74.

Abramson, P. P., Goldberg, P. A., Greenberg, J. H., & Abramson, L. M. (1977). The talking platypus phenomenon: Competency ratings as a function of sex and professional status. *Psychology of Women Quarterly, 2,* 114–124.

Abramson, P. R., & Mosher, D. L. (1979). An empirical investigation of experimentally induced masturbatory fantasies. *Archives of Sexual Behavior, 8,* 27–39.

Abzug, B., with Keller, M. (1984). *Gender gap: Bella Abzug's guide to political power for American women.* Boston: Houghton Mifflin.

Acock, A. C., & Ireland, N. K. (1983). Attribution of blame in rape cases: The impace of norm violation, gender, and sex-role attitude. *Sex Roles, 9,* 179–193.

Adams, D. B., Gold, A. R., & Burt, A. D. (1978). Cycles of sexual desire. *New England Journal of Medicine, 299*(21).

Adams, J. (1984). Women at West Point: A three-year perspective. *Sex Roles, 11,* 525–541.

Adams, K. A. (1980). Who has the final word? Sex, race, and dominance behavior. *Journal of Personality and Social Psychology, 38,* 1–8.

Adams, K. A. (1983). Aspects of social context as determinants of black women's resistance to challenges. *Journal of Social Issues, 39,* 69–78.

Adamsky, C. (1981). Changes in pronominal usage in a classroom situation. *Psychology of Women Quarterly, 5,* 773–779.

Adler, F. (1975). *Sisters in crime: The rise of the new female criminal.* New York: McGraw-Hill.

Adler, F. (Eds.) (1981). *The incidence of female criminality in the contemporary world.* New York: New York University Press.

AFDC cuts hurt. (1984, Spring/Summer). *ISR Newsletter,* p. 3.

African women seek larger role. (1985, January 6). *Allentown Call,* p. 5.

Agate, C., & Meacham, C. (1977). Women's equality: Implications of the law. In A. Sargent (Ed.), *Beyond sex roles* (pp. 434–450). St. Paul: West.

Agus, C. (1984, May 27). Mail-order Asian brides are filling the bill. *The Easton Express,* p. C2.

Ainsworth, M. D. S. (1979). Infant-mother attachment. *American Psychologist, 34,* 932–937.

Akert, R. M., & Chen, J. (1984, April.) *Gender display: The incidence of facial prominence in print and television media.* Paper presented at the meeting of the Eastern Psychological Association, Baltimore.

Alagna, S. W. (1982). Sex role identity, peer evaluation of competition and the responses of women and men in a competitive situation. *Journal of Personality and Social Psychology, 43,* 546–554.

Albert, A., & Porter, J. R. (1983). Age patterns in the development of children's gender-role stereotypes. *Sex Roles, 9,* 59–67.

Alberti, R., & Emmons, M. D. (1978). *Your perfect right.* San Luis Obispo, Calif.: Impact Press.

Albin, R. (1977, June). New look at single parenting: Focus on fathers. *APA Monitor,* pp. 7–8.

Aldous, J. (Ed.) (1982). *Two paychecks: Life in dual-earner families.* Beverly Hills, Calif.: Sage.

Al-Issa, I. (Ed.) (1983). *Gender and psychopathology.* New York: Academic Press.

Allen, I. L. (1984). Male sex roles and epithets for ethnic women in American slang. *Sex Roles, 11,* 43–50.

Allen, M. J., & Hogeland, R. (1978). Spatial problem solving strategies as a function of sex. *Perceptual and Motor Skills, 47,* 348–350.

Allgeier, E. R. (1981). The influence of androgynous identification on heterosexual relations. *Sex Roles, 7,* 321–330.

Alper, J. S. (1985). Sex differences in brain asymmetry: A critical analysis. *Feminist Studies, 11,* 7–37.

Alper, T. G. (1974). Achievement motivation in college women: A now-you-see-it-now-you-don't phenomenon. *American Psychologist, 29,* 194–203.

Alperson, B. L., & Friedman, W. J. (1983). Some aspects of the interpersonal phenomenology of heterosexual dyads with respect to sex-role stereotypes. *Sex Roles, 9,* 453–474.

Alternative families: So what's new? (1977, June). *APA Monitor,* p. 9.

American Psychological Association Task Force on Sex Bias and Sex Role Stereotyping. (1978). Source materials for nonsexist therapy. JSAS *Catalog of Selected Documents in Psychology, 8*(2), 40. (Ms. No. 1685)

Ames, N. R. (1984, Winter). The socialization of women into and out of sports. *Journal of the National Association for Women, Deans, Administrators, and Counselors, 47,* 3–8.

Amir, M. (1971, November). Forcible rape. *Sexual Behavior,* 26–36.

Anastas, J. W., & Reinharz, H. (1984). Gender differences in learning and adjustment problems in school: Results of a longitudinal study. *American Journal of Orthopsychiatry, 54,* 110–122.

Andelin, H. (1975). *Fascinating womanhood.* New York: Ravelle Books.

Anderegg, D., & Chess, J. (1983, April). *Sex differences in teachers' assessments of their students' social competence.* Paper presented at the meeting of the Eastern Psychological Association, Baltimore.

Andersen, M. L. (1983). *Thinking about women: Sociological and feminist perspectives.* New York: Macmillan.

Andersen, S., & Bem, S. L. (1981). Sex typing and androgyny in dyadic interaction: Individual differences in responsiveness to physical attractiveness. *Journal of Personality and Social Psychology, 41,* 74–86.

Anderson, L. (1984, November 20). Designers preview short skirts for spring. *The Easton Express,* p. A11.

Anderson, S. C. (1984). Alcoholic women: Sex-role identification and perceptions of parental personality characteristics. *Sex Roles, 11,* 277–287.

Andors, P. (1983). *The unfinished liberation of Chinese women.* Bloomington: Indiana University Press.

Antill, J. K. (1983). Sex role complementarity vs. similarity in married couples. *Journal of Personality and Social Psychology, 45,* 145–155.

Antill, J. K., & Cunningham, J. D. (1979). Self-esteem as a function of masculinity in both sexes. *Journal of Consulting and Clinical Psychology, 47,* 783–785.

Antill, J. K., & Cunningham, J. D. (1982). Sex differences in performance on ability tests as a function of masculinity, femininity and androgyny. *Journal of Personality and Social Psychology, 42,* 718–728.

Apao, W. K. (1982, April). *Women among men: Androgyny and sex-role attitudes of women in a military college.* Paper presented at the meeting of the Eastern Psychological Association, Baltimore.

Archer, C. J. (1984). Children's attitudes toward sex-role division in adult occupational roles. *Sex Roles, 10,* 1–10.

Archer, D., Iritani, B., Kimes, D. D., & Barrios, M. (1983). Face-isms: Five studies of sex differences in facial prominence. *Journal of Personality and Social Psychology, 45,* 725–735.

Aries, E. (1977). Male-female interpersonal styles in all male, all female and mixed groups. In A. Sargent (Ed.), *Beyond sex roles* (pp. 292–299). St. Paul: West.

Aries, E. J., & Johnson, F. L. (1983). Close friendship in adulthood: Conversational content between same-sex friends. *Sex Roles, 9,* 1183–1196.

Arkin, W., & Dobrofsky, L. R. (1978a). Job sharing. In R. Rapoport & R. Rapoport (Eds). *Working couples* (pp. 122–137). New York: Harper & Row.

Arkin, W., & Dobrofsky, L. (1978b) Military socialization and masculinity. *Journal of Social Issues, 34*(1), 131–168.

Arkkelin, D., & Simmons, R. (1985). The "good manager": Sex-typed, androgynous, or likable? *Sex Roles, 12,* 1187–1198.

Armitage, K. J., Schneiderman, L. J., & Bass, R. A. (1979). Response of physicians to medical complaints in men and women. *Journal of the AMA, 241,* 2186–2187.

Arms and the woman: Equal opportunity in the military. (1977, Spring). *WEAL Washington Report,* pp. 1–6.

Arnett, M. D., Higgins, R. B., & Priem, A. P. (1980). Sex and least preferred co-worker score effects in leadership behavior. *Sex Roles, 6,* 139–152.

Asch, S. E. (1956). Studies of independence and conformity: A minority of one against a unanimous majority. *Psychology Monographs, 70*(9, Whole No. 416).

Ashmore, R. D., & DelBoca, F. K. (1979). Sex stereotypes and implicit personality theory: Toward a cognitive-social psychological conceptualization. *Sex Roles, 5,* 219–248.

Ashmore, R. D., & Tumia, M. L. (1980). Sex stereotypes and implicit personality theory. I. A personality description approach to the assessment of sex stereotypes. *Sex Roles, 6,* 501–518.

Ashton, E. (1983). Measures of play behavior: The influence of sex-role stereotyped children's books. *Sex Roles, 9,* 43–47.

Astin, A. W. (1985, Jan. 16). Freshman characteristics and attitudes. *Chronicle of Higher Education,* p. 15–16.

Astrachan, A. (1984, August). Men: A movement of their own. *Ms.,* pp. 91–94.

Atkinson, J. W., & Feather, N. T. (1966). *A theory of achievement motivation.* New York: Wiley.

Atkinson, J., & Huston, T. L. (1984). Sex role orientation and division of labor early in marriage. *Journal of Personality and Social Psychology, 46,* 330–345.

Baber, K. M., & Dreyer, A. S. (in press). Delayed childbearing: Men's thinking about the fertility decision. In R. Lewis and R. Scott (Eds.), *Fatherhood.* Beverly Hills, Calif.: Sage.

Baber, K. M., & Dreyer, A. S. (in press). Gender-role orientations in older childfree and expectant couples. *Sex Roles.*

Babl, J. D. (1979). Compensatory masculine responding as a function of sex role. *Journal of Consulting and Clinical Psychology, 47,* 252–257.

Bailyn, L. (1970). Career and family orientations of husbands and wives in relation to marital happiness. *Human Relationships, 23*(2), 97–144.

Bakan, D. (1966). *The duality of human existence.* Chicago: Rand McNally.

Baldwin, R. O. (1984). Stability of masculinity-femininity scores over an eleven-year period. *Sex Roles, 10,* 257–260.

Bales, J. (1984, November). Men troubled by societal changes. *APA Monitor,* p. 22.

Balswick, J., & Ingoldsby, B. (1982). Heroes and heroines among American adolescents. *Sex Roles, 8,* 243–249.

Bandura, A. (1965). Influence of the model's reinforcement contingencies on the acquisition of imitative responses. *Journal of Personality and Social Psychology, 1,* 589–595.

Bandura, A. (1969). *Principles of behavior modification.* Stanford, Calif.: Stanford University Press.

Bandura, A. (1973). *Aggression: A social learning analysis.* Englewood Cliffs, N.J.: Prentice-Hall.

Bandura, A., & Walters, R. H. (1963). *Social learning and personality development.* New York: Holt, Rinehart & Winston.

Banner, L. (1977). *Women in the college curriculum.* Princeton, N.J.: Princeton Project on Women in College Curriculum.

Bannon, J. A., & Southern, M. L. (1980). Father-absent women: Self-concept and modes of relating to men. *Sex Roles, 6,* 75–84.

Bardwick, J. M. (1979). *In transition.* New York: Holt, Rinehart & Winston.

Barfield, A. (1976). Biological influences on sex differences in behavior. In M. S. Teitelbaum (Ed.), *Sex differences: Social and biological perspectives* (pp. 62–121). New York: Anchor Books.

Barnett, R. C. (1982). Multiple roles and well-being: A study of mothers of preschool age children. *Psychology of Women Quarterly, 7,* 175–178.

Barnett, R., & Baruch, G. K. (1978). Women in middle years: A critique of research and theory. *Psychology of Women Quarterly, 3,* 187–197.

Baron, J. N., & Brelby, W. T. (1985). Organizational barriers to gender equality: Sex segregation of jobs and opportunities. In A. Rossi (Ed.), *Gender and the life course* (pp. 233–251). New York: Aldine.

Barry, R. J. (1980). Stereotyping of sex role in preschoolers in relation to age, family structure, and parental sexism. *Sex Roles, 6,* 795–806.

Bart, P. (1972). Depression in middle aged women. In V. Gornick and B. K. Moran (Eds.), *Women in sexist society* (pp. 162–186). New York: Basic Books.

Bart, P. B., & O'Brien, P. H. (1984). Stopping rape: Effective avoidance strategies. *Signs, 10,* 83–101.

Bar-Tal, D., & Saxe, L. (1976). Physical attractiveness and its relationship to sex-role stereotyping. *Sex Roles, 2,* 123–133.

Bartol, K. M., & Wortman, M. S., Jr. (1979). Sex of leader and subordinate role stress: A field study. *Sex Roles, 5,* 513–518.

Bartolome, F. (1972, November-December). Executives as human beings. *Harvard Business Review,* pp. 62–69ff.

Baruch, G., & Barnett, R. (1981). Father's participation in the care of their preschool children. *Sex Roles, 7,* 1043–1055.

Baruch, G. K., & Barnett, R. C. (in press). Multiple role involvement and well-being. In F. Crosby (Ed.), *Women's multiple roles.* New Haven: Yale University Press.

Baruch, G., Barnett, R., & Rivers, C. (1983). *Lifeprints: New patterns of love and work for today's women.* New York: McGraw-Hill.

Basler, B. (1984, Feb. 12). Study finds sex stereotypes affect voters at polls. *The New York Times,* p. 4.

Basow, S. A. (1984a). Cultural variations in sex-typing. *Sex Roles, 10,* 577–585.

Basow, S. A., (1984b). Ethnic group differences in educational achievement in Fiji. *Journal of Cross-Cultural Psychology, 15,* 435–451.

Basow, S. A. (in press). Correlates of sex-typing in Fiji. *Psychology of Women Quarterly.*

Basow, S. A., & Crawley, D. M. (1982). Helping behavior: Effects of sex and sex typing. *Social Behavior and Personality, 10,* 69–72.

Basow, S. A., & Distenfeld, M. S. (1985). Teacher expressiveness: More important for male teachers than female teachers? *Journal of Educational Psychology, 77,* 45–52.

Basow, S. A., & Howe, K. G. (1979a). Model influence on career choices of college students. *The Vocational Guidance Quarterly, 27,* 239–243.

Basow, S. A., & Howe, K. G. (1979b). Sex bias and career evaluations. *Perceptual and Motor Skills, 49,* 705–706.

Basow, S. A., & Howe, K. G. (1980). Role model influence: Effects of sex and sex-role attitudes in college students. *Psychology of Women Quarterly, 4,* 558–572.

Basow, S. A., & Howe, K. G. (1982, April). *Evaluations of college professors: Effects of professor sex-type, professor sex, and student sex.* Paper presented at the meeting of the Eastern Psychological Association, Baltimore.

Basow, S. A., & Schneck, R. (1984). *Eating disorders among college women.* ERIC Document Reproduction Service No. ED 243 049.

Basow, S. A., & Silberg, N. T. (in press). Student evaluations of college professors: Are males prejudiced against women professors? *Journal of Educational Psychology.*

Basow, S. A., & Spinner, J. (1984). Social acceptability of college athletes: Effects of sport sex-typing, athlete sex, and rater sex. *International Journal of Sport Psychology, 15,* 79–87.

Baucom, D. H. (1983). Sex role identity and the decision to regain control among women: A learned helplessness investigation. *Journal of Personality and Social Psychology, 44,* 334–343.

Baucom, D. H., Besch, P. K., & Callahan, S. (1985). Relation between testosterone concentration, sex role identity, and personality among females. *Journal of Personality and Social Psychology, 48,* 1218–1226.

Baucom, D. H., & Danker-Brown, P. (1979). Influence of sex roles on the development of learned helplessness. *Journal of Consulting and Clinical Psychology, 47,* 928–936.

Baucom, D. H., & Danker-Brown, P. (1984). Sex role identity and sex stereotyped tasks in the development of learned helplessness in women. *Journal of Personality and Social Psychology, 46,* 422–430.

Baude, A. (1979). Public policy and changing family patterns in Sweden 1930–1977. In J. Lipman-Blumen & J. Bernard (Eds.), *Sex roles and social policy: A complex social science equation* (pp. 145–175). Beverly Hills, Calif.: Sage.

Baxter, S., & Lansing, M. (1983). *Women and politics: The invisible majority,* rev. ed. Ann Arbor: University of Michigan Press.

Bayes, M. (1981). Wife battering and the maintenance of gender roles: A sociopsychological perspective. In E. Howell & M. Bayes (Eds.), *Women*

and mental health (pp. 440–448). New York: Basic Books.

Bear, S., Berger, M., & Wright, L. (1979). Even cowboys sing the blues: Difficulties experienced by men trying to adopt nontraditional sex roles and how clinicians can be helpful to them. *Sex Roles, 5,* 191–198.

Bearison, D. J. (1979). Sex-linked patterns of socialization. *Sex Roles, 5,* 11–18.

Beattie, M. Y., & Diehl, L. A. (1979). Effects of social conditions on the expression of sex-role stereotypes. *Psychology of Women Quarterly, 4,* 241–255.

Beck, J. (1977). Sexist math: Why women don't count in classroom. *Chicago Tribune.* Reported in *ER-Monitor, 3*(2), p. 12.

Beck, J. (1984, November 15). Women made little gain in elections. *The Easton Express,* p. 10.

Becker, B. J., & Hedges, L. N. (1984). Meta-analysis of cognitive gender differences: A comment on an analysis by Rosenthal and Rubin. *Journal of Educational Psychology, 76,* 583–587.

Bee, H. L., Mitchell, S. K., Barnard, K. E., Eyres, S. J., & Hammond, M. A. (1984). Predicting intellectual outcomes: Sex differences in response to early environmental stimulation. *Sex Roles, 10,* 783–803.

Beit-Hallahmi, B., & Rabin, A. I. (1977). The kibbutz as a social experiment and as a child-rearing laboratory. *American Psychologist, 32,* 534–551.

Bell, A., & Weinberg, M. (1978). *Homosexualities.* New York: Simon & Schuster.

Bell, A. P., Weinberg, M. S., & Hammersmith, S. K. (1981). *Sexual preference: Its development in men and women.* Bloomington: Indiana University Press.

Bell, D. H. (1983, July 31). Conflicting interests. *The New York Times Magazine,* p. 32.

Bell, R. R. (1981). Friendships of women and of men. *Psychology of Women Quarterly, 5,* 402–417.

Belle, D. (Ed.) (1982). *Lives in stress: Women and depression.* Beverly Hills, Calif.: Sage.

Bellinger, D. C., & Gleason, J. B. (1982). Sex differences in parental directives to young children. *Sex Roles, 8,* 1123–1139.

Belsky, J., & Sternberg, J. L. (1978). The effects of day-care: A critical review. *Child Development, 49,* 920–949.

Belzer, E. (1981). Orgasmic expulsions of women: A review and heuristic inquiry. *Journal of Sex Research, 17,* 1–12.

Bem, D., & Allen, A. (1974). On predicting some of the people some of the time: The search for cross-situational consistencies in behavior. *Psychological Review, 81,* 506–520.

Bem, S. L. (1974). The measurement of psychological androgyny. *Journal of Consulting and Clinical Psychology, 42,* 155–162.

Bem, S. L. (1975a). Androgyny versus the tight little lives of fluffy women and chesty men. *Psychology Today, 9,* 58–59ff.

Bem, S. L. (1975b). Sex role adaptability: One consequence of psychological androgyny. *Journal of Personality and Social Psychology, 31,* 634–643.

Bem, S. L. (1976). Probing the promise of androgyny. In A. Kaplan & J. Bean (Eds.), *Beyond sex role stereotypes: Readings toward a psychology of androgyny* (pp. 47–62). Boston: Little, Brown.

Bem, S. L. (1977). On the utility of alternative procedures for assessing psychological androgyny. *Journal of Consulting and Clinical Psychology, 45,* 196–205.

Bem, S. L. (1979). Theory and measurement of androgyny: A reply to the Pedhazur-Tetenbaum and Locksley-Colton critiques. *Journal of Personality and Social Psychology, 37,* 1047–1054.

Bem, S. L. (1981). *Bem Sex-Role Inventory, professional manual.* Palo Alto, Calif.: Consulting Psychologists Press.

Bem, S. L. (1981a). The BSRI and gender schema theory: A reply to Spence and Helmreich. *Psychological Review, 88,* 369–371.

Bem, S. L.(1981b). Gender schema theory: A cognitive account of sex typing. *Psychological Review, 88,* 354–364.

Bem, S. L. (1982). Gender schema theory and self-schema theory compared: A comment on Markus, Crane, Bernstein, and Siladi's "self-schemas and gender." *Journal of Personality and Social Psychology, 43,* 1192–1194.

Bem, S. L. (1983). Gender schema theory and its implications for child development: Raising gender-aschematic children in a gender-schematic society. *Signs, 8,* 598–616.

Bem, S. L.(1984). Androgyny and gender schema theory: A conceptual and empirical integration. In T. B. Sonderegger (Ed.), *Nebraska Symposium on Motivation: Psychology of Gender.* Lincoln, Nebraska: University of Nebraska Press.

Bem, S. L., & Bem, D. J. (1970). Case study of a nonconscious ideology: Teaching the woman to know her place. In D. J. Bem (Ed.), *Beliefs, attitudes and human affairs.* Monterey, Calif.: Brooks/Cole.

Bem, S. L., & Lenney, E. (1976). Sex-typing and the avoidance of cross-sex behavior. *Journal of Personality and Social Psychology, 33,* 48–54.

Bem, S., Martyna, W., & Watson, C. (1976). Sex-typing and androgyny: Further exploration of the expressive domain. *Journal of Personality and Social Psychology, 34,* 1016–1023.

Benbow, C. P., & Stanley, J. C. (1980). Sex differences in mathematical ability: Fact or artifact? *Science, 210,* 1262–1264.

Benbow, C. P., & Stanely, J. C. (1982). Consequences in high school and college of sex differences in mathematical reasoning ability: A longitudinal perspective. *American Educational Research Journal, 19,* 598–622.

Benbow, C. P., & Stanley, J. C. (1983). Sex differences in mathematical reasoning ability: More facts. *Science, 222,* 1029–1031.

Benton, C. J., Hernandez, A. C. P., Schmidt, A., Schmidt, M. D., Stone, A. J., & Weiner, B. (1983). Is hostility linked with affiliation among males and with achievement among females? A critique of Pollak & Gilligan. *Journal of Personality and Social Psychology, 45,* 1167–1171.

Berch, B. (1982). *The endless day: The political economy of women and work.* New York: Harcourt Brace Jovanovich.

Berg, J. H., & Peplau, L. A. (1982). Loneliness: The relationship of self-disclosure and androgyny. *Personality and Social Psychology Bulletin, 8,* 624–630.

Berg, J. H., Stephan, W. G., & Dodson, M. (1981). Attributional modesty in women. *Psychology of Women Quarterly, 5,* 711–727.

Berger, C., & Gold, D. (1979). Do sex differences in problem solving still exist? *Personality and Social Psychology Bulletin, 5,* 109–113.

Berger, M. (1979). Men's new family roles—some implications for therapists. *The Family Coordinator, 28,* 638–646.

Berger, M., Wallston, B. S., Foster, M., & Wright, L. (1977). You and me against the world: Dual career couples and joint job seeking. *Journal of Research and Development in Education, 10*(4), 30–37.

Bergman, J. (1974). Are little girls being harmed by Sesame Street? In J. Stacey, S. Bereaud, & J. Daniels (Eds.), *And Jill came tumbling after: Sexism in American education.* New York: Dell.

Berkeley Men's Center Manifesto, 1973. (1974). In J. Pleck and J. Sawyer (Eds.), *Men and masculinity* (pp. 173–174). Englewood Cliffs, N.J.: Prentice-Hall.

Berman, P. W. (1976). Social context as a determinant of sex differences in adults' attraction to infants. *Developmental Psychology, 12,* 365–366.

Berman, P. W. (1980). Are women more responsive than men to the young? A review of developmental and situational variables. *Psychological Bulletin, 88,* 668–695.

Berman, P. W., & Smith, V. L. (1984). Gender and situational differences in children's smiles, touch, and proxemics. *Sex Roles, 10,* 347–356.

Bernard, J. (1971). *Women and the public interest.* Chicago: Aldine.

Bernard, J. (1973). *The future of marriage*. New York: Bantam.

Bernard, J. (1974). *Sex differences: An overview*. New York: MSS Modular Publications, Modular 26, 1–18.

Bernard, J. (1976a). Homosexuality and female depression. *Journal of Social Issues, 34*(4).

Bernard, J. (1976b). Change and stability in sex-role and behavior. *Journal of Social Issues, 32*(3), 207–223.

Bernard, J. (1979a). Policy and women's time. In J. Lipman-Blumen & J. Bernard (Eds.), *Sex roles and social policy: A complex social science equation* (pp. 303–333). Beverly Hills, Calif.: Sage.

Bernard, J. (1979b). Women as voters: From redemptive to futurist role. In J. Lipman-Blumen & J. Bernard (Eds.), *Sex roles and social science equation* (pp. 279–286). Beverly Hills, Calif.: Sage.

Bernard, J. (1981). The good-provider role. *American Psychologist, 36*, 1–12.

Bernard, L. C. (1981). The multidimensional aspect of masculinity-femininity. *Journal of Personality and Social Psychology, 41*, 797–802.

Berndt, S. M., Berndt, D. J., & Kaiser, C. F. (1982). Attributional styles for helplessness and depression: The importance of sex and situational context. *Sex Roles, 8*, 433–441.

Berry, J. W. (1966). Temne and Eskimo perceptual skills. *International Journal of Psychology, 1*, 207–229.

Berryman-Fink, C. L., & Wilcox, J. R. (1983). A multivariate investigation of perceptual attributions concerning gender appropriateness in language. *Sex Roles, 9*, 663–681.

Bersoff, D., & Crosby, F. (1984). Job satisfaction and family status. *Personality and Social Psychology Bulletin, 10*, 79–83.

Best, F. (1981). Changing sex roles and worklife flexibility. *Psychology of Women Quarterly, 6*, 55–71.

Best, R. (1983) *We've all got scars: What boys and girls learn in elementary school*. Bloomington, Ind.: Indiana University Press.

Bettelheim, B. (1962). *Symbolic wounds*. New York: Collier.

Biaggio, M. K., Mohan, P. J., & Baldwin, C. (1985). Relationships among attitudes toward children, women's liberation, and personality characteristics. *Sex Roles, 12*, 47–62.

Bianchi, S., & Spain, D. (1983). *American women: Three decades of change*. Washington, D.C.: U.S. Government Printing Office.

Big rise in female engineering major found. (1984, May 9). *Chronicle of Higher Education*, p. 14.

Biller, H. B. (1981a). Father absence, divorce, & personality development. In M. Lamb (Ed.), *The role of the father in child development*, 2nd ed. (pp. 489–552). New York: Praeger.

Biller, H. B. (1981b). The father and sex role development. In M. Lamb (Ed.), *The role of the father in child development*, 2nd ed. (pp. 319–358). New York: Wiley & Sons.

Bird, C. (1979, June). The best years of a woman's life. *Psychology Today, 13*, 20–66.

Birnbaum, D. W., & Croll, W. L. (1984). The etiology of children's stereotypes about sex differences in emotionality. *Sex Roles, 10*, 677–691.

Birnbaum, D. W., Nosanchuk, T. A., & Croll, W. L. (1980). Children's stereotypes about sex differences in emotionality. *Sex Roles, 6*, 435–443.

Black, S. M., & Hill, C. E. (1984). The psychological well-being of women in their middle years. *Psychology of Women Quarterly, 8*, 282–292.

Blackwood, E. (1984). Sexuality and gender in certain Native American tribes: The case of cross-gender females. *Signs, 10*(1), 27–42.

Blake, C., & Cohen, H. (1984, August). *A meta-analysis of sex differences in moral development*. Paper presented at the meeting of the American Psychological Association, Toronto, Canada.

Blakely, M. K. (1985, April). Is one woman's sexuality another woman's pornography? *Ms.*, pp. 37, 38, 40, 42, 46, 47, 120, 123.

Blanck, P. D., Rosenthal, R., Snodgrass, S. E., DePaulo, B. M., & Zuckerman, M. (1981). Sex differences in eavesdropping on nonverbal cues: Developmental changes. *Journal of Personality and Social Psychology, 41*, 391–396.

Blascovich, J., Major, B., & Katkin, E. S. (1981). Sex-role orientation and Type A behavior. *Personality and Social Psychology Bulletin, 7*, 600–604.

Blau, F. D. (1975). Women in the labor force: An overview. In J. Freeman (Ed.), *Women: A feminist perspective* (pp. 211–226). Palo Alto, Calif.: Mayfield.

Blaubergs, M. S. (1978). Changing the sexist language: The theory behind the practice. *Psychology of Women Quarterly, 2*, 244–261.

Bleier, R. (1979). Social and political bias in science: An examination of animal studies and their generalizations to human behaviors and evolution. In E. Tobach & B. Rosoff (Eds.), *Genes and Gender II* (pp. 49–69). Staten Island: Gordian Press.

Bleier, R. (1984). *Science and gender: A critique of biology and its theories on women*. New York: Pergamon.

Block, J. D. (1980). *Friendship*. New York: McMillan.

Block, J., Denker, E. R., & Tittle, C. K. (1981). Perceived influences on career choices of eleventh graders: Sex, SES, and ethnic group comparisons. *Sex Roles, 7*, 895–904.

Block, J. H. (1973). Conceptions of sex-roles: Some cross-cultural and longitudinal perspectives. *American Psychologist, 28,* 512–526.

Blumberg, R. L. (1977). Women and work around the world: A cross-cultural examination of sex division of labor and sex status. In A. Sargent (Ed.), *Beyond sex roles* (pp. 412–433). St. Paul: West.

Blumberg, R. L. (1979). A paradigm for predicting the position of women: Policy implications and problems. In J. Lipman-Blumen & J. Bernard (Eds.), *Sex roles and social policy: A complex social science equation* (pp. 113–142). Beverly Hills, Calif.: Sage.

Blumstein, P. W., & Schwartz, P. (1977). Bisexuality: Some social psychological issues. *Journal of Social Issues, 33*(2), 30–45.

Blumstein, P., & Schwartz, P. (1983). *American Couples.* New York: William Morrow.

Bohen, H. H., & Viveros-Long, A. (1981). *Balancing jobs and family life.* Philadelphia: Temple University Press.

Bond, L. A. (1981). Perceptions of sex-role deviations: An attributional analysis. *Sex Roles, 7,* 107–115.

Boneparth, E. (Ed.) (1982). *Women, power, and policy.* New York: Pergamon.

Booth, A. (1972). Sex and social participation. *American Sociological Review, 37,* 183–193.

Booth, A., & Edwards, J. N. (1980). Fathers: The invisible parent. *Sex Roles, 6,* 445–456.

Borges, M. A., Levine, J. R., & Dutton, L. J. (1984). Men's and women's ratings of life satisfaction by age of respondent and age interval judged. *Sex Roles, 11,* 345–350.

Borges, M. A., Levine, J. R., & Naylor, P. A. (1982). Self-ratings and projected rating of sex-role attitudes. *Psychology of Women Quarterly, 6,* 406–414.

Borges, M. A., & Vaughn, L. S. (1977). Cognitive differences between the sexes in memory for names and faces. *Perceptual and Motor Skills, 45,* 317–318.

Boserup, E. (1970). *Women's role in economic development.* London: Allen & Unwin.

Boswell, S. L. (1985). The influence of sex-role stereotyping on women's attitudes and achievement in mathematics. In S. Chipman, L. Brush, & D. Wilson (Eds.), *Women and mathematics: Balancing the equation* (pp. 175–197). Hillsdale, N.J.: Lawrence Erlbaum Associates.

Boulding, E. (1979). Introduction. In J. Lipman-Blumen and J. Bernard (Eds.), *Sex roles and social policy: A complex social science equation* (pp. 7–14). Beverly Hills, Calif.: Sage.

Bowles, G., & Duelli-Klein, R. (Eds.) (1983). *Theories of women's studies.* London: Routledge & Kegan Paul.

Bradbard, M. R., & Endsley, R. C. (1983). The effects of sex-typed labeling on preschool children's information-seeking and retention. *Sex Roles, 9,* 247–260.

Braito, R., Dean, D., Powers, E., & Bruton, B. (1981). The inferiority games: Perceptions and behavior. *Sex Roles, 7,* 65–72.

Bram, S. (1983). The effects of childbearing on woman's mental health: A critical review of the literature. In E. Tobach & B. Rosoff (Eds.), *Genes and Gender IV* (pp. 143–160). Staten Island: Gordian Press.

Bram, S. (1984). Voluntarily childless women: Traditional or nontraditional? *Sex Roles, 10,* 195–206.

Brannon, R. (1976). The male sex-role: Our culture's blueprint of manhood and what it's done for us lately. In D. David & R. Brannon (Eds.), *The forty-nine percent majority.* Reading, Mass.: Addison-Wesley.

Brannon, R. (1978). Measuring attitudes toward women (and otherwise): A methodological critique. In J. Sherman & F. Denmark (Eds.), *The future of women: Issues in psychology* (pp. 647–709). New York: Psychological Dimensions.

Brannon, R. (1981). Current methodological issues in paper-and-pencil measuring instruments. *Psychology of Women Quarterly, 5,* 618–627.

Brehm, S. S., Powell, L., & Coke, J. S. (1984). The effects of empathic instructions upon donating behavior: Sex differences in young children. *Sex Roles, 10,* 405–416.

Brehony, K. A., & Geller, E. S. (1981). Relationship between psychological androgyny, social conformity and perceived locus of control. *Psychology of Women Quarterly, 6,* 204–217.

Bremer, T. H., & Wittig, M. A. (1980). Fear of success: A personality trait or a response to occupational deviance and role overload? *Sex Roles, 6,* 27–46.

Brenner, M. H. (1973). *Mental illness and the economy.* Cambridge, Mass.: Harvard University Press.

Brenner, M. H. (1979). Influence of the social environment on psychopathology: The historic perspective. In J. S. Barrett (Ed.), *Stress and mental disorder.* New York: Raven Press.

Brewer, M. B., & Berk, R. A. (Eds.) (1982). Beyond nine to five: Sexual harassment on the job. *Journal of Social Issues, 38* (Whole No. 4).

Brewer, M. B., & Blum, M. W. (1979). Sex-role androgyny and patterns of casual attribution for academic achievement. *Sex Roles, 5,* 783–796.

Briere, J., Corne, S., Runta, M., & Malamuth, N. (1984, Aug.). *The rape arousal inventory: Predicting actual and potential sexual aggression in a university population.* Paper presented at the meeting of the American Psychological Association, Toronto, Canada.

Briere, J., & Lanktree, C. (1983). Sex-role related effects of sex bias in language. *Sex Roles, 9,* 625–632.

Briere, J., & Malamuth, N. M. (1983). Self-reported likelihood of sexually aggressive behavior: Attitudinal versus sexual explanations. *Journal of Research in Personality, 17,* 315–323,

Brinn, J., Kraemer, K., Warm, J. S., & Paludi, M. A. (1984). Sex-role preferences in four age levels. *Sex Roles, 11,* 901–910.

Briscoe, A. M. (1978). Hormones and behavior. In E. Tobach & B. Rosoff (Eds.), *Genes and Gender* (pp. 31–50). Staten Island, New York: Gordian Press.

Brodsky, A. M. (1980). A decade of feminist influence on psychotherapy. *Psychology of Women Quarterly, 4,* 331–344.

Brodsky, A. M., & Hare-Mustin, R. T. (Eds.) (1980). *Women and psychotherapy: An assessment of research and practice.* New York: Grulford.

Brodsky, A. M., Holroyd, J., Payton, C. R., Rubenstein, E. A., Rosenkrantz, P., Sherman, J., Zell, F., Cummings, T., & Suber, C. J. (1978). Source materials for nonsexist therapy. *JSAS catalog of selected documents in psychology, 8*(2), 40. (Ms. No. 1685).

Brody, J. E. (1979, May 8). Marriage is good for health and longevity, studies say. *The New York Times,* p. C1.

Brody, L. R. (1984). Sex and age variations in the quality and intensity of children's emotional attributions to hypothetical situations. *Sex Roles, 11,* 51–59.

Bronfenbrenner, U. (1974). Developmental research, public policy and the ecology of childhood. *Child Development, 45,* 1–5.

Bronfenbrenner, U. (1977). Toward an experimental ecology of human development. *American Psychologist, 32,* 513–531.

Bronstein, P. (1984a). Differences in mothers' and fathers' behaviors to children: A cross-cultural comparison. *Developmental Psychology, 20,* 995–1003.

Bronstein, P. (1984b, August). *Getting academic jobs: Are women equally qualified—and equally successful.* Paper presented at the meeting of the American Psychological Association, Toronto.

Brooks, A. (1983, Oct.). For the woman: Strides and snags. *The New York Times,* p. 31.

Brooks-Gunn, J., & Fisch, M. (1980). Psychological androgyny and college students' judgments of mental health. *Sex Roles, 6,* 575–580.

Broude, N., & Garrard, M. (1982). *Feminism and art history.* New York: Harper & Row.

Broverman, D. M., Klaiber, E. L., Kobayaski, Y., & Vogel, W. (1968). Roles of activation and inhibition in sex differences in cognitive abilities. *Psychological Review, 75*(11), 5–7, 23–50, 167.

Broverman, I., Broverman, D. M., Clarkson, F. E., Rosenkrantz, P. S., & Vogel, S. R. (1970). Sex-role stereotypes and clinical judgments of mental health. *Journal of Consulting and Clinical Psychology, 34,* 1–7.

Broverman, I., Vogel, S. R., Broverman, D. M., Clarkson, F. E., & Rosenkrantz, P. S. (1972). Sex role stereotypes: A current appraisal. *Journal of Social Issues, 28,* 59–78.

Brown, A., Larsen, M. B., Rankin, S. A., & Ballard, R. A. (1980). Sex differences in information processing. *Sex Roles, 6,* 663–673.

Brown, D., Fulkerson, K. F., Furr, S., Ware, W. B., & Voight, N. L. (1984). Locus of control, sex role orientation, and self-concept in black and white third- and sixth-grade male and female leaders in a rural community. *Developmental Psychology, 20,* 717–721.

Brown, D. G. (1956). Sex role preference in young children. *Psychological Monographs, 70*(14, Whole No. 42).

Brown, J. K. (1970). Economic organization and position of women among the Iroquois. *Ethnohistory, 17,* 151–167.

Brown, J. K. (1976). An anthropological perspective on sex roles and subsistence. In M. Teitelbaum (Ed.), *Sex differences: Social and biological perspectives* (pp. 122–137). New York: Anchor Press.

Brown, J. K., Kerns, V., & contributors. (1985). *In her prime: A new view of middle-aged women.* South Hadley, Mass.: Bergin & Garvey.

Brown, J. M. (1982, April). *Attitude towards violence and self reports of participation in contact sports.* Paper presented at the meeting of the Eastern Psychological Association, Baltimore.

Brown, J. M., & Davies, N. (1978, May). Attitude towards violence among college athletes. *Journal of Sport Behavior, 1,* pp. 67–70.

Brown, J. W., Aldrich, M. L., & Hall, P. Q. (1978). *The participation of women in scientific research.* Washington, D.C.: National Science Foundation.

Brown, L. M. (1975). Sexism in western art. In J. Freeman (Ed.), *Women: A feminist perspective* (pp. 309–322). Palo Alto, Calif.: Mayfield.

Brown, P., & Fox, H. (1979). Sex differences in divorce. In E. S. Gomberg & V. Franks (Eds.), *Gender and diosordered behavior: Sex differences in psychopathology* (pp. 309–322). New York: Brunner/Mazel.

Brown, S. M. (1979). Male versus female leaders: A comparison of empirical studies. *Sex Roles, 5,* 597–611.

Brown, V., & Geis, F. L. (1984). Turning lead into gold: Evaluations of men and women leaders and the alchemy of social consensus. *Journal of Personality and Social Psychology, 46,* 811–824.

Brownmiller, S. (1975). *Against our will: Men, women and rape.* New York: Simon & Schuster.

Brozan, N. A. (1979, January 19). A study of the American man. *The New York Times,* p. 47.

Brush, L., Gold, A., & White, M. (1983). The paradox of intention and effect: A women's studies course. *Signs, 3,* 870–883.

Bryant, F. B., & Veroff, J. (1982). The structure of psychological well-being: A sociohistorical analysis. *Journal of Personality and Social Psychology, 43,* 653–673.

Bryden, M. P. (1979). Evidence for sex-related differences in cerebral organization. In M. A. Wittig & A. C. Petersen (Eds.), *Sex-related differences in cognitive functioning: Developmental issues* (pp. 121–143). New York: Academic Press.

Bryden, M. P. (1983). *Sex-related differences in perceptual asymmetry.* Paper presented at the meeting of the American Psychological Association, Anaheim.

Buck, R. (1977). Nonverbal communication of affect in preschool children. Relationships with personality and skin conductance. *Journal of Personality and Social Psychology, 35,* 225–236.

Budd, B. E., Clance, P. R., & Simerly, D. E. (1985). Spatial configurations: Erikson reexamined. *Sex Roles, 12,* 571–577.

Bunch, C. (1975). Lesbians in revolt. In M. Myron & C. Bunch (Eds.), *Lesbianism and the women's movement* (pp. 29–38). Oakland, Calif.: Diana Press.

Bunker, B. B., Forcey, B., Wilderom, C. P. M., & Elgie, D. M. (1984, August). *The competitive behaviors of men and women: Is there a difference?* Paper presented at the meeting of the American Psychological Association, Toronto, Canada.

Bunker, B. B., & Seashore, E. W. (1977). Power; collusion; intimacy-sexuality; support. In A. G. Sargent (Ed.), *Beyond sex roles* (pp. 356–370). St. Paul: West.

Burchardt, C. J., & Serbin, L. A. (1982). Psychological androgyny and personality adjustment in college and psychiatric populations. *Sex Roles, 8,* 835–851.

Burda, P. C., Jr., Vaux, A., & Schill, T. (1984). Social support resources: Variation across sex and sex role. *Personality and Social Psychology Bulletin, 10,* 119–126.

Burgess, A. W., & Holmstrom, L. L. (1979). *Rape: Crisis and recovery.* Bowie, Md.: Robert J. Brady Co.

Burkhauser, R. V., & Holden, K. C. (Eds.). (1982). *A challenge to social security—The changing roles of women and men in American society.* New York: Academic.

Burleigh, N. (1983, November 22). Youngsters of working moms retain old ideas of sex roles. *Easton Express.*

Burlew, A. K. (1982). The experience of black females in traditional and nontraditional professions. *Psychology of Women Quarterly, 6,* 312–326.

Burt, M. R. (1980). Cultural myths and supports for rape. *Journal of Personality and Social Psychology, 38,* 217–230.

Buss, D. M. (1981). Sex differences in the evaluation and performance of dominant acts. *Journal of Personality and Social Psychology, 40,* 147–154.

Bussey, K., & Bandura, A. (1984). Influence of gender constancy and social power on sex-linked modeling. *Journal of Personality and Social Psychology, 47,* 1292–1302.

Bussey, K., & Maughan, B. (1982). Gender differences in moral reasoning. *Journal of Personality and Social Psychology, 42,* 701–706.

Bussey, K., & Perry, D. G. (1982). Same-sex imitation: The avoidance of cross-sex models or the acceptance of same-sex models? *Sex Roles, 8,* 773–784.

Butler, D., & Geis, F. (1985, March). *Nonverbal affective responses to male and female leaders.* Paper presented at the meeting of the Eastern Psychology Association, Boston.

Butler, M., & Paisley, W. (Eds.) (1980). *Women and the mass media: Sourcebook for research and action.* Beverly Hills, Calif.: Sage.

Byrne, Donn. (1977). Social psychology and the study of sexual behavior. *Personality and Social Psychology Bulletin, 3,* 3–30.

Cahill, S. E. (1983). Reexamining the acquisition of sex roles: A social interactionist approach. *Sex Roles, 9,* 1–15.

Calder, B. G., & Ross, M. (1977). Sexual discrimination and work performance. *Personality and Social Psychology Bulletin, 13,* 429–433.

Caldwell, M. A., & Peplau, L. A. (1982). Sex differences in same-sex friendship. *Sex Roles, 8,* 721–732.

Caldwell, M. A., & Peplau, L. A. (1984). The balance of power in lesbian relationships. *Sex Roles, 10,* 587–599.

Callahan-Levy, C. M., & Messe, L. A. (1979). Sex differences in the allocation of pay. *Journal of Personality and Social Psychology, 37,* 433–446.

Cambridge Women's Peace Collective (1984). *My country is the whole world: An anthology of women's work on peace and war.* Boston: Pandora Press/Routledge and Kegan Paul.

Cameron, E., Eisenberg, N., & Tryon, K. (1985). The relations between sex-typed play and preschoolers' social behavior. *Sex Roles, 12,* 601–615.

Campbell, A. (1975, May). The American way of mating. Marriage sí, children only maybe. *Psychology Today,* pp. 37–43.

Candy, S. G., Troll, L. E., & Levy, S. G. (1981). A developmental exploration of friendship functions in women. *Psychology of Women Quarterly, 5,* 456–472.

Cann, A., & Garnett, A. K. (1984). Sex stereotype impacts on competence ratings by children. *Sex Roles, 11,* 333–343.

Cann, A., & Haight, J. M. (1983). Children's perceptions of relative competence in sex-typed occupations. *Sex Roles, 9,* 767–773.

Cano, L., Solomon, S., & Holmes, D. S. (1984). Fear of success: The influence of sex, sex-role identity, and components of masculinity. *Sex Roles, 10,* 341–346.

Canter, R. J. (1979). Achievement-related expectations and aspirations in college women. *Sex Roles, 5,* 453–470.

Canter, R. J., & Ageton, S. S. (1984). The epidemiology of adolescent sex-role attitudes. *Sex Roles, 11,* 657–676.

Canter, R. J., & Meyerowitz, B. C. (1984). Sex-role stereotypes: Self-reports of behavior. *Sex Roles, 10,* 293–306.

Cantor, A. (1983). The Lilith question. In S. Heschel (Ed.), *On being a Jewish feminist: A reader* (pp. 40–50). New York: Schocken.

Cantor, M. G., & Pingree, S. (1983). *The soap opera.* Beverly Hills, Calif.: Sage.

Caplan, P. J., MacPherson, G. M., & Tobin, P. (1985). Do sex-related differences in spatial abilities exist? A multilevel critique with new data. *American Psychologist, 40,* 786–799.

Card, J. J., & Farrell, W. S., Jr. (1983). Nontraditional careers for women: A prototypical example. *Sex Roles, 9,* 1005–1022.

Cardell, M., Finn, S., & Maracek, J. (1981). Sex-role identity, sex-role behavior, and satisfaction in heterosexual, lesbian, and gay male couples. *Sex Roles, 5,* 488–494.

Carlson, B. E. (1984). The father's contribution to child care: Effects on children's perceptions of parental roles. *American Journal of Orthopsychiatry, 54,* 123–136.

Carlson, H. M., & Baxter, L. A. (1984). Androgyny, depression, and self-esteem in Irish homosexual and heterosexual males and females. *Sex Roles, 10,* 457–467.

Carlson, J. E. (1976). The sexual role. In F. I. Nye (Ed.), *Role structure and analysis of the family.* Beverly Hills, Calif.: Sage.

Carlson, R. (1965). Stability and change in the adolescent's self-image. *Child Development, 36,* 659–666.

Carroll, J. L, Volk, K. D., & Hyde, J. S. (1984). Differences between males and females in motives for engaging in sexual intercourse. *Archives of Sexual Behavior.*

Carroll, S. J. (1984a). Women candidates and support for feminist concerns: The closet feminist syndrome. *The Western Political Quarterly, 37,* 307–323.

Carroll, S. J. (1984b, August). *Women's autonomy and the gender gap.* Paper presented at the meeting of the American Psychological Association, Toronto, Ontario.

Carter, C. S., & Greenough, W. T. (1979, September). Sending the right sex message. *Psychology Today,* p. 112.

Carter-Saltzman, L. (1979). Patterns of cognitive functioning in relation to handedness and sex-related differences. In M. A. Wittig and A. C. Petersen (Eds.), *Sex-related differences in cognitive functioning: Developmental issues* (pp. 97–118). New York: Academic Press.

Cartwright, R. D., Lloyd, S., Nelson, J. B., & Bass, S. (1983). The traditional-liberated woman dimension: Social stereotype and self-concept. *Journal of Personality and Social Psychology, 44,* 581–588.

Cash, T. F., Gillen, B., & Burns, D. S. (1977). Sexism and "beautyism" in personnel consultant decision making. *Journal of Applied Psychology, 62,* 301–310.

Cash, T. F., & Trimer, C. A. (1984). Sexism and beautyism in women's evaluations of peer performance. *Sex Roles, 10,* 87–98.

Casualties on campus: Rape. (1983, August 31). *Chronicle of Higher Education,* p. 4.

Catalyst. (1983). *Why should companies think about women?* (Available from author, 14 E. 60th St., New York, N.Y. 10022.)

Cazenave, N. A. (1984). Race, socioeconomic status, and age: The social context of American masculinity. *Sex Roles, 11,* 639–656.

Center for the American Woman and Politics. (1984). *Women holding elective office.* (Available from author, Eagleton Institute of Politics, Rutgers University, New Brunswick, N.J. 08901).

Chafetz, J. (1984). *Sex and advantage: A comparative macro-structural theory of sex stratification.* Totowa, N.J.: Rowman & Allanheld.

Chafetz, J. S. (1978). *Masculine/feminine or human?* (2nd ed.). Itasca, Ill.: Peacock.

Change over a decade. (1985, March 10). *The New York Times,* p. 24E.

Chaplin, W. F., & Goldberg, L. R. (1985). A failure to replicate the Bem and Allen study of individual differences in cross-situational consistency. *Journal of Personality and Social Psychology, 47,* 1074–1090.

Chavez, D. (1985) Perpetuation of gender inequality: A content analysis of comic strips. *Sex Roles, 13,* 93–102.

Chavkin, W. (1984, September). Parental leave—What there is and what there should be. *Ms.,* pp. 115–118.

Cheatham, H. E. (1984). Integration of women into the U.S. military. *Sex Roles, 11,* 141–153.

Check, J. V. P., & Malamuth, N. M. (1983). Sex role stereotyping and reactions to depictions of stranger versus acquaintance rape. *Journal of Personality and Social Psychology, 45,* 344–356.

Chelune, G. J. (1976). Reactions to male and female disclosure at two levels. *Journal of Personality and Social Psychology, 34,* 1000–1003.

Cherry, F., & Deaux, K. (1978). Fear of success versus fear of gender-inappropriate behavior. *Sex Roles, 4,* 97–101.

Cherry, L. (1975). Teacher-child verbal interaction: An approach to the study of sex differences. In B. Thorne & N. Henley (Eds.), *Language and sex: Differences and dominance* (pp. 172–183). Rowley, Mass.: Newbury House.

Cherry, L., & Lewis, M. (1976). Mothers and two-year-olds: A study of sex-differentiated aspects of verbal interaction. *Developmental Psychology, 12,* 278–282.

Cherulnik, P. D. (1979). Sex differences in the expression of emotion in a structured social encounter. *Sex Roles, 5,* 413–424.

Chesler, P. (1971). Patient and patriarch: Women in the psychotherapeutic relationship. In V. Gornick & B. Moran (Eds.), *Woman in sexist society: Studies in power and powerlessness* (pp. 251–275). New York: Basic Books.

Chesler, P. (1972). *Woman and madness.* New York: Doubleday.

Chesler, P. (1978). *About men.* New York: Simon & Schuster.

Chesler, P., & Goodman, E. J. (1976). *Women, money and power.* New York: Morrow.

Chester, N. L. (1983). Sex differentiation in two high school environments: Implications for career development among black adolescent females. *Journal of Social Issues, 39*(3), 29–40.

Chino, A. F., & Funabiki, D. (1984). A cross-validation of sex differences in the expression of depression. *Sex Roles, 11,* 175–187.

Chipman, S. F., Brush, L. R., & Wilson, D. M. (Eds.). (1985). *Women and mathematics: Balancing the equation.* Hillsdale, N.J.: Lawrence Erlbaum.

Chodorow, N. (1978). *The reproduction of mothering: Psychoanalysis and the sociology of gender.* Berkeley: University of California Press.

Chusmir, L. H., & Parker, B. (1984). Dimensions of need for power: Personalized vs. socialized power in female and male managers. *Sex Roles, 11,* 759–769.

Cicirelli, V. G. (1982). Sibling influence throughout the lifespan. In M. Lamb and B. Sutton-Smith (Eds.), *Siblings relationships: Their nature and significance across the lifespan* (pp. 267–284). Hillsdale, N.J.: Lawrence Erlbaum.

Cicone, M. N., & Ruble, D. N. (1978). Beliefs about males. *Journal of Social Issues, 34*(1), 5–16.

Clancy, K., & Gove, W. (1974). Sex differences in mental illness: An analysis of response bias in self reports. *American Journal of Sociology, 80,* 205–216.

Clarke, A. E., & Ruble, D. N. (1978). Young adolescents' beliefs concerning menstruation. *Child Development, 49,* 231–234.

Clayton, O., Jr., Baird, A. C., & Levinson, R. M. (1984). Subjective decision making in medical school admissions: Potential for discrimination. *Sex Roles, 10,* 527–532.

Coates, S. (1974). Sex differences in field independence among preschool children. In R. C. Friedman et al. (Eds.), *Sex difference in behavior* (pp. 259–274). New York: Wiley.

Cobb, N. J., Stevens-Long, J., & Goldstein, S. (1982). The influence of televised models on toy preference in children. *Sex Roles, 8,* 1075–1080.

Cochran, S. D., & Hammen, C. L. (1985). Perceptions of stressful life events and depression: A test of attributional models. *Journal of Personality and Social Psychology, 48,* 1562–1571.

Cohen, D., & Wilkie, F. (1979). Sex-related differences in cognition among the elderly. In M. A. Wittig & A. C. Petersen (Eds.), *Sex-related differences in cognitive functioning: Developmental issues* (pp. 145–159). New York: Academic Press.

Coker, D. R. (1984). The relationship among concepts and cognitive maturity in preschool children. *Sex Roles, 10,* 19–31.

Colangelo, N., Rosenthal, D. M., & Dettmann, D. F. (1984). Maternal employment and job satisfaction and their relationship to children's perceptions and behaviors. *Sex Roles, 10,* 693–702.

Cole, J. R. (1979). *Fair science.* New York: Free Press.

Coleman, J. C. (with S. Basow & P. Railey). (1984). *Intimate relationships, marriage, and family.* Indianapolis, Ind.: Bobbs-Merrill.

Coleman, M., & Ganong, L. H. (1985). Love and sex-role stereotypes: Do "macho" men and "feminine" women make better lovers? *Journal of Personality and Social Psychology, 49,* 170–176.

College degrees awarded in 1980. (1981, November 10). *Chronicle of Higher Education,* p. 10.

College women and self-esteem. (1978, December 10). *The New York Times,* p. 85.

Collier, J. F., & Rosaldo, M. Z. (1981). Politics and gender in simple societies. In S. Ortner & H.

Whitehead (Eds.), *Sexual meanings: The cultural construction of gender and sexuality* (pp. 275–329). Cambridge: Cambridge University Press.

Collins, G. (1979, June 1). A new look at life with father. *The New York Times Magazine*, pp. 30–31ff.

Collins, G. (1984, February 13). New studies on "girl toys" and "boy toys." *New York Times*, p. A23.

Colten, M. A., & Marsh, J. C. (1984). A sex-roles perspective on drug and alcohol use by women. In C. Widom (Ed.), *Sex roles and psychopathology* (pp. 219–248). New York: Plenum.

Comes the revolution. (1978, July 26). *Time*, pp. 54–59.

Condry, J. C. (1984). Gender identity and social competence. *Sex Roles, 11*, 485–511.

Condry, J., & Dyer, S. (1976). Fear of success: Attribution of cause to the victim. *Journal of Social Issues, 32*(3), 63–83.

Condry, S. M., Condry, J. C., Jr., & Pogatshnik, L. W. (1983). Sex differences: A study of the ear of the beholder. *Sex Roles, 9*, 697–704.

Connell, D. M., & Johnson, J. E. (1970). Relationship between sex-role identification and self-esteem in early adolescence. *Developmental Psychology, 3*, 268.

Connor, J. M., & Serbin, L. A. (1978). Children's responses to stories with male and female characters. *Sex Roles, 4*, 637–645.

Connor, J. M., & Serbin, L. A. (1985). Visual-spatial skill: Is it important for mathematics? Can it be taught? In S. Chipman, L. Brush, & D. Wilson (Eds.), *Women and mathematics: Balancing the equation* (pp. 151–174). Hillsdale, N.J.: Lawrence Erlbaum & Associates.

Connor, J. M., Serbin, L. A., & Ender, R. A. (1978). Responses of boys and girls to aggressive, assertive, and passive behaviors of male and female characters. *Journal of Genetic Psychology, 133*, 59–69.

Constantinople, A. (1973). Masculinity-femininity: An exception to a famous dictum? *Psychological Bulletin, 80*, 389–407.

Constantinople, A. (1979). Sex-role acquisition: In search of the elephant. *Sex Roles, 5*, 121–133.

Cook, A. S., Fritz, J. J., McCornack, B. L., & Visperas, C. (1985). Early gender differences in the functional usage of language. *Sex Roles, 12*, 909–915.

Cook, L. (1981, February 7). Study: Women still do most housework. *Easton Express*, p. 1.

Cooke, R. A., & Rousseau, D. M. (1984). Stress and strain from family roles and work-role expectations. *Journal of Applied Psychology, 69*, 252–260.

Cooper, H. M. (1979). Statistically combining independent studies: A meta-analysis of sex differences in conformity research. *Journal of Personality and Social Psychology, 37*, 131–146.

Cooper, K., Chassin, L., & Zeiss, A. (1985). The relation of sex-role attitudes to the marital satisfaction and personal adjustment of dual-worker couples with preschool children. *Sex Roles, 12*, 227–241.

Corcoran, M., Duncan, G. J., & Hill, M. S. (1984). The economic fortunes of women and children: Lessons from the panel study of income dynamics. *Signs, 10*, 232–248.

Cordes, C. (1983a, August). Child advocates push for policy on infant leave. *APA Monitor*, pp. 19–21.

Cordes, C. (1983b, December). Researchers make room for father. *APA Monitor*, pp. 1, 9, 10.

Cordes, C. (1984a, August). The rise of one-parent black families. *APA Monitor*, pp. 16–17.

Cordes, C. (1984b, October). "Feminine" morality ignored by theorists. *APA Monitor*, p. 23.

Cordes, C. (1985, January). At risk in America. *APA Monitor*, pp. 9–11, 27.

Cornelius, R. R., & Averill, J. R. (1983). Sex differences in fear of spiders. *Journal of Personality and Social Psychology, 45*, 377–383.

Costrich, N., Feinstein, J., Kidder, L., Maracek, J., & Pascale, L. (1975). When stereotypes hurt: Three studies of penalties for sex-role reversals. *Journal of Experimental Psychology, 11*, 520–530.

Cotten-Huston, A. L., & Lunney, G. S. (1983, August). *Young children's attributions: Pink and blue are for adults only.* Paper presented at the meeting of the American Psychological Association, Anaheim.

Council on Interracial Books for Children, Inc. (1977). *Checklist: Rate your school for racism and sexism.* (Available from author, 1841 Broadway, New York, N.Y. 10023).

Courtney, A. E., & Whipple, T. W. (1983). *Sex stereotyping in advertising.* Lexington, Mass.: D. C. Heath & Company.

Cowan, C. P., & Cowan, P. A. (1983, August). *Men's involvement in the family: Implications for family well-being.* Paper presented at the meeting of the American Psychological Association, Anaheim.

Cowan, G., Drinkard, J., & MacGavin, L. (1984). The effects of target, age, and gender on use of power strategies. *Journal of Personality and Social Psychology, 47*, 1391–1398.

Cowan, G., & Kasen, J. H. (1984). Form of reference: Sex differences in letters of recommendation. *Journal of Personality and Social Psychology, 46*, 636–645.

Cox, S., & Radloff, L. S. (1984). Depression in relation to sex roles: Differences in learned susceptibility and precipitating factors. In C. Widom

(Ed.), *Sex roles and psychopathology.* (pp. 123–144). New York: Plenum.

Craig, T. J., & Lin, S. P. (1984). Sex differences in mortality rate among long-stay psychiatric inpatients. *Sex Roles, 10,* 725–732.

Crane, M., & Markus, H. (1982). Gender identity: The benefits of a self-schema approach. *Journal of Personality and Social Psychology, 43,* 1195–1197.

Crombie, G. (1983). Women's attribution patterns and their relation to achievement: An examination of within-sex differences. *Sex Roles, 9,* 1171–1182.

Cronkite, R. C., & Moos, R. H. (1984). Sex and marital status in relation to treatment and outcome of alcoholic patients. *Sex Roles, 11,* 93–112.

Crosby, F. (1982). *Relative deprivation and working women.* New York: Oxford University Press.

Crosby, F., Jose, P., & Wong-McCarthy, W. (1982). Gender, androgyny, and conversational assertiveness. In C. Mayo and N. Henley (Eds.), *Gender and nonverbal behavior* (pp. 151–169). New York: Springer-Verlag.

Croteau, J. M., & Burda, P. C., Jr. (1983). Structured group programming on men's roles: A creative approach to change. *The Personnel and Guidance Journal, 62,* 243–245.

Crovitz, E., & Steinmann, A. (1980). A decade later: Black-White attitudes toward women's familial role. *Psychology of Women Quarterly, 5,* 170–176.

Croxton, J. S., Chiacchia, D., & Wagner, C. (1984, April). *Gender differences in attitudes toward sports and reactions to competitive situations.* Paper presented at the meeting of the Eastern Psychological Association, Baltimore.

Croxton, J. S., & Klonsky, B. G. (1982). Sex differences in causal attributions for success and failure in real and hypothetical sport settings. *Sex Roles, 8,* 399–409.

Cruikshank, M. (1982). *Lesbian studies: Present and future.* Old Westbury, N.Y.: The Feminist Press.

Cuca, J. (1976, March). Women psychologists and marriage: A bad match? *American Psychologist,* p. 3.

Culp, R. E., Cook, A. S., & Housley, P. C. (1983). A comparison of observed and reported adult-infant interactions: Effects of perceived sex. *Sex Roles, 9,* 475–479.

Cunningham, J. D., & Antill, J. K. (1984). Changes in masculinity and femininity across the family life cycle: A reexamination. *Developmental Psychology, 20,* 1135–1141.

Cunningham, J. D., Braiker, H., & Kelley, H. H. (1982). Marital-status and sex differences in problems reported by married and cohabitating couples. *Psychology of Women Quarterly, 6,* 415–427.

Curtis, R. (1981). Success and failure, gender differences, and the menstrual cycle. *Psychology of Women Quarterly, 5,* 702–710.

Custody: Kramer vs. Kramer. (1980, February 4). *Time,* p. 40.

Dally, A. (1983). *Inventing motherhood: The consequences of an ideal.* New York: Schocken.

Dalton, K. (1969). *The menstrual cycle.* New York: Pantheon.

Daly, M. (1974). *Beyond God the father.* Boston: Beacon.

Daly, M. (1978). *Gyn/Ecology.* Boston: Beacon.

Dan, A. J. (1976). Patterns of behavioral and mood variation in men and women: Variability and the menstrual cycle. *Dissertation Abstracts International, 37*(6-B), 3145–3146.

Dan, A. J. (1979). The menstrual cycle and sex-related differences in cognitive variability. In M. A. Wittig and A. C. Petersen (Eds.), *Sex-related differences in cognitive functioning: Developmental issues* (pp. 241–260). New York: Academic Press.

Danziger, N. (1983). Sex-related differences in the aspirations of high school students. *Sex Roles, 9,* 683–695.

Darden, B. J. (1983). Sex, sex-role identity and self-control: Correlates of negative and positive assertion. *Dissertation Abstracts International, 43*(8-B), 2693–2694.

David, D. S., & Brannon, R. (Eds.) (1976). *The forty-nine percent majority: The male sex role.* Reading Mass.: Addison-Wesley.

David, H. P., & Baldwin, W. P. (1979). Childbearing and child development. *American Psychologist, 34,* 866–871.

Davidson, C. V., & Abramowitz, S. I. (1980). Sex bias in clinical judgment: Later empirical returns. *Psychology of Women Quarterly, 4,* 377–395.

Davidson, L. R. (1981). Pressures and pretense: Living with gender stereotypes. *Sex Roles, 7,* 331–347.

Davidson, L. R., & Duberman, L. (1982). Friendship: Communication and interactional patterns in same-sex dyads. *Sex Roles, 8,* 809–822.

Davidson, S., & Packard, T. (1981). The therapeutic value of friendship between women. *Psychology of Women Quarterly, 5,* 495–510.

Davis, A. J. (1984). Sex-differentiated behaviors in nonsexist picture books. *Sex Roles, 11,* 1–16.

Davis, K. E. (1985, February). Near and dear: Friendship and love compared. *Psychology Today,* pp. 22, 24–28, 30.

Davis, K. E., & Todd, M. J. (1982). Friendship and love relationships. *Advances in Descriptive Psychology, 2,* 79–122.

Davis, M., & Weitz, S. (1982). Sex differences in body movements and positions. In C. Mayo &

N. Henley, (Eds.), *Gender and nonverbal behavior* (pp. 81–92). New York: Springer-Verlag.

Davis, S. W., Williams, J. E., & Best, D. L. (1982). Sex trait stereotypes in the self- and peer descriptions of third grade children. *Sex Roles, 8,* 315–331.

Dayhoff, S. A. (1983). Sexist language and person perception: Evaluation of candidates from newspaper articles. *Sex Roles, 9,* 527–539.

Deaux, K. (1976). *The behavior of women and men.* Monterey, Calif.: Brooks/Cole.

Deaux, K. (1979). Self-evaluations of male and female managers. *Sex Roles, 5,* 571–580.

Deaux, K. (1984). From individual differences to social categories: Analysis of a decade's research on gender. *American Psychologist, 39,* 105–116.

Deaux, K., & Emswiller, T. (1974). Explanations of successful performance on sex-linked tasks: What's skill for the male is luck for the female. *Journal of Personality and Social Psychology, 29,* 80–85.

Deaux, K., & Hanna, R. (1984). Courtship in the personals column: The influence of gender and sexual orientation. *Sex Roles, 11,* 363–375.

Deaux, K., & Lewis, L. (1984). Structure of gender stereotypes: Interrelationships among components and gender label. *Journal of Personality and Social Psychology, 46,* 991–1004.

Deaux, K., & Major, B. (1977). Sex-related patterns in the unit of perception. *Personality and Social Psychology Bulletin, 3,* 297–300.

Deaux, K., White, L. J., & Farris, E. (1975). Skill or luck: Field and lab studies of male and female preferences. *Journal of Personality and Social Psychology, 32,* 629–636.

DeBeauvoir, S. (1953). *The second sex.* (H. M. Parshey, Trans.). New York: Knopf.

DeBold, J. F., & Luria, Z. (1983). Gender identity, interactionism, and politics: A reply to Rogers & Walsh. *Sex Roles, 9,* 1101–1108.

Deckard, B. S. (1983). *The women's movement: Political, socioeconomic, and psychological issues.* New York: Harper & Row.

DeGregorio, E., & Carver, C. S. (1980). Type A behavior pattern, sex role orientation, and psychological adjustment. *Journal of Personality and Social Psychology, 39,* 286–293.

Deitz, S. R., Littman, M., & Bentley, B. J. (1984). Attribution of responsibility for rape: The influence of observer empathy, victim resistance, and victim attractiveness. *Sex Roles, 10,* 261–280.

De Lacoste-Utamsing, C., & Holloway, R. L. (1982). Sexual dimorphism in the human corpus collosum. *Science, 216,* 1431–1432.

Del Boca, F. K., & Ashmore, R. D. (1980a). Sex stereotypes and implicit personality theory. II. A trait-inference approach to the assessment of sex stereotypes. *Sex Roles, 6,* 519–535.

Del Boca, F. K., & Ashmore, R. D. (1980b). Sex stereotypes through the life cycle. In L. Wheeler (Ed.), *Review of Personal and Social Psychology* (pp. 163–192). Vol. 1. Beverly Hills, Calif.: Sage.

Della Selva, P., & Dusek, J. B. (1984). Sex role orientation and resolution of Eriksonian crises during the late adolescent years. *Journal of Personality and Social Psychology, 47,* 204–212.

Denmark, F. (1977). The psychology of women: An overview of an emerging field. *Personality and Social Psychology Bulletin, 3,* 356–367.

Denmark, F. L., Shaw, J. S., & Ciali, S. J. (1985). The relationship among sex roles, living arrangements, and the division of household responsibilities. *Sex Roles, 12,* 617–625.

Depner, C. E., & Veroff, J. (1979). Varieties of achievement motivation. *Journal of Social Psychology, 107,* 283–284.

Derlega, V. J., & Chaikin, A. L. (1976). Norms affecting self-disclosure in men and women. *Journal of Consulting and Clinical Psychology, 44,* 376–380.

Derlega, V. J., Durham, B., Gockel, B., & Sholis, D. (1981). Sex differences in self-disclosure: Effects of topic content, friendship, and partner's sex. *Sex Roles, 7,* 433–447.

Deseran, F. A., & Falk, W. W. (1982). Women as generalized other and self theory: A strategy for empirical research. *Sex Roles, 8,* 283–297.

Despite gains, women, minority-group members lag in college jobs (1982, February 3). *Chronicle of Higher Education,* p. 4.

Deutsch, F. M., & Leong, F. T. L. (1983). Male responses to female competence. *Sex Roles, 9,* 79–91.

Devaluation in women's employment per year. (1983, Spring). *On Campus with Women, 12,* p. 3.

Devereaux, G. (1937). Institutionalized homosexuality of the Mohave Indians. *Human Biology, 9.*

Devlin, P. K., & Cowen, G. A. (1983, August). *Homophobia, perceived fathering and intimacy of male relationships.* Paper presented at the meeting of the American Psychological Association, Anaheim.

De Wolf, V. A. (1981). High school mathematics preparation and sex differences in quantitative abilities. *Psychology of Women Quarterly, 5,* 555–567.

Diamond, M. (1982). Sexual identity, monozygotic twins reared in discordant sex roles. A BBC follow-up. *Archives of Sexual Behavior, 11,* 181–186.

Division 35 Task Force. (1981). Guidelines for non-sexist research.

Dixon, M. (1983). *The future of women.* San Francisco: Synthesis.

Dobbins, G. H., Stuart, C., Pence, E. C., & Sgro, J. A. (1985). Cognitive mechanisms mediating the biasing effects of leader sex on ratings of leader behavior. *Sex Roles, 12,* 549–560.

Doering, C. H., Brodie, H. K. H., Kramer, H. C., Becker, H. B., & Hamburg, D. A. (1974). Plasma testosterone levels and psychological measurements in men over a 2-month period. In R. C. Friedman, R. M. Richart, & R. L. Vande Wiele (Eds.), *Sex differences in behavior* (pp. 413–421). New York: Wiley.

Doherty, W. J., & Baldwin, C. (1985). Shift and stability in locus of control during the 1970's: Divergence of the sexes. *Journal of Personality and Social Psychology, 48,* 1048–1053.

Dohrenwend, B. P., & Dohrenwend, B. S. (1976). Sex differences and psychiatric disorders. *American Journal of Sociology, 18,* 1447–1454.

Domhoff, W. (1981). *Bohemian Grove and other retreats.* New York: Harper & Row.

Dominick, J. R. (1979). The portrayal of women in prime time, 1953–1977. *Sex Roles, 5,* 405–411.

Donelson, E. (1977a). Development of sex-typed behavior and self concept. In E. Donelson & J. Gullahorn (Eds.), *Women: A psychological perspective* (pp. 119–139). New York: Wiley.

Donelson, E. (1977b). Social responsiveness and separateness. In E. Donelson & J. Gullahorn (Eds.), *Women: A psychological perspective* (pp. 140–153). New York: Wiley.

Donelson, E., & Gullahorn, J. E. (1977). Individual and interpersonal achievement. In E. Donelson & J. Gullahorn (Eds.), *Women: A psychological perspective* (pp. 168–184). New York: Wiley.

Donnerstein, E. (1980). Aggressive erotica and violence against women. *Journal of Personality and Social Psychology, 39,* 269–277.

Donnerstein, E. (1982). Aggressive pornography: Can it influence aggression against women. *Primary Prevention and Psychopathology, 7.*

Donnerstein, E., & Berkowitz, L. (1981). Victim reactions in aggressive erotic films as a factor in violence against women. *Journal of Personality and Social Psychology, 41,* 710–724.

Donnerstein, E., & Hallam, J. (1978). Facilitating effects of erotica on aggression against women. *Journal of Personality and Social Psychology, 36,* 1270–1277.

Donovan, J. (1985). *Feminist theory: The intellectual traditions of American feminism.* New York: Frederick Ungar.

Doudna, C. (1981, April 5). Male secretaries: New men of letters. *The New York Times Magazine,* pp. 121, 123, 134, 135.

Dowd, M. (1983, December 4). Many women in poll equate values of job and family life. *The New York Times,* pp. 1, 66.

Dowd, M. (1984, December 16). Singles show less support for Reagan. *The New York Times,* p. 12.

Dowling, C. (1981). *The Cinderella Complex.* New York: Summit.

Downey, A. (1984). The relationship of sex-role orientation to self-perceived health status in middle-aged males. *Sex Roles, 11,* 211–225.

Downs, A. C. (1983). Letters to Santa Claus: Elementary school-age children's sex-typed toy preferences in a natural setting. *Sex Roles, 9,* 159–163.

Downs, A. C., & Gowan, C. (1980). Sex differences in reinforcement and punishment on prime-time television. *Sex Roles, 6,* 683–694.

Downs, A. C., & Harrison, S. K. (1985). Embarrassing age spots or just plain ugly? Physical attractiveness stereotyping as an instrument of sexism on American television commercials. *Sex Roles, 134,* 9–19.

Doyle, J. A. (1983). *The male experience.* Dubuque, Iowa: Wm. C. Brown.

Drabman, R. A., Robertson, S. J., Patterson, J. N., Jarvie, G. J., Hammer, D., & Cordua, G. (1981). Children's perception of media-portrayed sex roles. *Sex Roles, 7,* 379–389.

Drummond, H. (1977, September-October). The epidemics nobody tries to treat. *Mother Jones,* pp. 11–12.

Dubbert, J. L. (1979). *A man's place: Masculinity in transition.* New York: Prentice-Hall.

Dubin, M. (1985, June 4). Latchkey kids well adjusted study says. *Easton Express,* p. A7.

Dullea, G. (1981, November 30). When motherhood doesn't mean marriage. *The New York Times,* p. B16.

Dullea, G. (1983, October 31). When parents work on different shifts. *The New York Times,* p. B12.

Dullea, G. (1985, June 3). On corporate ladder, beauty can hurt. *The New York Times,* p. C13.

Dunlop, K. H. (1981). Maternal employment and childcare. *Professional Psychology, 12,* 67–75.

Dweck, C. S. (1975). The role of expectations and attributions in the alleviation of learned helplessness. *Journal of Personality and Social Psychology, 31,* 674–685.

Dweck, C. S., & Bush, E. S. (1976). Sex differences in learned helplessness: I. Differential debilitation with peers and adult evaluators. *Developmental Psychology, 12,* 147–156.

Dweck, C. S., Davidson, W., Nelson, S., & Enna, B. (1978). Sex differences in learned helplessness. II. The contingencies of evaluative feedback in the classroom. III. An experimental analysis. *Developmental Psychology, 14,* 268–276.

Dweck, C. S., Goetz, T. E., & Strauss, N. L. (1980). Sex differences in learned helplessness: IV. An experimental and naturalistic study of failure generalization and its mediators. *Journal of Personality and Social Psychology, 38,* 441–452.

Dworkin, A. (1981). *Pornography: Men possessing women*. New York: Perigee/Putnam.

Dworkin, R. J., & Dworkin, A. G. (1983). The effect of intergender conflict on sex-role attitudes. *Sex Roles, 9,* 49–57.

Dwyer, C. A. (1979). The role of tests and their construction in producing apparent sex-related differences. In M. A. Wittig and A. C. Petersen (Eds.), *Sex-related differences in cognitive functioning: Developmental issues* (pp. 335–353). New York: Academic Press.

Dziech, B. W., & Weiner, L. (1984). *The lecherous professor: Sexual harassment on campus*. Boston: Beacon Press.

Eagly, A. H. (1983). Gender and social influence: A social psychological analysis. *American Psychologist, 38,* 971–981.

Eagly, A. H., & Carli, L. L. (1981). Sex of researchers and sex-typed communications as determinants of sex differences in influenceability: A meta-analysis of social influence studies. *Psychological Bulletin, 90,* 1–20.

Eagly, A. H., Renner, P., & Carli, L. L. (1983, August). *Using meta-analysis to examine biases in gender-difference research*. Paper presented at the meeting of the American Psychological Association, Anaheim.

Eagly, A. H., & Steffen, V. J. (1984). Gender stereotypes stem from the distribution of women and men into social roles. *Journal of Personality and Social Psychology, 46,* 735–754.

Eagly, A. H., & Wood, W. (1982). Inferred sex differences in status as a determinant of gender stereotypes about social influence. *Journal of Personality and Social Psychology, 43,* 915–928.

Eagly, A. H., & Wood, W. (1985). Gender and influenceability: Stereotype versus behavior. In V. O'Leary, R. Unger, B. Wallston (Eds.), *Women, gender, and social psychology* (pp. 225–256). Hillsdale, N.J.: Lawrence Erlbaum Associates.

Eagly, A. H., Wood, W., & Fishbaugh, L. (1981). Sex differences in conformity: Surveillance by the group as a determinant of male nonconformity. *Journal of Personality and Social Psychology, 40,* 384–394.

Eccles (Parsons), J. (1983). Expectancies, values, and academic behaviors. In J. T. Spence (Ed.), *Achievement and achievement motivation: Psychological and sociological approaches* (pp. 75–146). San Francisco: W. H. Freeman & Co.

Eccles (Parsons), J., Adler T., & Meece, J. L. (1984). Sex differences in achievement: A test of alternate theories. *Journal of Personality and Social Psychology, 46,* 26–43.

Egeland, J. A., & Hosteller, A. M. (1983). Amish study; 1: Affective disorders among the Amish. *American Journal of Psychiatry, 140,* 56–62.

Ehrenreich, B. (1979, May). Is success dangerous to your health? *Ms.,* pp. 4, 97–101.

Ehrenreich, B. (1983). *The hearts of men: American dreams and the flight from commitment*. Garden City, N.Y.: Anchor.

Ehrenreich, B. (1984, May 20). A feminist's view of the new man. *The NYT Magazine,* pp. 36–41, 44, 46, 48.

Ehrenreich, B., & English, D. (1978). *For her own good: 150 years of the experts' advice to women*. Garden City, N.Y.: Anchor.

Ehrhardt, A. A. (1985). Psychobiology of gender. In A. Rossi (Ed.), *Gender and the life course* (pp. 81–96). Hawthorne, N.Y.: Aldine.

Eisenberg, N., & Lennon, R. (1983). Sex differences in empathy and related capacities. *Psychological Bulletin, 94,* 100–131.

Eisenstein, Z. (Ed.) (1979). *Capitalist patriarchy and the case for socialist feminism*. New York: Monthly Review Press.

Eisenstein, Z. (1984). The patriarchal relations of the Reagan state. *Signs, 10,* 329–337.

Eisenstock. B. (1984). Sex-role differences in children's identification with counterstereotypical televised portrayals. *Sex Roles, 10,* 417–430.

Elder, G. H., Jr., & MacInnes, D. J. (1983). Achievement imagery in women's lives from adolescence to adulthood. *Journal of Personality and Social Psychology, 45,* 394–404.

Elpern, S., & Karp, S. A. (1984). Sex-role orientation and depressive symptomatology. *Sex Roles, 10,* 987–992.

Ember, C. R. (1981). A cross-cultural perspective on sex differences. In R. H. Munroe, R. L. Munroe, & B. B. Whiting (Eds.), *Handbook of cross-cultural human development*. New York: Garland STPM Press.

Eme, R. F. (1979). Sex differences in childhood psychopathology: A review. *Psychological Bulletin, 68,* 574–595.

Eme, R. F. (1984). Sex-related differences in the epidemiology of child psychopathology. In C. Widom (Ed.), *Sex roles and psychopathology* (pp. 279–316). New York: Plenum.

Emihovich, C. A., Gaier, E. L., & Cronin, N. C. (1984). Sex-role expectations changes by fathers for their sons. *Sex Roles, 11,* 861–868.

Emmerich, W., Goldman, K. L., Kirsh, B., & Sharabany, R. (1977). Evidence for a transitional phase in the development of gender constancy. *Child Development, 48,* 930–936.

Engels, F. (1972). *The origins of the family, private property, and the state*. New York: International Publishers.

Englander-Golden, P., & Barton, G. (1983). Sex differences in absence from work: A reinterpretation. *Psychology of Women Quarterly, 8,* 185–188.

Enlightened talk, chauvinist action. (1980, December). *Psychology Today,* pp. 24–25.

Entwisle, D. (1972). To dispel fantasies about fantasy-based measures of achievement motivation. *Psychological Bulletin, 77,* 377–391.

Erdwins, C. J., & Mellinger, J. C. (1984). Mid-life women: Relation of age and role to personality. *Journal of Personality and Social Psychology, 47,* 390–395.

Erikson, E. (1963). *Childhood and society.* (2nd ed.). New York: Norton.

Erikson, E. (1964). Inner and outer space: Reflections on womanhood. *Daedalus, 93,* 582–606.

Erkut, S. (1983). Exploring sex differences in expectancy, attribution, and academic achievement. *Sex Roles, 9,* 217–231.

Erkut, S., & Mokros, J. R. (1983). *Professors as models and mentors for college students.* (Working Paper No. 65). Wellesley, Mass.: Wellesley College Center for Research on Women.

Etaugh, C. (1980). Effects of nonmaternal care on children. *American Psychologist, 35,* 309–319.

Etaugh, C., & Foresman, E. (1983). Evaluations of competence as a function of sex and marital status. *Sex Roles, 9,* 759–765.

Etaugh, C., Houtler, B. D., & Ptasnik, P. (1984, August). *Evaluations of women: Effects of experimenter sex and group composition.* Paper presented at the meeting of the American Psychological Association, Toronto.

Etaugh, C., & Kasley, H. C. (1981). Evaluating competence: Effects of sex, marital status, and parental status. *Psychology of Women Quarterly, 6,* 196–203.

Etaugh, C., Levine, D., & Mennella, A. (1984). Development of sex biases in children: 40 years later. *Sex Roles, 10,* 913–924.

Etaugh, C., & Riley, S. (1983). Evaluating competence of women and men: Effects of marital and parental status and occupational sex-typing. *Sex Roles, 9,* 943–952.

Etaugh, C., & Spandikow, D. B. (1981). Changing attitudes toward women: A longitudinal study of college students. *Psychology of Women Quarterly, 5,* 591–594.

Etaugh, C., & Stern, J. (1984). Person-perception: Effects of sex, marital status, and sex-typing occupation. *Sex Roles, 11,* 413–424.

Etaugh, C., & Whittler, T. E. (1982). Social memory of preschool girls and boys. *Psychology of Women Quarterly, 7,* 170–174.

Etheredge, L. (1978). *A world of men: Private sources of American foreign policy.* Cambridge, Mass.: MIT Press.

Etienne, M., & Leacock, E. (1980). *Women and colonization.* New York: Praegis.

Evans, G., & Fields, C. M. (1985, February 20). Equal-employment agency to focus its probes on individual victims of bias. *Chronicle of Higher Education,* p. 25.

Evans, R. G. (1984). Hostility and sex guilt: Perceptions of self and others as a function of gender and sex-role orientation. *Sex Roles, 10,* 207–215.

Eysenck, H. J., & Nias, D. K. B. (1978). *Sex, violence and the media.* New York: Harper Colophon.

Fagot, B. I. (1977). Consequences of moderate cross gender behavior in preschool children. *Child Development, 48,* 902–907.

Fagot, B. I. (1978). The influence of sex of child on parental reaction to toddler behaviors. *Child Development, 49,* 459–465.

Fagot, B. I. (1981a). Male and female teachers: Do they treat boys and girls differently? *Sex Roles, 7,* 263–271.

Fagot, B. I. (1981b). Stereotypes versus behavioral judgements of sex differences in young children. *Sex Roles, 7,* 1093–1096.

Fagot, B. I. (1984). Teacher and peer reactions to boys' and girls' play styles. *Sex Roles, 11,* 691–702.

Fagot, B. I. (1985) A cautionary note: Parents' socialization of boys and girls. *Sex Roles, 12,* 471–476.

Fagot, B. I., & Hagan, R. (1985). Aggression in toddlers: Responses to the assertive acts of boys and girls. *Sex Roles, 12,* 341–351.

Falbo, T. (1982). PAQ types and power strategies used in intimate relationships. *Psychology of Women Quarterly, 6,* 399–405.

Falbo, T., & Peplau, L. A. (1980). Power strategies in intimate relationships. *Journal of Personality and Social Psychology, 38,* 618–628.

Falk, G. (1975). Sex discrimination in the trade unions: Legal resources for change. In J. Freeman (Ed.), *Women: A feminist perspective* (pp. 259–276). Palo Alto, Calif.: Mayfield.

'Family Circle' chief hits sexist advertising. (1982, February 16). *The Easton Express,* p. A–5.

Farrell, W. (1974). *The liberated man.* New York: Random House.

Farrell, W. (1982, April). Risking sexual rejection: Women's last frontier? *Ms.,* p. 100.

Fasteau, M. F. (1974). *The male machine.* New York: McGraw-Hill.

Faulkner, E. E., Holandsworth, J. G., Jr., & Thomas, L. M. (1983, November). *Social perceptions of Type A vs. Type B behavior: A replication and extension.* Paper presented at the meeting of the Association for the Advancement of Behavior Therapy.

Feather, N. T. (1984). Masculinity, femininity, psychological androgyny, and the structure of values. *Journal of Personality and Social Psychology, 47,* 604–620.

Feather, N. T. (1985). Masculinity, femininity, self-esteem, and subclinical depression. *Sex Roles, 12,* 491–500.

Feather, N. T., & Raphaelson, A. C. (1974). Fear of success in Australian and American student groups: Motive or sex-role stereotype? *Journal of Personality and Social Psychology, 42,* 190–201.

Feather, N. T., & Simon, J. C. (1975). Reactions to male and female success and failure in sex-linked occupations: Impressions of personality, causal attributions and perceived likelihood of different consequences. *Journal of Personality and Social Psychology, 31,* 20–31.

Federal Bureau of Investigation (1981). *Uniform crime reports.* Washington, D.C.: U.S. Government Office.

Fee, E. (Ed.) (1983). *Women and health: The politics of sex and medicine.* Farmingdale, N.Y.: Baywood.

Feild, H. S. (1978). Attitudes toward rape: A comparative analysis of police, rapist, crisis counselors, and citizens. *Journal of Personality and Social Psychology, 36,* 156–178.

Feild, H. S., & Caldwell, B. E. (1979). Sex of supervisor, sex of subordinate and subordinate job satisfaction. *Psychology of Women Quarterly, 3,* 391–399.

Fein, E. B. (1985, May 5). The choice: Women officers decide to stay in or leave. *The New York Times Magazine,* pp. 32–38, 40, 42, 45, 46.

Fein, R. (1974). Men and young children. In J. Pleck & J. Sawyer (Eds.), *Men and masculinity* (pp. 54–62). Englewood, N.J.: Prentice-Hall.

Fein, R. (1978). Research on fathering: Social policy, and an emergent perspective. *Journal of Social Issues, 34*(1), 122–135.

Feinman, S. (1981). Why is cross-sex-role behavior more approved for girls than for boys? A status characteristic approach. *Sex Roles, 7,* 289–300.

Feinman, S. (1984). A status theory of the evaluation of sex-role and age-role behavior. *Sex Roles, 10,* 445–456.

Feinsilber, M. (1982, June 27). ERA defeat expected; views vary on reasons. *The Easton Express,* pp. A10–12.

Feldberg, R. L. (1984). Comparable worth: Toward theory and practice in the United States. *Signs, 10,* 311–328.

Feldman, N. S., & Brown, E. (1984, April). *Male vs. female differences in control strategies: What children learn from Saturday morning television.* Paper presented at the meeting of the Eastern Psychological Association, Baltimore.

Feldman, S. S., & Nash, S. C. (1984). The transition from expectancy to parenthood: Impact of the first-born child on men and women. *Sex Roles, 11,* 61–78.

Feldman-Summers, S., & Ashworth, C. D. (1981). Factors related to intentions to report a rape. *Journal of Social Issues, 37,* 53–70.

Feldman-Summers, S., Montano, D. E., Kasprzyk, D., & Wagner, B. (1980). Influence attempts when competing views are gender-related: Sex as credibility. *Psychology of Women Quarterly, 5,* 311–320.

Feldstein, J. H., & Feldstein, S. (1982). Sex differences on televised toy commercials. *Sex Roles, 8,* 581–587.

Female science majors said to face strong pressures. (1984, Feb. 29). *Chronicle of Higher Education,* p. 2.

Feminism and Nonviolence Study Group (1983). *Piecing it together: Feminism and nonviolence.* Devon, England: Author.

Fennema, E., & Sherman, J. (1977). Sex-related differences in mathematics achievement, spatial visualization and affective factors. *American Educational Research Journal, 14,* 51–71.

Ferguson, A., Philipson, I., Diamond, I., Quinby, L., Vance, C. S., & Snitow, A. B. (1984). Forum: The feminist sexuality debates. *Signs, 10,* 106–135.

Ferguson, L. R. (1977). The woman in the family. In E. Donelson & J. Gullahorn (Eds.), *Women: A psychological perspective* (pp. 214–227). New York: Wiley.

Ferguson, M. (1983). *Forever feminine: Women's magazines and the cult of femininity.* Exeter, N.H.: Heinemann Educational Books.

Ferraro, G. A. (1983). Bridging the wage gap: Pay equity and job evaluations. *American Psychologist, 39,* 1166–1170.

Ferree, M. M. (1976, September). The confused American housewife. *Psychology Today,* pp. 76–80.

Ferree, M. M. (1983). The women's movement in the working class. *Sex Roles, 9,* 493–505.

Ferree, M. M. (1984). Class, housework, and happiness: Women's work and life satisfaction. *Sex Roles, 11,* 1057–1074.

Ferree, M. M., & Hess, B. B. (1985). *Controversy and coalition: The new feminist movement.* Boston: G. K. Hall/Twayne.

Fidell, L. S. (1976). Empirical verification of sex discrimination in hiring practices in psychology. In R. Unger & F. Denmark (Eds.), *Women: Dependent or independent variable?* (pp. 779–782). New York: Psychological Dimensions.

Fidell, L. S. (1980). Sex role stereotypes and the American physician. *Psychology of Women Quarterly, 4,* 313–330.

Fidell, L. S. (1981). Sex differences in psychotropic drug use. *Professional Psychology, 12,* 156–162.

Fidell, L. S. (1984). Sex roles in medicine. In C. Widom (Ed.), *Sex roles and psychopathology* (pp. 375–389). New York: Plenum.

Fink, D. (1983, April 19). The sexes agree more about sex. *USA Today*, 1D–2D.

Finlay, B., Starnes, C. E., & Alvarez, F. B. (1985). Recent changes in sex-role ideology among divorced men and women: Some possible causes and implications. *Sex Roles, 12*, 637–653.

Finn, J. D. (1980). Sex differences in educational outcomes. A cross-national study. *Sex Roles, 6*, 9–26.

Finney, J. C., Brandsma, J. M., Tondoro, M., & Lemaistre, G. (1975). A study of transsexuals seeking gender reassignment. *American Journal of Psychology, 132*, 962–967.

Fiorenza, E. S. (1983). *In memory of her: A feminist theological reconstruction of Christian origins*. New York: Crossroad.

Fiorenza, E. S. (1985). *Bread not stone: The challenge of feminist biblical interpretation*. Boston: Beacon.

Firestone, S. (1970). *The dialectic of sex*. New York: William Morrow & Co.

Firth, M. (1982). Sex discrimination in job opportunities for women. *Sex Roles, 8*, 891– 901.

Fischer, J. L., & Narus, L. R., Jr. (1981a). Sex roles and intimacy in same sex and other sex relationships. *Psychology of Women Quarterly, 5*, 444–455.

Fischer, J. L., & Narus, L. R., Jr. (1981b). Sex-role development in late adolescence and adulthood. *Sex Roles, 7*, 97–106.

Fisher, K. (1984, August). Role choice linked to health. *APA Monitor*, p. 39.

Fisher, S., & Greenberg, R. P. (1979). Masculinity-femininity and response to somatic discomfort. *Sex Roles, 5*, 453–485.

Fisher, W. R., & Byrne, D. (1978). Sex differences in response to erotica? Love versus lust. *Journal of Personality and Social Psychology, 36*, 117–125.

Fisk, W. R. (1985). Responses to "neutral" pronoun presentations and the development of sex-biased responding. *Developmental Psychology, 21*, 481–485.

Fiske, E. B. (1981, November 23). Scholars face a challenge by feminists. *The New York Times*, pp. B1, B6.

Fitzgerald, H. E. (1977). Infants and caregivers: Sex differences as determinants of socialization. In E. Donelson & J. Gullahorn (Eds.), *Women: A psychological perspective* (pp. 101–118). New York: Wiley.

Fitzpatrick, M. A., & Bochner, A. (1981). Perspectives on self and other: Male-female differences in perceptions of communication behavior. *Sex Roles, 7*, 523–535.

Flaherty, J. F., & Dusek, J. B. (1980). An investigation of the relationship between psychological androgyny and components of self-concept. *Journal of Personality and Social Psychology, 38*, 984–992.

Flax, J. (1981). A materialist theory of women's status. *Psychology of Women Quarterly, 6*, 123–136.

Fleischer, R. A., & Chertkoff, J. M. (in press). Effects of dominance and sex on leader selection in dyadic work groups. *Journal of Personality and Social Psychology*.

Fleishman, E. G. (1983a). Sex-role acquisition, parental behavior, and sexual orientation: Some tentative hypotheses. *Sex Roles, 9*, 1051–1059.

Fleishman, E. G. (1983b). A rejoinder. *Sex Roles, 9*, 1063–1065.

Fleming, J. (1978). Fear of success, achievement-related motives and behavior in black college women. *Journal of Personality, 46*, 694–716.

Fleming, J. (1982). Fear of success in black male and female graduate students: A pilot study. *Psychology of Women Quarterly, 6*, 327–341.

Fleming, J. (1983). Black women in black and white college environments: The making of a matriarch. *Journal of Social Issues, 39*(3), 41–54.

Fling, S., & Manosevitz, M. (1972). Sex typing in nursery school children's play interest. *Developmental Psychology, 7*, 146–152.

Fodor, I. G. (1983). Toward an understanding of male/female differences in phobic anxiety disorders. In I. Al-Issa (Ed.), *Gender and psychopathology*. New York: Academic Press.

Fogel, R., & Paludi, M. A. (1984). Fear of success and failure, or norms for achievement? *Sex Roles, 10*, 431–443.

Foot, H. C., Chapman, A. J., & Smith, J. R. (1977). Friendship and social responsiveness in boys and girls. *Journal of Personality and Social Psychology, 35*, 401–411.

Forden, C. (1981). The influence of sex-role expectations on the perception of touch. *Sex Roles, 7*, 889–894.

Foreit, K. G., Agor, T., Byers, J., Larue, J., Lokey, H., Palazzini, M., Patterson, M., & Smith, L. (1980). Sex bias in the newspaper treatment of male-centered and female-centered news stories. *Sex Roles, 6*, 475–480.

Foushee, H. C., Helmreich, R. L., & Spence, J. T. (1979). Implicit theories of masculinity and feminity: Dualistic or bipolar? *Psychology of Women Quarterly, 3*, 259–269.

Fox, L. H. (1981). *The problem of women and mathematics*. New York: Ford Foundation.

Fox, L. H., & Cohn, J. J. (1980). Sex differences in the development of precocious mathematical talent. In L. H. Fox, L. Brody, & D. Tobin (Eds.), *Women and the mathematical mystique* (pp. 94–112). Baltimore: Johns Hopkins University Press.

Fox, L. H., Tobin, D., & Brody, L. (1979). Sex role socialization and achievement in mathematics. In M. A. Wittig & A. C. Petersen (Eds.), *Sex-related differences in cognitive functioning: Developmental issues* (pp. 303–332). New York: Academic Press.

Fox, M. F., & Hesse-Biber, S. (1984). *Women at work.* Palo Alto, Calif.: Mayfield.

Frable, D. E. S., & Bem, S. L. (1985). If you're gender-schematic, all members of the opposite sex look alike. *Journal of Personality and Social Psychology, 49,* 459–468.

Frank, S. J., McLaughlin, A. M, & Crusco, A. (1984). Sex role attributes, symptom distress, and defensive style among college men and women. *Journal of Personality and Social Psychology, 47,* 182–192.

Frank, S. J., Towell, P. A., & Huyck, M. (1985). The effects of sex-role traits on three aspects of psychological well-being in a sample of middle-aged women. *Sex Roles, 12,* 1073–1087.

Franke, L. B. (1983, May 22). The sons of divorce. *The New York Times Magazine,* pp. 40–42, 54–57.

Franken, M. W. (1983). Sex role expectations in children's vocational aspirations and perceptions of occupations. *Psychology of Women Quarterly, 8,* 59–68.

Franklin, C. W., II. (1984). *The changing definition of masculinity.* New York: Plenum.

Franks, V. (1979). Gender and psychotherapy. In E. S. Gomberg & V. Franks (Eds.), *Gender and disordered behavior: Sex differences in psychopathology* (pp. 453–485). New York: Brunner/Mazel.

Franks, V., & Rothblum, E. D. (Eds.) (1983). *The stereotyping of women: Its effects on mental health.* New York: Springer.

Franzwa, H. H. (1975). Female roles in women's magazine fiction, 1940–1970. In R. Unger & F. Denmark (Eds.), *Women: Dependent and independent variable* (pp. 42–53). New York: Psychological Dimensions.

Frasher, J. M., Frasher, R. S., & Wims, F. B. (1982). Sex-role stereotyping in school superintendents' personnel decisions. *Sex Roles, 8,* 261–268.

Freedman, M. (1975, March). Homosexuals may be healthier than straights. *Psychology Today,* pp. 28–32.

Freeman, H. R. (1979). Sex-role stereotypes, self-concepts, and measured personality characteristics in college women and men. *Sex Roles, 5,* 99–103.

Freeman, J. (1975). The women's liberation movement: Its origins, structure, impact and ideas. In J. Freeman (Ed.), *Women: A feminist perspective* (pp. 460–484). Palo Alto, Calif.: Mayfield.

Freimuth, M., & Hornstein, G. A. (1982). A critical examination of the concept of gender. *Sex Roles, 8,* 515–532.

Freud, S. (1964a). The dissolution of the Oedipus Complex. In J. Strachey (Rev. and Ed.), *The standard edition of the complete works of Sigmund Freud* (Vol. 19). London: Hogarth. (Original work published 1924).

Freud, S. (1964b). Some psychological consequences of the anatomy. Distinction between the sexes. In J. Strachey (Rev. and Ed.), *The standard edition of the complete works of Sigmund Freud,* (Vol 19). London: Hogarth Press. (Original work published 1924).

Freud, S. (1964c). Three essays on the theory of sexuality. In J. Strachey (Rev. and Ed.), *The standard edition of the complete works of Sigmund Freud,* (Vol. 7). London: Hogarth Press. (Original work published 1905).

Freud, S. (1965). Femininity. In J. Strachey (Ed. and Trans.), *New introductory lectures on psychoanalysis.* New York: W. W. Norton & Co. (Original work published 1933).

Freudiger, P., & Almquist, E. (1978). Male and female roles in the lyrics of three genres of contemporary music. *Sex Roles, 4,* 51–65.

Freundl, P. C. (1981, August). *Influence of sex and status variables on perceptions of assertiveness.* Paper presented at the meeting of the American Psychological Association, Los Angeles.

Frevert, R. L. (1983, August). *Relationship between life roles and mental health across 25 years.* Paper presented at the meeting of the American Psychological Association, Anaheim.

Friedan, B. (1963). *The feminine mystique.* New York: Dell.

Friedan, B. (1981). *The second stage.* New York: Summit Books.

Friedan, B. (1983, February 27). Twenty years after the feminine mystique. *The New York Times Magazine,* pp. 38, 39, 42, 54–57.

Friedan, B. (1985, November 3). How to get the women's movement moving again. *The New York Times Magazine,* pp. 27, 28, 66, 67, 84, 85, 89, 98, 106, 108.

Friedl, E. (1975). *Women and men: An anthropologist's view.* New York: Holt, Rinehart & Winston.

Friedman, S. (1983, December 24). Polls: White males Reagan's biggest supporters. *The Easton Express.* p. A10.

Frieze, I. H., & Ramsey, S. J. (1976). Nonverbal maintenance of traditional sex roles. *Journal of Social Issues, 32*(3), 133–141.

Frieze, I. H., Whitley, B. E., Jr., Hanusa, B. H., & McHugh, M. C. (1982). Assessing the theoretical models for sex differences in causal attributions for success and failure. *Sex Roles, 8,* 333–343.

Frisch, H. L. (1977). Sex stereotypes in adult-infant play. *Child Development, 48,* 1671–1675.

Fritsche, J. M. (1985). *Toward excellence and equity: The scholarship on women as a catalyst for change in the university.* (Available from author, University of Maine, Orono, ME 04669).

Frodi, A., Macaulay, J., & Thome, P. R. (1977). Are women always less aggressive than men? A review of the experimental literature. *Psychological Bulletin, 84,* 634–660.

Gagnon, J. H., & Simon, W. (1973). *Sexual conduct: The social sources of human sexuality.* Chicago: Aldine.

Galper, R. E., & Luck, D. (1980). Gender, evaluation, and causal attribution: The double standard is alive and well. *Sex Roles, 6,* 273–283.

Garai, J. E., & Scheinfeld, A. (1968). Sex differences in mental and behavioral traits. *Genetic Psychology Monographs, 77,* 169–299.

Garcia, L. T. (1982). Sex-role orientation and stereotypes about male-female sexuality. *Sex Roles, 8,* 863–876.

Garcia, L. T., & Derfel, B. (1983). Perception of sexual experience: The impact of nonverbal behavior. *Sex Roles, 9,* 871–878.

Garfinkel, P. E., & Garner, D. M. (1982). *Anorexia nervosa: A multidimensional perspective.* New York: Brunner/Mazel.

Garfinkle, E., & Morin, S. (1978). Psychologists' attitudes toward homosexual psychotherapeutic clients. *Journal of Social Issues, 34*(3), 101–112.

Garland, H., Hale, K. F., & Burnson, M. (1982). Attribution for the success and failure of female managers: A replication and extension. *Psychology of Women Quarterly, 7,* 155–162.

Garland, H., & Smith, G. B. (1981). Occupational achievement motivation as a function of biological sex, sex-linked personality, and occupation stereotype. *Psychology of Women Quarterly, 5,* 568–585.

Garnets, L., & Pleck, J. H. (1979). Sex role identity, androgyny, and sex role transcendence: A sex role strain analysis. *Psychology of Women Quarterly, 3,* 270–283.

Garrett, C. D., Ein, P. L., & Tremaine, L. (1977). The development of gender-stereotyping of adult occupations in elementary school children. *Child Development, 48,* 507–517.

Gartrell, N., & Mosbacher, D. (1984). Sex differences in the naming of children's genitalia. *Sex Roles, 10,* 869–876.

Gary, L. E. (1981). *Black men.* Beverly Hills, Calif.: Sage.

Gauthier, J., & Kjervik, D. (1982). Sex-role identity and self-esteem in female graduate nursing students. *Sex Roles, 8,* 45–55.

Geffner, R., & Gross, M. M. (1984). Sex-role behavior and obedience to authority: A field study. *Sex Roles, 10,* 973–985.

Geis, F. L., Boston, M. B., & Hoffman, N. (1985). Sex of authority role models and achievement by men and women: Leadership performance and recognition. *Journal of Personality and Social Psychology, 49,* 636–653.

Geis, F. L., Brown, V., Jennings, J. W., & Corrado-Taylor, D. (1984). Sex vs. status in sex-associated stereotypes. *Sex Roles, 11,* 771–786.

Geis, F. L., Brown, V., Jennings, J., & Porter, N. (1984). T.V. commercials as achievement scripts for women. *Sex Roles, 10,* 513–525.

Geise, L. A. (1979). The female role in middle class women's magazines from 1955 to 1976: A content analysis of nonfiction selections. *Sex Roles, 5,* 51–62.

Gelbort, K. R., & Winer, J. L. (1985). Fear of success and fear of failure: A multitrait-multimethod validation study. *Journal of Personality and Social Psychology, 48,* 1009–1014.

Gerbner, G., & Gross, L. (1976, April). The scary world of TV's heavy viewer. *Psychology Today,* pp. 41–45ff.

Gerdes, E. P., & Garber, D. M. (1983). Sex bias in hiring: Effects of job demands and applicant competence. *Sex Roles, 9,* 307–319.

Gerdes, E. P., Gehling, J. D., & Rapp, J. N. (1981). The effects of sex and sex-role concept on self-disclosure. *Sex Roles, 7,* 989–998.

Gerdes, E. P., & Kelman, J. H. (1981). Sex discrimination: Effects of sex-role incongruence, evaluator sex, and stereotypes. *Basic and Applied Social Psychology, 2,* 219–226.

Gerrard, M. (1982). Sex, sex guilt, and contraceptive use. *Journal of Personality and Social Psychology, 42,* 153–158.

Gerson, J. M. (1985). Women returning to school: The consequences of multiple roles. *Sex Roles, 13,* 77–91.

Gerson, M. J. (1980). The lure of motherhood. *Psychology of Women Quarterly, 5,* 207–218.

Gerson, M. J. (1985). Feminism and the wish for a child. *Sex Roles, 11,* 389–399.

Gilbert, L. A., Deutsch, C. J., & Strahan, R. F. (1978). Feminine and masculine dimensions of the typical, desirable, and ideal woman and man. *Sex Roles, 4,* 767–778.

Gilbert, L. A., & Evans, S. L. (1985). Dimensions of same-gender student-faculty role-model relationships. *Sex Roles, 12,* 111–123.

Gilbert, L. A., Gallessich, J. M., & Evans, S. L. (1983). Sex of faculty role model and students' self-perceptions of competency. *Sex Roles, 9,* 597–607.

Gilbert, L. A., Holahan, C. K., & Manning, L. (1981). Coping with conflict between professional and maternal roles. *Family Relations, 30,* 419–426.

Gilder, G. (1979, January 28). The case against women in combat. *The New York Times Magazine,* pp. 29–30ff.

Gilkes, C. T. (1982). Successful rebellious professionals: The black women's professional identity and community commitment. *Psychology of Women Quarterly, 6,* 289–311.

Gillespie, D. L. (1971, August). Who has the power? The marital struggle. *Journal of Marriage and Family,* pp. 445–458.

Gilligan, C. (1977). In a different voice: Woman's conceptions of self and of morality. *Harvard Educational Review, 47,* 481–517.

Gilligan, C. (1982a). *In a different voice: Psychological theory and women's development.* Cambridge: Harvard University Press.

Gilligan, C. (1982b, June). Why should a woman be more like a man? *Psychology Today,* pp. 68, 70, 71, 73, 74–77.

Gitelson, I. B., Petersen, A. C., & Tobin-Richards, M. H. (1982). Adolescents' expectancies of success, self-evaluations, and attributions about performance on spatial and verbal tasks. *Sex Roles, 8,* 411–419.

Glass, S. P., & Wright, T. L. (1985). Sex differences in type of extramarital involvement and marital dissatisfaction. *Sex Roles, 12,* 1101–1120.

Glenn, N. D., & Weaver, C. N. (1979, May). Attitudes toward premarital, extramarital, and homosexual relations in the U.S. in the 1970's. *Journal of Sex Research, 15*(2), 108–118.

Goffman, E. (1979). *Gender advertisements.* New York: Harper & Row.

Gold, A. R., & Adams, D. B. (1981). Motivational factors affecting fluctuations of female sexual activity at menstruation. *Psychology of Women Quarterly, 5,* 670–680.

Gold, A. R., Brush, L. R., & Sprotzer, E. R. (1980). Developmental changes in self-perceptions of intelligence and self-confidence. *Psychology of Women Quarterly, 5,* 231–239.

Gold, D., & Berger, C. (1978). Problem-solving performance of young boys and girls as a function of task appropriateness and sex identity. *Sex Roles, 4,* 183–193.

Gold, D., & Reis, M. (1982). Male teacher effects on young children: A theoretical and empirical consideration. *Sex Roles, 8,* 493–513.

Gold, M. E. (1983). *A dialogue on comparable worth.* Ithaca, New York: ILR Press.

Goldberg, A. S., & Shiflett, S. (1981). Goal of male and female college students: Do traditional sex differences still exist? *Sex Roles, 7,* 1213–1222.

Goldberg, H. (1976). *The hazards of being male: Surviving the myth of masculine privilege.* New York: Nash.

Goldberg, H. (1980). *The new male: From self-destruction to self-care.* New York: New American Library.

Goldberg, H. (1983). *The new male female relationship.* New York: Wm. Morrow.

Goldberg, P. (1968). Are women prejudiced against women? *Trans-Action, 5*(5), 28–30.

Goldberg, S. (1974). *The inevitability of patriarchy.* New York: William Morrow.

Golden, G. A., & Cherry, F. (1982). Test performance and social comparison choices of high school men and women. *Sex Roles, 8,* 761–772.

Golding, J. M., & Singer, J. L. (1983). Patterns of inner experience: Daydreaming styles, depressive moods and sex roles. *Journal of Personality and Social Psychology, 45,* 663–675.

Goldman, J. D. G., & Goldman, R. J. (1983). Children's perceptions of parents and their roles: A cross-national study in Australia, England, North America, and Sweden. *Sex Roles, 9,* 791–812.

Goldman, N. L. (Ed.) (1982). *Female soldiers—combatants or noncombatants? Historical and contemporary perspectives.* Westport, Conn.: Greenwood Press.

Goldstein, E. (1979). Effect of same-sex and cross-sex role models on the subsequent academic prosperity of scholars. *American Psychologist, 34,* 407–410.

Goleman, D. (1978, June). Special abilities of the sexes: Do they begin in the brain? *Psychology Today,* pp. 48–59ff.

Goleman, D. (1984, August 21). As sex roles change, men turn to therapy to cope with stress. *The New York Times,* pp. C1, 5.

Golub, S., & Canty, E. (1982). Sex role expectations and the assumption of leadership by college women. *Journal of Social Psychology, 116,* 83–90.

Golub, S., & Harrington, D. M. (1981). Premenstrual and menstrual mood changes in adolescent women. *Journal of Personality and Social Psychology, 41,* 961–965.

Gomberg, E. S. (1981). Women, sex roles, and alcohol problems. *Professional Psychology, 12,* 146–155.

Gomberg, E. S. (1982). Historical and political perspective: Women and drug use. *Journal of Social Issues, 38*(2), 9–23.

Gomberg, E. S. (1984, August). *Femininity issues in women's alcohol abuse.* Paper presented at the meeting of the American Psychological Association, Toronto.

Gomberg, E. S., & Franks, V. (Eds.) (1979). *Gender and disordered behavior: Sex differences in psychopathology.* New York: Brunner/Mazel.

Good, P. R., & Smith, B. D. (1980). Menstrual distress and sex-role attributes. *Psychology of Women Quarterly, 4,* 482–491.

Goodchilds, J. D. (1979). Power: A matter of mechanics? *Society for the Advancement of Social Psychology Newsletter, 5*(3), p. 3.

Goodman, E. (1979). Who says feminists are anti-male? Boston.

Goodman, M. J., Griffin, P. B., & Estioko-Griffin, A. A., & Grove, J. S. (1985). The compatibility of hunting and mothering among the Agte hunter-gatherers of the Philippines. *Sex Roles, 12,* 1199–1209.

Gordon, S. (1983). What's new in endocrinology? Target: Sex hormones. In M. Fooden, S. Gordon, & B. Hughley (Eds.), *Genes and Gender IV* (pp. 39–48). Staten Island, New York: Gordian Press.

Gordon, S. (1985, July). Anger, power, and women's sense of self. *Ms.*, pp. 42–44.

Gough, K. (1975). The origin of the family. In J. Freeman (Ed.), *Women: A feminist perspective*. Palo Alto, Calif.: Mayfield.

Gove, W. (1972). The relationship between sex roles, marital status, and mental illness. *Social Forces, 51,* 34–44.

Gove, W. (1973). Sex, marital status and mortality. *American Journal of Sociology, 79,* 45–67.

Gove, W. (1979). Sex differences in the epidemiology of mental disorder: Evidence and explanations. In E. S. Gomberg & V. Franks (Eds.), *Gender and disordered behavior: Sex differences in psychopathology* (pp. 23–68). New York: Brunner/Mazel.

Gove, W. R. (1980). Mental illness and psychiatric treatment among women. *Psychology of Women Quarterly, 4,* 345–362.

Gove, W. R. (1985). The effect of age and gender on deviant behavior: A biopsychosocial perspective. In A. Rossi (Ed.), *Gender and the life course* (pp. 115–144). New York: Aldine.

Gove, W., & Geerken, M. (1977). Response bias in community surveys: An empirical investigation. *American Journal of Sociology, 82,* 1289–1317.

Gove, W., & Tudor, J. F. (1973). Adult sex roles and mental illness. In J. Huber (Ed.), *Changing women in a changing society*. Chicago: University of Chicago Press.

Gove, W., & Tudor, J. (1977). Sex differences in mental illness: A comment on Dohrenwend and Dohrenwend. *American Journal of Sociology, 82,* 1327–1336.

Graddick, M. M., & Farr, J. S. (1983). Professionals in scientific discipline: Sex-related differences in working life commitments. *Journal of Applied Psychology, 68,* 641–645.

Graduate women and men in science and engineering at Stanford: Very different experiences. (1985, Spring). *On Campus with Women*, p. 8.

Grady, K. E. (1981). Sex bias in research design. *Psychology of Women Quarterly, 5,* 628–636.

Graf, R. G., & Riddell, J. C. (1972). Sex differences in problem-solving as a function of problem context. *Journal of Educational Research, 65,* 451–452.

Gralewski, C., & Rodgon, M. M. (1980). Effect of social and intellectual instruction on achievement motivation as a function of role orientation. *Sex Roles, 6,* 301–309.

Gravenkemper, S. A., & Paludi, M. A. (1983). Fear of success revisited: Introducing an ambiguous cue. *Sex Roles, 9,* 897–900.

Graverholz, E., & Serpe, R. T. (1985). Initiation and response: The dynamics of sexual interaction. *Sex Roles, 12,* 1041–1059.

Gray, J. D. (1983). The married professional woman: An examination of her role conflicts and coping strategies. *Psychology of Women Quarterly, 7,* 235–243.

Gray, L. S. (1983, November 11). Schools that overcome girls' computer shyness. *The New York Times*, Sect. 12, p. 9.

Green, S. K., & Sandos, P. (1983). Perceptions of male and female initiators of relationships. *Sex Roles, 9,* 849–852.

Greenberg, M., & Morris, N. (1974). Engrossment: The newborn's impact upon the father. *American Journal of Orthopsychiatry, 44,* 520–531.

Greenberg, R. P., & Fisher, S. (1977). The relationship between willingness to adopt the sick role and attitudes toward women. *Journal of Chronic Diseases, 30,* 29–37.

Greendlinger, V., & Byrne, D. (in press). Coercive sexual fantasies of college males as predictors of self-reported likelihood to rape and overt sexual aggression. *Journal of Sex Research*.

Greene, A. L., Sullivan, H. J., & Beyard-Tyler, K. (1982). Attitudinal effects of the use of role models in information about sex-typed careers. *Journal of Educational Psychology, 74,* 393–398.

Greenfield, P. M. (1981). Childcare in cross-cultural perspective: Implications for the future organization of childcare in the U.S. *Psychology of Women Quarterly, 6,* 41–45.

Greenglass, E. R. (1984a, May–June). *Psychological implications of Type A behavior in employed women*. Paper presented at the meeting of the Canadian Psychological Association, Ottawa.

Greenglass, E. R. (1984b, June). *The impact of feminist values on organizations: Psychological consequences for female workers*. Paper presented at the meeting of the Canadian Psychological Association, Ottawa.

Greenglass, E. R., & Devins, R. (1982). Factors related to marriage and career plans in unmarried women. *Sex Roles, 8,* 57–71.

Greenstein, M., Miller, R. H., & Weldon, D. E. (1979). Attitudinal and normative beliefs as antecedents of female occupational choice. *Personality and Social Psychology Bulletin, 5,* 356–362.

Greer, G. (1984). *Sex and destiny: The politics of human fertility.* New York: Harper & Row.

Greif, G. (1985). *Single fathers.* Lexington, Mass.: Lexington Books.

Griffin, P. S. (1984, Winter). "But she's so feminine": Changing mixed messages we give to girls and women in sports. *Journal of the National Association for Women Deans, Administrators, and Counselors, 47,* 9–12.

Griffin, S. (1975). Rape: The All-American crime. In J. Freeman (Ed.), *Women: A feminist perspective* (pp. 25–40). Palo Alto, Calif.: Mayfield.

Griffin, S. (1979). *Rape: The power of consciousness.* San Francisco: Harper & Row.

Griffin, S. (1981). *Pornography and silence: Culture's revenge against nature.* New York: Harper & Row.

Griffith, W., & Hatfield, E. (1985). *Human sexual behavior.* Glenview, Ill.: Scott, Foresman.

Grimm, L., & Yarnold, P. R. (1985). Sex typing and the coronary-prone behavior pattern. *Sex Roles, 12,* 171–178.

Gross, A. E. (1978). The male role and heterosexual behavior. *Journal of Social Issues, 34*(1), 87–107.

Gross, A., Smith, R., & Wallston, B. (in press). The men's movement: Personal vs. political. In J. Freeman (Ed.), *The politics of social movements.* New York: Longmans.

Gross, L., & Jeffries-Fox, S. (1978). "What do you want to be when you grow up little girl?" In G. Tuchman, A. K. Daniels, & J. Benet (Eds.), *Hearth and home: Images of women in the mass media* (pp. 240–265). New York: Oxford University Press.

Gross, M. M., & Geffner, R. A. (1980). Are the times changing? An analysis of sex-role prejudice. *Sex Roles, 6,* 713–722.

Group consciousness. (1982, Spring/Summer). *Institute for Social Research Newsletter,* pp. 4–5.

Growth in homeownership credited to working wives. (1983, Apr. 16). *The Easton Express,* p. B5.

Grube, J. W., Kleinhesselink, R. R., & Kearney, K. A. (1982). Male self-acceptance and attraction toward women. *Personality and Social Psychology Bulletin, 8,* 107–112.

Gruber, K. J., & Gaebelein, J. (1979). Sex differences in listening comprehension. *Sex Roles, 5,* 299–310.

Grush, J. E., & Yehl, J. G. (1979). Marital roles, sex differences, and interpersonal attraction. *Journal of Personality and Social Psychology, 37,* 116–123.

Gulanick, N. A., Howard, G, S., & Moreland, J. (1979). Evaluation of a group program designed to increase androgyny in feminine women. *Sex Roles, 5,* 811–827.

Gullahorn, J. E. (1977a). Equality and social structure. In E. Donelson & J. Gullahorn (Eds.), *Women: A psychological perspective* (pp. 266–281). New York: Wiley.

Gullahorn, J. E. (1977b). Sex roles and sexuality. In E. Donelson & J. Gullahorn (Eds.), *Women: A psychological perspective* (pp. 226–281). New York: Wiley.

Gump, J. (1980). Reality and myth: Employment and sex role ideology in black women. In F. Denmark & J. Sherman (Eds.), *The psychology of women.* New York: Psychological Dimensions.

Gupta, N., Jenkins, D., Jr., & Beehr, T. A. (1983). Employee gender, gender similarity, and supervisor-subordinate cross-evaluations. *Psychology of Women Quarterly, 8,* 174–184.

Gurin, P. (1981). Labor market experiences and expectancies. *Sex Roles, 7,* 1079–1092.

Gurwitz, S. B., & Dodge, K. A. (1975). Adults' evaluation of a child as a function of sex of adult and sex of child. *Journal of Personality and Social Psychology, 33,* 822–828.

Gutek, B. A., & Nakamura, C. Y. (1980). Sexuality and the workplace. *Basic and Applied Social Psychology, 1,* 225–265.

Gutierres, S. E., Kenrick, D. T., & Goldberg, L. (1983, August). *Adverse effect of popular erotica on judgments of one's mate.* Paper presented at the meeting of the American Psychological Association, Anaheim.

Guttentag, M., & Bray, H. (1975, December). Tough to nip sexism in the bud. *Psychology Today,* p. 58.

Guttentag, M., & Bray, H. (1977). Teachers as mediators of sex-role standards. In A. Sargent (Ed.), *Beyond sex roles* (pp. 395–411). St. Paul: West.

Guttentag, M., & Secord, P. F. (1983). *Too many women? The sex ratio question.* Beverly Hills, Calif.: Sage.

Haas, A. (1979). Male and female spoken language differences: Stereotypes and evidence. *Psychological Bulletin, 86,* 616–626.

Haas, A. (1981). Partner influences on sex-associated spoken language of children. *Sex Roles, 7,* 925–935.

Haas, L. (1982). Determinants of role-sharing behavior: A study of egalitarian couples. *Sex Roles, 8,* 747–760.

Haavio-Mannila, E. (1975). Convergences between East and West: Traditional and modernity in sex role in Sweden, Finland and the Soviet Union. In M. Mednick, S. S. Tangri, and L. Hoffman (Eds.), *Women and achievement: Social and motivational analyses* (pp. 71–84). New York: Halsted Press.

Haccoun, D. M., & Stacy, S. (1980). Perceptions of male and female success or failure in relation to spouse encouragement and sex-association of occupation. *Sex Roles, 6,* 819–831.

Hacker, A. (1984, December 9). Women vs. men in the work force. *The New York Times Magazine,* 124–129.

Hacker, H. M. (1951). Women as a minority group. *Social Forces, 30,* 60–69.

Hacker, H. M. (1975). Women as a minority group twenty years later. In R. Unger & F. Denmark (Eds.), *Women: Dependent or independent variable?* (pp. 103–112). New York: Psychological Dimensions.

Hacker, H. M. (1981). Blabbermouths and clams: Sex differences in self-disclosure in same-sex and cross-sex friendship dyads. *Psychology of Women Quarterly, 5,* 385–401.

Hall, E. G., & Lee, A. M. (1984). Sex differences in motor performance of young children: Fact or fiction? *Sex Roles, 10,* 217–230.

Hall, J. A. (1980). Gender differences in nonverbal communication skills. In R. Rosenthal (Ed.), *Quantitative assessment of research domains.* San Francisco: Jossey-Bass.

Hall, J. A. (1985). *Nonverbal sex differences: Communication accuracy and expressive style.* Baltimore: Johns Hopkins University.

Hall, J. A., & Braunwald, K. G. (1981). Gender cues in conversations. *Journal of Personality and Social Psychology, 40,* 99–110.

Hall, J. A., & Halberstadt, A. G. (1981). Sex roles and nonverbal communication skills. *Sex Roles, 7,* 273–287.

Hall, J. A., & Taylor, M. C. (1985). Psychological androgyny and the masculinity × femininity interaction. *Journal of Personality and Social Psychology, 49,* 429–435.

Hall, R. M., & Sandler, B. R. (1984). *Out of the classroom: A chilly campus climate for women.* Washington, D.C.: Association of American Colleges.

Hall, T. (1984, October 10). Many women decide they want their careers rather than children. *Wall Street Journal,* p. 35.

Halmi, K. A., Falk, F. R., & Schwartz, E. (1981). Binge-eating and vomiting: A survey of a college population. *Psychological Medicine, 41,* 697–706.

Halpern, D. F. (1985). The influence of sex-role stereotypes on prose recall. *Sex Roles, 12,* 363–375.

Hamburg, D. A., & Lunde, D. T. (1966). Sex hormones in the development of sex differences in human behavior. In E. E. Maccoby (Ed.), *The development of sex differences* (pp. 1–24). Stanford, Calif.: Stanford University Press.

Hamilton, M. (1983, April). *Sex differences in memory for social stimuli.* Paper presented at the meeting of the Eastern Psychological Association, Philadelphia.

Handal, P. J., & Salit, E. D. (1985). Gender-role classification and demographic relationships: A function of type of scoring procedures. *Sex Roles, 12,* 411–419.

Haney, D. Q. (1984, May 27). Sharing chores said to help working couples. *The Easton Express,* p. A1.

Hanley, R. (1983, November 22). Panel in Jersey finds bias against women in the State's Courts. *The New York Times,* pp. 1, B2.

Hans, V. P., & Eisenberg, N. (1985). The effects of sex-role attitudes and group composition on men and women in groups. *Sex Roles, 12,* 477–490.

Hansen, G. L. (1985). Dating jealousy among college students. *Sex Roles, 12,* 713–721.

Hare-Mustin, R. T. (1978, June). A feminist approach to family therapy. *Family Process, 17,* 181–194.

Hare-Mustin, R. T. (1983). An appraisal of the relationship between women and psychotherapy: 80 years after the case of Dora. *American Psychologist, 38,* 593–601.

Harlow, H. F. (1958). The nature of love. *American Psychologist, 13,* 673–385.

Harlow, H. F. (1962). The heterosexual affectional system in monkeys. *American Psychologist, 17,* 1–9.

Harlow, H. F. (1965). Sexual behavior in the rhesus monkeys. In F. A. Beach (Ed.), *Sex and behavior.* New York: Wiley.

Harmon, L. W. (1981). The life and career plans of young adult college women: A follow-up study. *Journal of Counseling Psychology, 28,* 416–427.

Harren, V. A., Kass, R. A., Tinsley, H. E. A., & Moreland, J. R. (1978). Influence of sex role attitudes and cognitive styles on career decision-making. *Journal of Counseling Psychology, 25,* 390–398.

Harren, V. A., Kass, R. A., Tinsley, H. E. A., & Moreland, J. R. (1979). Influences of gender, sex-role attitudes and cognitive complexity on gender-dominant career choices. *Journal of Counseling Psychology, 26,* 227–234.

Harrington, D. M. & Andersen, S. M. (1981). Creativity, masculinity, femininity, and three models of psychological androgyny. *Journal of Personality and Social Psychology, 41,* 744–757.

Harris, L. J. (1977). Sex differences in the growth and use of language. In E. Donelson & J. E. Gullahorn (Eds.), *Women: A psychological perspective* (pp. 79–94). New York: Wiley.

Harris, L. J. (1981). Sex-related variations in spatial skill. In L. S. Liben, A. H. Patterson, & N. Newcombe (Eds.), *Spatial representation and behavior across the life span: Theory and application.* New York: Academic Press.

Harris, M. (1977a). *Cannibals and kings.* New York: Random House.

Harris, M. (1977b, November 13). Why men dominate women. *The New York Times Magazine,* p. 46ff.

Harris, M. (1981). *Why America changed: Our cultural crisis.* New York: Simon & Schuster.

Harrison, A. O., & Minor, J. H. (1983). Interrole conflict, coping strategies, and role satisfaction among single and married employed mothers. *Psychology of Women Quarterly, 6,* 354–360.

Harrison, J. (1978). Male sex role and health. *Journal of Social Issues, 34*(1), 65–86.

Hartley, R. E. (1959). Sex role pressures and the socialization of the male child. *Psychological Reports, 5,* 457–468.

Hartmann, H. (1976). Capitalism, patriarchy, and job segregation by sex. *Signs, 1*(3), 137–169.

Hartmann, H. I., & Treiman, D. J. (Eds.) (1981). *Women, work, and wages.* Washington, D.C.: National Academy Press.

Hartup, W. W. (1983). The peer system. In P. Mussen & E. Heatherington (Ed.), *Handbook of child psychology, 4th ed.,* Vol. 4. New York: Wiley.

Harway, M. (1980). Sex bias in educational-vocational counseling. *Psychology of Women Quarterly, 4,* 412–423.

Harway, M., & Astin, H. S. (1977). *Sex discrimination in career counseling and education.* New York: Praeger.

Haskell, M. (1983, January). Women in the movies grow up. *Psychology Today,* pp. 18–27.

Haskell, M. (1984, February). Good girls, earth mothers, and sluts in film. *Ms.,* pp. 35, 37.

Hatton, G. J. (1977). Biology and gender: Structure, sex and cycles. In E. Donelson & J. E. Gullahorn (Eds.), *Women: A psychological perspective* (pp. 49–64). New York: Wiley.

Haviland, J. J., & Malatesta, C. Z. (1982). The development of sex differences in nonverbal signals. In C. Mayo & N. Henley (Eds.), *Gender and nonverbal behavior* (pp. 183–208). New York: Springer-Verlag.

Hawkins, R. C., III, Turell, S., & Jackson, L. J. (1983). Desirable and undesirable masculine and feminine traits in relation to students' dieting tendencies and body image dissatisfaction. *Sex Roles, 9,* 705–718.

Hayduk, L. A. (1983). Personal space: Where we now stand. *Psychological Bulletin, 94,* 293–335.

Hayman, A. S. (1976). Legal challenge to discrimination against men. In D. David & R. Brannon (Eds.), *The forty-nine percent majority* (pp. 297–321). Reading, Mass.: Addison-Wesley.

Hechinger, F. M. (1981, April 28). About education. *The New York Times,* p. C5.

Heffner, E. (1983, May). Mother love: The tender trap. *Redbook,* pp. 112–115, 187.

Heilbrun, A. B., Jr. (1976). Measurement of masculine and feminine sex role identities as independent dimensions. *Journal of Consulting and Clinical Psychology, 44,* 183–190.

Heilbrun, A. B., Jr. (1981). Gender differences in the functional linkage between androgyny, social cognition, and competence. *Journal of Personality and Social Psychology, 41,* 1106–1118.

Heilbrun, A. B., Jr. (1984). Sex-based models of androgyny: A further cognitive elaboration of competence differences. *Journal of Personality and Social Psychology, 46,* 216–229.

Heilbrun, A. B., Jr., & Schwartz, H. L. (1982). Sex-gender differences in level of androgyny. *Sex Roles, 8,* 201–214.

Heilman, M. E., & Kram, K. E. (1983). Male and female assumptions about colleagues' views of their competence. *Psychology of Women Quarterly, 7,* 329–337.

Heilman, M. E., & Martell, R. F. (1986, in press). Exposure to successful women: Antidote to sex discrimination in applicant screening decisions? *Organizational behavior and human decision processes.*

Heilman, M. E., & Stopeck, M. H. (1985). Attractiveness and corporate success: Different casual attributions for males and females. *Journal of Applied Psychology, 70,* 379–388.

Heiman, J. R. (1975, April). The physiology of erotica: Women's sexual arousal. *Psychology Today,* pp. 90–94.

Heiser, P., & Gannon, L. (1984). The relationship of sex-role stereotype to anger expression and the report of psychosomatic symptoms. *Sex Roles, 10,* 601–611.

Helmreich, R. J., & Spence, J. T. (1978). The Work and Family Orientation Questionnaire. JSAS *Catalog of Selected Documents in Psychology, 8,* 35. (Ms. No. 1677).

Helmreich, R., Spence, J. T., Beane, W. E., Lucker, G. W., & Matthews, K. A. (1980). Making it in academic psychology: Demographic and personality correlates of attainment. *Journal of Personality and Social Psychology, 39,* 896–908.

Helmreich, R. L., Spence, J. T., & Gibson, R. H. (1982). Sex-role attitudes: 1972–1980. *Personality and Social Psychology, 8,* 656–663.

Helmreich, R. L., Spence, J. T., & Holahan, C. K. (1979). Psychological androgyny and sex role flexibility: A test of two hypotheses. *Journal of Personality and Social Psychology, 37,* 1631–1644.

Hemmer, J. D., & Kleiber, D. A. (1981). Tomboys and sissies: Androgynous children? *Sex Roles, 7,* 1205–1212.

Hemmons, W. M. (1980). The women's liberation movement: Understanding black women's attitudes. In L. F. Rodgers-Rose (Ed.), *The black woman* (pp. 285–299). Beverly Hills, Calif.: Sage.

Hendrick, S. S., Hendrick, C., Slapion-Foote, M. J., & Foote, F. F. (1985). Gender differences in sexual attitudes. *Journal of Personality and Social Psychology, 48,* 1630–1642.

Henley, N., & Thorne, B. (1977). Womanspeak and manspeak: Sex differences and sexism in communication, verbal and nonverbal. In A. Sargent (Ed.), *Beyond sex roles* (pp. 201–218). St. Paul: West, p. 57, 58, 73, 136, 137.

Henley, N. M. (1977). *Body politics: Power, sex and nonverbal communications.* Englewood Cliffs, N.J.: Prentice-Hall.

Hennig, M., & Jardim, A. (1977). *The managerial woman.* New York: Doubleday.

Hensley, K. K., & Borges, M. A. (1981). Sex role stereotyping and sex role norms: A comparison of elementary and college age students. *Psychology of Women Quarterly, 5,* 543–554.

Hepburn, C. (1985). Memory for the frequency of sex-typed versus neutral behaviors: Implications for the maintenance of sex stereotypes. *Sex Roles, 12, 7/8,* 771–776.

Heppner, P. P. (1981). Counseling men in groups. *Personnel and Guidance Journal, 60,* 249–252.

Herman, J., & Hirschman, L. (1981). *Father-daughter incest.* Cambridge, Mass.: Harvard University Press.

Herman, R. (1981, May 3). Men and women also grow old in different ways. *The New York Times,* p. E7.

Hersh, S. (1970). *My Lai 4.* New York: Random House.

Herzog, A. R., Bachman, J. G., & Johnson, L. D. (1983). Paid work, child care, and housework: A national survey of high school seniors' preferences for sharing responsibilities between husband and wife. *Sex Roles, 9,* 109–135.

Heschel, S. (Ed.) (1983). *On being a Jewish feminist: A reader.* New York: Schocken.

Hess, R. D., & Camara, K. A. (1979). Post-divorce family relationships as mediating factors in the consequences of divorce for children. *Journal of Social Issues, 35*(4), 79–96.

Hess, R. D., & Shipman, V. C. (1967). Cognitive elements in maternal behavior. In J. P. Hell (Ed.), *Minnesota symposia on child psychology* (Vol. 1). (pp. 57–81). Minneapolis: University of Minnesota Press.

Hetherington, E. M., Cox, M., & Cox, R. (1977, April). Divorced fathers. *Psychology Today,* pp. 42–46.

Hetherington, E. M., Cox, M., & Cox, R. (1979). Play and social interaction in children following divorce. *Journal of Social Issues, 35*(4), 26–49.

Hildebrandt, K. A., & Fitzgerald, H. E. (1979). Adults' perceptions of infant sex and cuteness. *Sex Roles, 5,* 471–481.

Hill, C. E., Hobbs, M. A., & Verble, C. (1974). A developmental analysis of the sex-role identification of school-related objects. *Journal of Educational Research, 67,* 205–206.

Hill, C. E., Tanney, M. F., Leonard, M. M., & Reiss, J. (1977). Counselor reaction to female clients: Type of problem, age of client, and sex of counselor. *Journal of Counseling Psychology, 24,* 60–65.

Hill, C. T., Peplau, S. A., & Rubin, Z. (1981). Differing perceptions in dating couples: Sex roles vs. alternative explanations. *Psychology of Women Quarterly, 5,* 418–434.

Hill, C. T., Rubin, Z., & Peplau, A. (1976). Breakups before marriage: The end of 103 affairs. *Journal of Social Issues, 32,* 147–168.

Hill, C. T., & Stull, D. E. (1981). Sex differences in effects of social and value similarity in same-sex friendship. *Journal of Personality and Social Psychology, 41,* 488–502.

Hiller, D. V. (1984). Power dependence and division of family work. *Sex Roles, 10,* 1003–1019.

Himadi, W. G., Arkowitz, H., Hinton, R., & Perl, J. (1980). Minimal dating and its relationship to other social problems and general adjustment. *Behavior Therapy, 11,* 345–352.

Hines, M. (1982). Prenatal gonadal hormones and sex differences in human behavior. *Psychological Bulletin, 92,* 56–80.

Hines, M., & Shipley, C. (1984). Prenatal exposure to diethylstilbestrol (DES) and the development of sexually dimorphic cognitive abilities and cerebral lateralization. *Developmental Psychology, 20,* 81–94.

Hirt, J., Hoffman, M. A., & Sedlacek, W. E. (1983, January). Attitudes toward changing sex-roles of male varsity athletes versus nonathletes: Developmental perspectives. *Journal of College Student Personnel,* pp. 33–38.

Hite, S. (1976). *The Hite report: A nationwide study of female sexuality.* New York: Macmillan.

Hite, S. (1981). *The Hite report on male sexuality.* New York: MacMillan.

Hodges, K. K., Brandt, D. A., & Kline, J. (1981). Competence, guilt, and victimization: Sex differences in attribution of causality in television dramas. *Sex Roles, 7,* 537–546.

Hodgson, J. W., & Fischer, J. L. (1981). Pathways of identity development in college women. *Sex Roles, 7,* 681–690.

Hoferek, M. J., & Hanick, P. L. (1985). Woman and athlete: Toward role consistency. *Sex Roles, 12,* 687–695.

Hoffman, D. M., & Fidell, L. A. (1979). Characteristics of androgynous, undifferentiated, masculine and feminine middle-class women. *Sex Roles, 5,* 765–781.

Hoffman, L. R., & Maier, N. R. F. (1966). Social factors influencing problem solving in women. *Journal of Personality and Social Psychology, 4,* 382–390.

Hoffman, L. W. (1977). Changes in family roles, socialization, and sex differences. *American Psychologist, 32,* 644–657.

Hoffman, L. W. (1979). Maternal employment: 1979. *American Psychologist, 34,* 859–865.

Hoffman, M. L. (1981). The role of the father in moral internalization. In M. Lamb (Ed.), *The role of the father in child development,* 2nd ed. (pp. 359–378). New York: Wiley & Sons.

Holahan, C. K. (1979). Stress experienced by women doctoral students, need for support, and occupational sex typing: An interactional view. *Sex Roles, 5,* 425–436.

Holahan, C. K., & Gilbert, L. A. (1979). Interrole conflict for working women: Careers versus jobs. *Journal of Applied Psychology, 64,* 86–90.

Holahan, C. K., & Stephan, C. W. (1981). When beauty isn't talent: The influence of physical attractiveness, attitudes toward women, and competence on impression formation. *Sex Roles, 7,* 867–876.

Hollander, N. (1979). *I'm in training to be tall and blonde.* New York: St. Martin's Press.

Hollender, J., & Shafer, L. (1981). Male acceptance of female career roles. *Sex Roles, 7,* 1199–1203.

Holmstrom, L. L., & Burgess, A. W. (1981). *The victim of rape: Institutional reactions* New York: John Wiley.

Honegger, B. (1983, Aug. 21). Reagan has not fulfilled his promise. *The Washington Post.*

Honig, A. S., & Wittmer, D. S. (1982). Teachers and low-income toddlers in metropolitan daycare. *Early Childhood Development and Care, 10,* 95–112.

Hooks, B. (1984). *Feminist theory: From margin to center.* Boston: South End.

Hopkins, J. R. (1977). Sexual behavior in adolescence. *Journal of Social Issues, 33*(2), 67–85.

Hopson, J., & Rosenfeld, A. (1984, August). PMS: Puzzling monthly symptoms. *Psychology Today,* pp. 30–35.

Horn, J. (1978, November). Drinking buddies and confidants. *Psychology Today,* p. 28.

Horner, M. J. (1968). *Sex differences in achievement motivation and performance in competitive-noncompetitive situations.* Unpublished doctoral dissertation, University of Michigan.

Horner, M. J. (1970). Femininity and successful achievement: A basic inconsistency. In J. M Bardwick, E. Douvan, M. S. Horner, & D. Gutman (Eds.), *Feminine personality and conflict.* Monterey, Calif.: Brooks/Cole.

Horner, M. J. (1972). Toward an understanding of achievement related conflicts in women. *Journal of Social Issues, 28,* 157–176.

Horner, M. J. (1978). The measurement and behavioral implications of fear of success in women. In J. W. Atkinson, & J. O. Raynor (Eds.), *Personality, motivation, and achievement* (pp. 41–70). Washington, D.C.: Hemisphere.

Horney, K. (1973). On the genesis of the castration complex in women. In J. B. Miller (Ed.), *Psychoanalysis and women.* New York: Brunner/Mazel. (Original work published 1922).

Hornung, C. A., & McCullough, B. C. (1981). Status relationships in dual-employment marriages: Consequences for psychological well-being. *Journal of Marriage and the Family,* 125–141.

Horwitz, A. V. (1982). Sex-role expectations, power, and psychological distress. *Sex Roles, 8,* 607–623.

Houghton, M. (1984, November/December). Women push Kunin, senators over the top. *Women's Political Times.* p. 1.

Houseknecht, S. K., & Macke, A. S. (1981). Combining marriage and career: The marital adjustment of professional women. *Journal of Marriage and the Family,* 651–661.

Houser, B. B., & Beckman, L. J. (1980). Background characteristics and women's dual-role attitudes. *Sex Roles, 6,* 355–366.

Houser, B. B., Berkman, S. L., & Beckman, L. J. (1984). The relative rewards and costs of childlessness for older women. *Psychology of Women Quarterly, 8,* 395–398.

Howard, J. A. (1984). Societal influences on attribution: Blaming some victims more than others. *Journal of Personality and Social Psychology, 47,* 494–505.

Howe, K. G. (1985, Spring). The psychological impact of a women's studies course. *Women's Studies Quarterly.*

Howell, E. (1981). Psychological reactions of postpartum women. In E. Howell & M. Bayes (Eds.), *Women and mental health* (pp. 340–346). New York: Basic.

How Title IX has helped. (1984, March/April). *Women's Political Times,* p. 3.

Hrdy, S. B. (1981). *The woman that never evolved.* Cambridge, Mass.: Harvard University Press.

Huber, J., & Spitze, G. (1983). *Sex stratification: Children, housework, and jobs.* New York: Academic Press.

Hull, G. T., Scott, P. B., & Smith, B. (Eds.) (1982). *But some of us are brave: Black women's studies.* Old Westbury, New York: The Feminist Press.

Hunt, M. (1974). *Sexual behavior in the 1970s.* Chicago: Playboy Press.

Huston, A. C., Greer, D., Wright, J. C., Welch, R., & Ross, R. (1984). Children's comprehension of televised formal features with masculine and feminine connotations. *Developmental Psychology, 20,* 707–716.

Hyde, J. S. (1981). How large are cognitive gender differences? A meta-analysis using ω and d. *American Psychologist, 36,* 892–901.

Hyde, J. S. (1984a). Children's understanding of sexist language. *Developmental Psychology, 20,* 697–706.

Hyde, J. S. (1984b). How large are gender differences in aggression? A developmental meta-analysis. *Developmental Psychology, 20,* 722–736.

Hyde, J. S., Rosenberg, B. G., & Behrman, J. (1977). Tomboyism. *Psychology of Women Quarterly, 2,* 73–75.

Hyland, D. A. (1978, January 26). Participation in athletics: Is it worth all the suffering? *The New York Times,* p. S2.

Ickes, W., & Barnes, R. D. (1977). The role of sex and self-monitoring in unstructured dyadic interaction. *Journal of Personality and Social Psychology, 35,* 315–330.

Ickes, W., & Barnes, R. D. (1978). Boys and girls together—and alienated: On enacting stereotyped sex roles in mixed-sex dyads. *Journal of Personality and Social Psychology, 36,* 669–683.

If women had a foreign policy. (1985, March). *Ms.,* pp. 42, 44, 46, 48, 49, 108.

Inderlied, S. D., & Powell, G. (1979). Sex-role identity and leadership style: Different labels for the same concept? *Sex Roles, 5,* 613–625.

Inequality of sacrifice: Impact of the Reagan budget on women. (1984, March/April). *National NOW Times,* p. 6.

Ingalls, Z. (1984, September 12). Women's colleges show renewed vigor after long, painful self-examination. *Chronicle of Higher Education,* pp. 1, 18, 19.

Inoff, G. E., Halverson, C. F., Jr., & Pizzigati, K. A. L. (1983). The influence of sex-role stereotypes on children's self- and peer-attributions. *Sex Roles, 9,* 1205–1222.

Instone, D., Major, B., & Bunker, B. B. (1983). Gender, self confidence, and social influence strategies: An organizational simulation. *Journal of Personality and Social Psychology, 44,* 322–333.

Ireson, C. J. (1984). Adolescent pregnancy and sex roles. *Sex Roles, 11,* 189–201.

Isaacs, M. B. (1981). Sex role stereotyping and the evaluation of the performance of women: Changing trends. *Psychology of Women Quarterly, 6,* 187–195.

Israel, J., & Eliasson, R. (1971). Consumption society, sex-role and sexual behavior. *Acta Sociologica, 14,* 68–82.

Israeli women insulted at return to stereotype. (1982, June 21). *Easton Express,* p. A–9.

Jackson, A. D. (1982). Militancy and black women's competitive behavior in competitive versus noncompetitive conditions. *Psychology of Women Quarterly, 6,* 342–353.

Jackson, L. A. (1983). The perception of androgyny and physical attractiveness: Two is better than one. *Personality and Social Psychology Bulletin, 9,* 405–413.

Jackson, L. A., & Cash, T. F. (1985). Components of gender stereotypes: Their implications for inferences on stereotypic and nonstereotypic dimensions. *Personality and Social Psychology Bulletin, 11,* 326–344.

Jackson, L. A., Ialongo, N., & Stollak, G. E. (1983, August). *Another look at parental antecedents of sex role development.* Paper presented at the meeting of the American Psychological Association, Anaheim.

Jackson, L. A., & Larrance, S. T. (1979). Is a "refinement" of attribution theory necessary to accommodate the learned helplessness reformulation? *Journal of Abnormal Psychology, 88,* 681–682.

Jacobs, J. A., & Powell, B. (1985). Occupational prestige: A sex-neutral concept. *Sex Roles, 12,* 1061–1071.

Jacobson, M. B., & Popovich, P. M. (1983). Victim attractiveness and perceptions of responsibility in an ambiguous rape case. *Psychology of Women Quarterly, 8,* 100–104.

Jagger, A. M., & Struhl, P. R. (1978). *Feminist frameworks: Alternative theoretical accounts of the relations between women and men.* New York: McGraw-Hill.

Jamison, W., & Signorella, M. L. (1980). Sex-typing and spatial ability: The association between masculinity and success on Piaget's water-level task. *Sex Roles, 6,* 345–353.

Jancar, B. W. (1978). *Women under communism.* Baltimore: Johns Hopkins Press.

Janda, L. H., O'Grady, K. E., & Capps, C. F. (1978). Fear of success in males and females in sex linked occupations. *Sex Roles, 4,* 43–50.

Janssen-Jurreit, M. (1982). *Sexism: The male monopoly on history and thought.* (Trans. by Verne Moberg). New York: Farrar, Straus, & Geroux.

Jaquette, J. S. (Ed.) (1974). *Women in politics.* New York: Wiley.

Jeffords, C. R. (1984). The impact of sex-role and religious attitudes upon forced marital intercourse norms. *Sex Roles, 11,* 543–552.

Jenkins, A. H. (1982). *The psychology of the Afro-American: A humanistic approach*. New York: Pergamon.

Jennings, J. W., Geis, F. L., & Brown, V. (1980). The influence of television commercials on women's self-confidence and independent judgment. *Journal of Personality and Social Psychology, 38,* 203–210.

Joesting, J. (1971). Comparison of women's liberation members with their nonmember peers. *Psychological Reports, 29,* 1291–1294.

Johnson, A. G. (1980). On the prevalence of rape in the United States. *Signs, 6,* 136–146.

Johnson, D. D. (1973–1974). Sex differences in reading across cultures. *Reading Research Quarterly, 9,* 67–86.

Johnson, M. (1982a). Research in teaching the psychology of women. *Psychology of Women Quarterly, 7,* 96–104.

Johnson, M. (Ed.) (1982b). Special issue: Teaching psychology of women. *Psychology of Women Quarterly, 7,* Whole No. 1.

Johnson, M. M., Stockard, J., Rothbart, M. K., & Friedmen, L. (1981). Sexual preference, feminism, and women's perceptions of their parents. *Sex Roles, 7,* 1–18.

Johnson, P. B. (1982). Sex differences, women's role and alcohol use: Preliminary national data. *Journal of Social Issues, 38*(2), 95–116.

Johnson, P. B., & Goodchilds, J. D. (1976, October). How women get their way. *Psychology Today,* pp. 69–70.

Johnson, S. J., & Black, K. N. (1981). The relationship between sex-role identity and beliefs in personal control. *Sex Roles, 7,* 425–431.

Jolly, E. J., & O'Kelly, C. G. (1980). Sex-role stereotyping in the language of the deaf. *Sex Roles, 6,* 285–292.

Jones, W. H., Chernovetz, M. E., & Hansson, R. O. (1978). The enigma of androgyny: Differential implications for males and females? *Journal of Consulting and Clinical Psychology, 46,* 298–313.

Jorgenson, C., Davis, J., Opella, J., & Angerstein, G. (1979, September). *Hemispheric asymmetry in the processing of Stroop stimuli: An examination of gender, hand-preference, and language differences.* Paper presented at the meeting of the American Psychological Association, New York.

Josefowitz, N. (1980). Management men and women: Closed vs. open doors. *Harvard Business Review, 58*(5), 56–62.

Jourard, S. (1971). *The transparent self.* New York: Van Nostrand.

Joy, S. S., & Wise, P. S. (1983). Maternal employment, anxiety, and sex differences in college students' self-descriptions. *Sex Roles, 9,* 519–525.

Judge blames sex assault on 5-year old victim. (1982, January/February). *National NOW Times,* p. 6.

Jung, C. G. (1956). *Two essays on analytical psychology.* New York: Meridian.

Kagan, J. (1964). Acquisition and significance of sex typing and sex role identity. In M. L. Hoffman & L. W. Hoffman (Eds.), *Review of child research* (Vol. 1) (pp. 137–169). New York: Russell Sage.

Kahn, A. (1979). From theories of equity to theories of justice: An example of demasculinization in social psychology, *Society for the Advancement of Social Psychology Newsletter, 5*(3), pp. 12–13.

Kahn, A. (1981). Reactions of profeminist and antifeminist men to an expert woman. *Sex Roles, 7,* 857–866.

Kahn, A. (1984). The power war: Male response to power loss under equality. *Psychology of Women Quarterly, 8,* 234–247.

Kahn, A., & Gaeddert, W. P. (1985). From theories of equity to theories of justice: The liberating consequences of studying women. In V. O'Leary, R. Unger, & B. Wallston (Eds.), *Women, gender, and social psychology* (pp. 129–148). Hillsdale, N.J.: Lawrence Erlbaum Associates.

Kahn, A., Nelson, R. E., & Gaeddert, W. P. (1980). Sex of subject and sex composition of the group as determinants of reward allocations. *Journal of Personality and Social Psychology, 38,* 737–750.

Kahn, A., O'Leary, V. E., Krulewitz, J. E., & Lamm, H. (1980). Equity and equality: Male and female means to a just end. *Basic and Applied Social Psychology, 1,* 173–197.

Kahn, S. E., & Richardson, A. (1983). Evaluation of a course in sex roles for secondary school students. *Sex Roles, 9,* 431–440.

Kalisch, P. A., & Kalisch, B. J. (1984). Sex-role stereotyping of nurses and physicians on prime-time television: A dichotomy of occupational portrayals. *Sex Roles, 10,* 533–553.

Kamerman, S. B. (1984). Women, children, and poverty: Public policies and female-headed families in industrialized countries. *Signs, 10,* 249–271.

Kandel, D. B. (1978). Similarity in real-life adolescent friendship pairs. *Journal of Personality and Social Psychology, 36,* 306–312.

Kanter, R. M. (1976, May). Why bosses turn bitchy. *Psychology Today,* pp. 56–59ff.

Kanter, R. M. (1977). *Men and women in the corporation.* New York: Basic Books.

Kanter, R. M. (1983). *The change masters: Innovation for productivity in the American corporation.* New York: Simon & Schuster.

Kanter, R. M., & Stein, B. (1980). *A tale of "O": On being different in an organization.* New York: Harper & Row.

Kaplan, A. (1979). Clarifying the concept of androgyny: Implications for therapy. *Psychology of Women Quarterly, 3*, 223–230.

Kaplan, A., & Bean, J. P. (1976). From sex stereotypes to androgyny: Considerations of societal and individual change. In A. Kaplan & J. Bean (Eds.), *Beyond sex-role stereotypes* (pp. 383–392). Boston: Little, Brown.

Kaplan, H. S. (1979). *Disorders of desire.* New York: Simon & Schuster.

Kaplan, M. (1983a). The issue of sex bias in DSM-III: Comments on the articles by Spitzer, Williams, & Kass. *American Psychologist, 38*, 802–803.

Kaplan, M. (1983b). A woman's view of DSM-III. *American Psychologist, 38*, 786–792.

Karabenick, S. A. (1983). Sex-relevance of content and influenceability: Sistrunk & McDavid revisited. *Personality and Social Psychology Bulletin, 9*, 243–252.

Karpoe, K. P., & Olney, R. L. (1983). The effect of boys' or girls' toys on sex-typed play in preadolescents. *Sex Roles, 9*, 507–518.

Karr, R. G. (1978). Homosexual labeling and the male role. *Journal of Social Issues, 34*(3), 73–83.

Kaschak, E. (1978). Sex bias in student evaluation of college professors. *Psychology of Women Quarterly, 3*, 235–243.

Kaschak, E. (1981a). Another look at sex bias in students' evaluation of professors: Do winners get the recognition that they have been given. *Psychology of Women Quarterly, 5*, 767–772.

Kaschak, E. (1981b). Feminist psychotherapy: The first decade. In S. Cox (Ed.), *Female psychology: The emerging self*, 2nd ed. (pp. 387–401). New York: St. Martin's.

Kasl, S. (1979). Changes in mental health status associated with job loss and retirement. In J. Barrett (Ed.), *Stress and mental disorder.* New York: Raven Press.

Kasl, S., & Cobb, S. (1979). Some mental health consequences of plant closing and job loss. In L. Ferman & J. Gordus (Eds.), *Mental health and the economy.* Kalamazoo, Mich.: Upjohn Institute.

Kassell, P. (1984, July/August). Equal pay. *New Directions for Women*, p. 7.

Katz, P. (1979). The development of female identity. *Sex Roles, 5*, 115–178.

Katzenstein, M. F. (1984). Feminism and the meaning of the vote. *Signs, 10*, 4–26.

Kaufman, C. G., & Shikiar, R. (1985). Sex of employee and sex of supervisor: Effect on attributions for the causality of success and failure. *Sex Roles, 12*, 257–269.

Keith, P. M., & Schafer, R. B. (1980). Role strain and depression in two-job families. *Family Relations, 29*, 483–488.

Keller, E. F. (1982). Feminism and science. *Signs, 7*, 589–602.

Keller, E. F. (1985). *Reflections on gender and science.* New Haven, Conn.: Yale University.

Keller, J. F., Elliott, S. S., & Gunberg, E. (1982). Premarital sexual intercourse among single college students: A discriminant analysis. *Sex Roles, 8*, 21–32.

Kelly, J. A., O'Brian, G. G., & Hosford, R. (1981). Sex roles and social skills considerations for interpersonal adjustment. *Psychology of Women Quarterly, 5*, 758–766.

Kelly, J. A., & Worell, J. (1976). Parent behaviors related to masculine, feminine, and androgynous sex role orientations. *Journal of Consulting and Clinical Psychology, 44*, 843–851.

Kelly, J. A., & Worell, J. (1977). New formulations of sex roles and androgyny: A critical review. *Journal of Consulting and Clinical Psychology, 45*, 1101–1115.

Kelly, K. E., & Houston, B. K. (1985). Type A behavior in employed women: Relation to work, marital, and leisure variables, social support, stress, tension and health. *Journal of Personality and Social Psychology, 48*, 1067–1079.

Kelly-Gadol, J. (1977). Did women have a renaissance? In R. Bridenthal & C. Koonz (Eds.), *Becoming visible: Women in European history* (pp. 137–164). Boston: Houghton Mifflin.

Kemper, S. (1984). When to speak like a lady. *Sex Roles, 10*, 435–443.

Kennelly, E. (1984, September/October). Republicans in fear of gender gap, feature women at convention. *National NOW Times*, p. 3.

Kenworthy, J. A. (1979). Androgyny in psychotherapy: But will it sell in Peoria? *Psychology of Women Quarterly, 3*, 231–240.

Kerr, C. D. (1985, June 16). The computer room at some schools is in danger of being a boy's domain. *The Philadelphia Inquirer*, p. 5 I.

Kerr, N. L., & Sullaway, M. E. (1983). Group sex composition and member task motivation. *Sex Roles, 9*, 403–417.

Kerr, P. (1984, September 16). Women in take-charge roles stride into TV's limelight. *The New York Times*, pp. H 29–30.

Kershner, J. R., & Ledger, G. (1985). Effect of sex, intelligence, and style of thinking on creativity: A comparison of gifted and average IQ children. *Journal of Personality and Social Psychology, 48*, 1033–1040.

Kessler, S. J., & McKenna, W. (1978). *Gender: An ethnomethodological approach.* New York: Wiley.

Keyes, S. (1983). Sex differences in cognitive abilities and sex-role stereotypes in Hong Kong Chinese adolescents. *Sex Roles, 9*, 853–870.

Kidder, L. H., Boell, J. L., & Moyer, M. M. (1983). Rights consciousness and victimization prevention: Personal defense and assertiveness training. *Journal of Social Issues, 39*(2), 155–170.

Kiesler, S., Sproull, L., & Eccles, J. S. (1983, March). Second-class citizens? *Psychology Today,* 41–48.

Kilpatrick, D. G., Resick, P. A., & Veronen, L. J. (1981). Effects of a rape experience: A longitudinal study. *Journal of Social Issues, 37*(4), 105–122.

Kimball, M. M., & Gray, V. A. (1982). Feedback and performance expectancies in an academic setting. *Sex Roles, 8,* 999–1007.

Kimble, C. E., Yoshikawa, J. C., & Zehr, H. D. (1981). Vocal and verbal assertiveness in same-sex and mixed-sex groups. *Journal of Personality and Social Psychology, 40,* 1047–1054.

Kimlicka, T., Cross, H., & Tarnai, J. (1983). A comparison of androgynous, feminine, masculine, and undifferentiated women on self-esteem, body satisfaction, and sexual satisfaction. *Psychology of Women Quarterly, 7,* 291–294.

King, D. A., & Buchwald, A. M. (1982). Sex differences in subclinical depression: Administration of the Beck Depression Inventory in public and private disclosure situations. *Journal of Personality and Social Psychology, 42,* 963–969.

King, M. C. (1973, April). The politics of sexual stereotypes. *The Black Scholar,* pp. 12–23.

Kingery, D. W. (1985). Are sex-role attitudes useful in explaining male/female differences in rates of depression? *Sex Roles, 12,* 627–636.

Kinsey, A. E., Pomeroy, W. B., & Martin, C. E. (1948). *Sexual behavior in the human male.* Philadelphia: Saunders.

Kinsey, A. E., Pomeroy, W. B., & Martin, C. E., & Gebhard, P. H. (1953). *Sexual behavior in the human female.* Philadelphia: Saunders.

Kirkpatrick, C. S. (1980). Sex roles and sexual satisfaction in women. *Psychology of Women Quarterly, 4,* 444–459.

Kirshner, L., & Johnston, L. (1983). Effects of gender on inpatient psychiatric hospitalization. *Journal of Nervous and Mental Disease, 171,* 651–657.

Kite, M. E., & Deaux, K. (1984, August). *Stereotypes of male and female heterosexuals.* Paper presented at the meeting of the American Psychological Association, Toronto, Canada.

Klein, S. S. (Ed.) (1985). *Handbook for achieving sex equity through education.* Baltimore, Md.: Johns Hopkins University.

Kleinke, C. L., & Hinrichs, C. A. (1983). College adjustment problems and attitudes toward drinking reported by feminine, androgynous, and masculine college women. *Psychology of Women Quarterly, 7,* 373–382.

Kleinke, C. L., Staneski, R. A., & Mason, J. K. (1982). Sex differences in coping with depression. *Sex Roles, 8,* 877–889.

Klemesrud, J. (1979, March 11). Women executives: View from the top. *The New York Times,* p. 50.

Klemesrud, J. (1983, November 28). Women study the art of politics. *The New York Times,* p. 10.

Klerman, G. L. (1979, April). The age of melancholy? *Psychology Today,* pp. 36–42, 88.

Knafo, D., & Jaffe, Y. (1984). Sexual fantasizing in males and females. *Journal of Research in Personality, 18,* 451–462.

Knopp, S. (1980). Sexism in the picture of children's readers: East and West Germany compared. *Sex Roles, 6,* 189–205.

The knot's being tied later in life. (1985, September 19). *Easton Express,* pp. A1–A2.

Koblinsky, S. A., & Sugawara, A. I. (1984). Nonsexist curricula, sex of teacher, and children's sex role learning. *Sex Roles, 10,* 357–367.

Kobrin, F. E., & Hendershot, G. E. (1977). Do family ties reduce mortality—evidence from United States, 1966–1968. *Journal of Marriage, 39,* 737–745.

Koeske, R. K., & Koeske, G. F. (1975) An attributional approach to moods and the menstrual cycle. *Journal of Personality and Social Psychology, 31,* 473–478.

Kohlberg, L. A. (1966). A cognitive-developmental analysis of children's sex-role concepts and attitudes. In E. E. Maccoby (Ed.), *The development of sex differences* (pp. 82–173). Stanford, Calif.: Stanford University Press.

Kohlberg, L. (1969). Stage and sequence: The cognitive-developmental approach to socialization. In D. A. Goslin (Ed.), *Handbook of socialization and research* (pp. 347–480). Chicago: Rand McNally.

Kohlberg, L., & Ullian, D. Z. (1974). Stages in the development of psychosexual concepts and attitudes. In R. C. Friedman, R. M. Richart, & R. L. Vande Wiele (Eds.), *Sex differences in behavior.* New York: Wiley.

Kolata, G. B. (1974). !Kung hunter-gatherers: Feminism, diet and birth control. *Science, 185,* 932–934.

Kolata, G. (1983). Math genius may have hormonal basis. *Science, 222,* 1312.

Komarovsky, M. (1946). Cultural contradictions and sex roles. *American Journal of Sociology, 52*(3), 184–189.

Komarovsky, M. (1973). Cultural contradictions and sex roles: The masculine case. *American Journal of Sociology, 78,* 873–874.

Komarovsky, M. (1974). Patterns of self-disclosure in male undergraduates. *Journal of Marriage and the Family, 36,* 677–687.

Komarovsky, M. (1976). *Dilemmas of masculinity: A study of college youth.* New York: Norton.

Komarovsky, M. (1982). Female freshmen view their future: Career salience and its correlates. *Sex Roles, 8,* 299–314.

Komisar, L. (1977, August). Right wingers and the ERA. *Do It NOW,* p. 1.

Koss, M. P., Leonard, K. E., Beezley, D. A., & Oros, C. J. (1985). Nonstranger sexual aggression: A discriminant analysis of the psychological characteristics of undetected offenders. *Sex Roles, 12,* 981–992.

Kotelchuck, M. (1976). The infant's relationship to the father: Experimental evidence. In M. E. Lamb (Ed.), *The role of the father in child development* (pp. 329–344). New York: Wiley.

Kotkin, M. (1983). Sex roles among married and unmarried couples. *Sex Roles, 9,* 975–985.

Krasnoff, A. G. (1981). The sex difference in self-assessed fears. *Sex Roles, 7,* 19–23.

Krause, N. (1983). Conflicting sex-role expectations, housework dissatisfaction, and depressive symptoms among full-time housewives. *Sex Roles, 9,* 1115–1125.

Kravetz, D. (1978). Consciousness-raising groups in the 1970s. *Psychology of Women Quarterly, 3,* 168–186.

Kravetz, D., Maracek, J., & Finn, S. E. (1983). Factors influencing women's participation in consciousness-raising groups. *Psychology of Women Quarterly, 7,* 257–271.

Krogh, K. M. (1985). Women's motives to achieve and to nurture in different life stages. *Sex Roles, 12,* 75–90.

Krulewitz, J. E. (1981). Sex differences in evaluations of female and male victims' responses to assault. *Journal of Applied Social Psychology, 11,* 460–474.

Krulewitz, J. E., & Nash, J. E. (1980). Effects of sex role attitudes and similarity on men's rejection of male homosexuals. *Journal of Personality and Social Psychology, 38,* 67–74.

Kuhn, D., Nash, S. C., & Brucken, L. (1978). Sex-role concepts of two- and three-year olds. *Child Development, 49,* 445–451.

Kulik, J. A., & Harackiewicz, J. (1979). Opposite-sex interpersonal attraction as a function of the sex roles of the perceiver and the perceived. *Sex Roles, 5,* 443–452.

Kunerth, J. (1984, November 18). Marriage gives signs of a comeback. *Easton Express,* p. C7.

Kupke, T., Lewis, R., & Rennick, P. (1979). Sex differences in the neuropsychological functioning of epileptics. *Journal of Consulting and Clinical Psychology, 47,* 1128–1130.

Kurdek, L. A., & Schmitt, J. P. (in press). Relationship quality of partners in heterosexual married, heterosexual cohabitating, gay, and lesbian relationships. *Journal of Personality and Social Psychology.*

Lacher, M. R. B. (1978). On advising undergraduate women: A psychologist's advice to academic advisors. *Journal of College Student Personnel, 19,* 488–493.

LaFrance, M. (1982). Gender gestures: Sex, sex-role, and nonverbal communication. In C. Mayo & N. Henley (Eds.), *Gender and nonverbal behavior* (pp. 129–150). New York: Springer-Verlag.

LaFrance, M., & Carmen, B. (1980). The nonverbal display of psychological androgyny. *Journal of Personality and Social Psychology, 38,* pp. 36–49.

Lakoff, R. (1975). *Language and woman's place.* New York: Harper & Row.

Lamb, M. C., & Sagi, A. (Eds.) (1983). *Fatherhood and family policy.* Hillsdale, N.J.: Lawrence Erlbaum Associates.

Lamb, M. E. (1979). Paternal influences and the father's role: A personal perspective. *American Psychologist, 34,* 938–943.

Lamb, M. E. (1981a). The development of father-infant relationship. In M. Lamb (Ed.), *The role of the father in child development,* 2nd ed. (pp. 459–488). New York: Praeger.

Lamb, M. E., (Ed.) (1981b). *The role of the father in child development* (2nd ed.). New York: Wiley.

Lancaster, J. B. (1985). Evolutionary perspectives on sex differences in the higher primates. In A. Rossi (Ed.), *Gender and the life course* (pp. 3–27). New York: Aldine.

Landers, A. D. (1977). The menstrual experience. In E. Donelson & J. Gullahorn (Eds.), *Women: A psychological perspective* (pp. 65–78). New York: Wiley.

Landy, F. J., & Farr, J. L. (1980). Performance rating. *Psychological Bulletin, 87,* 72–107.

Langland, E., & Gove, W. (Eds.) (1981). *A feminist perspective in the academy.* Chicago: University of Chicago Press.

Lapidus, G. W. (Ed.) (1982). *Women, work, and family in the Soviet Union.* White Plains, N.Y.: M. E. Sharpe.

L'Armand, K., & Pepitone, A. (1982). Judgments of rape: A study of victim-rapist relationship and victim sexual history. *Personality and Social Psychology Bulletin, 8,* 134–139.

Larrance, D., Pavelich, S., Storer, P., Polizzi, M., Baron, B., Sloan, S., Jordan, P., & Reis, H. T. (1979). Competence and incompetence: Asymmetric responses to women and men on a sex-linked task. *Personality and Social Psychology Bulletin, 5,* 363–366.

Larwood, L., & Gattiker, U. (1984, August). *A comparison of the career paths used by successful men and women.* Paper presented at the meeting of the American Psychological Association, Toronto.

Larwood, L., & Kaplan, M. (1980). Job tactics of women in banking. *Group and Organization Studies, 5,* 70–79.

LaTorre, R. A., Yu, L., Fortin, L., & Marrache, M. (1983). Gender-role adoption and sex as academic and psychological risk factors. *Sex Roles, 9,* 1127–1136.

Lavine, L. O., & Lombardo, J. P. (1984). Self disclosure: Intimate and nonintimate disclosures to parents and best friends as a function of Bem Sex-Role category. *Sex Roles, 11,* 735–744.

Laws, J. L., & Schwartz, P. (1977). *Sexual scripts: The social construction of female sexuality.* Hinsdale, Ill.: Dryden.

Leacock, E. (1978). Society and gender. In E. Tobach & B. Rosoff (Eds.), *Genes and gender* (pp. 75–85). Staten Island, N.Y.: Gordian Press.

Leahy, R. L., & Shirk, S. R. (1984). The development of classificatory skills and sex-trait stereotypes in children. *Sex Roles, 10,* 281–292.

Lee, A. G., & Scheurer, V. J. (1983). Psychological androgyny and aspects of self-image in women and men. *Sex Roles, 9,* 289–306.

Lee, R. B. (1972). !The Kung Bushmen of Botswana. In M. G. Bicchieri (Ed.), *Hunters and gatherers today.* New York: Holt, Rinehart & Winston.

Lefcourt, H. (1976). *Locus of control: Current trends in theory and research.* Hillsdale, N.J.: Lawrence Erlbaum Associates.

Leghorn, L., & Parker, K. (1981). *Woman's worth: Sexual economics and the world of women.* New York: Routledge and Kegan Paul.

Lehne, G. K. (1976). Homophobia among men. In D. David & R. Brannon (Eds.), *The forty-nine percent majority* (pp. 66–88). Reading, Mass.: Addison-Wesley.

Leibowitz, L. (1979). Universals and male dominance among primates: A critical examination. In E. Tobach & B. Rosoff (Eds.), *Genes and Gender II* (pp. 35–46). Staten Island, N.Y.: Gordian Press.

Leibowitz, L. (1983). Origins of the sexual division of labor. In M. Lowe & R. Hubbard (Eds.), *Women's nature: Rationalizations of inequality* (pp. 123–147). New York: Pergamon Press.

Lein, L. (1982). *Who does the housework? The allocation of work in the home as a reflection of family ideology.* (Working Paper No. 92). Wellesley, Mass.: Wellesley College Center for Research on Women.

Lemkau, J. P. (1983). Women in male-dominated professions: Distinguishing personality and background characteristics. *Psychology of Women Quarterly, 8,* 144–165.

Lenney, E. (1979a). Androgyny: Some audacious assertions toward its coming of age. *Sex Roles, 5,* 703–719.

Lenney, E. (1979b). Concluding comments on androgyny: Some intimation of its mature development. *Sex Roles, 5,* 829–840.

Lenney, E. (1981). What's fine for the gander isn't always good for the goose: Sex differences in self-confidence as a function of ability area and comparison with others. *Sex Roles, 7,* 905–924.

Lenney, E., Gold, J., & Browning, C. (1983). Sex differences in self-confidence: The influence of comparison to others' ability level. *Sex Roles, 9,* 925–942.

Lenney, E., Mitchell, L., & Browning, C. (1983). The effect of clear evaluation criteria on sex bias in judgments of performance. *Psychology of Women Quarterly, 7,* 313–328.

Lentz, M. E. (1982). Fear of success as a situational phenomenon. *Sex Roles, 8,* 987–997.

Leon, G. R., & Finn, S. (1984). Sex-role stereotypes and the development of eating disorders. In C. Widom (Ed.), *Sex roles and psychopathology* (pp. 317–338). New York: Plenum.

Lerner, R. M., Sorell, G. T., & Brackney, B. E. (1981). Sex differences in self-concept and self-esteem of late adolescents: A time-lag analysis. *Sex Roles, 7,* 709–722.

Lesser, G. L., Kravitz, R. N., & Packard, R. (1963). Experimental arousal of achievement motivation in adolescent girls. *Journal of Abnormal and Social Psychology, 66,* 59–66.

Lester, D. (1984). Suicide. In C. Widom (Ed.), *Sex roles and psychopathology* (pp. 145–156), New York: Plenum.

Lester, M. (1976, January 26). Rape: A report. *New York Times Magazine,* pp. 4–16.

Levin, J., & Arluke, A. (1985). An exploratory analysis of sex differences in gossip. *Sex Roles, 12,* 281–286.

Levine, L., & Barbach, L. (1984). *The intimate male.* New York: Doubleday.

Levine, M. P., & Leonard, R. (1984). Discrimination against lesbians in the work force. *Signs, 9,* 700–710.

Levine, R., Gillman, M. J., & Reis, H. (1982). Individual differences or sex differences in achievement attributions? *Sex Roles, 8,* 455–466.

Levinson, D. (1978). *The seasons of a man's life.* New York: Knopf.

Levi-Strauss, C. (1956). The family. In H. Shapiro (Ed.), *Man, culture, and society.* New York: Oxford University Press.

Levitin, R. E., Quinn, R. P., & Staines, G. L. (1973, March). A woman is 58% of a man. *Psychology Today,* pp. 89–91.

Levitz-Jones, E. M., & Orlofsky, J. L. (in press). Separation-individuation and intimacy capacity in college women. *Journal of Personality and Social Psychology.*

Levy, J., & Reid, M. (1978). Variations in cerebral organization as a function of handedness, hand posture in writing, and sex. *Journal of Experimental Psychology: General, 107,* 119–144.

Lewis, D. K. (1977). A response to inequality: Black women, racism, and sexism. *Signs, 3,* 339–361.

Lewis, L. L., & Deaux, K. (1983, August). *Gender stereotyping: Subcategories and their contents.* Paper presented at the meeting of the American Psychological Association, Anaheim.

Lewis, M. (1972). Parents versus children: Sex-role development. *School Review, 80*(2), 229–240.

Lewis, M., & Weinraub, M. (1979). Origins of early sex-role development. *Sex Roles, 5,* 135–153.

Lewis, R. A. (1978). Emotional intimacy among men. *Journal of Social Issues, 34*(1), 108–121.

Lewittes, H. J., & Bem, S. L. (1983). Training women to be more assertive in mixed-sex task-oriented discussions. *Sex Roles, 9,* 581–596.

Lewontin, R. C., Rose, S., & Kamin, L. J. (1984). *Not in our genes: Biology, ideology, and human nature.* New York: Pantheon.

Liben, L. S., & Signorella, M. L. (1980). Gender-related schemata and constructive memory in children. *Child Development, 51,* 11–18.

Lichenstein, G. (1981, February 8). The wooing of women athletes. *The New York Times Magazine,* pp. 27, 30, 33, 50, 52, 54, 55.

Licht, B. G., & Dweck, C. S. (1984). Determinants of academic achievement: The interaction of children's achievement orientations with skill area. *Developmental Psychology, 20,* 628–636.

Liden, R. C. (1985). Female perceptions of female and male managerial behavior. *Sex Roles, 12,* 421–432.

Lieberman, M. A., Solow, N., Bond, G. R., & Reibstein, J. (1979). The psychotherapeutic impact of women's consciousness-raising groups. *Archives of General Psychiatry, 36,* 161–168.

Lieblich, A., & Friedman, G. (1985). Attitudes toward male and female homosexuality and sex-role stereotypes in Israeli and American students. *Sex Roles, 12,* 561–570.

Liem, R., & Rayman, P. (1982). Health and social costs of unemployment: Research and policy considerations. *American Psychologist, 37,* 1116–1123.

Lifschitz, S. (1983). Male and female careers: Sex-role and occupational stereotypes among high school students. *Sex Roles, 9,* 725–735.

Lii, S., & Wong, S. (1982). A cross-cultural study on sex-role stereotypes and social desirability. *Sex Roles, 8,* 481–491.

Linehan, M. M., & Seifert, R. F. (1983). Sex and contextual differences in the appropriateness of assertive behavior. *Psychology of Women Quarterly, 8,* 79–88.

Linn, M. C., & Petersen, A. C. (1983, August). *Emergence and characterization of gender differences in spatial ability: A meta-analysis.* Paper presented at the meeting of the American Psychological Association, Anaheim.

Linscott, J. (1984, March 15). Road still rougher for career women. *Easton Express,* p. C2.

Linz, D., Donnerstein, E., & Penrod, S. (1984). The effects of multiple exposure to filmed violence against women. *Journal of Communications, 34*(3), 130–147.

Lipman-Blumen, J., & Bernard, J. (Eds.) (1979). *Sex roles and social policy: A complex social science equation.* Beverly Hills, Calif.: Sage.

Lipman-Blumen, J., Handley-Isaksen, A., & Leavitt, H. J. (1983). Achieving styles in men and women: A model, an instrument, and some findings. In J. T. Spence (Ed.), *Achievement and achievement motives: Psychological and sociological approaches* (pp. 147–204). San Francisco: W. H. Freeman.

Lipman-Blumen, J., & Leavitt, H. (1976). Vicarious and direct achievement patterns in adulthood. *The Counseling Psychologist, 6,* 26–32.

Lippa, R., & Beauvais, C. (1983). Gender jeopardy: The effects of gender, assessed femininity and masculinity and false success/failure feedback on performance in an experimental quiz game. *Journal of Personality and Social Psychology, 44,* 344–353.

Lips, H. M., & Myers, A. M. (1980). Subject reactions to a stimulus person as a function of sex of subject and sex-role appropriateness of stimulus person's career goal. *Sex Roles, 6,* 675–682.

Lipson, E. R. (1977, May 1). In the Carter administration, big jobs for young lawyers. *The New York Times,* Sec. 3, p. 1ff.

Lockheed, M. E. (1975). Female motive to avoid success: A psychological barrier or a response to deviancy? *Sex Roles, 1,* 41–50.

Lockheed, M. E., & Hall, K. P. (1976). Conceptualizing sex as a status characteristic and applications to leadership training strategies. *Journal of Social Issues, 32,* 111–124.

Locksley, A., Borgida, E., Brekke, N., & Hepburn, C. (1980). Sex stereotypes and social judgement. *Journal of Personality and Social Psychology, 39,* 821–831.

Locksley, A., & Colten, M. E. (1979). Psychological androgyny: A case of mistaken identity? *Journal of Personality and Social Psychology, 37,* 1017–1031.

Locksley, A., & Douvan, E. (1979). Problem behavior in adolescents. In E. S. Gomberg & V. Franks

(Eds.), *Gender and disordered behavior: Sex differences in psychopathology* (pp. 71–100). New York: Brunner/Mazel.

Loeb, R. C., & Horst, L. (1978). Sex differences in self and teacher's reports of self-esteem in preadolescents. *Sex Roles, 4,* 779–788.

Logan, D. D., & Kaschak, E. (1980). The relationship of sex, sex role, and mental health. *Psychology of Women Quarterly, 4,* 573–580.

Lombardo, J. P., & Lavine, L. O. (1981). Sex-role stereotyping and patterns of self-disclosure. *Sex Roles, 7,* 403–411.

Lombardo, W. K., Cretser, G. A., Lombardo, B., & Mathis, S. L. (1983). For cryin' out loud—there is a sex difference. *Sex Roles, 9,* 987–995.

LoPiccolo, J., & Heiman, J. (1977). Cultural values and the therapeutic definition of sexual function and dysfunction. *Journal of Social Issues, 33*(2), 166–183.

Lorde, A. (1984). *Sister outsider.* Trumensburg, New York: The Crossing Press.

Lott, B. (1978). Behavioral concordance with sex role ideology related to play areas, creativity and parental sex typing of children. *Journal of Personality and Social Psychology, 36,* 1087–1100.

Lott, B. (1985). The potential enrichment of social/personality psychology through feminist research, and vice versa. *American Psychologist, 40,* 155–164.

Lovenheim, B. (1981, January 29). Programs to develop skills of fatherhood. *The New York Times,* p. C3.

Lowe, M., & Hubbard, R. (1979). Sociobiology and biosociology: Can science prove the biological basis of sex differences in behavior? In E. Tobach & B. Rosoff (Eds.), *Genes and Gender II* (pp. 91–112). Staten Island, N.Y.: Gordian Press.

Lowe, M., & Hubbard, R. (Eds.) (1983). *Woman's nature: Rationalizations of inequality.* New York: Pergamon.

Lubinski, D., Tellegen, A., & Butcher, J. N. (1981). The relationship between androgyny and subjective indicators of emotional well-being. *Journal of Personality and Social Psychology, 40,* 722–730.

Lubinski, D., Tellegen, A., & Butcher, J. N. (1983). Masculinity, femininity, and androgyny viewed and assessed as distinct concepts. *Journal of Personality and Social Psychology, 44,* 428–439.

Lunneborg, P. W. (1979). The vocational interest inventory: Development and validation. *Educational and Psychological Measurement, 39*(2).

Lykes, B., Stewart, A., & LaFrance, M. (1981, April). *Control and aspirations in adolescents: A comparison by race, sex, and social class.* Paper presented at the meeting of the Eastern Psychological Association, New York.

Lykes, M. B. (1983). Discrimination and coping in the lives of black women: Analyses of oral history data. *Journal of Social Issues, 39*(3), 79–100.

Lynn, D. B. (1959). A note on sex differences in the development of masculine and feminine identification. *Psychological Review, 66,* 126–135.

Lynn, D. B. (1969). *Parental and sex role identification: A theoretical formulation.* Berkeley: McCutchan.

Lynn, D. B. (1979). *Daughters and parents: Past, present, and future.* Monterey, Calif.: Brooks/Cole.

Lynn, N. (1975). Women in American politics: An overview. In J. Freeman (Ed.), *Women: A feminist perspective* (pp. 364–385). Palo Alto, Calif.: Mayfield.

Lyons, R. D. (1983, October 4). Sex in America. *The New York Times,* p. C1.

MacArthur, R. S. (1967). Sex differences in field dependence for the Eskimo. *International Journal of Psychology, 2,* 139–140.

Macaulay, J. (1979, October 8). *Response to Marwell et al.* Unpublished letter to the Editor. (Available from author, 314 Shepard Terrace, Madison, WI 53705).

Maccoby, E. E. (1966). Sex differences in intellectual functioning. In E. E. Maccoby (Ed.), *The development of sex differences* (pp. 25–55). Stanford, Calif.: Stanford University Press.

Maccoby, E. E., & Jacklin, C. M. (1974). *The psychology of sex differences.* Stanford, Calif.: Stanford University Press.

Maccoby, E. E., Snow, M. E., & Jacklin, C. N. (1984). Children's dispositions and mother-child interaction at 12 and 18 months: A short term longitudinal study. *Developmental Psychology, 20,* 459–472.

Maccoby, M. (1976, December). The corporate climber. *Fortune,* pp. 98–101, 104–108.

MacCormack, C., & Strathern, M. (1981). *Nature, culture and gender.* Cambridge: Cambridge University Press.

MacDonald, N. E., & Hyde, J. S. (1980). Fear of success, need for achievement, and fear of failure: A factor analytic study. *Sex Roles, 6,* 695–711.

MacKay, D. G. (1980). Psychology, prescriptive grammar, and the pronoun problem. *American Psychologist, 35,* 444–449.

Mackey, W. C. (1985). A cross-cultural perspective on perceptions of paternalistic deficiencies in the United States: The myth of the derelict Daddy. *Sex Roles, 12,* 509–534.

MacKinnon, C. A. (1979). *Sexual harassment of working women: A case of sex discrimination.* New Haven: Yale University Press.

MacKinnon, C. A. (1982). Feminism, Marxism, method, and the state: An agenda for theory. *Signs, 7,* 515–544.

Macklin, E. D. (1980). Nontraditional family forms: A decade of research. *Journal of Marriage and the Family, 42,* 905–922.

Madden, J. M. (1981). Using policy-capturing to measure attitudes in organizational diagnosis. *Personnel Psychology, 34,* 341–350.

Madden, M. E. (1983). Perceived control and power in marriage: A study of marital decision making and task performance. *Dissertation Abstracts International, 43*(8-B), 2744.

Madden, M. E., Brownstein, A. D., & Marshall, T. (1985, March). *Influence strategies in same-sex and opposite-sex friendships.* Paper presented at the meeting of the Eastern Psychological Association, Boston.

Mader, D. R. D., & Pollack, R. H. (1984, April). *Sexual arousal to hostility in sexual fantasy: A test of Stoller's theory.* Paper presented at the meeting of the Eastern Psychological Association, Baltimore.

Maier, N. R. F., & Casselman, G. C. (1970). The SAT as a measure of problem-solving ability in males and females. *Psychological Reports, 26,* 927–939.

Maihoff, N., & Forrest, L. (1982). Sexual harassment in higher education: An assessment study. *Journal of the National Association for Women Deans, Administrators, and Counselors, 46*(2), 3–8.

Major, B. (1979). Sex-role orientation and fear of success: Clarifying an unclear relationship. *Sex Roles, 5,* 63–70.

Major, B. (1982). Gender patterns in touching behavior. In C. Mayo & N. Henley (Eds.), *Gender and nonverbal behavior* (pp. 15–38). New York: Springer-Verlag.

Major, B., & Adams, J. B. (1983). Role of gender, interpersonal orientation, and self-presentation in distributive-justice behavior. *Journal of Personality and Social Psychology, 45,* 598–608.

Major, B., & Adams, J. B. (1984). Situational moderators of gender differences in reward allocations. *Sex Roles, 11,* 869–880.

Major, B., Carnevale, P. J. D., & Deaux, K. (1981). A different perspective on androgyny: Evaluation of masculine and feminine personality characteristics. *Journal of Personality and Social Psychology, 41,* 988–1001.

Major, B., McFarlin, D., & Gagnon, D. (1984). Overworked and underpaid: On the nature of gender differences in personal entitlement. *Journal of Personality and Social Psychology, 47,* 1399–1412.

Makosky, V. P. (1976). Sex role compatibility of task and of competitor, and fear of success as variables affecting women's performance. *Sex Roles, 2,* 237–248.

Malamuth, N. M. (1981). Rape proclivity among males. *Journal of Social Issues, 37*(4), 138–157.

Malamuth, N. M. (1983). Factors associated with rape as predictors of laboratory aggression against women. *Journal of Personality and Social Psychology, 45,* 432–442.

Malamuth, N. M., & Donnerstein, E. (Eds.) (1984). *Pornography and sexual aggression.* New York: Academic Press.

Malamuth, N. M., Feshbach, S., & Jaffe, Y. (1977). Sexual arousal and aggression: Recent experiments and theoretical issues. *Journal of Social Issues, 33*(2), 110–133.

Malamuth, N. M., Haber, S., & Feshbach, S. (1980). Testing hypotheses regarding rape: Exposure and sexual violence, sex differences and the "normality" of rapists. *Journal of Research in Personality, 14*(1), 121–137.

Malamuth, N. M., Heim, M., & Feshbach, S. (1980). Sexual responsiveness of college students to rape depictions: Inhibitory and disinhibitory effects. *Journal of Personality and Social Psychology, 38,* 399–408.

Malchon, M. J., & Penner, L. A. (1981). The effects of sex and sex-role identity on the attribution of maladjustment. *Sex Roles, 1,* 363–378.

Malinowski, B. (1932). *The sexual life of savages.* London: Routledge.

Malson, M. R. (1983). Black women's sex roles: The social context for a new ideology. *Journal of Social Issues, 39,* 101–113.

Mamary, P. D., & Simpson, R. L. (1981). Three female roles in television commercials. *Sex Roles, 7,* 1223–1232.

Mamonova, T. (Ed.) (1984). *Women and Russia: Feminist writings.* (R. Park & C. A. Fitzpatrick, Trans.). Boston: Beacon.

Mancini, J. A., & Orthner, D. K. (1978). Recreational sexuality preferences among middle-class husbands and wives. *Journal of Sex Research, 14*(2), 96–106.

Mandel, R. (1981). *In the running: The new woman candidate.* New York: Ticknor and Fields.

Mann, C. R. (1984). *Female crime and delinquency.* University, Alabama: University of Alabama Press.

Marcus, S., & Overton, W. F. (1978). The development of cognitive gender constancy and sex role preferences. *Child Development, 49,* 434–444.

Maracek, J., & Ballou, D. J. (1981). Family roles and women's mental health. *Professional Psychology, 12,* 39–46.

Margolis, M. L. (1984). *Mothers and such: View of American women and why they changed.* Berkeley: University of California Press.

Marini, M. M. (1978). Sex differences in the determination of adolescent aspirations: A review of research. *Sex Roles, 4,* 723–753.

Mark, E. W., & Alper, T. G. (1985). Women, men, and intimacy motivation. *Psychology of Women Quarterly, 9,* 81–88.

Markowitz, J. (1984). The impact of the sexist-language controversy and regulation on language in university documents. *Psychology of Women Quarterly, 8,* 337–347.

Markus, H., Crane, N., Bernstein, S., & Siladi, M. (1982). Self-schemas and gender. *Journal of Personality and Social Psychology, 42,* 38–50.

Marmor, J. (Ed.) (1980). *Homosexual behavior.* New York: Basic Books.

Marolla, J. A., & Scully, D. H. (1979). Rape and psychiatric vocabularies of motive. In E. S. Gomberg & V. Franks (Eds.), *Gender and disordered behavior: Sex differences in psychopathology* (pp. 301–318). New York: Brunner/Mazel.

Marriage: It's back in style. (1983, June 20). *U.S. News and World Report,* pp. 44–50.

Marshall, D. S. (1971, February). Too much in Mangaia. *Psychology Today, 4,* pp. 43–44.

Martin, C. L. (1984, August). *Assessing the accuracy of sex stereotypes and their relation to individual self concepts.* Paper presented at the meeting of the American Psychological Association, Toronto, Canada.

Martin, C. L., & Halverson, C. F., Jr. (1983). Gender constancy: A methodological and theoretical analysis. *Sex Roles, 9,* 775–790.

Martinac, P. (1984, March). The trade in wives. *Womanews,* pp. 1, 21.

Martinko, M. J., & Gardner, W. L. (1983). A methodological review of sex-related access discrimination problems. *Sex Roles, 9,* 825–839.

Marwell, G., Rosenfeld, R., & Spilerman, S. (1979). Geographic constraints on women's careers in academia. *Science, 205,* 1225–1231.

Marx, J. (1982). Autoimmunity in left-handers. *Science, 217,* 141–144.

Maslin, J. (1984, August 26). Men and women in film: A war zone update. *The New York Times,* pp. H1, 19.

Maslow, A. H. (1942). Self-esteem (dominance-feeling) and sexuality in women. *Journal of Social Psychology, 16.*

Maslow, A. H. (1962). *Toward a psychology of being.* Princeton, N.J.: Van Nostrand.

Massengill, D., & DiMarco, N. (1979). Sex-role stereotypes and requisite management characteristics: A current replication. *Sex Roles, 5,* 561–570.

Masters, W. H., & Johnson, V. (1966). *Human sexual response.* Boston: Little, Brown.

Masters, W. H., & Johnson, V. (1970). *Human sexual inadequacy.* Boston: Little, Brown.

Masters, W. H., & Johnson, V. (1974). *The pleasure bond: A new look at sexuality and commitment.* Boston: Little, Brown.

Masters, W. H., & Johnson, V. (1979). *Homosexuality in perspective.* Boston: Little, Brown.

Matteo, S. (1984, August). *The effect of sex role stereotyping on sport participation.* Paper presented at the meeting of the American Psychological Association, Toronto, Canada.

Mayo, C., & Henley, N. (1981). *Gender and nonverbal behavior.* New York: Springer-Verlag.

McAllister, P. (Ed.) (1982). *Reweaving the web of life: Feminism and nonviolence.* Philadelphia: New Society.

McArthur, L. Z., & Eisen, S. V. (1976). Achievements of male and female storybook characters as determinants of achieving behavior by boys and girls. *Journal of Personality and Social Psychology, 33,* 467–473.

McBride, A. B., & Black, K. N. (1984). Differences that suggest female investment in, and male distance from, children. *Sex Roles, 10,* 231–246.

McBroom, W. H. (1981). Parental relationships, socioeconomic status, and sex role expectations. *Sex Roles, 7,* 1027–1033.

McBroom, W. H. (1984). Changes in sex-role orientations: A five-year longitudinal comparison. *Sex Roles, 11,* 583–592.

McCain, N. (1983, November 2). Female faculty members and students at Harvard report sexual harassment. *Chronicle of Higher Education,* pp. 1, 14.

McClelland, D. C. (1980). Motive dispositions: The merits of operant and respondent measures. In L. Wheeler (Ed.), *Review of personality and social psychology,* Vol. 1 (pp. 10–41). Beverly Hills, Calif.: Sage.

McClelland, D. C., Atkinson, J. W., Clark, R. A., & Lowell, E. G. (1953). *The achievement motive.* New York: Appleton-Century-Crofts.

McCoy, N. L. (1977). Innate factors in sex differences. In A. Sargent (Ed.), *Beyond sex roles.* St. Paul: West.

McDonald, K. (1984, March 21). Female athletes are competing at levels close to those of men in some sports. *Chronicle of Higher Education,* p. 23.

McElroy, M. A. (1983). Parent-child relations and orientations toward sport. *Sex Roles, 9,* 997–1004.

McGhee, P. E., & Frueh, T. (1980). Television viewing and the learning of sex-role stereotypes. *Sex Roles, 6,* 179–188.

McGlone, J. (1980). Sex differences in human brain asymmetry: A critical survey. *Behavioral and Brain Sciences, 3,* 215–263.

McGuinness, D., & Pribram, K. (1978). The origins of sensory bias in the development of gender differences in perception and cognition. In M. Bortner (Ed.), *Cognitive growth and development—Essays in honor of Herbert G. Birch.* New York: Brunner/Mazel.

McHugh, M. C., Frieze, I. H., & Hanusa, B. H. (1982). Attributions and sex differences in achievement: Problems and new perspectives. *Sex Roles, 8,* 467–479.

McKelvey, B. (1984, January 20). The big brushoff. *The Easton Express,* pp. S 10–11.

McKenna, W., & Kessler, S. (1977). Experimental design as a source of sex bias in social psychology. *Sex Roles, 3,* 117–128.

McMahan, I. (1982). Expectancy of success on sex-linked tasks. *Sex Roles, 8,* 949–958.

McMillan, J. A., Clifton, A. K., McGrath, C., & Gale, W. S. (1977). Women's language: Uncertainty of interpersonal sensitivity and emotionality? *Sex Roles, 3,* 545–559.

Mead, M. (1935). *Sex and temperament.* New York: William Morrow.

Mednick, M., Carr, P., & Thomas, V. (1983, April). *Evaluations of sex-typed tasks by Black men and women: A second look.* Paper presented at the meeting of the Eastern Psychological Association, Philadelphia.

Mednick, M. T. S., & Puryear, G. R. (1975). Motivational and personality factors related to career goals of Black college women. *Journal of Social and Behavioral Sciences, 12,* 1–30.

Megargee, E. (1969). Influence of sex roles on the manifestation of leadership. *Journal of Applied Psychology, 53,* 377–382.

Meillassoux, C. (1981). *Maidens, meal and money: Capitalism and the domestic community.* Cambridge: Cambridge University Press.

Mellen, J. (1973). *Women and their sexuality in the new film.* New York: Dell.

Mellen, J. (1978a). *Big bad wolves; Masculinity in the American film.* New York: Pantheon.

Mellen, J. (1978b, April 23). Hollywood rediscovers the American Woman. *The New York Times,* Sect. 2, p. 1ff.

Mellon, P. M., Crano, W. D., & Schmitt, N. (1982). An analysis of the role and trait components of sex-biased occupational beliefs. *Sex Roles, 8,* 533–541.

Men get twice what women do. (1984, July 26). *The Easton Express,* p. 2.

Mendonsa, E. L. (1981). The status of women in Sisala society. *Sex Roles, 7,* 607–625.

Meredith, D. (1985, June). Dad and the kids. *Psychology Today,* pp. 63–67.

Meredith, N. (1984, January). The Gay dilemma. *Psychology Today,* pp. 56–62.

Merriam, S. B., & Hyer, P. (1984). Changing attitudes of women towards family related tasks in young adulthood. *Sex Roles, 10,* 825–835.

Merritt, S. (1982). Sex roles and political ambition. *Sex Roles, 8,* 1025–1036.

Messe, L. A., & Watts, B. (1980). Self-pay behavior: Sex differences in reliance on external cues and feelings of comfort. *American Psychology Bulletin, 2*(1), 83–88.

Messing, K. (1982). Women have different jobs because of their biological differences. In E. Fee (Ed.), *Women and health: The politics of sex in medicine* (pp. 139–148). Farmingdale, N.Y.: Baywood.

Meyer-Bahlburg, F. L. (1974). Aggression, androgens and the XYY syndrome. In R. C. Friedman et al. (Eds.), *Sex differences in behavior* (pp. 433–454). New York: Wiley.

Michelini, R. L., Eisen, D., & Snodgrass, S. R. (1981). Success orientation and the attractiveness of competent males and females. *Sex Roles, 7,* 391–401.

Milgram, S. (1965). Some conditions of obedience and disobedience to authority. *Human Relations, 18,* 57–76.

Miller, C. T. (1984). Self-schemas, gender, and social comparison: A clarification of the related attributes hypothesis. *Journal of Personality and Social Psychology, 46,* 1222–1229.

Miller, F. D., & Zeitz, B. (1978). A women's place is in the footnotes. *Personality and Social Psychology Bulletin, 4,* 511–514.

Miller, M. S. (1985, March). *Personal, motivational, and attitudinal correlates and discriminators of academic success among women psychology faculty.* Paper presented at the meeting of the Eastern Psychological Association, Boston.

Miller, S. (1983). *Men and friendship.* New York: Houghton Mifflin.

Millet, K. (1970). *Sexual politics.* New York: Doubleday.

Mills, C. J. (1983). Sex-typing and self-schemata effects on memory and response latency. *Journal of Personality and Social Psychology, 45,* 163–172.

Mills, C. J., & Bohannon, W. E. (1983). Personality, sex-role orientation, and psychological health in stereotypically masculine groups of males. *Sex Roles, 9,* 1161–1169.

Mills, C. J., & Tyrrell, D. J. (1983). Sex-stereotypic encoding and release from proactive interference. *Journal of Personality and Social Psychology, 45,* 772–781.

Milton, C., Pierce, C., & Lyons, M. (1977). *Little sisters and the law.* Washington, D.C.: American Bar Association Commission on Correctional Services and Facilities.

Minturn, L. (1984). Sex-role differentiation in contemporary communes. *Sex Roles, 10,* 73–85.

Mirande, A., & Enriquez, E. (1980). *La Chicana— The Mexican-American woman.* Chicago: University of Chicago Press.

Mischel, W. (1966). A social learning view of sex differences in behavior. In E. E. Maccoby (Ed.), *The development of sex differences* (pp. 56–81). Stanford, Calif.: Stanford University Press.

Mischel, W. (1968). *Personality and assessment.* New York: Wiley.

Mitchell, J. (1971). *Women's estate.* New York: Pantheon.

Moely, B. E., Skarin, K., & Weil, S. (1979). Sex differences in competition-cooperation behavior of children at two age levels. *Sex Roles, 5,* 329–342.

Monagan, D. (1983, March). The failure of coed sports. *Psychology Today,* 58–63.

Monahan, L. (1983). The effects of sex differences and evaluation on task performance and aspiration. *Sex Roles, 9,* 205–215.

Monahan, L., Kuhn, D., & Shaver, P. (1974). Intrapsychic versus cultural explanations of the fear of success motive. *Journal of Personality and Social Psychology, 29,* 60–64.

Money, J. (1963). Developmental differentiation of femininity and masculinity compared. In Farber & Wilson (Eds.), *Man and civilization: The potential of women.* New York: McGraw-Hill.

Money, J. (1978, April). *Sex determinants and sex stereotyping: Aristotle to H-Y androgen.* Invited address at the meeting of the Western Psychological Association, San Francisco.

Money, J., & Ehrhardt, A. A. (1972). *Man and woman, boy and girl.* Baltimore: Johns Hopkins University Press.

deMonteflores, C., & Schultz, S. (1978). Coming out: Similarities and differences for lesbians and gay men. *Journal of Social Issues, 34*(3), 59–72.

Moore, D. E. (Ed.). (1979). *Battered women.* Beverly Hills, Calif.: Sage.

Moos, R., Kopell, B., Melges, F., Yalum, I., Lunde, D., Clayton, R., & Hamburg, D. (1969). Variations in symptoms and mood during the menstrual cycle. *Journal of Psychosomatic Research, 13,* 37–44.

Moraga, C., & Anazaldua, G. (Eds.) (1981). *This bridge called my back: Writings by radical women of color.* Watertown, Mass: Persephone Press.

More women delay having children into their 30s. (1984, October 13). *The Easton Express,* p. 10.

Moreland, J. (1980). Age and change in the adult male sex role. *Sex Roles, 6,* 807–818.

Moreland, J. R. (1983, August). *Nuclear family break-up as an impetus for male change.* Paper presented at the meeting of the American Psychological Association, Anaheim.

Morelock, J. C. (1980). Sex differences in susceptibility to social influence. *Sex Roles, 6,* 537–548.

Morgan, C. S. (1980). Female and male attitudes toward life: Implications for theories of mental health. *Sex Roles, 6,* 367–380.

Morgan, M. (1975). *The total woman.* New York: Pocket Book.

Morgan, M. (1982). Television and adolescents' sex role stereotypes: A longitudinal study. *Journal of Personality and Social Psychology, 43,* 947–955.

Morgan, R. (Ed.) (1984). *Sisterhood is global: The international women's movement anthology.* Garden City, New York: Anchor.

Morin, S. F., & Garfinkle, E. M. (1978). Male homophobia. *Journal of Social Issues, 34*(1), 29–47.

Morokoff, P. J. (1985). Effects of sex, guilt, repression, sexual arousability, and sex experience on female sexual arousal during erotica and fantasy. *Journal of Personality and Social Psychology, 49,* 177–187.

Moses, A. E., & Hawkins, R. O., Jr. (1982). *Counseling lesbian women and gay men: A life-issues approach.* St. Louis: C. V. Mosby Company.

Mosher, D. L., & Abramson, P. R. (1977). Subjective sexual arousal to films of masturbation. *Journal of Consulting and Clinical Psychology, 45,* 796–807.

Moss, H. (1967). Sex, age, and state as determinants of mother-infant interaction. *Merrill-Palmer Quarterly, 13,* 19–36.

Motowidlo, S. J. (1982). Sex role orientation and behavior in a work setting. *Journal of Personality and Social Psychology, 42,* 935–945.

Moulton, J., Robinson, G. M., & Elias, C. (1978). Sex bias in language use. *American Psychologist, 33,* 1032–1036.

Moyer, K. E. (1974). Sex differences in aggression. In R. C. Friedman et al. (Eds.), *Sex differences in behavior* (pp. 149–163). New York: Wiley.

Mulac, A., Incontro, C. R., & James, M. R. (1985). A comparison of the gender-linked language effect and sex-role stereotypes. *Journal of Personality and Social Psychology, 49,* 1098–1109.

Mulhern, R. K., Jr., & Passman, R. H. (1981). Parental discipline as affected by the sex of the parent, the sex of the child, and the child's apparent responsiveness to discipline. *Developmental Psychology, 17,* 604–613.

Munroe, R. L., & Munroe, R. H. (1969). A cross-cultural study of sex, gender and social structure. *Ethnology, 8*(2), 206–211.

Munroe, R. L., & Munroe, R. H. (1980). Perspectives suggested by anthropological data. In H. C. Triandis & W. W. Lambert (Eds.), *Handbook of cross-cultural psychology* (Vol. I). Boston: Allyn & Bacon.

Munroe, R. H., Shimmin, H. S., & Munroe, R. L. (1984). Gender understanding and sex role preference in four cultures. *Developmental Psychology, 20,* 673–682.

Murray, S. R. (1981). Who is that person? Images and roles of black women. In S. Cox (Ed.), *Female psychology,* 2nd ed. (pp. 113–123). New York: St. Martin's.

Murray, S. R., & Scott, P. B. (Eds.) (1982). A special issue on black women. *Psychology of Women Quarterly, 6,* (whole No. 3).

Musante, L., MacDougall, J. M., Dembroski, T. M., & Van Horn, A. E. (1983). Component analysis of the Type A coronary-prone behavior pattern in male and female college students. *Journal of Personality and Social Psychology, 45,* 1104–1117.

Myers, A. M., & Gonda, G. (1982a). Empirical validation of the Bem Sex-Role Inventory. *Journal of Personality and Social Psychology, 43,* 304–318.

Myers, A. M., & Gonda, G. (1982b). Utility of the masculinity-femininity construct: Comparison of traditional and androgyny approaches. *Journal of Personality and Social Psychology, 43,* 514–522.

Myers, A. M., & Lips, H. M. (1978). Participation in competitive amateur sports as a function of psychological androgyny. *Sex Roles, 4,* 571–588.

Myers, B. J., Weinraub, M., & Shelter, S. (1979, September). *Preschoolers' knowledge of sex role stereotypes: A developmental study.* Paper presented at the American Psychological Association convention, New York.

Nadelman, L. (1974). Sex identity in American children: Memory, knowledge, and preference tests. *Developmental Psychology, 10,* 413–417.

Nadler, A., Maler, S., & Friedman, A. (1984). Effects of helper's sex, subjects' androgyny, and self-evaluation on males' and females' willingness to seek and receive help. *Sex Roles, 10,* 327–339.

Nardi, B. A. (1981). [Review of *Gender and culture: Kibbutz women revisited*]. *Sex Roles, 7,* 670–676.

Narus, L. R., Jr., & Fischer, J. L. (1982). Strong but not silent: A reexamination of expressivity in the relationships of men. *Sex Roles, 8,* 159–168.

Nash, J., & Fernandez-Kelly, M. P. (Eds.) (1983). *Women, men, and the international division of labor.* Albany: State University of New York Press.

Nash, S. C. (1975). The relationship among sex-role stereotyping, sex-role preference, and sex differences in spatial visualization. *Sex Roles, 1,* 15–32.

Nash, S. C. (1979). Sex role as a mediator of intellectual functioning. In M. A. Wittig & A. C. Petersen (Eds.), *Sex-related differences in cognitive functioning: Developmental issues* (pp. 263–302). New York: Academic Press.

Nash, S. C., & Feldman, S. S. (1981). Sex-related differences in the relationship between sibling status and responsibility to babies. *Sex Roles, 7,* 1035–1042.

Nassi, A. J., & Abramowitz, S. I. (1978). Raising consciousness about women's groups: Process and outcome research. *Psychology of Women Quarterly, 3,* 139–156.

Nathan, S. (1981). Cross-cultural perspectives on penis envy. *Psychiatry, 44*(1), 39–44.

National Center for Education Statistics. (1983). *Faculty salaries, tenure, and benefits survey.* Washington, D.C.: Author.

National Center for Education Statistics. (1985, September 9). 1,345,900 degrees will be awarded in 1985–1986. *Chronicle of Higher Education,* p. 11.

National Science Foundation. (1984, March). Women and minorities in science and engineering. *Manpower Comments.*

Nemy, E. (1979, April 29). Networks: New concepts for top-level women. *The New York Times,* p. 60.

Ness, S. (1980, December). The judiciary. *Women's Political Times,* p. 10.

Nettles, E. J., & Loevinger, J. (1983). Sex role expectations and ego level in relation to problem marriages. *Journal of Personality and Social Psychology, 45,* 676–687.

Neugarten, B. L. & Gutmann, D. L. (1968). Age, sex-roles and personality in middle-age: A thematic apperception study. In B. L. Neugarten (Ed.), *Middle age and aging: A reader in social psychology.* Chicago: University of Chicago Press.

New edition of the Bible to eliminate many masculine references. (1977, June 5). *The New York Times,* p. B6.

New report on rape shows underreporting. (1978, August 26). *The New York Times.*

Newcombe, N. (1982). Sex-related differences in spatial ability: Problems and gaps in current approaches. In M. Potegal (Ed.), *Spatial abilities: Development and physiological foundations.* New York: Academic Press.

Newcombe, N. (1983). *Issues in the study of the development of sex-related differences.* Paper presented at the meeting of the American Psychological Association, Anaheim.

Newcombe, N., & Arnkoff, D. B. (1979). Effects of speech style and sex of speaker on person perception. *Journal of Personality and Social Psychology, 37,* 1293–1303.

Newcombe, N., & Bandura, M. M. (1983). Effect of age at puberty on spatial ability: A question of mechanism. *Developmental Psychology, 19,* 215–224.

Newcombe, N., Bandura, M. M., & Taylor, D. G. (1983). Sex differences in spatial ability and spatial activities. *Sex Roles, 9,* 377–386.

Nicholson, L. (1984, September/October). *AFCSME v. Washington State* briefs due soon. *National NOW Times.* p. 5.

Nielsen Media Research. (1985). *'85 Nielsen Report on television.* Northbrook, Ill.: Author.

Noller, P. (1980). Misunderstandings in marital communication: A study of couples' nonverbal communication. *Journal of Personality and Social Psychology, 39,* 1135–1148.

Noller, P. (1981). Gender and marital adjustment level differences in decoding messages from spouses and strangers. *Journal of Personality and Social Psychology, 41,* 272–278.

Norton, E. H. (1985, June 2). Restoring the traditional Black family. *The New York Times Magazine,* pp. 43, 79, 93, 96, 98.

Notes on computers. (1984, October 10). *Chronicle of Higher Education,* p. 26.

Notman, M. T. (1981). Midlife concerns of women: Implications of the menopause. In E. Howell & M. Bayes (Eds.), *Women and Mental Health* (pp. 385–394). New York: Basic.

Nyquist, L., Slivken, K., Spence, J. T., & Helmreich, R. L. (1985). Household responsibilities in middle-class couples: The contribution of demographic and personality variables. *Sex Roles, 12,* 15–34.

Nyquist, L. V., & Spence, J. T. (in press). Effects of dispositional dominance and sex-role expectations on leadership behaviors. *Journal of Personality and Social Psychology.*

Oakes, R. (1984). Sex patterns in DSM III: Bias or basis for theory development. (Letter to the Editor). *American Psychologist, 39,* 1320–1322.

Oakley, A. (1972). *Sex, gender and society.* New York: Harper & Row.

O'Brien, M. (1981). *The politics of reproduction.* Boston: Routledge & Kegan Paul.

O'Connell, A. N., & Russo, N. F. (Eds.) (1983). *Models of achievement: Reflections of eminent women in psychology.* New York: Columbia University Press.

Ogilvie, B. C., & Tutko, T. (1971, October). Sport: If you want to build character, try something else. *Psychology Today,* p. 61ff.

Ogintz, E. (1983, December 8). 19 million mothers juggling jobs, homelife. *The Easton Express,* pp. C1–C2.

O'Keefe, E. S. C., & Hyde, J. S. (1983). The development of occupational sex-role stereotypes: The effects of gender stability and age. *Sex Roles, 39,* 481–492.

O'Kelly, C. (1980). Sex-role imagery in modern art: An empirical examination. *Sex Roles, 6,* 99–111.

Olds, D. E., & Shaver, P. (1980). Masculinity, femininity, academic performance, and health: Further evidence concerning the androgyny controversy. *Journal of Personality, 48,* 323–341.

O'Leary, V. (1974). Some additional barriers to occupational aspirations in women. *Psychological Bulletin, 81,* 809–826.

O'Leary, V., & Donoghue, J. M. (1978). Latitudes of masculinity: Reactions to sex-role deviance in man. *Journal of Social Issues, 34*(1), 17–28.

O'Leary, V. E., Unger, R. K., & Wallston, B. S. (Eds.) (1985). *Women, gender, and social psychology.* Hillsdale, N.J.: Lawrence Erlbaum Associates.

Olejnik, A. B., Tompkins, B., & Heinbuck, C. (1982). Sex differences, sex-role orientation, and reward allocations. *Sex Roles, 8,* 711–719.

Olstad, K. (1975). Brave new man: A basis for discussion. In J. W. Petras (Ed.), *Sex: Male; gender: masculine* (pp. 160–178). Port Washington, N.Y.: Alfred.

One-parent families singled out for trouble. (1983, September). *Dollars and Sense,* pp. 12–14.

O'Neil, J. M. (1981a). Male sex-role conflicts, sexism, and masculinity: Psychological implications for men, women and the counseling psychologist. *The Counseling Psychologist, 9,* 61–80.

O'Neil, J. M. (1981b). Patterns of gender role conflict and strain: The fear of femininity in men's lives. *Personnel and Guidance Journal, 60,* 203–210.

O'Neil, J. M. (1982). Gender role conflict and strain in men's lives: Implications for psychiatrists, psychologists, and other human service providers. In K. Solomon & N. B. Levy (Eds.), *Men in transition: Changing male roles, theory, and therapy* (pp. 5–44). New York: Plenum.

O'Neil, J. M., Helms, B. J., Gable, R., Stillson, R., David, L., & Wrightsman, L. S. (1984, August). *Data on college men's gender role conflict and strain.* Paper presented at the meeting of the American Psychological Association, Toronto, Canada.

O'Neil, J. M., Ohlde, C., Barke, C., Prosser-Gelwick, B., & Garfield, N. (1980). Research on a workshop to reduce the effects of sexism and sex-role socialization on women's career planning. *Journal of Counseling Psychology, 27,* 355–363.

O'Neil, J. M., Ohlde, C., Tollefson N., Barke, C., Piggott, T., & Watts, D. (1980). Factors, correlates, and problem areas affecting career decision making of a cross-sectional sample of students. *Journal of Counseling Psychology, 27,* 571–580.

Oppenheimer, V. K. (1975). The sex labeling of jobs. In M. S. Mednick, S. S. Tangri, & L. W. Hoffman (Eds.), *Women and achievement: Social and motivational analyses* (pp. 307–325). New York: Halsted.

Orlinsky, D., & Howard, K. (1976). The effects of sex of therapist on the therapeutic experience of women. *Psychotherapy: Theory, research, and practice, 13,* 82–88.

Orlofsky, J. L. (1979). Parental antecedents of sex-role orientation in college men and women. *Sex Roles, 5,* 495–512.

Orlofsky, J. L. (1981a). A comparison of projective and objective fear-of-success and sex-role orientation measures as predictors of women's performance on masculine and feminine tasks. *Sex Roles, 7,* 999–1018.

Orlofsky, J. L. (1981b). Relationship between sex role attitudes and personality traits and the Sex Role Behavior Scale—1: A new measure of masculine and feminine role behaviors and interests. *Journal of Personality and Social Psychology, 40,* 927–940.

Orlofsky, J. L. (1982). Psychological androgyny, sex typing, and sex-role ideology as predictors of male-female interpersonal attraction. *Sex Roles, 8,* 1057–1073.

Orlofsky, J. L., & Stake, J. E. (1981). Psychological masculinity and femininity: Relationship to striving and self-concept in the achievement and interpersonal domains. *Psychology of Women Quarterly, 6,* 218–233.

Ortner, S. B. (1974). Is female to male as nature is to culture? In M. Z. Rosaldo & L. Lamphere (Eds.), *Women, culture, and society.* Stanford, Calif.: Stanford University Press.

Ortner, S. B. (1981). Gender and sexuality in hierarchical societies. In S. B. Ortner & H. Whitehead (Eds.), *Sexual meanings: The cultural construction of gender and sexuality* (pp. 359–409). Cambridge: Cambridge University Press.

Ortner, S. B., & Whitehead, H. (Eds.) (1981). *Sexual meanings: The cultural construction of gender and sexuality.* Cambridge: Cambridge University Press.

Packwood, R. (1983, November/December). ERA: Debunking the myths. *Women's Political Times,* pp. 11, 14.

Padesky, C. A., & Hammen, C. L. (1981). Sex differences in depressive symptom expression and help-seeking among college students. *Sex Roles, 7,* 309–320.

Paige, K. E. (1971). The effects of oral contraceptives on affective fluctuations associated with the menstrual cycle. *Psychosomatic Medicine, 33,* 515–537.

Paige, K. E. (1973). Women learning to sing the menstrual blues. *Psychology Today, 7,* 41–43ff.

Paige, K. E., & Paige, J. M. (1973). The politics of birth practices: A strategic analysis. *American Sociological Review, 38,* 663–676.

Paikoff, R. L., & Savin-Williams, R. C. (1983, October). An exploratory study of dominance interactions among adolescent females at a summer camp. *Journal of Youth and Adolescence, 12,* 419–433.

Palkovitz, R. (1984). Parental attitudes and fathers' interactions with their 5-month-old infants. *Developmental Psychology, 20,* 1054–1060.

Paludi, M. A. (1984a). A comment on the measure of the Chi-square statistics in research with the IT Scale for Children. *Sex Roles, 8,* 791–793.

Paludi, M. A. (1984b). Psychometric properties and underlying assumptions of four objective measures of fear of success. *Sex Roles, 10,* 765–781.

Paludi, M. A., & Bauer, W. D. (1983). Goldberg revisited: What's in an author's name. *Sex Roles, 9,* 387–390.

Paludi, M. A., & Strayer, L. A. (1985). What's in an author's name? Differential evaluations of performance as a function of author's name. *Sex Roles, 12,* 353–361.

Parachini, A. (1985, May 9). Study: Turnover of women in "men's" jobs isn't high. *Easton Express,* p. C10.

Parke, R. (1981). *Fathers.* Cambridge, Mass.: Harvard University Press.

Parke, R. D., & O'Leary, S. E. (1976). Father-mother-infant interactions in the new-born period. In K. Riegel & J. Meacham (Eds.), *The developing individual in a changing world.* The Hague, Netherlands: Mouton.

Parke, R. D., & Sawin, D. B. (1977). Fathering: Its major role. *Psychology Today, 11*(6), 108–112.

Parke, R. D., & Tinsley, B. R. (1981). The father's role in infancy: Determinants of involvement in caregiving and play. In M. Lamb (Ed.), *The role of the father in child development.* 2nd ed. (pp. 429–457). New York: Wiley & Sons.

Parker, M., Peltier, S., & Wolleat, P. (1981, September). Understanding dual career couples. *The Personnel and Guidance Journal,* 14–18.

Parlee, M. B. (1973). The premenstrual syndrome. *Psychological Bulletin, 80,* 454–465.

Parlee, M. B. (1979, May). Conversational politics. *Psychology Today, 12,* 48–56.

Parlee, M. B. (1981). Appropriate control groups in feminist research. *Psychology of Women Quarterly, 5,* 637–644.

Parlee, M. B. (1982a). Changes in moods and activation levels during the menstrual cycle in experimentally naive subjects. *Psychology of Women Quarterly, 7,* 119–131.

Parlee, M. B. (1982b, September). New findings: Menstrual cycles and behavior. *Ms.,* pp. 126–128.

Parsons, J. E., Adler, T. F., & Kaczala, C. M. (1982). Socialization of achievement attitudes and beliefs: Parental influences. *Child Development, 53,* 310–321.

Parsons, J. E., & Bryan, J. (1978). Adolescence: Gateway to androgyny. *Michigan Occasional Paper.* No. VIII.

Parsons, J. E., Meece, J. L., Adler, T. F., & Kaczala, C. M. (1982). Sex differences in attributions and learned helplessness. *Sex Roles, 8,* 421–432.

Parsons, J. E., Ruble, D. N., Hodges, K. L., & Small, A. W. (1976). Cognitive-developmental factors in sex differences in achievement-related expectancies. *Journal of Social Issues, 32*(3), 47–61.

Parsons, T., & Bales, R. F. (1955). *Family, socialization and interaction process.* Glencoe, Ill.: Free Press.

Pattison, P., & Grieve, N. (1984). Do spatial skills contribute to sex differences in different types of mathematical problems? *Journal of Educational Psychology, 76,* 678–689.

Pawlicki, R. E., & Almquist, C. (1973). Authoritarianism, locus of control and tolerance of ambiguity as reflected in membership and nonmembership in a women's liberation group. *Psychological Reports, 32,* 1331–1337.

Payne, B. D. (1981). Sex and age differences in the sex-role stereotyping of third- and fifth-grade children. *Sex Roles, 7,* 135–144.

Pear, R. (1983, September 9). Reagan's record on women still being debated. *The New York Times,* p. A20.

Pearce, D. M. (1985). Toil and trouble: Women workers and unemployment compensation. *Signs, 10,* 439–459.

Pedersen, F. A. (Ed.) (1980). *The father-infant relationship: Observational studies in the family setting.* New York: Praeger.

Pedhazur, E. J., & Tetenbaum, T. J. (1979). Bem Sex Role Inventory: A theoretical and methodological critique. *Journal of Personality and Social Psychology, 37,* 996–1016.

Peevers, B. H. (1979). Androgyny on the TV screen: An analysis of sex-role portrayal. *Sex Roles, 5,* 797–809.

Pepitone-Rockwell (Ed.) (1980). *Dual-career couples.* Beverly Hills, Calif.: Sage.

Peplau, L. A. (1976). Impact of fear of success and sex-role attitude on women's competitive achievement. *Journal of Personality and Social Psychology, 34,* 561–568.

Peplau, L. A. (1979). Power in dating relationships. In J. Freeman (Ed.), *Women: A feminist perspective.* (2nd ed.). Palo Alto: Mayfield.

Peplau, L. A. (1981, March). What do homosexuals want. *Psychology Today, 15*(3), 28–38.

Peplau, L. A., Cochran, S., Rook, K., & Padesky, C. (1978). Loving women: Attachment and autonomy in lesbian relationships. *Journal of Social Issues, 34*(3), 7–28.

Peplau, L. A., Rubin, Z., & Hill, C. T. (1976, November). The sexual balance of power. *Psychology Today,* p. 142ff.

Peplau, L. A., Rubin, Z., & Hill, C. T. (1977). Sexual intimacy in dating relationships. *Journal of Social Issues, 33*(2), 86–109.

Perlez, J. (1984, June 24). Women power and politics. *The New York Times Magazine,* pp. 22–27, 29, 31, 72, 76.

Perry, D. G., & Bussey, K. (1979). The social learning theory of sex differences: Imitation is alive and well. *Journal of Personality and Social Psychology, 37,* 1699–1712.

Perry, J., & Whipple, B. (1981). Pelvic muscle strength of female ejaculators: Evidence in support of a new theory of orgasm. *Journal of Sex Research, 17,* 22–39.

Perry, M. (1982, April 21). Being 'macho' can be a short-lived experience. *The Easton Express.* A-14.

Persell, C. H. (1983). Gender rewards and research in education. *Psychology of Women Quarterly, 8,* 33–47.

Peters, L. H., O'Connor, E. J., Weekley, J., Pooyan, A., Frank, B., & Erenkrantz, B. (1984). Sex bias and managerial evaluations: A replication and extension. *Journal of Applied Psychology, 69,* 349–352.

Peters, T. J., & Waterman, R. H., Jr. (1982). *In search of excellence: Lessons from American's best-run companies.* New York: Warner.

Petersen, A. C. (1976). Physical androgyny and cognitive functioning. *Developmental Psychology, 12,* 524–533.

Petersen, A. C. (1979). Hormones and cognitive functioning in normal development. In M. A. Wittig & A. C. Petersen (Eds.), *Sex-related differences in cognitive functioning: Developmental issues* (pp. 189–214). New York: Academic Press.

Petersen, A. C. (1982). A biopsychosocial perspective on sex differences in the human brain. *Behavioral and Brain Sciences, 2,* 312.

Petersen, A. C. (1983). *The development of sex-related differences in achievement.* Invited address at the meeting of the American Psychological Association, Anaheim.

Petersen, A. C., Crockett, L., & Tobin-Richards, M. H. (1982). Sex differences. In H. E. Mitzel (Ed.), *Encyclopedia of education research* (5th ed.). New York: Free Press.

Petersen, A. C., & Wittig, M. A. (1979). Sex-related differences in cognitive functioning: An overview. In M. A. Wittig & A. C. Petersen (Eds.), *Sex-related differences in cognitive functioning: Developmental issues* (pp. 1–17). New York: Academic Press.

Peterson, R. A. (1983). Attitudes toward the childless spouse. *Sex Roles, 9,* 321–331.

Pflafflin, S. M. (1984). Women, science, and technology. *American Psychologist, 39,* 1183–1186.

Phelps, S., & Austin, N. (1975). *The assertive woman.* San Luis Obispo, Calif.: Impact Press.

Phillips, D., King, S., & DuBois, L. (1978). Spontaneous activities of female versus male newborns. *Child Development, 48*(3).

Phillips, D., & Segal, B. (1969). Sexual status and psychiatric symptoms. *American Sociology Review, 34,* 58–72.

Phillips, E. B. (1978). Magazine heroines: Is *Ms.* just another member of the *Family Circle?* In G. Tuchman, A. K. Danials & J. Benet (Eds.), *Hearth and home: Images of women in the mass media* (pp. 116–129). New York: Oxford University Press.

Phillips, R. (1981, March 10). Caring for babies just one more part of a busy boy's life. *The Easton Express,* p. A12.

Phillips, R. D., & Gilroy, F. D. (1985). Sex-role stereotypes and clinical judgements of mental health: The Broverman's findings reexamined. *Sex Roles, 12,* 179–193.

Pidano, A. E., & Tennen, H. (1985). Transient depressive experiences and their relationship to gender and sex-role orientation. *Sex Roles, 12,* 97–110.

Pierce, K., Smith, H., & Akert, R. M. (1984, April). *Terminating adult same-sex friendships: The role of gender and decision to terminate in the break-up process.* Paper presented at the meeting of the Eastern Psychological Association, Baltimore.

Pietropinto, A., & Simenauer, J. (1977). *Beyond the male myth: What women want to know about men's sexuality.* New York: Times Books.

Piliavin, J. A, & Unger, R. K. (1985). The helpful but helpless female: Myth or reality? In V. O'Leary, R. Unger, B. Wallston (Eds.), *Women, gender, and social psychology* (pp. 149–189). Hillsdale, N.J.: Lawrence Erlbaum Associates.

Pines, A., & Kafry, D. (1981). Tedium in the life and work of professional women as compared with men. *Sex Roles, 7,* 963–977.

Pingree, S. (1978). The effects of nonsexist TV commercials and perceptions of reality on children's attitudes about women. *Psychology of Women Quarterly, 2,* 262–277.

Playboy. (1982, October). Sex on campus.

Pleck, J. H. (1976a). My male sex role and ours. In D. David & R. Brannon (Eds.), *The forty-nine percent majority* (pp. 253–264). Reading, Mass.: Addison-Wesley.

Pleck, J. H. (1976b). The male sex role: Definitions, problems and sources of change. *Journal of Social Issues, 32*(3), 155–164.

Pleck, J. H. (1978). The work family role system. *Social Problems, 24,* 417–427.

Pleck, J. (1981a). *Changing patterns of work and family roles.* (Working Paper No. 81). Wellesley, Mass.: Wellesley College Center for Research on Women.

Pleck, J. H. (1981b). *The myth of masculinity.* Cambridge, Mass.: The MIT Press.

Pleck, J. H., & Sawyer, J. (Eds.) (1974). *Men and masculinity.* Englewood Cliffs, N.J.: Prentice-Hall.

Plumb, P., & Cowan, G. (1984). A developmental study of stereotyping and androgynous activity preferences of tomboys, nontomboys, and males. *Sex Roles, 10,* 703–712.

Pogrebin, L. C. (1981). *Growing up free: Raising your child in the 80's.* New York: Bantam.

Pogrebin, L. C. (1982a, February). Are men discovering the joys of fatherhood? *Ms.,* pp. 41–45.

Pogrebin, L. C. (1982b, April). A feminist in Sweden. *Ms.,* pp. 66–70, 82–88.

Pogrebin, L. C. (1983). *Family politics: Love and power on an intimate frontier.* New York: McGraw Hill.

Polatnick, M. (1973–1974). Why men can't rear children: A power analysis. *Berkeley Journal of Sociology, 18,* 45–86.

Polk, B. B. (1976). Male power and the women's movement. In S. Cox (Ed.), *Female psychology: The emerging self* (pp. 400–413). Chicago: SRA.

Poll rates candidates by gender. (1985, January 20). *The New York Times,* p. 45.

Pollak, S., & Gilligan, C. (1982). Images of violence in Thematic Apperception Test stories. *Journal of Personality and Social Psychology, 42,* 159–167.

Pollak, S., & Gilligan, C. (1983). Differing about differences: The incidence and interpretation of violent fantasies in women and men. *Journal of Personality and Social Psychology, 45,* 1172–1175.

Polyson, J. (1978). Sexism and sexual problems: Societal censure of the sexually troubled male. *Psychological Reports, 42,* 843–850.

Pope, K. S., Levenson, H., & Schover, L. R. (1979). Sexual intimacy in psychology training. *American Psychologist, 34,* 682–689.

Porter, J. R., & Washington, R. E. (1979). Black identity and self-esteem: A review of studies of Black self-concept 1968–1978. *Annual Review of Sociology, 5,* 53–74.

Porter, N., & Geis, F. (1982). Women and nonverbal leadership cues: When seeing is not believing. In C. Mayo & N. Henley (Eds.), *Gender and Nonverbal Behavior* (pp. 39–61). New York: Springer-Verlag.

Porter, N., Geis, F. L., Cooper, E., & Newman, E. (1985). Androgyny and leadership in mixed-sex groups. *Journal of Personality and Social Psychology, 49,* 808–823.

Porter, N., Geis, F., & Jennings (Walstedt), J. (1983). Are women invisible as leaders? *Sex Roles, 9,* 1035–1049.

Post, R. D. (1981). Causal explanations of male and female academic performance as a function of sex-role biases. *Sex Roles, 7,* 691–698.

Potkay, C. E., Potkay, C. R., Boynton, G. J., & Klingbeil, J. A. (1982). Perceptions of male and female comic strip characters using the Adjective Generation Technique (AGT). *Sex Roles, 8*, 185–200.

Potkay, C. R., & Potkay, C. E. (1984). Perceptions of female and male comic strip characters. II: Favorability and identification are different dimensions. *Sex Roles, 10*, 119–128.

Poverty statistics seen worsening for women. (1983, April 12). *The Easton Express*, p. 5.

Powell, G. N., & Butterfield, D. A. (1984). If "good managers" are masculine, what are "bad managers"? *Sex Roles, 10*, 477–484.

Power, T. G., & Parke, R. D. (1984). Social network factors and the transition to parenthood. *Sex Roles, 10*, 949–972.

Powers, E., & Bultena, G. (1976). Sex differences in intimate friendships of old age. *Job, Marriage and the Family, 38*, 739–747.

Pressler, E. J., & Blanchard, F. A. (1984, April). *Dimensions of mentor-protege relationships.* Paper presented at the meeting of the Eastern Psychological Association, Baltimore.

Probber, J., & Ehrman, L. (1978). Pertinent genetics for understanding gender. In E. Tobach & B. Rofsoff (Eds.), *Genes and Gender* (pp. 13–30). Staten Island, N.Y.: Gordian Press.

Proctor, E. B., Wagner, N. M., & Butler, J. C. (1974). The differentiation of male and female orgasms: An experimental study. In N. M. Wagner (Ed.), *Perspectives in human sexuality.* New York: Human Sciences.

Progress slow for women in network news. (1985, January 1). *TV Guide*, p. A-1.

Project on the Status and Education of Women. (1982). *The classroom climate: A chilly one for women?* Washington, D.C.: Association of American Colleges.

Project on the Status and Education of Women. (1983, Fall). *Academic mentoring for women students and faculty: A new look at an old way to get ahead.* Washington, D.C.: Association of American Colleges.

Project on the Status and Education of Women. (1984, Spring). Women get less financial aid than men. *On Campus with Women*, p. 6.

Proportion of degrees awarded to women. (1978, November 13). *Chronicle of Higher Education*, p. 13.

Pursell, S., Banikiotes, P. G., & Sebastian, R. J. (1981). Androgyny and the perception of marital roles. *Sex Roles, 7*, 201–215.

Pyke, S. W., & Kahill, S. P. (1983). Sex differences in characteristics presumed relevant to professional productivity. *Psychology of Women Quarterly, 8*, 189–192.

Quante, A. L. (1981, April). *Attitudes toward sexually assertive women.* Paper presented at the meeting of the Eastern Psychological Association, New York.

Radin, N. (1981). The role of the father in cognitive, academic, and intellectual development. In M. Lamb (Ed.), *The role of the father in child development*, 2nd ed. (pp. 379–427). New York: Wiley Sons.

Radloff, L. S. (1980). Depression and the empty nest. *Sex Roles, 6*, 775–781.

Radway, J. R. (1984). *Reading the romance: Women, patriarchy, and popular literature.* Chapel Hill, N.C.: University of North Carolina Press.

Raines, H. (1983, November 27). Poll shows support for political gains by women in the U.S., *The New York Times*, pp. 1, 40.

Ramey, E. R. (1972, Spring). Men's cycles (they have them too, you know). *Ms.*, pp. 8–14.

Ramey, E. R. (1973). Sex hormones and executive ability. *Annals of the N.Y. Academy of Sciences, 208*, 237–245.

Rao, V. V. P., & Overman, S. J. (1984). Sex-role perceptions among black female athletes and nonathletes. *Sex Roles, 11*, 601–614.

Rao, V. V. P., & Rao, V. N. (1985). Sex-role attitudes: A comparison of sex-race groups. *Sex Roles, 12*, 939–953.

Raskin, P. A., & Israel, A. C. (1981). Sex-role imitation in children: Effects of sex of child, sex of model, and sex-role appropriateness of modeled behavior. *Sex Roles, 7*, 1067–1077.

Raymond, J. G. (1979). Transsexualism: An issue of sex-role stereotyping. In E. Tobach & B. Rosoff (Eds.), *Genes and Gender II* (pp. 131–141). Staten Island, N.Y.: Gordian Press.

Reagan judges: Where's the women? (1985, January/February). *Women's Political Times*, p. 5.

Reagan's credibility gap on women's rights. (1984, January/February). *Women's Political Times*, p. 5, 12.

Rebecca, M., Hefner, R., & Olenshansky, B. (1976). A model of sex role transcendence. *Journal of Social Issues, 32*(3), 197–206.

The registration and drafting of women in 1980. (1980, March). *National NOW Times*, pp. 1, 4–9.

Reid, P. T. (1984). Feminism versus minority group identity: Not for Black women only. *Sex Roles, 10*, 247–255.

Reinartz, K. F. (1975). The paper doll: Images of American women in popular songs. In J. Freeman (Ed.), *Women: A feminist perspective* (pp. 293–308). Palo Alto, Calif.: Mayfield.

Reinisch, J. M., Gandelman, R., & Spiegel, F. S. (1979). Prenatal influences on cognitive abilities: Data from experimental animals and syndromes. In M. A. Wittig & A. C. Petersen (Eds.), *Sex-related differences in cognitive functioning: Develop-*

mental issues (pp. 215-239). New York: Academic Press.

Reinisch, J. M., & Karow, W. A. (1977). Prenatal exposure to synthetic progestins and estrogens: Effects of human development. *Archives of Sexual Behavior, 6,* 257–288.

Reinke, B. J., Holmes, D. S., & Harris, R. L. (1985). The timing of psychological changes in women's lives: The years 25 to 45. *Journal of Personality and Social Psychology, 48,* 1353–1364.

Reis, H. T., & Jackson, L. A. (1981). Sex differences in reward allocation: Subjects, partners, and tasks. *Journal of Personality and Social Psychology, 40,* 465–478.

Reis, H. T., & Jelsma, B. (1978). A social psychology of sex differences in sport. In W. Straub (Ed.), *Sport psychology: An analysis of athlete behavior* (pp. 178–188). Ithaca, N.Y.: Mouvement.

Reis, H. T., Senchak, M., & Solomon, B. (1985). Sex differences in the intimacy of social interaction: Further examination of potential explanations. *Journal of Personality and Social Psychology, 48,* 1204–1217.

Reis, H. T., & Wright, S. (1982). Knowledge of sex-role stereotypes in children aged 3 to 5. *Sex Roles, 8,* 1049–1056.

Remick, H. (Ed.) (1984). *Comparable worth and wage discrimination.* Philadelphia: Temple University Press.

Rendely, J. G., Holmstrom, R. M., & Karp, S. A. (1984). The relationship of sex-role identity, lifestyle, and mental health in suburban American homemakers: 1. Sex role, employment and adjustment. *Sex Roles, 11,* 839–848.

Renwick, P. A., & Lawler, E E. (1978). What you really want from a job. *Psychology Today, 11*(12), 53–65ff.

Repetti, R. L. (1984). Determinants of children's sex-stereotyping: Parental sex-role trait and television viewing. *Personality and Social Psychology Bulletin, 10,* 457–468.

Resick, P. A. (1983). Sex-role stereotypes and violence against women. In V. Franks, & E. Rothblum (Eds.), *The stereotyping of women: Its effects on mental health* (pp. 230–256). New York: Springer.

Reskin, B. F. (1984, Fall). Gender hierarchies and sex segregation in the workplace. *The Committee for Gender Research,* pp. 1, 4, 5.

Revell, J. E. (1976, February 9/23). WACS in combat. *The Army Times Magazine,* pp. 7–12/9–13.

The revolution is over. (1984, April 9). *Time,* pp. 74–83.

Rhodes, A. L. (1983). Effects of religious denominations on sex differences in occupational expectations. *Sex Roles, 9,* 93–108.

Rhue, J. W., Lynn, S. J., & Garske, J. P. (1984). The effects of competent behavior on interpersonal attraction and task leadership. *Sex Roles, 10,* 925–937.

Rice, D. G. (1979). *Dual career marriage: Conflict and treatment.* New York: Free Press.

Rice, R. W., Instone, D., & Adams, J. (1984). Leader sex, leader success, and leadership process: Two field studies. *Journal of Applied Psychology, 69,* 12–31.

Rice, R. W., Yoder, J. D., Adams, J., Priest, R. F., & Prince, H. T. II. (1984). Leadership ratings for male and female military cadets. *Sex Roles, 10,* 885–901.

Rich, A. (1980). Compulsory heterosexuality and lesbian existence. *Signs, 5,* 631–660.

Rich. F. (1984, September 30). Theater's gender gap is a chasm. *The New York Times,* pp. H1, 4.

Rich, S. (1984, November 14). Study finds significance in delay of motherhood. *Easton Express,* p. 7.

Rich, S. (1985, January 22). 46.8% of mothers with infants work. *Easton Express,* p. A-3.

Richardson, D., Vinsel, A., & Taylor, S. P. (1980). Female aggression as a function of attitudes toward women. *Sex Roles, 6,* 265–271.

Richardson, J. G., & Mahoney, E. R. (1981). The perceived social status of husbands and wives in dual-work families as a function of achieved and deprived occupational status. *Sex Roles, 7,* 1189–1198.

Richardson, M. S., & Alpert, J. L. (1980). Role perceptions: Variations by sex and roles. *Sex Roles, 6,* 783–793.

Ricks, F., & Pyke, S. (1973). Teacher perceptions and attitudes that foster or maintain sex role differences. *Interchange, 4,* 26–33.

Riddle, D. I., & Morin, S. F. (1977, November). Removing the stigma: Data from individuals. *APA Monitor,* pp. 16, 28.

Riddle, D. I., & Sang, B. (1978). Psychotherapy with lesbians. *Journal of Social Issues, 34*(3), 84–100.

Riess, B. F., & Safer, J. M. (1979). Homosexuality in females and males. In E. S. Gomberg & V. Franks (Eds.), *Gender and disordered behavior: Sex differences in psychopathology* (pp. 257–286). New York: Brunner/Mazel.

Reiss, M., & Salzer, S. (1981, August). *Individuals avoid invading the space of males but not females.* Paper presented at the meeting of the American Psychological Association, Los Angeles.

Riger, S., & Galligan, P. (1980). Women in management. *American Psychologist, 35,* 902–910.

Riger, S., & Gordon, M. T. (1981). The fear of rape: A study in social control. *Journal of Social Issues, 37,* 71–92.

Ritter, M. (1984, August 28). Active women gain self-esteem, handle stress better, study shows. *The Easton Express,* p. A11.

Roache, J. P. (1972, November). Confessions of a house husband. *Ms., 1,* 25–27.

Robbins, J. H., & Siegel, R. J. (Eds.) (1983). *Women changing therapy: New assessments, values and strategies in feminist therapy.* New York: Haworth.

Roberts, S. V. (1984, May 6). Congress stages a preemptive strike on the gender gap. *The New York Times,* p. E24.

Roberts, S. V. (1985, July 14). "Machismo" on Capitol Hill. *The New York Times,* Sect. 4, p. 1.

Roders-Rose, L. (Ed.) (1980). *The Black woman.* Beverly Hills, Calif.: Sage.

Rodman, H., Pratto, D. J., & Nelson, R. S. (1985). Child care arrangements and children's functioning: A comparison of self-care and adult-care children. *Developmental Psychology, 21,* 413–418.

Rogan, H. (1984, October 30). Executive women find it difficult to balance demands of job, home. *Wall Street Journal,* pp. 35, 55.

Rogers, L., & Walsh, J. (1982). Shortcomings of the psychomedical research of John Money and co-workers in sex differences in behavior: Social and political implications. *Sex Roles, 8,* 269–281.

Rogers, L. J. (1983). Hormonal theories for sex differences—Politics disguised as science: A reply to DeBold and Luria. *Sex Roles, 9,* 1109–1113.

Rohrbaugh, J. B. (1979, August). Femininity on the line. *Psychology Today,* p. 30ff.

Roman, M., & Haddad, W., (1978). The case for joint custody. *Psychology Today, 12*(4), 96–105.

Romer, N., & Cherry, D. (1980). Ethnic and social class differences in children's sex-role concepts. *Sex Roles, 6,* 245–263.

Rooney, J. F., Volpe, J. N., & Suziedelis, A. (1984). Changes in femininity, masculinity, and self-regard among women alcoholics in residential treatment. *Sex Roles, 11,* 257–267.

Rose, R. M., Gordon, T. P., & Bernstein, I. (1972). Plasma testosterone levels in the male rhesus: Influence of sexual and social stimuli. *Science, 178,* 643–645.

Rose, R. M., Holaday, J. W., & Bernstein, I. (1971). Plasma testosterone, dominant rank, and aggression behavior in male rhesus monkeys. *Nature, 231,* 366–368.

Rose, S. M. (1983, August). *Friendship termination patterns of college women and men.* Paper presented at the meeting of the American Psychological Association, Anaheim.

Rose, S. M. (1985). Same-sex and cross-sex friendships and the psychology of homosociality. *Sex Roles, 12,* 63-74.

Rosenbach, W. E., Dailey, R. C., & Morgan, C. B. (1979). Perceptions of job characteristics and affective work outcomes for women and men. *Sex Roles, 5,* 267–277.

Rosenberg, B. G., & Sutton-Smith, B. (1972). *Sex and identity.* New York: Holt, Rinehart & Winston.

Rosenberg, M. (1973). The biological basis for sex role stereotypes. *Contemporary Psychoanalysis, 9,* 374–391.

Rosenfeld, L. B., Civikly, J. M., & Herron, J. R. (1979, May). *Anatomical sex and self-disclosure: Topic, situation and relationship considerations.* Paper presented at the meeting of the International Communications Association, Philadelphia.

Rosenkrantz, P., Vogel, S. R., Bee, H., Broverman, I. K., & Broverman, D. M. (1968). Sex role stereotypes and self-concepts in college students. *Journal of Consulting and Clinical Psychology, 32,* 287–295.

Rosenstein, M., & Milazzo-Sayre, L. J. (1981). *Characteristics of admissions to selected mental health facilities, 1975: An annotated book of charts and tables.* Washington, D.C.: U.S. Government Printing Office.

Rosenthal, D., & Hansen, J. (1981). The impact of maternal employment on children's perceptions of parents and personal development. *Sex Roles, 7,* 593–598.

Rosenthal, K., & Keshet, H. F. (1981). *Fathers without partners: A study of fathers and the family after marital separation.* Totowa, N.J.: Rowman and Littlefield.

Rosenthal, N. B. (1984). Consciousness raising: From revolution to re-evaluation. *Psychology of Women Quarterly, 8,* 309–326.

Rosenthal, R. (1966). *Experimenter effects in behavioral research.* New York: Appleton-Century-Crofts.

Rosenthal, R., & DePaulo, B. M. (1979). Sex differences in eavesdropping on nonverbal cues. *Journal of Personality and Social Psychology, 37,* 273–285.

Rosenthal, R., Hall, J. A., DiMatteo, M. R., Rogers, P. L., & Archer, D. (1979). *Sensitivity to nonverbal communication: The PONS test.* Baltimore, Md.: Johns Hopkins University Press.

Rosenthal, R., & Jacobson, L. (1968). *Pygmalion in the classroom: Teacher expectation and pupil's intellectual development.* New York: Holt, Rinehart & Winston.

Rosenthal, R., & Rubin, D. B. (1982). Further meta-analytic procedures for assessing cognitive gender differences. *Journal of Educational Psychology, 74,* 708–712.

Rosewater, L. B., & Walker, L. E. A. (Eds.) *Handbook of feminist therapy: Women's issues in psychotherapy.* New York: Springer.

Ross, C. E., Mirowsky, J., & Huber, J. (1983). Dividing work, sharing work, and in-between: Marriage patterns and depression. *American Sociological Review, 48,* 809–823.

Ross, J., & Kahan, J. P. (1983). Children by choice or by chance: The perceived effects of parity. *Sex Roles, 9,* 69–77.

Ross, L., Anderson, D. R., & Wisocki, P. A. (1982). Television viewing and adult sex-role attitudes. *Sex Roles, 8,* 589–592.

Rossi, A. S. (1985). Gender and parenthood. In A. Rossi (Ed.), *Gender and the life course* (pp. 161–191). Hawthorne, N.Y.: Aldine.

Rossi, J. D. (1983). Ratios exaggerate gender differences in mathematical ability. *American Psychologist, 38,* 348. (Comment).

Rotenberg, K. J. (1984). Sex differences in children's trust in peers. *Sex Roles, 11,* 953–957.

Rothblum, E. D. (1983). Sex-role stereotypes and depression in women. In V. Franks and E. Rothblum (Eds.), *The stereotyping of women: Its effects on mental health* (pp. 83–111). New York: Springer.

Rotheram, M. J., & Weiner, N. (1983). Androgyny, stress, and satisfaction: Dual-career and traditional relationships. *Sex Roles, 9,* 151–158.

Rothschild, J. (Ed.) (1983). *Machina ex dea: Feminist perspectives on technology.* New York: Pergamon.

Rotkin, K. F. (1972). The phallacy of our sexual norm. *RT: A Journal of Radical Therapy, 3*(11).

Rotter, N. G., & O'Connell, A. N. (1982). The relationship among sex-role orientation, cognitive complexity, and tolerance for ambiguity. *Sex Roles, 8,* 1209–1220.

Rubenstein, C. (1982). Real men don't earn less than their wives. *Psychology Today, 16*(11), 36–41.

Rubenstein, J. L., & Howes, C. (1979). Caregiving and infant behavior in day care and in homes. *Developmental Psychology, 15,* 1–24.

Rubin, G. (1975). The traffic in women. In R. Reiter (Ed.), *Toward an anthropology of women* (pp. 157–211). New York: Monthly Review.

Rubin, J. Z., Provenzano, F. J., & Luria, Z. (1974). The eye of the beholder: Parents' views on sex of newborns. *American Journal of Orthopsychiatry, 44,* 512–519.

Rubin, L. B. (1983). *Intimate strangers: Men and women together.* New York: Harper and Row.

Rubin, L. B. (1985). *Just friends: The role of friendship in our lives.* New York: Harper & Row.

Rubin, Z. (1982a, June). Fathers and sons: The search for reunion. *Psychology Today,* pp. 22–33.

Rubin, Z. (1982b, November). Reagan's women problem. *Psychology Today,* pp. 12, 13, 92.

Rubin, Z. (1983). Are working wives hazardous to their husbands' mental health? *Psychology Today,* pp. 70–72.

Rubin, Z., Peplau, L. A., & Hill, C. T. (1981). Loving and leaving: Sex differences in romantic attachments. *Sex Roles, 7,* 821–835.

Ruble, D. N. (1977). Premenstrual symptoms: A reinterpretation. *Science, 197,* 291–292.

Ruble, D. N., Boggiano, A. K., & Brooks-Gunn, J. (1982). Men's and women's evaluations of menstrual-related excuses. *Sex Roles, 8,* 625–638.

Ruble, D. N., & Ruble, T. L. (1982). Sex stereotypes. In A. G. Miller (Ed.), *In the eye of the beholder: Contemporary issues in stereotyping* (pp. 188–252). New York: Praeger.

Ruble, T. L. (1983). Sex stereotypes: Issues of change in the 1970's. *Sex Roles, 9,* 397–402.

Ruch, L. O. (1984). Dimensionality of the Bem Sex Role Inventory: A multidimensional analysis. *Sex Roles, 10,* 99–117.

Ruether, R. R. (1983). *Sexism and God-talk: Toward a feminist theology.* Boston: Beacon.

Ruether, R. R. (1985). *Womanguides: Readings toward a feminist theology.* Boston: Beacon.

Ruggiero, J. A., & Weston, L. C. (1985). Work options for women in women's magazines: The medium and the message. *Sex Roles, 12,* 535–547.

Rumenik, D. K., Capasso, D. R., & Hendrick, C. (1977). Experimenter sex effects in behavioral research. *Psychological Bulletin, 84,* 852–877.

Rush, F. (1980). *The best kept secret: Sexual abuse of children.* Englewood Cliffs, N.J.: Prentice-Hall.

Russell, D. E. H. (1984). *Sexual exploitation: Rape, child sexual abuse and workplace harassment.* Beverly Hills, Calif.: Sage.

Russell, D. E. H., & Howell, N. (1983). The prevalence of rape in the United States revisited. *Signs, 8,* 688–695.

Russell, J. (1981, February 1). How the arts mirror the retreat of manhood. *The New York Times,* sect. 2, pp. 1, 12.

Russell, J. (1983, July 24). It's not 'women's art', it's good art. *The New York Times,* sect. 2, pp. 1, 25.

Russo, N. F. (1976). The Motherhood Mandate. *Journal of Social Issues, 32*(3), 143–153.

Russo, N. F., & Sobel, S. B. (1981). Sex differences in the utilization of mental health facilities. *Professional Psychology, 12,* 7–19.

Rustad, M. (1982). *Women in Khaki: The American enlisted women.* New York: Praeger.

Ryan, S. (1975, January). Gynecological considerations. *Journal of Health, Physical Education, and Recreation.* pp. 40–44.

Rytina, N. F., & Bianchi, S. M. (1984, March). Occupational reclassification and changes in distribution by gender. *Monthly Labor Review, 107*(3), 11–17.

Rywick, T. (1984, April). *A SYMLOG analysis of friendship.* Paper presented at the meeting of the Eastern Psychology Association, Baltimore.

Saario, T. N., Jacklin, C. N., & Tittle, C. K. (1973). Sex role stereotypes in the public schools. *Harvard Educational Review, 43*(3), 386–416.

Sadd, S. Lenauer, M., Shaver, P., & Dunivant, N. (1978). Objective measurement of fear of success and fear of failure: A factor analytic approach. *Journal of Consulting and Clinical Psychology, 46,* 405–416.

Sadd, S., Miller, F. D., & Zeitz, B. (1979). Sex roles and achievement conflicts. *Personality and Social Psychology Bulletin, 5,* 352–355.

Sadker, M., & Sadker, D. (1985, March). Sexism in the schoolroom of the '80s. *Psychology Today,* pp. 54, 56, 57.

Safer, M. A. (1981). Sex and hemisphere differences in access to codes for processing emotional expressions and faces. *Journal of Experimental Psychology, 110,* 86–100.

Safilios-Rothschild, C. (1975). A cross-cultural examination of women's marital, educational, and occupational options. In M. S. Mednick, S. S. Tangri, & L. W. Hoffman (Eds.), *Women and achievement: Social and motivational analyses* (pp. 48–70). New York: Halsted.

Safilios-Rothschild, C. (1977). *Love, sex, and sex roles.* Englewood Cliffs, N.J.: Prentice-Hall.

Safilios-Rothschild, C. (1979). Women as change agents: Toward a conflict theoretical model of sex role change. In J. Lipman-Blumen & J. Bernard (Eds.), *Sex roles and social policy: A complex social science equation* (pp. 287–301). Beverly Hills, Calif.: Sage.

Safilios-Rothschild, C. (Ed.) (1981). Relationships. *Psychology of Women Quarterly, 5* (Whole No. 3).

Salk, L. (1982). *My father, my son: Intimate relationships.* New York: Putnam.

Samuelson, R. J. (1983, July 19). Frustration deepens for working woman. *The Washington Post,* p. D1.

Sanday, P. R. (1973). Toward a theory of the status of women. *Anerican Anthropologist, 75,* 1682–1700.

Sanday, P. R. (1974). Female status in the public domain. In M. Z. Rosaldo & L. Lamphere (Eds.), *Women, culture, and society* (pp. 189–207). Stanford, Calif.: Stanford University Press.

Sanday, P. R. (1981a). *Female power and male dominance: On the origins of sexual inequality.* Cambridge: Cambridge University Press.

Sanday, P. R. (1981b). The socio-cultural context of rape: A cross-cultural study. *Journal of Social Issues, 37*(4), 5–27.

Santrock, J. W., & Warshak, P. A. (1979). Father custody and social development in boys and girls. *Journal of Social Issues, 35*(4), 112–125.

Sarri, R. C. (1979). Crime and the female offender. In E. S. Gomberg & V. Franks (Eds.), *Gender and disordered behavior: Sex differences in psychopathology* (pp. 159–203). New York: Brunner/Mazel.

Savage, J. E., Jr., Stearns, A. D., & Friedman, P. (1979). Relationship of internal-external locus of control, self-concept, and masculinity-femininity to fear of success in Black freshmen and senior college women. *Sex Roles, 5,* 373–383.

Savell, J. M., Woelfel, J. C., Collins, B. E., & Bentler, P. M. (1979). A study of male and female soldiers' beliefs about the "appropriateness" of various jobs for women in the Army. *Sex Roles, 5,* 41–62.

Sawyer, J. (1970, August-October). On male liberation. *Liberation, 15*(6–8), 32–33.

Scarf, M. (1979). The more sorrowful sex. *Psychology Today, 12*(11), pp. 44–52, 89–90.

Scarr, S. (1984). *Mother care/Other care.* New York: Basic.

Schacter, S., & Singer, J. E. (1962). Cognitive, social and physiological determinants of emotional state. *Psychological Review, 63,* 379–399.

Schau, C. G., & Scott, K. P. (1984). Impact of gender characteristics of instructional materials: An integration of the research literature. *Journal of Educational Psychology, 76,* 183–193.

Schaupp, D. L., O'Connell, A. N., & Haupt, E. J. (1985, March). *Sex-role self-concepts, marital adjustment, and self-actualization in long term marriages.* Paper presented at the meeting of the Eastern Psychological Association, Boston, Mass.

Scheppele, K. L., & Bart, P. B. (1983). Through women's eyes: Defining danger in the wake of sexual assault. *Journal of Social Issues, 39*(2), 63–81.

Scher, D. (1984). Sex-role contradictions: Self-perceptions and ideal perceptions. *Sex Roles, 10,* 651–656.

Scher, M. (Ed.) (1981). Special issue: Counseling males. *Personnel and Guidance Journal, 60.*

Schichman, S., & Cooper, E. (1984). Life satisfaction and sex-role concept. *Sex Roles, 11,* 227–240.

Schlafly, P. (1977). *The power of the positive woman.* New Rochelle, N.Y.: Arlington House.

Schmich, M. T. (1984, November 12). Young teenage girls find that stereotypes die hard. *Easton Express,* p. 3.

Schmid, R. E. (1984, April 11). Gains seen for women on the job. *Philadelphia Inquirer,* p. 3A.

Schmidlin, A. M., & Major, B. (1983, April). *The impact of setting on gender differences in touch.* Paper presented at the meeting of the Eastern Psychological Association, Philadelphia.

Schmidt, G. (1975). Male-female differences in sexual arousal and behavior during and after exposure to sexually explicit stimuli. *Archives of Sexual Behavior, 4,* 353–364.

Schmidt, G., & Sigusch, V. (1973). Women's sexual arousal. In J. Zubein & J. Money (Eds.), *Contemporary sexual behavior: Critical issues in the 1970's* (pp. 117–143). Baltimore: Johns Hopkins Press.

Schneider, F. W., & Coutts, L. M. (1985). Person orientation of male and female high school students: To the educational disadvantage of males? *Sex Roles, 13*, 47–63.

Schreiber, C. T. (1979). *Changing places.* Boston: MIT Press.

Schroeder, P. (1982, January). Patriotism is not sex specific. *Women's Political Times*, pp. 4, 14,

Schullo, S. A., & Alperson, B. L. (1984). Interpersonal phenomenology as a function of sexual orientation, sex, sentiment, and trait categories in long-term dyadic relationships. *Journal of Personality and Social Psychology, 47*, 983–1002.

Schwartz, L. A., & Markham, W. T. (1985). Sex stereotyping in children's toy advertisements. *Sex Roles, 12*, 157–170.

Sciolino, E. (1985, June 23). U.N. finds widespread inequality for women. *The New York Times*, p. 10.

Scott, H. (1979). Women in Eastern Europe. In J. Lipman-Blumen & J. Bernard (Eds.), *Sex roles and social policy: A complex social science equation* (pp. 177–197). Beverly Hills, Calif.: Sage.

Scott, H. (1984). *Working your way to the bottom: The feminization of poverty.* London/Boston: Pandora Press/Routledge & Kegan Paul.

Scott, W. J., & Morgan, C. S. (1983). An analysis of factors affecting traditional family expectations and perceptions of ideal fertility. *Sex Roles, 9*, 901–914.

Seaman, B. (1972). *Free and female.* Greenwich, Conn.: Fawcett Crest.

Secord, P. F. (1983). Imbalanced sex ratios: The social consequences. *Personality and Social Psychology Bulletin, 9*, 525–543.

Sedney, M. A. (1981). Comments on median split procedures for scoring androgyny measures. *Sex Roles, 7*, 217–222.

Segal, J., & Yahraes, H. (1978). Bringing up mother. *Psychology Today, 12*(6), 90–96.

Seggar, J. F., Hafen, J. K., & Hannonen-Gladden, H. (1981). Television's portrayal of minorities and women in drama and comedy drama 1971–1980. *Journal of Broadcasting, 25*, 277–288.

Seiden, A. M. (1979). Gender differences in psychophysiological illness. In E. S. Gomberg & V. Franks (Eds.), *Gender and disordered behavior: Sex differences in psychopathology* (pp. 426–449). New York: Brunner/Mazel.

Seidenberg, R. (1973). *Marriage between equals.* Garden City, N.Y.: Anchor Press.

Seidman, C. (1979, December 30). Women athletes gained recognition and also respect. *The New York Times*, p. S7.

Selkow, P. (1984). Effects of maternal employment on kindergarten and first-grade children's vocational aspirations. *Sex Roles, 11*, 677–690.

Sells, L. W. (1980). The mathematics filter and the education of women and minorities. In L. H. Fox, L. Brody, and D. Tobin (Eds.), *Women and the mathematical mystique.* Baltimore: Johns Hopkins University Press.

Selnow, G. W. (1985). Sex differences in uses and perceptions of profanity. *Sex Roles, 12*, 303–312.

Senneker, P., & Hendrick, C. (1983). Androgyny and helping behavior. *Journal of Personality and Social Psychology, 45*, 916–925.

Senour, M. N. (1981). Psychology of the Chicana. In S. Cox (Ed.), *Female psychology*, 2nd ed. (pp. 136–148). New York: St. Martin's.

Serbin, L. A., & Connor, J. M. (1979). Sex-typing of children's play preference and patterns of cognitive performance. *Journal of Genetic Psychology, 134*, 315–316.

Serbin, L. A., Connor, J. M., & Citron, C. C. (1981). Sex differentiated free play behavior: Effects of teacher modeling, location, and gender. *Developmental Psychology, 17*, 640–646.

Serbin, L. A., O'Leary, K. D., Kent, R. N., & Tonick, I. J. (1973). A comparison of teacher response to the pre-academic and problem behavior of boys and girls. *Child Development, 44*, 796–804.

Serrin, W. (1984a, April 10). Unions success at Yale: New focus on white-collar women. *The New York Times*, p. D24.

Serrin, W. (1984b, December 9). White men discover it's a shrinking job market. *The New York Times*, p. E2.

Sharabany, R., Gershoni, R., & Hofman, J. E. (1981). Girl friend, boy friend: Age and sex differences in development of intimate friendships. *Developmental Psychology, 17*, 800–808.

Sharing chores said to help working couples. (1984, May 27). *The Easton Express*, p. A1.

Sharp, C., & Post, R. (1980). Evaluation of male and female applicants for sex-congruent and sex-incongruent jobs. *Sex Roles, 6*, 391–401.

Shaw, J. S. (1982). Psychological androgyny and stressful life events. *Journal of Personality and Social Psychology, 43*, 145–153.

Sheehy, G. (1976). *Passages: Predictable crises of adult life.* New York: Bantam.

Shehan, C. L. (1984). Wive's work and psychological well-being: An extension of Gove's social role theory of depression. *Sex Roles, 11*, 881–899.

Shepard, W. (1980). Mothers and fathers, sons and daughters: Perceptions of young adults. *Sex Roles, 6*, 421–433.

Shepelak, N. J., Ogden, D., & Tobin-Bennett, D. (1984). The influence of gender labels on the sex typing of imaginary occupations. *Sex Roles, 11,* 983–996.

Sherfey, M. J. (1974). *The nature and evolution of female sexuality.* New York: Aronson.

Sherif, C. W. (1979). Bias in psychology. In J. Sherman & E. Beck (Eds.), *The prison of sex: Essays in the sociology of knowledge.* Madison: University of Wisconsin Press.

Sherif, C. W. (1982). Needed concepts in the study of gender identity. *Psychology of Women Quarterly, 6,* 375–398.

Sherman, J. (1967). Problems of sex differences in space perception and aspects of intellectual functioning. *Psychological Review, 74,* 290–299.

Sherman, J. (1976). Social values, femininity and the development of female competence. *Journal of Social Issues, 32,* 181–195.

Sherman, J. (1978). *Sex-related differences in cognition: An essay on theory and evidence.* Springfield, Ill.: Charles C. Thomas.

Sherman, J. (1979). Cognitive performance as a function of sex and handedness: An evaluation of the Levy hypothesis. *Psychology of Women Quarterly, 3,* 378–390.

Sherman, J. (1981). Girls' and boys' enrollment in theoretical math courses: A longitudinal study. *Psychology of Women Quarterly, 5,* 681–689.

Sherman, J. (1982a). Continuing in mathematics: A longitudinal study of the attitudes of high school girls. *Psychology of Women Quarterly, 7,* 132–140.

Sherman, J. A. (1982b). Mathematics, the critical filter: A look at some residues. *Psychology of Women Quarterly, 6,* 428–444.

Sherman, J. (1983a). Factors predicting girls' and boys' preparatory mathematics. *Psychology of Women Quarterly, 7,* 272–281.

Sherman, J. (1983b). Girls talk about mathematics and their future: A partial replication. *Psychology of Women Quarterly, 7,* 338–342.

Sherman, J., & Fennema, E. (1978). Distribution of spatial visualization and mathematical problem-solving scores: A test of Stafford's X linked hypotheses. *Psychology of Women Quarterly, 3,* 157–167.

Sherman, S. R., & Rosenblatt, A. (1984). Women physicians as teachers, administrators, and researchers in medical and surgical specialties. *Sex Roles, 11,* 203–209.

Shields, S. (1975). Functionalism, Darwinism and the psychology of women: A study in social myth. *American Psychologist, 30,* 739–754.

Shigetomi, C. C., Hartmann, D. P., & Gelfand, D. N. (1981). Sex differences in children's altruistic behavior and reputations for helpfulness. *Developmental Psychology, 19,* 434–437.

Shinar, E. H. (1978). Person perception as a function of occupation and sex. *Sex Roles, 4,* 679–693.

Shinedling, M., & Pedersen, D. M. (1970). Effects of sex of teacher versus student on children's gain in quantitative and verbal performance. *Journal of Psychology, 76,* 79–84.

Shinn, M. (1978). Father absence and children's cognitive development. *Psychological Bulletin, 85,* 295–324.

Short, J. F., Jr., & Strodtbeck, F. L. (1976). Why gangs fight. In D. S. David & R. Brannon (Eds.), *The forty-nine percent majority: The male sex role* (pp. 131–137). Reading, Mass.: Addison-Wesley.

Siegfried, W. D. (1982). The effects of specifying job requirements and using explicit warnings to decrease sex discrimination in employment interviews. *Sex Roles, 8,* 73–82.

Signorella, M. L., & Vegega, M. E. (1984). A note on gender stereotyping of research topics. *Personality and Social Psychology Bulletin, 10,* 107–109.

Signorella, M. L., Vegega, M. E., & Mitchell, M. E. (1981). Subject selection and analyses for sex-related differences: 1968–1970 and 1975–1977. *American Psychologist, 36,* 988–990. (Comment).

Silbert, M. H., & Pines, A. M. (1984). Pornography and sexual abuse of women. *Sex Roles, 10,* 857–868.

Silver, G. A., & Silver, M. (1981). *Weekend fathers.* Los Angeles, Calif.: Stratford Press.

Silver, R. L., Boon, C., & Stones, M. H. (1983). Searching for meaning in misfortune: Making sense of incest. *Journal of Social Issues, 39*(2), 81–101.

Silverman, L. H., & Fisher, A. K. (1981). The Oedipus complex: Studies in adult male behavior. In L. Wheeler (Ed.), *Review of Personality and Social Psychology* (pp. 43–67). Vol. 2. Beverly Hills, Calif.: Sage.

Silvern, L. E. (1977). Children's sex-role preferences: Stronger among girls than boys. *Sex Roles, 3,* 159–171.

Silvern, L. E., & Ryan, V. L. (1979). Self-related adjustment and sex-typing on the Bem Sex Role Inventory: Is masculinity the primary predictor of adjustment? *Sex Roles, 5,* 739–763.

Silvern, L. E., & Ryan, V. L. (1983). A reexamination of masculine and feminine sex-role ideals and conflicts among ideals for the man, woman, and person. *Sex Roles, 9,* 1223–1248.

Simari, C. G., & Baskin, D. (1983). Sex-role acquisition, parental behavior, and sexual orientation: Some tentative hypotheses—A critique. *Sex Roles, 9,* 1061–1062.

Simpson, G. (1984). The daughters of Charlotte Ray: The career development process during the exploratory and establishment stages of black women attorneys. *Sex Roles, 11,* 113–139.

Sinott, J. D. (1984). Older men, older women: Are their perceived sex roles similar? *Sex Roles, 10,* 847–856.

Sistrunk, F., & McDavid, J. W. (1971). Sex variables in conforming behavior. *Journal of Personality and Social Psychology, 17,* 200–207.

Skelly, G., & Lundstrom, W. (1981). Male sex roles in magazine advertising, 1959–1979. *Journal of Communication, 31,* 52–57.

Skinner, D. A. (1980). Dual-career family stress and coping: A literature review. *Family Relations, 29,* 473–480.

Skrypnek, B. J., & Snyder, M. (1982). On the self-perpetuating nature of stereotypes about women and men. *Journal of Experimental Social Psychology, 18,* 277–291.

Slaby, R. G., & Frey, K. S. (1975). Development of gender constancy and selective attention to same-sex models. *Child Development, 46,* 849–856.

Slife, B. D., & Rychlak, J. F. (1982). Role of affects assessment in modeling aggressive behavior. *Journal of Personality and Social Psychology, 43,* 861–868.

Sloane, B. K. (1983, November). In brief. *National NOW Times,* p. 16.

Slobogin, K. (1977, November 20). Stress. *The New York Times Magazine,* pp. 48–55ff.

Small, A., Gessner, T., & Ferguson, T. (1984). Sex role and dysphoric mood. *Sex Roles, 11,* 627–638.

Smeal, E. (1984). *Why and how women will elect the next president.* New York: Harper & Row.

Smetana, J. G., & Letourneau, K. J. (1984). Development of gender constancy and children's sex-typed free play behavior. *Developmental Psychology, 20,* 691–696.

Smith, A. (1983). Nonverbal communication among black female dyads: An assessment of intimacy, gender, and race. *Journal of Social Issues, 39,* 55–67.

Smith, A., & Stewart, A. J. (Eds.) (1983). Racism and sexism in black women's lives. *Journal of Social Issues, 39* (Whole No. 3).

Smith, B. (1982). Racism and women's studies. In G. Hull, P. Scott, & B. Smith (Eds.), *But some of us are brave* (pp. 48–51). Old Westbury, New York: Feminist Press.

Smith, B. (Ed.) (1983). *Home girls: A black feminist anthology* (pp. xix–1vi). New York: Kitchen Table: Women of Color Press.

Smith, E. J. (1982). The Black female adolescent: A review of the educational, career, and psychological literature. *Psychology of Women Quarterly, 6,* 261–288.

Smith, H. L., & Grenier, M. (1982). Sources of organizational power for women: Overcoming structural obstacles. *Sex Roles, 8,* 733–746.

Smith, J. (1984). The paradox of women's poverty: Wage-earning women and economic transformation. *Signs, 10,* 291–310.

Smith, P. A., & Midlarsky, E. (1985). Empirically derived conceptions of femaleness and maleness: A current view. *Sex Roles, 12,* 313–328.

Smith, R. E. (Ed.) (1979). *The subtle revolution: Women at work.* Washington, D.C.: The Urban Institute.

Smith, S. H., Whitehead, G. I., & Sussman, N. M. (1984). Perception of female and male success in the United States and Third World Nations. *Sex Roles, 10,* 903–911.

Smye, M. D., & Wine, J. D. (1980). A comparison of female and male adolescents' social behaviors and cognitions: A challenge to the assertiveness literature. *Sex Roles, 6,* 213–230.

Snarey, J., Friedman, K., & Blasi, J. (1985). *Sex role strain among Kibbutz women: A developmental perspective.* (Working Paper No. 151). Wellesley, Mass.: Center for Research on Women.

Snitow, A., Stansell, C., & Thompson, S. (Eds.) (1983). *Powers of desire: The politics of sexuality.* New York: Monthly Review Press.

Snodgrass, S. E. (1985). Women's intuition: The effect of subordinate role upon interpersonal sensitivity. *Journal of Personality and Social Psychology, 49,* 146–155.

Snow, K. (1975). Women in the American novel. In J. Freeman (Ed.), *Women: A feminist perspective* (pp. 279–292). Palo Alto, Calif.: Mayfield.

Snow, L. J., & Parsons, J. L. (1983). Sex role orientation and female sexual functioning. *Psychology of Women Quarterly, 8,* 133–143.

Snyder, M., Tanke, E. D., & Berscheid, E. (1977). Social perception and interpersonal behavior: On the self-fulfilling nature of social stereotypes. *Journal of Personality and Social Psychology, 35,* 656–666.

Social security is a women's issue. (1985, May). *National NOW Times,* p. 10.

Sohn, D. (1980). Critique of Cooper's meta-analytic assessment of the findings on sex differences in conformity behavior. *Journal of Personality and Social Psychology, 39,* 1215–1221.

Sohn, D. (1982). Sex differences in achievement self-attributions: An effect-size analysis. *Sex Roles, 8,* 345–357.

Sollie, D. L., & Fischer, J. L. (1985). Sex-role orientation, intimacy of topic, and target person differences in self-disclosure among women. *Sex Roles, 12,* 917–929.

Solomon, K., & Levy, N. (Eds.) (1982). *Men in transition: Changing male roles, theory, and therapy.* New York: Plenum.

Solomon, L. C. (1978). Attracting women to psychology: Effects of university behavior and the labor market. *American Psychologist, 33,* 990–999.

Sommer, B. (1984, August). PMS in the courts: Are all women on trial? *Psychology Today,* pp. 36–38.

Son, L., & Schmitt, N. (1983). The influence of sex bias upon compliance with expert power. *Sex Roles, 9,* 233–246.

Spence, J. T. (1983). Commenting on Lubinski, Tellegen, and Butcher's "Masculinity, femininity and androgyny viewed and assessed as distinct concepts." *Journal of Personality and Social Psychology, 44,* 440–446.

Spence, J. T., & Helmreich, R. (1972). Who likes competent women? Competence, sex-role congruence of interests, and subjects' attitude toward women as determinants of interpersonal attraction. *Journal of Applied Social Psychology, 2*(3), 197–213.

Spence, J. T., & Helmreich, R. (1978). *Masculinity and femininity: The psychological dimensions, correlates and antecedents.* Austin: University of Texas Press.

Spence, J. T., & Helmreich, R. L. (1979a). On assessing "androgyny." *Sex Roles, 5,* 721–738.

Spence, J. T., & Helmreich, R. L. (1979b). The many faces of androgyny: A reply to Locksley and Colten. *Journal of Personality and Social Psychology, 37,* 1032–1046.

Spence, J. T., and Helmreich, R. L. (1980). Masculine instrumentality and feminine expressiveness: Their relationships with sex role attitudes and behavior. *Psychology of Women Quarterly, 5,* 147–163.

Spence, J. T., & Helmreich, R. L. (1981). Androgyny versus gender schema: A comment on Bem's gender schema theory. *Psychological Review, 88,* 365–368.

Spence, J. T. & Helmreich, R. L. (1983). Achievement-related motives and behaviors. In J. T. Spence (Ed.), *Achievement and achievement motivation: Psychological and sociological approaches.* (pp. 7–74). San Francisco: W. H. Freeman.

Spence, J. T., Helmreich, R. L., & Holahan, C. K. (1979). Negative and positive components of psychological masculinity and femininity and their relationship to self-reports of neurotic and acting out behaviors. *Journal of Personality and Social Psychology, 37,* 1673–1682.

Spence, J. T., Helmreich, R., & Stapp, J. (1974). The Personal Attributes Questionnaire: A measure of sex role stereotyping and masculinity and femininity. *JSAS Selected Documents in Psychology,* (Ms. No. 617).

Spence, J. T., Helmreich, R., & Stapp, J. (1975). Ratings of self and peers on sex role attributes and the relation to self-esteem and conceptions of masculinity and femininity. *Journal of Personality and Social Psychology, 32,* 29–39.

Spence, J. T., & Sawin, L. L. (1985). Images of masculinity and femininity: A reconceptualization. In V. O'Leary, R. Unger, & B. Wallston (Eds.), *Women, gender and social psychology* (pp. 35–66). Hillsdale, N.J.: Lawrence Erlbaum Associates.

Sprafkin, J. N., & Liebert, R. M. (1978). Sex-typing and children's television preferences. In G. Tuchman, A. K. Daniels, & J. Benet (Eds.), *Hearth and home: Images of women in the mass media* (pp. 228–239). New York: Oxford University Press.

Sprecher, S. (1984). Sex differences in bases of power in dating relationships. *Sex Roles, 12,* 449–462.

Stacey, J. (1983). *Patriarchy and socialist revolution in China.* Berkeley, Calif.: University of California Press.

Staines, G. L., Tavris, C., & Jayaratne, T. E. (1974, January). The Queen Bee Syndrome. *Psychology Today,* pp. 55–60.

Stake, J. E. (1979). The ability/performance dimension of self-esteem: Implications for women's achievement behavior. *Psychology of Women Quarterly, 3,* 365–377.

Stake, J. E. (1983). Ability level, evaluative feedback, and sex differences in performance expectancy. *Psychology of Women Quarterly, 8,* 48–58.

Stake, J. E. (1985). Exploring the basis of sex differences in third-party allocations. *Journal of Personality and Social Psychology, 48,* 1621–1629.

Stake, J. E., & Orlosky, J. L. (1981). On the use of global and specific measures in assessing the self-esteem of males and females. *Sex Roles, 7,* 653–662.

Stake, J. E., Walker, E. F., & Speno, M. V. (1981). The relationship of sex and academic performance to quality of recommendations for graduate school. *Psychology of Women Quarterly, 5,* 515–522.

Stallard, K., Ehrenreich, B., & Sklar, H. (1983). *Poverty in the American dream: Women and children first.* New York: South End.

Stanley, A. D. (1983, September 19). High-tech will hurt women. *The New York Times,* p. A19.

Stanwick, K. A., & Kleeman, K. E. (1983). *Women make a difference.* New Brunswick, N.J.: Center for the American Woman and Politics, Eagleton Institute of Politics, Rutgers University.

Stapp. J. (1979). Minorities and women: Caught in an academic revolving door. *APA Monitor, 10*(11), p. 14.

Star, S. L. (1979). Sex differences and the dichotomization of the brain: Methods, limits and problems in research on consciousness. In E. Tobach & B.

Rosoff (Eds.), *Genes and Gender II* (pp. 113–130). Staten Island, N.Y.: Gordian Press.

Starer, R., & Denmark, F. (1974). Discrimination against aspiring women. *International Journal of Group Tensions, 4,* 65–71.

Starr, P. (1978, July 16). Hollywood's new ideal of masculinity. *The New York Times,* Sect. 2, p. 1ff.

Starting up an old girls' network. (1983, April 18). *Newsweek,* pp. 88–89.

Steffensmeier, R. H. (1984). Suicide and the contemporary women: Are male and female suicide rates converging? *Sex Roles, 10,* 613–631.

Steiger, J. C. (1981). The impact of the feminist subculture in changing sex-role attitudes. *Sex Roles, 7,* 627–633.

Stein, J. S., & Yaworsky, K. B. (1983, August). *Menstrual cycle and memory for affective and neutral words.* Paper presented at the meeting of the American Psychological Association, Anaheim.

Stein, P. J., & Hoffman, S. (1978). Sports and male role strain. *Journal of Social Issues, 34*(1), 136–150.

Steinem, G. (1972). The myth of the Masculine Mystique. *International Education, 1,* 30–35.

Steinem, G. (1984, July). How women live, vote, think . . . . *Ms.,* pp. 51–54.

Stephen, T. D., & Harrison, T. M. (1985). A longitudinal comparison of couples with sex-typical and non-sex typical orientations to intimacy. *Sex Roles, 12,* 195–206.

Stericker, A. B., & Kurdek, L. A. (1982). Dimensions and correlates of third through eighth graders' sex-role self-concepts. *Sex Roles, 8,* 915–929.

Stericker, A., & LeVesconte, S. (1982). Effect of brief training on sex-related differences in visual-spatial skill. *Journal of Personality and Social Psychology, 43,* 1018–1029.

Sterling, B. S., & Owen, J. W. (1982). Perceptions of demanding versus reasoning male and female police officers. *Personality and Social Psychology Bulletin, 8,* 336–340.

Sternglanz, S. H., & Serbin, L. A. (1974). Sex role stereotyping in children's TV programs. *Developmental Psychology, 10,* 710–715.

Stewart, V. (1976). Social influences on sex differences in behavior. In M. Teitelbaum (Ed.), *Sex differences: Social and biological perspectives.* New York: Anchor Press.

Stiehm, J. (Ed.) (1983). *Women and men's wars.* Oxford: Pergamon Press.

Stier, D. S., & Hall, J. A. (1984). Gender differences in touch: An empirical and theoretical review. *Journal of Personality and Social Psychology, 47,* 440–459.

Stipek, D. J. (1984). Sex differences in children's attributions for success and failure on math and spelling tests. *Sex Roles, 11,* 969–981.

Stitt, C., Schmidt, S., Price, K., & Kipnis, D. (1983). Sex of leader, leader behavior, and subordinate satisfaction. *Sex Roles, 9,* 31–42.

Stock, W. E. (1984). Sex roles and sexual dysfunction. In C. Widom (Ed.), *Sex roles and psychopathology.* (pp. 249–275). New York: Plenum.

Stockard, J., & Dougherty, M. (1983). Variations in subjective culture: A comparison of females and males in three settings. *Sex Roles, 9,* 953–974.

Stockard, J., & Johnson, M. M. (1979). The social origins of male dominance. *Sex Roles, 5,* 199–218.

Stoller, R. J. (1968). *Sex and gender: On the development of masculinity and femininity.* New York: Science House.

Stone, E. (1979, May 13). Mothers and daughters: Taking a new look at Mom. *The New York Times Magazine,* pp. 14–17ff.

Stone, I. F. (1974). Machismo in Washington. In J. Pleck & L. Sawyer (Eds.), *Men and masculinity* (pp. 130–133). Englewood Cliffs, N.J.: Prentice-Hall.

Stoppard, J. M., & Kalin, R. (1983). Gender typing and social desirability of personality in person evaluation. *Psychology of Women Quarterly, 7,* 209–218.

Storms, M. D. (1980). Theories of sexual orientation. *Journal of Personality and Social Psychology, 38,* 783–792.

Storms, M. D., Stivers, M. L., Lambers, S. M., & Hill, C. A. (1981). Sexual scripts for women. *Sex Roles, 7,* 699–707.

Strahan, R. F. (1981). Remarks on scoring androgyny as a single continuous variable. *Psychological Reports, 49,* 887–890.

Strommen, E. A. (1977). Friendship. In E. Doneleon & J. Gullahorn (Eds.), *Women: A psychological perspective.* New York: Wiley.

Study of Black females cites role of praise. (1985, June 25). *The New York Times,* p. C5.

Study finds new mothers get limited time off from work. (1983, December 25). *The New York Times.*

Study: Many support payments are unpaid. (1983, July 8). *The Easton Express,* p. A-5.

Study: Married mothers feel more stress than unmarried. (1982, July 2). *The Easton Express,* p. A5.

Study shows births up in women in their 30's. (1984, May 9). *The New York Times,* p. A7.

Study: Women's role in car buying ignored. (1985, March 13). *The Easton Express,* p. C11.

Suchner, R. W. (1979). Sex ratios and occupational prestige: Three failures to replicate a sexist bias. *Personality and Social Psychology Bulletin, 5,* 236–239.

Sugg, R. S. (1978). *Motherteacher: The feminization of American education.* Charlottesville: University Press of Virginia.

Survey finds "male stronghold" persists in schools. (1979, Sept. 5). *The New York Times,* p. A16.

Survey: Women writers skirted on front pages. (1985, April 14). *Easton Express*, p. D5.

Sussman, B. (1983, April 17). Women at bottom as acceptable candidates. *The Easton Express*, p. A4.

Sussman, N. M., & Rosenfeld, H. M. (1982). Influences of culture, language, and sex on conversational distance. *Journal of Personality and Social Psychology, 42,* 66–74.

Swanson, M. A., & Tjosvold, D. (1979). The effects of unequal competence and sex on achievement and self-presentation. *Sex Roles, 5,* 279–285.

Swap, W. C., & Rubin, J. Z. (1983). Measurement of interpersonal orientation. *Journal of Personality and Social Psychology, 44,* 208–219.

Sweeney, P. D., Moreland, R. L., & Gruber, K. L. (1982). Gender differences in performance attributions: Students' explanations for personal success or failure. *Sex Roles, 8,* 359–373.

Symons, D. (1979). *The evolution of human sexuality.* Oxford, England: Oxford University Press.

Tauber, M. A. (1979). Parental socialization techniques and sex differences in children's play. *Child Development, 50,* 225–234.

Tavris, C. (1973). Who likes women's liberation and why: The case of the unliberated liberals. *Journal of Social Issues, 29*(4), 175–194.

Tavris, C., & Offir, C. (1977). *The longest war: Sex differences in perspective.* New York: Harcourt Brace Jovanovich.

Taylor, D. (1984). Concurrent validity of the Bem Sex Role Inventory: A person-environment approach. *Sex Roles, 10,* 713–723.

Taylor, M. C. (1979). Race, sex, and the expression of self-fulfilling prophecies in a laboratory teaching situation. *Journal of Personality and Social Psychology, 37,* 897–912.

Taylor, M. C., & Hall, J. A. (1982). Psychological androgyny: Theories, methods, and conclusions. *Psychological Bulletin, 92,* 347–366.

Taynor, J., & Deaux, K. (1973). When women are more deserving then men: Equity, attribution and perceived sex differences. *Journal of Personality and Social Psychology, 28,* 360–367.

Taynor, J., & Deaux, K. (1975). Equity and perceived sex differences: Role behavior as defined by the task, the mode, and the action. *Journal of Personality and Social Psychology, 32,* 381–390.

Teen moods, hormones linked. (1985, July). *APA Monitor,* p. 11.

Tennov, D. (1975). *Psychotherapy: The hazardous cure.* New York: Abelard-Schuman.

Terborg, J. R., & Shingledecker, P. (1983). Employee reactions to supervision and work evaluation as a function of subordinate and manager sex. *Sex Roles, 9,* 813–824.

Teri, L. (1982). Effects of sex and sex-role style on clinical judgement. *Sex Roles, 8,* 639–649.

"That's women's work." (1985, Winter). *On Campus with Women,* p. 8.

Thom, M. (1984, July). The all-time definitive map of the gender gap. *Ms.,* pp. 55–60.

Thomas, A. H., & Stewart, N. R. (1971). Counselor ratings to female clients with deviate and conforming career goals. *Journal of Counseling Psychology, 18,* 352–357.

Thompson, H. L., & Richardson, D. R. (1983). The Rooster effect: Same-sex rivalry and inequity as factors in retaliative aggression. *PSPB, 9,* 415–425.

Thompson, M. E. (1981). Sex differences: Differential access to power or sex-role socialization? *Sex Roles, 7,* 413–424.

Thompson, N. L., McCandless, B. R., & Strickland, B. B. (1971). Personal adjustment of male and female homosexuality and heterosexuality. *Journal of Abnormal Psychology, 78,* 237–240.

Thorne, B., Kramarae, C., & Henley, N. (Eds.) (1983). *Language, gender and society.* Rowley, Mass.: Newbury House.

Tice, D. M., & Baumeister, R. F. (1985). Masculinity inhibits helping in emergencies: Personality does predict the bystander effect. *Journal of Personality and Social Psychology, 49,* 420–428.

Tidball, E. M. (1976). Of men and research: The 1973 dominant themes in American higher education include neither teaching nor women. *Journal of Higher Education, 47,* 373–389.

Tiger, L. (1969). *Men in groups.* New York: Random House.

Tilby, P. J., & Kalin, R. (1980). Effects of sex-role deviant lifestyles in otherwise normal persons on the perception of maladjustment. *Sex Roles, 6,* 581–592.

Timnick, L. (1985, August 25). Poll: 22% of children in U.S. sexually abused. *The Easton Express,* p. A10.

Tinsley, E. G., Sullivan-Guest, S., & McGuire, J. (1984). Feminine sex role and depression in middle-aged women. *Sex Roles, 11,* 25–32.

Tittle, C. K. (1981). *Careers and family: Sex roles and adolescent life plans.* Beverly Hills, Calif.: Sage, 1981.

Tobias, S. (1978). *Overcoming math anxiety.* New York: Norton.

Tobias, S. (1982, January). Sexist equations. *Psychology Today,* pp. 14–17.

Toder, N. L. (1980). The effect of the sexual composition of a group on discrimination against women and sex-role attitudes. *Psychology of Women Quarterly, 5,* 292–310.

Tolchin, M. (1979, April 22). U.S. search for women and Blacks to serve as judges is going slowly. *The New York Times*, p. 1.

Tolson, A. (1977). *The limits of masculinity: Male identity and women's liberation*. New York: Harper & Row.

Toth, E. (1984, February). Who'll take romance? *The Women's Review of Books*, pp. 11–13.

Touhey, J. C. (1974). Effects of additional women professionals on ratings of occupational prestige and desirability. *Journal of Personality and Social Psychology, 29*, 86–89.

Townsend, R. C. (1977). The competitive male as loser. In A. Sargent (Ed.), *Beyond sex roles* (p. 228–242). St. Paul: West.

Townsley, C. J., Scruggs, M. M., Callsen, M. S., & Warde, W. D. (1984, Fall). Incomes of home economists employed full-time. *Journal of Home Economics, 76*, 19–21.

Towson, S. M. J., & Zanna, M. P. (1982). Toward a situational analysis of gender differences in aggression. *Sex Roles, 8*, 903–914.

Travis, C. B., Burnett-Doering, J., & Reid, P. T. (1982). The impact of sex, achievement domain, and conceptual orientation on causal attributions. *Sex Roles, 8*, 443–454.

Trebilcot, J. (1977). Two forms of androgynism. *Journal of Social Philosophy, 8*(1).

Trebilcot, J. (Ed.) (1984). *Mothering: Essays in feminist theory*. Totowa, N.J.: Rowman and Allanheld.

Tremaine, L. S., Schau, C. G., & Busch, J. W. (1982). Children's occupational sex-typing. *Sex Roles, 8*, 691–710.

Tresemer, D. W. (1977). *Fear of success*. New York: Plenum Press.

Troll, L. E., & Turner, B. F. (1979). Sex differences in problems of aging. In E. S. Gomberg & V. Franks (Eds.), *Gender and disordered behavior: Sex differences in psychopathology* (pp. 124–156). New York: Brunner/Mazel.

Trotter, R. J. (1983, August). Baby face. *Psychology Today*, 15–20.

True, R. H. (1981). The profile of Asian American women. In S. Cox (Ed.), *Female psychology*, 2nd ed. (pp. 124–135). New York: St. Martin's.

Tucker, D. (1983, May 21). Women's sports entering new era. *The Easton Express*, p. C-6.

Tucker, L. A. (1982a). Effect of a weight-training program on the self-concepts of college males. *Perceptual and Motor Skills, 54*, 1055–1061.

Tucker, L. A. (1982b). Relationship between perceived somatotype and body cathexis of college males. *Psychological Reports, 50*, 983–989.

Tucker, L. A. (1983a). Effect of weight training on self-concept: A profile of those influenced most. *Research Quarterly for Exercise and Sport, 54*, 389–397.

Tucker, L. A. (1983b). Muscular strength and mental health. *Journal of Personality and Social Psychology, 45*, 1355–1360.

Tunnell, G. (1981). Sex role and cognitive schemata: Person perception in feminine and androgynous women. *Journal of Personality and Social Psychology, 40*, 1126–1136.

Tuohy, W. (1985, May 31). What makes British soccer fans violent? *The Easton Express*, p. 1–2.

Turkewitz, G., & Ross-Kossak, P. (1984). Multiple modes of right-hemisphere information processing: Age and sex differences in facial recognition. *Developmental Psychology, 20*, 95–103.

Turkington, C. (1985, April). Women drinkers' unique problems no longer ignored. *APA Monitor*, pp. 16–18.

Turkle, S. (1984). *The second self: The computer and the human spirit*. New York: Simon & Schuster.

Two-income couples are the norm. (1984, April 2). *The Easton Express*, p. A2.

Tzuriel, D. (1984). Sex role typing and ego identity in Israeli, Oriental, and Western adolescents. *Journal of Personality and Social Psychology, 46*, 440–457.

Uleman, J. S., & Weston, M. (1984, April). *Changing social roles changes BSRI masculinity and femininity*. Paper presented at the meeting of the Eastern Psychological Association, Baltimore.

Ullian, D. Z. (1976). The development of conceptions of masculinity and femininity. In B. Lloyd & J. Archer (Eds.), *Exploring sex differences*. New York: Academic Press.

Ullian, D. (1984). "Why girls are good": A constructivist view. *Sex Roles, 11*, 241–256.

Umstot, M. E. (1980). Occupational sex-role liberality of third-, fifth-, and seventh-grade females. *Sex Roles, 6*, 611–617.

Ungar, S. B. (1982). The sex-typing of adult and child behavior in toy sales. *Sex Roles, 8*, 251–260.

Unger, M. (1984, April 6). Women's lung cancer rate doubled. *Easton Express*, A-8.

Unger, R. K. (1979). Toward a redefinition of sex and gender. *American Psychologist, 34*, 1085–1094.

Unger, R. K. (1981). Sex as a social reality: Field and laboratory research. *Psychology of Women Quarterly, 5*, 645–653.

Unger, R. K. (1983). Through the looking glass: No wonderland yet! (The reciprocal relationship between methodology and models of reality). *Psychology of Women Quarterly, 8*, 9–32.

Unger, R. K., & Denmark, F. L. (Eds.) (1975). *Women: Dependent or independent variables?* New York: Psychological Dimensions.

Unger, R. K., & Siiter, R. (1975). Sex role stereotypes: The weight of a "grain of truth." In R. Unger (Ed.), *Sex-role stereotypes revisited: Psychological approaches to women's studies* (pp. 10–13). New York: Harper & Row.

Union wins funds to correct male-female pay disparities. (1981, July 15). *The New York Times*, p. 1.

U.S. Bureau of the Census. (1977; 1979). *Statistical abstract of the United States*. Washington, D.C.: U.S. Government Printing Office.

U.S. Bureau of the Census. (1982). *Statistical abstracts of the United States, 1982–1983*, (103rd ed. Washington, D.C.: U.S. Government Printing Office

U.S. Bureau of the Census. (1983, October). *School enrollment: Social and economic characteristics*. Washington, D.C.: Author.

U.S. Commission on Civil Rights. (1977). *Window dressing on the set: Woman and minorities on television*. Washington, D.C.: U.S. Government Printing Office.

U.S. Commission on Civil Rights. (1979). *Window dressing on the set: An update*. Washington, D.C.: U.S. Government Printing Office.

U.S. Commission on Civil Rights. (1980). *More hurdles to clear: Women and girls in competitive athletics*. Washington, D.C.: Clearinghouse. no. 63.

U.S. Department of Commerce, Bureau of the Census. (1984). *Statistical abstracts of the United States, 1984*.

U.S. Department of Health, Education and Welfare, Bureau of Occupational and Adult Education. (1979). *Summary data vocational education, project year 1978*. Washington, D.C.: U.S. Government Printing Office.

U.S. Department of Labor, Women's Bureau. (1975). *1975 handbook on women workers*. Bulletin 297. Washington, D.C.: U.S. Government Printing Office.

U.S. Department of Labor, Women's Bureau. (1976a). *The earnings gap between women and men*. Washington, D.C.: U.S. Government Printing Office.

U.S. Department of Labor, Women's Bureau. (1976b). *Women workers today*. Washington, D.C.: U.S. Government Printing Office.

U.S. Department of Labor, Women's Bureau. (1977a). *U.S. working women: A datebook*. Washington, D.C.: U.S. Government Printing Office.

U.S. Department of Labor, Women's Bureau. (1977b). *Women in the labor force, 1976–1977, April*. Washington, D.C.: U.S. Government Printing Office.

U.S. Department of Labor, Bureau of Labor Statistics. (1979a). *Employment and earnings, November 1979*. Washington, D.C.: U.S. Government Printing Office.

U.S. Department of Labor, Bureau of Labor Statistics. (1979b). *Employment and earnings, 1979, February*. Washington, D.C.: U.S. Government Printing Office.

U.S. Department of Labor, Women's Bureau. (1980). *20 facts on women workers*. Washington, D.C.: U.S. Government Printing Office.

U.S. Department of Labor, Bureau of Labor Statistics. (1983). *Women at work: A chartbook*. Washington, D.C.: U.S. Government Printing Office.

U.S. Department of Labor, Bureau of Labor Statistics. (1985). *Employment and Earnings, April, 1985*. Washington, D.C.: U.S. Government Printing Office.

U.S. Merit Systems Protection Board. (1981). *Sexual harassment in the federal workplace: Is it a problem?* Washington, D.C.: Author.

U.S. support for equality is growing, study reveals. (1983, August 31). *The Easton Express*, p. A10.

Urberg, K. A. (1982). The development of the concepts of masculinity and femininity in young children. *Sex Roles, 8*, 659–668.

Vance, C. S. (Ed.) (1984). *Pleasure and danger: Exploring female sexuality*. Boston: Routledge & Kegan Paul.

Vandenberg, S. G., & Kuse, A. R. (1979). Spatial ability: A critical review of the sex-linked major gene hypothesis. In M. A. Wittig & A. C. Petersen (Eds.), *Sex-related differences in cognitive functioning: Developmental issues* (pp. 67–95). New York: Academic Press.

Van Dusen, R. R., & Sheldon, E. B. (1976). The changing status of American women: A life cycle perspective. *American Psychologist, 31*, 106–117.

Van Gelder, L. (1985, January). Help for technophobes. *Ms.*, pp. 89–91.

Van Hecke, M., Tracy, R. J., Cotler, S., & Ribordy, S. C. (1984). Approval versus achievement motives in seventh-grade girls. *Sex Roles, 11*, 33–41.

Van Hecke, M. T., Van Keep, P. A., & Kellerhals, J. M. (1975). The aging woman. *Acts Obstietrica et Gynecologia, 51*, Scandinavica Supplement, 17–27.

Vecsey, G. (1979, October 2). Quest for equality in Church dividing Catholic women. *The New York Times*, p. A12.

Vedovato, S., & Vaughter, R. M. (1980). Psychology of women courses changing sexist and sex-typed attitudes. *Psychology of Women Quarterly, 4*, 587–590.

Veitch, R., & Griffitt, W. (1980). The perception of erotic arousal in men and women by same and opposite-sex peers. *Sex Roles, 6*, 723–733.

Vener, A. M., & Snyder, C. (1966). The preschool child's awareness and anticipation of adult sex roles. *Sociometry, 29*, 159–168.

Ventura, S. J., Taffel, S., & Mosher, W. D. (1985). Estimates of pregnancies and pregnancy rates for the U.S., 1976–1981. *Public Health Reports, 100*(1), 31–34.

Verbrugge, L. M. (1982). Sex differences in legal drug use. *Journal of Social Issues, 38*(2), 59–76.

Verbrugge, L. M., & Madans, J. H. (1985, March). Women's roles and health. *American Demographics, 7*(3), 36–39.

Verbrugge, L. M., & Steiner, R. P. (1984). Another look at physicians' treatment of men and women with common complaints. *Sex Roles, 11,* 1091–1109.

Veroff, J., Depner, C., Kulka, R., & Douvan, E. (1980). Comparison of American motives: 1957 versus 1976. *Journal of Personality and Social Psychology, 39,* 1249–1262.

Veroff, J., Wilcox, S., & Atkinson, J. W. (1953). Achievement motivation in high school and college age women. *Journal of Abnormal and Social Psychology, 48,* 108–119.

Veterans preference hurts women. (1978, August). *National NOW Times,* p. 15.

Views of younger generation surveyed. (1983, December 7). *The New York Times,* p. C15.

Villemur, N. K., & Hyde, J. S. (1983). Effects of sex of defense attorney, sex of juror, and age and attractiveness of the victim on mock juror decision making in a rape case. *Sex Roles, 9,* 879–889.

Vogel, S. R. (1979). Discussant's comments. Symposium: Applications of androgyny to the theory and practice of psychotherapy. *Psychology of Women Quarterly, 3,* 255–258.

Vollmer, Fred. (1984). Sex differences in personality and expectancy. *Sex Roles, 11,* 1121–1139.

Volsky, G. (1983, December 26). Chastity rule evokes anger. *The New York Times,* p. 28.

von Baeyer, C. L., Sherk, D. L., & Zanna, M. P. (1981). Impression management in the job interview: When the female applicant meets the male (chauvinist) interviewer. *Personality and Social Psychology Bulletin, 7,* 45–51.

Voydanoff, P. (1980). Perceived job characteristics and job satisfaction among men and women. *Psychology of Women Quarterly, 5,* 177–185.

Voydanoff, P. (Ed.) (1984). *Work and family: Changing roles of men and women.* Palo Alto, Calif.: Mayfield.

Vredenburg, K., Flett, G. L., Krames, L., & Pliner, P. (1984, August). *Sex differences in attitudes, feelings, and behaviors, and behaviors toward computers.* Paper presented at the meeting of the American Psychological Association, Toronto, Canada.

Waber, D. P. (1976). Sex differences in cognition: A function of maturation rate? *Science, 192,* 572–574.

Waber, D. P. (1977). Sex differences in mental abilities, hemispheric lateralization, and rate of physical growth at adolescence. *Developmental Psychology, 13,* 29–38.

Waber, D. P. (1979). Cognitive abilities and sex-related variations in the maturation of cerebral cortical functions. In M. A. Wittig & A. C. Petersen (Eds.), *Sex-related differences in cognitive functioning: Developmental issues* (pp. 161–186). New York: Academic Press.

Wagner, J. (1982). *Sex roles in contemporary American communes.* Bloomington, Ind.: Indiana University Press.

Waldron, I. (1976). Why do women live longer than men? *Journal of Human Stress, 2,* 1–13.

Waldron, I. (1978). Type A behavior pattern and coronary heart disease in men and women. *Social Science and Medicine, 12,* 167–170.

Waldron, I. (1983). Employment and women's health: An analysis of causal relationships. In E. Fee (Ed.), *Women and health: The politics of sex and medicine* (pp. 119–138). Farmingdale, N.Y.: Baywood.

Waldron, I., & Herold, J. (1984, May). *Employment, attitudes toward employment and women's health.* Paper presented at the meeting of the Society of Behavioral Medicine, Philadelphia.

Walker, E., Bettes, B. A., Kain, E. L., & Harvey, P. (1985). Relationship of gender and marital status with symptomatology in psychotic patients. *Journal of Abnormal Psychology, 94,* 42–50.

Walker, L. E. (1979). *The battered woman.* New York: Harper & Row.

Walker, L. E. (1984). *The battered woman syndrome.* New York: Springer.

Wallace, J. R., & Richardson, A. (1984, April). *Intellectual competition: Self-confidence and performance in males and females.* Paper presented at the meeting of the Eastern Psychological Association, Baltimore.

Wallace, M. (1979). *Black macho and the myth of the superwoman.* New York: Dial Press.

Wallerstein, J. S., & Kelly, J. B. (1980). *Surviving the break-up: How children and parents cope with divorce.* New York: Basic Books.

Wallston, B. S., DeVellis, B. M., & Wallston, K. (1983). Licensed practical nurses' sex role stereotypes. *Psychology of Women Quarterly, 7,* 199–208.

Wallston, B. S., & Grady, K. E., (1985). Integrating the feminist critique and the crisis in social psychology: Another look at research methods. In V. O'Leary, R. Unger, & B. Wallston (Eds.), *Women, gender, and social psychology* (pp. 7–33). Hillsdale, N.J.: Lawrence Erlbaum Associates.

Wallston, B. S., & O'Leary, V. (1981). Sex makes a difference: Differential perceptions of women and men. In L. Wheeler (Ed.), *Review of personality and social psychology,* Vol. 2 (pp. 9–41). Beverly Hills, Calif.: Sage.

Ward, C. (1981). Prejudice against women: Who, when, and why? *Sex Roles, 7,* 163–171.

Ward, C. (1985). Sex trait stereotypes in Malaysian children. *Sex Roles, 12,* 35–45.

Ward, E. E., Dworkin, S., Powers-Alexander, S., & Dowd, E. T. (1983, August). *Cognitive and emotional changes associated with premenstrual syndrome.* Paper presented at the meeting of the American Psychological Association, Anaheim.

Wardle, J., & Beinart, H. (1981). Binge-eating: A theoretical review. *British Journal of Clinical Psychology, 20,* 97–109.

Warr, P., & Parry, G. (1982a). Depressed mood in working-class mothers with and without paid employment. *Social Psychiatry, 17,* 161–165.

Warr, P., & Parry, G. (1982b). Paid employment and women's psychological well-being. *Psychological Bulletin, 91,* 498–516.

Warren, L. W., & McEachren, L. (1985). Derived identity and depressive symptomatology in women differing in marital and employment status. *Psychology of Women Quarterly, 9,* 133–144.

Warren, M Q. (Ed.) (1981). *Comparing female and male offenders.* Beverly Hills, Calif.: Sage.

Wasserman, G. A., & Lewis, M. (1985). Infant sex differences: Ecological effects. *Sex Roles, 12,* 665–675.

Waterman, A., & Whitbourne, S. K. (1980). Androgyny and psychosocial development among college students and adults. *Journal of Personality, 50,* 121–133.

Watkins, B. T. (1985, Sept. 18). Number of women college presidents has doubled in decade, study finds. *Chronicle of Higher Education,* p. 1.

Wattenawaha, N., & Clements, M. A. (1982). Qualitative aspects of sex-related differences in performances on pencil-and-paper spatial questions, grades 7–9. *Journal of Educational Psychology, 74,* 878–887.

Watts, B. L., Messe, L. A., & Vallacher, R. R. (1982). Toward understanding sex differences in pay allocation: Agency, communion, and reward distribution behavior. *Sex Roles, 8,* 1175–1187.

Weaver, J. L., & Garrett, S. D. (1983). Sexism and racism in the American health care industry: A comparative analysis. In E. Fee (Ed.), *Women and health: The politics of sex and medicine* (pp. 79–116). Farmingdale, N.Y.: Baywood.

Webb, N. M. (1984). Sex differences in interaction and achievement in cooperative small groups. *Journal of Educational Psychology, 76,* 33–44.

Webb, T. E., & VanDevere, C. A. (1985). Sex differences in the expression of depression: A developmental interaction effect. *Sex Roles, 12,* 91–95.

Weimann, G. (1985). Sex differences in dealing with bureaucracy. *Sex Roles, 12,* 777–790.

Weisberg, D. K. (Ed.) (1982). *Women and the law: The social historical perspective. Vol. I. Women and the criminal law.* Cambridge, Mass.: Schenkman.

Weisheit, R. A. (1984). Women and crime: Issues and perspectives. *Sex Roles, 11,* 567–581.

Weiss, M. (1974). Unlearning. In J. Pleck & J. Sawyer (Eds.), *Men and masculinity* (pp. 162–170). Englewood Cliffs, N.J.: Prentice-Hall.

Weissman, M. M., & Klerman, G. L. (1977). Sex differences and the epidemiology of depression. *Archives of General Psychiatry, 34,* 98–111.

Weisstein, N. (1969, October). Woman as nigger. *Psychology Today,* p. 22ff.

Weitz, R. (1982). Feminist consciousness raising, self-concept, and depression. *Sex Roles, 8,* 231–241.

Weitz, S. (1977). *Sex roles: Biological, psychological and social foundations.* New York: Oxford University Press.

Weitzman, L. J. (1975). Sex-role socialization. In J. Freeman (Ed.), *Women: A feminist perspective* (pp. 105–144). Palo Alto, Calif.: Mayfield.

Weitzman, L. J. (1985). *The divorce revolution: The unexpected social and economic consequences for women and children in America.* New York: Free Press.

Weitzman, L. J., & Rizzo, D. (1974). *Images of males and females in elementary school text books.* New York: NOW Legal Defense & Education Fund.

Welch, M. R., & Page, B. M. (1981). Sex differences in childhood socialization patterns in African societies. *Sex Roles, 7,* 1163–1173.

Welch, R. L., Huston-Stein, A., Wright, J. C., & Plehal, R. (1979). Subtle sex-role cues in children's commercials. *Journal of Communication, 29,* 202–209.

Wentworth, D. K., & Anderson, L. R. (1984). Emergent leadership as a function of sex and task type. *Sex Roles, 11,* 513–524.

Werner, D. (1984). Child care and influences among the Mekranoti of Central Brasil. *Sex Roles, 10,* 395–404.

Werner, P. D., & LaRussa, G. W. (1985). Persistence and change in sex-role stereotypes. *Sex Roles, 12,* 9/10, 1089–1100.

Weston, L. C., & Ruggiero, J. A. (1978). Male-female relationships in best-selling "Modern Gothic" novels. *Sex Roles, 4,* 647–655.

Wetter, B. (1966). The cult of true womanhood, 1820–1860. *American Quarterly, 18,* 244–256.

Wetzsteon, R. (1977, November). The feminist man? *Mother Jones,* pp. 52–59.

Wheeler, L., Reis, H., & Nezlek, J. (1983). Loneliness, social interactions, and sex roles. *Journal of Personality and Social Psychology, 45,* 943–953.

White, A. (1985). Women as authors and editors of psychological journals: A 10-year perspective. *American Psychologist, 40,* 527–530.

White, M. S. (1979). Measuring androgyny in adulthood. *Psychology of Women Quarterly, 3,* 293–307.

Whiting, B., & Edwards, C. P. (1973). A cross-cultural analysis of sex differences in the behavior of children aged three through eleven. *Journal of Social Psychology, 91* (Second Half), 171–188.

Whitley, B. E., Jr. (1983). Sex role orientation and self-esteem: A critical meta-analytic review. *Journal of Personality and Social Psychology, 44,* 765–778.

Whitley, B. E., Jr. (1984). Sex-role orientation and psychological well-being: Two meta-analyses. *Sex Roles, 12,* 207–225.

Widom, C. S. (1978). Toward an understanding of female criminality. In B. A. Maher (Ed.), *Progress in Experimental Personality Research,* Vol. 8 (pp. 245–308). New York: Academic.

Widom, C. S. (1979). Female offenders: Three assumptions about self-esteem, sex-role identity, and feminism. *Criminal Justice and Behavior, 6,* 365–382.

Widom, C. S. (Ed.) (1984a). *Sex roles and psychopathology.* New York: Plenum.

Widom, C. S. (1984b). Sex roles, criminology, and psychopathology. In Widom, C. S. (Ed.), *Sex roles and psychopathology* (pp. 183–217). New York: Plenum.

Wiggins, J. S., & Holzmuller, A. (1978). Psychological androgyny and interpersonal behavior. *Journal of Consulting and Clinical Psychology, 46,* 40–52.

Wiggins, J. S., & Holzmuller, A. (1981). Further evidence on androgyny and interpersonal flexibility. *Journal of Research in Personality, 15,* 67–80.

Wilborn, B. L. (1978). The myth of the perfect mother. In L. Harmon, J. Bert, L. Fitzgerald, & M. F. Tanney (Eds.), *Counseling women* (pp. 241–249). Monterey, Calif.: Brooks/Cole.

Wiley, M. G., & Eskilson, A. (1985). Speech style, gender stereotypes, and corporate success: What if women talk more like men? *Sex Roles, 12,* 993–1007.

Williams, D. G. (1985). Gender, masculinity-femininity, and emotional intimacy in same-sex friendship. *Sex Roles, 12,* 587–600.

Williams, F., LaRose, R., & Frost, F. (1981). Children, television and sex-role stereotyping. New York: Praeger.

Williams, J. B. W., & Spitzer, R. L. (1983). The issue of sex bias in DSM-III. *American Psychologist, 38,* 793–798.

Williams, J. E., & Best, D. L. (1982). *Measuring sex stereotypes: A thirty-nation study.* Beverly Hills, Calif.: Sage.

Williams, J. E., & Best, D. L. (1984, August). *Sex stereotypes and masculinity-femininity in cross-cultural perspectives.* Paper presented at the meeting of the American Psychological Association, Toronto, Canada.

Williams, J. H. (1973). Sexual role identification and personality functioning in girls: A theory revisited. *Journal of Personality, 41*(1), 1–8.

Williams, S. W., & McCullers, J. C. (1983). Personal factors related to typicalness of career and success in active professional women. *Psychology of Women Quarterly, 7,* 343–357.

Williamson, N. E. (1976). *Sons and daughters: A cross-cultural survey of parental preferences.* Beverly Hills, Calif.: Sage.

Wilson, D. G., & Stokes, J. P. (1983, August). *Gender differences in social support.* Paper presented at the meeting of the American Psychological Association, Anaheim.

Wilson, F. R., & Cook, E. P. (1984). Concurrent validity of four androgyny instruments. *Sex Roles, 11,* 813–837.

Wilson, J. (1977, May 29). Hollywood flirts with the New Woman. *The New York Times,* Sect. 2, p. 1ff.

Wilson, J. (1978). *Religion in American society.* Englewood Cliffs, N.J.: Prentice-Hall.

Wilson, J. G. (1984, December). Are newswomen changing the news? *Ms.,* pp. 45–50, 124–126.

Wilson, L. K., & Gallois, C. (1985). Perceptions of assertive behavior: Sex combination, role appropriateness, and message type. *Sex Roles, 12,* 125–141.

Winick, C. (1968). *The new people and desexualization in American life.* New York: Pegasus.

Winnett, R. A., & Neale, M. S. (1980). Results of experimental study on flextime and family life. *Monthly Labor Review, 103,* 29–32.

Winstead, B. A. (1984). Hysteria. In C. Widom (Ed.), *Sex roles and psychopathology* (pp. 73–100). New York: Plenum.

Winstead, B. A., Derlega, V. J., & Wong, P. T. P. (1984). Effects of sex-role orientation on behavioral self-disclosure. *Journal of Research in Personality, 18,* 541–553.

Winter, D., Stewart, A., & McClelland, D. (1977). Husband's motive and wife's career level. *Journal of Personality and Social Psychology, 35,* 154–166.

Wise, E., & Rafferty, J. (1982). Sex bias and language. *Sex Roles, 8,* 1189–1196.

Wise, P. S., & Joy, S. S. (1982). Working mothers, sex, differences, and self-esteem in college students' self-descriptions. *Sex Roles, 8,* 785–790.

Witelson, S. F. (1976). Sex and the single hemisphere: Specialization of the right hemisphere for spatial processing. *Science, 193,* 425–427.

Witkin, H. A., Dyk, R. B., Faterson, H. F., Goodenough, D. R., & Karp, S. A. (1962). *Psychological differentiation.* New York: Wiley.

Witkin, H. A., & Goodenough, D. R. (1981). *Cognitive styles: Essence and origins.* New York: International Universities Press.

Witt, S. H. (1981). The two worlds of native women. In S. Cox (Ed.), *Female psychology*, 2nd ed. (pp. 149–155). New York: St. Martin's.

Wittig, A. F. (1984). Sport competition anxiety and sex role. *Sex Roles, 10,* 469-473.

Wittig, M. A. (1979). Genetic influences of sex-related differences in intellectual performance: Theoretical and methodological issues. In M. A. Wittig and A. C. Petersen (Eds.), *Sex-related differences in cognitive functioning: Developmental issues* (pp. 21–66). New York: Academic Press.

Wittig, M. A. (1985b). Metatheoretical dilemmas in the psychology of gender. *American Psychologist, 40,* 800–811.

Wittig, M. A. (1985b). Sex-role norms and gender-related attainment values: Their role in attributions of success and failure. *Sex Roles, 12,* 1–13.

Wittig, M. A., & Petersen, A. C. (Eds.) (1979). *Sex-related differences in genetic functioning: Developmental issues.* New York: Academic Press.

Woelfel, J. C. (1981). Women in the United States Army. *Sex Roles, 7,* 785–800.

Woelfel, J. C., & Savell, J. M. (1981). Marital satisfaction, job satisfaction, and retention in the army. In E. Hunter & D. Nice (Eds.), *Military families: Adaptation to change.* New York: Praeger, 1981.

Wojcicka-Sharff, J. (1981, March). Free enterprise and the ghetto family. *Psychology Today,* p. 41, 43, 44, 46–48.

Wolfe, B. E. (1984). Gender ideology and phobias in women. In C. Widom (Ed.), *Sex roles and psychopathology* (pp. 51–72). New York: Plenum.

Women gaining in senior administrative posts. (1985, Spring). *On Campus with Women,* p. 5.

Women have the best sniffers, study indicates. (1984, December 15). *The Easton Express,* p. B7.

Women hold their own. (1981, December/January). *WEAL Washington Report,* pp. 1–2.

Women in Transition, Inc. (1975). *Women in transition.* New York: Scribner.

Women on Words and Images. (1972). *Dick and Jane as victims.* Princeton, N.J.: Author.

Women on Words and Images. (1975a). *Channeling children.* Princeton, N.J.: Author.

Women on Words and Images. (1975b). *Dick and Jane as victims: An update.* Princeton, N.J.: Author.

Women on Words and Images. (1975c). *Doctor, lawyer, Indian chief . . . ? Sex stereotyping in career education materials.* Princeton, N.J.: Author.

Wong, P. T. P., Kettlewell, G., & Sproule, C. F. (1985). On the importance of being masculine: Sex role, attribution, and women's career achievement. *Sex Roles, 12,* 757–769.

Wood, W., & Karten, S. J. (1984, August). *Sex differences in interaction style as a product of perceived sex differences in competence.* Paper presented at the meeting of the American Psychological Association, Toronto.

Woody, B., & Malson, M. (1984). *In crisis: Low income Black employed women in the U.S. workplace* (Working Paper No. 131). Wellesley, Mass.: Wellesley College Center for Research on Women.

Worell, J. (1978). Sex roles and psychological well-being: Perspectives on methodology. *Journal of Consulting and Clinical Psychology, 46,* 777–791.

Wright, C. T., Meadow, A., Abramowitz, S. I., & Davidson, C. V. (1980). Psychiatric diagnosis as a function of assessor profession and sex. *Psychology of Women Quarterly, 5,* 240–254.

Wright, P. H. (1982). Men's friendships, women's friendships and the alleged inferiority of the latter. *Sex Roles, 8,* 1–20.

Wrightsman, L. (1977). *Social psychology* (2nd ed.). Monterey, Calif.: Brooks/Cole.

Wyer, R. S., Bodenhauser, G. V., & Gorman, T. F. (1985). Cognitive mediators of reactions to rape. *Journal of Personality and Social Psychology, 48,* 324–338.

Yablonsky, L. (1982). *Fathers and sons.* New York: Simon & Schuster.

Yankelovich, D. (1981, April). New rules in American life: Searching for self-fulfillment in a world turned upside down. *Psychology Today,* 35–92.

Yarczower, M., & Daruns, L. (1982). Social inhibition of spontaneous facial expressions in children. *Journal of Personality and Social Psychology, 43,* 831–837.

Yarkin, K. L., Town, J. P., & Wallston, B. S. (1982). Blacks and women must try harder: Stimulus persons' race and sex attributions of causality. *Personality and Social Psychology Bulletin, 8,* 21–24.

Yoder, J. D. (1983). Another look at women in the United States Army: A comment on Woelfel's article. *Sex Roles, 9,* 285–288.

Yogev, S. (1982). Happiness in dual-career couples: Changing research, changing values. *Sex Roles, 8,* 593–605.

Yogev, S. (1983). Judging the professional woman: Changing research, changing values. *Psychology of Women Quarterly, 7,* 219–234.

Yogev, S., & Vierra, A. (1983). The state of motherhood among professional women. *Sex Roles, 9,* 391–396.

Yoshihashi, P. (1984, April 15). New boy on campus: Men's studies. *The New York Times,* Higher Education Supplement, pp. 2–3.

Yost, P. (1985, August 2). Jobless rate stuck at 7.3%. *The Easton Express,* p. 1.

Young, C. J., MacKenzie, D. L., & Sherif, C. W. (1980). In search of token women in academia. *Psychology of Women Quarterly, 4,* 508–525.

Young, R. A. (1984). Vocational choice and values in adolescent women. *Sex Roles, 7/8,* 485–492.

Youssef, N. H., & Hartley, S. F. (1979). Demographic indicators of the status of women in various societies. In J. Lipman-Bluman & J. Bernard (Eds.), *Sex roles and social policy: A complex social science equation* (pp. 83–112). Beverly Hills, Calif.: Sage.

You've come a long way, baby—But not as far as you thought. (1984, October 1). *Business Week,* p. 126–128.

Zanna, J. J., & Pack, S. J. (1975). On the self-fulfilling nature of apparent sex differences in behavior. *Journal of Experimental Social Psychology, 11,* 583–591.

Zarbatany, L., Hartmann, D. P., Gelfand, D. M., & Vinciguerra, P. (1985). Gender differences in altruistic reputation: Are they artifactual? *Developmental Psychology, 21,* 97–101.

Zaslow, M. J., & Pedersen, F. A. (1981). Sex role conflicts and the experience of childbearing. *Professional Psychology, 12,* 47–55.

Zeldow, P. B. (1976). Effects of nonpathological sex-role stereotypes on student evaluations of psychiatric patients. *Journal of Consulting and Clinical Psychology, 44,* 304.

Zeldow, P. B., Clark, D., & Daugherty, S. R. (1985). Masculinity, femininity, Type A behavior, and psychosocial adjustment in medical students. *Journal of Personality and Social Psychology, 48,* 481–492.

Zern, D. S. (1984). Relationships among selected child-rearing variables in a cross-cultural sample of 110 societies. *Developmental Psychology, 20,* 683–690.

Ziegler, M. (1983, Aug.). *Assessing parents' and children's time together.* Paper presented at the meeting of the American Psychological Association, Anaheim.

Zigler, E., & Muenchow, S. (1983). Infant day care and infant-care leaves. *American Psychologist, 38,* 91–94.

Zilbergeld, B. (1978). *Male sexuality: A guide to sexual fulfillment.* Boston: Little, Brown.

Zuckerman, D. M. (1981). Family background, sex-role attitudes, and life goals of technical college and university students. *Sex Roles, 7,* 1109–1126.

Zuckerman, D. M. (1983). Women's studies, self-esteem, and college women's plans for the future. *Sex Roles, 9,* 633–642.

Zuckerman, D. M., & Sayre, D. H. (1982). Cultural sex-role expectations and children's sex-role concepts. *Sex Roles, 8,* 853–862.

Zuckerman, D. M., Singer, D. S., & Singer, J. L. (1980). Children's television viewing, racial and sex-role attitudes. *Journal of Applied Social Psychology, 10,* 281–294.

Zuckerman, M., DeFrank, R. S., Spiegel, N. H., & Larrance, D. T. (1982). Masculinity-femininity and encoding of nonverbal cues. *Journal of Personality and Social Psychology, 42,* 548–556.

Name Index

Subject Index